Chris Payne

Teach Yourself

.NET Windows Forms in 21 Days

SAMS

201 West 103rd St., Indianapolis, Indiana, 46290 USA

Sams Teach Yourself .NET Windows Forms in 21 Days

Copyright © 2002 by Sams Publishing

International Standard Book Number: 0-672-32320-6

Library of Congress Catalog Card Number: 2001094777

Printed in the United States of America

First Printing: May, 2002

04   03   02   01   4   3   2   1

Trademarks

Warning and Disclaimer

ASSOCIATE PUBLISHER
Michael Stephens

ACQUISITIONS EDITORS
Shelley Kronzek
Neil Rowe

DEVELOPMENT EDITOR
Songlin Qiu

MANAGING EDITOR
Charlotte Clapp

PROJECT EDITOR
Andy Beaster

COPY EDITORS
Maryann Steinhart
Chuck Hutchinson
Matt Wynalda
Karen Gill

INDEXER
Tom Dinse

PROOFREADER
Suzanne Thomas

TECHNICAL EDITOR
Mark Nicholson

TEAM COORDINATOR
Lynne Williams

MEDIA DEVELOPER
Dan Scherf

INTERIOR DESIGNER
Gary Adair

COVER DESIGNER
Aren Howell

PAGE LAYOUT
Michelle Mitchell

Contents at a Glance

Contents

About the Author

 **CHRIS PAYNE,** author of *Sams Teach Yourself ASP.NET in 21 Days,* has had a passion for computers and writing since a young age. He holds a Bachelor of Science in Biomedical Engineering from Boston University and supported himself through college as an independent consultant and writer of technical articles, focused on Web development. Currently making his home in Orlando, Florida, with his wife, Eva, he works as a Web developer and is continuing his career as an author, both of technical and fictional material.

Dedication

This one is for my parents.

Acknowledgments

Again I must thank Shelley Kronzek for her help and dedication in getting this book (and my writing career) going. I wish her the best in her new endeavors.

Thanks to Songlin Qiu for helping me stay on track with this book and for understanding when I didn't. Thanks to Mark Nicholson for calling me on numerous inconsistencies and for making this a very strong book technically. Thanks to Neil Rowe for stepping in at the last moment—my thoughts and prayers are with you and your family.

I can't forget all the little people (wink, wink) who helped in one way or another on this book: my friends at the Golf Channel for help on research; Enrique Iglesias for inspirational music as I wrote this; and Maggie, for distracting me.

Finally, I must extend my biggest thanks to my wife, Eva, for being eternally patient as I wrote this book; for understanding about the many evenings and weekends that I didn't get to spend with you; for being positive about the future. I love you.

Tell Us What You Think!

As the reader of this book, *you* are our most important critic and commentator. We value your opinion and want to know what we're doing right, what we could do better, what areas you'd like to see us publish in, and any other words of wisdom you're willing to pass our way.

As an Associate Publisher for Sams, I welcome your comments. You can fax, e-mail, or write me directly to let me know what you did or didn't like about this book—as well as what we can do to make our books stronger.

Please note that I cannot help you with technical problems related to the topic of this book, and that due to the high volume of mail I receive, I might not be able to reply to every message.

When you write, please be sure to include this book's title and author as well as your name and phone or fax number. I will carefully review your comments and share them with the author and editors who worked on the book.

Fax: 317-581-4770

E-mail: feedback@samspublishing.com

Mail: Michael Stephens, Associate Publisher
          Sams Publishing
          201 West 103rd Street
          Indianapolis, IN 46290 USA

Introduction

Welcome to *Sams Teach Yourself .NET Windows Forms in 21 Days*. This book will guide you step by step from the basics of Microsoft's .NET Windows Forms to quite advanced topics. You're in for a very informative and exciting adventure over the next 21 days.

Windows Forms technology is a part of Microsoft's .NET initiative—it allows you to build powerful Windows applications very easily using nearly any programming language you are familiar with. You can build everything from simple calculators to multi-threaded database-driven Web services (if you don't know the first thing about multi-threading or database access, keep reading). Simply put, if you want to develop Windows applications in the future, you're going to be using Windows Forms.

As you move through the tutorial-style lessons in this book, you'll discover just how easily these tasks can be accomplished. And not only will you see examples and learn how to build these and other applications, but you'll gain understanding that will enable you to be confident in any endeavor you choose to pursue in Windows programming.

Who Is This Book's Intended Audience?

This book is intended to completely familiarize newcomers to Windows Forms with this wonderful technology. "Newcomers" is a broad term, though. Specifically, you should pick this book up if you want to learn how to make Windows applications in .NET, whether or not you've had any experience building them in another environment. And because Microsoft's future is based on .NET, every Windows application developer will need to move to Windows Forms.

That said, even if you are familiar with Windows Forms, you will find this book an invaluable resource that can help you brush up on forgotten basics and prepare you for advanced projects.

Those familiar with other methods of building Windows applications will find Windows Forms refreshing, as they make previously tedious tasks, such as memory management, a snap. You'll find that many of the skills you've already learned still apply in this new framework.

Finally, if you're simply curious about the .NET Framework, this book provides an excellent introduction and takes you through many of the major topics as they relate to application development.

What Do You Need to Know Prior to Reading This Book?

The only absolute requirement is that you are familiar with using the Windows operating system, from interacting with the command prompt to working with application windows.

Knowing a .NET programming language such as C# or Visual Basic.NET will help immensely, but is not required. This book quickly introduces you to the basics of these two languages, and introduces each new topic before they are used. If you can follow along in the code and text (and both C# and Visual Basic.NET are very easy to read), you'll be fine.

No knowledge of the .NET Framework is necessary. This book thoroughly discusses the framework, and will point you to further resources when necessary.

What Software Will You Need to Complete the Examples Provided with This Book?

The only required software (aside from Windows XP, Windows 2000, or Windows NT with Service Pack 6) is the .NET Framework and Notepad. The .NET Framework is necessary to build Windows Forms applications, and can be had for free at Microsoft's Web site: http://www.Microsoft.com/net.

To build applications, you only need a word processor capable of creating plain text files, and Notepad is excellent for that. If you are more comfortable with another processor, such as Word or WordPad, or even FrontPage, feel free to use it.

Visual Studio.NET is not required here, and in fact, is used very seldom throughout this book. While it is true that Visual Studio.NET provides a lot of excellent functionality when building applications, we find that it is best to learn how to do things manually before you let an IDE do them for you. You'll appreciate this in the long run.

Finally, to take advantage of the database examples, you'll need some form of OLE DB–compliant database system, such as Microsoft Access or SQL Server. Without these, you won't be able to play around with the related examples.

How This Book Is Organized

The book is organized as a series of tutorials. Each day's lesson builds on the lesson previous to it, so it may be helpful to proceed in a linear fashion, although it is certainly not required. In general, topics are discussed first, followed by some examples (which are accompanied with analyses). Each day's lesson concludes with answers to commonly asked questions, a short quiz to test your new knowledge (no cheating!), and an exercise for you to play with on your own. All of these are carefully chosen to further your knowledge and extend your experience with the technology.

This book is divided into three logical sections, spanning a week each, and a set of three appendixes:

- Week 1 will be spent learning the fundamentals of .NET and Windows Forms. You'll see what it means to build a Windows Forms application, find out how to get started, and play with the controls that will make your applications fully functional. The strong foundation you'll build during this week will help you as you continue on.

- Week 2 focuses on technologies that will enhance the functionality of your Windows Forms application, from ActiveX to ADO.NET. These technologies aren't necessarily a part of Windows Forms, but you'll most likely need to use them in one way or another as you build Windows applications.

- Week 3 delves into advanced Windows Forms topics. You'll learn how to completely customize your applications, from building unique (and marketable) controls to configuring deployment options and languages. You'll also learn several techniques that can vastly improve the performance of your applications, from multithreading to profiling.

Note

At the end of each week you'll spend some time reviewing, and then apply that week's knowledge to an actual project. You'll build a Word processing application similar to Microsoft Word from scratch, adding new features and technologies as you learn them. Each week's review builds on the week's lessons. These week-in-review projects give you an opportunity to apply and solidify the skills you've learned in each week.

- Finally, the appendixes provide a complete reference section for the topics covered in the book. You can refer to these for answers to quizzes, or for refreshers on all the controls and objects used in this book.

Where to Download the Code for This Book

All of the code in this book is available for download on the Sams Publishing Web site at http://www.samspublishing.com/. Enter this book's ISBN (0672323206—don't use the hyphens) in the Search box and click Search. When the book's title is displayed, click the title to go to a page where you can download the code.

| **Note** | For additional resources, go to my Web site, `http://www.clpayne.com`, You'll find links to relevant information (source code, articles, errata, and so on). |

Conventions Used in This Book

The following typographic conventions are used in this book:

- Code lines, commands, statements, variables, and any text you type or see onscreen appears in a monospace typeface. **Bold monospace** typeface is often used to represent the user's input.

- Placeholders in syntax descriptions appear in an *italic monospace* typeface. Replace the placeholder with the actual filename, parameter, or whatever element it represents.

- *Italics* highlight technical terms when they're being defined.

- The ➡ icon is used before a line of code that is really a continuation of the preceding line. Sometimes a line of code is too long to fit as a single line on the page. If you see ➡ before a line of code, remember that it's part of the line immediately above it.

- The **ANALYSIS** sections following code listings discuss in detail the code in this book. Here you will find a discussion on what a particular piece of code does, how it works, and often a line-by-line analysis.

- The book contains Notes, Tips, and Cautions to help you spot important or useful information more quickly. These often include shortcuts to help you work more efficiently. Also, you'll find helpful Do/Don't sections throughout the book that provide helpful suggestions on the proper (or improper) way to accomplish a task.

Finally...

I hope you have a wonderful time learning this exciting technology. With it, you can do many amazing things with Windows, many of which are in high demand in the technology market. Without further ado, let's get on with the lessons!

WEEK 1

At a Glance

Learning the Basics

The first week of your journey through Windows Forms will be spent learning the basics. You'll get a solid foundation from the first seven lessons so that you'll be able to move onto more advanced topics in weeks two and three.

Day 1, "Getting Started with Windows Forms," introduces you to the .NET Framework, Windows Forms, and Windows programming. You'll also see your first application in this lesson. In Day 2, "Building Windows Forms Applications," you'll build your own Windows application from scratch, and learn more about how to compile and run that application.

Day 3, "Working with Your Windows Forms," is a very important lesson. You'll learn all about the Form object, the central part of any Windows Forms application. You'll also start to take a look at handling events—making your applications respond to users.

In Day 4, "Adding Menus and Toolbars to Your Windows Forms," you'll learn about many of the controls in the Windows Forms framework that will make your life as a developer much easier. Day 5, "Handling Events in Your Windows Forms," teaches you how to react to various occurrences in your application, such as button or menu clicks. In Day 6, "Enhancing Your Windows Forms with More Controls," you'll greatly enlarge your repertoire of Windows Forms controls by learning all of the major controls not covered in Day 4.

1

2

3

4

5

6

7

Finally, Day 7, "Working with Dialog Boxes," teaches you all about a special type of Windows Form. There are quite a few types of dialog boxes that are very useful in Windows programming. At the end of the week, you'll recap everything you learned in these first seven days and apply them to build a working application.

Without further ado, let's get on with it!

DAY 1

Getting Started with .NET Windows Forms

Welcome to Day 1, your first step into Windows Forms! Windows Forms is a new technology (part of Microsoft .NET) that allows you to build Windows applications quickly and easily. Today you'll get started by learning what is involved with Windows Forms and .NET, and you'll also get to see some real code!

Today, you will

- Discover what Windows programming means to developers
- Learn what .NET and Windows Forms are
- Find out the advantages that .NET and Windows Forms provide you
- Learn how the Common Language Runtime and the Microsoft Intermediate Language work
- Learn how to install the .NET Framework
- Examine a simple Windows Forms application

Introduction to Windows Programming

First things first: What is a Windows program? Perhaps we should take another step back and ask, What is Microsoft Windows? Now that you're on your way to becoming a programmer, you'll have to think of Windows in a different way. If you're already a programmer, then you've already learned how to control an operating system (OS).

From a normal user's perspective, Microsoft Windows is an operating system that makes your computer run. It allows you to create and save documents, perform calculations, browse the Internet, print files, and so on. If you're reading this book, that description most likely does not suit you, because you want to know more: how things work under the hood, and how you can make Windows do things for you.

Underneath the pretty exterior, Microsoft Windows (as well as any other operating system) is an environment for translators, and occasionally a translator itself. Windows and its applications take input from a user and translates it into something a computer processor can understand (1s and 0s) and vice versa. Figure 1.1 shows this layered paradigm. Windows doesn't know how to translate every input by itself, and that's where Windows applications step in.

FIGURE 1.1

Windows acts as a translator between the user and the CPU.

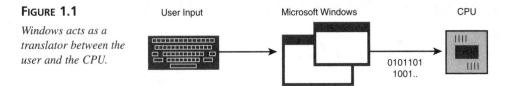

User Input   Microsoft Windows   CPU

0101101
1001..

NEW TERM A Windows program is written by a programmer and tells Windows what to do in response to input. That input may be a key press, a mouse click, or simply starting the program. Using a *programming language*—a collection of keywords, statements, phrases, and so on that hold special meaning for a computer—a programmer writes instructions for the OS, so it knows how to translate input into machine language.

So what is a Windows program? It is a set of instructions that tells Windows what to do and how to react to user input. You, as a programmer, will write those instructions—and trust me, it's easier than you think. We'll examine some more of the process when you build your first applications later today and tomorrow.

Programming Languages

As mentioned in the previous section, a programming language is what a programmer uses to instruct the OS. It contains special keywords and syntax that may not make much sense to an untrained eye, but is often constructed in a beautifully logical way.

Even if you have never programmed before, you probably heard about several programming languages: C, C++, C# (pronounced *see-sharp*), Visual Basic, Pascal, Java, and so on. Why so many? Each language approaches things in a slightly different manner and provides different options to the programmer; their applications are very similar to spoken languages. For example, an Eskimo may have tens of ways to say the word "snow," whereas the English language only has a few at most. Likewise, C++ may have several ways to say "function pointer," while Visual Basic has few or none. This doesn't mean that either language is deficient or lacking, but rather that they have evolved from different roots.

In addition, most languages (with exceptions you'll learn about in the "What Is .NET?" section later today) use different paradigms to build Windows applications. C and C++ programs often use the Microsoft Foundation Classes (MFC), while Visual Basic has its own internal forms designer. This meant that learning a new language often also meant learning a new method of building Windows applications (which is no longer so with .NET—more on that later).

Programming languages aren't typically understood by the OS. Rather, an intermediate program, called a compiler, translates the programming language into machine language—something the OS does understand. You could, theoretically write in machine language as well, but most humans don't understand binary commands. For example, the sequence "01010111101010101011" may look like gibberish to you but may actually hold meaning to the computer.

The languages you'll be using in this book are C# and Visual Basic .NET (VB .NET); the former because it was developed especially for use with the .NET environment, and the latter because it is an easy-to-learn language that most beginners will use. In many cases, it is a simple matter to translate from one to the other. For example, the following code snippet shows two lines of code—one in C# and one in VB .NET—that do that same thing.

```
C#
System.Console.WriteLine("Hello World!");
```

```
VB.NET
System.Console.WriteLine("Hello World!")
```

In this case, the only difference is the semicolon at the end of the statement. Throughout this book, code examples are provided in both languages, so you can choose the one you prefer.

Note

It's probably a good idea to know either C# or VB .NET before you start this book. You can pick up either language from the examples in this book, but you would miss out on many of the elements of learning the languages explicitly.

Win32 Programming

Often, you'll see the term Win32 tossed around in programmer jargon. Win32 applications are simply applications that are built for (and probably using) a 32-bit version of Windows (for example, Windows 95, 98, ME, 2000, or XP). Older versions of Windows were 16 bits, and are referred to as Win16.

The move from 16 to 32 bits allows you much greater processing power and control over the computer. Win16 programs will work on a Win32 OS, but not the other way around because of the processing limitations and no backwards compatibility.

Note

In simple terms, 32 bits is better than 16 bits because it allows you to do more processing in the same amount of time. For a computer processor, 32 bits means that it can access and manipulate information in memory that is 32 bits in length, which is more "space" than 16 bits.

In today's computing world, most of the applications you'll come across are Win32, and all the applications you'll build in this book are Win32 as well.

Note

Win16 programs are often referred to as "legacy" programs as well, because they hark back to olden days. Many developers refer to legacy applications in a derisive tone, because those programs are usually very old and lack modern processing mechanisms.

What Is .NET?

.NET is Microsoft's initiative to bring about a new generation of Windows applications. .NET simplifies many of the disparaging concepts in Windows programming into a simple architecture, and tightly integrates the Internet into its applications. While .NET is a conceptual initiative, the .NET Framework is magic that makes it all happen—you'll use the Framework extensively with Windows Forms.

Simply put, the .NET Framework is an architecture with which applications (both Internet and desktop-based) can be built and executed. It represents a completely new way for Windows to operate by providing a standard, unified system that all applications can use, instead of the many disparate frameworks available today. .NET also provides a new environment for those applications to run in, which is inherently more efficient, secure, and capable. That's a mouthful, but it boils to down this: with .NET, you can build applications easier than ever before.

NEW TERM One of the main goals of .NET is to deliver applications, or pieces of applications, over the Internet as *services*. A service is an application that is available to you over the Internet and can be used directly by you or by other applications. These services would be available to anyone who needs them—you'd simply log on to the Internet and connect to the service. Imagine not having to install programs such as Microsoft Word on your computer. Rather, you get online and use it from Microsoft's Web site just as you would if it were on your own computer. Figure 1.2 illustrates this concept.

FIGURE 1.2

A Web service is an application or part of an application that is available for use over the Internet.

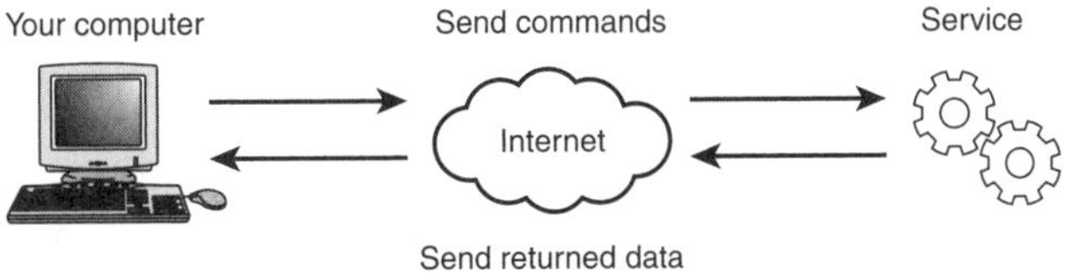

Your computer   Send commands   Service

Internet

Send returned data

This paradigm saves both end users and developers from headaches. The end users don't have to worry about messy installation procedures or maintaining their applications, applying upgrades, and so on. The developer doesn't have worry about deployment issues or maintaining multiple versions of the program on potentially thousands of users' computers. He simply builds it and makes it available over the Internet, for users to come along and use whenever they need it. When the developer creates a new version, users simply connect to use new features.

In the next few sections, you'll learn about the components of .NET and how they work together to make your job as a developer easier. It may be a bit dry at first, but you'll need this foundation before you begin building applications.

.NET Compilation

A traditional (that is, before .NET) application works in the following way: it's written in a programming language by a developer and then compiled into an executable application (this is a very important concept). The OS provides the environment for the application to run in, allowing it resources when the need arises. In a multitasking OS, such as Windows, you can run multiple applications at once because each application has its own set of operating system resources. Usually, each application respects other applications' resources, and you don't run into conflicts. Each application also has to maintain itself; that is, it runs and then cleans up after itself, properly disposing of resources when they are no longer needed.

This is generally a good way to operate. Applications are typically self-contained and don't care about what another application does. Application A could crash while application B continues on, because no resources are being shared. The OS has to invest only minimal resources to maintain the application (other than supplying processor power needed to run the program).

However, there are some drawbacks as well. The OS must register most applications so that it can maintain settings, determine resource boundaries, and allow the programs to interact with the OS and other applications when necessary. This can lead to a rather convoluted registration process, requiring hefty installation procedures.

Additionally, since each application has to maintain its own resources, the developer is left to properly handle them. You must write code that is often tedious to make sure you properly acquire and dispose of resources to avoid creating conflicts.

The Common Language Runtime (CLR) is .NET's form of a mananger. The CLR manages all aspects of the applications that run in .NET. Because of this, things in .NET work a bit differently than in traditional environments. When you create a .NET application, it is not compiled into a directly executable program. Rather, your code is translated into something called the Microsoft Intermediate Language (MSIL), which is essentially a shorthand way of representing your code. Then, when you execute your program, it is compiled into machine code by a *just-in-time* (*JIT*) compiler, which is then executed by the CLR.

This two-step process is slower than the one-step process prior to .NET, but not as much as you may think. First of all, MSIL is very easy for the JIT to understand and, thus, more efficient to compile than a straight programming language. Second, this process provides a large benefit over the previous method: cross-platform compatibility.

Machine languages depend on the machine used. Windows x86-based computers (computers based on the Windows operating system and Intel x86 processors) speak different languages than Unix platforms. Thus, every time you wanted to port an application to another platform, it meant, at a minimum, recompiling the source code to run on the new platform. More often it meant large rewrites to support the new system.

However, MSIL is MSIL no matter what platform it's on. Something that works in MSIL on Windows will work on Unix. The only requirement is that there be an appropriate JIT compiler to perform the final step of compilation to machine language—something you don't typically have to worry about. Large corporations such as Microsoft most likely have a JIT compiler for each platform before you ever need to transfer your applications.

Another benefit of .NET's paradigm over the traditional one is that MSIL contains special attributes, called *metadata*, that allow a piece of code to describe itself to the operating system. Recall that traditional applications were often required to register themselves in a central repository so the OS can keep track of them. This is no longer necessary because all relevant information is kept with the application. This information could include things like where to look for dependencies, the security requirements, version numbers, authors, and so on. This bundling of information is very useful, as you'll see once you start writing code.

> **Note** Not all programming languages or compilers can create MSIL and metadata. Therefore, a new class of compilers has been created by Microsoft that supports the .NET Framework, enabling all your favorite programming languages to support .NET. As time goes on and .NET becomes more popular, expect to see more compilers created by different companies.

Let's focus now on what happens after compilation: executing the program.

The Common Language Runtime

CLR is the heart of the .NET Framework. Think of it as the central processor for your applications; it handles all execution and maintenance of your applications. It has quite a few features, but there are only a few you need to know to get started with Windows Forms.

First, CLR handles all resource needs for your application. It doles out memory and processor time to parts of your application, and cleans them up when they are no longer in use. This process is known as *garbage collection*. Programmers with prior experience (especially in C and C++) will recall the complex and tedious routines that had to be written just to manage memory resources. Thankfully, these procedures are no longer necessary.

Second, the CLR provides a unified architecture. This means that no matter which programming language you use, you can always target the same framework. C++ applications can easily use components created in VB .NET, and vice versa.

Third, CLR uses the metadata created with your MSIL to ensure proper execution. For example, one feature of metadata is that it contains information on the environment (component versions, resources, and so on) that was used to build your application. The CLR can examine this data, and if the current system does not have the same required resources, it can automatically update those components.

Code that is built for CLR is known as *managed code* (simply because CLR manages every aspect of its execution). Code that does not target the CLR (pre-.NET applications) is known as *unmanaged code*. We'll be using these terms from now on. Unmanaged code can still be run in the CLR, but special considerations must be taken (we'll examine that in Day 14, "Using ActiveX.") Figure 1.3 shows the paths that managed and unmanaged code take to the CLR.

Figure 1.3

The CLR manages all execution of managed code, ensuring security, compatibility, and functionality.

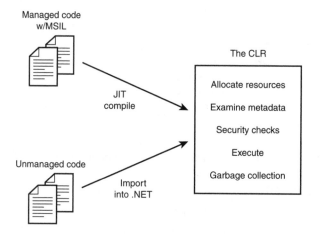

Installing the .NET Framework

Before you can start using the CLR and writing Windows Forms, you have to install the .NET Framework Software Development Kit (SDK). This SDK is available free at www.Microsoft.com/net, but beware that it is more than 100MB and can take more than 6 hours to download on a 56K modem. You can also order the SDK on CD-ROM from Microsoft's Web site for a nominal shipping charge. The .NET Framework SDK requires Windows NT 4.0 with Service Pack 6, Windows 2000, or Windows XP to run properly— if you're running any other operating system, you're out of luck (you may be able to get some examples to work, but you'll receive no support from Microsoft if you can't).

Once you have a copy of the .NET Framework SDK, run the setup program (see Figure 1.4). Click Next to begin installation, and accept the license agreement. Click Next three more times and sit back while the world of .NET opens to you (in other words, while the SDK is installed).

FIGURE 1.4

The .NET Framework SDK installation process begins with the setup screen.

After installation is complete, a shortcut to the .NET Framework overview appears on your desktop. This Web page has links to set up the .NET samples (assuming you chose to install them in the previous step), as well as links to more documentation.

Development Environments

A development environment is where you'll be doing all of your work—building applications and writing code. For Windows Forms development, you need some form of text editor to write your code. Many development environments offer, in addition to the text editor, complex user interfaces that provide advanced capabilities for managing code and projects. These features are often helpful, but not required.

All of the source code in this book (and at the associated Web site, www. samspublishing.com) is plain text, which means you can use an editor such as Notepad for your development environment. (Note that the files you create in this book will have the extensions .cs and .vb, but they will still be plain text.)

Visual Studio. NET (VS .NET) is also an excellent editor for the applications you'll be creating. VS .NET color-codes your code and provides context-sensitive features, such as pop-up boxes that complete sentences for you. In addition, VS .NET has numerous wizards that help you get on your way creating Windows Forms applications.

While there are many features in VS .NET that are of value to developers, this book won't focus on them—it concentrates on the Windows Forms technology, rather than on how to make VS .NET do certain tasks for you. After all, the best way to learn to program Windows Forms is to build them yourself, not rely on a graphical interface to build it for you. Once you've become comfortable writing source code yourself, though, you'll appreciate the features VS .NET provides even more.

In summary, use any editor that you are comfortable with—this book requires only Notepad.

Tip

In this book we'll create a new directory for each day's lessons, to keep things easy to find. For example, Day 2's files will be placed in c:\winforms\day2. So when you write your own code from the examples in this book (or you download the exercises from Sams Web site, www. samspublishing.com, you can create these directories and place the applicable files in them. Stick to this naming scheme, and you'll be able to follow along easily.

What Is .NET Windows Forms?

You may be wondering if the title for this section should be, "What *are* Windows Forms?" The answer is no, because Windows Forms is not a collection of forms used in Windows, but a single technology that helps you design Windows applications. This technology is the new platform from Microsoft for developing Windows applications, based on the .NET Framework.

Let's dissect the words Windows Forms. You already know what Windows is: an operating system that collects user input and performs tasks based on them. A form, then, is exactly like its paper-based namesake: something you fill out with information in order to accomplish something. A paper form can be used to obtain a passport, take a test, or apply for employment. A digital form is typically used for submitting information or interacting with an application.

If you've used the Internet at all, you've already seen digital forms many times. Many Web sites provide forms to collect information, often to register you for one service or another. You've probably filled out dozens if not hundreds of these forms. Figure 1.5 shows an example of a digital form.

The advantage of a digital form over a paper form is that a digital one can interact with you. As soon as you enter any information, the form can perform some processing or make other options available to you. The form reacts to your actions.

The Windows Forms technology is based on this exact idea. Windows Forms uses digital forms—interestingly enough called Windows Forms—to collect data. A Windows Form is a window onscreen that a user interacts with. It can be used to gather or display data, provide alerts, or any number of other functions. The point is that a Windows Form is a window that interacts with users. It's as simple as that. (Note that as we discuss Windows Forms, we'll often refer to the technology itself and the actual Windows Form window interchangeably. We can do so because the former is comprised mainly of the latter.)

FIGURE 1.5

A typical Web form has text fields and a button.

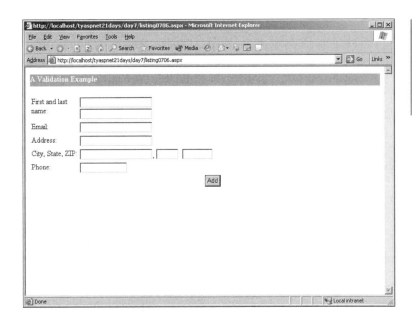

That description may give the impression that a Windows Form isn't very functional, but in reality it provides you with a lot of power and flexibility. Because Windows Forms technology is based on the .NET Framework, it has available to it a large library of useful objects and methods, allowing a Windows Form window to do just about anything you could possibly want.

Thus, a Windows Form may simply be an interface to interact with the user, but the technology behind the form delivers the power.

Integration with .NET

.NET and CLR provide a bevy of features to make developing applications much easier. As we discussed previously, garbage collection ensures that any unused or discarded resources that your application no longer needs are adequately disposed of and released for other applications to use.

Integration with .NET allows your Windows Forms to use the extensive .NET Framework class library. This library contains almost all the objects you'll ever need for your applications, pre-built and ready for you to use. Need a component that accesses databases? .NET has several for you to choose from. How about XML files? .NET has those, too. Part of learning to program with Windows Forms is to build your repertoire of these objects as large as possible—a factor that separates the novices from experts. And best of all, this framework is available no matter what programming language you choose.

Speaking of database access, with Windows Forms you have the power of ADO.NET, the next generation of ActiveX Data Objects. This evolution introduces many features that extend your application's reach and flexibility. You can access existing data sources or create your own, use disconnected data sets, read and write XML files, and more. You'll learn more about these features in Day 9, "Using ADO.NET."

.NET also has strong security measures built into the framework. These allow you to let the operating system know how secure your application is even before you execute it. It also can prevent unauthorized users from accessing your applications, and prevent authorized users from executing unauthorized applications (such as computer viruses).

Configuring and deploying your applications is also a snap. Configuration often only involves creating a single text file with the .config extension. Deployment simply means copying your files to the target computer—no need to register or install your applications. This is all possible due to CLR and metadata.

As the moniker ".NET" suggests, Windows Forms is also tightly integrated with the Internet and Web services. Web services are pieces of applications online that you can connect to in order to take advantage of their functionality, freeing you from having to build the functionality yourself.

GDI+ (the Graphical Device Interface) allows you to use Windows graphical capabilities to create visually interactive applications. With GDI+, you can color your applications, load and manipulate images, and even make windows transparent—but more on GDI+ in Day 13, "Creating Graphical Applications with GDI+."

We'll cover all of these features in the next 20 days, so by the time you've finished this book, you'll be an expert Windows Forms programmer.

Windows Forms Controls

A Windows Form by itself isn't very interactive. As you'll see in "Building Your First Application" later today, there's a limited number of things a user can do with just a form. Windows Forms controls (all of which are part of the .NET Framework class library) can greatly enhance your applications, by providing you with interactive objects, such as buttons, text fields, menus, status bars, and so on.

All Windows Forms controls work from a common architecture, which makes learning new ones very easy. Each control is completely controllable through properties it provides. And when there are no existing controls to suit your needs, you can easily create your own custom ones. Additionally, most common HTML controls have counterparts in Windows Forms.

You'll take a look at a few controls starting tomorrow, with in-depth study beginning in Day 4, "Adding Menus and Toolbars to Your Windows."

The Object-Oriented Way

The .NET Framework is completely object-oriented. So what does that mean? Object-oriented programming (OOP) is a programming paradigm that provides a logical way to develop your applications; it relates programming concepts to real life.

In true OOP, everything is an object, just like everything you interact with daily is an object (your car, your toaster, your chair—these are all objects). Every object has certain properties that make it what it is. For example, your car has a color property, a mileage property, a manufacturer property, and so on. All of these things can be used to describe and uniquely identify the object. Most things you deal with in OOP are objects. A Windows Form is an object, as is an ASP.NET page. These things have properties such as size, color, and name.

Objects also have methods, or actions. Your car has methods to start, to brake, to stop, to turn on the headlights, and so on. A Windows Form has methods to start, close, resize, change color, and many other actions.

Figure 1.6 shows examples of objects and some of their properties and methods.

FIGURE 1.6

A car has many properties and methods, as well as sub-objects, each with its own properties and methods.

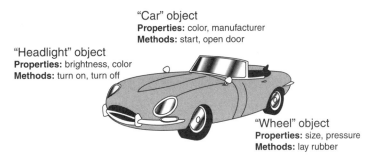

"Car" object
Properties: color, manufacturer
Methods: start, open door

"Headlight" object
Properties: brightness, color
Methods: turn on, turn off

"Wheel" object
Properties: size, pressure
Methods: lay rubber

In addition, you often have objects that are based upon the same underlying concept. Both cars and trucks are motor vehicles, but very different in the details. Sometimes you even have objects that are based on another object—the new Volkswagen Beetle is based on the original Beetle, for example. These are principles (known as interfaces and inheritance, respectively) in OOP as well, and they provide you with the flexibility to enhance your existing objects when one doesn't exactly meet your needs.

Windows Forms is based on OOP principles; every part of a Windows Forms application is an object, from the window you see to the buttons you click, the text fields you fill out, and even the time of day you use the application.

Even if you've never used OOP before, this should make a lot of sense to you, and you'll catch on quickly. As long as you think of everything as a self-contained object, you'll be fine. Since everything in .NET is an object, once you understand how to interact with one object, you'll know how to do so for all objects, simplifying your life as a developer.

We'll examine this topic more in Day 3, "Working with Your Windows Forms," after you've seen a few examples of the objects in Windows Forms.

Building Your First Application

It's time to start digging into some code! Enter the code from Listing 1.1 into Notepad, and save it as `c:\winforms\day1\helloworld.vb`.

> **Tip**
>
> Remember to set the Save as Type field in the Save window to All Files instead of `.txt` files. Otherwise, you may end up with a file called `helloworld.vb.txt`!

LISTING 1.1   Your First VB .NET Windows Forms Application

```
1:   Imports System
2:   Imports System.Windows.Forms
3:
4:   Public Class HelloWorld : Inherits Form
5:
6:       Public Shared Sub Main()
7:           Application.Run(New HelloWorld)
8:       End Sub
9:
10:      Public Sub New()
11:          Me.Text = "Hello World!"
12:      End Sub
13:
14:   End Class
```

ANALYSIS   Don't worry if you don't understand this code—you'll learn what this all means tomorrow (we'll also examine the C# source code tomorrow). For now, let's just take a quick overview. Lines 1 and 2 use special syntax to allow your application to use the `System` and `System.Windows.Forms` namespaces, or groups of objects (these are part of the .NET Framework class library). The `Imports` keyword references these namespaces for easier use. On line 4, you declare your class, or object. Lines 6–8 provide the starting point for your application, and lines 10–12 are a constructor. Finally, you end your class on line 14.

Much of this code is used to set up your application. The only actual custom execution done in this code is on line 11, which looks like it displays "Hello World!" somewhere in the application.

The next step is to compile your application into MSIL. Open a command prompt window (Start Menu, Programs, Accessories, Command Prompt), and navigate to the directory in which you saved this file. Type the following command into the window, and press Enter.

```
vbc /t:winexe /r:System.dll /r:System.Windows.Forms.dll helloworld.vb
```

Again, don't worry about the syntax now. Just know that this command compiles a VB .NET application into an executable MSIL file. You should see this output:

```
C:\winforms\day1>vbc /t:winexe /r:system.dll
[ic:ccc]/r:system.windows.forms.dll helloworld.vb
Microsoft (R) Visual Basic.NET Compiler version 7.00.9254
for Microsoft (R) .NET CLR version 1.00.2914.16
Copyright (C) Microsoft Corp 2001. All rights reserved.


C:\winforms\day1>
```

If no error messages are displayed, your application is ready to be executed! Type **helloworld** into the command prompt, and you should see the window in Figure 1.7.

FIGURE 1.7

Here's your first "Hello World" Windows Forms application.

This application isn't very functional yet, but notice the title bar. It says "Hello World!" Congratulations on building your first, albeit simple, Windows Forms application!

Tomorrow, you'll reexamine this code, and enhance it as well. In no time you'll be writing your own code.

Summary

Today was a short lesson to get you started with the .NET Framework and Windows Forms. These background topics needed to be discussed first so that code will make more sense to you when you delve into it.

Today you learned what an operating system is and how it interacts with your applications and user input. The .NET Framework is a new architecture for building Windows applications. With it, you can build an application using any programming language you want, all the while building from the same standardized architecture.

Common Language Runtime allows your applications to be compiled into Microsoft Intermediate Language rather than directly into an executable. MSIL contains metadata, which provides information about your application, such as version numbers and security data, to the CLR. Metadata frees you from having to register your applications with an operating system.

Windows Forms is part of .NET. It is a framework for building Windows applications that utilize the CLR. The advantage of Windows Forms over traditional Windows programming is the unified, object-oriented architecture that can take advantage of the .NET Framework class libraries.

Finally, from your first Windows Forms application, you learned that the source code is plain text that can be created in Notepad. It must be compiled to MSIL in order to be used; you did so using a command prompt compiler.

Tomorrow, we'll dissect the application you built today and enhance it with some Windows Forms controls. By the end of tomorrow's lesson, you'll understand all of the parts of a Windows Forms application, why you need them, and what they do for you.

Q&A

Q Can I really use any programming language I want to build Windows Forms?

A In theory, yes; but in practice, not exactly. You must have a compiler available that will compile your code into MSIL, and emit metadata. Currently, the languages that are capable of this are limited to C++, C#, and VB .NET, although development is underway for many other languages as well.

Q What is ASP.NET?

A ASP.NET is another facet of .NET; it allows you to create interactive Web pages and Web services. ASP.NET is very similar to Windows Forms—they share many of the same concepts and frameworks—but the former is used to build Internet applications, while the latter is for Windows applications.

Workshop

This workshop will help reinforce the concepts covered in today's lesson. It is very helpful to understand fully the answers before moving on. Answers to the quiz questions and the exercise are in Appendix A.

Quiz

1. True or false: Windows Forms is Win32 programming.

2. True or false: Metadata contains information about the environment in which an application was built.

3. How does MSIL allow cross-platform operation?

4. What is the next evolution of ActiveX Data Objects called?

5. True or false: You can create Windows Forms applications with any text editor you're comfortable with.

6. What is a Windows Forms control?

7. What does the `Imports` statement do?

Exercise

What would the following code do when compiled and executed?

```
1:  Imports System
2:  Imports System.Windows.Forms
3:
4:  Public Class MyApp : Inherits Form
5:
6:      Public Shared Sub Main()
7:          Application.Run(New MyApp)
8:      End Sub
9:
10:     Public Sub New()
11:         Me.Height = 100
12:         Me.Width = 50
13:     End Sub
14:
15: End Class
```

DAY 2

Building Windows Forms Applications

Now that you understand the basics, it's time to dive headfirst into building Windows Forms applications. In today's lesson, you'll take another look at yesterday's application and concentrate on the different elements of a Windows Forms application.

You'll also take a look at building Windows Forms with C#, the language many developers prefer for Windows Forms. You'll examine the differences in code between VB.NET and C#, and by the end of today's lesson you'll be able to easily translate one language to the other.

Today, you'll learn

- What classes, assemblies, and namespaces are
- How inheritance works
- How to use the Main method
- What constructors and destructors are
- How to compile your source code
- How to put everything together to make an application

Another Look at Your First Application

Before you dissect yesterday's code, let's recap a bit. First, you know that Windows Forms is a framework for building Windows applications. It is integrated with the .NET Framework, and as such, can take advantage of the Common Language Runtime (CLR) and the .NET Framework class library.

Windows Forms source code is just plain text that must be compiled into MSIL. CLR can then use a just-in-time (JIT) compiler to compile it again to machine code, which is then executed and managed by the CLR.

There are a few key concepts that will be useful to keep in mind as you examine and write code:

- The Windows Forms technology is object oriented, so everything you deal with is an object with properties and methods. Even the Windows Form you create is an object.
- The .NET class library also contains many objects that you'll use in your applications. In fact, some of these objects are required by Windows Forms.
- All Windows Forms and objects have standard formats.

Now let's take a look at the code. Listing 2.1 shows the code from yesterday's lesson, and Listing 2.2 shows the same code in C#. Because all Windows Forms applications use the same .NET Framework, the VB.NET and C# source codes are almost exactly the same, with some syntactical differences; all concepts in one apply to the other as well.

LISTING 2.1 Your First VB.NET Windows Forms Application

```
1:  Imports System
2:  Imports System.Windows.Forms
3:
4:  Public Class HelloWorld : Inherits Form
5:
6:      Public Shared Sub Main()
7:          Application.Run(New HelloWorld)
8:      End Sub
9:
10:     Public Sub New()
11:         Me.Text = "Hello World!"
12:     End Sub
13:
14: End Class
```

LISTING 2.2 Your First C# Windows Forms Application

```
 1:  using System;
 2:  using System.Windows.Forms;
 3:
 4:  public class HelloWorld : Form {
 5:
 6:      public static void Main() {
 7:          Application.Run(new HelloWorld());
 8:      }
 9:
10:      public HelloWorld() {
11:          this.Text = "Hello World!";
12:      }
13:
14:  }
```

Caution Note that C# is case-sensitive, so the code must be written exactly as shown in Listing 2.2, or you'll get errors.

We won't cover the code in depth here, but you'll notice several similarities. There are namespaces, classes, methods, and a Main method in both Listings 2.1 and 2.2. In the following sections, we'll address each of these concepts in detail.

Classes

If you've never used an OOP language before, the previous code may look strange to you. To start, let's look at line 4 in either Listing 2.1 or 2.2 because it contains the most important concepts. This line declares our class, called HelloWorld. A class is essentially the definition of an object; in the class you define custom properties and functionality that other objects may end up using.

Imagine a class as a blueprint for a house. The blueprint isn't exactly functional—you can't really do anything with it. However, it does define everything that the house needs to be—where the doors and light fixtures should go, the size of the rooms, the plumbing, and all the other inner workings of a house. A builder uses the blueprint to construct the actual house, which is a functional object; you can open and close doors, look at (and change) the color of the walls, and so on.

Like a blueprint, a class defines all the inner workings of an object. The builder in our case would be the CLR because it examines the blueprints and makes something useful out of them—an object or application. Thus, the users of your object can execute methods you've defined and examine available properties.

To summarize, you build a class that CLR turns into something useful. Whoever uses this object doesn't need to worry about how things inside it are defined, he just uses it—just like a user of a house generally doesn't need to know how the air conditioning unit or the plumbing works, as long as they do work.

NEW TERM This abstraction of complexity is known as *encapsulation*. With classes, you encapsulate the particulars and implementation details so that the user need not bother himself with it. As with the house, the user doesn't care how the functionality works, as long as it does.

Figure 2.1 illustrates this concept of encapsulation.

FIGURE 2.1

The CLR encapsulates your class blueprints into an object.

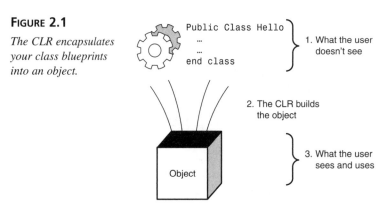

If this concept is still fuzzy, don't worry. As we examine this and other classes, you'll quickly gain a fundamental understanding. The words class and object are often used interchangeably, and as long as you know the difference—that is, that a class defines the inner workings of an object—then you'll be fine.

Going back to line 4, we still have two parts to examine. The `Public` keyword means that this class is accessible by other classes. Conversely, if you use the `Private` keyword, no other classes can see or use this class. We want this class to be public so that the CLR can make a useable object out of it. If it were not public, you would not be able to use your application. There are a few other keywords that can be used here, such as `Protected` and `Friend`, but we'll examine those as we need to use them.

The last part of line 4, `Inherits Form`, is something special to object oriented programming (the C# version does not use the `Inherits` keyword; it simply uses a colon). Remember that everything in .NET is an object (or class)? Well, there is also a class named `Form`. This class is the base class for all Windows Forms applications: it contains functionally that allows a form to display onscreen, to be closed, to move around and be resized, and so on. Thus, every Windows Forms application that you build must access this `Form` class (unless, of course, you want to rebuild all this functionality yourself, but why bother?).

The `Inherits` keyword tells the CLR that all properties and methods in the `Form` class should be added to our `HelloWorld` class automatically; the `HelloWorld` class *inherits* them from the `Form` class. Just like you inherited your blue or brown eyes from your parents, the `HelloWorld` class inherits the ability to display a window onscreen from its parent, `Form`.

The `Form` class, in turn, inherits from another class, `ContainerControl`, which inherits from the `Control` class, which inherits from the `Component` class, and on and on. At the very base is the `Object` class, the ancestor of all .NET classes. It contains properties that all other classes share in common, which means that if you know how to interact with an `Object`, you'll have an idea on how to interact with its descendants. Each descendant inherits things from all its predecessors.

Inheritance saves us from a lot of rewriting of code; after all, if it's already done, why reinvent the wheel? It also makes learning new classes easier. As long as you got along with its parents, you'll understand how to get along with it. We examine the `Form` class in more depth in Day 3, "Working with Your Windows Forms."

> **Tip**
>
> Now that you know something about classes, you should know that the `Form` class is also `Public`; otherwise your `HelloWorld` class wouldn't be able to access it! Only non-`Private` members of the `Form` class are inherited.
>
> Also, classes aren't the only things that can inherit; methods can as well, using the same syntax.

Classes and inheritance are two of the major concepts in OOP, and once you understand them, you'll have a much easier time with the rest of it. You'll learn more about these topics throughout the rest of the book.

Namespaces and Assemblies

 Lines 1 and 2 of Listing 2.1 contain another crucial element of Windows Forms applications: the `Imports` keyword (`using` in C#, as you can see in Listing 2.2). As you learned earlier, this keyword allows you to use collections of other classes in your application. These collections are called *namespaces*. They serve to group related classes together.

In line 1, the application imports the namespace `System`. Inside the `System` namespace are many, many objects and classes that your application uses, even though you may not know it. For example, the common data types `Integer` and `String` are part of the `System` namespace. Thus, if you are using any of these objects, it's a good idea to import the `System` namespace (a good idea certainly, but not necessary —you'll see why in a moment).

Line 2 imports the `System.Windows.Forms` namespace, which, as you may have guessed, contains the `Form` class. The `Forms` namespace is just one of many in the `Windows` namespace, and the `Windows` namespace, in turn, is just one of many in the `System` namespace. Namespaces are organized in this hierarchical fashion to make it more intuitive to use them, especially once you've understood the concepts of OOP.

A few of the more common namespaces are

- `System`
- `System.Data`
- `System.Drawing`
- `System.Net`
- `System.Security`
- `System.Web`
- `System.Web.UI`
- `System.Web.Services`
- `System.Windows`
- `System.Windows.Forms`
- `System.Xml`

Although the namespaces are grouped hierarchically, with one under another, it does not necessarily mean that one inherits anything from the one above it. Namespaces are different than classes; they are merely collections of objects, and are not built into any sort of useable object. Namespaces are used solely for organizational purposes.

You can easily create your own namespaces as well. At this early stage, it may not be necessary, but once you start creating complex applications that consist of more than one source code file, you may want to group them in a namespace. For example:

```
Namespace MyNamespace
   Public Class MyClass : Inherits Form
      'some more code
   End Class
End Namespace
```

The rest of your code stays exactly the same—you've just added a namespace around it. In this case, the namespace is called `MyNamespace`. You can even add to existing name-spaces if you want:

```
Namespace System.Windows.Forms
```

It all depends on how you want to group things.

Recall that we said that you don't need to import namespaces. What importing these namespaces does is allow you to use shortcuts further on in your code. For example, if you removed line 2 from Listing 2.1, you'd have to change line 4 from

```
Public Class HelloWorld: Inherits Form
```

to

```
Public Class HelloWorld: Inherits System.Windows.Forms.Form
```

In other words, you had to specify the entire namespace name for the `Form` class. The same goes for the `System` class; if you didn't import it, your data types would look like `System.Integer` instead of just `Integer`.

Do	Don't
Do: Import namespaces with the `Imports` keyword when you're going to be using classes contained within that namespace; it helps with organization and saves you time.	**Don't:** Rely on using the full namespace name for all your objects, even if you think it may help you distinguish classes—it clutters your code and makes it difficult to reference your object in the hierarchy. Occasional use is okay, but don't overdo it.

If you don't specify a namespace in your application, a default one is created for you. This default namespace, sometimes referred to as the global namespace, doesn't have an actual name, but is used to group those classes not explicitly declared in a namespace.

Namespaces are conceptual groupings of related classes, but they don't say much about the physical location of the classes. You could have several source code files located in different parts of your computer, but all belonging to the same namespace.

NEW TERM In order to consolidate multiple files and namespaces into a single location, we have *assemblies*. Assemblies are physical files on your computer that contain the classes you've built (typically with the `.dll` file extension). You can have multiple class-es or namespaces in a single assembly.

For example, in the `c:\Winnt\Microsoft.NET\Framework\`*version*`\` folder, you'll notice
the `system.dll` file. This assembly actually contains the namespaces `System`,
`System.CodeDom` (and its sub-namespaces), `System.ComponentModel`, `System.Net` (and
its sub-namespaces), and a few others. We'll examine how to use these assemblies later
today in "Compiling Your Windows Forms." Table 2.1 lists the various .NET assemblies
and the namespaces they contain.

TABLE 2.1   .NET Assemblies and Namespaces

Assembly	*Namespaces*
`Custommarshalers.dll`	`Runtime.InteropServices.CustomMarshalers`
`mscorlib.dll`	`Collections`, `Configuration.Assemblies`, `Diagnostics.SymbolStore`, `Globalization`, `IO`, `IO.IsolatedStorage`, `Reflection`, `Reflection.Emit`, `Resources`, all `Runtime.*` namespaces (except those in `CustomMarshalers.dll`, `System.Runtime.Remoting.dll`, and `System.Runtime.Serialization.Formatters.Soap.dll`), `Security`, `Security.Cryptography`, `Security.Cryptography.X509Certificates`, `Security.Permissions`, `Security.Policy`, `Security.Principal`, `Text`, `Threading`
`system.dll`	`System`, `CodeDom`, `CodeDom.Compiler`, `Collections.Specialized`, `ComponentModel`, `ComponentModel.Design`, `Configuration`, `Diagnostics`, `Net`, `Net.Sockets`, `Text.RegularExpressions`, `Timers`
`system.configuration.install.dll`	`Configuration.Install`
`system.data.dll`	`Data`, `Data.Common`, `Data.OleDb`, `Data.SqlClient`, `Data.SqlTypes`
`system.design.dll`	`ComponentModel.Design.Serialization`, `Web.UI.Design`, `Web.UI.Design.WebControls`, `Windows.Forms.Design`
`system.directoryservices.dll`	`DirectoryServices`
`system.drawing.dll`	`Drawing`,`Drawing.Drawing2D`, `Drawing.Imaging`, `Drawing.Printing`, `Drawing.Text`
`system.drawing.design.dll`	`Drawing.Design`
`system.enterpriseservices.dll`	`EnterpriseServices`, `System.EnterpriseServices.CompensatingResourceManager`
`system.management.dll`	`Management`, `Management.Instrumentation`

TABLE 2.1   continued

Assembly	Namespaces
system.messaging.dll	Messaging
system.runtime.remoting.dll	Runtime.Remoting.Channels, Runtime.Remoting.Channels.Http, Runtime.Remoting.Channels.Tcp, Runtime.Remoting.MetadataServices
	system.runtime.serialization.formatters.soap.dll Runtime.Serialization.Formatters.Soap
system.security	Security.Cryptography.Xml
system.serviceprocess.dll	ServiceProcess
system.web.dll	Web, Web.Caching, Web.Configuration, Web.Hosting, Web.Mail, Web.Security,Web.SessionState, Web.UI, Web.UI.HtmlControls, Web.UI.WebControls
system.web.services.dll	Web.Services, Web.Services.Configuration, Web.Services.Description, Web.Services.Discovery, Web.Services.Protocols
system.windows.forms.dll	Windows.Forms
system.xml.dll	Xml, Xml.Schema, Xml.Serialization, Xml.XPath, Xml.Xsl

(Unless otherwise specified, all namespaces are sub-namespaces to the System namespace.)

There are a lot of namespaces in Table 2.1, many of which you'll never use in this book. However, you may often need to know which assemblies they belong to in order to compile your applications.

Note

If you are familiar with previous forms of Windows programming, you may recognize the .dll extension that is used for dynamically linked libraries, which are similar to assemblies. They provided objects that could be used by other applications.

DLL files are used both in .NET and pre-.NET. Remember, though, that .NET .dll files are written in MSIL, and are completely object-oriented. Pre-.NET .dlls are neither and, unfortunately, there's no way to tell the difference from first glance.

Assemblies are not just used for grouping namespaces. They are an essential component of the .NET Framework because they provide the boundaries between applications that the CLR uses to enforce security, versioning, and metadata scopes. You'll be using assemblies very often when developing Windows Forms, as you'll see in the rest of today's lesson.

The Main Method

Let's look at lines 6, 7, and 8 in Listing 2.1 once again:

```
6:      Public Shared Sub Main()
7:          Application.Run(New HelloWorld)
8:      End Sub
```

If you know what methods are, then you're more than halfway to understanding this bit of code. A method is a piece of code that performs some function; it does something. Code that performs any function, from the simplest addition to the most complex threading routines, must always be placed in a method.

In VB.NET, there are two types of methods: Sub and Function A Sub does something, and then stops. A Function does something, and then sends some data back to whatever called it. (There is nothing stopping you from creating a Function that doesn't return anything, but the inverse is not possible; a Sub cannot return data.)

In C#, a method is a method. There is no distinction drawn on whether the method returns data. However, in C#, you do need to specify the type of data to be returned, or void if data is not to be returned. For example, line 6 of Listing 2.2

```
6:      public static void Main() {
```

says that this method returns nothing, while the following code line would return an integer:

```
6:      public static int Main() {
```

Here, you can automatically deduce a few things: you're declaring a void function (Sub in VB.NET), it is called Main, and it is public (Public in VB.NET), which means it can be accessed by other classes. The static (Shared) keyword is something new, and to understand it, we have to revisit objects and classes.

Object Instances

NEW TERM   From a single class (or blueprint) you can create multiple objects of that class. Each individual object is referred to as an *instance*. The car object—an actual, physical, useable item—would be an instance of the car concept, or class. You have one concept, but you can have many instances: a Ford Thunderbird, a Toyota Corolla, a Dodge Intrepid—these are all instances of a car. None of them are exactly alike, but they all share the fundamental concept of being a car.

For example, Figure 2.2 shows two instances of a "clock" object. Note that they don't display the same time, yet somehow, you know they are both clocks. Thus, you can have many instances of a concept, each with different properties.

FIGURE 2.2

Two instances of a clock object can have different properties.

Clock A: 1:27   Clock B: 9:54

The same can be said about OOP and objects. The class defines the theoretical concept of a `HelloWorld` object, but doesn't create any instances. It is left to other objects to create those instances when they are needed (more on that in the next section).

When you use the `Shared` or `static` keyword in front of a method, it means that the method or property is available to all instances of that object, and is the same for all instances. For example, let's say that all cars are made of metal, and for simplicity's sake, we'll assume the metal is the same for every car. This would be a `static` property; the type of metal does not change from one car to another. All cars also share the same concept of color, but the color is not the same for all cars; this would not be `static`. The keywords are self-descriptive: a single value or method can be `Shared` (VB.NET) by all objects (meaning each object does not have its own copy), or `static` (C#), which means they do not change from one instance to another.

The `Shared` and `static` concepts are somewhat common in the .NET Framework, so it's essential you gain a solid understanding of their meanings. For now, know that your `Main` method must always be `static` or `Shared`.

Your Code's Entry Point

The `Main` method is known as the entry point for your application. This means that whenever you start your program, the `Main` method is always the first thing that is executed. If your program doesn't have a `Main` method, it simply won't do anything (in fact, you'll probably get an error way before you can even try to execute it).

The Main method is also the last thing that executes. When your code is done executing, it always returns to this method.

This places a lot of responsibility on Main. Your entire program's code can be placed in the Main method, or, Main can call other methods. From Main, you can determine which form to display (many applications can contain more than one Windows Form object), set up variables that will be used by the rest of your application, or perform any other preparation work.

In our Main method, we execute one line of code:

```
Application.Run(New HelloWorld)
```

NEW TERM   This line calls the Run method of the Application object (part of the System.Windows.Forms namespace). The Run method tells your application to enter a *message loop*. A message loop is essentially a program's way of waiting for input from the user—entering a message loop is almost always the start of your application from the user's perspective. We'll talk more about message loops tomorrow.

You give the Run method an instance of your HelloWorld object (note that we've moved from a class to an object now—the New keyword creates an object instance for you). This tells the Run method to display your form on screen for the user to interact with.

Wait a second. Why do we have to pass an instance of the HelloWorld class to HelloWorld class? Won't this end up in an infinite loop because the Main method will execute again, and pass a new instance, and so on?

Not exactly. To understand why not, you have to make the distinction between a class and an application. When a new instance of a class is created, nothing occurs (unless you've created a constructor, but we're getting ahead of ourselves). When the application starts, it looks for a Main method—it doesn't care where it finds the method or what class it is in, as long as it's there and inside any class. Main only gets executed once, when your application is started, and not ever again. In other words, Main is executed every time the application is started, but not every time the class is created. In fact, even though the Main method looks like any other method, any attempt to call it from elsewhere in your program results in an error, as shown in Figure 2.3.

FIGURE 2.3

An error occurs if you try to execute the Main method in your code.

So although line 7 of Listing 2.1

```
Application.Run(New HelloWorld)
```

creates a new instance of the `HelloWorld` class, the `Main` method will not execute again.

To further illustrate the separation between your `HelloWorld` class and the `Main` method, you could put the `Main` method in a completely different class, and it would still work, as shown in Listing 2.3. The key is that you need a `Main` method for an application, and it must be contained in a class—but the class you choose is arbitrary.

LISTING 2.3   The `Main` Method Can Go in Any Class

```
1:  Imports System
2:  Imports System.Windows.Forms
3:
4:  Public Class HelloWorld : Inherits Form
5:      Public Sub New()
6:          Me.Text = "Hello World!"
7:      End Sub
8:  End Class
9:
10: Public Class MyMainClass
11:     Public Shared Sub Main()
12:         Application.Run(New HelloWorld)
13:     End Sub
14: End Class
```

ANALYSIS   Listing 2.3 may make a little more sense because it clearly shows how the `Main` method and the Windows Form class are separate entities. The `Run` method on line 12 creates a new instance of your Windows Form class (`HelloWorld`), and causes it to display onscreen.

NEW TERM   The `New` (or `HelloWorld` in C#) method in the last part of Listing 2.3 is called a constructor. A *constructor* is a method that is executed when a new instance of a class is created. It has a "partner" method called a destructor. These two methods are discussed in the following section.

Constructors and Destructors

A constructor is normally used to initialize the instance, set up any variables that will be needed, and so on. In VB.NET, a constructor is always named `New`, as these lines (10–12) from Listing 2.3 show:

```
10:     Public Sub New()
11:         Me.Text = "Hello World!"
12:     End Sub
```

This makes sense; recall from Listing 2.1 (line 7) how you used `New` `classname`:

```
Application.Run(New HelloWorld)
```

This calls the `New` method. In C#, the constructor takes on the same name as the class itself, as these lines (10–12) from Listing 2.2 show:

```
public HelloWorld() {
    this.Text = "Hello World!";
}
```

The `Me` variable in Listing 2.1

```
11:        Me.Text = "Hello World!"
```

and `this` variable in Listing 2.2

```
11:        this.Text = "Hello World!";
```

are special keywords that refer to whatever object the code is in. In this case, they refer to the `HelloWorld` Windows Form object. This is an easy way to refer to the containing object. Line 11 in Listings 2.1 and 2.2 simply assigns the string "Hello World!" to the `Text` property of the `HelloWorld` class, which, as you've seen, sets the caption on the Windows Form.

A destructor, conversely, is called whenever an object of the class is disposed of. In VB.NET, this is done by setting the object equal to `Nothing`:

```
ObjHelloWorld = new HelloWorld()
objHelloWorld = Nothing
```

In C#, by setting the class to `null`:

```
HelloWorld objHelloWorld = new HelloWorld();
objHelloWorld = null;
```

In VB.NET, however, you cannot create a custom destructor—whenever you set your object to `Nothing`, VB.NET takes care of the disposal for you. C# allows you to define your own destructor, which is declared using the same name as the constructor, prefixed by a tilde (~):

```
~HelloWorld() {
    'do some processing
}
```

Inheriting Constructors

As a rule in OOP, a class's constructor must always call its parent's constructor. For example, the `HelloWorld` class inherits from the `Form` class. Therefore, your class must call the `Form` class's constructor. The `Form` class's constructor must call the constructor of its parent, ContainerControl, and so on until you reach the base of the family tree, Object. Let's examine why this is necessary.

Remember that when an object inherits from another (a parent), it inherits all the properties and methods of the other. Some of those methods and properties may depend on certain variables that must be initialized. For example, imagine a class that inherits a Color property, which sets the background color of the form. This property must be assigned an actual value before it can be used, or you'll get an error (after all, you can't set the color of your form to nothing). This Color property would be initialized in your parent class's constructor. Therefore, you must call the parent's constructor for the Color property to hold any meaning.

For another example, consider your eye color, which you inherited from one of your parents. For the sake of analogy, let's consider your conception to be your constructor. Your eye color is determined at conception, and for you to have inherited it from your parents, they both must have eye colors; your color depends on theirs, and their eye colors depended on their conceptions, which depended on their parents' conceptions, and on and on. Your eye color depends on your entire ancestry! The same applies for classes in OOP.

This reliance on parent classes tells us two things. First, many classes that inherit from others depend upon their parents for information. And second, it means you can write less initialization code in your constructor, because so much has already been done in your class's parents' constructors.

The call to your parent's constructor must be the first thing you do in your constructor. In VB.NET, this is done by calling the MyBase.New method; in C# by making your constructor execute the base() method:

```
'VB.NET
Public Sub New()
   MyBase.New
End Sub

'C#
public HelloWorld(): base() {
}
```

All the code you've written today (Listings 2.1, 2.2, and 2.3) is missing these calls, so why don't we get errors? If you only have one constructor in your class (you'll learn about multiple constructors in the next section), then the CLR automatically calls your parent's constructor for you. Thus, you can leave these lines out.

Overloading Constructors

Sometimes you may want to have more than one constructor. A useful example of this is
when you want to allow the user to be able to initialize your class in more than one way:
one requiring a value to be supplied for a variable, and one that doesn't require a value,
for instance. You can do this through a process called overloading. It's often easier to
understand this concept by first looking at code, so take a look at Listing 2.4.

LISTING 2.4   Overloading Constructors in C#

```
1:   using System;
2:   using System.Windows.Forms;
3:
4:   public class HelloWorld : Form {
5:
6:      public static void Main() {
7:         Application.Run(new HelloWorld());
8:      }
9:
10:     public HelloWorld(): this("Hello World!") {}
11:
12:     public HelloWorld(string strText): base() {
13:        this.Text = strText;
14:     }
15:
16:  }
```

ANALYSIS   Let's skip down to line 12 first. Here we see a constructor that takes a `string`
value for a parameter. The `Text` property of the form is set to this parameter on
line 13. Finally, this constructor calls the parent constructor, by invoking from the `base()`
method. Nothing new here.

On line 10, we see what at first appears to be another constructor. This one, however,
doesn't take any parameters, and doesn't contain any initialization code. Notice, however, the list after the colon. It calls `this`, which we know is a reference to the current
object, and passes in a string "Hello World!" What does this do?

Line 10 says that should this constructor be called, call the constructor on line 12 instead
and pass in "Hello World!" as the parameter. Execution then passes to line 12 and 13,
and the `Text` property is set to "Hello World!" Thus, you are effectively saying that the
`strText` parameter is optional; if one is not supplied, it uses the default string, "Hello
World!" Line 7, which calls a constructor, could now read either

```
Application.Run(new HelloWorld());
```

or

```
Application.Run(new HelloWorld("I love NY"));
```

The appropriate constructor is called depending on whether parameters were passed in. The constructor on line 10 could even perform its own initialization routines, and doesn't need to call the constructor on line 12 if you don't want it to.

In VB.NET, the syntax is a bit different, as shown in Listing 2.5.

LISTING 2.5   Overloading Constructors in VB.NET

```
 1:  Imports System
 2:  Imports System.Windows.Forms
 3:
 4:  Public Class HelloWorld : Inherits Form
 5:
 6:      Public Shared Sub Main()
 7:          Application.Run(New HelloWorld)
 8:      End Sub
 9:
10:      Public Sub New()
11:          Me.New("Hello World!")
12:      End Sub
13:
14:      Public Sub New(strText as String)
15:          Me.Text = strText
16:      End Sub
17:
18:  End Class
```

ANALYSIS   On line 11 you use the Me keyword and call the New method, supplying a default string. The concepts behind Listing 2.5 are identical to Listing 2.4.

Note   Note that it is not necessary for you to create a constructor at all. If you do not create one, then VB.NET (or C#) automatically creates one for you. This auto-generated one calls only the constructor of the parent class.

Constructors are not the only methods you can overload. In VB.NET, however, you need to put the Overloads keyword in front of any methods that are overloaded (aside from constructors, of course), before the Public keyword.

A Final Look at the Code

Now that you've examined every part of the source code, let's recap. Listing 2.1 is shown again in Listing 2.6.

LISTING 2.6   Your First VB.NET Windows Forms Application

```
1:  Imports System
2:  Imports System.Windows.Forms
3:
4:  Public Class HelloWorld : Inherits Form
5:
6:      Public Shared Sub Main()
7:          Application.Run(New HelloWorld)
8:      End Sub
9:
10:     Public Sub New()
11:         Me.Text = "Hello World!"
12:     End Sub
13:
14: End Class
```

ANALYSIS   Lines 1 and 2 define the namespaces that are imported into your application. Members of these namespaces are available to your application using their short names (in other words, Form instead of System.Windows.Forms.Form).

Line 4 declares your class and that it inherits from the Form class—the base class for all Windows Forms applications.

Line 6 starts the Main method, the entry point to your application. It calls the Run method, which causes the form to display on screen and wait for user input. You pass in a new instance of your class to tell it which form to display.

Lines 10–12 represent a constructor for the HelloWorld class. On line 11, you simply assign the string "Hello World!" to the Text property of your form, which causes the caption on the application to change.

Once you understand the fundamentals, you can see how simple this source code was. You now know all the necessary components to building Windows Forms, and can start building your own!

Compiling Your Windows Forms

The next step in building an executable Windows Forms application is to compile your source code into MSIL. This procedure varies depending on the programming language you're using, but all are very similar.

The easiest way to compile your code is to use Visual Studio.NET. VS.NET is an integrated development environment (IDE) that allows you to create all types of applications from a central location, no matter what programming language you use. Let's take a brief tour of this environment and examine how to write and compile your code.

Open VS.NET and open a new project by selecting New, Project from the File Menu. The New Project dialog, shown in Figure 2.4, appears.

FIGURE 2.4

The New Project dialog allows you to choose a VB.NET or C# application.

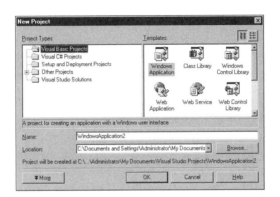

2

Use this dialog to choose a number of different options, both for C# and VB.NET. For now, just click on Visual Basic Projects in the left pane, and click Windows Application in the right pane. Choose an appropriate name and location for the project, and click OK.

When VS.NET finishes processing, a new project will be displayed in the solution explorer (right upper corner of the VS.NET application), with several files under it. First is a References folder that shows all the namespaces your application will use—note that when you expand this folder by clicking the plus sign, there are a few default references to namespaces already created for you. If you use the using or Imports statements with a namespace that isn't listed in the references folder, you'll need to add it by right-clicking on the folder and selecting Add Reference. A dialog will appear helping you to select an assembly. Next is AssemblyInfo.vb, used to provide information about your assembly. Finally, there is a file named Form1.vb, which is where all your code will go. Open this file by right-clicking on it and selecting View Code. Your window should look similar to Figure 2.5.

VS.NET comes with a very intuitive source code editor. It groups like items (such as classes), and allows you to hide them from view (by clicking on the minus signs to the left of the code) to prevent a cluttered environment. Also note that VS.NET created some code for you, shown under the Windows Form Designer generated code region. We won't cover the auto-generated code here, but if you glance through it, you'll see at least one method you recognize: the class's constructor. The rest of the code is necessary for VS.NET to integrate your application into the studio environment. (That doesn't mean you can't, however, delete the code if you want.)

FIGURE 2.5

Your empty Windows Forms application is displayed in the Solutions Explorer.

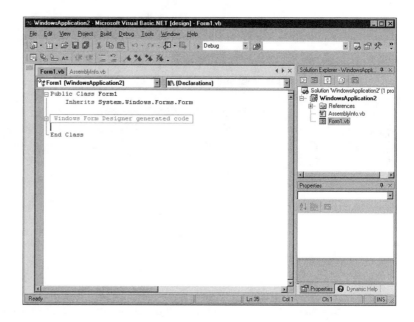

You can now insert your code anywhere between the `Public Class` and `End Class` lines, or even modify the name of the class. The properties box in the lower right window allows you to customize the saved filename, the author's name, and other attributes.

Once you've written the code, select Build from the Build menu to create your application. If there are any errors in your code, they'll be displayed in an Output window. If all is successful, VS.NET creates an `.exe` file (the name of the file depends on what you've named your project) that you can execute like any other application.

VS.NET provides a lot of features that aren't covered here. Feel free to explore the environment and use it to write your code.

If you prefer not to use VS.NET or don't have access to it, you can compile your code using the command-line compilers. These are simple executable programs that take a few parameters (including your source code file) and spit out a compiled `.exe` executable file.

The compiler command to use is either `vbc.exe` (for VB.NET source code), or `csc.exe` (for C# source code). The syntax for both methods is the same, so we'll only examine the first here:

```
vbc options source code file
```

At its simplest, your command would look like:

```
vbc helloworld.vb
```

Table 2.2 lists the common command-line options available to you. Type **vbc** **/?** or **csc** **/?** at the command line to view all the options.

TABLE 2.2 Common Command-Line Compiler Options

Option	Description
@	Specifies a text file that contains the options to use for the command. You must supply a filename: `@filename`.
/bugreport	Creates a bug report file. Must specify a filename: `/bugreport:filename`.
/debug	Emits various debugging information. Use: `/debug+` to emit information `/debug-` to emit no information `/debug:full` to emit all debugging info default) `/debug:pdbonly` to create the pdb symbols file only
/main	Specifies the class that contains the Main method. Use /m for short.
/nologo	Suppresses the Microsoft logo.
/optioncompare	Use binary or text to specify how all string comparisons in your code should be performed.
/optionexplicit	Requires explicit declaration of all variables before use. Use `/optionexplicit+` or `/optionexplicit-`.
/optionstrict	Enforces strict language semantics. Use `/optionstrict+` or `/optionstrict-`.
/out	Specifies the output location and name for your compiled MSIL file.
/reference	Specifies assemblies to reference in your application (those specified by the using or Imports keywords). Use /r for short.
/target	Specifies the type of output file to be generated. Use /t for short. Use: `/t:exe` for an executable console app `/t:library` for a DLL `/t:winexe` for a Windows executable app `/t:module` for a module
/win32icon	Specifies the icon (.ico file) to use for the applications icon.
/win32resource	Specifies resource files (.res files) to use.

2

For our applications, we'll typically only use two of the options: /target (/t) and
/reference (/r). For example, to compile the HelloWorld application, the target should
be winexe, and we must add references to the assemblies that will be needed (these are
determined by the namespaces we've imported). Looking back to our source code and
Table 2.1 (I told you that table would come in handy!), you see that we use the System
and System.Windows.Forms namespaces, which are located in the system.dll and
system.windows.forms.dll assemblies respectively. Thus, our final command looks
like:

```
vbc /t:winexe /r:system.dll /r:system.windows.forms.dll HelloWorld.vb
```

Tip

The compiler also allows you to combine multiple references into a single
list. For example:

```
vbc /t:winexe /r:system.dll,system.windows.forms.dll
➥HelloWorld.vb
```

Note

The mscorlib.dll assembly from Table 2.1 is automatically available to all
applications—it is the foundation assembly for .NET. Therefore, you don't
have to add an explicit reference to it.

Running in your command prompt, the command would generate the output shown in
Figure 2.6.

FIGURE 2.6

*Successful compilation
produces this result.*

Whatever way you choose to do it, compilation is a necessary step for your Windows
Forms applications. Throughout the rest of this book we'll be using the command-line
method unless otherwise specified. From the commands, you can easily determine which
references to add to your VS.NET project.

Building a Complete Application

Now that you have all the parts of a Windows Forms application under your belt, you can begin to build a functional application—something more useful than the "Hello World" program. In this section, we're going to build a simple calculator application that you'll enhance in Days 5, "Handling Events in Your Windows Forms" and 6, "Enhancing Your Windows Forms with More Controls."

To build a calculator, you need at least three things (in addition to your Windows Form):

- A place for the user to enter a number(s).
- A place for the user to see the result (possibly the same place as the first item).
- A button(s) that allows the user to perform a mathematical operation. To keep it simple, we'll only allow the addition operation in this application.

These components will be handled by Windows Forms controls—interactive UI (user interface) elements. You'll examine these controls in great detail beginning in Day 4, "Adding Menus and Toolbars to Your Windows," so we won't spend too much time on them here.

First, let's set up the basic frame for your application—this involves all pieces you learned about earlier today. Take a look at Listing 2.7 (the full C# source code will be shown later today).

LISTING 2.7   The Calculator Application Foundation

```
 1:  Imports System
 2:  Imports System.Windows.Forms
 3:
 4:  Namespace TYWinforms.Day2
 5:
 6:     Public Class Calculator : Inherits Form
 7:
 8:        Public Shared Sub Main()
 9:           Application.Run(New Calculator)
10:        End Sub
11:
12:        Public Sub New()
13:
14:        End Sub
15:
16:     End Class
17:
18:  End Namespace
```

ANALYSIS Save this code as `Listing2.7.vb`. There's nothing new with this listing. It is nearly identical to Listing 2.1, with the addition of a namespace declaration on line 4. This declaration tells the CLR that this class belongs to the `TYWinforms.Day2` namespace.

The `Calculator` class is declared on line 6, inheriting from the `System.Windows.Forms.Form` class. Lines 8–10 contain the `Main` method, and it simply calls the `Run` method, passing a new instance of the current class as a parameter. Lines 12–14 contain a constructor method, which is left blank for now—we'll add to it in a moment.

We need to use four Windows Forms controls in this application: two `TextBoxes` for the user to enter numbers, a `Label` to display the answer, and a `Button` to perform the addition. All of these controls belong to the `System.Windows.Forms` namespace, so you can use them just as you do the `Form` class. Add the following code on line 7 of your `Listing2.7.vb` file:

```
Private WithEvents btnAdd as Button
Private tbNumber1 as TextBox
Private tbNumber2 as TextBox
Private lblAnswer as Label
```

This section declares four variables as controls. The `WithEvents` keyword essentially means that a particular control can perform actions.

Next, Listing 2.8 shows the complete constructor method.

LISTING 2.8   Initializing Your Application

```
12:   Public Sub New()
13:       Me.btnAdd = New Button
14:       Me.tbNumber1 = New TextBox
15:       Me.tbNumber2 = New TextBox
16:       Me.lblAnswer = New Label
17:
18:       tbNumber1.Location = New Point(0,0)
19:       tbNumber2.Location = New Point(100,0)
20:
21:       btnAdd.Location = New Point(0,25)
22:       btnAdd.Text = "Add"
23:       AddHandler btnAdd.Click, new EventHandler(AddressOf Add)
24:
25:       lblAnswer.Location = New Point(0,75)
26:
27:       Me.Controls.Add(btnAdd)
28:       Me.Controls.Add(tbNumber1)
29:       Me.Controls.Add(tbNumber2)
```

LISTING 2.8   continued

```
30:      Me.Controls.Add(lblAnswer)
31:  End Sub
```

 ANALYSIS   Add this code into your `Listing2.7.vb` file. Again, we won't get into the specifics of each control here, but let's cover the basics. Lines 13–16 create new instances of each control.

Note

You may be wondering why lines 13–16 are necessary when we declared the variables earlier. The reason is because in the previous code snippet, we created variables, set their names, and told the CLR what type of variables they are. We did not, however, actually assign any values to those variables. This is what lines 13–16 do: they assign objects to the variables (as indicated by the equals signs). Creating any object (whether it be a control, a form, or any other object) is a two-step process: declaration of the variable and assignment of a value.

It is possible, however, to do both steps on one line:

```
dim btnAdd as Button = New Button
```

Or even simpler:

```
dim btnAdd as New Button
```

We'll be using this short version from now on.

Lines 18, 19, 21, and 25 all do the same thing: they set the locations for the controls on our Windows Form. The `Location` property takes a single parameter of type `Point` that describes the location where the control should be placed. The constructor for `Point`, in turn, takes two parameters (an x and a y coordinate). It is possible to place controls on top of each other, but that's often not very useful. We'll examine this topic in further detail tomorrow.

You should already know what line 22 does; it sets the `Text` property of the button to the word "Add." Recall that the `Text` property for the form sets a caption; the same property for a `Button` sets the text that will be displayed on the button.

Line 23 is something new. We'll learn exactly what it means in Day 5. For now, you should know that this line tells the CLR that when this button is clicked, the `Add` method (see Listing 2.9) should be executed.

Finally, lines 27–30 add each of the controls to your form. This step is necessary or the CLR won't know where to display the controls—they would simply exist in memory taking up valuable resources.

Listing 2.9 shows the final part of our code, the Add method. Place this code after line 31, but before the end of the class.

LISTING 2.9   Adding the Numbers

```
33:  Public Sub Add(ByVal Sender as Object, ByVal e as EventArgs)
34:      lblAnswer.Text = CStr(CInt(tbNumber1.Text) +
➥CInt(tbNumber2.Text))
35:  End Sub
```

ANALYSIS This method takes two parameters that we'll ignore for now—they aren't of any use for this simple application. Line 34 takes the values from the two textboxes (using their respective Text properties), adds them, and displays them in the label, using its Text property. The CStr and CInt functions convert user input into strings and integers respectively. This is necessary because the CLR doesn't know how to interpret user input values. For example, 9 could be interpreted as a number or string, so we must provide an explicit type. Line 34 performs the following steps:

1. Retrieves the values from the two textboxes
2. Converts those values into integers using CInt
3. Adds the two integers
4. Converts the result to a string for display in the label (a required step because the Text property always expects a string, and will balk at integers)

That's all there is to it. Save the combined code as calculator.vb in your c:\winforms\day2 directory, and compile it using VS.NET or the command-line command:

```
vbc /t:winexe /r:system.dll /r:system.windows.forms.dll
➥/r:system.drawing.dll Calculator.vb
```

This command uses the VB.NET compiler, spits out a Windows executable file, and references the system.dll, system.windows.forms.dll, and system.drawing.dll assemblies (these were determined using Table 2.1) to compile the application. Figure 2.7 shows an example output.

Listing 2.10 shows the same source code in C#.

FIGURE 2.7

The application successfully adds two numbers.

LISTING 2.10   A C# Calculator

```
 1: using System;
 2: using System.Windows.Forms;
 3: using System.Drawing;
 4:
 5: namespace TYWinforms.Day2 {
 6:
 7:    public class Calculator : Form {
 8:       private Button btnAdd;
 9:       private TextBox tbNumber1;
10:       private TextBox tbNumber2;
11:       private Label lblAnswer;
12:
13:       public static void Main() {
14:          Application.Run(new Calculator());
15:       }
16:
17:       public Calculator() {
18:          this.btnAdd = new Button();
19:          this.tbNumber1 = new TextBox();
20:          this.tbNumber2 = new TextBox();
21:          this.lblAnswer = new Label();
22:
23:          tbNumber1.Location = new Point(0,0);
24:          tbNumber2.Location = new Point(100,0);
25:
26:          btnAdd.Location = new Point(0,25);
27:          btnAdd.Text = "Add";
28:          btnAdd.Click += new EventHandler(this.Add);
29:
30:          lblAnswer.Location = new Point(0,75);
31:
32:          this.Controls.Add(btnAdd);
33:          this.Controls.Add(tbNumber1);
```

2

LISTING 2.10 continued

```
34:            this.Controls.Add(tbNumber2);
35:            this.Controls.Add(lblAnswer);
36:         }
37:
38:         public void Add(object Sender, EventArgs e) {
39:            lblAnswer.Text = Convert.ToString(Convert.ToInt32
40:               (tbNumber1.Text) + Convert.ToInt32(tbNumber2.Text));
41:         }
42:      }
43:   }
```

ANALYSIS Aside from the semantic differences from the VB.NET code, there are a few other things you need to know about. Everything is the same until line 28. Notice that you don't use the AddHandler method any more and that the WithEvents keyword is gone as well from line 8. C# has a different method to make objects perform actions, and we'll get to those in Chapter 5.

The only other difference is on lines 39 and 40. Instead of using the CStr and CInt functions to transform the data types, you use the Convert.ToString and Convert.ToInt32 methods.

Note

If you're familiar with C#, you may be wondering why we didn't just use the casting operator to convert data types (for example, (string) and (int) placed before the variable names: (int)tbNumber1.Text, and so on). This is because, in C#, you cannot implicitly or explicitly convert a string to any other base data type.

The System.Convert class, however, has all the necessary methods to convert any built-in data type to another (ToInt32, ToString, ToDouble, and so on).

The command to compile the code is the same except that you use the C# compiler instead:

```
csc /t:winexe /r:system.dll /r:system.windows.forms.dll
➥/r:system.drawing.dll Calculator.cs
```

Summary

Today was a very intensive lesson. By examining some simple source code, you learned a lot about the .NET framework and how it works, including classes, namespaces, assemblies, and methods.

Classes are blueprints for objects. In a class you define the properties, methods, and events that a user of an object can use. These exposed members are declared using the `public` keyword. Members you do not want exposed require the `private` keyword.

You also learned about class inheritance. One class can inherit from another to take advantage of the latter's functionality, saving you from rewriting code. All your Windows Forms classes will inherit from the `System.Windows.Forms.Form` class. Classes also have constructors and destructors—methods that initialize and dispose of the resources used by a class. In C#, the constructor shares the same name as the class itself, and the destructor is the same, but with a tilde in front of the name. VB.NET does not have destructors, and the constructor always uses the name `New`.

Namespaces are groupings of classes, and assemblies are physical files that group namespaces. Assemblies end in the `.dll` extension, and can be referenced from your applications using the `/r` option of the compiler.

The `Main` method is always the starting point for your application. It must be located in a class, but it does not matter which class. Typically, this method invokes the `Application.Run` method, which displays a form onscreen and waits for user input.

Finally, you learned how to put everything together by building a functional Windows Forms application. With this knowledge you can now identify nearly every part of a Windows Forms application as well as create your own.

Tomorrow we're going to focus on the `Form` object and learn how to control its various properties. We've only touched the tip of what this object can do—you'll be surprised at how much functionality this little object contains!

Q&A

Q Does importing namespaces incur additional overhead for my application?

A Not necessarily. The objects in imported namespaces are only loaded when needed, rather than all at once. So while using outside objects does utilize resources, it's only a very small amount.

Workshop

This workshop will help reinforce the concepts we've covered in today's lesson. It is very helpful to understand fully the answers before moving on. Answers can be found in Appendix A.

Quiz

1. What is the base class that all other classes inherit from?

2. What does the `Shared` or `static` keyword do?

3. True or false: You can extend existing namespaces with your own classes.

4. True or false: The `Main` method will execute every time a new instance of your class is created.

5. Why is the following code not sufficient? What else must be used?

   ```
   dim MyObject as Button
   ```

6. What is wrong with the following compilation command? (Hint: there may be more than one thing wrong with it.)

   ```
   csc /type:windowsexe /r:system.dll /r:system.drawing.dll
   /r:system.drawing.text.dll filename.vb
   ```

7. Infer the meaning of the following properties:

   ```
   Button.CanSelect
   ```

   ```
   Button.Cursor
   ```

   ```
   Form.AllowDrop
   ```

   ```
   Form.Visible
   ```

8. Name three differences in semantics between C# and VB.NET.

9. True or false: Every class must have a constructor.

Exercise

Expand on the calculator example from today's lesson. Add additional buttons to perform other arithmetic operations: subtraction, multiplication, and division. Try building the application in both C# and VB.NET. Also enhance the UI with liberal use of `Labels`.

DAY 3

Working with Your Windows Forms

In the first two days you learned quite a bit about the way Windows Forms applications work. You can identify and describe each part of a Windows Forms application, and how it works with .NET, and you can infer the usage from those you don't know.

Since you have the basics now on how to construct Windows Forms, it's time to get into the details. Today's lesson focuses on all aspects of the `System.Windows.Forms.Form` object, and shows you the multitude of ways that you can customize your applications.

Today you will learn

- How to use the `Object` object
- How to control a form's layout and appearance
- How to control interactivity in your forms
- What the message loop is and how it works with the CLR
- How to handle keyboard and mouse input
- How to make your forms work with drag-and-drop

The Object-Oriented Windows Form

If you haven't started thinking of your forms as objects yet, now is a good time to start. Imagine the Windows Form on your screen as an actual window in your house. You can change the color of the window, the opacity (how transparent the window is), the type of knobs and locks, curtain dressing, type of glass, and on and on. You can do virtually anything you want to your window (assuming you have the necessary resources).

The same statement can be said about Windows Forms. You know from yesterday's lesson that you can change the caption and size of a form. You can also change the title bar, the way objects inside the form are arranged, the color, the opacity and visibility, the borders, the buttons, and so on. Figure 3.1 shows just a few styles your form can take on.

FIGURE 3.1

Forms can be transparent, have no borders, and be resized.

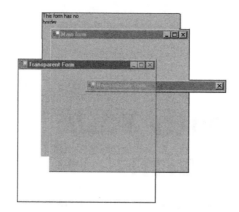

Thus, it is helpful to think of Windows Forms as generic objects that can be manipulated and customized however you want. You can go to the .NET Class Library "store" and pick out a `Form` object, and then tailor it as you see fit.

Working with the `Object` Object

You worked with a few objects in Days 1 and 2, but you haven't yet examined the `Object` object, the base class for all .NET classes, including Windows Forms. Because it is inherited by every class, you will deal it with from now on, so it's a good idea to learn a bit more about it—specifically, the methods it provides you.

`Object` is the most generic class you can use in .NET. As such, it is used to represent any otherwise unknown object. For example, if you use the following statement to create a variable, CLR doesn't know what type to create it as, and just creates an `Object`:

```
dim MyObjectVariable
```

Because your variable is just an Object, you lose a lot of functionality that you would gain from declaring an explicit data type. For example, you can add an integer to an integer, but you cannot add Objects together; doing so would result in an error no matter your intentions. Therefore it's a good idea to always declare a specific type, rather than using Object for everything.

 Note   By default, your applications must always declare a type for your variables to prevent misuse and increase performance. However, you can turn this safety feature off by disabling the Option Strict feature. See the "Compiling Your Windows Forms" section in Day 2 for more information on how to do this.

3

There are many functions you'll use in Windows Forms programming that create objects for you. For example, the ConfigurationSettings.GetConfig method retrieves configuration settings from a file. This function returns an Object data type, because it doesn't know specifically what you're going to do with the returned results. By returning an Object, you are free to transform the results to any data type you want by casting, a process that transforms one data type into another. In C#, you cast a variable with the following:

```
myDataType myVariable;     //declare variable of myDataType
myVariable = (myDataType) ConfigurationSettings.GetConfig
➥("some setting"); //retrieve settings and cast to myDataType
```

There are five key methods of the Object object: Equals, ReferenceEquals, GetHashCode, GetType, and ToString. These all come in handy, so let's cover them individually. Remember that every object inherits from Object, so these methods are available to every object you use.

The Equals method is both a static and non-static member. This means that you can call it from either a specific instance of an object, or from the Object type itself. For example, Listing 3.1 shows a snippet using both static and non-static versions of the Equals method.

LISTING 3.1   Using the Equals Method

```
1:  int intA;
2:  int intB;
3:
4:  intA = 4;
5:  intB = 5;
6:
```

LISTING 3.1   continued

```
7:  Console.WriteLine("{0}", intA.Equals(intB));  //non-static method
8:
9:  Console.WriteLine("{0}", Object.Equals(intA, intB)); //static method
```

 Lines 7 and 9 will both print "False" to the command line because the intA and intB objects are not equal (intA is 4, and intB is 5). Line 7, however, calls the Equals method from an instance, while line 9 calls Equals from the Object class itself. There are many times you need to compare two objects, so this method will prove useful.

> **Tip**
>
> The Console.Writeline method prints a string to the command line. The first parameter is the string to be printed. A number in brackets means the method should refer to one of the additional supplied parameters: {0} means print the next parameter, {1} means print the parameter after that, and so on. You could also simply use the parameter in place of the numeric identifiers.
>
> To use this method, you must compile your application as a regular executable file (use the /t:exe option when compiling).

The ReferenceEquals method is a static-only member that is similar to the Equals method. The difference is that ReferenceEquals compares two objects to see if they are the same *instance*, rather than the same value. This can be done because an instance in computer terms is defined by a location in memory. Therefore, two objects that point to the same memory location are the same instance. Two different memory locations can have the same value, but they are not the same instance. (Note that null—or Nothing in VB.NET—always equals the same instance as another null.) Take a look at Listing 3.2, which compares different variables.

LISTING 3.2   Comparing References

```
1:  object a = null;
2:  object b = null;
3:  object c = new Object();
4:
5:  Console.WriteLine(Object.ReferenceEquals(a, b));
6:  Console.WriteLine(Object.ReferenceEquals(a, c));
7:  a = c;
8:  Console.WriteLine(Object.ReferenceEquals(a, c));
```

ANALYSIS Line 5 returns `true`, because all `null` values equate to the same instance. Line 6 returns `false` because a and c are two different objects. Line 7 looks like it sets a and c to the same value, but when you do an assignment of one variable to another, you're actually setting the memory locations equal, and therefore, line 8 returns `true`.

> **Note**
> If you have previous programming experience, you'll know where the name `ReferenceEquals` comes from: this method compares the variables' memory locations (or references) rather than simply their values.

Most often, the `Equals` method suffices, but it is useful to have the `ReferenceEquals` method around as well.

The next three methods are all non-static. `GetHashCode` returns a hash code for your object. A hash code is a numeric representation of an object; it doesn't actually hold any meaning. Objects A and B may be different objects but generate the same hash code, for example, the number 7. However, you cannot reverse the process and go from the number 7 to an object. Thus, hashing is a one-way mechanism.

`GetType`, as the name implies, simply returns the specific data type of an object. This is very useful when you don't know what kind of data you're dealing with; for instance, when a function returns an unidentifiable object:

```
string a = "hi";
Console.WriteLine(a.GetType());
```

This snippet will return `System.String`, the data type of the variable a. Note that this method returns a *type* of data, rather than just the type's name. In other words, it returns a type, and not a string. This method is often used to compare data types. For example, using the `GetConfig` method discussed previously:

```
myType myVariable;
if (myVariable.GetType() != ConfigurationSettings.GetConfig
➥("my settings").GetType()) return false;
```

This code snippet tests whether the type returned by the `GetConfig` method (a `Type` object) is of the same type as `myVariable`. And in this case, it is not.

Finally, probably the most common method, `ToString`, returns a string representation of a variable's type. For example, the following code snippet would print "system.object" to the command line:

```
Object objA = new Object();
Console.WriteLine(objA.ToString());
```

Note that it does not print out an object's value, but the name of the type. Sometimes the `ToString` method is overridden for a particular class. The `string` data type, for instance, overrides `ToString` so that it prints out the actual value of the variable, rather than the name of the type. The following code prints out "hello world."

```
string strA = "hello world";
Console.WriteLine(strA.ToString());
```

Form Properties

The `System.Windows.Forms.Form` object has 101 properties (no exaggeration!) that let you control nearly every imaginable aspect of the form. That's too many to cover in just one day, so let's just look a few of the more useful ones here, grouping by function.

Controlling Size and Location

You already know two ways to control the size of your form: the `Width` and `Height` properties. These properties simply take numeric values to set the size of the form in pixels. For example:

```
form1.Width = 100
form1.Height = 200
```

You can also set the size using the `Size` property and a `Size` object:

```
form1.Size = New Size(100, Form1.Size.Height)
form1.Size = New Size(100, Form1.Size.Width)
```

Both methods do the same thing, but you'll typically use the first method because it's simpler.

You can set the size relative to the user's screen as well by using the `Screen` object. Listing 3.3 shows an example.

LISTING 3.3   Setting Form Height Based on Screen Size in VB.NET

```
1:  Imports System
2:  Imports System.Windows.Forms
3:
4:  Public Class MultiForm : Inherits Form
5:     Public Sub New()
6:        Me.Text = "Main form"
7:        Me.Height = Screen.GetWorkingArea(Me).Height / 2
8:     End Sub
9:  End Class
10:
11:  Public Class StartForm
12:     Public Shared Sub Main()
```

LISTING 3.3   continued

```
13:        Application.Run(New MultiForm)
14:    End Sub
15: End Class
```

ANALYSIS   This code should be familiar to you by now, so the only line we'll examine is line 7. The GetWorkingArea method of the Screen object returns a Rectangle object that represents the user's screen. You pass in the current form object (using the Me keyword) to tell the CLR which screen to use (this is just in case the user has more than one monitor). Rectangle objects in turn have Height and Width properties that return integers describing the height and width of the screen. We then divide the height value by two. Compile this application and run it; note that the window now takes up half the vertical height of your screen!

To control where the form pops up on the screen, you can use the Location, DesktopLocation, Top, or Left properties. The last two set the position of the upper left corner of your form to a location on the user's desktop. They work just like the Height and Width properties. Note that you can set these properties to some location way off the user's screen, such as Top = 9999 and Left = 9999, but that's generally not a good idea.

The Location and DesktopLocation properties are similar. For a Form object, they do the same thing: set the starting location for the top left corner of your form. For example, both of the following lines do the same thing:

```
Form1.DesktopLocation = New Point(100,300)
```

```
Form1.Location = New Point(100,300)
```

Location is a property inherited from the Form's great-grandparent class, Control. This property is used to set the location of a control within another control. In this case, the containing control for the form is simply the user's desktop. You could use the Location property for any other object that inherits from the Control object, such as the TextBox or Label controls, to set its location within another object, such as your form. The DesktopLocation property, however, only applies to the Form object. For consistency, we'll use the Location property from now on, so you only need to use one property for all Windows Forms objects.

Controlling Appearance

You already know about the Text property, which controls the text displayed in the form's title bar, so let's examine a few things you can do with font (the typeface in which the text appears).

3

The Font property sets the font that will be used on the form, unless otherwise overridden by a control's Font property. The ForeColor property then sets the color of that text. Take a look at the following code snippet:

```
Form1.Font = New Font(new FontFamily("Wingdings"), 23)
Form1.ForeColor = Color.Blue
```

The first line creates a new Font object (you're now beginning to see how *everything* in .NET is an object, even fonts and colors). There are quite a few different ways to create Font objects (in other words, it has many constructors), and this is just one method. You specify the font face by using the FontFamily object, which contains predefined font names. The second parameter is the size of the font. The second line sets the text color to blue, using the Blue property of the Color object. This code, when used in a Windows Form, produces the output shown in Figure 3.2 (you'll have to trust my word that the color is really blue).

FIGURE 3.2

Font face and colors are specified in properties.

The BackColor and BackgroundImage properties enable you to change the default appearance of the form. BackColor is used just like ForeColor:

```
Form1.BackColor = Color.LightSalmon
```

The BackgroundImage property takes an Image object as a parameter. Typically, you'll use the Image's FromFile method to load an image; you must provide a path name. For example:

```
Form1.BackgroundImage = Image.FromFile("c:\winforms\day3\coffee bean.bmp")
```

FromFile is a static method, as you've probably inferred since you don't have to create a new Image instance to use it. Using the form from Figure 3.2, we now have a tiled background, as shown in Figure 3.3.

FIGURE 3.3

You can use a graphic to tile a background in your form.

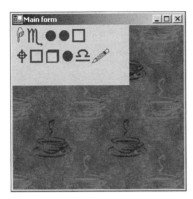

The background color of the `Label` is still gray, but you'll learn how to change that in Day 6, "Enhancing Your Windows Forms with More Controls."

Another image property you can customize is the `Icon` property. This icon is used in the upper left of your form's title bar, as well as in any other representation of your application, such as in the taskbar. Here's how you set this property:

```
Me.Icon = New Icon("c:\winforms\day3\VSProjectApplication.ico")
```

You must create a new instance of the `Icon` object, supplying a valid path to an image. The image you select must be an icon file (`.ico`) or your application will generate an error.

The mouse cursor image can be controlled via the `Cursor` property:

```
Me.Cursor = Cursors.Hand
```

The `Cursors` object has quite a few built-in properties for the default set of Windows cursors, such as `Arrow`, `IBeam`, `WaitCursor`, and `Help`. See the .NET Framework documentation for more cursors. You can also load a custom cursor from a file:

```
Me.Cursor = New Cursor("path name")
```

The cursor file must be a `.cur` file. Animated cursors (those with the `.ani` extension) are not supported by the CLR.

The `ShowInTaskBar` property determines if your application should be shown in the Windows taskbar (this doesn't affect the onscreen window, only the taskbar button). The default value is `true`. Occasionally you may want to change this to not allow a user to select your form. For example, if you create a "splash screen" that displays your company's logo, you probably don't want the user to be able to select it. Simply set the `ShowInTaskBar` property to `false`, and the user won't be able to select it from the taskbar.

The FormBorderStyle property represents the type of border around a Windows Form. The main reason you modify this property is to allow or disallow resizing of the form, although changing border styles sometimes also changes the form's appearance. For example:

```
Form1.FormBorderStyle = FormBorderStyle.Sizable
```

The FormBorderStyle enumeration (not to be confused with the Form.FormBorderStyle property) has several predefined styles to choose from, as shown in Table 3.1. (An enumeration is simply a collection of properties or styles.) Figure 3.4 shows a collection of the different styles.

FIGURE 3.4

There are seven prede-fined border styles available.

TABLE 3.1   FormBorderStyle Styles

Style	Description
Fixed3D	Non-resizable. 3D border around form.
FixedDialog	A thick border, non-resizable.
FixedSingle	Thin border, non-resizable.
FixedToolWindow	Form with a smaller title bar, useful for displaying ToolTips and Help windows. Non-resizable. Does not include minimize or maximize buttons.
None	No border and non-resizable.
Sizable	Resizable form. The default style.
SizableToolWindow	Form with a smaller title bar, useful for displaying ToolTips and Help windows. Resizable. Does not include minimize or maximize buttons.

Finally, there are three properties that control how, and if, your form is displayed on screen. First, the Visible property determines if your form is visible to the user. If a form is not visible, the user cannot interact with it. This is a good way to hide things from the user—if you want your application to stay open but don't want it interfering with the user's desktop, for example. By default, a form is not visible.

To make a form partially visible (in other words, transparent), you must set the Visible property to true, and use the Opacity property. This property takes a value from 1 (fully opaque—in other words, fully visible) to 0.0 (invisible). To perform some really interesting transparency techniques, you can use the TransparencyKey property to specify that only a certain color should be transparent. For example, the following code will make all gray areas on the form invisible, while everything else remains opaque:

```
Form1.TransparencyKey = Color.Gray
```

If you set the form's BackColor to gray as well, then you'll end up with a form like the one shown in Figure 3.5 (the form is placed over a command prompt window to show the effect of transparency.

FIGURE 3.5

Use the TransparencyKey property to make only a certain color invisible.

Controlling Interactivity

When you look at any Windows application, you'll notice that most of them have standard features: Minimize, Maximize, Close, and sometimes Help buttons in the upper right corner of the window, and a "gripper" on the bottom right to resize the form. These control boxes are shown in Figure 3.6.

Each of these control boxes can be hidden or shown on your forms with the following properties:

- MaximizeBox
- MinimizeBox

- HelpButton
- ControlBox
- SizeGripStyle

FIGURE 3.6

These control boxes are among standard Windows features.

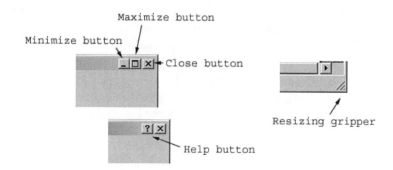

The first four properties simply take a `true` or `false` value. `ControlBox` determines whether the previous buttons should be shown at all. Be careful, though; if you set `ControlBox` to `false`, you may not be able to close your application!

 Note

The Help button appears only if the Maximize and Minimize buttons are not visible. This is a standard feature of .NET.

The `SizeGripStyle` property takes a `SizeGripStyle` enumeration value: `Auto`, `Hide`, or `Show`. `Auto` displays the sizing grip when necessary (in other words, depending on the `FormBorderStyle`), while `Hide` and `Show` prevent display of and display the sizing grips, respectively.

There are often two special keys associated with applications: the Enter key and the Esc (Escape) key. For example, many applications exit if you press the Esc key. You can control these functions with the `AcceptButton` and `CancelButton` properties. Listing 3.4 shows an example in C# of using these properties.

LISTING 3.4   The `AcceptButton` and `CancelButton` Properties

```
1:   using System;
2:   using System.Windows.Forms;
3:   using System.Drawing;
4:
5:   namespace TYWinForms.Day3 {
```

LISTING 3.4   continued

```
6:
7:     public class Listing34 : Form {
8:        Button btAccept = new Button();
9:        Button btCancel = new Button();
10:       Label lblMessage = new Label();
11:
12:       public Listing34() {
13:          lblMessage.Location = new Point(75,150);
14:          lblMessage.Width = 200;
15:
16:          btAccept.Location = new Point(100,25);
17:          btAccept.Text = "Accept";
18:          btAccept.Click += new EventHandler(this.AcceptIt);
19:
20:          btCancel.Location = new Point(100,100);
21:          btCancel.Text = "Cancel";
22:          btCancel.Click += new EventHandler(this.CancelIt);
23:
24:          this.AcceptButton = btAccept;
25:          this.CancelButton = btCancel;
26:          this.Text = "Accept and Cancel Button Example";
27:          this.Height = 200;
28:          this.Controls.Add(lblMessage);
29:          this.Controls.Add(btAccept);
30:          this.Controls.Add(btCancel);AcceptButton and
31:       }
32:
33:       public void AcceptIt(Object Sender, EventArgs e) {
34:          lblMessage.Text = "Accept button pressed";
35:       }
36:
37:       public void CancelIt(Object Sender, EventArgs e) {
38:          lblMessage.Text = "Cancel button pressed";
39:       }
40:    }
41:
42:    public class StartForm {
43:       public static void Main() {
44:          Application.Run(new Listing34());
45:       }
46:    }
47:
48: }
```

ANALYSIS   Much of this code should already look familiar, so we can just breeze through most of it. Lines 1–3 import the necessary namespaces. Line 5 declares the namespace this application belongs to; following our naming scheme, the namespace is TYWinForms.Day3. Line 6 declares the Windows Form class.

Lines 8–10 declare the controls we'll be using in our form. Note that these are declared outside of any method, but inside the class so that they can be used from every method in the class.

The constructor, beginning on line 12, is where most of the work takes place. The code on lines 13–22 simply sets a few properties for our controls. Take special note of lines 18 and 22, which point to methods that will be executed when either button on the form is clicked. These methods, AcceptIt and CancelIt, are on lines 33 and 37, and simply print a message in the Label control.

Lines 24–30 set some properties and add the controls to the form. Lines 24 and 25 set the AcceptButton and CancelButton properties to the accept and cancel buttons respectively. Essentially, this means that clicking the Accept and Cancel buttons with your mouse will do the same thing as pressing the Enter and Esc keys.

Finally, lines 42–46 contain another class that is used simply to hold our Main method and call the Application.Run method. The output of the application after pressing the Esc key is shown in AcceptButton and Figure 3.7.

Note

If the Cancel button on the form gets the focus, then pressing Enter causes that button to be pressed and, consequently, the CancelIt method to execute. In other words, the button receives the input before the form does. Unfortunately, there's no easy way to get around this. Some controls, such as the Button and RichTextBox controls, automatically handle the Enter key press when they have the focus, before anything else can execute. As a result, once you give the Cancel button focus (by clicking it, or tabbing to it), pressing the Enter key always causes the CancelIt method to execute.

If you're curious, you can override this behavior by overriding the Button control itself. We'll cover that in Day 18, "Building Custom Windows Forms Controls."

Note that although the AcceptButton and CancelButton properties need to point to Button controls, those Buttons do not have to necessarily be visible to the user. By setting their Visible properties to false, the buttons will be invisible, but you can still retain their functionality.

Finally, the AllowDrop property specifies whether the form can handle drag-and-drop functionality—that is, when a user drags some item into the form and releases it there. This property accepts a true or false value. We'll discuss how to make your forms actually do something when this event occurs in the "Form Events" section later today.

FIGURE 3.7

Pressing the Esc key has the same effect as clicking the Cancel button.

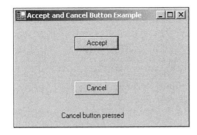

For a complete reference on the properties of the Form object, see Appendix B, "Windows Forms Controls."

Form Methods

The Form object has quite a few methods as well—57 of them to be precise. Most of them are inherited from the Object and Control classes, so they will be common to almost all the objects you work with in Windows Forms. Again, we'll cover a few of them here, grouped by category.

In addition to the methods discussed here, don't forget the Object methods such as Equals and ToString that we talked about earlier today. The Form object can take advantage of these as well.

Dealing with Display Issues

The first two methods you should learn are Show and Hide. These two functions make your form visible and invisible, respectively, by modifying the Visible property. These functions don't do anything to the form—such as removing it from memory or activating other functions—they only control what the user sees.

The Close method, on the other hand, completely gets rid of a form (and its controls), removing it from memory. Use this method when you want to close your application or simply when you don't need a form anymore.

Since Windows is a multitasking environment, you can have many windows open at once. Each window must compete for the user's attention. The Form object has a few methods that help you deal with this issue.

The Activate method "activates" your form. This can mean two different things:

1. If your application is the active one (the one the user happens to be using at the moment), Activate brings the form to the front of the screen, ensuring it is on top of all other forms.

2. If it is not the active application, the title bar and taskbar icon flash, grabbing the user's attention. More than likely you've seen this type of attention grabber before; the most common usage is for instant messaging applications. If someone sends you an instant message while you're working on another application, the IM window pops up in the background and flashes its title bar.

The BringToFront and SendToBack methods are more direct than Activate at getting a user's attention. The first method brings your form to the front of all other windows on screen, forcing the user to look at it. This is useful, for example, when something happens with your application that demands the user's attention (like getting an instant message popup). SendToBack, conversely, places your form behind all others on screen. SendToBack isn't used as often, but it's there just in case.

Tip

> You can set the TopMost property to true to have your form *always* stay on top of other windows. This is especially useful for forms that deliver error or warning messages.

Finally, the Refresh method works much like the Refresh button on your Web browser; it simply redraws everything on the form, updating if necessary. We'll talk more about this method when you deal with GDI+ in Day 13, "Creating Graphical Applications with GDI+."

Resetting Properties

The Form object has a series of reset methods that enable you to change modified properties back to their default values. All of these methods follow the naming scheme Reset*property*. A few of the more common ones are

- ResetBackColor
- ResetCursor
- ResetFont
- ResetForeColor
- ResetText

These methods are very convenient when you've modified something and need to go back, but don't know or don't care what the original value was. For example, if in a word processor the user changes the font several times, but then wants to go back to default values, you could use ResetFont.

Event Handling

An *event* is something that happens as a result of an action. Going back to the car object analogy, imagine that you press the brake (an action). The car stops (an event). If you press the gas pedal (an action), the car moves (an event). An event is always the effect of some action taking place.

Windows Forms have events too, although many of them may not seem very obvious. For example, open and close are two events that occur when you start and stop your application. When you move your mouse cursor into the form, an event takes place, and when your mouse cursor leaves the form, another event occurs. Without events, Windows Forms would be very bland because they would never do anything, no matter what the user tried.

In this section, we'll take a brief look at how events are handled with Windows Forms and .NET. You'll examine events in more detail, and learn how to take advantage of them, in Day 5, "Handling Events in Your Windows Forms."

3

The Message Loop

Events are wonderful ways of dealing with user input. Let's look at two different application models—one with events and one without events—before we examine how applications use events.

First, imagine an event-driven application. Event-driven means that the application responds to events caused by user actions. In fact, without these events, the application would do nothing. The events *drive* the application.

In this model, an application sits around and waits for things to happen. It uses events as its cues to perform actions. For example, a user presses a letter on the keyboard. The application sees that an event has occurred (the key being pressed), performs an action to display that letter on screen, and then waits for another event.

A non–event-driven application doesn't allow users free reign of the application—they can only respond to prompts from the application. With an event-driven application, users can interact with any part of the application they wanted, in any order or time they wanted.

Imagine a non–event-driven calculator application. When you start the application, it retrieves two values from textboxes, performs the mathematical calculations, and spits out the result. If there are no values in the textboxes, the calculator does nothing. The calculator cannot detect when a number has changed because it isn't aware of events. Anytime you want to change the numbers to calculate a different value, you have to change the numbers first, and then run the application again.

Classic Active Server Pages (in other words, prior to ASP.NET) also work in this way. An ASP application runs when a user requests the page from a browser, spits out the necessary HTML, and then stops. ASPs do not care what happens after that since they don't need to wait for any events. For the ASP application to deal with user input, a user has to enter all values into a Web form *before* posting it back to the ASP for processing. The ASP has no knowledge other than what is given to it at the start of execution. Figure 3.8 illustrates this process.

FIGURE 3.8

Non–event-driven applications involve a three-step process.

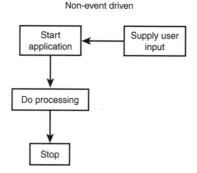

Both models have their advantages and disadvantages. Non-event driven applications, once started, can execute without user intervention. Event-driven applications typically require user input, but are often more interactive. Since interactivity is a must with any Windows-based application, all your programs will use the event-driven model.

NEW TERM So how does an application detect events? When a typical Windows application starts, it enters a *message loop*. A message loop is simply a period of time when the application is waiting for input, or messages from the user. This period continues until the application quits, so it is known as a loop. During this loop, the application does nothing except wait for user input (the period of non-activity is known is idling). When some input is received, the application does some work, and then goes back into the message loop. This cycle continues over and over again until the application is closed.

 Note

When you provide some input, the Windows OS is the first stop for processing. Windows determines to what application the event applies, and sends it along to the application. These communications are known as *Windows messages*, hence, the name *message loop*.

For example, when you first open a Microsoft Word document, nothing happens; Word just idles, waiting for you to type. When you hit a key, an event occurs, a method is executed (to display the character onscreen), and Word goes back into the message loop waiting for more input. Every time you press a key, the message loop stops for a moment to do some processing, and then continues the wait. Figure 3.9 illustrates this cycle.

FIGURE 3.9

The message loop waits for user input.

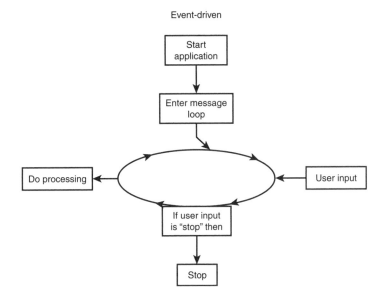

3

Windows Forms are typically the main user interface for your applications. Thus, they'll be dealing with quite a few different events.

Form Events

You've already seen how to handle a few events. In the calculator example from yesterday's lesson, you took advantage of the `Button` object's `Click` event. Handling events in Windows Forms, no matter what objects they belong to, is pretty much all the same.

In Day 5 we'll have an in-depth discussion about events, how to handle them, and the differences between various events. For now, though, let's take a look at a few of the 71 events of the `Form` object.

Controlling Execution

In order to give you, the developer, the most control over your applications, some events fire both before and after an action occurs. For example, when you close your form, the `Closing` event occurs immediately before the form begins to close, and the `Closed` event occurs immediately after.

> **Tip**
>
> These types of event names always follow the gerund/pluperfect grammar rules (using *ing* and *ed* suffixes—`Closing` and `Closed`). Not all events come in pairs like this. If you see an *ing* event name, though, you can be sure there's also an *ed* event as well, but not the other way around.

Why this two-event-per-action approach? Imagine a grocery store that closes at 10 p.m. Five minutes before the stores actually closes, a message is played over the intercom alerting customers to move to the checkout lanes. This pre-closing event is used to alert customers that something is about to occur. After 10 p.m., the store closes, all customers are kicked out (okay, so it's not a very friendly grocery store), and the doors are locked. This two-step approach allows both the store manager and customers to prepare for the actual closing event.

Windows applications are similar. For example, if a user makes a large number of changes to a word-processing document, and then closes the application using the Close control box but forgets to save the document, what would happen? If you waited for the `Closed` event to fire before doing anything, it would be too late; the document would have closed and all changes would be lost. With .NET, however, the `Closing` event fires before closing actually takes place. Here you can prompt the user to save her document before changes are lost, and conditionally save the changes. After the window closes, the `Closed` event fires, and then you can do whatever other processing you need to (display a message to the user, for instance).

Let's take a look at an example using this two-step process. Listing 3.5 uses the `Closing` and `Closed` events of the `Form` object to illustrate the previous example.

LISTING 3.5　Controlling Execution with Events in VB.NET

```
1:  Imports System
2:  Imports System.Windows.Forms
3:  Imports System.Drawing
4:  Imports System.ComponentModel
5:
6:  Namespace TYWinForms.Day3
7:
8:      public class Listing35 : Inherits Form
9:          public sub New()
10:             Me.Text = "Event Example"
11:             AddHandler Me.Closing, AddressOf Me.ClosingMsg
12:             AddHandler Me.Closed, AddressOf Me.ClosedMsg
13:         end sub
14:
```

LISTING 3.5   continued

```
15:        public sub ClosingMsg(Sender as Object, e as
➥CancelEventArgs)
16:            Microsoft.VisualBasic.MsgBox("Form closing")
17:        end sub
18:
19:        public sub ClosedMsg(Sender as Object, e as EventArgs)
20:            Microsoft.VisualBasic.MsgBox("Form closed")
21:        end sub
22:
23:     end class
24:
25:     public class StartForm
26:        public shared sub Main()
27:            Application.Run(new Listing35)
28:        end sub
29:     end class
30:
31:  End Namespace
```

ANALYSIS   On line 4 we import a namespace we haven't seen before:
System.ComponentModel. This namespace has objects that apply to events that
you'll need later in the code. Lines 6–10 are all standard fare. Lines 11 and 12 use the
AddHandler method (which you've seen in Days 1 and 2) to tell the CLR to execute the
ClosingMsg and ClosedMsg methods (on lines 15 and 19) when the Closing and Closed
events fire respectively. Let's skip down to line 15 and the ClosingMsg method, which is
executed when the Closing event fires and before the form actually closes.

First, look at the signature (the first line) of this method. It takes two parameters: an
Object and a System.ComponentModel.CancelEventArgs object. You already know what
the Object object is. The second parameter is a specialized object that applies only to
events, and only to Closing events in particular. It has a special property, Cancel, to
interrupt the process—the form's closing in this case—should that be necessary (like in
the word processor example discussed earlier). If you determine that the closing should
be stopped (if, for example, the user forgot to save her document), set the Cancel property to true:

```
e.Cancel = true
```

The application will stop closing and go back into the message loop.

In this case, we're not concerned about stopping the form from closing. On line 16, we
call a method to display a message to the user onscreen. The MsgBox method of the
Microsoft.VisualBasic simply presents a pop-up box to the user with the specified
text. (Note that instead of using the MsgBox method's full name on line 16, we could have
imported the Microsoft.VisualBasic namespace using Imports.)

The ClosedMsg method beginning on line 19 executes after the form has closed. Note that it takes an EventArgs object instead of CancelEventArgs for the second parameter. We'll discuss why in Day 5. This method again calls the MsgBox function to display another message, alerting the user that the form has already closed.

Finally, compile this code from VS.NET or with the following command:

```
vbc /t:winexe /r:system.dll /r:system.windows.forms.dll
➥/r:system.drawing.dll listing3.5.vb
```

Recall from Day 2 that the System.ComponentModel namespace is in the System.dll assembly, so we didn't need to reference any new assemblies here. Figure 3.10 shows the output after the Close control box is clicked.

FIGURE 3.10

The Closing event enables you to intercept the Closed event.

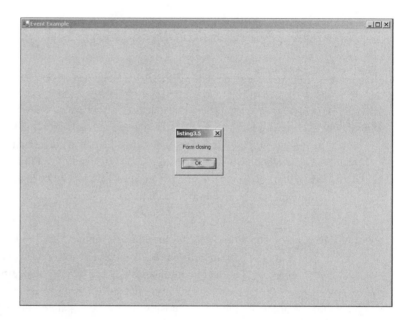

Not all events follow this two-step process, but a few of the Form object's do. Table 3.2 describes these.

TABLE 3.2   Events with Pre-Cursor Events

Event	Description
Closed	Occurs when a form closes
InputLanguageChanged	Occurs when the user attempts to change the language of the form
Validated	Occurs when the control's input is validated

There are a few important events that you should know about when dealing with Windows Forms. You've already learned about Closed, which fires when a form closes. There is also a Load event, which fires immediately before a form is displayed for the first time. The event handler for this event is often a good place to initialize components on your form that you haven't already initialized in the constructor.

The Activated event occurs when your form gains focus and becomes the active application—it corresponds to the Activate method. Deactivate, on the other hand, is fired when your form is deactivated, that is, when it loses focus or another application become the active one.

Mouse and Keyboard Events

Mouse and keyboard actions are one of the most important types of events—after all, those are typically the only forms of user input. As such, there are quite a few events that pertain to these two input devices. Let's begin with the keyboard events.

First is the KeyPress event. This occurs anytime a key is pressed, no matter what key it is (we'll see in a moment how to determine which key it was). If this event doesn't provide enough control, there are also the KeyDown and KeyUp events, which fire when a key is pressed down, and then released, respectively.

These events, due to their nature, provide additional information (such as the specific key that is pressed) that you can use in your application. As such, their event handlers (the methods that execute when the event is fired) are specialized. Declaring these handlers in VB.NET is the same process that you're used to:

```
'VB.NET
AddHandler Form1.KeyPress, AddressOf methodName
AddHandler Form1.KeyDown, AddressOf methodName
AddHandler Form1.KeyUp, AddressOf methodName
```

In C#, however, you need to take note of the specialized handlers. Instead of using EventHandler as you did on line 18 of Listing 3.4:

```
18:        btAccept.Click += new EventHandler(this.AcceptIt);
```

you need to use the KeyPressEventHandler and KeyEventHandler objects:

```
//C#
Form1.KeyPress += new KeyPressEventHandler(methodName)
Form1.KeyDown += new KeyEventHandler(methodName)
Form1.KeyUp += new KeyEventHandler(methodName)
```

Like the CancelEventArgs object, the KeyPressEventHandler and KeyEventHandler objects have special properties that aid your application in determining what action caused the event.

The `KeyPressEventHandler` has two properties: `Handled` and `KeyChar`. The first method is simply a `true` or `false` value indicating if your method has handled the key press (if it hasn't, the key press is sent to the Windows OS for processing). Most of the time you'll want to set this property to `true`, unless you specifically want the OS to process that specific key (for example, if you don't need to handle the PrintScrn button, pass it to the OS). `KeyChar` simply returns the key that was pressed. Listing 3.6 shows an example in VB.NET.

LISTING 3.6 Handling Key Presses

```
1:  Imports System
2:  Imports System.Windows.Forms
3:  Imports System.Drawing
4:  Imports System.ComponentModel
5:
6:  Namespace TYWinForms.Day3
7:
8:      public class Listing36 : Inherits Form
9:          public sub New()
10:             Me.Text = "Keypress Example"
11:             AddHandler Me.KeyPress, AddressOf Me.KeyPressed
12:         end sub
13:
14:         public sub KeyPressed(Sender as Object, e as
    KeyPressEventArgs)
15:             Microsoft.VisualBasic.MsgBox(e.KeyChar)
16:             e.Handled = True
17:         end sub
18:
19:         public shared sub Main()
20:             Application.Run(new Listing36)
21:         end sub
22:     end class
23:  End Namespace
```

On line 11, you see the event handler, `KeyPressed`, for the `KeyPress` event assigned to the event. On line 14 you declare the event handler. Note that it takes a `KeyPressEventArgs` object parameter—this name corresponds to the `KeyPressEventHandler` object discussed earlier. On line 15 you simply display the character pressed in a message box, and then set the `Handled` property to `true` on line 16. Figure 3.11 shows the output when the capital A key is pressed (Shift+a).

Note, however, that only character, numeric, and the Enter keys fire the `KeyPress` event. To handle other keys (such as Ctrl, Alt, and the F1–F12 function keys), you need to use the `KeyUp` and `KeyDown` events. Recall that these events use handlers of type

`KeyEventHandler`, so the second parameter of your event handler methods must be `KeyEventArgs`:

```
public sub KeyReleased(Sender as Object, e as KeyEventArgs)
    'some code
end sub
```

FIGURE 3.11

As long as your form has the focus, any key press executes the `KeyPressed` *method.*

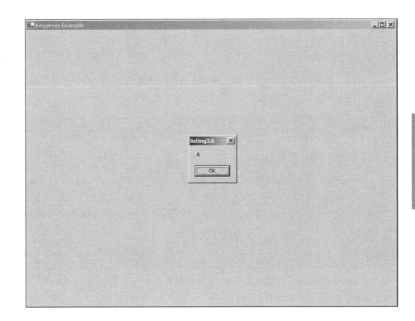

The `KeyEventArgs` object has several properties that are useful in determining which key was pressed:

- `Alt`—True or false value that indicates if the Alt key was pressed
- `Control`—Indicates if the Ctrl key was pressed
- `Handled`—Just like the `KeyPressEventArgs` object's `Handled` property
- `KeyCode`—The keyboard code for the key pressed
- `KeyData`—The key data for the key pressed
- `KeyValue`—The keyboard code for the key pressed
- `Modifiers`—Returns flags indicating which keys and modifiers (such as Shift, Ctrl, or Alt) were pressed
- `Shift`—Indicates if the shift key was pressed

Every key on the keyboard has unique `KeyCode`, `KeyData`, and `KeyValue` values. The `KeyCode` and `KeyValue` properties are typically the same. `KeyData` is the same as the other two for most keys, but different on modifier keys (see the Keys enumeration in the .NET Framework documentation for a complete reference).

Mouse events occur in a standard order:

1. MouseEnter—When the mouse cursor enters the form
2. MouseMove—When the mouse cursor moves over the form
3. MouseHover—When the cursor simply hovers over the form (without moving or clicking)
4. MouseDown—When you press a mouse button on the form
5. MouseUp—When you release the mouse button
6. MouseLeave—When the mouse cursor leaves the form (moves out from over the form)

The MouseEnter, MouseLeave, and MouseHover events don't provide any special information, and therefore use the standard EventHandler event handler and EventArgs event parameter objects. The MouseMove, MouseDown, and MouseUp events, however, provide special information, and all use the MouseEventHandler MouseEventArgs objects:

```
public sub MouseClick(Sender as Object, e as MouseEventHandler)
```

The MouseEventHandler object provides information such as the cursor's exact position onscreen, which button was clicked, and so on. The properties are summarized in Table 3.3.

TABLE 3.3 MouseEventHandler Properties

Property	Description
Button	Gets which mouse button was pressed (MouseButtons.Left, MouseButtons.Middle, MouseButtons.None, MouseButtons.Right, MouseButtons.XButton1, or MouseButtons.XButton2)
Clicks	The number of times the mouse was clicked (an integer value)
Delta	The number of detents (or rotational notches) the mouse wheel has moved
X	The x screen coordinate of the mouse cursor
Y	The y screen coordinate of the mouse cursor

Drag-and-Drop

Drag-and-drop, a feature introduced with Windows, allows users to take shortcuts with applications by dragging an icon on their computer onto an application. The application takes the file represented by that icon, and does some processing. For example, if you have Microsoft Word open and drag an icon of a Word document into it, Word automatically opens that document for editing. Drag-and-drop also allows you to move and copy files from one folder to another using just the mouse.

Making your Windows Forms applications take advantage of drag-and-drop is a simple process. First, you must set the DragDrop property of the form to true, and then write code for the DragDrop, DragEnter, DragLeave, or DragOver events. The DragEnter, DragLeave, and DragOver events are much like to the similarly named mouse events; they occur when an icon is moved into, out of, or over your form. All of these events use the DragEventHandler object handler, and the DragEventArgs event parameter. Let's take a look at the properties of this parameter.

The AllowedEffect property is an indicator telling you what drag-and-drop actions can take place. For example, if you try to drag and drop a read-only file, you only copy, not move, that file. The actions are indicated by the DragDropEffects enumeration: DragDropEffects.All, DragDropEffects.Copy, DragDropEffects.Link, DragDropEffects.Move, DragDropEffects.None, and DragDropEffects.Scroll. All of these effects correspond to simple Windows functions.

The DragEventArgs.Effect property, then, indicates the effect that is taking place. This is one of the DragDropEffects values listed previously. For example, if the user is dragging a file and holds down the Ctrl key, a copy operation will attempt to be performed, and the Effect property will indicate DragDropEffects.Copy.

The Data property contains the item that is being dragged-and-dropped. This item, whatever it may be, is represented by the IdataObject object, which can represent many different types of objects. See the .NET Framework documentation for more information.

The KeyState property tells you if the Shift, Ctrl, or Alt keys are pressed, just like the Alt, Control, and Shift properties of the KeyUp and KeyDown events.

Finally, the X and Y properties are the same as those for the mouse events; they indicate at which point an item was located at the time of the event.

Changing Events

Any time one of Form's properties changes, there's usually an event associated with it. For example, when you change the Text property of the form, the TextChanged event fires.

Most of the time, these types of events are used for validation routines. For instance, if you want to limit the available fonts for use with your form, you could create a handler for the FontChanged event that overrides invalid user choices.

I won't list all of these events here. You can determine them simply by adding the word "Changed" to each of the properties you learned about earlier today—TextChanged, CursorChanged, VisibleChanged, and so on. All of these methods use a handler of type EventHandler.

Summary

The base object for all other objects in the .NET Framework is, appropriately titled, the Object object. Because it is so generic, it is used in several places where a specialized object is either not needed or unable to be determined. Object has five methods— Equals, ReferenceEquals, GetHashCode, GetType, and ToString—that all other .NET objects inherit.

The System.Windows.Forms.Form object, derived indirectly from Object, is typically the main piece of your Windows Forms applications. It provides the frame and background for other user interface pieces, and it provides a lot of functionality by itself.

The Form object has 101 properties that enable you to control nearly every single visual aspect of the UI. You can make your form transparent with the Opacity property, make it non-resizable with the FormBorderStyle property, and control how the user can interact with the form by modifying the MaximizeBox, MinimizeBox, HelpButton, ControlBox, or SizeGripStyle properties.

Additionally, Form has many methods, such as BringToFront and Focus, that you can execute to control the display.

Finally, you learned about events and the message loop, which enables an application to sit idly by until a user provides some input. The Form object has events that fire for many user actions, including mouse clicks, key presses, and dragging-and-dropping.

Tomorrow you'll learn to enhance your Windows Forms by adding menus and toolbars— standard features on almost every commercial application—to your applications. Then in Day 5, you'll examine events in more detail, and make your menus and toolbars functional!

Q&A

Q Can I inherit from a form I created? How are properties dealt with?

A Absolutely, you can inherit from any class unless it is declared with the NotInheritable keyword (sealed in C#).

Dealing with inherited properties is often a complex issue. For example, look at the following code:

```
1:  Imports System
2:  Imports System.Windows.Forms
3:  Imports System.Drawing
4:
5:  Public Class ClassA : Inherits Form
6:      private lblMessage as New Label
7:
8:      Public Sub New()
9:          lblMessage.Location = new Point(100,100)
10:         lblMessage.Height = 100
11:         lblMessage.Width = 200
12:         lblMessage.Text = "Hello World!"
13:         Me.Controls.Add(lblMessage)
14:     End Sub
15: End Class
16:
17: Public Class ClassB : Inherits ClassA
18:     private lblMessage as New Label
19:
20:     Public Sub New()
21:         lblMessage.Location = new Point(100,100)
22:         lblMessage.Height = 100
23:         lblMessage.Width = 200
24:         Me.Controls.Add(lblMessage)
25:     End Sub
26: End Class
27:
28: Public Class StartForm
29:     Public Shared Sub Main()
30:         Application.Run(New ClassB)
31:     End Sub
32: End Class
```

When you compile and run this application, the form defined by ClassB will display. Note that nowhere in this class do you set the Text property of the label declared on line 18. However, when you run the application, the label contains the text "Hello World!" This text is set in ClassA on line 12.

This is not because the label from ClassB was inherited from ClassA, but rather because in ClassA's constructor, a label is created with the text in question, and added to the form. Recall that the first thing that occurs in any constructor is a call to its parent's constructor. Thus, by the time ClassB's constructor executes, there's already a label there with the words "Hello World!" You cannot, however, modify that label from ClassB because on line 6, it is declared as private, and therefore only accessible from ClassA. If you changed it to public, then you would receive an error because ClassB would have inherited the label lblMessage, and line 18 is trying to re-declare it—not a valid task.

The bottom line is to be careful when inheriting from your own classes, and pay attention to the security context in which variables are declared.

Workshop

This workshop will help reinforce the concepts covered in today's lesson. It is very helpful to understand fully the answers before moving on. Answers can be found in Appendix A.

Quiz

Questions 1–3 refer to the following code snippet:

```
1:  using System;
2:  using System.Windows.Forms;
3:  using System.Drawing;
4:
5:  public class MyForm : Form {
6:     private Label lblMessage = new Label();
7:
8:     public MyForm() {
9:        this.Text = "Hello World!";
10:    }
11: }
12:
13: public class StartForm {
14:    public static void Main() {
15:       Application.Run(new MyForm());
16:    }
17: }
```

1. What would the following statement return if placed after line 9?

   ```
   Console.Write(this.ToString());
   ```

2. What would the following code return if placed after line 9?

   ```
   Label lblTemp = new Label();
   Console.Write(lblTemp.Equals(this.lblMessage).ToString());
   ```

3. What would the following code return if placed after line 9?

   ```
   Label lblTemp = new Label();
   Console.Write(Object.ReferenceEquals(lblTemp, this.lblMessage)
   ➡.ToString());
   ```

4. True or false: The KeyPress event takes a handler of type KeyEventHandler.

5. What are the five properties of the MouseEventArg object?

6. Write a single statement in VB.NET that will set the width of a form to 1/3 of the height of the screen.

7. What property controls which button will be activated when the user presses the Escape key?

8. What is the default `FormBorderStyle`?

9. Which three events use the two-event for a single action paradigm?

Exercises

1. Build an application, in C#, that monitors all six of the mouse events. Display a message in a label when each of the events occurs.

2. Build an application in VB.NET that allows users to customize the `Text`, `Height`, `Width`, and `Opacity` properties by entering values in a `TextBox`, and pressing a Submit `Button`.

3

DAY 4

Adding Menus and Toolbars to Your Windows

By this time you should feel comfortable working with the Form object and creating Windows Forms applications. You've learned how to manipulate the user interface by adding a few controls such as the Label and TextBox, and by changing form properties. Now let's look at some more advanced controls.

Menus and toolbars are standard UI features—nearly every Windows application has them, and users know how to use them. Additionally, they give your applications a more finished and professional look. Today you'll see how to build these common UI elements and allow the user to interact with them.

Today you will learn

- What Windows Forms controls are
- How to add interactive menus to your forms
- How to make your application context-sensitive

- How to add toolbar buttons
- How to display information in status bars
- How to add scroll bars to your application

Introduction to Windows Forms Controls

You've worked with a few controls in Days 1–3, but you haven't really examined what a control is. Let's take a step back and look what controls are and why you use them.

A Windows Forms control, to the user, is a self-contained piece of the UI. Buttons, menus, and list boxes are all controls. Some, such as buttons, are interactive, while others, such as labels, are not. The user often doesn't care about the specifics of each control—he or she can just use them intuitively to get their work done.

Imagine a control as a clock. The user sees only the outside of the clock and therefore only external properties, including the color of the clock and the time. The user can push and pull the clock, and place things on top of the clock—the clock is a physical entity that can be manipulated.

The developer sees the clock (control) a bit differently, because he is able to open up the clock and mess with its innards, setting the time, winding the clock, changing the gears, setting the pendulum in motion, and so on. The "clock" still represents a piece of the UI, but it is also an object with properties, methods, and events. A control can be controlled just like the Form object. Each control is built from a class, just like the ones you've been creating, and inherits from other classes in the .NET Framework.

The clock, and Windows Forms controls, present two faces (see Figure 4.1): an exterior for the user, and a deeper interior for the developer. (In turn, there are even deeper faces. After all the manufacturer of the gears can control things the developer doesn't have access to—but you need not worry about those. This is part of the beauty of encapsulation with OOP.)

You know Forms, controls, and Objects are all objects that you can manipulate via properties and methods. Let's compare our favorite object, the Form, with form controls.

Forms and controls are very similar. They both inherit (directly or indirectly) from the Control class, which means they share many common properties and methods (ToString, Equals, and GetType, for instance). Since you know how to use the Form object, you know the basics of using all controls. Controls are stored in the System.Windows.Forms namespace as well.

FIGURE 4.1

A control provides an external face and an internal face.

Developer can work with innards

User sees exterior

The difference between a Form and a control is that a control must be contained within another component—typically, although not necessarily, a Form. Controls are the focus of a user's interaction—the background of an application (the blank Form area) is typically ignored by the user. Let's take a brief look at the types of controls (we'll examine many of these in more detail in Day 6, "Enhancing Your Windows Forms with More Controls"):

- **Container controls.** There are a few controls that are designed exclusively to hold other controls (hence the name container controls). These controls, such as the Panel control, group things not only for a cleaner UI presentation, but to make it easier for the developer to modify them. For example, when you add controls to a Panel, you can change their common properties with a single command, rather than having to issue one command for each control.

- **Button controls.** You've already worked with the Button control. This category also includes other controls such as CheckBox and RadioButton that may not seem like buttons but, in fact, behave as buttons. For example, a CheckBox (like those you use when filling out forms on the Internet) can be clicked, has an associated text message, and can perform an action when clicked, just like a regular Button. These are among the most common controls you'll use in Windows Forms.

- **List controls.** List controls are typically used to display data, often from databases. This category includes controls such as the ComboBox and ListBox. These controls are also one of the more complex types to work with, due to the nature of dealing with collections of data (that doesn't, however, mean that they're difficult to learn or use!). We'll skip detailed discussion on these until you learn how to work with data and databases in Day 9, "Using ADO.NET."

4

- **Menu controls.** Menus, along with buttons, are some of the most common controls in any application, from regular toolbar menus to context-sensitive menus. Much of the rest of this chapter is devoted to examining the way these controls work.

- **Other controls.** There are quite a few other controls not listed in the preceding categories, simply because they don't fit there. These include the `Label` control, date and time controls, and the `TreeView` control, among others. Just because they don't belong in a category, however, doesn't mean they're any less important. The `Label` control, as you've already seen, is one of the most commonly used controls.

Without further ado, let's learn how to build menus!

Adding Menus

We all know conceptually what menus are and how to use them, but let's recap a bit. A menu is a group of similar commands located in a bar located directly under the title bar in an application. The main menu heading typically serves only as a category grouping, and doesn't perform any functionality. The subitems are the worker bees of menus. Sometimes even subitems can serve as menus, further grouping commands into subcategories. Figure 4.2 shows a typical menu.

FIGURE 4.2

The File menu of Internet Explorer is a typical menu.

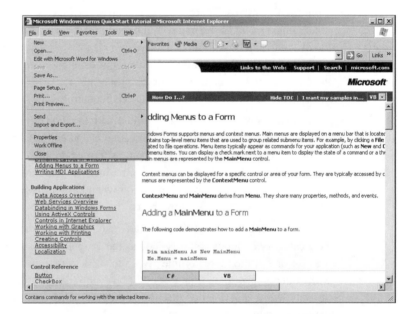

Note

In Figure 4.2, notice the horizontal lines separating groups of menu items in the File menu. These lines are called separator bars, and they help users navigate around application menus. You'll learn how to include separator bars in your menus in the "Customizing Menus" section later today.

In .NET, the menu headings are represented by the `MainMenu` object, while subitems are represented by `MenuItem` controls. These controls are similar to ones you've already worked with, so let's dive straight into some code. Listing 4.1 is your first foray into menu territory.

LISTING 4.1   Your First Menu Example in VB.NET

```
1:  Imports System
2:  Imports System.Windows.Forms
3:
4:  Namespace TYWinForms.Day4
5:
6:      public class Listing41 : Inherits Form
7:          private mnuFile as new MainMenu
8:          private lblMessage as new Label
9:
10:        public sub New()
11:            Me.Text = "Listing 4.1"
12:            Me.Menu = mnuFile
13:
14:            dim miFile as MenuItem = mnuFile.MenuItems.
➥Add("&File")
15:            miFile.MenuItems.Add(new MenuItem("&Open..."))
16:
17:            lblMessage.Text = "I love WinForms"
18:            lblMessage.Width = 200
19:            lblMessage.Height = 200
20:
21:            Me.Font = new System.Drawing.Font(new System.
➥Drawing.FontFamily("Arial"), 15)
22:            Me.Controls.Add(lblMessage)
23:        End Sub
24:
25:        public Shared Sub Main()
26:            Application.Run(new Listing41)
27:        end sub
28:    end class
29:
30:  End Namespace
```

4

ANALYSIS   Beginning on line 7, we create an instance of our first new object, `MainMenu`. As of line 7, there are no menus yet—we've just created the framework for adding menus by instantiating a `MainMenu` object. Adding the menus and commands comes later.

On line 12 you're introduced to a new property of the `Form` object: `Menu`. `Menu` must always point to a `MainMenu` object—specifically, the `MainMenu` that will be displayed on the form. By doing it this way, you can create as many menus as you like, and then switch the one that is displayed by simply modifying the `Menu` property.

On line 14 you see the first instance of the `MenuItem` object. This object is very versatile; it can represent any menu item, whether it's the top level or three levels down. You use the `MainMenu`'s `Add` method to add new `MenuItems` to the `MenuItems` collection. This `MenuItem` will represent the top level, or heading for one menu. In this case, we've named it "File," a typical menu used in applications.

> **Tip**
>
> The ampersand (&) in the menu name means that the character immediately following will be keyboard accessible. This is known as an *access key*. On line 14 the ampersand is followed by the letter F. Thus, the user can access the file menu with the keyboard shortcut Alt+F. You can only have one keyboard shortcut per menu item.
>
> You can also set the caption of a menu item after you've created it by using the `Text` property.

On line 15, you add a new `MenuItem` object to `MenuItem` object you created on line 14. Because this new object belongs to another `MenuItem` object instead of the `MainMenu` object, it will appear as an item in the menu rather than the menu heading. The new `MenuItem` is named Open.

That's all there is to it! Figure 4.3 shows the output from this code.

FIGURE 4.3

Listing 4.1 creates a File menu with one menu item, Open.

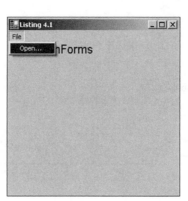

When you click on the menu item, nothing happens—that's because we still have to create a handler for this item. To do so, simply change line 15 to read

```
miFile.MenuItems.Add(new MenuItem("&Open...", new
➥EventHandler(AddressOf Me.Open_Clicked)))
```

or, in C#:

```
miFile.MenuItems.Add(new MenuItem("&Open...", new
➥EventHandler(this.Open_Clicked)));
```

And then create the Open_Clicked method. Place the following code somewhere between the end of the New method and the beginning of the Main method:

```
public sub Open_Clicked(Sender As Object, e as EventArgs)
   Microsoft.VisualBasic.MsgBox("Open menu clicked!")
end sub
```

Instead of using the familiar AddHandler method, just specify the method that should be executed on the menu selection as another parameter in the creation of the menu item (although you could use AddHandler if you wanted to). Figure 4.4 shows the modified output.

FIGURE 4.4

Adding handlers enable the menu items to be functional.

I told you that adding menus was easy! Let's take a look at one more example, this time creating submenus. Listing 4.2 shows the application in C#.

LISTING 4.2   An Extended Menu in C#

```
1:  using System;
2:  using System.Windows.Forms;
3:
4:  namespace TYWinForms.Day4 {
5:
```

LISTING 4.2 continued

```
6:      public class Listing42 : Form {
7:          private MainMenu mnuFile = new MainMenu();
8:          private Label lblMessage = new Label();
9:
10:         public Listing42() {
11:             this.Text = "Listing 4.2";
12:             this.Menu = mnuFile;
13:
14:             MenuItem miFile = mnuFile.MenuItems.Add("&Windows");
15:             miFile.MenuItems.Add(new MenuItem("&Forms"));
16:             miFile.MenuItems[0].MenuItems.Add(new
➥MenuItem("&Menus"));
17:             miFile.MenuItems[0].MenuItems[0].MenuItems.Add(new
➥MenuItem("&Are"));
18:             miFile.MenuItems[0].MenuItems[0].MenuItems.Add(new
➥MenuItem("As"));
19:             miFile.MenuItems[0].MenuItems[0].MenuItems[1].
➥MenuItems.Add(new MenuItem("&Easy"));
20:             miFile.MenuItems[0].MenuItems[0].MenuItems[1].
➥MenuItems.Add(new MenuItem("As pie"));
21:
22:         }
23:
24:         public static void Main() {
25:             Application.Run(new Listing42());
26:         }
27:     }
28:
29: }
```

ANALYSIS Listing 4.2 is the same as Listing 4.1 until line 14, where it starts to get interesting. Lines 14 and 15 add MenuItem objects to your MainMenu just as before. At this point, you have two levels: the menu heading (which we'll call Item A), and a single menu item, Windows (which will be called Item B).

Remember that the MenuItems property is a collection, which means you can reference each item in the collection by using an index number (0 is always the first member in the collection). On line 16, you access the first element in Item B's MenuItems collection, which itself is another MenuItem. We'll call this MenuItem Item C. You then add a new MenuItem to Item C just as you did for other menu items. Because you added this menu to Item C, it becomes another submenu. We now have three menu levels: Windows, Forms, and Menus.

> **Tip**
>
> To access a member of a collection in VB.NET, you need to use the `Item` property:
>
> ```
> miFile.MenuItems.Item(0).MenuItems.Add(new etc etc)
> ```

On line 17 you extend this concept a bit further. You access Item C's `MenuItems` collection, and add a new `MenuItem`, gaining you a fourth menu level. Line 18 does the same thing, adding another `MenuItem` to the fourth level.

Lines 19 and 20 keep the process going by adding submenus to the second item (as denoted by the index 1).

After all this we end up with five levels of menus, as shown in Figure 4.5.

FIGURE 4.5

Nesting menus makes for interesting code.

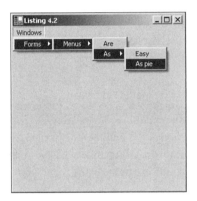

4

This process of nesting menus may be a bit confusing, but just remember that the first `MenuItem` you add to another `MenuItem` always creates a submenu.

You can also add submenus by explicitly creating a new `MenuItem` for each item in the menu. For example, examine the following code snippet:

```
MenuItem miFile = mnuFile.MenuItems.Add("&Windows");
MenuItem miForms = miFile.MenuItems.Add("&Forms");
MenuItem miMenus = miForms.MenuItems.Add("&Menus");
MenuItem miAre = miMenus.MenuItems.Add("Are");
...
```

The first line creates the menu header item as normal. The next menu item is created as a new `MenuItem`, and added to the previous level's `MenuItems` collection, just as you did for the menu header. Note that each subsequent line adds the new `MenuItem` to the previous line's `MenuItems` collection.

Both methods of creating menus are efficient at getting the job done. This second method, however, has a couple benefits: it creates a name for each menu item so that we can easily refer to it later if need be (rather than by using its index number); and the code is easier to read as well. In the end, the choice is yours.

Customizing Menus

Menus are highly customizable. You can group menus together, add visual enhancements and shortcuts, and so on. These tweaks often provide a better experience for the end user, so let's take a look at a few of them.

The easiest way to customize your menus is by grouping similar items together. The Internet Explorer File menu shown in Figure 4.2 illustrated how menu items can be grouped together; a separator bar divides one set of menu items from the next. Adding a separator bar is straightforward and a good way to help users navigate through your menus. Look at the following code snippet:

```
MenuItem miFile = mnuFile.MenuItems.Add("&File");
MenuItem miOpen = miFile.MenuItems.Add("&Open");
MenuItem miSave = miFile.MenuItems.Add("&Save");
miFile.MenuItems.Add("-");
MenuItem miExit = miFile.MenuItems.Add("Exit");
```

The first three lines add simple menu items to an existing `MainMenu` object. To add the separator bar, all you have to do is call the `Add` method, passing in a hyphen (-). The CLR understands this to mean you want to separate whatever menu items follow into a different grouping. This simple addition produces the menu shown in Figure 4.6.

FIGURE 4.6

Separator bars help organize your menus.

In addition to access keys, you can add shortcuts for your menu items as well. For example, Microsoft Word uses Ctrl+S as a shortcut to save documents, and most applications use the F1 function key as a shortcut to a Help menu item.

```
MenuItem.miOpen = miFile.MenuItems.Add("Open", this.Open_Clicked,
➥Shortcut.CtrlS)
```

The new third parameter that you see here is the `Shortcut` property. You can use the `Shortcut` enumeration to specify the shortcut you want. This enumeration has values for most keyboard combinations, such as `Ctrl`x where x is any number or character, `F`x where x is any number, `CtrlShift`x where x is any number or character, and so on. See the .NET documentation for full information.

If you don't want to specify the shortcut while creating a new `MenuItem`, you can do so afterward via the `MenuItem`'s `Shortcut` property:

```
miFile.Shortcut = Shortcut.ShiftF9
```

Set the `ShowShortcut` property to `true` if you want the associated shortcut key to appear in the menu next to the menu item:

```
MiFile.ShowShortcut = true
```

Finally, there are a few simple Boolean properties you can customize for each menu item:

- `Enabled` dictates whether the user can select the menu item (disabled items will appear grayed out).
- `Visible` indicates whether the user can see the item (note that even if a menu item is invisible, it can still be accessed via shortcut keys, so be sure to set both `Enabled` and `Visible` to `false` if you don't want users to see or select a menu item).
- `Checked` indicates whether there is a check next to the menu item. This is useful if, for example, you want to indicate that a menu item has been selected.
- `DefaultItem` indicates whether the menu item is the default choice (default items will appear in bold text).

See Appendix B, "Windows Forms Controls," for further information on `MenuItem` properties.

Context Menus

If you've right-clicked on a form, you'll know that nothing happens—no pop-up menu appears as they do in many Windows applications. This right-click pop-up menu, which often has context-sensitive menu items to choose from (for example, `Cut`, `Paste`, and so on), is known as a context menu. If you've spent time working with Windows applications, this menu is often indispensable to your productivity. Luckily, context menus are just as easy to add to your forms as regular menus are.

All context menus are represented by the ContextMenu object, which is very similar to the MainMenu object. In fact, menu items in the ContextMenu are represented by MenuItem objects, so everything you've learned so far applies to context menus as well.

The easiest way to create a context menu is to make a copy of the regular menu you've already made. This can be done with the CloneMenu method. For example, the following code creates a new ContextMenu object, and adds a copy of an existing menu:

```
ContextMenu mnuContext = new ContextMenu();
Form1.ContextMenu = mnuContext
MenuItem miContext = miFile.CloneMenu();
mnuContext.MenuItems.Add(miContext);
```

After adding this code to your form, a right-click on your form would produce a pop-up menu exactly the same as your File menu.

This example is the most simple context menu. But the reason they're called *context* menus is that the application can detect what part of the form the mouse cursor was on when you right-clicked and can provide a specialized menu for that spot. For instance, right-clicking over a blank area on the form can bring up the File menu, and right-clicking on a TextBox can bring up a specialized context menu with Cut and Paste options.

To provide this functionality, every Windows Forms control (including the Form object) has a ContextMenu property that specifies the menu that will pop up when the control is right-clicked, making it easy for you to greatly customize your context menus. Let's look at an example, shown in Listing 4.3.

LISTING 4.3   Customized Context Menus

```
 1:  using System;
 2:  using System.Windows.Forms;
 3:  using System.Drawing;
 4:
 5:  namespace TYWinForms.Day4 {
 6:
 7:      public class Listing43 : Form {
 8:          private MainMenu mnuFile = new MainMenu();
 9:          private ContextMenu ctmTextBox = new ContextMenu();
10:          private ContextMenu ctmLabel = new ContextMenu();
11:          private Label lblMessage = new Label();
12:          private TextBox tbMessage = new TextBox();
13:
14:          public Listing43() {
15:              this.Text = "Listing 4.3";
```

LISTING 4.3   continued

```
16:             this.Menu = mnuFile;
17:
18:             AddMenus();
19:
20:             lblMessage.Text = "I love Windows Forms";
21:             lblMessage.Location = new Point(100,75);
22:             lblMessage.Width = 150;
23:
24:             tbMessage.Text = "I love Windows Forms";
25:             tbMessage.Location = new Point(75,125);
26:             tbMessage.Width = 150;
27:
28:             this.Controls.Add(lblMessage);
29:             this.Controls.Add(tbMessage);
30:         }
31:
32:         public void AddMenus() {
33:             MenuItem miFile = mnuFile.MenuItems.Add("&File");
34:             MenuItem miOpen = miFile.MenuItems.Add("&Open");
35:             MenuItem miSave = miFile.MenuItems.Add("&Save");
36:             miFile.MenuItems.Add("-");
37:             MenuItem miExit = miFile.MenuItems.Add("Exit");
38:
39:             MenuItem ctiLabel = ctmLabel.MenuItems.Add
    ➥("Label menu");
40:             lblMessage.ContextMenu = ctmLabel;
41:
42:             MenuItem ctiTextBox = ctmTextBox.MenuItems.Add
    ➥ ("Textbox menu");
43:             tbMessage.ContextMenu = ctmTextBox;
44:         }
45:
46:         public static void Main() {
47:             Application.Run(new Listing43());
48:         }
49:     }
50: }
```

4

ANALYSIS   Lines 1–30 are nothing new. Note, though, that lines 9 and 10 instantiate ContextMenu objects; we'll use those in a moment. Line 18 calls the AddMenus method, which begins on line 32.

Lines 33–37 create a standard File menu for your application (you saw this code in Listing 4.2). Line 39 creates a new MenuItem for the ctmLabel ContextMenu object; its caption is "Label menu." On line 40, you assign this ContextMenu object (and thus its MenuItem child object) to the Label control. This context menu now applies only to that

Label (you could, however, also add this context menu to other controls if you wanted to).

Lines 42 and 43 do the same for the TextBox object, creating a menu item captioned "Textbox menu." Since nowhere do you assign a ContextMenu to the Form object, a right-click on the blank areas of the form will produce no pop-up menu.

This listing produces the output shown in Figure 4.7.

FIGURE 4.7

Right-clicking on the label displays the associated context menu.

In this example, right-clicking on the text box displays the "Textbox menu" menu. If you comment out lines 42 and 43 of Listing 4.3 and recompile, a right-click on the text box produces another context menu associated with it—one that provides options to copy and paste. This is because TextBox (and RichTextBox) controls already have default context menus, and by creating your own, you override the existing menus.

Adding Toolbars, Status Bars, and Scroll Bars

Toolbars, status bars, and scroll bars, like menus, are all familiar pieces of any Windows application. A toolbar is usually located at the top of an application window, just below the menu bar, and contains buttons with images that represent functionality in the application. For example, Word has an open-folder picture button to signify opening a file, and a floppy-disk picture button to save files. A status bar is located at the bottom of the application window, and provides processing information to the user; its only interactivity is to provide messages. Finally, scroll bars allow users to scroll through a form in case all of the controls don't fit in the existing window space. Figure 4.8 shows all three types of bars.

FIGURE **4.8**

You find toolbars, status bars, and scroll bars in most applications.

Despite the similar names, these three controls are very different when it comes to implementation. The toolbar acts as a single control (although it contains other controls) and is associated with an `ImageList` object, while the status bar acts as a container for other controls, much like a form. The scroll bar is an entirely different beast altogether, and doesn't have many custom properties. We'll take a look at each of these controls in turn.

Toolbars

A toolbar is collection of buttons (usually represented by images) that provide shortcuts to the functionality of your application. You've most likely worked with toolbars for a long time, so we won't spend much time examining the conceptual details.

The toolbar and its buttons are represented by the `ToolBar` and `ToolBarButton` objects. These two objects behave very much like the `MainMenu` and `MenuItem` objects; you create and add the latter object to the former object. Let's take a look at Listing 4.4, which shows some code that creates a simple toolbar.

LISTING 4.4   Adding a Simple Toolbar

```
1:  using System;
2:  using System.Windows.Forms;
3:
4:  namespace TYWinForms.Day4 {
5:
6:      public class Listing44 : Form {
7:          private ToolBar tlbStandard = new ToolBar();
8:
9:          public Listing44() {
10:             ToolBarButton tbbOpen = new ToolBarButton();
```

LISTING 4.4   continued

```
11:             tbbOpen.Text = "Open";
12:
13:             tlbStandard.Buttons.Add(tbbOpen);
14:
15:             this.Controls.Add(tlbStandard);
16:         }
17:
18:         public static void Main() {
19:             Application.Run(new Listing44());
20:         }
21:     }
22: }
```

ANALYSIS On line 7 you create a new ToolBar object just as you created the MainMenu object. Then on line 15 you add it to your form like any other control. On line 10 you create a new ToolBarButton control—this will be what the user is able to click on. On line 11 you set the Text property to display the word "Open" (you'll see in a moment that this Text property isn't exactly what you may think it is). Finally, you add the ToolBarButton control to your ToolBar object. Without this step, your toolbar would be empty and collapse in on itself.

Compile and execute this application. The result should be similar to what's shown in Figure 4.9.

FIGURE 4.9

Listing 4.4 produces a simple toolbar with one button.

We now have a toolbar button, but there are a few things missing or wrong. First, the text seems to be off-center. Second, there is no image associated with the button. And finally, nothing happens when you click the button. These are all easy things to fix.

First, the Text property isn't exactly what we're used to. For example, the Text property on a Button displays a caption in the center of the button. The Text property for the ToolBarButton, however, is used to supplement the button's image (think of the Back button in Internet Explorer). That's why our caption appears off-center; it's leaving room for an image.

Second, to add an image to the button, we need to learn about a new object, ImageList. ImageList is used mainly by other controls, such as the ToolBar control, to associate images to a collection of some sort (such as ToolBarButtons). ImageList has methods to add, remove, and reorder the images it contains.

After you've added images to an ImageList (which you'll see in a moment), the buttons in a toolbar will reference the images through their ImageIndex property. For example:

```
MyToolbar.ImageList = myImageList;
MyToolbarButton.ImageIndex = 1;
```

Let's use a new method, AddToolbar, to handle the creation of your toolbar. Replace lines 10–13 in Listing 4.4 with a call to this method:

```
AddToolbar();
```

And then add the code shown in Listing 4.5 to your application between the constructor and the Main method.

LISTING 4.5 Associating Images with Toolbar Buttons

```
1:   private ImageList ilstToolbar = new ImageList();
2:
3:   public void AddToolbar() {
4:      ilstToolbar.Images.Add(Image.FromFile("i_open.bmp"));
5:      ilstToolbar.Images.Add(Image.FromFile("i_maximize.bmp"));
6:      ilstToolbar.Images.Add(Image.FromFile("i_happy.bmp"));
7:
8:      ToolBarButton tbbOpen = new ToolBarButton();
9:      tbbOpen.ImageIndex = 0;
10:      tbbOpen.Text = "Open";
11:
12:      ToolBarButton tbbMaximize = new ToolBarButton();
13:      tbbMaximize.ImageIndex = 1;
14:      tbbMaximize.Text = "Maximize";
15:
16:      ToolBarButton tbbHappy = new ToolBarButton();
17:      tbbHappy.ImageIndex = 2;
18:      tbbHappy.Text = "Get happy!";
19:
20:      tlbStandard.ImageList = ilstToolbar;
21:      tlbStandard.Buttons.Add(tbbOpen);
```

LISTING 4.5   conrinued

```
22:        tlbStandard.Buttons.Add(tbbMaximize);
23:        tlbStandard.Buttons.Add(tbbHappy);
24:    }
```

 ANALYSIS   Line 1 creates a new `ImageList` object. Lines 4–6 add images to this object using the static `FromFile` method of the `Image` object. (Note that you should change the filenames specified here to files you actually have!) This method loads the specified file and passes it into the `ImageList`'s `Images` collection.

Note

Since you are using the `Image` object in Listing 4.5, don't forget to import the `System.Drawing` namespace as well! For example, add the following code near the top of your file:

`using System.Drawing;`

Lines 8–18 create three new `ToolBarButton` objects, specifying the `ImageIndex` and `Text` properties. The `ImageIndex` points to the index of the image in the `ImageList` that you want to associate with the button (the first index is always `0`).

Finally, on line 20 you associate the `ImageList` created on line 1 to the `ToolBar` object by using the latter's `ImageList` property. Lines 21–23 simply add the newly created buttons to the toolbar.

Figure 4.10 shows the output of this file.

FIGURE 4.10

Now the toolbar has buttons with icons and captions.

The application is now looking more filled out. There is still the matter, however, of making your buttons do stuff. Remember I said that the `ToolBar` acts as a single control? Well, now you'll see why.

ToolBarButton objects do not have events you can handle (aside from the Disposed event, but that's inherited from another object). By themselves, they have no way of knowing when they have been clicked. So if you want to control the actions when a user clicks on a toolbar button, you have to go to the ToolBar object.

ToolBar has a ButtonClick event this is fired whenever any of the ToolBarButtons it contains is clicked. Thus, all events and actions must go through the ToolBar. To add a handler to your ToolBar, use the following code:

```
tlbStandard.ButtonClick += new ToolBarButtonClickEventHandler
➡(this.MyToolBarHandler);
```

Listing 4.6 shows the MyToolBarHandler.

LISTING 4.6   Handling Toolbar Events in C#

```
 1:  private void MyToolBarHandler(Object Sender,
➡ToolBarButtonClickEventArgs e) {
 2:      switch(tlbStandard.Buttons.IndexOf(e.Button)) {
 3:          case 0:
 4:              //code goes here;
 5:              break;
 6:          case 1:
 7:              //code goes here;
 8:              break;
 9:          case 2:
10:              //code goes here;
11:              break;
12:      }
13:  }
```

The ToolBarButtonClickEventArgs parameter object has a Button property, as shown on line 2, that indicates which button was clicked. We use the IndexOf property of the Buttons collection to return a numeric representation of each button, which we can use to determine what code to execute.

The switch statement (Select Case in VB.NET) evaluates the supplied condition against each case item, and when the values match, the code inside that particular case is executed. IndexOf determines which item in the ToolBar's Buttons collection matches the one specified in the parameter object, and returns the index of that control in the collection. That index is evaluated to see what code should be executed. Break is required to tell the CLR not to execute or evaluate any more case statements after one has executed. Listing 4.7 shows the same code in VB.NET.

LISTING 4.7   Handling Toolbar Events in VB.NET

```
 1:  private Sub MyToolBarHandler(Sender as Object, e as
➥ToolBarButtonClickEventArgs)
 2:      Select Case tlbStandard.Buttons.IndexOf(e.Button)
 3:          Case 0
 4:              'execute some code
 5:          Case 1
 6:              'execute some code
 7:          Case 2
 8:              'execute some code
 9:      end Select
10:  End Sub
```

Customizing Your Toolbars

ToolBar and ToolBarButton controls have a few properties that allow you to customize their appearances. Let's take a quick look at them, starting with the ToolBar control properties.

The Appearance property specifies whether your toolbar buttons should appear as normal 3D objects (raised buttons) or flat (what is known as browser-style because it is used in Internet Explorer). The best way to understand the difference is to look at both styles—they're shown in Figure 4.11.

FIGURE 4.11

Normal toolbar buttons have a 3D look to them; flat buttons are just that—flat.

Appearance can be set to one of two values: Normal (3D) or Flat. Both values belong to the ToolBarAppearance enumeration. For example, the following code snippet makes the buttons appear flat:

```
tlbStandard.Appearance = ToolBarAppearance.Flat;
```

Functionally, there is no difference between the two styles, it's just a matter of visual preference.

The `ToolBar` control's `AutoSize` property indicates whether the `ToolBar` should resize based on the size of the `ToolBarButtons` it contains. Similarly, there is the `ButtonSize` property, which dictates the size of the buttons in your `ToolBar`.

Note

> The default size for a button is 24 pixels wide by 22 pixels high, but if `ButtonSize` is not otherwise specified, the buttons will resize to the largest image and text associated with them.

To control the boundaries of your toolbar, you have the `Divider` and `BorderStyle` properties. `Divider` indicates if a divider should be drawn between the toolbar and other controls, such as a menu. `BorderStyle` can be `BorderStyle.FixedSingle`, `BorderStyle.Fixed3D`, or `BorderStyle.None`. This property works much the way it did for the `Form` object.

The `ToolBarButton` control has only one main property, `Style`, and several others that support that property. `Style` indicates the type of button that will be shown to the user. It can be one of the following `ToolBarButtonStyle` enumeration values:

4

- `DropDownButton`—Displays a drop-down menu when clicked. Use the `DropDownMenu` property to assign a `MenuItem` to be displayed when clicked. Use the `ToolBar` object's `DropDownArrows` property to indicate whether an arrow that can be clicked to pull down the menu should be displayed.

- `PushButton`—The standard 3D button as determined by your operating system. (For instance, the button may appear flat instead of 3D in some versions of Windows.)

- `Separator`—A dividing line between two buttons.

- `ToggleButton`—A button that stays pushed in when clicked. Use the `Pushed` property to indicate if the button is currently pushed in. `PartialPush` is similar to `Pushed` except the button is not pushed in, but rather grayed over.

Figure 4.12 shows examples of all of these styles.

Status Bars

A status bar on a Windows Forms application is represented by a `StatusBar` object and any number of `StatusBarPanels`. The `StatusBar` itself looks just like a `Label` control—

it doesn't have any borders or separators. Therefore, it uses StatusBarPanels to separate and display information. There's no rule that says you have to add StatusBarPanels to your StatusBar—after all, the StatusBar has a Text property that will display text to the user—but the standard look for a status bar is to contain panels.

FIGURE 4.12

The DropDown, PushButton, *and* ToggleButton *button styles in action.*

StatusBar and StatusBarPanel controls are very similar to the menu and toolbar controls you've learned today, so you should be able to grasp them easily. Let's dive into some code—Listing 4.8 (we'll use VB.NET for this example) shows how to add a status bar.

LISTING 4.8 Adding a Status Bar to Your Application in VB.NET

```
1:  Imports System
2:  Imports System.Windows.Forms
3:
4:  Namespace TYWinForms.Day4
5:
6:     public class Listing48 : Inherits Form
7:        private sbrMain as new StatusBar
8:        private lblMessage as new Label
9:
10:       public sub New()
11:          Me.Text = "Listing 4.8"
12:
13:          AddStatusBar
14:
15:          lblMessage.Text = "I love WinForms"
16:          lblMessage.Width = 200
17:          lblMessage.Height = 200
18:          lblMessage.Font = new System.Drawing.Font(new
➥System.Drawing.FontFamily("Arial"), 15)
19:
```

LISTING 4.8   continued

```
20:              Me.Controls.Add(lblMessage)
21:              Me.Controls.Add(sbrMain)
22:
23:         End Sub
24:
25:         public sub AddStatusBar()
26:             dim sbpName as StatusBarPanel = sbrMain.Panels.
➡Add("Welcome User")
27:             sbpName.Width = 100
28:             sbpName.BorderStyle = StatusBarPanelBorderStyle.
➡Raised
29:
30:             dim sbpTime as StatusBarPanel = sbrMain.Panels.
➡Add("")
31:             sbpTime.Text = Datetime.Now.ToString
32:             sbpTime.AutoSize = StatusBarPanelAutoSize.Spring
33:             sbpTime.Alignment = HorizontalAlignment.Right
34:
35:             sbrMain.ShowPanels = true
36:         end sub
37:
38:         public Shared Sub Main()
39:             Application.Run(new Listing48)
40:         end sub
41:     end class
42:
43:   End Namespace
```

ANALYSIS   This listing demonstrates quite a few properties of the StatusBar and
StatusBarPanel controls. On line 7 you create the first new object, the
StatusBar. In order to logically group the code (and preserve our sanity!), we placed the
status bar initialization code in a method called AddStatusBar, called from line 13. Line
21 adds the status bar to the form.

The first line of AddStatusBar (line 26) creates a new StatusBarPanel object and adds
it to the StatusBar's Panels collection. (This code is nearly identical to the code you
used to add ToolBarButtons to a ToolBar.) Line 27 sets the width of the panel, and line
28 sets the BorderStyle to Raised (a value in the StatusBarPanelBorderStyle enumeration; the other values you could use are None or Sunken, which is the default style).

Line 30 creates another StatusBarPanel. The Text property is initially set to an empty
string. On line 21 you set it to the current time using the DateTime.Now function (use
ToString to return the time as a string—the default return type is a DateTime object).

Line 32 sets the `AutoSize` property, which indicates how the panel will resize given its contents and/or the size of the form. `Spring` means that it will spring to fill up whatever space is not already taken by other panels. `AutoSize` can also be `None` or `Contents`, which will resize the panel to fit whatever is inside of it.

Line 33 uses the `Alignment` property to make the contents of the panel align to the right. This value can be `Left`, `Center`, or `Right`, all from the `HorizontalAlignment` enumeration.

Finally, on line 35 you set the `ShowPanels` property of the `StatusBar` control to `true`, so that the panels you've created will be displayed to the user.

Figure 4.13 shows the appearance of this application.

FIGURE 4.13

Your first status bar contains a message and the date and time.

You can add as many panels as you like to your status bar. Just remember not to add so many that the user can't see them all!

The `StatusBarPanel` control has one more important custom property we haven't yet covered: `Icon`. This property can be used to show an image in the status bar instead of just text (like, for example, the icon in Word's status bar that indicates the status of your document). This image file must be an icon (`.ico`) file. For instance, adding the following code snippet to the `AddStatusBar` method in Listing 4.8 adds a new panel:

```
dim sbpIcon as StatusBarPanel = sbrMain.Panels.Add("")
sbpIcon.AutoSize = StatusBarPanelAutoSize.Contents
sbpIcon.Icon = new Icon("VSProjectApplication.ico")
```

Scroll Bars

Scroll bars allow you (or your users) to move around your form when the controls contained within are too large to fit in the current window. There are two types of scroll bars: horizontal (moves the form from side to side), represented by the HScrollBar control; and vertical (moves the form up and down), represented by VScrollBar.

Scroll bars are very easy to add to your forms, but they are a bit more complex to make functional. To learn how to use scroll bars, look at the code in Listing 4.9 (a modified version of yesterday's Listing 3.4).

LISTING 4.9   Implementing Scroll Bars

```
1:  using System;
2:  using System.Windows.Forms;
3:  using System.Drawing;
4:
5:  namespace TYWinForms.Day4 {
6:
7:      public class Listing49 : Form {
8:          Button btAccept = new Button();
9:          Button btCancel = new Button();
10:         Label lblMessage = new Label();
11:         VScrollBar vbarForm = new VScrollBar();
12:         HScrollBar hbarForm = new HScrollBar();
13:
14:         public Listing49() {
15:             lblMessage.Location = new Point(75,150);
16:             lblMessage.Width = 200;
17:
18:             btAccept.Location = new Point(100,25);
19:             btAccept.Text = "Accept";
20:             btAccept.Click += new EventHandler(this.AcceptIt);
21:
22:             btCancel.Location = new Point(100,100);
23:             btCancel.Text = "Cancel";
24:             btCancel.Click += new EventHandler(this.CancelIt);
25:
26:             vbarForm.Dock = DockStyle.Right;
27:             vbarForm.Visible = false;
28:             hbarForm.Dock = DockStyle.Bottom;
29:             hbarForm.Visible = false;
30:
31:             this.Resize += new EventHandler(this.Resized);
32:             this.AcceptButton = btAccept;
33:             this.CancelButton = btCancel;
34:             this.Text = "Accept and Cancel Button Example";
35:             this.Height = 200;
36:             this.Controls.Add(lblMessage);
37:             this.Controls.Add(btAccept);
38:             this.Controls.Add(btCancel);
39:             this.Controls.Add(vbarForm);
40:             this.Controls.Add(hbarForm);
```

4

LISTING 4.9   continued

```
41:            }
42:
43:        public void Resized(Object Sender, EventArgs e) {
44:            if (this.Height < lblMessage.Top + lblMessage.Height) {
45:                vbarForm.Visible = true;
46:            } else {
47:                vbarForm.Visible = false;
48:            }
49:
50:            if (this.Width < btAccept.Left + btAccept.Width) {
51:                hbarForm.Visible = true;
52:            } else {
53:                hbarForm.Visible = false;
54:            }
55:            this.Refresh();
56:        }
57:
58:        public void AcceptIt(Object Sender, EventArgs e) {
59:            lblMessage.Text = "Accept button pressed";
60:        }
61:
62:        public void CancelIt(Object Sender, EventArgs e) {
63:            lblMessage.Text = "Cancel button pressed";
64:        }
65:    }
66:
67:    public class StartForm {
68:        public static void Main() {
69:            Application.Run(new Listing49());
70:        }
71:    }
72: }
```

ANALYSIS   There's a lot of code here, but most of it we covered yesterday. Briefly, lines
15–24 create and display a label and two button controls. Lines 32–38 add these
controls to the form, and lines 58–65 handle the buttons' events. (For more detail, check
out yesterday's lesson.)

Lines 11 and 12 contain the first new code; they create new VScrollBar and HScrollBar
controls. Lines 26–29 set the Dock and Visible properties. Because we know the form
will be large enough to display its contents, we want the scroll bars to be invisible initially. We'll examine the Dock property more on Day 6, "Enhancing Your Windows Forms
with More Controls." For now, just know that our scroll bars are locked to the right and
bottom sides of our form.

On line 31 you handle a new event of the Form object: Resize. This event fires, appropriately enough, whenever the form is resized. Line 31 says that whenever this occurs, execute the Resized method, shown on lines 43–56.

The Resized method needs to do two things. First, whenever the form is resized, it has to reevaluate the size of the form (both horizontally and vertically) and determine if the form is large enough to display the contents. If not, then it displays the scroll bars. Second, it needs to call the Refresh method to redraw the form so that the newly modified scroll bars can be drawn or erased.

The minimum height the form should be before displaying vertical scroll bars is the bottom of the lowest control, lblMessage in this case. Summing the Top and Height properties of the label gives us the proper height. The if statement on line 44 performs the comparison between the height of the form, and the minimum height. If the form's height is smaller, you show the vertical scroll bar (line 45). Conversely, if the form is larger than the minimum height, you hide the scroll bar, as shown on line 47. Lines 50–54 do the same thing in the horizontal direction. In this case, the minimum width is the Left property of the further right control, plus that control's Width.

Finally, you call the Refresh method on line 55.

Compile this application and try resizing the form to smaller than the minimum boundaries. Figure 4.14 shows a typical example.

FIGURE 4.14

The appropriate scroll bars appear when the form is resized.

Notice, however, that when you click on the scroll bars, nothing happens! Your form does not move around as it should. There are two ways to fix this. The first, and easier way, is to simply set the AutoScroll property of the form to true:

```
this.AutoScroll = true;
```

Your form now scrolls around properly.

The second is the manual way, which is done by handling the scroll bars' events to produce the scrolling effect. You usually only do it this way when you don't know how big your form is going to be ahead of time (for example, if the user can dynamically increase its size).

Let's examine what, exactly, you want to scroll when the scroll bars are clicked. Your first guess may be to scroll the Form object, but that would be incorrect. Remember that the Form's location is measured against the desktop, so if you try to scroll the form object, it will move all around your desktop, but its contents would still be in the same spot relatively—meaning that you wouldn't see the controls move around as expected. (I'll show you exactly what this procedure does in a moment.)

You want to scroll the controls *inside* the form, rather than the form itself. That way, the form stays put, but its contents will move around. For example, when the user clicks the down arrow on the vertical scroll bar, all controls must move up (clicking down means you want to see what's under the current view, therefore everything must move up). Similarly, when the user clicks right on the horizontal scroll bar, all controls must move to the left.

With only three controls in our example that must move, this may not be such a big deal. But what if you have more? It becomes a pain to have to reposition every single control on a form. Our trick is to use another container control—a Panel to hold all the controls that need to be moved. Then, you can scroll the Panel around, and all its child controls will move with it! Imagine the Panel as a sort of mini-Form, or a form inside of a Form. By grouping the controls into a Panel, you can manipulate them as a group, which is exactly what you want to do when scrolling.

Creating the panel is simple; add the following code somewhere between lines 8 and 13 of Listing 4.9:

```
Panel pnlForm = new Panel();
```

You'll want to make sure the panel is the same size as the form so all controls will be displayed as normal. In the constructor, add the code:

```
pnlForm.Height = this.Height;
pnlForm.Width = this.Width;
```

Next, replace lines 36–38 with the following:

```
pnlForm.Controls.Add(lblMessage);
pnlForm.Controls.Add(btAccept);
pnlForm.Controls.Add(btCancel);
```

Now the Label and two Button controls no longer are attached to the Form, but to the Panel instead. Next, add the Panel to the Form's constructor:

```
this.Controls.Add(pnlForm);
```

To handle the scrolling events, you need to add event handlers to the scroll bars' Scroll event in the constructor, like so:

```
vbarForm.Scroll += new ScrollEventHandler(this.HandleVScroll);
hbarForm.Scroll += new ScrollEventHandler(this.HandleHScroll);
```

Note the use of the `ScrollEventHandler` object, which means you'll use a `ScrollEventArgs` parameter object for your methods. Finally, you need to build the `HandleVScroll` and `HandleHScroll` methods, as shown in Listing 4.10.

LISTING **4.10** Methods to Handle Scrolling

```
1:  public void HandleVScroll(Object Sender, ScrollEventArgs e) {
2:      pnlForm.Top = 0 - e.NewValue;
3:  }
4:
5:  public void HandleHScroll(Object Sender, ScrollEventArgs e) {
6:      pnlForm.Left = 0 - e.NewValue;
7:  }
```

These two functions do two simple things: move the panel up or down, and left or right, using the `Top` and `Left` properties, respectively, of the panel. The difficult part of these methods is determining how much to move the panel around in each direction.

The panel should always be moved in reference to its starting position. For example, when the scroll bar is moved x spaces down, the panel should move x spaces up *from its original position*. In this case, the initial position of the panel is the x-y coordinates (0,0), which is why you see the zeroes on lines 2 and 6. From this initial position, you want to subtract the amount the scroll bar has moved. By subtracting you ensure that the panel moves in the opposite direction of the scrolling (recall that if the user clicks down, the controls move up). Table 4.1 shows an example situation.

TABLE **4.1** Example Scrolling Movements

	Action	*Result*
1.	User clicks up arrow 10 units. (Scroll bar value = 10)	Panel moves down 10 units. New `Panel.Top` value is -10, `Panel.Left` = 0.
2.	User moves scroll bar all the way down (scroll bar value = `Form.Height`)	Panel moves up all the way New `Panel.Top` = 0 - `Form.Height`. `Left` = 0. (Note that since the movement is relative to the initial position, movements are not cumulative. That is, the `Top` value in this step is not -10 -`Form.Height`.)

TABLE 4.1   continued

	Action	Result
3.	User moves scroll bar left 20 units.	Panel moves right 20 units. `Top = 0 - Form.Height. Left` value = -20.

So what units do the scroll bars use? By default, the `Minimum` property is set to `0` (this is the initial position of the scroll bar; at the top for a vertical scroll bar, at the far left for a horizontal one). `Maximum` defaults to 100, which means that there are 100 "units" for the scroll bars to move. You can modify both `Minimum` and `Maximum`, but no matter what values you set them to, `Minimum` is always at the top or far left of the bars, and `Maximum` is always at the bottom or far right.

The `NewValue` property of the `ScrollEventArgs` parameter is the new position of the scroll bar (what the user has changed the position to). According to lines 2 and 6 of Listing 4.10, the farthest the panel can move around is ±100 units up, down, left, or right.

For forms with more complicated size requirements, you may have to adjust the amount the panel can move; in other words, normalize the movement against the size of the form. For example, if your form is 1,000 pixels in height, the ±100 units is not going to be enough for your vertical scroll bar. Thus, each 1-unit movement of the scroll bar should move more than just 1 unit of panel height. The following code could accomplish this normalization:

```
int normalizedHeight = pnlForm.Height / vbarForm.Maximum;
pnlForm.Top = 0 - (e.NewValue * normalizedHeight);
```

Note

Remove the word `pnlForm` from lines 2 and 6 of Listing 4.10 to see the example discussed earlier, where the form moves around the desktop.

Tip

`Forms` aren't the only objects that can have scroll bars; you can add scroll bars to almost any control you want, such as `PictureBoxes` or even `Buttons`. This provides you great versatility in designing your application and in how you let users interact with it.

Let's examine a few more properties that you can employ with your scroll bars. `LargeChange` and `SmallChange` properties can be used to adjust the number of units the scroll bar moves when clicked. `SmallChange` usually is used when the user clicks one of the arrows at the end of the scroll bar or presses the up or down arrow keys, and LargeChange is used when the scroll bar itself is clicked or the Page Up or Page Down keys are pressed.

The ScrollEventArgs parameter object's Type property tells you what actually happened during the scroll event, such as a large move, small move, or where the scroll bar moved to. Table 4.2 lists its values, all of which belong to the ScrollEventType enumeration.

TABLE 4.2 ScrollEventType Values

Value	Description
EndScroll	The scroll box (the box that indicates the position of the scroll bar) has stopped moving.
First	The scroll box has moved to the Minimum value.
LargeDecrement	The scroll box has moved the LargeChange value up or to the left (the contents would scroll down or to the right).
LargeIncrement	The scroll box has moved the LargeChange value down or to the right (the contents would scroll up or to the left).
Last	The scroll box has moved to the value specified by Maximum.
SmallDecrement	The scroll box has moved the SmallChange value up or to the left (the contents would scroll down or to the right).
SmallIncrement	The scroll box has moved the SmallChange value down or to the right (the contents would scroll up or to the left).
ThumbPosition	The scroll box itself was moved.
ThumbTrack	The scroll box is still moving.

Listing 4.10 shows a brief (at least in terms of complexity) example of using these values.

LISTING 4.10 Determining the Type of Scroll that Occurred

```
1:  using System;
2:  using System.Windows.Forms;
3:  using System.Drawing;
4:
5:  namespace TYWinForms.Day4 {
6:
7:      public class Listing410 : Form {
8:          Label lblMessage = new Label();
9:          VScrollBar vbarForm = new VScrollBar();
10:         HScrollBar hbarForm = new HScrollBar();
11:
```

LISTING **4.10**   continued

```
12:          public Listing410() {
13:              lblMessage.Location = new Point(75,75);
14:              lblMessage.Width = 200;
15:
16:              vbarForm.Dock = DockStyle.Right;
17:              vbarForm.Visible = true;
18:              vbarForm.Scroll += new ScrollEventHandler
➥(this.HandleScroll);
19:              hbarForm.Dock = DockStyle.Bottom;
20:              hbarForm.Visible = true;
21:              hbarForm.Scroll += new ScrollEventHandler
➥(this.HandleScroll);
22:
23:              this.Text = "ScrollEventType Value Example";
24:              this.Height = 200;
25:              this.Controls.Add(lblMessage);
26:              this.Controls.Add(vbarForm);
27:              this.Controls.Add(hbarForm);
28:          }
29:
30:          public void HandleScroll(Object Sender,
➥ScrollEventArgs e) {
31:              switch(e.Type) {
32:                  case ScrollEventType.EndScroll:
33:                      lblMessage.Text = "Scroll box has stopped
➥moving";
34:                      break;
35:                  case ScrollEventType.First:
36:                      lblMessage.Text = "Scroll box is at " +
➥((ScrollBar)Sender).Minimum.ToString();
37:                      break;
38:                  case ScrollEventType.LargeDecrement:
39:                      lblMessage.Text = "Scroll box has moved -" +
➥ ((ScrollBar)Sender).LargeChange.ToString();
40:                      break;
41:                  case ScrollEventType.LargeIncrement:
42:                      lblMessage.Text = "Scroll box has moved " +
➥ ((ScrollBar)Sender).LargeChange.ToString();
43:                      break;
44:                  case ScrollEventType.Last:
45:                      lblMessage.Text = "Scroll box is at " +
➥ ((ScrollBar)Sender).Maximum.ToString();
46:                      break;
47:                  case ScrollEventType.SmallDecrement:
48:                      lblMessage.Text = "Scroll box has moved -" +
➥ ((ScrollBar)Sender).SmallChange.ToString();
49:                      break;
50:                  case ScrollEventType.SmallIncrement:
```

LISTING **4.10**   continued

```
51:                    lblMessage.Text = "Scroll box has moved " +
 ➡ ((ScrollBar)Sender).SmallChange.ToString();
52:                    break;
53:                case ScrollEventType.ThumbPosition:
54:                    lblMessage.Text = "Scroll box was moved";
55:                    break;
56:                case ScrollEventType.ThumbTrack:
57:                    lblMessage.Text = "Scroll box is moving";
58:                    break;
59:            }
60:        }
61:    }
62:
63:    public class StartForm {
64:        public static void Main() {
65:            Application.Run(new Listing410());
66:        }
67:    }
68: }
```

ANALYSIS   The constructor should look very familiar; it simply creates your scroll bars and a label, and adds the controls to the form. The Scroll event handler, HandleScroll, is where the interesting part takes place.

This method, beginning on line 30, evaluates the Type property of the ScrollEventArgs parameter. Using a switch statement, it compares the Type value to each of the ScrollEventType values shown in Table 4.2. For each case, it prints out an appropriate string to the Label control.

There are a couple things to notice about this listing. First, you are required to convert variables on lines 36, 39, 42, 45, 48, and 51. The variable Sender is an Object type (as indicated by the method declaration on line 30). We know two things about this Object: it represents the scroll bar that was clicked (you'll explain why tomorrow), and as such, it should contain the various scroll bar properties, such as Minimum, Maximum, and so on. An Object, however, doesn't have these properties (see yesterday's discussion on the Object object), so you must convert it to the proper type—a ScrollBar—in order to access the appropriate properties. (Don't worry if this doesn't make much sense now—it leads into the tomorrow's discussion, and by the end of it all you'll know it all like the back of your hand.)

The second thing to notice is that you convert to a ScrollBar instead of a VScrollBar or HScrollBar control (both of these inherit all of their properties from the ScrollBar control). It's irrelevant, then, whether the control that was clicked is a VScrollBar or

4

HScrollBar, because all we need is access to the appropriate properties, which the ScrollBar class provides. Again, this will be discussed more in tomorrow's lesson.

Figure 4.15 shows this example when the scroll bar below the scroll box is clicked.

FIGURE 4.15

Clicking below the scroll box moves the LargeChange *value.*

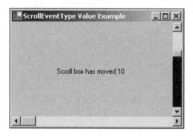

Summary

You learned about three very important and common types of controls today: menus, toolbars, and scroll bars. They are all very similar in terms of function, and even share many similar properties, but they are very different in implementation.

A Windows Forms control is an object that presents an interface to the user, and often can be interacted with. There are several types of controls, including container controls, buttons, and menus.

Menus are represented with the MainMenu and MenuItem controls. The MainMenu acts as the holder for MenuItems, which in turn represent the captions that users see and interact with in menus. Context menus—those that pop up when you right-click a control—also use MenuItem controls, but use ContextMenu in place of MainMenu.

A toolbar is similar to a menu, except that you use a ToolBar control as the parent object, and ToolBarButton controls as the children (ToolBarButtons can even have child MenuItem controls, as in the case of drop-down buttons). The ToolBar is the only one of the two that has useable events, so each button click must be handled in its event handler, typically with a switch or Select Case statement.

A status bar is another type of container, using StatusBar and StatusBarPanel controls. Status bars are usually not interactive, but rather just display data. Both StatusBars and StatusBarPanels have properties that can be used to display information, but the usual procedure is to use only the StatusBarPanel as a display mechanism, and the StatusBar control as a container.

Finally, scroll bars come in two flavors: HScrollBar and VSCrollBar, for representing horizontal and vertical scroll bars respectively. You learned that adding these to your forms is relatively easy, but handling their events takes some careful planning, especially when trying to figure out what needs to be scrolled, by how much, and in which directions. Both of these controls inherit from the base `ScrollBar` class.

Tomorrow you'll learn more about how to handle events. As you'll see, there is quite a bit of complexity behind the event-handling mechanism in .NET, so it's essential that you learn it before you learn too many more controls.

Q&A

Q Is there an event that signals when a menu is about to pop up?

A Yes, there is an event: `PopUp`. You can create a handler for this event if you want to perform any actions immediately before the menu pops up, such as hiding or displaying menu items.

Q How is the `NewValue` property of the `ScrollEventArgs` object different than the `Value` property?

A `NewValue` specifies the value the scroll bar is changed to during an event. `Value` specifies the static value. Often, these values are the same, but sometimes they are not.

For example, when the scroll bar or arrows are clicked, these values are the same. However, when the scroll box itself is dragged around, `Value` is the previous position, while `NewValue` is the current position. When the scroll box is released, both values become equal.

Workshop

This workshop will help reinforce the concepts you learned in today's lesson. It is very helpful to understand fully the answers before moving on. Answers can be found in Appendix A.

Quiz

1. True or false? All controls, including the `Form` object, inherit from the `Control` class.

2. What object must be associated to toolbars to display images in the toolbar buttons?

3. What are the three optional parameters for a `MenuItem` constructor, and what are their types?

4. What character is used to provide a keyboard shortcut for a letter in a menu item's caption?

5. Write a line of code in C# that instructs a `ToolBarButton` control named `myFirstButton` to use the fourth image in the associated `ImageList`.

6. True or false? The event that is used to handle toolbar button clicks is called `Click`.

7. What are the default values for a scroll bar's `Minimum`, `Maximum`, `SmallChange`, and `LargeChange` properties?

Exercise

Create an application in VB.NET that uses a personalized menu like those introduced with Microsoft Office 2000 and Windows 2000. These menus display only the most recently used menu items, hiding others, and allowing users to click an arrow to display the seldom-used choices. Your application should provide a menu that has hidden items. When a particular menu item is clicked, the hidden items should be displayed. Don't worry about adding event handlers for every menu item.

Your menu can be rather simple—it doesn't need to remember which items the user chooses most often, and it won't display hidden menu items simply by hovering over the menu. Finally, once the user clicks on the "more" button, she will have to reopen to menu to see the newly discovered items. (You'll see how to perform some more advanced functionality when you learn about GDI+ in Day 13, "Creating Graphical Applications with GDI+.")

DAY 5

Handling Events in Your Windows Forms

One of the most important things in any application, aside from the visual interface, is how it interacts with users. As you already know, this interaction is carried out by events and their handlers.

An event is the result of an action—a message created to signal the occurrence of an action—that can be caused by a user or the application itself. An event handler is the method that responds when an event occurs.

Today we'll discuss events and their methods, how they apply to your applications, and why you need them. And I'll introduce you to a new type of class, called a `Delegate`, that helps your application with its events.

Today you will learn

- What, technically, an event handler is
- How to "wire" your events
- How to use delegates

- How to create your own custom events and event parameters
- What each parameter of an event handler does, where it comes from, and how to use it

What Are Event Handlers?

You already have a bit of experience dealing with events from previous chapters. You know what an event is, and, in general, what an event handler is. Let's expand a bit on the latter.

Objects are full of events. Events fire when you start your application, when you close it, when you click buttons, when you press a key, and so on. Just because an event is raised, however, doesn't mean anything needs to happen. In fact, many of the simple applications you've already built don't do anything in response to events.

New Term   To make your application respond to an event, you have to build an *event handler*. The event handler is a piece of code that is executed only when an event occurs.

When you press the gas pedal in your car, for example, you expect the car to start moving. From a conceptual point of view, you take an action (stepping on the gas), an event fires (the car alerts the fuel injection system to start pumping gas to the engine), and something happens (the car moves). This last step, however, is dependent on a crucial factor: the wiring between the gas tank and the engine. If there were no gas line, the car would not move no matter how much you pressed the gas pedal—the wiring must be there.

New Term   The same can be said for events in .NET. An action may occur and an event will be raised, but unless there is wiring, nothing will happen (unlike cars, however, you won't ruin your applications if the wiring isn't there). Appropriately enough, then, the process of creating an event handler for an event is known as *wiring* the event.

Handling Events

Let's look at an application that handles some events created by menu items, shown in Listing 5.1.

LISTING 5.1   Working with Event Handlers

```
1:  Imports System
2:  Imports System.Windows.Forms
3:  Imports System.Drawing
4:
```

LISTING 5.1 continued

```
5:   Namespace TYWinForms.Day5
6:
7:     public class Listing51 : Inherits Form
8:         private mnuFont as new MainMenu
9:         private lblMessage as new Label
10:
11:      public sub New()
12:          Me.Text = "Listing 5.1"
13:          Me.Menu = mnuFont
14:
15:          lblMessage.Text = "Testing events"
16:          lblMessage.Location = new Point(75,75)
17:          lblMessage.Height = 50
18:          lblMessage.Width = 150
19:          lblMessage.BackColor = Color.LightBlue
20:
21:          dim miFont as MenuItem = mnuFont.MenuItems.
➥Add("Font")
22:          dim miTimes as MenuItem = miFont.MenuItems.
➥Add("Times Roman")
23:          AddHandler miTimes.Click, new EventHandler
➥ (AddressOf Me.TimesClicked)
24:
25:          dim miArial as MenuItem = miFont.MenuItems.
➥Add("Arial")
26:          AddHandler miArial.Click, new EventHandler
➥ (AddressOf Me.ArialClicked)
27:
28:          dim miWing as MenuItem = miFont.MenuItems.
➥Add("Wingdings")
29:          AddHandler miWing.Click, new EventHandler
➥ (AddressOf Me.WingClicked)
30:
31:          Me.Controls.Add(lblMessage)
32:        End Sub
33:
34:      public sub TimesClicked(Sender as Object, e as
➥EventArgs)
35:          lblMessage.Font = new Font("Times", 15)
36:          mnuFont.MenuItems(0).MenuItems(0).Checked = True
37:          mnuFont.MenuItems(0).MenuItems(1).Checked = False
38:          mnuFont.MenuItems(0).MenuItems(2).Checked = False
39:        end sub
40:
41:      public sub ArialClicked(Sender as Object, e as
➥EventArgs)
42:          lblMessage.Font = new Font("Arial", 15)
43:          mnuFont.MenuItems(0).MenuItems(0).Checked = False
44:          mnuFont.MenuItems(0).MenuItems(1).Checked = True
```

5

LISTING 5.1   continued

```
45:            mnuFont.MenuItems(0).MenuItems(2).Checked = False
46:         end sub
47:
48:         public sub WingClicked(Sender as Object, e as
➥EventArgs)
49:            lblMessage.Font = new Font("Wingdings", 15)
50:            mnuFont.MenuItems(0).MenuItems(0).Checked = False
51:            mnuFont.MenuItems(0).MenuItems(1).Checked = False
52:            mnuFont.MenuItems(0).MenuItems(2).Checked = True
53:         end sub
54:
55:         public Shared Sub Main()
56:            Application.Run(new Listing51)
57:         end sub
58:      end class
59:
60:   End Namespace
```

ANALYSIS This application displays some text and allows the user to change the font through a menu. First, let's cover the basics. Lines 1–3 import the namespaces we'll be using. Lines 8 and 9 declare the two main controls in this application: a MainMenu and a Label control. Line 11 begins the constructor for the Windows Forms class. Lines 15–19 initialize the properties of the label, settings its size, location, and Text properties.

The next set of code should look familiar from yesterday's lesson. Line 21 adds a menu item with the caption Font to the MainMenu object. This first menu item will be the header of the menu. Line 22 adds a menu item—the first of our font choices—to this menu header. Line 23 uses the AddHandler method to add an event handler to the menu item's Click event, which occurs, easily enough, whenever a menu item is clicked. In essence, this line is alerting the application of an event handler named TimesClicked that should be used for this event (we'll learn more about this process later today in "Understanding Delegates").

Lines 25–29 do the same thing as lines 22 and 23—that is, create new menu items for more font choices (Arial and Wingdings) and assign event handlers to those menu items' Click events. In essence, these lines "wire" the events. Whenever one of these menu items is clicked, the appropriate method (TimesClicked, ArialClicked, or WingClicked) will be executed. The process is actually very simple, although the code may look a little strange.

The TimesClicked method on line 34 changes the font of the label on line 35. We examined how to modify fonts in Day 3's lesson using the Font and FontFamily objects.

Today, you're learning a new way. Instead of using the `FontFamily` object, we're just passing in a string of the font we want to change to—`Times` in this case. The second parameter, again, is the size of the font to display.

To let the user know which font is currently being used, we want to check the menu items `miTimes`, `miArial`, or `miWing` when each item is selected. The following line literally means that the first `MenuItem` added to the `mnuFont MainMenu` object should be checked. In other words, the `miTimes` menu item:

```
mnuFont.MenuItems(0).MenuItems(0).Checked = True
```

Similarly, the next two lines (37 and 38) refer to the `miArial` and `miWing` items (the second and third menu items added to the first `MenuItem` added to the `mnuFont MainMenu` object). Since these options are obviously not selected (since the user just chose the Times Roman menu item, they should not be checked, and their `Checked` values should be `False`:

```
mnuFont.MenuItems(0).MenuItems(1).Checked = False
mnuFont.MenuItems(0).MenuItems(2).Checked = False
```

Because you don't know which one of these menu items was previously checked, you set them both to `False` to cover all your bases. The `ArialClicked` and `WingClicked` methods on lines 41 and 48 respectively do the same thing as the `TimesClicked` method except, of course, using Arial and Wingdings fonts instead of Times Roman.

Finally, line 55 declares the entry point to the application, the `Main` method, which simply calls the `Run` method.

Figure 5.1 shows this application in action.

5

FIGURE 5.1

The font changes in response to events.

Let's go back to the `TimesClicked` method for a moment. Notice the signature of this event handler:

```
public sub TimesClicked(Sender as Object, e as EventArgs)
```

This is the standard event handler signature (or, in other words, declaration). All event handlers have nearly identical signatures. The only things that typically change are the name of the method—TimesClicked in this case—and, rarely, the final parameter type, EventArgs (you'll see why this might change in the "Understanding Delegates" section later today).

The first parameter, Sender, represents the object that generated the event. It would be the miTimes MenuItem object in Listing 5.1. The second parameter contains any special information about the event. These parameters are used to aid your event handler in doing its job. Most of the time you'll use this standard signature for all your event handlers, which makes them very easy to write as well as easy to pick out from previously written code.

That was a very simple example of using event handlers. We created a single event handler for each event that we cared about—one wire per event. For all other events, we don't create handlers, which effectively ignores those events.

Handling Multiple Events

A very interesting feature of .NET is that each event does not have to have its own event handler—they can share handlers! A wire can lead from one handler to multiple events. In our car analogy, this means that more than one thing can start the car moving, such as pushing it, or releasing the brake on a steep hill.

However, with so many events that can trigger an event handler, it becomes more important to figure out which object generated the event. This is where using the event handler parameters comes in handy. Listing 5.2 shows an example of one event handler handling multiple events. Make a copy of Listing 5.1 and replace lines 34–53 with the code in this listing.

LISTING 5.2 Handling Multiple Events with One Handler

```
1:  public sub FontClicked(Sender as Object, e as EventArgs)
2:     dim item as MenuItem
3:
4:     if Sender is mnuFont.MenuItems(0).MenuItems(0) then
5:        lblMessage.Font = new Font("Times", 15)
6:     elseif Sender is mnuFont.MenuItems(0).MenuItems(1) then
7:        lblMessage.Font = new Font("Arial", 15)
8:     elseif Sender is mnuFont.MenuItems(0).MenuItems(2) then
9:        lblMessage.Font = new Font("Wingdings", 15)
10:     end if
11:
12:     for each item in mnuFont.MenuItems(0).MenuItems
```

LISTING 5.2   continued

```
13:          item.Checked = False
14:       next item
15:       CType(Sender, MenuItem).Checked = True
16:    end sub
```

ANALYSIS   The FontClicked method will replace the TimesClicked, ArialClicked, and WingClicked methods from Listing 5.1—it does the same thing, but in a slightly different way. Notice the signature on line 1—it's still the same standard signature. In Listing 5.1, we didn't use any of the parameters, but this time, we'll use them to determine what object generated the event.

On line 2 you declare a new MenuItem object—we'll use that in a moment. Lines 4–10 determine what menu item generated the event that this method is responding to. It does so by evaluating the Sender parameter, and comparing it to each of the MenuItem objects contained in the miFont.MenuItems collection. Remember that Sender represents the object that generated the event; the font in the label is changed depending on the value of Sender.

Note   We don't use an equals sign (=) to evaluate the comparison on lines 4, 6, and 8, because the equals operator only works with simple data types, such as numbers or strings. With objects, we need to use the is keyword.

Next, we check the current menu item and uncheck the rest. To do this, we use a for each loop, shown on line 12. This loop takes each MenuItem in the miFont.MenuItems collection, assigns it to the variable item that we created on line 2, and then sets the Checked property of that variable to False, effectively unchecking all of the MenuItems. The for each loop could have been accomplished using a simple for loop as well:

```
for i = 0 to mnuFont.MenuItems(0).MenuItems.Count - 1
   mnuFont.MenuItems(0).MenuItems(i).Checked = False
next i
```

The for loop uses a variable, i, to iterate through the total number of menu items. Don't forget to declare the variable i if you use this method.

Now that all of the MenuItems are unchecked, we have to check only the current one. This is done on line 15. Using the CType method, we convert the Sender parameter into a MenuItem object (to understand why, see the "Event Handlers" section later today). Since Sender represents the current menu item, we can set its Checked property to True.

5

Finally, you'll have to change lines 23, 26, and 29 of Listing 5.1 to take advantage of your new, all-in-one event handler:

```
23:  AddHandler miTimes.Click, new EventHandler(AddressOf
➥Me.FontClicked)
...
26:  AddHandler miArial.Click, new EventHandler(AddressOf
➥Me.FontClicked)
...
29:  AddHandler miWing.Click, new EventHandler(AddressOf
➥Me.FontClicked)
...
```

Running the modified code produces the same results as the original Listing 5.1. The only difference is that you have one event handler doing the work of three.

You're almost a veteran at handling events, but there are a few other pieces that we haven't yet put together. For instance, where do the Sender and EventArgs parameters come from? We'll spend the rest of the day examining those, and learning the mechanisms behind events, and learning how to create your own custom events.

Understanding Delegates

An *event*, you'll recall, is a message sent by an object to signal the occurrence of an action. For example, when a button is clicked, it sends an "I've been clicked" message to the Common Language Runtime. Every object is responsible for alerting the CLR about events—otherwise nothing would ever happen.

The object that raises the event—the button in the preceding example—is known as the *sender* (you've been using a Sender parameter when declaring event handlers; now you know why). The object that receives the event message and responds to it is called the *receiver*.

In .NET, things are very flexible, meaning that any object can raise an event, and any object can receive an event—there are almost no limitations whatsoever. This flexibility, however, comes at a price; the sender never knows ahead of time who or what will be the receiver, nor does it care. All the sender knows is that it raises an event for something else to handle. You need an intermediary—something to be the go-between from the sender to the receiver.

NEW TERM   Luckily, .NET provides a *delegate*, a special type for this intermediary. A delegate is a class that can hold a reference to a method. That may not make much sense yet. Simply speaking, a delegate acts as a pointer for an event sender—it points the way to the receiver.

For example, in a simplistic football game, play starts when the quarterback (the sender) has the ball. He must pass the ball to someone else (a receiver) on his team. When play begins, the quarterback has any number of potential receivers. The way in which the current play unfolds dictates who actually will receive the ball. The quarterback surveys the field trying to figure out to whom to pass the ball. Sometimes members of the opposing team may block some of the receivers, and sometimes the quarterback just may not be able to see all of the available receivers. Until just before he throws the ball, the quarterback doesn't know who will receive it (sometimes, in fact, he doesn't know who will receive it even *after* he throws the ball, but that's beside the point).

In our simplistic game, however, the coach on the sidelines sees everything at a much better angle, and therefore sees (better than the quarterback can) who should be the receiver. Through a radio embedded in the quarterback's helmet, the coach yells, "Throw the ball to number 66!" (For the purposes of this example, ignore whether this is legal.) The quarterback then throws the ball to the receiver indicated by the coach. Figure 5.2 illustrates this concept.

FIGURE 5.2

A quarterback, or sender, has any number of potential receivers.

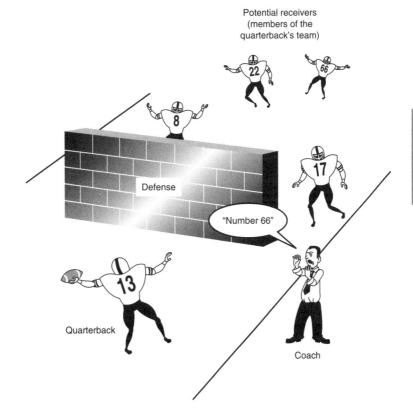

In this example, the coach is the delegate—the intermediary between the sender and receiver, pointing the event (the ball) in the proper direction.

In .NET, an object (the sender) can "throw" an event. The event's receiver can be any other member of the sender's team, or the class that the object belongs to. A delegate guides the event message to the proper receiver. When you think about it in terms of football, it makes more sense!

So what exactly does a delegate look like in your code? You may be surprised to learn that you've used quite a few of them already. Look at this code snippet:

```
'VB.NET
AddHandler Button.Click, new EventHandler(AddressOf method)
```

```
//C#
Button.Click += new EventHandler(this.method);
```

Remember, the definition of a delegate is a *class* that can hold a reference to a method. And the implementation of a class is an object. The delegates in this code snippet are the EventHandler objects. The ScrollEventHandler, ToolBarButtonClickEventHandler, and KeyPressEventHandler objects that you've used in previous lessons are also delegates. In fact, every class that you come across in .NET with the words EventHandler in its name is a delegate.

So, the effect of the preceding code snippet is to add delegates to the Button control's Click event. These delegates point the way to the receiver of the event, the *method* parameter in this case, which is just a method.

Let's talk a moment about the different implementations in VB.NET and C#. In C#, the only way to add a delegate to an event is with the += operator. (For those not familiar with C++ and C, += is a shortcut for summing and assigning.) For example,

```
myInteger += 1;
```

is the same as

```
myInteger = myInteger + 1;
```

 Tip

> To remove a delegate from an event, you use the -= operator (or RemoveHandler method in VB.NET).

In VB.NET, on the other hand, you have a couple more options. The first option—and the one you've been using for a while now—is using AddHandler method. The syntax is fairly straightforward. The `AddHandler` method adds the delegate (pointing to *method*) to the `Button` object's `Click` event. The `AddressOf` operator is simply a keyword that generates a programmatic equivalent of a pointer to the supplied method.

The second, and least common, option VB.NET allows is to use the `Handles` keyword. In a method's declaration, add the `Handles` keyword followed by the event that is to be handled, like Listing 5.3.

LISTING 5.3   Another Way to Wire Events

```
1:  public sub MyEventHandler(Sender as Object, e as EventArgs)
➥Handles btTemp.Click
2:      'do something
3:  end sub
```

This works the same as the other methods.

Do	**DON'T**
Do use the `AddHandler` method in VB.NET most of the time. Not only is the clearest method, but it also allows you to use the same handler for many different events.	**Don't** use the `Handles` method often. It limits you to just one event per handler, and it makes code less readable.
Do try to name your event handlers with a standard naming convention. It makes it much easier to read and understand your code later.	

Note   If you are coming from a background in C++, then you should be familiar with delegates; they are equivalent to function pointers in C++.

Events and Objects

Now let's look at implementing delegates. All predefined delegates in .NET have two parameters: an `Object` that represents the object that generated the event, and a second parameter that provides specifics on the event that occurred.

5

The most common delegate in .NET is EventHandler—you've already seen it in action
many times. When an event occurs, this delegate creates two objects (an Object and an
EventArgs object) and passes them to the event handler, or receiver, that can do with
them what it wants.

The following sections discuss creating delegates and custom events.

Event Handlers

Listing 5.4 shows a typical event handler in VB.NET. It assumes that you've already created a Button control and added to it a delegate pointing to the HandleClick method.
Note that the Button.Click event uses the standard EventHandler delegate.

LISTING 5.4   A Typical Event Handler

```
1:  private sub HandleClick(Sender as Object, e as EventArgs)
2:     Microsoft.VisualBasic.MsgBox(CType(Sender, Button).Text)
3:  end sub
```

Remember that every delegate creates two objects and passes them to the event handler.
The event handler, regardless of whether or not it uses them, must take those two objects
as parameters, as shown on line 1. The first object, which we've named Sender on line 1,
represents the object that generated the event. In this case, that object would be the
Button previously created. Because the delegate that calls this method is of type
EventHandler, the second parameter is of type EventArgs. This second parameter is
used to hold additional information about the event, but in the case of EventArgs, it
holds nothing; it's just used as a placeholder.

(Thankfully, the people at Microsoft who developed .NET and its class libraries used
standard naming conventions. Whatever your delegate name is, the second parameter follows the same naming scheme. For example, EventHandler and EventArgs;
ScrollEventHandler and ScrollEventArgs, and so on.)

In our football analogy, these two parameters wouldn't make much sense. The first parameter could be a picture of the quarterback taped to the ball. The second parameter
would be information such as the radial velocity of the ball as it flies to the receiver, or
maybe the number of fingers the quarterback had on the ball before he let it go. The
receiver wouldn't necessarily do anything with the information, but it's there nonetheless.
There may be times, however, when the receiver will care, and that's why these parameters are there.

You may be wondering why, if the first parameter represents the object that created the
event, the delegate doesn't create that type of object instead. For example, create a

`Button` object in Listing 5.4 instead of an `Object` object. The reason is flexibility. If the delegate passed an actual `Button` type, you would have to have many types of delegates—one for every type of object that could generate an event. The standard `EventHandler` delegate wouldn't be sufficient. Therefore, a delegate wraps the `Button` object up in the guise of an `Object`.

To make more sense of this, imagine that you receive a book in the mail. Most likely, the book is contained in a box for shipping. This box represents the `Object` in our discussion. The shipping company puts the book in a generic box that can be used to send anything. This saves the company from creating a different type of box for every different item it sells. *You* know it's a book in the box, but you can't exactly do much with the box, and never mind about reading it. You must open the box and retrieve the book—in very crude terminology, you *transform* the box into a book.

This is the same thing that happens in the method in Listing 5.4. The first parameter is passed as an `Object` that, as you'll recall from Day 3, "Working with Your Windows Forms," doesn't have many useful properties. Therefore, if you want to use this first parameter, you must first convert it to the type you need—in other words, open the box. For example, on line 2 of Listing 5.4, you use the `CType` method to convert the first parameter from an `Object` to a `Button` type, which then has a `Text` property you can access. In C#, you use the *casting* operator, which is simply a pair of parentheses enclosing the type to transform to:

```
((Button) Sender).Text;
```

Note

It's a good idea to always explicitly convert the sender object to the type you need. VB.NET can (depending on the complexity of the type of object generating the event) perform this conversion for you automatically, but it's not a good idea to rely on VB.NET to do your work.

5

Creating Custom Events

Let's take your knowledge of what classes are, how to use them, and how to consume events to the next step. In this section we'll create a custom class that has its own events that you, or any other developer, can provide handlers for. Because you don't yet know how to create your own UI controls, this example is rather contrived, but it's a good learning exercise nonetheless (you'll find out about creating your own controls in Day 18, "Building Custom Windows Forms Controls").

In this example, we need two things: a custom class that will raise the custom event, and another class that contains the handler for the custom event (this can be a normal

Windows Forms class). We'll create a simple golf ball class in this example as our custom event-generating class. The code for this class is shown in Listing 5.5.

LISTING 5.5 The `GolfBall` Class

```
1:  using System;
2:  using System.Windows.Forms;
3:
4:  namespace TYWinforms.Day5 {
5:     public class GolfBall {
6:        public event EventHandler Sunk;
7:
8:        protected virtual void OnSunk(EventArgs e) {
9:           if (Sunk != null) {
10:              Sunk(this, e);
11:           }
12:        }
13:
14:        public void Putt(int intStrength) {
15:           if (intStrength == 5) {
16:              OnSunk(new EventArgs());
17:           }
18:        }
19:     }
```

ANALYSIS There's a lot of new stuff in this code. On line 5 you declare your custom `GolfBall` class. This class is used to represent a real-world golf ball. For simplicity's sake, we'll only create one method for it, `Putt`, which simulates putting a golf ball. This method is shown on lines 14–18—more on that method in a moment. Consequently, the only event will be raised when the putt makes it into the hole.

Line 6 declares the custom event for this class, `Sunk`. Notice how simple this code line is; it consists of only four words. The event is declared just like a class, but instead of using the `class` keyword, you use the `event` keyword. Additionally, you don't need to provide any functionality for it—after all, it's not up to you to handle the event, it's up to the implementer. You must also specify the type of delegate that will be used to handle your event—in this case, we've used the standard `EventHandler` delegate, although we could have created our own custom one as well—more on that later.

Lines 8–12 declare a peculiar type of method. This method has the same name as our custom event, preceded by the word `On`. Every custom event must have a corresponding `OnEventName` method. The sole purpose of this method is to raise the event, as shown on line 10—no other methods can call the event directly; they must go through this `On` method.

The On method is particularly interesting. The first thing to note is that it takes a parameter of type EventArgs—the type that corresponds to the type of EventHandler used on line 6. You'll see where this parameter comes from in a moment. The second thing to notice is that it seems to evaluate, on line 9, the value of Sunk, our event. What exactly does this mean?

On line 6 you declared a new event, but you didn't provide any implementation for it, nor did you create an instance of it. Recall that you have to create instances of most objects before you can use them—an Event is the same way. By your not creating an instance here, you leave it up to the user of the GolfBall class. With events, the user of your GolfBall class creates an instance by assigning a delegate to the event. For example:

```
GolfBall myGolfBall = new GolfBall();
myGolfBall.Sunk += new EventHandler(this.someMethod)
```

Until the event is assigned a delegate, it is not instantiated, and thus evaluates to null (or Nothing in VB.NET).

The OnSunk method is there to check whether a delegate has been assigned or not. This is what's done on line 9. If Sunk, the event, is not equal to null, then it means a delegate has been assigned, and the event can be raised. If you didn't perform this check, and a delegate is not assigned, you'd receive an error the first time the event needed to be raised.

Note that the event declared on line 6 uses a delegate of type EventHandler. Recall from previous event handlers you've created that the EventHandler delegate (and any delegate, in fact) sends two parameters to the event handler: an Object representing the object that raises the event, and an EventArgs parameter.

So what object here raises our event? Naturally, it's the GolfBall object, the class all of this code is contained in. Therefore, the first parameter you pass to the event is simply this, which represents the current class. The first parameter for raising an event this way is always this (or Me in VB.NET). To learn about the second parameter, we need to skip down to line 14.

This method, Putt, conditionally executes the OnSunk method. If there were any event specific information you wanted to pass, you would create it here. Since there isn't any specific information for this event, we simply create a new EventArgs parameter, and pass it to the OnSunk method.

Let's summarize. First, the user of our GolfBall class creates an instance of this class, and a delegate is assigned to the Sunk event. The user calls the Putt method to try and "sink the golf ball." If it is determined that the proper strength was applied to the putt (as

5

indicated by the intStrength parameter) then the OnSunk method is executed and passed an EventArgs parameter. The OnSunk method, in turn, determines if a delegate has been assigned, and if so, raises the Sunk event, passing it a representation of the current object and the EventArgs parameter. When the Sunk event is raised, the delegate causes the event handler, assigned by the user, to execute.

Let's next look at the GolfBall class user (as opposed to the end-user) side of the code, shown in Listing 5.6.

LISTING 5.6   The User Side of the GolfBall Example

```
 1:    public class MainForm : Form {
 2:        private Button btPutt = new Button();
 3:        private Label lblStrength = new Label();
 4:        private TextBox tbStrength = new TextBox();
 5:        private GolfBall gfBall = new GolfBall();
 6:
 7:        public MainForm() {
 8:            lblStrength.Text = "Strength:";
 9:            lblStrength.Location = new Point(50,50);
10:
11:            tbStrength.Text = 0.ToString();
12:            tbStrength.Location = new Point(125, 50);
13:
14:            btPutt.Text = "Putt the ball";
15:            btPutt.Location = new Point(100, 100);
16:            btPutt.Click += new EventHandler(this.PuttBall);
17:
18:            gfBall.Sunk += new EventHandler(this.BallSunk);
19:
20:            this.Text = "Custom event example";
21:            this.Controls.Add(btPutt);
22:            this.Controls.Add(tbStrength);
23:            this.Controls.Add(lblStrength);
24:        }
25:
26:        public void PuttBall(Object Sender, EventArgs e) {
27:            gfBall.Putt(Convert.ToInt32(tbStrength.Text));
28:        }
29:
30:        public void BallSunk(Object Sender, EventArgs e) {
31:            MessageBox.Show("Sunk!");
32:        }
33:
34:        public static void Main() {
35:            Application.Run(new MainForm());
36:        }
37:    }
38: }
```

Save this listing and Listing 5.5 in a single file.

ANALYSIS There's nothing special about Listing 5.6. On lines 2–5 you create a few controls, including an instance of the GolfBall class. Lines 8–16 simply place the controls on the form and set a few properties. The controls allow the end-user to enter a strength value and click a button to putt the ball.

On line 18 you add a delegate to the Sunk method of the GolfBall class just like you would any other class. Lines 20–23 then add all the controls to your form.

The PuttBall method on line 26 is executed whenever the button declared on line 2 is clicked. It simply executes the Putt method of the GolfBall class, which was defined way back on line 14 of Listing 5.5. It passes the strength value the user has entered into the textbox. The BallSunk method is executed whenever the Sunk event is fired. In this case, Sunk is raised whenever the Putt method is called with a strength value of 5. BallSunk calls the Show method of the MessageBox class (this is different than the MsgBox function of the Microsoft.VisualBasic namespace) to display a simple message indicating that the ball was sunk.

Compile and execute this application. Enter different values into the textbox and notice that nothing happens when you click the button, unless you enter a strength value of 5. The output is shown in Figure 5.3.

FIGURE 5.3

Our custom Sunk *event in action—the user wins!*

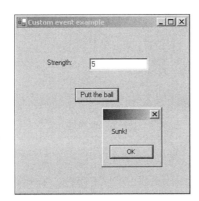

5

Dissecting Controls

With the knowledge that you now have, you can hypothesize about how objects you are already familiar with are implemented (which will help you when creating your own controls). Take the Button control, for instance. Even though you don't know how exactly it was built, you can extrapolate from what you learned today to make a good guess. Let's examine one property, Text, and one event, Click (we'll ignore the process of actually displaying the control, which we'll discuss in Day 13).Specifically, we'll examine how what we learned today is applied in useful objects.

First, you can guess that the Text property is a simple variable, declared in the Button's source code as follows:

```
public string Text;
```

Next, the Button class must declare the Click event, as shown in the following code snippet:

```
public event EventHandler Click;
```

Since all events must have corresponding *On* methods. We declare that next, following the example set in Listing 5.5:

```
protected virtual void OnClick(EventArgs e) {
   if (Click != null) {
      Click(this, e);
   }
}
```

That's all there is to it! Listing 5.7 puts it all together.

LISTING 5.7   The Extrapolated Button Class

```
 1:  using System;
 2:  using System.Windows.Forms;
 3:
 4:  namespace System.Windows.Forms {
 5:     public class Button : ButtonBase {
 6:        public string Text;
 7:        public event EventHandler Click;
 8:
 9:        protected virtual void OnClick(EventArgs e) {
10:           if (Click != null) {
11:              Click(this, e);
12:           }
13:        }
14:
15:        public Button() {
16:           //code to initialize and display the button
17:        }
18:     }
19:  }
```

This is, of course, simplified, since we know the Button control has more than just one property and one event. And, in fact, the Click event is inherited from the Control class, so we wouldn't need to declare it here, but this gives you a good idea what it means to create controls.

Creating Custom Delegates

In creating your own custom events, you'll often need to create your own custom delegate and EventArgs object as well. Creating the delegate is easy; the EventArgs object is a bit more complex, but nothing you aren't ready to tackle.

The delegate declaration consists of one line with the delegate keyword:

```
public delegate void MyEventHandler(Object Sender, MyEventArgs e);
```

This line creates a new delegate named MyEventHandler that can be used in any of your custom events. It provides a MyEventArgs parameter, a custom object that we'll have to create as well (note that both these objects follow the standard naming conventions). Just like an event, you don't need to provide any implementation or code for this delegate; the CLR handles it all for you.

Creating the second parameter consists of building your own custom class with the properties needed by your event, as demonstrated in Listing 5.8.

LISTING 5.8   Creating a Custom EventArgs Class

```
 1:  using System;
 2:  using System.Windows.Forms;
 3:
 4:  namespace TYWinforms.Day5 {
 5:      public class GolfBallEventArgs : EventArgs {
 6:          public readonly int Feet;
 7:          public readonly bool Save;
 8:
 9:          public GolfBallEventArgs(int Feet, bool Save) {
10:              this.Feet = Feet;
11:              this.Save = Save;
12:          }
13:      }
14:  }
```

ANALYSIS   This class, GolfBallEventArgs, will be used to provide custom event information to an event handler. It inherits from the EventArgs class, so that we don't have to duplicate any of the latter's functionality.

On line 6 and 7 you declare two properties: Feet, which tells from how far away the putt was sunk, and Save, which indicates if the putt saved for par. These values are readonly,

5

meaning they cannot be modified by anything other than the constructor. Making these values readonly is a standard practice—after all, once they are set, there is no reason for them to be modified. In VB.NET, these lines would look like:

```
ReadOnly Feet as Integer
ReadOnly Save as Boolean
```

On line 9 we have the constructor for our GolfBallEventArgs class. It takes two parameters, Feet and Save, which correspond to the readonly properties you just created. All this constructor does is assign the parameter values to the appropriate properties of the class.

Let's modify our GolfBall class to use this new delegate and EventArgs object. The new code, modified from Listing 5.5, is shown in Listing 5.9.

LISTING 5.9   Using the Custom Delegate

```
1:  using System;
2:  using System.Windows.Forms;
3:  using System.Drawing;
4:
5:  namespace TYWinforms.Day5 {
6:     public class GolfBallEventArgs : EventArgs {
7:        public readonly int Feet;
8:        public readonly bool Save;
9:
10:        public GolfBallEventArgs(int Feet, bool Save) {
11:           this.Feet = Feet;
12:           this.Save = Save;
13:        }
14:     }
15:
16:     public delegate void GolfBallEventHandler(Object Sender,
    ➥GolfBallEventArgs e);
17:
18:     public class GolfBall {
19:        public event GolfBallEventHandler Sunk;
20:
21:        protected virtual void OnSunk(GolfBallEventArgs e) {
22:           if (Sunk != null) {
23:              Sunk(this, e);
24:           }
25:        }
26:
27:        public void Putt(int intStrength) {
28:           if (intStrength == 5) {
29:              Random rndGen = new Random();
30:              OnSunk(new GolfBallEventArgs(rndGen.Next(1,101),
```

LISTING 5.9   continued

```
➥Convert.ToBoolean(rndGen.Next(0,2))));
31:                }
32:            }
33:        }
```

ANALYSIS Lines 5–14 contain the GolfBallEventArgs class we just developed (Listing 5.8). Line 16 contains the delegate declaration that uses our GolfBallEventArgs class. Inside the GolfBall class, there have only been a few changes. On line 19 you declare the Sunk event using the GolfBallEventHandler delegate instead of EventHandler. Similarly, on lines 21 and 30 you use the GolfBallEventArgs instead of EventArgs. The Putt method, however, does things a bit differently now.

Because it must supply the GolfBallEventArgs object with two values now—Feet and Save—we have to do a little extra work. In this case, we don't actually care what the values are, just as long as they are returned. Therefore, we'll just pass random numbers. On line 29 we create an instance of the Random class, which contains all sorts of methods to generate random numbers, including the method we'll use, Next. The Next method takes two parameters, both integers, that specify a range of values from which to return a random number (Next returns an integer—no decimal places).

For the first parameter, Feet, we'll choose any number from 1 to 100 (any more than that and most people can't sink a putt). For the second parameter, we need a Boolean value. Booleans can be True, False, 1, or 0. Therefore, we use Next to return a random number in the range of 0 to 1 (and since Next returns only integers, it must return either 0 or 1, and nothing in between). Using the Convert.ToBoolean method, we convert the returned random number into a Boolean value to pass to the GolfBallEventArgs constructor.

We can modify the event handler for the Sunk event to take advantage of this new object. For example, using the same MainForm class from Listing 5.6, change line 31 to read:

```
MessageBox.Show("Sunk from " + e.Feet.ToString() + " feet!");
```

Figure 5.4 shows the output of this last modification.

5

FIGURE 5.4

Our custom Sunk *event with the* GolfBallEventArgs *object gives the user something to cheer about.*

Summary

Today's lesson was filled with good technical information. Events are a key part of Windows Forms application, without them, nothing would get done. You now know how the event system works from both the user's and developer's perspective.

An event handler is the method that executes whenever an event is raised. Creating the handler also involves wiring the event to the handler using the AddHandler method in VB.NET, or the += operator in C#. Event handlers have a standard signature, with a few variations.

A delegate is a class that holds a reference to an event handler. It represents the "wires" between an event and its handlers. In .NET, all delegates follow the naming scheme *Name*EventHandler. Delegates provide two parameters to the event handlers: an Object object representing the object that raised the event, and an EventArgs parameter that provides additional information. The EventArgs parameter follows the same naming schemes as the delegate.

To create your own events, you only need to declare it using the event keyword, and choose an appropriate delegate. All events must have a corresponding On*EventName* method, which is used to raise the event. This method can also check to see if a delegate has been wired by checking whether the event evaluates to null (or Nothing in VB.NET).

You can create your own delegates, using the delegate keyword, in much the same way you create a custom event. A delegate doesn't need to have any code or implementation—the CLR creates it for you. Your custom delegates can use a predefined EventArgs parameter, or you can create your own by creating a class that inherits from the EventArgs object. Your custom EventArgs object only needs to provide the custom read-only properties you want, and a constructor to assign values to those properties.

Tomorrow you'll learn about a bevy of new Windows Forms controls that can greatly enhance the UI of your applications. You'll also learn how to arrange those controls on your form in an organized way.

Q&A

Q How do I know what type of delegate to use for an event?

A Unfortunately, there isn't an easy way to tell. Most of the time, you use the standard `EventHandler` delegate, so that's usually a safe bet. If that's not the correct one, your compiler (Visual Studio.NET or the command line compilers, `csc.exe` and `vbc.exe`) will usually tell you the proper one to use.

Throughout this book, I'll point out when you must use a non-standard delegate.

Q Can I assign more than one delegate to a single event?

A Absolutely. You may do this if you want a single event to execute more than action. In our car analogy, it is equivalent to your taking one action (pressing the gas pedal), the car doing multiple actions (moving, the speedometer moving, the cruise control turning off, and so on).

This isn't a very common practice, however, since one event handler can usually perform all the actions you need. However, this is a sly way to "extend" event handlers. For example, assume you have two events: `ShowText` and `ShowTextAndAlert`. Both events need to cause text to be displayed in a label, but the second event also needs to display a message box with an alert. There's no reason to duplicate the code that displays the text, so both events can have a single delegate assigned to it. The `ShowTextAndAlert` event would have another delegate assigned to it as well, that pops up the message box. When the `ShowTextAndAlert` event fires, both event handlers would execute, causing text to be displayed and a message box to pop up.

The event handlers execute in the order they are assigned by the delegates.

Workshop

This workshop helps reinforce the concepts we've covered in today's lesson. It will be very helpful to you to fully understand the answers before moving on. Answers can be found in Appendix A.

5

Quiz

1. What is the standard event handler signature?

2. Create an event named ShowText in C# that uses the KeyPressEventHandler delegate.

3. Create a custom delegate that uses the KeyPressEventArgs object.

4. True or false: To compare object types, you use the equals (=) operator.

5. Which of the following statements is incorrect?

```
AddHandler btOne.Click, new EventHandler(AddressOf btOne_Click)
public sub MyEventHandler(Sender as Object, e as EventArgs)
➥Handles btTemp.Click

AddHandler btOne.Click += new EventHandler(AddressOf btOne.Click)
```

6. Why should the properties of a custom EventArgs object be readonly?

7. Is the following code snippet correct? What, if anything, needs to be changed?

```
public virtual void OnMyEvent(EventArgs e) {
   MyEvent(this, e);
}
```

8. Where must custom events and delegates be declared (in what part of your code)?

Exercise

Create a calculator application in C# like the Windows calculator. It should have numeric buttons that display numbers when pushed, and operator buttons that perform calculations when clicked. Use one event handler for all numeric buttons, and one handler for all operator buttons. (Hint: use hidden controls—controls with their Visible property set to false—to store temporary variables.)

DAY 6

Enhancing Your Windows Forms with More Controls

In today's lesson you will round out your growing repertoire of Windows Forms controls. So far, you've seen the menu, scroll bar, status bar, toolbar, textbox, label, and button controls. Today you'll learn about combo boxes and radio buttons that let users make choices, timers that you can use to keep track of events, treeviews to explore the file system, and many others.

You'll also learn how to use the automatic layout features of Windows Forms to present a cleaner and easier-to-maintain user interface.

Today you will learn how to

- Collect information from and display it logically to the user
- Force the user to make choices
- Format user input
- Display images in your applications
- Build time-keeping applications
- Use the many enumerations available to customize your controls
- Control the positioning of your controls

As you go through today's lesson, there are a few key points to keep in mind about Windows Forms controls.

First, every Windows Forms control in the .NET Framework inherits, directly or indirectly, from the `Control` class, which in turns inherits indirectly from the `Object` class. This means that there are quite a few common properties and methods among these controls, such as the `GetType` method, the `Height` and `Width` properties, the `Click` event, and others you'll learn about later today. For a full listing of these common members, turn to Appendix B, "Windows Forms Controls."

Also, all of these controls share a similar set of rules for usage. You'll find that after you learn one, you'll immediately know the basics of using the others. Of course, each control has its own peculiarities and custom members, but they all follow the same pattern.

Finally, keep in mind that .NET does a lot of the background work for you, to simplify your development. Prior to Windows Forms programming, developers had to know the intricacies of how controls were rendered and their modes. For instance, controls were sometimes put into states that made them immutable. If you attempted to make changes, an error would occur, sometimes causing your application to crash. With Windows Forms, these immutable states still exist, but the CLR takes the necessary steps to prevent any problems from occurring for you.

Without further ado, let's get on with the controls.

The `Button` Control

Let's start with a brief discussion of one that you've already used a few times, `Button`. The most basic property of the `Button` control is `Text`. This property simply sets the caption that is displayed on the button, giving hints to the user as to what the button does. `TextAlign` positions the caption in the button, and can be one of the following `ContentAlignment` enumeration values: `BottomCenter`, `BottomLeft`, `BottomRight`, `MiddleCenter`, `MiddleLeft`, `MiddleRight`, `TopCenter`, `TopLeft`, and `TopRight`—a value for every spot on the button.

The `FlatStyle` property allows you to customize the appearance of the button. This property can be any of the `FlatStyle` enumeration values: `Flat`; `Popup`, where the button appears flat until your mouse moves over the button; `Standard`, the default value; or `System`, where the button appearance is whatever is specified by default by your operating system (which must be one of the preceding three). Figure 6.1 shows the first three styles, as well as the use of the `TextAlign` properties.

FIGURE 6.1

Notice the button text is in different positions in these FlatStyle *value examples. That's a function of the* TextAlign *property.*

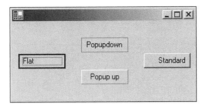

Button controls also allow you to display images in two different ways. You can use the Image and ImageAlign properties, or you can use the ImageList and ImageIndex properties like you did for the toolbars (see Day 4, "Adding Menus and Toolbars to Your Windows Forms," for more information on these latter two). ImageAlign uses the same ContentAlignment enumeration values as TextAlign, while Image takes an Image object:

```
button1.Image = Image.FromFile("C:\WinForms\Day6\MyBitmap.bmp")
```

You already know how to handle the Button control's main event: Click. The following code snippet shows the assignment of a delegate to the Click method, and an example event handler:

```
AddHandler Button1.Click, new EventHandler(AddressOf
➥Me.Button1_Click)
...
private sub Button1_Click(Sender as Object, e as EventArgs)
   MessageBox.Show("You clicked: " & CType(Sender, Button).
➥ToString)
end sub
```

The Button control has a method, PerformClick, that allows you to simulate a button click. In other words, you can raise the Click event just as if the user clicked the button. You don't need to provide any parameters for this method; the CLR will generate them for you:

```
Button1.PerformClick
```

This is useful if you need to invoke the Click event's handler; with PerformClick, you don't have to worry about creating EventArgs objects and such.

The CheckBox and RadioButton Controls

The CheckBox and RadioButton controls are very similar. They both allow the user to select a choice (or choices) from a group of similar items. Chances are you've used these controls when filling out forms on the Internet. The difference is that the CheckBox allows the user to select more than one item from a group, while the RadioButton only allows one selection. Listing 6.1 is an example of using these controls.

6

LISTING 6.1 RadioButton and CheckBox Example

```
 1:  Imports System
 2:  Imports System.Windows.Forms
 3:  Imports System.Drawing
 4:
 5:  namespace TYWinforms.Day6
 6:
 7:    public class Listing61 : Inherits Form
 8:        private lblColor as new Label
 9:        private lblSex as new Label
10:
11:        private chkColorBlue as new CheckBox
12:        private chkColorRed as new CheckBox
13:        private chkColorYellow as new CheckBox
14:        private chkColorGreen as new CheckBox
15:        private rbSexMale as new RadioButton
16:        private rbSexFemale as new RadioButton
17:
18:        public sub New
19:           lblColor.Text = "Choose your favorite color(s)"
20:           lblColor.Location = new Point(10,10)
21:           lblColor.AutoSize = True
22:
23:           chkColorBlue.Text = "Blue"
24:           chkColorBlue.Location = new Point(10,25)
25:           chkColorBlue.Width = 50
26:
27:           chkColorRed.Text = "Red"
28:           chkColorRed.Location = new Point(60,25)
29:           chkColorRed.Width = 50
30:
31:           chkColorYellow.Text = "Yellow"
32:           chkColorYellow.Location = new Point(110,25)
33:           chkColorYellow.Width = 60
34:
35:           chkColorGreen.Text = "Green"
36:           chkColorGreen.Location = new Point(170,25)
37:           chkColorGreen.Width = 60
38:
39:           lblSex.Text = "Choose your gender"
40:           lblSex.Location = new Point(10,50)
41:           lblSex.AutoSize = True
42:
43:           rbSexMale.Text = "Male"
44:           rbSexMale.Location = new Point(10,75)
45:           rbSexMale.Width = 50
46:
47:           rbSexFemale.Text = "Female"
48:           rbSexFemale.Location = new Point(60,75)
```

LISTING 6.1   continued

```
49:              rbSexFemale.Width = 60
50:
51:            Me.Controls.Add(lblColor)
52:            Me.Controls.Add(lblSex)
53:            Me.Controls.Add(chkColorBlue)
54:            Me.Controls.Add(chkColorRed)
55:            Me.Controls.Add(chkColorYellow)
56:            Me.Controls.Add(chkColorGreen)
57:            Me.Controls.Add(rbSexMale)
58:            Me.Controls.Add(rbSexFemale)
59:         end sub
60:
61:         public shared sub Main()
62:             Application.Run(new Listing61)
63:          end sub
64:      end class
65:  end namespace
```

ANALYSIS This listing is very simple. All of the controls used here are declared on lines 8–16, and the `Text`, `Location`, and `Width` properties are set on lines 19–49. The controls are then added to the form on lines 51–58.

Listing 6.1 produces the output shown in Figure 6.2.

FIGURE 6.2

RadioButton*s and* CheckBox*es are very useful in forms.*

`CheckBox` controls allow you to select any combination of boxes in the container control, which happens to be the form in this case. `RadioButtons`, on the other hand, allow only one selection *per parent control*—per form in this case. To create separate groups of `RadioButtons` that each has one selectable value, group the buttons by placing them on a `Panel` control (a `Panel` simply allows you to group controls together; group each set of `RadioButtons` that describe the same value on a single `Panel`). `RadioButtons` contained on separate parent controls are mutually exclusive.

6

There are a few properties the CheckBox and RadioButton controls have in common. The Checked property can be used to check or determine if the specified control is selected. The CheckAlign property is similar to the TextAlign property from the Button control; it determines how the selection box is aligned relative to the text. CheckAlign also uses the ContentAlignment enumeration.

The AutoCheck property determines if the control's appearance should change automatically when clicked. In other words, should a check mark appear when the selection is clicked? Set this property to False if you want to check the control yourself using the Checked property. You'd typically do this if you need to perform some type of validation before allowing a control to be clicked (such as verifying user-entered information).

Appearance is another property that is common to many controls. Using values from the Appearance enumeration (Button or Normal), it determines if the control appears as normal (default), or as a button that can be toggled on or off. The functionality is the same, but it provides a slightly different interface for users.

There is one event the two controls have in common: CheckChanged. This occurs, as the name implies, when the control is checked or unchecked.

The CheckBox, due to its more complex features, has a few additional properties. CheckState property is similar to the Checked property, but provides slightly more advanced capabilities. The CheckState property must be one of the CheckState enumeration values: Checked, Unchecked, or Indeterminate. The first two provide the same functionality as the Checked property. Indeterminate, however, is a third state of a CheckBox control; the control is checked, but shaded, so that it gives the impression of being only partially checked. Add the following line to Listing 6.1 (after line 25) and recompile the application to see this new state:

```
chkColorBlue.CheckState = CheckState.Indeterminate
```

By default, you can only select this "indeterminate" state in code. However, if you set the ThreeState property to True, then the user can toggle into this mode as well.

Finally, to go along with the CheckState property, the CheckStateChanged event is raised whenever this property changes, much like CheckChanged is raised for changes of Checked.

Since both of the CheckBox and RadioButton controls inherit from the same class as the Button control (ButtonBase), they share many of the same properties—Text, TextAlign, PerformClick, and FlatStyle, for example.

The ComboBox Control

The ComboBox control is an interesting one; it combines an editable text field (like a TextBox) and a drop-down list from which the user can use to choose predefined options. Because of this dual functionality, it has quite a few properties to set its appearance and assign choices.

The next few sections describe in detail how to use this peculiar control.

Instantiating the ComboBox

Creating this control is just like creating any other control:

```
dim cboMyList as new ComboBox
```

You can use the Top and Left or Location properties to position the control on its form, and the Font, BackColor, and other properties that are available to all controls to customize its appearance. You can even use the Text property to display a string in the textbox-like portion of this control. The interesting properties, however, deal with the population of the drop-down list part.

The simplest way to add items to the ComboBox is to use the Items collection and the Add or AddRange method. The first adds a single item to the list, and the second adds an entire array of objects. Listing 6.2 shows both methods.

LISTING 6.2   Adding Items to a ComboBox Drop-Down List

```
 1:  Imports System
 2:  Imports System.Windows.Forms
 3:  Imports System.Drawing
 4:
 5:  namespace TYWinforms.Day6
 6:
 7:     public class Listing62 : Inherits Form
 8:        private cboMyList as new ComboBox
 9:
10:        public sub New
11:           cboMyList.Location = new Point(75,50)
12:           cboMyList.Text = "Select an Item"
13:           cboMyList.Items.Add("Single Item")
14:           cboMyList.Items.AddRange(new Object() _
➥{"1st in Range", "2nd in Range", "3rd in Range"})
15:
16:           Me.Text = "Listing 6.2"
17:           Me.Controls.Add(cboMyList)
18:        end sub
19:
```

6

LISTING 6.2   continued

```
20:        public shared sub Main()
21:            Application.Run(new Listing62)
22:        end sub
23:    end class
24: end namespace
```

ANALYSIS   We start adding items in lines 13 and 14—we'll get to those in a moment. Line 12 sets the text that is displayed in the textbox portion of the control. This text appears when no other item in the list has been selected; in this way, it often substitutes as a default value or selection.

Line 13 adds a single item to the list using the Add method. Line 14 adds an array to the ComboBox. Both the Add and AddRange methods take Object data types as parameters. Here, you are creating objects of type string, the most common type, but you could easily add other types. If you do assign another type of object to the ComboBox, be sure to set the DisplayMember property to the property of the object you want to display. For example, the Text property of a Button object:

```
cboMyList.Items.Add(new Button())
cboMyList.DisplayMember = "Text"
```

If you don't specify a property to display, the CLR automatically executes the ToString method on the object in question and displays the result.

Note that line 14 creates a new Object array and populates it with values on the same line. You could have done the same by using the following two lines instead:

```
dim arrList as Object() = {"1st in Range", "2nd in Range",
➡"3rd in Range"}
cboMyList.Items.AddRange(arrList)
```

Some people prefer doing things one way, and some, the other. The choice is yours.

Figure 6.3 shows the output of this listing.

Instead of using the AddRange method to add multiple values at once, you can also set the DataSource property to an object array. The following code snippet does the same thing as line 14 in Listing 6.2:

```
cboMyList.DataSource = new Object() {"1st in Range",
➡"2nd in Range", "3rd in Range"}
```

Using DataSource, you can easily set the ComboBox's items to any collection of objects. In Day 9, "Using ADO.NET," you'll see another wonderful use for this property involving databases.

FIGURE 6.3

You can see the single item and the range items we added to our ComboBox *control example.*

Tip

> If you're going to add many items to the ComboBox by using the Add method, first call the BeginUpdate method:
>
> cboMyList.BeginUpdate()
>
> This method forces the application to stop updating the UI of the ComboBox until all items are added. Updating the UI is a time-consuming process, and if you have to add many items one at a time, the updates could slow your application to a crawl. When you're done adding items, call the EndUpdate method:
>
> cboMyList.EndUpdate()

Controlling the Display

DropDownStyle is the first property you need to know about for controlling the ComboBox display. It controls the look and feel of the UI for the control, and may alter the way your user interacts with the ComboBox. This property must be set to one of the ComboBoxStyle enumeration values:

- DropDown—The default value. The textbox portion is editable by the user, and she must click an arrow to see the drop-down contents.

- DropDownList—The user cannot edit the textbox portion. The drop-down portion is the same as with the DropDown value.

- Simple—The user can edit the textbox portion, and the drop-down list is always displayed (there is no arrow to click to display more items, although there may be a scroll bar).

6

Once you've set this property, there are several others you can use to customize the look of the textbox portion. MaxLength sets the maximum number of characters that can be entered in the text area (note, however, that if the user selects an item from the list that is longer than MaxLength, the item's entire text will still be shown). SelectedText returns whatever value is currently selected in the text area.

To control what part of the displayed text is selected, use the SelectionStart and SelectionLength properties. The first takes an integer that specifies the character to start the selection. The second property determines how many characters after the SelectionStart position will be selected.

The Select and SelectAll methods allow you to select a part or all of the text in the text area. SelectAll takes no parameters, but Select takes two integer values specifying the range of characters to select. Selecting text is often useful if you need to update or insert new items into the ComboBox.

The drop-down list also has several custom properties. First, DroppedDown, simply enough, indicates if the drop-down list is currently displayed. DropDownWidth, similar to the MaxLength property, indicates the number of characters that can be displayed in the list. DropDownWidth, however, is measured in pixels rather than characters. MaxDropDownItems indicates the number of items that will be displayed at once when the user clicks the drop-down list. If you have more items in the list than MaxDropDownItems, a scroll bar appears on the list allowing the user to view more items.

Two properties have to do with the height of the ComboBox. ItemHeight is the height, in pixels, of each item in the list. This property does not let you adjust the height, only view it (that is, unless you override the control's default behavior, but we'll learn about that in Day 18, "Building Custom Windows Forms Controls"). PreferredHeight is assigned by the user's operating system, and indicates the actual height of the control.

Finally, you can use the Sorted property to tell the ComboBox to automatically sort (alphabetically) the items in the list. Items already in the list will be sorted, and newly added items will be placed in the proper alphabetic position. Set Sorted to True if you want this functionality, or False otherwise.

Using the ComboBox

Now that you have all the values in the ComboBox for the user to choose from, you'll need to know how to control and monitor the selection. Two of the most common members of ComboBox you'll use are the SelectedIndex property and SelectedIndexChanged event. Listing 6.3 shows an example using these members.

LISTING 6.3 Monitoring the User's Selection

```
1:  Imports System
2:  Imports System.Windows.Forms
3:  Imports System.Drawing
4:
5:  namespace TYWinforms.Day6
6:
7:      public class Listing63 : Inherits Form
8:          private cboMyList as new ComboBox
9:
10:         public sub New
11:             cboMyList.Location = new Point(75,50)
12:             cboMyList.Text = "Select an Item"
13:             dim arrList as Object() = {"1st in Range",
➥"2nd in Range", "3rd in Range"}
14:             cboMyList.Items.AddRange(arrList)
15:             AddHandler cboMyList.SelectedIndexChanged, new
➥EventHandler(AddressOf Me.HandleSelect)
16:
17:             Me.Text = "Listing 6.3"
18:             Me.Controls.Add(cboMyList)
19:         end sub
20:
21:         public sub HandleSelect(Sender as Object, e as
➥EventArgs)
22:             MessageBox.Show("You have selected item: " &
➥ cboMyList.SelectedIndex.ToString)
23:         end sub
24:
25:         public shared sub Main()
26:             Application.Run(new Listing63)
27:         end sub
28:     end class
29: end namespace
```

ANALYSIS This listing is similar to Listing 6.2. The ComboBox is populated on lines 13 and 14, this time using only an array. A delegate is then assigned to the SelectedIndexChanged event on line 15, which occurs whenever the user selects a new item from the list.

The handler for this event, HandleSelect, begins on line 21, and consists of a single line of code. Using the MessageBox.Show method, you display a message to the user indicating which item he selected. Remember that all lists in .NET are zero-based (meaning they start at zero instead of one) so if the user selects the second item, the message box will show item 1 selected.

Figure 6.4 shows the output from Listing 6.3.

6

FIGURE 6.4

SelectedIndex *displays the index number of the selected item.*

Most of the time, these two members will be enough to give you the control you need. There are, however, a few more useful methods that may come in handy: FindString and FindStringExact. The first method finds and returns the index for the first item in the list that begins with the string you specify. For example, using Listing 6.3, the following code snippet would return the number 0:

```
cboMyList.FindString("1st")
```

FindStringExact, however, returns the first item in the list that matches the string exactly. The previous code snippet would return nothing, because there are no items with only the text "1st". This method is useful if you need to search a ComboBox for a particular value (and even more useful for your users when you have a very long listing).

The ComboBox is a very powerful control; you just have to know how to use it.

The DateTimePicker Control

The DateTimePicker control, by default, behaves very much like the ComboBox control; it has an editable text portion and a drop-down list. Only with the DateTimePicker the text portion is a modifiable date, and the drop-down is an interactive calendar. Figure 6.5 shows a typical DateTimePicker control.

This single control presents a very powerful user interface. The user can change the date in the control by entering it directly into the text portion, or by selecting one from the calendar portion. The calendar provides buttons that allow the user to move back and forth in time by months, or select months from a list by clicking on the title bar. Best of all, the DateTimePicker only allows real, valid dates to be entered or chosen. Thus, a user can't enter the date "July 57th, 1345" no matter how much he tries.

FIGURE 6.5

A DateTimePicker *allows you to select dates and times.*

The DateTimePicker has a number of properties that can be used to customize the appearance of the calendar:

Property	Used To Set
CalendarFont	Font used in the calendar
CalendarForeColor	Color of the text
CalendarMonthBackground	Color behind the month
CalendarTitleBackColor	Color behind the title
CalendarTitleForeColor	Color of the text of the title
CalendarTrailingForeColor	Color of the trailing dates in the calendar

You can tailor the display to your heart's content!

In addition, the Format property allows you to control how the dates are displayed in the text area. These must be the values in the DateTimePickerFormat enumeration:

- Custom—A custom display format; use the CustomFormat property.
- Long—The long date time format chosen by the user's operating system. For example, "Wednesday, November 07, 2001."
- Short—The short date time format chosen by the user's operating system. For example, "11/7/01."
- Time—The time formatting according to the user's operating system. For example, "9:48:25 PM."

6

When the Format is set to DateTimePickerFormat.Custom, you can use the CustomFormat property to tailor the display of the date and time. This property uses specially formatted strings to display date/time information. For example, the following code snippet would display the date "June, 01, 0930":

```
dtpMyDate.CustomFormat = "MMMM, dd, HHmm"
```

Table 6.1 shows all of the strings available (the string values are case-sensitive).

TABLE 6.1   CustomFormat Date/Time Strings

Format String	Description
d	One or two-digit day
dd	Two-digit day
ddd	Three-character day of week name abbreviation
dddd	Full day of week name
h	One or two-digit hour in 12-hour format (for example, 1 PM)
hh	Two-digit hour in 12-hour format
H	One- or two-digit hour in 24-hour format (for example, 1300 hours)
HH	Two-digit hour in 24-hour format
m	One- or two-digit minute
mm	Two-digit minute
M	One- or two-digit month
MM	Two-digit month
MMM	Three-character month name abbreviation
MMMM	Full month name
s	One- or two-digit second
ss	Two-digit second
t	One-letter AM/PM abbreviation (for example, "AM" is displayed as "A")
tt	Two-letter AM/PM abbreviation
y	One-digit year (for example, 2001 is displayed as "1")
yy	Last two digits of the year
yyyy	All four digits of the year

The Value property returns a DateTime object representing the time currently displayed on the control. MaxDate and MinDate specify the maximum (furthest in the future) and minimum (furthest in the past) dates that the user can select from the calendar. These properties take `DateTime` objects as values. For example, the following code snippet sets the minimum date to June 20, 1985:

```
dtpMinDate = new DateTime(1985, 6, 20)
```

`DropDownAlignment` takes a `LeftRightAlignment` enumeration value to specify which side of the text area the calendar should be aligned with. Possible values are `LeftRightAlignment.Left` (the default value) and `LeftRightAlignment.Right`.

There are a couple ways you can allow the user to change the date in the text area. The first, which is the default, is to let the user type in the value. The `DateTimePicker` allows only valid entries (the exact type may depend on the `Format` property), so you don't have to worry about invalid data. The second method is to allow the user to use an up/down control (sort of like a very small scroll bar) to modify the values. For this method, you must set the `ShowUpDown` property to `True`.

Setting `ShowCheckBox` to `True` displays a check box next to the date in the text area, allowing the user to signify that he is explicitly "choosing" the date being displayed. This can be useful when you require the user to enter ranges of date values—by leaving the check box unchecked, the user could specify an open-end or beginning date. Use the `Checked` property to see if the check box is currently checked.

There are a few important events to the `DateTimePicker` control. `Checked` property`ValueChanged` is fired when the value in the text area changes, whether by direct editing or a selection from the calendar.

The `CloseUp` and `DropDown` events fire when the calendar portion of the control is closed or opened, respectively. You may want to take advantage of these events to perform validation checks—to see if, for example, a selected date falls in a valid range before allowing the user to continue.

The `ImageList` Control

We discussed the `ImageList` control in Day 4, "Adding Menus and Toolbars to Your Windows," so we won't spend much time with it here.

Recapping, the most prevalent property of the `ImageList` is `Images`, which holds a collection of images that may be used by other parts of your application. To add images, simply use the `Add` method. For example:

```
private ImageList ilstToolbar = new ImageList();
ilstToolbar.Images.Add(Image.FromFile("i_open.bmp"));
ilstToolbar.Images.Add(Image.FromFile("i_maximize.bmp"));
```

6

To remove images, use Remove, specifying the index of the image to remove. There are only a few other ImageList control properties: ColorDepth, which returns the number of colors available for each image in the list (in bits—4 bits, 8 bits, and so on); ImageSize, which can be used to resize the images in the list; and TransparentColor, which makes a color in the image transparent, allowing things behind the image to be seen. Listing 6.4 shows a typical example of an ImageList interacting with a Button control.

LISTING 6.4   Using the ImageList in C#

```
1:   using System;
2:   using System.Windows.Forms;
3:   using System.Drawing;
4:
5:   namespace TYWinForms.Day6 {
6:
7:      public class Listing64 : Form {
8:         private ImageList ilstButton = new ImageList();
9:         private Button btImage = new Button();
10:
11:         public Listing64() {
12:            ilstButton.Images.Add(Image.FromFile
➥("i_open.bmp"));
13:            ilstButton.Images.Add(Image.FromFile
➥ ("i_maximize.bmp"));
14:            ilstButton.Images.Add(Image.FromFile
➥ ("i_happy.bmp"));
15:
16:            btImage.ImageList = ilstButton;
17:            btImage.ImageIndex = 0;
18:            btImage.Location = new Point(100,100);
19:            btImage.Click += new EventHandler
➥ (this.CycleImages);
20:
21:            this.Text = "Listing 6.4";
22:            this.Controls.Add(btImage);
23:         }
24:
25:         public void CycleImages(Object Sender, EventArgs e) {
26:            if (btImage.ImageIndex ==
➥ilstButton.Images.Count-1) {
27:               btImage.ImageIndex = 0;
28:            } else {
29:               btImage.ImageIndex += 1;
30:            }
31:         }
32:
33:         public static void Main() {
34:            Application.Run(new Listing64());
```

LISTING 6.4   continued

```
35:           }
36:       }
37:   }
```

ANALYSIS   The ImageList is populated with images on lines 12–14 (make sure you change these lines to point to images you have available on your computer!). Button, like many Windows Forms controls, has an ImageList property, which lets you assign an ImageList to that control. Line 16 assigns the ImageList to the Button. Line 17 sets the button to initially display the first image in the list.

Line 18 positions the button on the form, and line 19 adds a delegate to the Click event.

The event handler, CycleImages on line 25, changes the image displayed in the Button, but performs some checks first. When the user clicks the button, you want the next image to be displayed. This is done by simply incrementing the ImageIndex property, as shown on line 29. Once you come to the last image in the list, however, the image won't change anymore because there are no more images available. In this case, you want to reset the ImageIndex property to 0, so that the images start from the beginning and cycle again. On line 26 a check is performed to see if the ImageIndex value is currently on the last image in the list (Count - 1). If so, restart ImageIndex on 0; otherwise, increment to the next value.

Figure 6.6 shows the output from this example.

FIGURE 6.6

Assigning an ImageList *to a* Button *causes images to be displayed instead of text.*

6

The ListBox Control

The ListBox control is very much like the ComboBox control (in fact, a ComboBox is a combination of a ListBox and TextBox). They share members such as Items, DataSource, DisplayMember, SelectedIndex, FindString, and so on. After all, both ListBox and ComboBox derive from the same parent, ListControl. The ListBox, because it is not a combination of anything, is more specialized in its job than the ComboBox is, so it has a few more members.

The ListBox is used to display a list of items to the user. A ListBox is always displayed—it doesn't hide like the drop-down in a ComboBox. And, unlike ComboBox, users can select multiple items in a ListBox at once by holding the Ctrl or Shift key as they select items. Being able to select many items means that the ListBox has to have some more complex functionality.

The example in Listing 6.5 uses most of the available properties of the ListBox.

LISTING 6.5   Using the ListBox Control in C#

```
 1:  using System;
 2:  using System.Windows.Forms;
 3:  using System.Drawing;
 4:
 5:  namespace TYWinForms.Day6 {
 6:
 7:     public class Listing65 : Form {
 8:        private ListBox lbItems = new ListBox();
 9:
10:        public Listing65() {
11:           lbItems.Location = new Point(75,75);
12:           lbItems.MultiColumn = true;
13:           lbItems.ColumnWidth = 75;
14:           lbItems.SelectedIndexChanged += new
➥EventHandler(this.HandleSelect);
15:           lbItems.SelectionMode = SelectionMode.MultiExtended;
16:
17:           Object [] arrColors = {"White", "Red", "Orange",
➥"Yellow", "Green", "Blue", "Indigo", "Violet", "Black"};
18:           lbItems.Items.AddRange(arrColors);
19:
20:           this.Text = "Listing 6.5";
21:           this.Controls.Add(lbItems);
22:        }
23:
24:        public void HandleSelect(Object Sender, EventArgs e) {
25:           ListBox lbTemp = (ListBox)Sender;
26:           int i;
27:
28:           if (lbTemp.SelectedIndices.Count == 1 ) {
29:              lbItems.BackColor = Color.FromName(lbTemp.
➥SelectedItem.ToString());
30:           } else {
31:              for (i = 0; i < lbTemp.SelectedIndices.Count;
➥i++) {
```

LISTING 6.5   continued

```
32:                      MessageBox.Show("You selected: " +
➥lbTemp.SelectedItems[i].ToString());
33:               }
34:            }
35:         }
36:
37:      public static void Main() {
38:         Application.Run(new Listing65());
39:      }
40:   }
41: }
```

ANALYSIS Lines 11–18 contain most of the properties we're interested in. Line 11 you already know; it sets the position of the control on the form.

The ListBox can display multiple columns of items at once. When you set MultiColumn to true, as on line 12, the ListBox creates as many columns as necessary to accommodate its items, so that the user won't have to scroll down (note that the scrolling functionality is already built into the ListBox, so you don't have to handle any of those events). Figure 6.7 shows an example of this concept.

FIGURE 6.7

MultiColumn *specifies if items can scroll horizontally or vertically.*

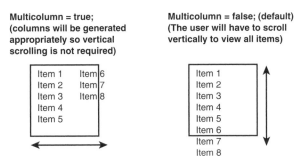

Multicolumn = true;
(columns will be generated appropriately so vertical scrolling is not required)

Multicolumn = false; (default)
(The user will have to scroll vertically to view all items)

Line 13 simply sets the width of each column when MultiColumn is set to true. Line 14 assigns a delegate to the SelectedIndexChanged event, exactly like the event of the same name for the ComboBox control.

Line 15 sets the SelectionMode of the ListBox. This property determines how the user can select items (multi-selects, single selects, and so on). The possible values of the SelectionMode enumeration are

6

- `MultiExtended`—The user can select multiple items by using the Shift, Ctrl, and arrow keys. (This is the typical way of allowing multi-select.)
- `MultiSimple`—The user can select multiple items simply by clicking on them one at a time. Each subsequent click adds a new selected item—no modifier key (such as Shift or Ctrl) is necessary.
- `None`—No selections are allowed.
- `One`—Only one item is selectable at a time.

Finally, on lines 17 and 18 you create an array of string objects and assign it to the `ListBox` using the `AddRange` method. Note that we use color names here, and in a moment you'll see how these colors are used.

Let's skip down to line 24, the event handler for the `SelectedIndexChanged` event. The first thing to do in this method is to create two variables: a `ListBox` and an integer. The first variable is used as a shortcut to the object that generated the event. Recall that the `Sender` variable must be cast to the appropriate type whenever you want to use it:

```
((ListBox)Sender).property
```

To save yourself from having to type the cast every single time, do it once on line 25 and use the new `lbTemp` variable from now on, which now is identical to the object that generated the event, `lbItems`. This isn't a necessary step, but does save some typing.

There are two possible situations: The user has selected one item, and the user has selected more than one item. In the one-item case, we want to set the background color of the `ListBox` to the selected color. In the multiple-items case, we obviously can't set the background of the `ListBox` to more than one color at a time; instead, we simply display a message box alerting the user to his selections (actually, only the user's last selection is displayed in the message box).

So on line 28, you use the `SelectedIndices` property that returns the item indices that have been selected, no matter how many items were selected. If the number of `SelectedIndices` (as specified by the `Count` property) equals one, then you know only one item has been selected. On line 29, then, you use the `FromName` method of the `Color` object to return the appropriate `Color` value based on the selected item. Remember that the `SelectedItem` property returns a string object, so you need to use the `ToString` method to get the string representation instead.

Lines 30–33 handle the case where there is more than one selection. Using the integer variable, `i`, that you created earlier, you loop through each of the selected items. The `for` loop sets the variable `i` to `0`, and continues to increment it (and execute the code in the loop), until it no longer is less than the number of selected indices (as specified by

`SelectedIndices.Count`). The code in the loop uses the `MessageBox.Show` method to display an alert to the user. `SelectedItems` is a collection of the selected items (much like `SelectedIndices` is a collection of the index numbers of the selected items).

That's all there is to it. Figure 6.8 shows the output after a single color has been selected (the background color of the `ListBox` has changed), and then multiple items.

FIGURE 6.8

The `ListBox` allows multiple selections.

There are just a few more members of the `ListBox` to learn about. `ScrollAlwaysVisible` can be set to `true` to cause a vertical scroll bar to always be displayed on the `ListBox`, even if all of the items are visible without scrolling.

`UseTabStops` is an interesting property. If the item or text you want to display in the `ListBox` contains tabs, setting this property to `true` causes those tabs to be displayed as normal. Setting `UseTabStops` to `false` converts the tabs to single spaces.

Finally, the `ListBox` has a `Text` property that's a little different from the `Text` property of all the other controls. If an item has already been selected, then `Text` returns the text of that item. If multiple items have been selected, `Text` returns the text of the first selected item. However, if you try to set `Text` equal to a value, it performs a search for the text and selects that item, just like the `FindStringExact` method. For example, the following code would select the item with the text "Hello World" (assuming, of course, there is an item with that text):

```
lbTemp.Text = "Hello World";
```

The **PictureBox** Control

The `PictureBox` control is a very simple one; its only job is to display an image to the user. Let's take a look at a few of its properties.

6

First, and probably most importantly, is the `Image` property, which indicates what image the `PictureBox` will display. This image can be almost any graphic file, such as `GIF`, `JPEG`, or `BMP`. For example:

```
dim pbMyPicture as new PictureBox
pbMyPicture.Image = Image.FromFile("i_happy.bmp")
```

Just make sure that the image you use is a valid one, and that you provide the proper path for it (image files are typically placed in the same directory as the application).

`SizeMode` controls how the images are displayed, and takes any of the `PictureBoxSizeMode` enumeration values:

- `AutoSize`—The `PictureBox` changes size to equal the size of the picture inside it.
- `CenterImage`—The picture is centered in the `PictureBox`. If the picture is larger than the `PictureBox`, the outside edges are cropped.
- `Normal`—The picture is aligned in the upper-left corner of the `PictureBox`. If the image is larger than the `PictureBox`, the outside edges are cropped.
- `StretchImage`—The picture will be shrunk or stretched to completely fill the `PictureBox`.

In Day 13, "Creating Graphical Applications with GDI+," you'll see how to use scroll bars in combination with the `PictureBox` to move around an image that is larger than the `PictureBox`.

The `TabControl` Control

In the Windows operating system, it is very common to see "tabbed" windows—windows that have numerous tabs that group functionality. For example, Figure 6.9 shows Windows' Display Properties dialog box, which has five tabs.

Prior to .NET, creating this type of interface was often a chore, requiring many different controls and maintenance of the order in which tab pages displayed. With the `TabControl`, it's now a snap to build these interactive windows.

Like the `Toolbar` and `MainMenu` controls, `TabControl` consists of the main control and several child controls. Each of the tabs (and pages) is represented by a `TabPage` control. To add a new tab to the `TabControl`, simply call the `Add` method:

```
TabControl tcMain = new TabControl();
tcMain.TabPages.Add(new TabPage("Tab 1"));
```

The easiest way to understand these controls is through an example. It's a rather long example, so I'll split it into sections to make it easier to dissect. The first part, the application framework, is shown in Listing 6.6.

FIGURE 6.9

You can use TabControl *to create tabbed windows.*

LISTING 6.6 Creating Tabs in Your Application in C#

```
1:  using System;
2:  using System.Windows.Forms;
3:  using System.Drawing;
4:
5:  namespace TYWinForms.Day6 {
6:
7:      public class Listing66 : Form {
8:          private TabControl tcMain = new TabControl();
9:          private TabPage tpGeneral = new TabPage("General");
10:          private TabPage tpDisplay = new TabPage("Display");
11:          private TabPage tpLocation = new TabPage("Location");
12:          private TabPage tpAdvanced = new TabPage("Advanced");
13:
14:          private Label lbl1Name = new Label();
15:          private TextBox tb2Color = new TextBox();
16:          private Button bt2Color = new Button();
17:          private TextBox tb3Top = new TextBox();
18:          private TextBox tb3Left = new TextBox();
19:          private Button bt3Location = new Button();
20:          private TextBox tb4Tab = new TextBox();
21:          private Button bt4Tab = new Button();
22:
23:          public static void Main() {
24:              Application.Run(new Listing66());
25:          }
26:      }
27:  }
```

ANALYSIS This listing is very simple. The appropriate namespaces are imported on lines 1–3. The class and namespace are declared on lines 5 and 7, and all the controls we'll need are declared on lines 8–21. These include a TabControl, four TabPages, and several Buttons and Labels. Line 23 declares the Main method, which, as usual, just calls the Run method.

Listing 6.7 shows the constructor for this class, which should be placed between lines 22 and 23 in Listing 6.6.

LISTING 6.7   The TabControl Constructor Example

```
1:  public Listing66() {
2:      // Tab Page 1
3:      lbl1Name.Text = "Listing 6.6: Teach Yourself Windows Forms in 21 Days";
4:      lbl1Name.AutoSize = true;
5:      lbl1Name.Location = new Point(10,75);
6:
7:      // Tab Page 2
8:      tb2Color.Location = new Point(25,75);
9:
10:      bt2Color.Text = "Change!";
11:      bt2Color.Location = new Point(125,75);
12:      bt2Color.Click += new EventHandler(this.ChangeColor);
13:
14:      // Tab Page 3
15:      tb3Top.Text = this.DesktopLocation.Y.ToString();
16:      tb3Top.Location = new Point(25,50);
17:      tb3Left.Text = this.DesktopLocation.X.ToString();
18:      tb3Left.Location = new Point(25,75);
19:
20:      bt3Location.Text = "Change!";
21:      bt3Location.Location = new Point(125,75);
22:      bt3Location.Click += new EventHandler(this.
➥ChangeLocation);
23:
24:      // Tab Page 4
25:      tb4Tab.Location = new Point(25,50);
26:
27:      bt4Tab.Text = "Add Tab!";
28:      bt4Tab.Location = new Point(75,75);
29:      bt4Tab.Click += new EventHandler(this.AddTab);
30:
31:      tpGeneral.Controls.Add(lbl1Name);
32:      tpDisplay.Controls.Add(tb2Color);
33:      tpDisplay.Controls.Add(bt2Color);
34:      tpLocation.Controls.Add(tb3Top);
35:      tpLocation.Controls.Add(tb3Left);
36:      tpLocation.Controls.Add(bt3Location);
37:      tpAdvanced.Controls.Add(tb4Tab);
38:      tpAdvanced.Controls.Add(bt4Tab);
39:
```

LISTING 6.7 continued

```
40:     tcMain.Width = this.Width;
41:     tcMain.Height = this.Height;
42:     tcMain.TabPages.Add(tpGeneral);
43:     tcMain.TabPages.Add(tpDisplay);
44:     tcMain.TabPages.Add(tpLocation);
45:     tcMain.TabPages.Add(tpAdvanced);
46:
47:     this.Text = "Listing 6.6";
48:     this.Controls.Add(tcMain);
49:  }
```

ANALYSIS This part of the code is divided into sections for each of the tabs. Our design calls for four tabs: "General," which displays general information about the application; "Display," which allows the user to customize the color of the application; "Location," which allows the user to programmatically adjust the location of the application on the desktop; and "Advanced," which allows users to add new TabPages to the application.

Lines 2–5 set up the controls that will appear on the first tab page. Here we only have a Label control. Lines 8–12 contain the initialization for the second tab page. We create a TextBox that the user can enter a new color in, and a Button that allows him to submit the value. (The event handler, ChangeColor, is shown in Listing 6.8—we'll get there in a moment.)

Tab page 3, on lines 15–22, contain two TextBoxes (one for the top of the application and one for the left), and a Button to submit the new values. Tab page 4 is has one TextBox and a Button. (Both event handlers for these controls are in Listing 6.8.)

There's been nothing new or difficult in the code yet. Once we have all the controls, we have to add them to the appropriate tab pages. This is done the same way controls are added to the form: using the Controls.Add method. Lines 31–38 add the controls we've just discussed to all the appropriate tabs.

Lines 40–45 set up the properties for the main TabControl object. We have to add all the TabPages to the TabControl just as all the other controls were added to the TabPages. Then on line 48 you have to add the TabControl to the Form.

You can compile this application as is to see the application so far (don't forget to first comment out lines 12, 22, and 29 in Listing 6.7—these lines will raise errors because we haven't yet created these event handler methods). Note that the tabs are already fully functional—you can move around the tabs without having written any code to do so!

6

Let's examine the event handlers, shown in Listing 6.8. This code should be placed after the constructor, but before the Main method in Listing 6.6 (note that it doesn't actually have to go here, it's just a good suggestion).

LISTING 6.8   Handling Events with the `TabControl`

```
1:  public void ChangeColor(Object Sender, EventArgs e) {
2:      int i;
3:
4:      for (i = 0; i < tcMain.TabPages.Count; i++) {
5:          tcMain.TabPages[i].BackColor = Color.FromName
➥(tb2Color.Text);
6:      }
7:  }
8:
9:  public void ChangeLocation(Object Sender, EventArgs e) {
10:      this.DesktopLocation = new Point(Convert.ToInt32
➥ (tb3Top.Text), Convert.ToInt32(tb3Left.Text));
11:  }
12:
13:  public void AddTab(Object Sender, EventArgs e) {
14:      tcMain.TabPages.Add(new TabPage(tb4Tab.Text));
15:  }
```

ANALYSIS   Lines 1–7 contain the `ChangeColor` method, which is responsible for taking the color a user has specified and applying it to the application. The method is executed when the `bt2Color` button is clicked on the second tab page.

Changing the color, however, isn't as easy as it seems. You could set the form's `BackColor` property to the new color, but since the `TabPages` are covering the entire form, the color change would not be shown. Therefore, you need to change the color of the `TabPages` themselves. Line 4 uses another `for` loop to count from the first tab page to the last (as specified by `TabPages.Count`). For each `TabPage` in the `TabControl` control, you set the `BackColor` to the color specified by the user. Use the `FromName` method of the `Color` object to transform the given text into a `Color` value.

Lines 9–11 contain the `ChangeLocation` method, which moves the form around the user's desktop, given values from the third tab page. This method is actually very simple: just use the `DesktopLocation` property of the `Form` object to position the form to the coordinates specified by the user. Remember to convert the text in the textboxes to an integer using the `Convert.ToInt32` method, as shown on line 10.

Finally, the `AddTab` method on line 13 is the simplest of them all. It just creates and adds a new tab to the `TabControl` object. The text specified by the user in `tb4Tab` will be used as the title of the tab.

Compile this complete application and experiment with the functionality. Figure 6.10 shows the output after adding a new tab.

FIGURE 6.10

You can dynamically create new tabs with the TabControl *control.*

There are a few more TabControl properties of which you should be aware. First, the TabControl has the same SelectedIndex and SelectedIndexChanged members that the ComboBox and ListBox controls had, so you already know how to use them. In addition, it has a SelectedTab property that returns the TabPage object that is currently selected.

TabControl can also use images in the tabs' titles rather than text like you used in Listings 6.6–6.8. Simply create an ImageList like always and assign it to the ImageList property of the TabControl.

You can change the location of the tabs on your form by using the Alignment property. This property takes one of the TabAlignment enumeration values: Bottom, Left, Right, or Top. A simple change here can give an entirely different look to your application.

Like many other controls, the TabControl also has an Appearance property. This time around, it uses values from the TabAppearance enumeration and determines how the individual tabs should be displayed. Possible values are Buttons, FlatButtons, and Normal. The first two options give the visual impression of being buttons rather than tabs, but the functionality is still the same.

There are a few properties that deal with sizing of the tabs. ItemSize gets or sets the width and height of the tabs. The default functionality is to automatically fit whatever content is contained in the tab. Padding changes the amount of space between the content contained in the tab and the edge of the tab. This property doesn't take an integer value, though; it uses a Point value:

```
tcMain.Padding = new Point(20,20);
```

6

Imagine creating a new `Point` object of size 20 pixels by 20 pixels that will sit on each side of the tab's title. This causes the tab to expand in size.

Then there is the `SizeMode` property, that determines how far across a `TabControl` the tabs should expand. This property uses `TabSizeMode` enumeration values: `FillToRight`, which causes the tabs to expand to fill the entire width of the `TabControl`; `Fixed`, where each tab has the same, fixed size; and `Normal`, where the size of each tab is controlled by the `ItemSize` and `Padding` properties you just learned about.

If you create more tabs than can be displayed at once, arrows appear on the `TabControl` that allow the user to scroll to see all of the tabs. If you set the `Multiline` property to `true`, the tabs that would normally be hidden move to another row, so that they are always displayed—as many rows as necessary will be created to display all of the tabs.

To keep track of your controls, there are the `RowCount` and `TabCount` properties, which, when Multiline is set to `true`, return the number of rows of tabs and the total number of tabs, respectively.

Finally, the `HotTrack` property causes the tabs to change appearance (specifically, the title text changes color) when the mouse is moved over them.

The `TextBox` and `RichTextBox` Controls

You've seen the `TextBox` control quite a few times already. Most of the time you've only used its `Text` property, and often, that's all you'll need. There are a few more properties, however, that may come in handy. Let's take a brief look at them, and then I'll discuss how they apply to the `RichTextBox` control.

`AcceptsReturn` and `AcceptsTab` are two properties that indicate if the Enter and Tab keys will cause line breaks and tab indents in the `TextBox`. By default, when the user hits the Tab key, the focus will move to the next control, and the Enter key will activate the default button (if there is one). By setting them to `true`, you can enhance the functionality of your control.

When you allow `AcceptsReturn`, you may hope to end up with more than one line of data. If so, don't forget to set `Multiline` to `true`, otherwise `AcceptsReturn` may be useless. `Lines`, then, returns an array of strings containing the text from each line in the `TextBox`. `WordWrap` indicates if the text should wrap to the next line when the `TextBox` isn't large enough to display it all at once. If `WordWrap` is `false` and `Multiline` is `true`, the user will have to press the Enter key to move to the next line.

You can modify the way the user interacts with the `TextBox` as well. The `CharacterCasing` property takes a `CharacterCasing` enumeration value (yes, the property name is the same as the enumeration name) that indicates how capitalization should be handled when the user enters text. It can be one of three values: Lower, which converts all input to lowercase; Normal, which leaves text as it is typed; or Upper, which converts all input to uppercase.

CanUndo allows users to undo recent actions they've performed (a big bonus to many users!). The Undo method causes the undo to occur, and ClearUndo clears the undo history, meaning that users won't be able to undo past actions. Modified indicates if the text in the TextBox has been changed. This property is often used to see if content should be saved before closing an application. ReadOnly means the text cannot be edited. PasswordChar indicates the character that should mask user input. For example, many times when typing in passwords, you'll notice that asterisks (*) appear instead of what you're typing. PasswordChar can give you this functionality.

Finally, the TextBox has a number of methods that deal with text. Clear erases all of the text in the TextBox. Copy, Cut, and Paste all follow the familiar cut, copy, and paste operations common in Windows. AppendText appends a given string onto the end of the content in the TextBox.

Rich Text

The TextBox control is great for handling user input. Its main drawback is that it can only handle plain text, or text without any formatting. (If you've ever used WordPad instead of Notepad, you know the difference. With WordPad, you can make text bold or italic, change font sizes and colors, enter bullets and numbering, apply different alignment rules, and so on. None of this is possible in Notepad. This is because WordPad deals with what is known as rich text, whereas Notepad deals only with plain text.)

At its simplest, the RichTextBox is just like any other control. It shares many members with its brethren, including the AcceptsTab, CanUndo, and Multiline properties from the TextBox. However, the RichTextControl offers much more functionality, including saving and loading files.

Let's take a look at a simple RichTextBox control example that allows the user to format some text. Again I'll split up the code to dissect it easier; Listing 6.9 contains the first part of this application.

LISTING 6.9   Using the RichTextBox Control in VB.NET

```
1:  Imports System
2:  Imports System.Windows.Forms
3:  Imports System.Drawing
4:
```

6

LISTING 6.8   continued

```
5:   Namespace TYWinForms.Day6
6:
7:     Public Class Listing69 : Inherits Form
8:         private rtbText as New RichTextBox
9:         private intFontSize as Integer
10:        private strFontColor as String
11:        private strFontStyle as String
12:
13:        private cmnuText as New ContextMenu
14:        private cmniFont as New MenuItem
15:        private cmniBold as New MenuItem
16:        private cmniItalics as New MenuItem
17:        private cmniNormal as New MenuItem
18:        private cmniFontSize as New MenuItem
19:        private cmniSize8 as New MenuItem
20:        private cmniSize10 as New MenuItem
21:        private cmniSize12 as New MenuItem
22:        private cmniSize14 as New MenuItem
23:        private cmniColor as New MenuItem
24:        private cmniColorRed as New MenuItem
25:        private cmniColorBlue as New MenuItem
26:        private cmniColorGreen as New MenuItem
27:        private cmniColorBlack as New MenuItem
28:
29:        public shared sub Main()
30:            Application.Run(new Listing69)
31:        end sub
32:     End Class
33:   End Namespace
```

ANALYSIS Listing 6.9 shows the basic frame for our application. Lines 8–27 show quite a few variables, many of which are ContextMenus and MenuItems, which the user will use to change the font in the RichTextBox control. The three variables on lines 9–11 are global variables that will keep track of what size, color, and style the current font is; these values will be very handy later on.

Tip

> As your applications get more and more complex, your code is getting longer and longer. Now, more than ever, it's essential to follow a good naming scheme and code layout!

Listing 6.10 shows the constructor for this example application.

LISTING 6.10   The `RichTextBox` Application Constructor

```
1:  public sub New()
2:      intFontSize = 10
3:      strFontColor = "Black"
4:      strFontStyle = "Normal"
5:
6:      rtbText.Dock = DockStyle.Fill
7:      rtbText.ScrollBars = RichTextBoxScrollBars.Both
8:      rtbText.ContextMenu = cmnuText
9:
10:     cmnuText.MenuItems.Add(cmniFont)
11:     cmnuText.MenuItems.Add(cmniFontSize)
12:     cmnuText.MenuItems.Add(cmniColor)
13:
14:     cmniFont.Text = "Font"
15:     cmniBold.Text = "Bold"
16:     cmniFont.MenuItems.Add(cmniBold)
17:     cmniItalics.Text = "Italics"
18:     cmniFont.MenuItems.Add(cmniItalics)
19:     cmniNormal.Text = "Normal"
20:     cmniNormal.Checked = true
21:     cmniFont.MenuItems.Add(cmniNormal)
22:     AddHandler cmniBold.Click, new EventHandler(AddressOf
➡Me.HandleFont)
23:     AddHandler cmniItalics.Click, new EventHandler(AddressOf
➡Me.HandleFont)
24:     AddHandler cmniNormal.Click, new EventHandler(AddressOf
➡Me.HandleFont)
25:
26:     cmniFontSize.Text = "Size"
27:     cmniSize8.Text = "8"
28:     cmniFontSize.MenuItems.Add(cmniSize8)
29:     cmniSize10.Text = "10"
30:     cmniSize10.Checked = true
31:     cmniFontSize.MenuItems.Add(cmniSize10)
32:     cmniSize12.Text = "12"
33:     cmniFontSize.MenuItems.Add(cmniSize12)
34:     cmniSize14.Text = "14"
35:     cmniFontSize.MenuItems.Add(cmniSize14)
36:     AddHandler cmniSize8.Click, new EventHandler(AddressOf
➡Me.HandleFontSize)
37:     AddHandler cmniSize10.Click, new EventHandler(AddressOf
➡Me.HandleFontSize)
38:     AddHandler cmniSize12.Click, new EventHandler(AddressOf
➡Me.HandleFontSize)
39:     AddHandler cmniSize14.Click, new EventHandler(AddressOf
➡Me.HandleFontSize)
40:
41:     cmniColor.Text = "Color"
```

6

LISTING 6.10   continued

```
42:     cmniColorRed.Text = "Red"
43:     cmniColor.MenuItems.Add(cmniColorRed)
44:     cmniColorBlue.Text = "Blue"
45:     cmniColor.MenuItems.Add(cmniColorBlue)
46:     cmniColorGreen.Text = "Green"
47:     cmniColor.MenuItems.Add(cmniColorGreen)
48:     cmniColorBlack.Text = "Black"
49:     cmniColorBlack.Checked = true
50:     cmniColor.MenuItems.Add(cmniColorBlack)
51:     AddHandler cmniColorRed.Click, new EventHandler(AddressOf
➥Me.HandleFontColor)
52:     AddHandler cmniColorBlue.Click, new EventHandler(AddressOf
➥Me.HandleFontColor)
53:     AddHandler cmniColorGreen.Click, new EventHandler(AddressOf
➥Me.HandleFontColor)
54:     AddHandler cmniColorBlack.Click, new EventHandler(AddressOf
➥Me.HandleFontColor)
55:
56:     Me.Text = "Listing 6.9"
57:     Me.Font = New Font("Times New Roman", intFontSize)
58:     Me.Controls.Add(rtbText)
59:  end sub
```

ANALYSIS   This is a standard constructor, but it has a lot of code to cover. Lines 2–4 set initial values for the font styles for our application. Lines 6–8 define properties for the RichTextBox control. Dock indicates how the control moves in relation to the form (you'll learn more about that later today in the "Controlling Layout" section. ScrollBars dictates how and if scroll bars should be displayed for the RichTextBox control. This property can be any of the RichTextBoxScrollBar enumeration values:

- Both—Horizontal and vertical scroll bars will appear when necessary
- ForcedBoth—Horizontal and vertical scroll bars will always appear, whether needed or not
- ForcedHorizontal—A horizontal scroll bar will always be present
- ForcedVertical—A vertical scroll bar will always be present
- Horizontal—A horizontal scroll bar will appear as necessary
- None—No scroll bars will be displayed
- Vertical—A vertical scroll bar will appear as necessary

Line 8 simply assigns a context menu to this control, so that users can right-click and change the font properties.

Lines 10–12 add the top-level menu items to the ContextMenu control. Almost all of the rest of the listing deals with the properties of these MenuItems. Lines 14–24 initialize the menu items that control font style (bold, italics, or regular). Lines 26–39 initialize the items that deal with the font size, and lines 41–54 deal with the items that control font color. Note that each group of code uses only one event handler—lines 14–24 use HandleFont, 26–39 use HandleFontSize, and 41–54 use HandleFontColor.

Finally, lines 56–59 initialize the Form, setting the default font to be used.

Listing 6.11 shows the application's event handlers and miscellaneous functions.

LISTING 6.11   Handling the RichTextBox Events

```
1:  public sub HandleFont(Sender as Object, e as EventArgs)
2:      strFontStyle = CType(Sender, MenuItem).Text
3:      rtbText.SelectionFont = new Font("Times New Roman",
➥intFontSize, ConvertToFontStyle(strFontStyle))
4:
5:      cmniBold.Checked = false
6:      cmniItalics.Checked = false
7:      cmniNormal.Checked = false
8:
9:      CType(Sender, MenuItem).Checked = true
10: end sub
11:
12: public sub HandleFontSize(Sender as Object, e as EventArgs)
13:     intFontSize = Convert.ToInt32(CType(Sender, MenuItem).Text)
14:     rtbText.SelectionFont = new Font("Times New Roman",
➥intFontSize, ConvertToFontStyle(strFontStyle))
15:
16:     cmniSize8.Checked = false
17:     cmniSize10.Checked = false
18:     cmniSize12.Checked = false
19:     cmniSize14.Checked = false
20:
21:     CType(Sender, MenuItem).Checked = true
22: end sub
23:
24: public sub HandleFontColor(Sender as Object, e as EventArgs)
25:     strFontColor = CType(Sender, MenuItem).Text
26:     rtbText.SelectionColor = Color.FromName(strFontColor)
27:
28:     cmniColorRed.Checked = false
29:     cmniColorBlue.Checked = false
30:     cmniColorGreen.Checked = false
31:     cmniColorBlack.Checked = false
32:
33:     CType(Sender, MenuItem).Checked = true
```

6

LISTING 6.11 continued

```
34:   end sub
35:
36:   private function ConvertToFontStyle(strStyle) as FontStyle
37:      select strStyle
38:         case "Bold"
39:            return FontStyle.Bold
40:         case "Italics"
41:            return FontStyle.Italic
42:         case "Normal"
43:            return  FontStyle.Regular
44:      end select
45:   end function
```

ANALYSIS First, note that none of these methods handles any of the RichTextBox's events directly. Rather, we are handling the MenuItems controls' events, which modify the RichTextBox's properties accordingly.

Next, let's skip down to the ConvertToFontStyle function beginning on line 36. This function, as you can tell from its declaration, returns a FontStyle enumeration value. As you handle each event, you'll notice that it becomes necessary to convert the menu item that the user selected into an appropriate type that can be used by the RichTextBox. For instance, you can't create a Font with the command:

```
new Font("Times New Roman", 8, "Bold")
```

Instead, you have to use a FontStyle enumeration value:

```
new Font("Times New Roman", 8, FontStyle.Bold)
```

The ConvertToFontStyle converts the text "Bold" into a FontStyle.Bold value that you to use elsewhere in your code. You'll see exactly how in a moment.

Moving back to line 1 and the HandleFont method, recall that this method handles the Click event for the cmniBold, cmniItalics, and cmniNormal MenuItems, which should bold, italicize, and return the font to normal respectively. On line 2, you retrieve the text value from the MenuItem that was selected and put in the strFontStyle variable (remember to cast the Sender variable to an appropriate type—MenuItem in this case); this value will be "Bold," "Italics," or "Normal," as shown on lines 15, 17, and 19 of Listing 6.10.

On line 3 you use the SelectionFont property of the RichTextBox. This property retrieves and sets information about the font currently used in the RichTextBox—specifically, the currently selected (or highlighted) text. If no text is currently selected, this property affects all new text that is entered by the user. Line 3 assigns a new Font object to `SelectionFont`, using the values set in `intFontSize` and `strFontStyle` variables. Now you see why these global variables are important—without them, it would require more work to set new font styles.

Note

Lack of global variables would mean more work, yes, but it would not be more difficult. If you didn't want to use these global variables, you could change line 3 to read:

```
rtbText.SelectionFont = new Font("Times New Roman",
➥rtbText.SelectionFont.Size, ConvertToFontStyle
➥(CType(Sender, MenuItem).Text))
```

In other words, the global variables substitute for values of the `SelectionFont` property and `Sender` variable.

Let's return to the `ConvertToFontStyle` function for a moment. Remember, you can't use the string passed in from the select menu item directly. Therefore, this method returns the proper `FontStyle` enumeration value to properly set the font.

Recall from Day 4, "Adding Menus and Toolbars to Your Windows Forms," that when you allow menu items to be checked, you need to make sure that non-apropos items are unchecked. Lines 5–9 uncheck all of the font style menu items, and then the appropriate menu item is checked, based on the `Sender` variable.

The `HandleFontSize` and `HandleFontColor` methods do virtually the same thing as `HandleFont`. They both retrieve the selected menu item's text (lines 13 and 25 respectively). `HandleFontSize` assigns a new `Font` to the `SelectionFont` property, using the global variables, and then checks and unchecks menu items as necessary. `HandleFontColor` uses a slightly different property, `SelectionColor`. This property retrieves or sets the color used for the currently selected text (or all new text if none is currently selected). On line 26 you use the `FromName` method of the `Color` object to assign the color. Checks and unchecks are performed on lines 28–33.

This application contained a lot of code—in fact, it was the longest code example you've yet seen—but most of it was very simple, consisting mostly of initialization code in the constructor. Combine these three listings by placing Listings 6.10 and 6.11 on line 28 of Listing 6.9. Figure 6.11 shows some typical output from this application.

6

FIGURE 6.11

The fully functional `RichTextBox` *application provides users with lots of choices.*

Much of the process of using `RichTextBox` controls is simply providing user interfaces to modify font properties. The two major properties you learned about—`SelectionFont` and `SelectionColor`—deal with the currently selected text. The `RichTextBox` control has many other such properties, including `SelectionAlignment`, which indicates how to align the currently selected text; `SelectionBullet`, which determines if the text should be in a bulleted list; and `SelectionIndent`, which determines how large indents should be. There are quite a few other properties, as well. For more information on these properties, see Appendix B, "Windows Forms Controls."

Before we move on, there are three more `RichTextBox` members everyone should know. The first, `DetectUrls`, is an interesting one whose functionality is becoming more and more prevalent in today's applications. When this property is set to `true`, the `RichTextBox` control automatically formats any text that "looks" like an Internet URL (for example, `http://www.clpayne.com`) so that it is clickable, just like a normal link in a Web browser. The text in point automatically turns blue and is underlined (depending on your Internet settings). To handle clicks of these links, you need to add a delegate to the `LinkClicked` event for the `RichTextBox` control, and add an event handler, like the following code snippet:

```
public Sub Link_Clicked(Sender As Object, e As
➥LinkClickedEventArgs)
    System.Diagnostics.Process.Start(e.LinkText)
End Sub
```

The `Start` method in this snippet launches the user's default Web browser with the link he clicked on (actually, it launches the application that is configured to handle Internet links, which is typically a Web browser—but that's beyond the scope of this chapter).

The second `RichTextBox` member to know is the `Find` method. This method simply searches the `RichTextBox` for a specified string—a very useful function for any word processor-like application. This method can take quite a few different types of parameters, but the most common are a string, and a string and a character index to start from.

The last member is really two that perform similar functions. `Rtf` and `SelectedRtf` return all of text (or just the selected text) in the `RichTextBox`, including all rich text formatting. The `Copy` method (also available for the `TextBox` control) simply copies the text, and you lose all formatting such as font size, color, and style. Use `Rtf` or `SelectedRtf` to maintain the formatting if you need to transfer the text to another application (such as Microsoft Word).

You'll learn more about this control at the end of the week in "Week 1 in Review: Creating a Word Processor," when you create your own word processor.

The `Timer` Control

The `Timer` control is one of the most useful controls you'll come across. Very simply, it allows you to raise an event at a specific interval of time. Until now, you had no way to keep track of time in an application. It may not sound like much, but think of all the opportunities this affords you: you can create an application that reminds users to save their documents every five minutes, provide real-time clocks and counters to keep track of time, and create performance monitors. Basically any interactive task that you want to automate needs the `Timer` control.

Because it doesn't actually do much besides keep time, the `Timer` control has very few members. In fact, it has just two properties: `Enabled` indicates whether the `Timer` should run, and `Interval` sets the amount of time in milliseconds that the `Timer` should "tick" at. At each "tick," the `Timer` raises an event, appropriately called `Tick`, that you can use to perform your custom automated routines. Finally, it has only two methods of interest, `Start` and `Stop`, which, oddly enough, start and stop the `Timer`.

One of the best applications of the `Timer` control is an alarm clock. Listing 6.12 shows such an application.

6

LISTING 6.12   An Alarm Clock

```
1:  Imports System
2:  Imports System.Windows.Forms
3:  Imports System.Drawing
4:
5:  namespace TYWinForms.Day6
6:
7:     public class Listing612 : Inherits Form
8:        private tmrClock as New Timer
```

LISTING 6.12   continued

```
 9:        private tmrAlarm as New Timer
10:         private lblClock as New Label
11:         private intSnoozeTime as Integer
12:         private intSnoozeCounter as Integer
13:
14:        public sub New()
15:            intSnoozeTime = 10000    '10 seconds
16:
17:            tmrClock.Interval = 1000
18:            tmrClock.Enabled = true
19:            AddHandler tmrClock.Tick, new
➥EventHandler(AddressOf Me.UpdateClock)
20:
21:            tmrAlarm.Interval = 1000
22:            tmrAlarm.Enabled = true
23:            AddHandler tmrAlarm.Tick, new
➥EventHandler(AddressOf Me.CheckAlarm)
24:
25:            lblClock.Width = 300
26:            lblClock.Height = 150
27:            lblClock.Location = new Point(0,100)
28:            lblClock.Text = DateTime.Now.ToString
29:
30:            Me.Text = "Listing 6.12"
31:            Me.Font = new Font("Arial", 20)
32:            Me.Controls.Add(lblClock)
33:        end sub
34:
35:        public sub UpdateClock(Sender as Object, e
➥as EventArgs)
36:            lblClock.Text = DateTime.Now.ToString
37:        end sub
38:
39:        public sub CheckAlarm(Sender as Object, e
➥as EventArgs)
40:            intSnoozeCounter += tmrAlarm.Interval
41:
42:            if intSnoozeCounter = intSnoozeTime then
43:                intSnoozeCounter = 0
44:                MessageBox.Show("Wake up sleepy head!!!")
45:            end if
46:        end sub
47:
48:        public shared sub Main()
49:            Application.Run(new Listing612)
50:        end sub
51:    end class
52: end namespace
```

In this application, you create two `Timer` controls—one to update a clock visible to the user, and one to control the "alarm." On lines 8–12 these two `Timer`s, as well as a few other variables, are declared.

On line 15, in the constructor, you set the "snooze period," or the time before the alarm goes off—10 seconds in this case (10,000 milliseconds). On lines 17–19 you set the clock `Timer`'s `Interval` to one second (1000 milliseconds), enable it (in other words, start it), and give it an event handler. Lines 21–23 do the same for the alarm `Timer`. Lines 25–28 set a few properties for a `Label` that will display the clock, and lines 30–32 set some general properties for the form. Note that you use the `DateTime.Now` method to return the current time as defined by the user's computer's clock, and the `ToString` method converts that `DateTime` object into text for display in the `Label`.

The `UpdateClock` method on line 35 is executed every 1000 milliseconds by the `tmrClock` `Timer`. It simply calls `DateTime.Now` over and over again to update the visible clock.

`CheckAlarm` executes every 1000 milliseconds also, and determines if the predetermined snooze interval has passed. On line 40 it increments the `intSnoozeCounter` variable, which is compared to the `intSnoozeTime` variable on line 42. If both are equal—meaning 10 seconds have passed—then a message box is displayed with a nice wake-up call. The counter variable is then reset to `0` to start the alarm all over again. Otherwise, nothing happens, and the `Timer` keeps ticking away.

Figure 6.12 shows the output after 10 seconds.

Figure 6.12

Your simple alarm clock has a quiet alarm!

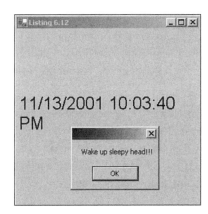

6

The `TreeView` Control

The `TreeView` control is used to display hierarchical lists of information. The most common usage is to display Windows Explorer-type interfaces that allow you to browse through a directory structure, as shown in Figure 6.13.

FIGURE 6.13

The Explorer interface uses a tree view.

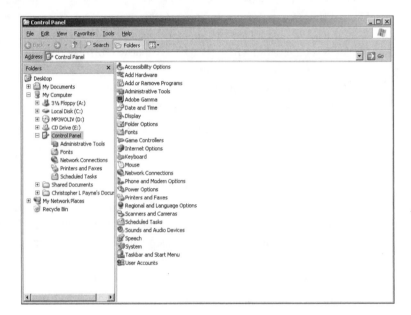

A directory structure, however, is not the only thing a `TreeView` control can represent. Any hierarchical information—customer and order data, family trees, restaurant menus, and so forth—can be handled by `TreeView`. (We'll delve into using `TreeView` for a directory explorer after you learn about file input and output in Day 11, "Working with Windows Input/Output.")

Each item, or node, in the `TreeView` list is represented by a `TreeNode` object. Each `TreeNode` can have `TreeNodes` under it as well, thereby giving the control its hierarchical nature—the first node is known as the root node. Because you have to create each and every node in the `TreeView`, setting this control up can be tedious, but luckily it's not difficult. For example, the following code snippet simply creates new nodes using simple loops:

```
dim myTreeView as new TreeView
For i = 0 to 20
   MyTreeView.Nodes.Add(New TreeNode("Node" & i.ToString))

   For j = 0 to 20
```

```
        MyTreeView.Nodes(i).Nodes.Add(New TreeNode
➡("SubNode" & j.ToString))

        For k = 0 to 20
            MyTreeView.Nodes(i).Nodes(j).Nodes.Add(New TreeNode
➡ ("SubSubNode" & k.ToString))
        Next k
    Next j
Next i
```

In this snippet, you loop through three different variables from 0 to 20. The result is a
TreeView control three layers deep, each with 21 nodes. To add new nodes you simply
use the Nodes.Add method (similar to the Controls.Add method you've used for the
Form object), passing in a new TreeNode object with a specified label. This label can also
be accessed using the Text property of each node.

The TreeView control is highly customizable; each aspect of the UI is controllable. Table
6.2 shows TreeView's most common properties.

TABLE 6.2   Common TreeView properties

Property	Description
CheckBoxes	Indicates whether checkboxes should be displayed next to each node. This allows the user to select specific nodes for manipulation. Use the Checked property of the TreeNode object to determine if an object is checked.
FullRowSelect	Indicates whether the highlight that appears when a node is selected should span the entire width of the control, or just the label of the node.
HotTracking	Makes the nodes change appearance when mouse-overed (the text changes to blue).
ImageList	An ImageList control that can be used to display images for the node icons. Use this with the ImageIndex property like other controls.
Indent	The amount of pixels each child node should be indented from its parent.
LabelEdit	Indicates whether the nodes' labels may be edited.
Nodes	Returns a collection of TreeNodes.
PathSeparator	The character used to separate nodes (more on this later).
ShowLines	Indicates whether lines are drawn between nodes in the TreeView, connecting them.
ShowPlusMinus	Indicates whether plus (+) and minus (–) signs should be shown next to those nodes that have children.

6

TABLE 6.2   continued

Property	Description
ShowRootLines	Indicates whether lines should be drawn between the nodes at the root of the tree.
Scrollable	Indicates whether scroll bars should be shown when necessary.
VisibleCount	The number of nodes that can be visible at once.
TopNode	Returns the topmost visible TreeNode object.

The TreeNode object has a few useful properties as well. FullPath combines the labels of all the nodes that must be navigated to reach the current node, separated by the PathSeparator character (\ by default). For example, the FullPath of the 3rd root node's 2nd child's 14th child node using the default PathSeparator is:

"Node2\SubNode1\SubSubNode13"

The IsEditing, IsExpanded, IsSelected, and IsVisible properties return true or false values indicating whether the current TreeNode is in the process of being edited, is expanded, selected, or visible.

To navigate around TreeNodes, you have the NextNode and NextVisibleNode properties and the PrevNode and PrevVisibleNode properties. These properties return the specified TreeNodes.

Two useful methods of the TreeView are CollapseAll and ExpandAll, which, respectively, collapse all of the expanded nodes and expand all of the collapsed nodes. The TreeNode similarly has Collapse, Expand, and ExpandAll, and Toggle. The last method toggles between the expanded and collapsed states.

Finally, the TreeView control has a series of events that fire both before and after certain actions happen. These events use the prefixes Before and After. For example, BeforeCheck, BeforeCollapse, BeforeExpand, BeforeLabelEdit, and BeforeSelect (along with each of the corresponding After methods).

Additional Useful Controls

We've only scratched the surface of Windows Forms controls in today's lesson. We explored the most common ones here, but there are quite a few other controls that will help you build your applications (42 in total). Here's a sampling of the other controls:

- CheckListBox—Similar to the ListBox control, but places checkboxes next to each list item. Being a combination of a CheckBox and a ListBox, you can imagine the properties contained in this control.

- `DataGrid`—Very useful for displaying information from stored data sources, such as databases. We'll cover this control more in Day 9, "Using ADO.NET."

- `ProgressBar`—Similar to the "bar" controls you learned about in Day 4. This one displays a bar that fills up as a task is being completed, providing the user with progress updates.

- `ToolTip`—Represents a ToolTip that is displayed when the user's mouse hovers over another control. Windows is filled with ToolTips, so this control can be very useful.

The key to becoming an expert in Windows Forms programming is to have an arsenal of controls at your disposal, to know when each is appropriate, and how to use them. For more information on these controls, see the .NET Framework documentation or QuickStart guide.

Controlling Layout

It's necessary to learn how to arrange all of these controls neatly on your forms. Otherwise you'd end up with an incomprehensible jumble of controls! You've already seen one method of organization: adding controls to other, parent controls, such as `Panels` and `TabControls`. These two allow you to logically group controls into manageable (and easily presentable) groups.

There are a few other ways to organize controls as well. One is to use the `Dock` property of the `Control` class. (Note that since every Windows Forms control inherits from `Control`, every Windows Forms control has the `Dock` property.) `Dock` is used to specify the position and manner in which a given control is locked to its containing control. Using values from the `DockStyle` enumeration, you can make controls stick to the top or bottom of a form or `Panel` control (like toolbars and status bars), or fill the entire container. The `DockStyle` values are

- `Bottom`—Docks the control to the bottom of the containing control.
- `Fill`—Each of the control's edges is docked to the corresponding edge of the container, causing the control to fill the entire container, even when the container is resized.
- `Left`—Docks the control to the left side of the containing control.
- `None`—The default value; the control is not docked to anything.
- `Right`—Docks the control to the right side of the container.
- `Top`—Docks the control to the top of the container.

6

Another layout-defining property is Anchor, also available on every control. This property is similar to Dock in that it defines which edges of a control should be linked with the parent form, but unlike Dock, the controls aren't necessarily stuck, or "docked," to the edges of the form. Rather, the specified side of the control will stay in its location relative to the edge of the form, no matter where on the form it is, or how the form is resized. Anchor uses one of the AnchorStyle enumeration values: Bottom, Left, None, Right, or Top. To get a control to resize along with the form, set the anchor to opposite sides of the form using the Or operator in VB.NET, or the | operator in C#, like this:

```
textBox1.Anchor = AnchorStyles.Top Or AnchorStyles.Bottom
textBox1.Anchor = AnchorStyles.Top | AnchorStyles.Bottom;
```

Listing 6.13 shows a good example of manipulating the Dock and Anchor properties.

LISTING 6.13   Dynamically Changing Layout of a Control

```
 1:  Imports System
 2:  Imports System.Windows.Forms
 3:  Imports System.Drawing
 4:
 5:  Namespace TYWinForms.Day6
 6:
 7:      Public Class Listing613 : Inherits Form
 8:          Private WithEvents pnlButton As New Panel
 9:          Private WithEvents pnlControls As New Panel
10:          Private WithEvents gboxAnchor As New GroupBox
11:          Private WithEvents gboxDock As New GroupBox
12:          Private WithEvents btnDemo As New Button
13:          Private WithEvents rbNone As New RadioButton
14:          Private WithEvents rbTop As New RadioButton
15:          Private WithEvents rbLeft As New RadioButton
16:          Private WithEvents rbBottom As New RadioButton
17:          Private WithEvents rbRight As New RadioButton
18:          Private WithEvents rbFill As New RadioButton
19:          Private WithEvents chkTop As New CheckBox
20:          Private WithEvents chkLeft As New CheckBox
21:          Private WithEvents chkBottom As New CheckBox
22:          Private WithEvents chkRight As New CheckBox
23:
24:          Public Sub New()
25:              rbRight.Location = New Point(8,120)
26:              rbRight.Size = New Size(72,24)
27:              rbRight.Text = "Right"
28:
29:              rbNone.Location = New Point(8,24)
30:              rbNone.Size = New Size(72,24)
31:              rbNone.Text = "None"
32:              rbNone.Checked = True
33:
```

LISTING 6.13   continued

```
34:              rbBottom.Location = New Point(8,96)
35:              rbBottom.Size = New Size(72,24)
36:              rbBottom.Text = "Bottom"
37:
38:              rbTop.Location = New Point(8,48)
39:              rbTop.Size = New Size(72,24)
40:              rbTop.Text = "Top"
41:
42:              rbLeft.Location = New Point(8,72)
43:              rbLeft.Size = New Size(72,24)
44:              rbLeft.Text = "Left"
45:
46:              rbFill.Location = New Point(8,144)
47:              rbFill.Size = New Size(72,24)
48:              rbFill.Text = "Fill"
49:
50:              gboxAnchor.Location = New Point(16,16)
51:              gboxAnchor.Size = New Size(88,128)
52:              gboxAnchor.Text = "Anchor"
53:
54:              gboxDock.Location = New Point(16,152)
55:              gboxDock.Size = New Size(88,176)
56:              gboxDock.Text = "Dock"
57:
58:              btnDemo.Size = New Size(120,24)
59:              btnDemo.Anchor = AnchorStyles.None
60:              btnDemo.Location = New Point(64,72)
61:              btnDemo.Text = "Play with Me!"
62:
63:              chkBottom.Location = New Point(8,72)
64:              chkBottom.Size = New Size(72,24)
65:              chkBottom.Text = "Bottom"
66:
67:              chkLeft.Location = New Point(8,48)
68:              chkLeft.Size = New Size(72,24)
69:              chkLeft.Text = "Left"
70:
71:              chkTop.Location = New Point(8,24)
72:              chkTop.Size = New Size(72,24)
73:              chkTop.Text = "Top"
74:
75:              chkRight.Location = New Point(8,96)
76:              chkRight.Size = New Size(72,24)
77:              chkRight.Text = "Right"
78:
79:              pnlButton.BorderStyle = FormBorderStyle.Fixed3D
80:              pnlButton.Dock = DockStyle.Fill
81:              pnlButton.Size = New Size(448,400)
82:              pnlButton.Text = "ButtonPanel"
83:              pnlButton.Controls.Add(btnDemo)
84:
```

6

LISTING 6.13   continued

```
85:            pnlControls.BorderStyle = FormBorderStyle.Fixed3D
86:            pnlControls.Dock = DockStyle.Right
87:            pnlControls.Location = New Point(328,0)
88:            pnlControls.Size = New Size(120,400)
89:            pnlControls.Text = "ControlsPanel"
90:            pnlControls.Controls.Add(gboxAnchor)
91:            pnlControls.Controls.Add(gboxDock)
92:
93:            gboxAnchor.Controls.Add(chkRight)
94:            gboxAnchor.Controls.Add(chkBottom)
95:            gboxAnchor.Controls.Add(chkLeft)
96:            gboxAnchor.Controls.Add(chkTop)
97:            gboxDock.Controls.Add(rbBottom)
98:            gboxDock.Controls.Add(rbLeft)
99:            gboxDock.Controls.Add(rbNone)
100:           gboxDock.Controls.Add(rbRight)
101:           gboxDock.Controls.Add(rbFill)
102:           gboxDock.Controls.Add(rbTop)
103:
104:           Me.Text = "Listing 6.13"
105:           Me.Size = New Size(800,600)
106:           Me.Controls.Add(pnlButton)
107:           Me.Controls.Add(pnlControls)
108:        End Sub
109:
110:        Private Sub AnchorClicked(Sender As Object,e
➥As EventArgs) Handles chkBottom.Click,chkLeft.Click,
➥chkRight.Click,chkTop.Click
111:           If chkTop.Checked Then
112:               btnDemo.Anchor = btnDemo.Anchor Or
➥AnchorStyles.Top
113:           End If
114:
115:           If chkLeft.Checked Then
116:               btnDemo.Anchor = btnDemo.Anchor Or
➥AnchorStyles.Left
117:           End If
118:
119:           If chkBottom.Checked Then
120:               btnDemo.Anchor = btnDemo.Anchor Or
➥AnchorStyles.Bottom
121:           End If
122:
123:           If chkRight.Checked Then
124:               btnDemo.Anchor = btnDemo.Anchor Or
➥AnchorStyles.Right
125:           End If
126:        End Sub
127:
```

LISTING 6.13 continued

```
128:        Private Sub DockClicked(Sender As Object,e As
➥EventArgs) Handles rbBottom.Click,rbFill.Click,
➥rbLeft.Click,rbRight.Click,rbTop.Click,rbNone.Click
129:            dim rbSet as RadioButton =
➥CType(sender,RadioButton)
130:
131:            If rbSet Is rbNone Then
132:                btnDemo.Dock = DockStyle.None
133:            ElseIf rbSet Is rbTop Then
134:                btnDemo.Dock = DockStyle.Top
135:            ElseIf rbSet Is rbLeft Then
136:                btnDemo.Dock = DockStyle.Left
137:            ElseIf rbSet Is rbBottom Then
138:                btnDemo.Dock = DockStyle.Bottom
139:            ElseIf rbSet Is rbRight Then
140:                btnDemo.Dock = DockStyle.Right
141:            Else
142:                btnDemo.Dock = DockStyle.Fill
143:            End If
144:        End Sub
145:
146:        public shared sub Main()
147:            Application.Run(New Listing613)
148:        end sub
149:    End Class
150: End Namespace
```

ANALYSIS

Whoa, that's a lot of code! Let's take it step by step.

On lines 8–22 you simply set up some controls that allow the user to modify the Anchor and Dock properties; you need one radio button or checkbox for each of the values in the DockStyle and AnchorStyle enumerations (use radio buttons for DockStyle because only one can be applied at any given time; CheckBoxes are used for AnchorStyle because you can have multiple anchors at once). Note the use of the WithEvents keyword—this tells CLR that each of these controls will raise events (in C#, it's not necessary to include such keywords).

On lines 25–107, the bulk of the code, we simply initialize and place the controls on the form. There is another new control in this listing, a GroupBox. This control is like a Panel in that it contains other controls, but it draws a box around its child controls, providing further visual cues to the user that certain controls are separate from others. On lines 93–102 the individual controls are added to these GroupBoxes, which are in turn added to Panels on lines 90 and 91, which are finally added to the form on lines 106 and 107.

6

There are only two methods left to examine: AnchorClicked on line 110, and DockClicked on line 128. Note that these methods use the Handles keyword to tell the CLR which events these methods should be executed upon (see Day 5, "Handling Events in Your Windows Forms," for more information). In this case, the AnchorClicked method handles all of the CheckBoxes Click events, and DockClicked handles all of the RadioButton Click events.

Note

> We could use the delegate adding method we're used to
>
> AddHandler *control*.Click, new EventHandler
>
> ➥(AddressOfAnchorClicked)
>
> instead of the method in Listing 6.13 with the Handles keyword. However, using the previous method saves several lines of code by combining all of the delegate additions into two lines.

Let's examine AnchorClicked first. Because Anchors can be applied cumulatively to a control, you have to evaluate each and every anchor CheckBox. If the AnchorStyles.Top Checkbox is checked, you need to apply the AnchorStyles.Top value, and similarly so with the other values. This is easily done by adding the values in if statements to the button's Anchor property using the Or operator. The effect of this method is that each AnchorStyles value is evaluated and applied cumulatively, if necessary, in the order of the if statements.

DockClicked is similar, but since DockStyles can only be applied one at a time, you don't need to add the styles together. Using if statements, you simply determine which RadioButton was clicked, and apply the appropriate DockStyle (note the use of the Is keyword—remember to use this operator instead of the equals sign (=) when you're evaluating objects).

After all that, you're left with the application shown in Figure 6.14. To get the full experience, play with the controls and notice how the button is affected.

Although the TabStop and TabIndex properties don't directly deal with control layout, they do permit navigation among controls, so this is an excellent place to discuss them. If you're familiar with Windows applications, then you know you can use the Tab key to move from one control to another. This allows users to maneuver through an application without having to use the mouse.

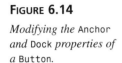

Figure 6.14

Modifying the Anchor *and* Dock *properties of a* Button.

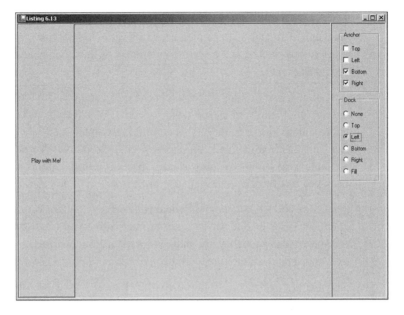

The TabIndex property indicates the order in which controls are traversed as the Tab key is pressed. A control with a TabIndex of 0 is the first control to be highlighted when the Tab key is hit, TabIndex 1 is the next one, and so on. Every control on the form can be traversed in this way. If you don't assign TabIndexes explicitly, the CLR assigns them for you based on the order in which the controls were added to the form (and if you mistakenly skip a tab index number, the CLR will ignore it and just move to the next available index). This is an important UI element to keep in mind.

There are times, however, when you don't want the user to be able to tab onto a control. For example, users often don't need to manipulate a Label control, so it shouldn't be selectable. In these cases, set the TabStop property to false.

You can define custom layout routines and properties in addition to those discussed here. However, this is an advanced topic best learned after you know about GDI+ and developing custom controls.

Summary

Whew, today was a long lesson, but you've made it to the end! Remember, the key to becoming an expert in Windows Forms being able to use and apply different controls to attack problems at hand; a developer who knows more controls is likely be more valuable. We covered a lot of material today, but don't feel that you have to memorize it all at once—use this chapter as a reference, and soon you'll know these controls by heart.

6

You learned about a few different types of button controls: Button, RadioButton, and CheckBox. Although their implementations vary slightly, they each allow the user to select an option. The most common members of these controls are the Text property and the Click event.

DateTimePicker enables a user to choose times and dates by entering them manually or by selecting them from a drop-down calendar. Which leads us to the next control you learned about: the ComboBox. This control is a combination of a TextBox and ListBox; a user can enter text manually, or choose from a drop-down list of items. The ListBox control, unlike the ComboBox, allows users to select multiple items at once. It is very useful when you want to give the user several choices.

ImageList and PictureBox both deal with images, but are very different from one another. ImageList is essentially an array of images that you can associate with other controls to display images (such as the buttons for a ToolBar control). A PictureBox is simply used to display a single image to the user.

TabControl enables you to group controls logically by using tabbed pages. This tab type interface is very common in Windows, and is intuitive for users to navigate.

The TextBox and RichTextBox controls both allow the user to enter text into a box. The RichTextBox provides much greater functionality, allowing the user to change fonts, colors, sizes, and so on. This type of control is similar to the WordPad application bundled with Windows.

With the Timer control, events can be raised at specific intervals. Among other things, you can use it to portray realistic time-keeping clocks or perform automated scheduled backups.

TreeView is an interesting control you can use to display hierarchical information in an easy to use tree structure. This type of control is used most often in the Windows Explorer type interface, but can be used for any type of information; it's not limited to just the file system.

Finally, you learned how to control layout of controls on forms using Anchor, Dock, TabIndex, and TabStop. The first two properties perform similar functionality; the difference is that Dock actually moves a control to an edge of the form, and Anchor fixes a control's location relative to the form's edges, without having to dock to the edge.

Tomorrow we're going to take a look at a special type of Windows form, the dialog box. You've already seen and used dialog boxes when you used the MessageBox.Show method, but dialog boxes are much more functional than this simple method implies.

Q&A

Q GDI+ was mentioned several times today. What is it?

A GDI+ is the enhanced Graphics Device Interface that allows you to deal with and draw different types of graphics and handle the Windows drawing procedures.

GDI+ was developed to allow developers to concentrate on graphics functionality without having to worry about the thousands of different types of graphics hardware (such as 3D video cards) and drivers. It abstracts the complex routines of dealing with hardware intricacies, much like classes hide implementation information from subclasses that inherit from them. We'll spend a lot of time with GDI+ in Day 13.

Q Does Microsoft Word use a `RichTextBox` control as its interface?

A Actually, no. Microsoft Word uses a special, custom-developed type of control that is not available to the general public. (After all, if it were, everyone on the planet could create his own word processor, costing Microsoft beaucoup bucks.) Also, rich text is represented in plain text with some special codes for formatting text. Word uses a binary format for its files (consisting of 1s and 0s) that makes them useable only by Microsoft Word (and other programs that have licensed this format).

In short, if you want to create an application as functional as Word, you'll have to either create your own custom control, or start building on the `RichTextBox` control.

Workshop

This workshop will help reinforce the concepts we covered today. It is very helpful to understand fully the answers before moving on. Answers can be found in Appendix A.

Quiz

1. How are `RadioButton` selections limited?

2. What does the following custom date/time string mean?

   `"hh:MM:yy-dddd"`

3. What object is associated with the `TreeView` control?

4. For a `Button` control named `btHappy`, set properties that will cause it to expand vertically when its container form is resized.

5. Name ten members that are shared by every control discussed today.

6

6. What are the five members of the `Timer` control discussed today?

7. How do you add "tabs" to the `TabControl` control? Describe in words and with a line of code.

8. What two methods should you execute when you plan on adding many items to a `ComboBox` control using the `Add` method? Given what you know about Windows Forms controls, what other controls (discussed today) do you think also have these methods?

9. True or false: The `PictureBox` control can only display bitmap (`BMP`) and `GIF` images.

Exercise

Create an application in C# that allows users to insert and view their CD collections. They must be able to enter new artists/albums/songs, and view them using a hierarchical list. (Don't worry about saving the input just now—we'll learn how to do that in Day 9, "Using ADO.NET.")

Remember to make sure that albums are only added to artists, and songs are only added to albums.

DAY 7

Working with Dialog Boxes

Dialog boxes are special types of Windows Forms that are used mainly for interacting with the user and providing alerts. You've probably seen thousands of them while working with Windows, from messages in Microsoft Word that say "Do you want to save the changes you made?" to prompts that ask for your username and password when you log into Windows.

Dialog boxes are a very versatile tool in Windows Forms, and as such provide a lot of complex options for your applications and their users. We'll spend this entire day studying the intricacies of dealing with dialog boxes and the special types of dialogs included with Windows Forms.

Today you will learn about the various kinds of dialog boxes used throughout Windows and how to:

- Determine a dialog box's "result"
- Customize any dialog box
- Perform commonly used tasks in Windows with dialog boxes

Retrieving and Displaying Information

The primary purpose of a dialog box is to prompt the user for information. This is different from simply obtaining information through your main Windows form object because it allows you to grab the user's attention in a direct way. Although users might just glance over requested information on your form, you can be pretty sure that they'll enter the requested information in a dialog box.

Because dialog boxes are very good at catching a user's attention (Windows often accompanies the initial display of a dialog box with an alert sound), they are perfect for *displaying* important information as well. In yesterday's alarm clock example, you used a message box—a special type of dialog box—to provide an alert for the user to wake up. Similarly, in yesterday's exercise (building a music catalog), you used dialog boxes to alert users when they try to add objects where they don't belong (adding an artist to an album, rather than the other way around, for instance). Whether displaying or retrieving information, a dialog box always sends data back to the main form (you'll learn about this in "Using Dialog Boxes" later today).

After the requested information is obtained, the dialog box's caller—typically a `Form` object—can use that information to perform some actions. For example, if you edit a document in Word and try to close the application without saving, a dialog box prompts you to save the document, as shown in Figure 7.1. Depending on what button the user clicks (Yes, No, or Cancel), Word takes the appropriate action (saving, not saving, or stopping the closing, respectively). In this way, the dialog box both alerts and retrieves information.

FIGURE 7.1

*This dialog box from
Microsoft Word
requires user response.*

As you'll see later today, dialog boxes can be a lot more complex than this simple example lets on. They provide you, the developer, a bevy of options for retrieving information, and the best part is that most of the common complex tasks are already done for you by .NET.

A dialog box is, for all intents and purposes, a `Form` object with its `FormBorderStyle` property set to `FixedDialog`. (Recall from Day 3, "Working with Your Windows Forms," this means that the window appears much like your typical Windows Forms window, but is non-resizable—try to remember when the last time you were able to resize a message box!). This, along with a property known as modality (which you'll learn about later today), makes dialog boxes that much more efficient at gathering user input—users cannot continue what they're doing until they answer the dialog box, and "get it out of the way."

While it's true that the most basic dialog box simply contains some text and OK/Cancel buttons, this doesn't stop you from adding your own controls to the box. In fact, you can add any Windows Forms control—even menus and status bars—to your dialog boxes just as if they were Form objects!

So why would you want to build an entire application out of a dialog box? Well, obviously, you wouldn't want to for a complex application, such as Word. But for very simple applications, such as a calculator or temperature converter, a dialog box would often suffice.

In general, however, you're better off creating your applications with a Form rather than a dialog box—after all, Forms are designed to act as applications, and dialog boxes are not.

Do	Don't
Do use Forms, just as we've been doing, to create your applications, unless you have a specific reason not to.	**Don't** rely on dialog boxes to gather all of your user input. Instead, only use them when you need to alert the user.

The Different Types of Dialogs

Although the most common dialog box you see is the standard "OK/Cancel" box, there are several different types available. In fact, the .NET Framework provides different dialog boxes for most of the common tasks in Windows that require user interaction. And, optionally, you can force a user to respond to a dialog box before he can do anything else. Let's take a look at the properties that control dialog boxes.

Modal Versus Modeless

NEW TERM A *modal* form or dialog box is one that requires users to respond before allowing them to continue on in the application. The "save changes" dialog from Word that we discussed earlier today is just such a dialog. When it appears, you cannot do anything else in Word until you answer Yes, No, or Cancel. If you try to go back to the main document window without answering the box, you typically hear an error sound and the dialog box prompts you again. Thus, a modal dialog *requires* user input.

7

Note

Modal dialogs prevent you from going back to the application you were using, but not to other applications. For example, not responding to Word's modal "save changes" dialog will prevent you from using Word, but you can switch to Excel or Photoshop at any time.

NEW TERM A *modeless* dialog, then, is just the opposite; it doesn't require any user input, and the user can move back and forth between it and the application at will. A typical use for this type of dialog is a "help" window that sits alongside your application and contains answers to commonly asked questions about the application. If you've use the Office Assistant bundled with Microsoft Office (the all-too-familiar paperclip), you understand what modeless dialogs are. The "assistant" simply sits on the side of any Office application and reacts with context sensitive information whenever the user starts to perform a common task. These dialogs don't require you to interact with them, although you may do so.

Modeless dialogs are often more difficult to work with than modal ones because the developer has to essentially keep track of two forms at once, passing appropriate data back and forth. With a modal dialog, you are dealing with either the dialog or the application, but never both at the same time, which makes things easier. It is for this reason that modeless dialogs are often used only to present information rather than to collect data.

The Common Dialog Boxes

Common dialog boxes, as the name implies, are dialog boxes that allow you to perform common tasks such as opening and saving files, choosing fonts, and so on. Because they perform common tasks, they are used in many places. Think of all the applications you've used that allow you to open files (Microsoft Office, Photoshop, Notepad, Media Player—the list goes on and on). Most of these applications present the same interface for opening files; they all use the same "open file" common dialog box to allow a user to choose a file to open. This helps developers tremendously because you don't have to build a new "open file" interface for every single application you write.

The .NET Framework comes with seven common dialog box classes that you can use in your applications:

- `ColorDialog`—Allows the user to choose a color from a specified palette (for example, to change font colors).

- `FontDialog`—Allows the user to choose a font to use.

- `OpenFileDialog`—Allows the user to choose a file to open. This dialog box does not open the file for you, but only lets you choose which one to open. It is up to you and your application to retrieve the file the user selected and open it; the dialog box won't do it automatically.

- `PageSetupDialog`—Allows the user to format documents in Windows (set page margins, select paper size, and so forth).

- `PrintDialog`—Allows the user to choose a printer, set print options, and print a document.

- `PrintPreviewDialog`—Allows the user to see what a document will look like on paper before printing it.

- `SaveFileDialog`—Allows the user to save files in a chosen directory (much like the "Save As" dialog in Word).

These classes are just like any other Windows Forms control or dialog box, so you should be able to learn them very quickly.

We'll revisit these controls later today. For now, let's examine how to use basic dialog boxes.

Using Dialog Boxes

The simplest dialog box is the `MessageBox` class. We've already used this one quite a bit because it's so easy. This class only has one available (non-inherited) member, the `Show` method, which causes the box to pop up on screen, with an OK button:

```
MessageBox.Show("Hello World")
```

This code snippet displays a dialog box with the text "Hello World," and an OK button. For many situations, this simple functionality will suffice. However, the `Show` method has a few optional parameters that allow you to further customize the dialog box.

Note

> You cannot create an instance of the `MessageBox` class directly. For example, the following code produces an error:
>
> ```
> dim msgMyMessage as New MessageBox
> ```
>
> The only way you can interact with the `MessageBox` is by calling its `Show` method:
>
> ```
> MessageBox.Show("Hello world!")
> ```

7

Table 7.1 lists the various parameters to this Show method, in the order that they must appear in the method call (all parameters are optional except number two in Table 7.1).

TABLE 7.1 MessageBox.Show Parameters

Parameter Number	Type	Description
1	Iwin32Window	The window to display the dialog box in front of (for example, Me in VB.NET, or this in C#).
2	String	The text to display in the dialog box. This is the only required parameter.
3	String	The text to display in the caption of the dialog box.
4	MessageBoxButtons	The number and type of buttons to display.
5	MessageBoxIcon	The icon to display for the dialog box.
6	MessageBoxDefaultButton	Specifies the default button (the pre-selected button) of the dialog box.
7	MessageBoxOptions	Various options for the dialog box.

For example, you could display the message box in any of the following ways:

```
MessageBox.Show(Me, "Hello World", "My Dialog Box")

MessageBox.Show("Hello World", "My Dialog Box",
➥MessageBoxButtons.OKCancel)

MessageBox.Show(Me, "Hello World", "My Dialog Box",
➥MessageBoxButtons.OKCancel, MessageBoxIcon.Hand)
```

These three calls produce the three dialogs shown in Figure 7.2.

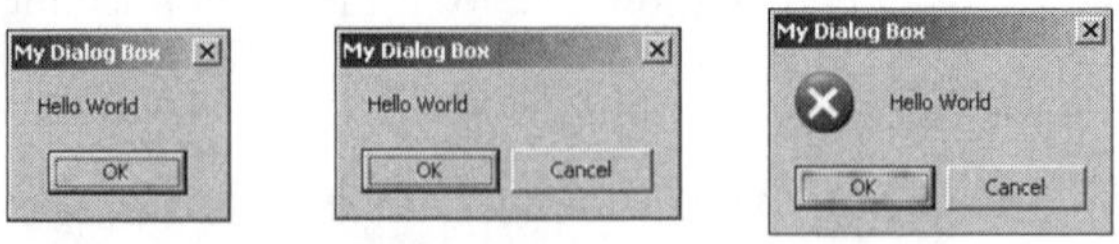

FIGURE 7.2

You can add easily add buttons (up to a maximum of three) and an icon to a message box.

The first three parameters listed in Table 7.1 are easy to understand. The last four, however, are all enumerations that specify display options of the dialog box. Let's examine them one by one.

The MessageBoxButtons enumeration contains the values AbortRetryIgnore, OK, OKCancel, RetryCancel, YesNo, and YesNoCancel. The purpose of each is rather easy to determine: `AbortRetryIgnore` displays three buttons with the captions Abort, Retry, and Cancel; `OK` simply displays an "OK" button; and so on.

`MessageBoxIcon` displays an icon next to the text in the message box. Values can be `Asterisk`, `Error`, `Exclamation`, `Hand`, `Information`, `None`, `Question`, `Stop`, or `Warning`. The actual images displayed may vary from operating system to operating system (and it just so happens that in Windows many of the images used for the different icons are the same). Figure 7.3 shows each of these icons in Windows XP.

FIGURE 7.3

The ninth `MessageBoxIcon` *enumeration value is* `None`.

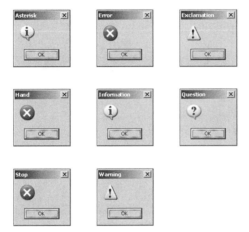

`MessageBoxDefaultButton` is an easy property to learn; it has only three values: `Button1`, `Button2`, and `Button3`. The property determines which button on the dialog box is the default one. This button is pre-selected when the dialog box is shown, and also is the one that is clicked should the user press the Enter key. (Note that there is a maximum of possible three buttons on a message box.)

Finally, `MessageBoxOptions` has four non-related values. `DefaultDesktopOnly` and `ServiceNotification` specify that the message box should appear on the active desktop (for those with more than one monitor). `RightAlign` specifies that the text in the message box is right-aligned, and `RtlReading` specifies that the text should be formatted for right-to-left reading order (some foreign languages require this value). You can combine these values much like you combined `Anchor` values in yesterday's lesson, by using the `Or` or `|` operators:

```
MessageBox.Show("Hello World", "My Dialog Box",
➥MessageBoxButtons.OKCancel, MessageBoxIcon.None,
➥MessageBoxDefaultButton.Button1,
➥MessageBoxOptions.RightAlign Or
➥MessageBoxOptions.ServiceNotification)
```

7

Creating Your Own Dialog Boxes

The MessageBox class is a great, pre-built dialog control that provides quite a few options. Sometimes, though, the MessageBox is simply not adequate for your needs. In these cases, you can easily build your own dialog box class.

Building a dialog box class is almost exactly like building a Windows Form class; you inherit from System.Windows.Forms.Form, create and add controls to your form, and add event handlers as well. The only difference is that you must make available to the parent form (the form that displays the dialog box) any necessary properties. For example, let's dissect the common "open file" dialog, shown in Figure 7.4.

FIGURE 7.4

The Open file dialog box includes several types of controls.

You can guess the types of controls that are needed to build this dialog box: a ComboBox for the directory drop-down and the file type drop-down, a couple of Buttons for the Open and Cancel buttons, a few Labels, possibly some type of TreeView control, and a few TextBoxes. After the user picks a file, the main application is interested in only one thing: What file did the user select? Then, the chosen file name is displayed in the File Name text box. Thus, the main application needs to know the Text property of that TextBox, so it can appropriately handle the file.

To expose these types of properties to the main form, we need to build properties (just like the Text property). Listing 7.1 shows a custom dialog box class that allows the user to change the caption of the form.

LISTING 7.1   Your First Custom Dialog Box Application

```
1:  Imports System
2:  Imports System.Windows.Forms
3:  Imports System.Drawing
4:
```

LISTING 7.1 continued

```
5:  namespace TYWinForms.Day7
6:
7:      public class ChangeCaption : Inherits Form
8:          private btnChange as new Button
9:          private tbCaption as new TextBox
10:
11:         public readonly property Caption as String
12:             Get
13:                 Return tbCaption.Text
14:             End Get
15:         end property
16:
17:         public sub New
18:             tbCaption.Location = new Point(10,10)
19:
20:             btnChange.Text = "Change!"
21:             btnChange.Location = new Point(125,10)
22:             AddHandler btnChange.Click, new EventHandler
➥(AddressOf Me.Clicked)
23:
24:             Me.Text = "Change Caption"
25:             Me.Size = new Size(250,100)
26:             Me.Controls.Add(btnChange)
27:             Me.Controls.Add(tbCaption)
28:         end sub
29:
30:         private sub Clicked(Sender as Object, e as EventArgs)
31:             Me.Hide
32:         end sub
33:     end class
34: End Namespace
```

ANALYSIS Save this file as listing7.1.vb. At first glance, this looks like any other Windows Forms application. You create two controls on lines 8 and 9, set properties in a constructor on lines 18–27, and have an event handler on lines 30–32.

The main difference is that there is no Main method in this code. That's because this class should never be run on its own—it should only be used from another form or application.

Take a look at line 30 and the event handler. This handler does only one thing: call the Hide method for the form. Without it, nothing would happen after the user clicks the "Change Caption" button. Since we want to create a modal dialog box, this would mean that the user could never go back to the originating application. By calling Hide, we cause the dialog box to disappear and bring the originating application to the front, allowing interaction again.

7

Finally, notice lines 11–15, which illustrate creating a property of a class. The declaration looks similar to a function, but uses the keyword `property` instead of `function`. Inside this property, there are two special keywords: `Get` and `Set`. The code inside `Get` is executed whenever another class tries to access this property. `Set`, on the other hand, is used whenever a value for this property is set by another class. Here, we don't need a `Set` portion, so we only write the `Get` and make sure that the property is marked as `readonly` (line 11). You can put whatever code you want in the `Get` and `Set` portions; here, we only want to return the value that is in the `TextBox`, using the `Return` keyword. In C#, this property would look like the following code snippet:

```
public string Caption {
   get {
      return tbCaption.Text;
   }
}
```

Note that C# doesn't require the `property` or `readonly` keywords.

When you want to set the property value, use the `value` keyword:

```
'VB.NET
Set
   tbCaption.Text = value
End Set

//C#
set { tbCaption.Text = value; }
```

 Note

> The only `public` members in the `ChangeCaption` class are the constructor and the `Caption` property. We don't want other classes accessing the rest of the members directly, so we make them all `private`.
>
> Also, you can use this method of declaring public and private variables to create properties for your regular classes as well.

Next, let's look at the application that will use this custom dialog box class. Listing 7.2 shows a simple application that allows the user to change the caption of the form using the `ChangeCaption` dialog box created in Listing 7.1 and its `Caption` property.

LISTING 7.2   Using the Custom Dialog Box

```
1:  Imports System
2:  Imports System.Windows.Forms
3:  Imports System.Drawing
4:
```

LISTING 7.2   continued

```
 5:   namespace TYWinForms.Day7
 6:
 7:     public class Listing72 : Inherits Form
 8:        private btnChange as new Button
 9:
10:          public sub New
11:             btnChange.Text = "Change caption"
12:             btnChange.Location = new Point(75,75)
13:             btnChange.Size = new Size(100,75)
14:             AddHandler btnChange.Click, new EventHandler
➥(AddressOf Me.ShowChangeBox)
15:
16:             Me.Text = "Change Caption"
17:             Me.Controls.Add(btnChange)
18:          end sub
19:
20:          public sub ShowChangeBox(Sender as Object, e
➥as EventArgs)
21:             dim dlgChangeCaption as new ChangeCaption
22:             dlgChangeCaption.ShowDialog
23:
24:             Me.Text = dlgChangeCaption.Caption
25:          end sub
26:
27:          public shared sub Main()
28:             Application.Run(new Listing72)
29:          end sub
30:       end class
31:   End Namespace
```

ANALYSIS   Save this file as `Listing7.2.vb`. Listing 7.2 shows another simple Windows Forms class, except that this one represents the main application, and consequently, has a `Main` method. Lines 1–18 are typical; they create and instantiate the form and its controls. The interesting part begins on line 20.

The `ShowChangeBox` method handles the `Click` event of the `btnChange` button. On line 21 you create a new instance of the `ChangeCaption` class you created in Listing 7.1. Notice that this procedure is exactly like creating any other .NET object. On line 22 you call the `ShowDialog` method, which causes the dialog box to be shown modally.

Wait a second! You didn't create a `ShowDialog` method in your `ChangeCaption` class. So where did it come from? The `System.Windows.Forms.Form` class has the `ShowDialog` method, which means that your custom dialog box class inherited it. It also means that *any* Windows Form can be used as a dialog box! This provides you a lot of flexibility when designing your applications.

7

After line 22 executes and the dialog box is displayed, control of the application passes to the modal dialog box, and until that box closes, the main application can't do anything else.

Once you type something in the dialog box and click the Change! button, control moves back to the application, and execution picks up on line 24. This line retrieves the Caption property of the dialog box, and assigns it to the Text property of the current form. Now you see how the Caption property in Listing 7.1 is utilized.

One more thing before we're done. Since these two listings are stored in two separate files (Listing7.1.vb and Listing7.2.vb), you'll have to compile them both into one application. With Visual Studio.NET, this is easy—just make sure that both files are in the same project, and compile as normal (by selecting Build from the Build menu). If you're using the command-line compiler, just specify both files in the command:

```
vbc /t:winexe /r:system.dll /r:system.windows.forms.dll
➥/r:system.drawing.dll listing7.1.vb listing7.2.vb
```

As long as these two files are in the same directory, the preceding command works, and you'll end up with one executable file, Listing7.1.exe (the order in which you name the files to be compiled determines what the executable name is). And that's all there is to it! Figure 7.5 shows the output.

FIGURE 7.5

A custom, modal dialog box is fairly easy to create.

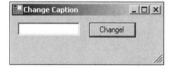

Note that you didn't have to set any special properties for your custom dialog box class. By calling its ShowDialog method, the Common Language Runtime (CLR) automatically presents it as a modal dialog box. However, just as for a normal form, you can modify any properties you want, such as SizeGripStyle to change the resizing grip on the lower right corner of the form, ControlBox to change the buttons available in the upper right corner, and so on.

If you want to display your custom dialog box as a modeless form, call the Show method instead of the ShowDialog method. The user will be able to switch back and forth between the application and dialog window. In the application you just built, this would cause a couple of problems:

- Because the execution doesn't stop in the main form when the Show method is called, line 24 of Listing 7.2 (which retrieves the caption from the dialog box) will execute immediately and the form's caption will change to a blank string. After all, when you first create your dialog box, the tbCaption TextBox is blank, and line 24 executes before you get a chance to enter any text and click the Change! button.

- The user can keep clicking the Change Caption button on the main form, which will cause many dialog boxes to display at once.

In this case, when the user enters text in the tbCaption box and presses the Change! button, the dialog box disappears and nothing else happens; the caption of the form doesn't change because line 24 has already executed, long before the Change! button was pressed. To set the caption then, you need to somehow be able to access the dialog box's tbCaption.Text property. You can do so by creating a new public property:

```
Public property Caption As String
   Get
      return tbCaption.Text
   End Get
   Set
      tbCaption.Text = value
   End Set
End Property
```

The solution to the second problem is to use a modal dialog box. But then the user must explicitly close the dialog box before being allowed to go back to the main form. Be sure to only use modal dialog boxes when you want this kind of functionality.

Retrieving Information

We've already seen how to retrieve data from a dialog box using properties. These properties, though, are sometimes not enough to give you all the information you need. Occasionally you'll also need to know how the user closed the dialog box: did he click the OK button? Did he click the Cancel button? These facts, known as the *result* of the dialog box, may change the operation of your application, so you need to retrieve these values as well.

The DialogResult enumeration holds several values that allow you to determine the result of a dialog box. The ShowDialog returns a value from this enumeration, so you can do with it what you will. For example:

```
dim objDR as DialogResult
objDR = dlgChangeCaption.ShowDialog
if objDR = DialogResult.OK then
   'change the caption
elseif objDR = DialogResult.No then
   'don't do anything
end if
```

7

Depending on the result returned from the dialog box, you can perform conditional execution. There is a `DialogResult` value for each of the possible buttons on a dialog box,
and then some:

- `Abort`
- `Cancel`
- `Ignore`
- `No`
- `None`
- `OK`
- `Retry`
- `Yes`

Listing 7.3 shows a simple example of using `DialogResult` with a message box.

LISTING 7.3   Retrieving the Result of a Dialog Box in C#

```
 1:  using System;
 2:  using System.Windows.Forms;
 3:  using System.Drawing;
 4:
 5:  namespace TYWinForms.Day7 {
 6:
 7:     public class Listing73 : Form {
 8:         public Listing73() {
 9:             if (MessageBox.Show("Do you want this application
➥to open full screen?", "Listing 7.3",
➥MessageBoxButtons.YesNo) == DialogResult.Yes) {
10:                 this.Size = Screen.GetWorkingArea(this).Size;
11:                 this.DesktopLocation = new Point(0,0);
12:             }
13:         }
14:
15:         public static void Main() {
16:             Application.Run(new Listing73());
17:         }
18:     }
19:  }
```

ANALYSIS On line 9 you test the result of the `MessageBox.Show` method. If it equals
`DialogResult.Yes`—that is, if the user clicked the Yes button—then you execute
the code on lines 10–11, which sets the size of the form to the size of the user's desktop,
and sets its location to the upper left corner of the desktop. Alternatively, you could
replace lines 10 and 11 with the following code to maximize the application:

```
this.WindowState = FormWindowState.Maximized;
```

Because you displayed the `MessageBox` using the `MessageBoxButtons.YesNo` button set, then the CLR knows that the Yes button should return `DialogResult.Yes`, and the No button should return the `DialogResult.No` value.

Recall the example of "Do you want to save the changes" Microsoft Word dialog box. When you click Yes, the dialog box returns `DialogResult.Yes`, and Word knows to execute the code that will save the document and then closes. If you click No, then `DialogResult.No` is passed, the document is not saved, and Word closes. If you click cancel, `DialogResult.Cancel` is passed and nothing happens (the document is neither saved nor closed, and Word doesn't close).

Retrieving a dialog's result this way is a great, standardized way to alert applications of a user's actions. What happens, however, when you've created your own custom dialog box? How does the CLR know that your `Change!` button is supposed to return `DialogResult.Yes`?

Actually, it's much easier than you think. Buttons and forms have a `DialogResult` property that allows you to specify what result should be returned. Let's take a look at a modified version of the custom dialog box you built in Listing 7.1, shown here in Listing 7.4 and in C#.

LISTING 7.4   A Modified Custom Dialog Box in C#

```
1:  using System;
2:  using System.Windows.Forms;
3:  using System.Drawing;
4:
5:  namespace TYWinForms.Day7 {
6:
7:      public class ChangeCaption2 : Form {
8:          private Button btnChange = new Button();
9:          private TextBox tbCaption = new TextBox();
10:
11:         public String Caption {
12:            get {
13:               return tbCaption.Text;
14:            }
15:         }
16:
17:         public ChangeCaption2() {
18:            tbCaption.Location = new Point(10,10);
19:
20:            btnChange.Text = "Change!";
21:            btnChange.Location = new Point(125,10);
```

7

LISTING 7.4   continued

```
22:            btnChange.DialogResult = DialogResult.OK;
23:
24:            this.Text = "Change Caption";
25:            this.Size = new Size(250,100);
26:            this.Controls.Add(btnChange);
27:            this.Controls.Add(tbCaption);
28:        }
29:    }
30: }
```

ANALYSIS   Aside from the language (and the name change of the class on line 7), there are only two differences in this listing (aside from the programming language) versus Listing 7.1. First, the Clicked event handler is now gone, as well as the assignation of a delegate to the button. I'll explain why in a moment.

The second change is the addition of line 22. Here you assign the DialogResult.OK value to the btnChange Button. This does two things. First, it returns DialogResult.OK to the parent form, just like the MessageBox returned DialogResult.Yes in Listing 7.3. Second, when this button is clicked, the CLR automatically closes the form for you—you don't need to call the Hide method anymore, and consequently, you don't need an event handler for the Clicked event. Thus, by specifying the DialogResult property, the CLR knows that this class is a dialog box, and makes it perform as such.

The main application needs to change slightly as well. The ShowChangeBox method from Listing 7.2 needs to look like the following code snippet:

```
public void ShowChangeBox(Object Sender, EventArgs e) {
   DialogResult objDR;
   ChangeCaption2 dlgChangeCaption = new ChangeCaption2();

   objDR = dlgChangeCaption.ShowDialog();

   if (objDR == DialogResult.OK) {
      this.Text = dlgChangeCaption.Caption;
   }

   this.Text = dlgChangeCaption.Caption;
}
```

(Don't forget to change the rest of the listing to C# as well!) The result of the new dialog box is stored in the objDR variable created on the second line. This value is then compared to DialogResult.OK, and, if they are equal, the caption of the form is changed. If not, then no action is taken.

Do	Don't
Do assign `DialogResult` values to the buttons in your custom dialog boxes. This is a standard convention, and makes the use of those custom dialog boxes easier for you and others who are using your class.	**Don't** rely on the parent form to interpret your dialog result, even if you are the only one who will ever see it. Assigning `DialogResult` values ensures that your application uses standardized values that are easy to evaluate.

Using Common Dialog Boxes

As mentioned earlier, there are seven common dialog boxes in .NET: `OpenFileDialog`, `SaveFileDialog`, `ColorDialog`, `FontDialog`, `PageSetupDialog`, `PrintDialog`, and `PrintPreviewDialog`. All of these dialogs are pre-built to make performing these common tasks easier (this doesn't prohibit you from creating your own versions of these controls if you want to).

You've probably seen all of these types of dialog boxes in Windows, and are somewhat familiar with their look and functionality. In the following sections, we'll spend some time with each, and learn the most common functionality. (For more detailed reference, see Appendix B, "Windows Forms Controls.")

 Tip

There are two members that all of the following common dialog boxes (except `PrintPreviewDialog`) have in common: `ShowHelp` and `Reset`. The first indicates whether a Help button should be displayed in the dialog box. The `Reset` method changes all properties of the specified dialog back to their default values. This method is especially useful when dealing with these rather complex controls.

File Input/Output

The two common dialogs that deal with file input and output (I/O) are the `OpenFileDialog` and `SaveFileDialog` controls, which have a lot of similar functionality. Most of the properties we cover in this section apply to both controls.

The most important property, obviously, of these two controls is `FileName` (and `FileNames`), which specifies the file that the user has selected to open or save. Your main form can retrieve this value and open or save the file as necessary—we'll cover those functions in Day 11, "Working with Windows Input/Output." Instantiating and displaying these controls is easy:

7

```
dim dlgOpen as new SaveFileDialog
dlgOpen.ShowDialog
```

This code produces the dialog shown in Figure 7.6.

FIGURE 7.6

The Save file dialog control can be found in most Windows applications.

Both dialogs return either `DialogResult.OK` or `DialogResult.Cancel` depending on whether the user clicked Save (or Open) or Cancel. You can then retrieve the `FileName` property:

```
if dlgOpen.ShowDialog = DialogResult.OK then
   Me.Text = dlgOpen.FileName
end if
```

For the `OpenFileDialog`, you can allow the user to select more than one file at a time by setting `MultiSelect` to `true`. The `FileNames` property will then hold an array of strings representing those files.

In addition to these main properties (`FileName` and `FileNames`), there are quite a few you can use to customize the functionality of these dialog boxes. The `Filter` property can be used to determine the types of files that appear in the "Save as (file) type" or "Files of Type" boxes; these filters essentially limit the types of files the user can open or save. This filter is a specially formatted string. For example, the following code snippet allows only Word document (`.doc`) and text files (`.txt`) to be opened:

```
dlgOpen.Filter = "Text files (*.txt)|*.txt|Word documents
➥(*.doc)|*.doc"
```

The string is essentially broken down into the following parts:

Description (extension) | *filter string*

The description is the user-friendly text the user sees in the Save or Open file type box. The pipe symbol (|) separates fields in this string. The filter string is used by the dialog to filter file extensions; `*.txt` means only files with the `.txt` extension will appear. Subsequent types can be separated by the pipe symbol.

`FilterIndex` can then be used to specify the default filter that is pre-selected. `InitialDirectory` is a string that specifies the initial directory the dialog will start in.

There are also quite a few properties that deal with prompting the user upon certain conditions. Setting the `CheckPathExists` property of either control to `true` prompts users with a warning if the path they have specified doesn't exist. The `OpenFileDialog`'s `CheckFileExists` property does the same except for a specific file. `CreatePrompt` and `OverwritePrompt` of the `SaveFileDialog` are similar; the first prompts the user for permission to create a file if it does not already exist, and the second prompts them when the file does exist, asking whether it should be overwritten or not.

We'll revisit these controls again in Day 11 when we discuss File I/O in .NET.

Choosing Colors and Fonts

The `ColorDialog` control is one of the easiest common dialog controls to learn. It only has a few properties that you need to know about. Listing 7.5 shows an example of using this control to set the background color of your form.

LISTING 7.5   Using the `ColorDialog` Control

```
 1: using System;
 2: using System.Windows.Forms;
 3: using System.Drawing;
 4:
 5: namespace TYWinForms.Day7 {
 6:    public class Listing75 : Form {
 7:       public Button btColor = new Button();
 8:
 9:       public Listing75() {
10:          btColor.Text = "Change Color!";
11:          btColor.Location = new Point(100,100);
12:          btColor.Size = new Size(100,25);
13:          btColor.Click += new EventHandler(this.ChangeColor);
14:
15:          this.Controls.Add(btColor);
16:       }
17:
18:       public void ChangeColor(Object Sender, EventArgs e) {
19:          ColorDialog dlgColor = new ColorDialog();
20:
```

LISTING 7.5   continued

```
21:              if (dlgColor.ShowDialog() == DialogResult.OK) {
22:                  this.BackColor = dlgColor.Color;
23:              }
24:          }
25:
26:          public static void Main() {
27:              Application.Run(new Listing75());
28:          }
29:      }
30: }
```

ANALYSIS   This listing presents a simple application with a single button that displays the common color dialog box.

When the user selects a color in the ColorDialog, it is placed into the ColorDialog.Color property. On line 22, we take that color and assign it to the BackColor value of the main form.

Figure 7.7 shows the output from this application and the ColorDialog dialog box.

FIGURE 7.7

ColorDialog *is an easy-to-use dialog box control.*

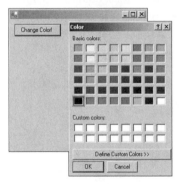

That's all you need to use ColorDialog. However, this control is a bit more functional, allowing the user to select more colors than just those presented. If you set AllowFullOpen to true, the user can open an additional window (by clicking the Define Custom Colors button, which is shown near the bottom of the Color dialog in Figure 7.7) to create custom colors from all available colors on the system. (If you don't want this functionality, set AllowFullOpen to false and set FullOpen, which causes the Define Custom Colors button to be shown, to false as well.) After the user has defined some custom colors, you can use the CustomColors property to return an array of Color objects.

The `FontDialog` is a bit more complex because there are many different styles of fonts; the color blue is blue, but the font Arial may be Arial bold, italics, regular; 10 points, 20 points, 36 points; and on and on. And then there are the different styles of fonts, from scripts (non-OEM and ANSI), vector fonts, vertical fonts, fixed pitch, and so forth.

If you don't care about that, then you can simply use the `FontDialog.Font` property to return the font the user chose, as you may have already guessed:

```
if (dlgFont.DialogResult == DialogResult.OK) {
   this.Font = dlgFont.Font;
}
```

This is a lot easier than having to create a new `Font` object every time you want to change the font! Figure 7.8 shows the default font dialog box.

FIGURE 7.8

`FontDialog`'s *default dialog box offers many choices.*

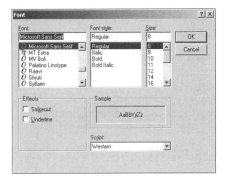

Each of the fields in the font dialog (effects, size, scripts, and so forth) is customizable. `AllowScriptChange` allows the user to change the default script, while `ScriptsOnly` only displays script fonts. `AllowSimulations`, `AllowVectorFonts`, and `AllowVerticalFonts` allow the different types of fonts (these are all set to `true` by default).

`FixedPitchOnly` only allows fixed pitch fonts to be displayed. `ShowColor` allows the user to change the color of the font (the `Color` property returns that color), and `ShowEffects` displays the effects box (underline or strikeout).

Finally, you can set the `MaxSize` and `MinSize` to set the maximum and minimum font size the user can select. Setting these properties to `0` allows the system to control these values—it will usually allow the entire range of sizes.

Printing

The last set of common controls we'll examine deals with printing pages: `PageSetupDialog`, `PrintDialog`, and `PrintPreview` dialog. All of these should be familiar to anyone who's ever dealt with printing documents.

7

`PageSetupDialog` allows you to set the margins for a document, change the orientation (portrait or landscape), change the size of paper being printed to, and so on.

Before you can use a `PageSetupDialog`, however, you have to have something to apply your settings to. This is done by creating a `PageSettings` object and assigning it to the `PageSetupDialog`'s `PageSettings` property, which indicates what object should have the properties applied to it. Listing 7.6 shows an example application that does just this.

LISTING 7.6   Setting up a Page

```
1:  using System;
2:  using System.Windows.Forms;
3:  using System.Drawing;
4:  using System.Drawing.Printing;
5:
6:  namespace TYWinForms.Day7 {
7:     public class Listing76 : Form {
8:        private PageSettings objPageSettings;
9:        private Button btShowDialog = new Button();
10:
11:        public Listing76() {
12:           btShowDialog.Text = "Page Settings";
13:           btShowDialog.Click += new EventHandler
➥(this.ShowSettings);
14:
15:           this.Controls.Add(btShowDialog);
16:        }
17:
18:        private void ShowSettings(Object Sender,
➥EventArgs e) {
19:           if (objPageSettings == null) {
20:              objPageSettings = new PageSettings();
21:           }
22:
23:           PageSetupDialog dlgSettings = new
➥PageSetupDialog();
24:           dlgSettings.PageSettings = objPageSettings;
25:           dlgSettings.ShowDialog();
26:        }
27:
28:        public static void Main() {
29:           Application.Run(new Listing76());
30:        }
31:     }
32:  }
```

ANALYSIS Managing page properties is somewhat complex. First, create a
System.Drawing.Printing.PageSettings object (line 8; notice the new using
statement on line 4). This object will be used throughout your application, so it's necessary to create an object that is available to the entire class. In the ShowSettings method
on line 18, you must check this PageSettings object. If it's null (or Nothing in
VB.NET), then no properties have yet been assigned to this document, so you must
instantiate the PageSettings object, as shown on line 20. If it is not null, then the
PageSettings object has already been instantiated and properties assigned, so we want
to use it over and over again.

Line 23 creates a new PageSetupDialog. Line 24 then assigns the PageSettings object
(whether newly created or already used) to the PageSettings property. Now the settings
the user chooses can be stored, and applied as necessary to the document. ShowDialog is
called on 25; notice that you don't need to check its DialogResult value. This is because
the PageSetupDialog takes care of applying the settings for you depending on the button
the user clicked. Thus, we don't care whether the user clicked OK or Cancel; the
PageSetupDialog handles it internally.

Compile this application and execute it. (Recall from Day 2, "Building Windows Forms
Applications," that the System.Drawing.Printing namespace is located in the
System.Drawing.dll assembly, so you don't need to add any additional references when
compiling.) Click the Page Settings button and modify some page properties. Close the
dialog, and then open it again with the button. Notice how the changes you made are still
reflected in the PageSetupDialog. This is because the changes you made were assigned
to the PageSettings object that is being used over and over again. Figure 7.9 shows the
output of this application.

FIGURE 7.9

PageSetupDialog *pro-
vides a Page Setup dia-
log box.*

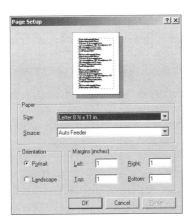

7

Like the other common dialog controls we've discussed today, the PageSetupDialog also has quite a few properties that allow you to customize the dialog box. AllowMargins, AllowOrientation, AllowPaper, and AllowPrinter show the boxes that let the user change margins, page orientation, paper size, and print settings, respectively. When modifying the AllowPrinter setting, you want to use a PrinterSettings object, but we'll discuss that when we talk about file I/O in Day 11. MinMargins specifies the smallest margins allowable by your application. Finally, Document specifies the PrintDocument object to get page settings from.

The PrintDialog control is easier to deal with. Like the PageSetupDialog, it contains Document and PrinterSettings properties to keep track of settings. You have to assign a PrinterSettings object to the PrinterSettings property for this control to work. Unlike the PageSetupDialog, however, here you want to check the DialogResult property when the dialog box is opened. We'll hold off further discussion of this control until Day 11. Figure 7.10 shows the typical Print dialog box.

FIGURE 7.10

The PrintDialog control provides a useful Print dialog box.

The last common dialog we'll discuss today is the PrintPreviewDialog object. This control is not like most of the controls discussed today. It doesn't inherit from the CommonDialog class like all the other common dialog controls. It doesn't even resemble a standard dialog box. Its DialogResult also doesn't need to be monitored.

There are only three properties of the PrintPreviewDialog control that we need to worry about. The first, Document, specifies the document to be previewed. Beware, though, that this property doesn't take just any type of document; it's very finicky. You must assign it a PrintDocument object, which in turns represents the document to be previewed. Again, we'll cover this object in Day 11.

The next two properties are simple. PrintPreviewControl returns, naturally, the PrintPreviewControl on the PrintPreviewDialog box. This control is what displays the actual preview—the rest of the PrintPreviewDialog's buttons and controls are separate items. If you wanted to build your own custom print-previewing dialog, you'd most likely use the `PrintPreviewControl` to do so.

`UseAntiAlias` specifies if the previewed document should be anti-aliased—that is, should the edges of the document be "smoothed out" so that no "jaggies" or harsh edges appear. Anti-aliasing often makes things easier and smoother to look at, at a cost of sharpness (in fact, the sharpness control on your television can be thought of as the degree of anti-aliasing).

Figure 7.11 shows the `PrintPreviewDialog` control at work.

FIGURE 7.11

You can use the `PrintPreviewDialog` dialog box to preview a document.

Summary

As you learned today, dialog boxes can be a lot more complex and functional than the simple `MessageBox` you've been using. Dialog boxes are used for collecting user input, whether it's a simple yes or no, or a selection of `Fonts` and `Colors`.

The first thing to remember about dialog boxes is that they can be modal or modeless. A modal dialog doesn't allow the user to switch to the parent application without first responding to the dialog box. Modeless dialogs do allow switching, but this type of dialog can often lead to problems because you need to manage more than one form at once. Therefore, use modeless dialogs only if you just need to present information to the user, without necessarily collecting any information.

7

The dialog you're most familiar with is the MessageBox. This control has one method, Show, that can take up to seven parameters to specify things such as the icon that appears in the box, the buttons available, and the text and caption to display.

If you need more functionality than the simple MessageBox, you must create your own dialog box classes. These classes are created just like regular Form classes; you inherit from the System.Windows.Forms.Form class and provide constructors and event handlers. You can expose values of the custom dialog to your parent form by creating public properties (with Get and/or Set statements).

Your dialog boxes can also return values indicating what button (such as OK or Cancel) the user clicked to close the dialog box. These values are in the DialogResult enumeration. The parent form can then test for this DialogResult to see what the user did with the dialog box.

You also learned about the many different common dialog controls offered by .NET. These controls encapsulate common Windows functionality, such as choosing fonts or colors, printing or print previewing, and so on.

You've reached the end of Week 1! Next week will cover topics that make your applications more functional, such as adding databases and graphics capabilities. Don't forget to check out the Bonus Project, "Creating a Word Processor," at the end of this week before you move ahead.

Q&A

Q What's the difference between the properties we created today and public variables?

A Both allow you to pass data from one class to another. For example, in Listing 7.1 we could have declared the property with the following line:

```
public Caption as String
```

And as long as you assign the tbCaption.Text property to this variable, then the functionality would be exactly the same. The difference between using properties and public variables is that with the property, you can execute additional code in the get and set statements. This is useful if, for example, you need to verify values before you return them:

```
public property Caption as String
   Get
      if tbCaption.Text <> "" then
         return tbCaption.Text
      else
```

```
            return "Nothing here!"
        end if
    End Get
End Property
```

With a public variable, you can't perform any additional functionality.

Q How do I get the actual document to show up in my `PrintPreviewDialog` control?

A This one's a bit more complicated. It involves a new class called `PrintDocument`, and requires some new skills we haven't talked about yet. For more information, check out Day 11, "Working with Windows I/O."

Workshop

This workshop helps reinforce the concepts we covered today. It is very helpful to understand fully the answers before moving on. Answers can be found in Appendix A.

Quiz

1. True or false: Any `Form` object can be a dialog box.

2. How do you make a dialog modal? Modeless?

3. True or false: You can directly instantiate a `MessageBox` object.

4. What are the seven parameters that the `MessageBox.Show` method can take? (Just list their types and a short description.)

5. Assigning a `DialogResult` value in your custom dialog class does what two things for you?

6. Is the following code snippet correct? If not, what's wrong with it?
```
public property IsClicked as string
    Get
        return blnClicked
end property
```

7. What two members are common to almost all common dialog controls? Name the exception(s).

8. Write a filter string for an `OpenFileDialog` control that displays: `.txt` files, `.gif` files, and all files.

9. Name the main properties (that is, the properties you are most interested in when the user makes a selection) for the `OpenFileDialog`, `SaveFileDialog`, `ColorDialog`, and `FontDialog` controls.

7

Exercise

Create a fully-featured application in C#, using menus, that uses all of the common dialog controls. Also, use a modeless dialog to display context-related help information. When a user moves from one menu item to another, the content in this dialog should change. (Hint: use the `MenuItem.Select` event to determine which menu item the mouse is currently over.)

WEEK 1

In Review

Project 1: Creating a Word Processor

Congratulations on making it through your first week! You should now be familiar with writing Windows Forms applications in C# and Visual Basic.NET, and should be aware of many of the intricacies of dealing with events and Windows Forms controls. With the knowledge you've gained so far, you're ready to tackle nearly any simple application, as well as a few more complex ones.

As a recap of the past seven days, this review section (and the ones following Weeks 2 and 3) will guide you through the process of creating your own word processing application—one that might even rival Microsoft Word! You'll build the foundation of the application in this lesson, the project at the end of Week 2 will add data and file I/O capabilities, and project 3 will add some more advanced features.

It's recommended that you work through these projects. They will better familiarize you with Windows Forms concepts because you'll be using real-world situations. Let's get started on your application.

About the Word-Processing Project

The purpose of this project is to give you the opportunity to work on an application at every stage of development. In his lesson, you start with a simple design, set up the basic functionality, and then add bells and whistles. This project also helps to hone your Windows Forms development skills so that you can be comfortable in your other projects. At the end of weeks 2 and 3, you will revisit this project to incorporate your new lessons.

Word processors are very useful applications; you'd be hard-pressed to find someone who *hasn't* used one. These applications use a wide range of technologies, from file I/O to Internet capabilities and search functionality.

This application, which we'll call *NetWord*, will allow users to edit and save documents, perform searches, format text, and eventually print documents and browse the Internet. In this lesson, however, we'll keep it simple and only build the basic framework and user interface for the application. Let's examine what you'll need to build in this lesson.

What You Need

The most important part of any word processor is the main interface—the text area that allows users to type and edit documents. You get three guesses as to how to build this interface....

I hope you guessed "using the `RichTextBox` control" on your first try. We've already seen (in Day 6, "Enhancing Your Windows Forms with More Controls") that this control allows you to perform nearly all of the functions of a word processor—from formatting text to performing searches—easily and without much effort.

Setting up the `RichTextBox` control will only be half the battle. You'll need to add menus to allow the user to open and save files, format text, choose colors, and so on. The menu and the `RichTextBox` control represent the bulk of this application (at least in this project).

To make your application more user-friendly, you'll want to add a few more controls, such as a status bar and context menus. These will be described in the "Adding Some Bells and Whistles" section later in this lesson.

Note

Even though most word processors are MDI (multiple-document interface) applications—meaning they can contain more than one open document at a time, à la Word—ours will remain a single document interface for now. We'll revisit MDI applications in Week 2.

Let's not delay—the dirty work awaits!

Building the User Interface

Listing P1.1 shows the basic framework for our application.

LISTING P1.1   The NetWord Class

```
 1:  using System;
 2:  using System.Windows.Forms;
 3:  using System.Drawing;
 4:
 5:  namespace TYWinforms.P1 {
 6:     public class NetWord : Form {
 7:        public NetWord() {
 8:           this.Text = "NetWord v.1";
 9:           this.Size = new Size(800,600);
10:        }
11:
12:        public static void Main() {
13:           Application.Run(new NetWord());
14:        }
15:     }
16:  }
```

Save this listing as NetWord.cs. As you can see, there's almost nothing to this listing—just a Main method and a simple constructor.

Compiling and running this application will result in an empty application (see Figure P1.1).

Next, let's build the user interface. We'll need to add the RichTextControl and all other controls that deal with it, such as the menus. Take a look at Listing P1.2.

FIGURE P1.1

The beginnings of NetWord.

LISTING P1.2   The Document Class

```
1:   using System;
2:   using System.Windows.Forms;
3:   using System.Drawing;
4:   using System.Drawing.Printing;
5:   using System.ComponentModel;
6:
7:   namespace TYWinforms.P1 {
8:      public class NetWord : Form {
9:         private RichTextBox rtbDocument = new RichTextBox();
10:
11:           private MainMenu mnuMain = new MainMenu();
12:           private MenuItem mniFile = new MenuItem("File");
13:           private MenuItem mniOpen = new MenuItem("Open...");
14:           private MenuItem mniSave = new MenuItem("Save");
15:           private MenuItem mniPageSetup = new MenuItem
➥("Page Setup...");
16:           private MenuItem mniPrintPreview = new MenuItem
➥ ("Print Preview");
17:           private MenuItem mniPrint = new MenuItem("Print...");
18:           private MenuItem mniExit = new MenuItem("Exit");
19:
20:           private MenuItem mniEdit = new MenuItem("Edit");
21:           private MenuItem mniUndo = new MenuItem("Undo");
22:           private MenuItem mniCut = new MenuItem("Cut");
```

LISTING P1.2   continued

```
23:          private MenuItem mniCopy = new MenuItem("Copy");
24:          private MenuItem mniPaste = new MenuItem("Paste");
25:          private MenuItem mniFind = new MenuItem("Find...");
26:
27:          private MenuItem mniFormat = new MenuItem("Format");
28:          private MenuItem mniFont = new MenuItem("Font...");
29:
30:          private Font fntCurrent = new Font("Times New Roman",
➥10);
31:          private Color fntColor = Color.Black;
32:          private FontDialog dlgFont = new FontDialog();
33:          private OpenFileDialog dlgOpen = new OpenFileDialog();
34:          private SaveFileDialog dlgSave = new SaveFileDialog();
35:          private PrintPreviewDialog dlgPrintPreview = new
➥PrintPreviewDialog();
36:          private PageSetupDialog dlgPageSetup = new
➥PageSetupDialog();
37:          private PrintDialog dlgPrint = new PrintDialog();
38:          private PageSettings objPageSettings = new
➥PageSettings();
39:          private PrinterSettings objPrintSettings = new
➥PrinterSettings();
40:
41:          public NetWord() {
42:              rtbDocument.Dock = DockStyle.Fill;
43:              rtbDocument.Font = fntCurrent;
44:              rtbDocument.HideSelection = false;
45:
46:              mniOpen.Click += new EventHandler(this.FileClicked);
47:              mniSave.Click += new EventHandler(this.FileClicked);
48:              mniPageSetup.Click += new EventHandler
➥ (this.FileClicked);
49:              mniPrintPreview.Click += new EventHandler
➥ (this.FileClicked);
50:              mniPrint.Click += new EventHandler(this.FileClicked);
51:              mniExit.Click += new EventHandler(this.FileClicked);
52:
53:              mniUndo.Click += new EventHandler(this.EditClicked);
54:              mniCut.Click += new EventHandler(this.EditClicked);
55:              mniCopy.Click += new EventHandler(this.EditClicked);
56:              mniPaste.Click += new EventHandler(this.EditClicked);
57:              mniFind.Click += new EventHandler(this.EditClicked);
58:
59:              mniFont.Click += new EventHandler
➥ (this.FormatClicked);
60:
61:              mnuMain.MenuItems.Add(mniFile);
62:              mnuMain.MenuItems.Add(mniEdit);
63:              mnuMain.MenuItems.Add(mniFormat);
64:
```

LISTING P1.2   continued

```
65:            mniFile.MenuItems.Add(mniOpen);
66:            mniFile.MenuItems.Add(mniSave);
67:            mniFile.MenuItems.Add("-");
68:            mniFile.MenuItems.Add(mniPageSetup);
69:            mniFile.MenuItems.Add(mniPrintPreview);
70:            mniFile.MenuItems.Add(mniPrint);
71:            mniFile.MenuItems.Add("-");
72:            mniFile.MenuItems.Add(mniExit);
73:
74:            mniEdit.MenuItems.Add(mniUndo);
75:            mniEdit.MenuItems.Add("-");
76:            mniEdit.MenuItems.Add(mniCut);
77:            mniEdit.MenuItems.Add(mniCopy);
78:            mniEdit.MenuItems.Add(mniPaste);
79:            mniEdit.MenuItems.Add("-");
80:            mniEdit.MenuItems.Add(mniFind);
81:
82:            mniFormat.MenuItems.Add(mniFont);
83:
84:            this.Text = "NetWord v.1";
85:            this.Name = "NetWord";
86:            this.Size = new Size(800,600);
87:            this.Menu = mnuMain;
88:            this.Closing += new CancelEventHandler
➥(this.DocumentClosing);
89:
90:            this.Controls.Add(rtbDocument);
91:        }
```

ANALYSIS This entire listing is simply the constructor and initialization of our application. By now, you should be aware of the fact that most of the code we'll write (at least in this first week) consists mainly of initialization and the user interface.

This code is very easy to follow. Line 9 creates the RichTextBox control that will be used for the main interface of this application. Lines 11–28 set up the various menus, and lines 30–39 declare settings that will be used throughout your application (the current font, color, printer settings, and so on). Lines 42–90 simply set up some general properties and assign delegates to the menu items.

There are just a couple of things to note here. First, line 44 sets HideSelection to false, which means that selected text in the RichTextBox will still appear as selected, even when this control doesn't have focus (this will be important when we build the search feature). Second, line 88 assigns a delegate for the form's Closing event. We want to monitor this event to see whether the content has changed before closing—if it has, we want to allow the user a chance to save the document.

Next, let's look at the event handlers, shown in Listing P1.3.

LISTING P1.3   The Event Handlers for NetWord

```
1:   private void FileClicked(Object Sender, EventArgs e) {
2:      MenuItem mniTemp = (MenuItem)Sender;
3:
4:      switch (mniTemp.Text) {
5:         case "Open...":
6:
7:             if (dlgOpen.ShowDialog() == DialogResult.OK) {
8:                //open file
9:             }
10:            break;
11:        case "Save":
12:
13:            if (dlgSave.ShowDialog() == DialogResult.OK) {
14:               //save file
15:            }
16:            break;
17:        case "Page Setup...":
18:
19:            dlgPageSetup.PageSettings = objPageSettings;
20:            dlgPageSetup.ShowDialog();
21:            break;
22:        case "Print Preview":
23:
24:            dlgPrintPreview.Document = new PrintDocument();
25:            dlgPrintPreview.ShowDialog();
26:            break;
27:        case "Print...":
28:
29:            dlgPrint.PrinterSettings = new PrinterSettings();
30:            if (dlgPrint.ShowDialog() == DialogResult.OK) {
31:               //print
32:            }
33:            break;
34:        case "Exit":
35:            this.Close();
36:            break;
37:      }
38:   }
39:
40:   private void EditClicked(Object Sender, EventArgs e) {
41:      MenuItem mniTemp = (MenuItem)Sender;
42:
43:      switch (mniTemp.Text) {
44:         case "Undo":
45:            rtbDocument.Undo();
46:            break;
```

LISTING P1.3   continued

```
47:         case "Cut":
48:             if (rtbDocument.SelectedRtf != "") {
49:                 rtbDocument.Cut();
50:             }
51:             break;
52:         case "Copy":
53:             if (rtbDocument.SelectedRtf != "") {
54:                 rtbDocument.Copy();
55:             }
56:             break;
57:         case "Paste":
58:             rtbDocument.Paste();
59:             break;
60:         case "Find...":
61:             FindDialog dlgFind = new FindDialog(rtbDocument);
62:             dlgFind.Show();
63:             break;
64:     }
65: }
66:
67: private void FormatClicked(Object Sender, EventArgs e) {
68:     MenuItem mniTemp = (MenuItem)Sender;
69:
70:     switch (mniTemp.Text) {
71:         case "Font...":
72:             dlgFont.ShowColor = true;
73:             if (dlgFont.ShowDialog() == DialogResult.OK) {
74:                 fntCurrent = dlgFont.Font;
75:                 fntColor = dlgFont.Color;
76:                 rtbDocument.SelectionFont = fntCurrent;
77:                 rtbDocument.SelectionColor = fntColor;
78:             }
79:             break;
80:     }
81: }
82:
83: private void DocumentClosing(Object Sender,
➥CancelEventArgs e) {
84:     if (rtbDocument.Modified) {
85:         DialogResult dr = MessageBox.Show("Do you want to
➥save the changes?", this.Name,
➥MessageBoxButtons.YesNoCancel);
86:
87:         if (dr == DialogResult.Yes) {
88:             MessageBox.Show("Too bad!", this.Name);
89:         } else if (dr == DialogResult.Cancel) {
90:             e.Cancel = true;
91:         }
92:     }
```

LISTING P1.3   continued

```
93:  }
94:
95:  public static void Main() {
96:      Application.Run(new NetWord());
97:  }
98:      }
99:  }
```

ANALYSIS   If you recall what you learned during Day 4, "Adding Menus and Toolbars to Your Windows," most of this code should look familiar. You have the method that handles all the MenuItems in the File menu on line 1, the event handler for the Edit menu on line 40, the event handler for the Format menu on line 67, and the event handler for the Closing event of the form on line 83. Much of this code is used to evaluate exactly which menu item was clicked.

Lines 4–36 should be familiar—they are almost direct copies from Day 7's lesson about dialog boxes. The only difference is the addition of an Exit menu, which simply calls the Close method. You create a FileOpenDialog, FileSaveDialog, PageSetupDialog, PrintPreviewDialog, or PrintDialog depending which menu item was clicked, and then display each of them using the ShowDialog method. For the Open, Save, and Print menu items, you evaluate the result of the dialog box using the DialogResult enumeration, and perform an action based on this result.

Lines 43–63 are very similar. They perform the Undo, Cut, Copy, and Paste operations by calling the various methods of the RichTextBox control. For the Cut and Copy methods, you first need to check whether any text is selected by evaluating the SelectedRtf property. The Find menu item on line 60 is a special case; it creates and displays a custom dialog box that you'll build in the next section.

Lines 70–78 are exactly like all of the other cases. You show the FontDialog dialog box and allow the user to choose a new font and font color to use. These values are stored in the global settings we created on lines 30 and 31, and then applied to the font in the RichTextBox.

Finally, you have the DocumentClosing method on line 83. Recall that the Closing event occurs immediately *before* the document closes, which means that you can use it to evaluate any last-minute conditions. Line 84 checks the Modified property of the RichTextBox, which tells you whether the document has been changed since the last save (or in this case, since it was opened). Line 85 displays a MessageBox asking the user whether she wants to continue without saving the changes. Depending on the answer, you do one of three things:

1. Don't save the document.

2. Stop the application from closing (by setting the `CancelEventArgs.Cancel` property to `true`).

3. Save the document (you don't actually save the document, but at least you'll have a place to put the code once you learn how).

That's all there is to it. That's not all there is, however, to the application. If you try to run this, you'll get an error because you haven't yet created the `FindDialog` object as required by line 61. This class is shown in Listing P1.4.

LISTING P1.4   The `FindDialog` Class

```
1:  using System;
2:  using System.Windows.Forms;
3:  using System.Drawing;
4:
5:  namespace TYWinforms.P1 {
6:     public class FindDialog : Form {
7:        private Label lblFind = new Label();
8:        private Label lblReplace = new Label();
9:        private TextBox tbFind = new TextBox();
10:        private TextBox tbReplace = new TextBox();
11:        private Button btFind = new Button();
12:        private Button btReplace = new Button();
13:        private Button btReplaceAll = new Button();
14:        private Button btCancel = new Button();
15:
16:        private RichTextBox rtbDoc;
17:
18:        public FindDialog(RichTextBox rtbParentDoc): base() {
19:           rtbDoc = rtbParentDoc;
20:
21:           lblFind.Text = "Find:";
22:           lblFind.Location = new Point(10,10);
23:           lblFind.Width = 50;
24:
25:           lblReplace.Text = "Replace:";
26:           lblReplace.Location = new Point(10,35);
27:           lblReplace.Width = 50;
28:
29:           tbFind.Width = 100;
30:           tbFind.Location = new Point(60,10);
31:
32:           tbReplace.Width = 100;
33:           tbReplace.Location = new Point(60,35);
34:
35:           btFind.Size = new Size(75,25);
```

```
36:              btFind.Text = "Find";
37:              btFind.Location = new Point(170,10);
38:              btFind.Click += new EventHandler(this.ButtonClicked);
39:
40:              btReplace.Size = new Size(75,25);
41:              btReplace.Text = "Replace";
42:              btReplace.Location = new Point(170,35);
43:              btReplace.Click += new EventHandler
➥(this.ButtonClicked);
44:
45:              btReplaceAll.Size = new Size(75,25);
46:              btReplaceAll.Text = "Replace All";
47:              btReplaceAll.Location = new Point(170,60);
48:              btReplaceAll.Click += new EventHandler
➥ (this.ButtonClicked);
49:
50:              btCancel.Size = new Size(75,25);
51:              btCancel.Text = "Cancel";
52:              btCancel.Location = new Point(170,85);
53:              btCancel.Click += new EventHandler
➥ (this.ButtonClicked);
54:
55:              this.Text = "Find";
56:              this.Size = new Size(255,140);
57:              this.MaximizeBox = false;
58:              this.MinimizeBox = false;
59:              this.FormBorderStyle = FormBorderStyle.
➥FixedDialog;
60:              this.TopMost = true;
61:
62:              this.Controls.Add(lblFind);
63:              this.Controls.Add(lblReplace);
64:              this.Controls.Add(tbFind);
65:              this.Controls.Add(tbReplace);
66:              this.Controls.Add(btFind);
67:              this.Controls.Add(btReplace);
68:              this.Controls.Add(btReplaceAll);
69:              this.Controls.Add(btCancel);
70:          }
71:
72:        private void ButtonClicked(Object Sender,
➥EventArgs e) {
73:              Button btTemp = (Button)Sender;
74:              int intLocation;
75:              int intCount = 0;
76:
77:              switch (btTemp.Text) {
78:                  case "Find":
```

LISTING P1.4   continued

```
79:                    intLocation = rtbDoc.Find(tbFind.Text,
➥rtbDoc.SelectionStart + rtbDoc.SelectionLength,
➥RichTextBoxFinds.None);
80:                    if (intLocation != -1) {
81:                        rtbDoc.SelectionStart = intLocation;
82:                        rtbDoc.SelectionLength =
➥tbFind.Text.Length;
83:                        rtbDoc.Focus();
84:                    }
85:                    break;
86:                case "Replace":
87:                    intLocation = rtbDoc.Find(tbFind.Text,
➥rtbDoc.SelectionStart + rtbDoc.SelectionLength,
➥RichTextBoxFinds.None);
88:                    if (intLocation != -1) {
89:                        rtbDoc.SelectionStart = intLocation;
90:                        rtbDoc.SelectionLength =
➥tbFind.Text.Length;
91:                        rtbDoc.SelectedText = tbReplace.Text;
92:                        rtbDoc.SelectionStart = intLocation;
93:                        rtbDoc.SelectionLength =
➥tbReplace.Text.Length;
94:                    }
95:                    break;
96:                case "Replace All":
97:                    intLocation = rtbDoc.Find(tbFind.Text);
98:                    while (intLocation != -1) {
99:                        rtbDoc.SelectionStart = intLocation;
100:                        rtbDoc.SelectionLength =
➥tbFind.Text.Length;
101:                        rtbDoc.SelectedText = tbReplace.Text;
102:                        intCount += 1;
103:                        intLocation = rtbDoc.Find
➥ (tbFind.Text, rtbDoc.SelectionStart +
➥rtbDoc.SelectionLength, RichTextBoxFinds.None);
104:                    }
105:                    MessageBox.Show(intCount.ToString() +
➥" occurrences replaced","Find");
106:                    break;
107:                case "Cancel":
108:                    this.Close();
109:                    break;
110:            }
111:        }
112:    }
113: }
```

ANALYSIS This listing defines a custom dialog box with Find and Replace text boxes and Find, Replace, and Replace All buttons. The code in this listing is a bit more complex than what we've covered before, but it's still not difficult.

Lines 1–70 contain the constructor and initialization code. This is just like every other constructor you've seen, so we'll skip most of it. There are only a few things you need to note. First, the declaration of a RichTextBox control on line 16; this control is then assigned the control passed into the constructor on line 18. Going back to line 61 of Listing P1.3, you see that we pass in the main RichTextBox to the constructor of the FindDialog class. This is done so that you'll have an easy reference to the control to search from your Find dialog control. You'll see how it's used in a moment. Then in the constructor on line 18, you have a call to the base method. This means that the constructor on line 18 should inherit from the RichTextBox control's constructor, and any necessary initialization procedures will be performed. It's not necessary to put this here, because .NET will do it for you, but it makes things a bit clearer.

ButtonClicked on line 72 uses a switch statement to evaluate the button that was clicked; nothing new there. On line 79 you see the Find method, which, as you know, finds specified text in the RichTextBox control. But this Find method has a few additional parameters: tbFind.Text is the text to search for, rtbDoc.SelectionStart is the location to start searching for the text from (in other words, the current cursor position in the RichTextBox), and RichTextBoxFinds.None specifies how the search should be conducted. The RichTextBoxFinds enumeration contains the values MatchCase, NoHighlight, None, Reverse, and WholeWord. These can be combined like Anchor values:

RichTextBoxFinds.MatchCase | RichTextBoxFinds.Reverse

Using RichTextBoxFinds you can allow the user to perform specialized searches, but for now, we don't need to worry about that.

If the Find method doesn't find the text it's looking for, it returns the value –1. We check this on line 80 and, if text was found, highlight it using the SelectionStart and SelectionLength properties. Finally, you hand the focus back to the RichTextBox. (Note, however, that because we've set TopMost to true for the FindDialog class—line 60—it won't disappear, but user input will still go to the RichTextBox.)

Note

> Note that for the Find and Replace cases, the search starts *after* the current position of the cursor (SelectionStart + SelectionLength). If some text is selected, it starts immediately after the selection. You can change this behavior by changing the second parameter of the Find method to the number 1, or simply omitting the second two parameters, as the Replace All case does on line 97.

The next two cases, Replace and Replace All, function similarly. Replace uses the `Find` method, selects the specified text, and replaces it using the `SelectedText` property. It then selects the newly replaced word. Replace All does the same thing except that it does so in a `while` loop, which allows you to replace all the occurrences instead of just one. Through each iteration of the loop, you find the specified text, select and replace it, and then move on to the next occurrence, until there are no more (that is, until `Find` returns –1). A `MessageBox` is then displayed to alert the user how many occurrences were replaced.

Finally, your application is complete. Compile and run it, and enjoy the fruits of your labor. Figure P1.2 shows the output from this application.

FIGURE P1.2

NetWord in action.

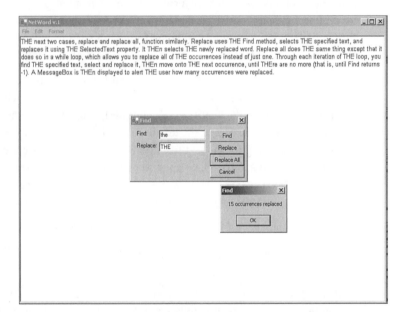

Adding Some Bells and Whistles

Your application is complete, but it's not especially user-friendly. Let's add some extra features to liven up NetWord.

First, we'll add shortcuts to your menu items. Add the following code snippet to the constructor of NetWord:

```
mniOpen.Shortcut = Shortcut.CtrlO;
mniSave.Shortcut = Shortcut.CtrlS;
mniPrint.Shortcut = Shortcut.CtrlP;
mniUndo.Shortcut = Shortcut.CtrlZ;
```

```
mniCut.Shortcut = Shortcut.CtrlX;
mniCopy.Shortcut = Shortcut.CtrlC;
mniPaste.Shortcut = Shortcut.CtrlV;
mniFind.Shortcut = Shortcut.CtrlF;

mniOpen.ShowShortcut = true;
mniSave.ShowShortcut = true;
mniPrint.ShowShortcut = true;
mniUndo.ShowShortcut = true;
mniCut.ShowShortcut = true;
mniCopy.ShowShortcut = true;
mniPaste.ShowShortcut = true;
mniFind.ShowShortcut = true;
```

The shortcuts we've assigned here are the standard Windows shortcuts for the menu
options in question.

Next, we'll create a context menu based on the `MenuItems` we've already created.
Depending on what the user has selected, different options will appear. Creating the
`ContextMenu` is simple; determining what items should appear in it is a bit more complex. Take a look at the following code:

```
'inside the class
private ContextMenu cmnuDocument = new ContextMenu();
...
'in the constructor
cmnuDocument.MenuItems.Add(mniCut.CloneMenu());
cmnuDocument.MenuItems.Add(mniCopy.CloneMenu());
cmnuDocument.MenuItems.Add(mniPaste.CloneMenu());
cmnuDocument.MenuItems.Add("-");
cmnuDocument.MenuItems.Add(mniFont.CloneMenu());
cmnuDocument.Popup += new EventHandler(this.HandleContext);
rtbDocument.ContextMenu = cmnuDocument;
...
'a new method
private void HandleContext(Object Sender, EventArgs e) {
   if (rtbDocument.SelectionLength == 0) {
      cmnuDocument.MenuItems[0].Enabled = false;
      cmnuDocument.MenuItems[1].Enabled = false;
   } else {
      cmnuDocument.MenuItems[0].Enabled = true;
      cmnuDocument.MenuItems[1].Enabled = true;
   }
}
```

The first line creates the `ContextMenu` object, and the next set of lines assigns various
`MenuItems` to it (a user should only be able to cut, copy, paste, and change the font from
the context menu). Note that you use the `CloneMenu` method to make copies of the menu
items in question. If you don't do this, you'll mess up your regular menu items. You need

to customize the context menu based on the context of the application (that is, what the user is currently doing). The Popup event allows you to do just this; it fires immediately before the menu is displayed. Let's look at the HandleContext method that handles the Popup event.

There are two simple cases to evaluate. If no text is selected in the RichTextBox, you want to disable the Cut and Copy menu items; after all, if nothing is selected then there's nothing to cut or copy. This is done by simply setting the Enabled property to false—the menu items will still be visible, but the user won't be able to select them.

If some text is selected, you want to make sure these two menu items are enabled; they are by default, but if the user opens the context menu without selecting any text first, you disable them. In the else condition, you simply re-enable them.

Finally, let's add a status bar that provides information such as the line the user is currently on and the current character in the line. We need a status bar and a status bar panel:

```
private StatusBar sbarMain = new StatusBar();
private StatusBarPanel spnlLine = new StatusBarPanel();
```

Next, initialize these controls in the constructor:

```
sbarMain.ShowPanels = true;
sbarMain.Panels.Add(spnlLine);
spnlLine.AutoSize = StatusBarPanelAutoSize.Spring;
spnlLine.Alignment = HorizontalAlignment.Right;
```

Now your status bar is all set, but it doesn't exactly do anything yet. Because you want to keep track of the current line and character, you need to update the status bar every time something in the RichTextBox changes. The SelectionChanged event is perfect for this; it fires every time the user changes the cursor position (by typing, clicking with the mouse, pressing Enter, and so on). Add a delegate to this event of the RichTextBox:

```
rtbDocument.SelectionChanged += new EventHandler(this.UpdateStatus);
```

The first part of the UpdateStatus method is to find the line number. This is a very simple process, and can be done using the following code:

```
private void UpdateStatus(Object Sender, EventArgs e) {
    String text = rtbDocument.Text;

    int intLine = rtbDocument.GetLineFromCharIndex
➥(rtbDocument.SelectionStart) + 1;
```

First, you retrieve the text contained in the RichTextBox for easier manipulation. The RichTextBox has a neat little method called GetLineFromCharIndex that tells you what line the cursor is currently on. This gives you the right number even if there are no line breaks. For example, if the first line in the control wraps to two lines, those two lines will return 1 and 2. The RichTextBox control's Lines property, on the other hand, can't be used to count lines because it doesn't take into account line wraps (it counts two wrapped lines as a single line).

Getting the character position in the current line is a bit more difficult. To determine when you are at the beginning of a line, you can use the RichTextBox's GetPositionFromCharIndex method, which will return a Point with the coordinates of the cursor. When the X coordinate is 1, you are at the left-most edge of the text box, or in other words, at the beginning of a line.

The following code snippet does this procedure:

```
int i = rtbDocument.SelectionStart;
while (rtbDocument.GetPositionFromCharIndex(i).X > 1)
    --i;
String strChar = (rtbDocument.SelectionStart - i + 1).ToString();
```

First we set the variable i to the current position of the cursor. Then, in a while loop, we decrement i as long as the X coordinate for the Point at the character i is greater than 1. Finally we subtract i from our starting position to determine how far the starting position is from the beginning of the line.

Finally, assign the string to the status bar panel:

```
spnlLine.Text = "Line " + intLine.ToString() + " Char " + strChar;
```

Figure P1.3 shows the output.

 Note

> Future projects will enhance this application further. In the project following Week 2, you'll add Internet capabilities and transform NetWord into an MDI application. After that, you'll learn about deploying your application and making it work with other Windows applications. But first, you've got to get through Week 2.

FIGURE P1.3

The current line number and character position are now accurately displayed in the status bar.

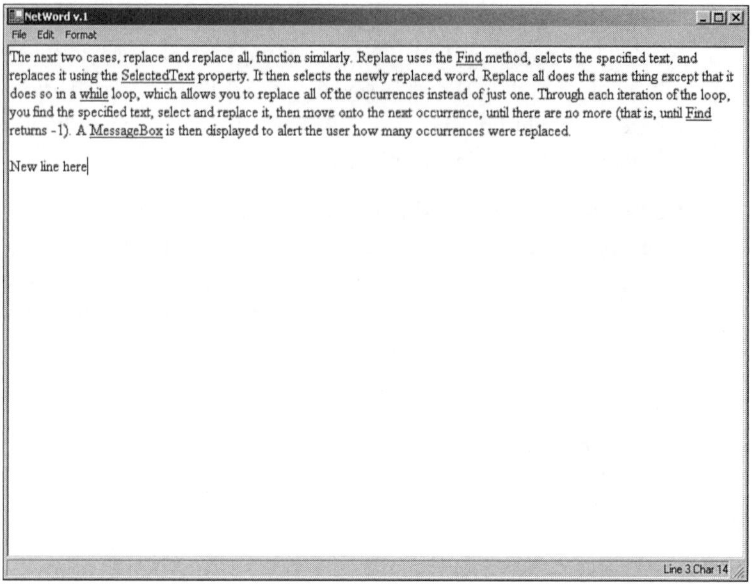

NetWord v.1

File   Edit   Format

The next two cases, replace and replace all, function similarly. Replace uses the <u>Find</u> method, selects the specified text, and replaces it using the <u>SelectedText</u> property. It then selects the newly replaced word. Replace all does the same thing except that it does so in a <u>while</u> loop, which allows you to replace all of the occurrences instead of just one. Through each iteration of the loop, you find the specified text, select and replace it, then move onto the next occurrence, until there are no more (that is, until <u>Find</u> returns -1). A <u>MessageBox</u> is then displayed to alert the user how many occurrences were replaced.

New line here

Line 3 Char 14

WEEK 2

At a Glance

Adding Functionality

Welcome to your second week through Windows Forms. Last week was spent introducing you to the various concepts required in Windows Forms. You learned what Windows Forms are, how to build them, and how to use Windows Forms controls. Now that you have the basics, it's time to move onto more advanced topics.

This week you'll learn how to add powerful features to your applications such as adding database capabilities and many other features used by today's applications. Then, in Week 3, you'll examine the complex inner workings of Windows Forms and learn how to take advantage of them to create advanced applications.

Day 8, "Databinding in Your Windows Forms," teaches you how Windows Forms are designed to handle all types of data without having to access databases. You can manipulate this data in many wonderful ways. In Day 9, "Using ADO.NET," you learn how to incorporate databases into your application using the knowledge from Day 8.

Day 10, "Creating MDI Applications," focuses on multiple document interface applications, a type of application that allows you to have many windows open at once. Then in Day 11, "Working with Windows Input/Output," you learn all about interacting with Windows files—saving, opening, over-writing, and so on—as well as printing.

8

9

10

11

12

13

14

You see how to take advantage of the Internet in your applications in Day 12, "Internet-Enabling Your Forms." You'll build a simple Web browser and surf to your heart's content. Day 13, "Creating Graphical Applications with GDI+," teaches you about GDI+, the paradigm for handling Windows graphics. Not only will you learn how to build "drawing" applications, but also how GDI+ affects your normal applications.

Finally, in Day 14, "Using ActiveX," you learn how to use other applications and components in your own Windows Forms applications!

Now, on to Week 2!

DAY 8

Databinding in Your Windows Forms

Databinding is an interesting concept in .NET; it allows you to associate data with controls in your Windows Forms. This capability, in turn, allows you to more easily display and manipulate that data. After today's lesson, you'll see that databinding is a powerful ally to have.

Today you'll learn

- What databinding is
- How to associate data with your controls
- What a `DataGrid` is
- How to determine what data a user has selected in a control

Introduction to Databinding

Grasping the concept of databinding is sometimes difficult, so let's spend a few moments exploring it in detail. First, let's examine the term *data*.

When discussing databinding, data is information of any type that is applicable to your application (often called your data model). It could be anything from the colors used in your application to a list of customers in your database to the `Text` property of your form. All these examples are pieces of information that you use in your applications.

Most of the time, you want to display such data to the user. For example, if you build a CD cataloging application, the user needs to be able to see what she's entered. You can add such a capability by assigning values to the `Text` properties of various controls, adding `ComboBox` or `ListBox` controls, and so on.

The definition of *data* is fuzzy; providing an exact explanation is difficult because data comes in so many forms. This, among other reasons, is why databinding is so important and powerful.

Simply put, databinding allows you to tie a piece (or pieces) of data together with a Windows Forms control. This bond creates a read/write relationship between the data and the control; the control displays the data in a user-friendly manner, and changes in the control are reflected in the data. By databinding a control, you are essentially making that control a vehicle for data display and manipulation.

So, how is databinding different from simply assigning values to a control? For simple databinding, there's not much difference. When you start more complex databinding, however, it saves you a lot of hassle when building your user interface and makes your code smaller and much easier to read. Believe me, after you start using databinding, you'll wonder how you ever did without it.

Imagine a typical scenario, such as a music cataloging application. When a user enters information on a new album, you can display it immediately in a `TreeView` control (see Day 6, "Enhancing Your Windows Forms with More Controls," for more information). This process is easy and quick, but unfortunately, you lose some functionality when you display information this way. One, you don't have a good record of the data except in the `TreeView` control, which admittedly isn't a good storage mechanism. Two, after the data is displayed in the `TreeView` control, it's there for good. You cannot manipulate it except by using lengthy and convoluted procedures.

Instead of displaying the information directly, you can enter it into a database as the user enters it. You then have a record of the data that you can manipulate easily as you see fit and display in as many different controls as you want rather than in a single `TreeView` control.

With this paradigm, you now have two distinct objects: the data and the controls with which to display it. You can bind the data to the control, and the control can then handle all aspects of its display for you. Interaction with the control directly affects the data.

8

This latter model has several benefits. You achieve a separation between the data in your application and the user interface (often called the data and UI layers). If you've studied application development scenarios, you know about the three-layer paradigm—one layer consisting only of the UI, one of data, and one to handle logic and the relationships between the data and UI. With this separation, your applications become much more elegant and yet sophisticated. This model is easier to build and easier to follow. Also, should one layer become dated or obsolete, you can easily replace it without having to rewrite your entire application. Thus, separation between your data and your UI should always be one of your goals when you're building applications, and databinding is an excellent tool to help you do so.

Data from Any Source

As you know, data can come in many different forms and in many different vehicles. Whether your data comes from a database or is entered arbitrarily by the user, it can be bound to Windows Forms controls. This immense flexibility saves you, the developer, a lot of work of having to marshal (in other words, transform) data types and forms. You can simply bind the data and go.

XML data and data from a relational database, for example, are treated almost exactly the same. It doesn't matter that some data came from a text file and the rest from Oracle or SQL Server; both types of data can be easily bound to controls for quick display. Changes in the control can be written back to the XML file or the database, so you never lose any information.

As you learn about ADO.NET tomorrow, you'll see how this read/write link works with databases. Right now, let's examine how to bind other types of data.

Simple Databinding

As mentioned previously, to use databinding, you need some data and a control to bind it to. The only restriction on the data is that it be in a form that implements the IList interface. Recall that interfaces are simply like a requirements list: They tell you everything a class needs to have but don't tell you how to build them. The IList interface defines the requirements for any object that can contain data. More than 40 objects use IList, from arrays and StringCollections to more obscure objects such as EventDescriptorCollection, so you usually don't have to worry about finding an object that uses IList.

To bind data, you add a new Binding object to a control's DataBindings collection. This process is exactly like adding new controls to a form's Controls collection. All Windows

Forms controls have a DataBindings collection, so they all can take advantage of data-binding. Let's look at the syntax:

```
control.DataBindings.Add("property", object, "field")
```

control is, obviously, the control you want to databind to. The first parameter, property, indicates what property of the control you want to bind to. It can vary, depending on what data you're trying to bind. For example, you might want to bind a list of names to the Text property of a Button but a list of colors to the BackColor property. Databinding is flexible enough that you can do both. The second parameter, then, is the data source—where your data is coming from. As mentioned earlier in this section, this source can be an array, a database, a StringCollection, and so on. The third parameter specifies what part (or field) of the data source should be bound. For an array, specifying this information doesn't make much sense; after all, an array just holds arbitrary data. For a database, however, you might want to bind the Name field of a table. Thus, in this third parameter, you would specify "Name".

In the next few sections, you'll see a more concrete example of databinding and learn how to edit bound data.

Binding a Button

Let's start with a simple example using an array to practice databinding. Listing 8.1 shows such an example.

LISTING 8.1 Databinding a Button

```
1:  using System;
2:  using System.Windows.Forms;
3:  using System.Drawing;
4:
5:  namespace TYWinforms.Day8 {
6:     public class Listing81 : Form {
7:        private Button btData = new Button();
8:        private Color[] arrColors = {Color.Green, Color.Blue,
➥Color.Red, Color.Orange};
9:
10:       public Listing81() {
11:          btData.Location = new Point(100,100);
12:          btData.DataBindings.Add("BackColor", arrColors,
➥"");
13:          btData.DataBindings.Add("Text", arrColors, "");
14:
15:          this.Controls.Add(btData);
16:       }
17:
```

LISTING 8.1   continued

```
18:         public static void Main() {
19:             Application.Run(new Listing81());
20:         }
21:     }
22: }
```

ANALYSIS   On line 7, you create the control, a `Button`, to bind the data to. Line 8 creates
and instantiates an array of `Color` objects: `Green`, `Blue`, `Red`, and `Orange`. You
have your control and your data, so now you can bind them.

On line 12, you use the syntax described previously to bind the array to the `Button`.
Notice the three parameters. The first specifies the property of the control to bind to;
because you're using an array of `Colors`, you bind to the `BackColor` property. The second parameter specifies the data source—the array created on line 8. Finally, the third
parameter is simply an empty string because no particular property of the array needs to
be bound; instead, the whole array should be bound. You've now bound the colors to the
`Button`.

Wait a moment, though. Line 13 appears to have another binding procedure. This time,
you bind the same array of colors to the `Button`'s `Text` property. The Common Language
Runtime (CLR) automatically calls a `ToString` method on the objects in the array to
properly match the `Text` property to the colors. Finally, the `Button` is added to the form
as normal on line 15.

Figure 8.1 shows the output of this application.

FIGURE 8.1

*Binding a property
causes the control to
display the data.*

So, what happened? First, the `Button`'s `BackColor` is set to the first color in the array,
`Green` (even though it appears a shade of gray in print, trust me, it's green). This color is
set without your ever having to assign a color to the `BackColor` property manually. The

databinding takes care of everything for you. Second, the word Green—which is what you see when you call Color.Green.ToString()—is displayed as the caption of the Button. Again, you don't have to assign this property yourself; this task is done for you.

This process, by itself, is great, but you can do even more. Because the array bound to the Button has more than color in it, you can cycle through all the colors in the Button. To do so, you first need to learn about a new object, the BindingContext.

The BindingContext for a control manages the relationship between the data and the bound property of the control. It specifies how and which item in the data collection should be displayed. To see it in use, add the following code to Listing 8.1:

```
//in the constructor
btData.Click += new EventHandler(this.Cycle);
...
//new method
public void Cycle(Object Sender, EventArgs e) {
    btData.BindingContext[arrColors].Position += 1;
}
```

The first line adds an event handler for the Click event. You use this event to cycle through the elements in the array. The event handler, Cycle, uses the BindingContext of the Button to change the bound value. BindingContext contains a list of all the objects bound to the control, so you need to specify the correct one; this one references the array of colors. The Position property indicates which item is currently being displayed, so you simply increment it by one here to move to the next item.

Now recompile the application and click the button. The BackColor and Text properties of the Button change with each click—all without your ever having to deal with those properties individually. This example may be a bit contrived, but when you have a database containing thousands of customers, you can imagine how this simple binding procedure can make life easy for developers.

Also, any changes you make to the array are automatically reflected in the Button. For example, you could add

```
arrColors[2] = Color.Purple;
```

anywhere in your application, and the button would adjust accordingly without a hiccup. That's all there is to simple databinding.

Editing Bound Data

Let's look at a slightly more complex example, using a ComboBox and enabling the user to edit items. With ComboBoxes and other controls designed for displaying lists, dealing with the data is a bit easier. Rather than assign databindings, you can simply set the

DataSource property to bind the default property of the control to the default property of the data in question.

In Listing 8.2's example, the application presents two controls: a ComboBox to display the data and a Button to change the data. When users select a color, they can change it by typing a new color value into the text box portion of the combo box.

LISTING 8.2   Complex Databinding

```
 1:  using System;
 2:  using System.Windows.Forms;
 3:  using System.Drawing;
 4:
 5:  namespace TYWinforms.Day8 {
 6:      public class Listing82 : Form {
 7:          private ComboBox cboData = new ComboBox();
 8:          private Button btChange = new Button();
 9:          private Color[] arrColors = {Color.Green,
➥Color.Blue, Color.Red, Color.Orange};
10:          private int intLastIndex;
11:
12:          public Listing82() {
13:              cboData.Location = new Point(50,75);
14:              cboData.DropDownStyle = ComboBoxStyle.Simple;
15:              cboData.DataBindings.Add("BackColor",
➥arrColors, "");
16:              cboData.DataSource = arrColors;
17:              cboData.SelectedIndexChanged += new
➥EventHandler(this.ChangeColor);
18:
19:              btChange.Location = new Point(175,75);
20:              btChange.Text = "Change";
21:              btChange.Click += new EventHandler(this.EditColor);
22:
23:              this.Controls.Add(cboData);
24:              this.Controls.Add(btChange);
25:          }
26:
27:          public void ChangeColor(Object Sender, EventArgs e) {
28:              cboData.BindingContext[arrColors].Position =
➥cboData.SelectedIndex;
29:              intLastIndex = cboData.SelectedIndex;
30:          }
31:
32:          public void EditColor(Object Sender, EventArgs e) {
33:              if (Color.FromName(cboData.Text).IsKnownColor) {
34:                  arrColors[intLastIndex] = Color.FromName
➥ (cboData.Text);
35:
```

LISTING 8.2   continued

```
36:                     cboData.SelectedText = Color.FromName
➡ (cboData.Text).ToString();
37:                     cboData.SelectedIndex = intLastIndex;
38:             }
39:         }
40:
41:         public static void Main() {
42:             Application.Run(new Listing82());
43:         }
44:     }
45:  }
```

ANALYSIS   The beginning of this listing is largely similar to Listing 8.1; you create an array of colors on line 9 and a Button on line 8. You don't bind any data to the button this time, however; rather, you bind to the ComboBox created on line 7.

On line 16, you set the DataSource property to the array of colors. That's all you need to do to bind the data. When you view this control, the items in the list are the colors in the array (and the displayed text is the text representation of those colors). To liven up the control, however, you also bind the BackColor property of the ComboBox like you did with the Button in Listing 8.1. Whenever the selected index changes, you want to change the color of the combo box, so you add an event handler to the SelectedIndexChange event.

On lines 19–21, you set up the button control. The user will use this button to confirm the changes he's made to the data in the combo box. When the user clicks this button, you modify the data and update the combo box as necessary.

The ChangeColor method—the event handler for the SelectedIndexChanged event—is very simple. Using the BindingContext property of the ComboBox, you set the position to the currently selected index. You then store this index for use later; when the user begins to type something in the combo box, the currently selected item becomes deselected. This causes problems when you try to modify items, so you need to keep an accurate record of the last selected item.

In the EditColor method, the interesting stuff happens. The first thing you do is change the array; you grab the new color entered by the user in the combo box, retrieve the associated Color object by using the Color.FromName method, and assign it to the selected index in the array. When a user clicks that item again, the background color will change to the new value.

You'll notice, however, that the text displayed in the combo box doesn't change, even though the actual color value does. The text doesn't change because the ComboBox doesn't have a mechanism to detect changes in the object set in its DataSource property. Therefore, you simply need to update the text by using the Color.FromName method once again. Finally, you set the currently selected item to the last item the user selected, which is now the new value.

Compile this Listing 8.2 and try it out. Figure 8.2 shows the output.

FIGURE 8.2

The ComboBox *uses bound data for its background color.*

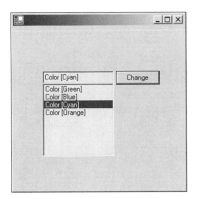

Binding to Forms

Often, you'll want to associate a data source with an entire application. For example, say you've created an application used solely to display a user's CD catalog. The application has multiple controls that are all bound to different aspects of an individual CD—one label for the artist, a text box for the title of the album, a text box for the running time, and so on. When the user moves to the next record, instead of having to change the BindingContext.Position value of every control on the form, you can simply change it for the Form object:

```
'VB.NET
Me.BindingContext[object].Position += 1
//C#
this.BindingContext[object].Position += 1;
```

BindingContext then changes for every single control bound on the form.

The DataGrid Control

The powerful DataGrid control was designed especially for use with databinding. It is efficient at displaying data in all different formats and has a bevy of display options that you can use to customize your UI. The DataGrid even has built-in capabilities for editing, adding, and deleting items.

Setting up the control is easy: Simply set its DataSource property to the data source, and you're ready to go. Listing 8.3 shows a simple example following the lead of Listings 8.1 and 8.2.

LISTING 8.3   Binding a DataGrid

```
 1:  using System;
 2:  using System.Windows.Forms;
 3:  using System.Drawing;
 4:
 5:  namespace TYWinforms.Day8 {
 6:     public class Listing83 : Form {
 7:        private DataGrid dgData = new DataGrid();
 8:        private Color[] arrColors = {Color.Green,
➥Color.Blue, Color.Red, Color.Orange};
 9:
10:        public Listing83() {
11:           dgData.DataSource = arrColors;
12:           dgData.Size = new Size(800,600);
13:
14:           this.Size = new Size(800,600);
15:           this.Controls.Add(dgData);
16:        }
17:
18:        public static void Main() {
19:           Application.Run(new Listing83());
20:        }
21:     }
22:  }
```

This code is nearly identical to Listing 8.1. The only difference is that you use a DataGrid control here instead of a ComboBox. Compile this listing and look at the output, shown in Figure 8.3.

Whoa, what happened? You assigned only an array of colors to the DataGrid, so where did all that extra information come from? The IsEmpty, A, B, IsNamedColor, IsKnownColor, Name, G, R, and IsSystemColor columns shown in Figure 8.3 are all properties of the Color object. Every Color object, no matter what color, has these properties. Thus, the DataGrid assumed that, because you gave it a collection of Color objects, you wanted to display all the properties. If you passed in an array of strings, it would simply display the length of the text content of those strings. Pretty nifty, eh?

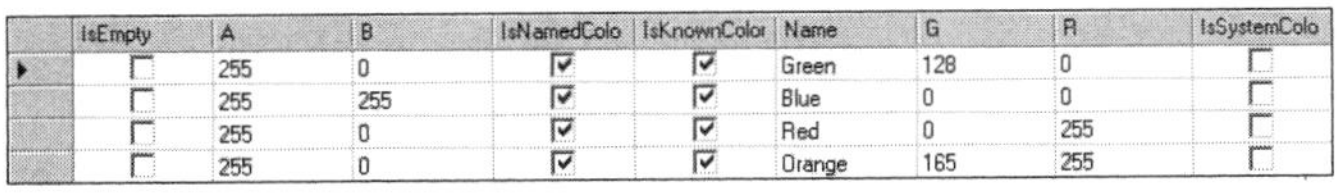

FIGURE 8.3

The DataGrid *easily displays copious amounts of information.*

	IsEmpty	A	B	IsNamedColo	IsKnownColor	Name	G	R	IsSystemColo
▶	☐	255	0	☑	☑	Green	128	0	☐
	☐	255	255	☑	☑	Blue	0	0	☐
	☐	255	0	☑	☑	Red	0	255	☐
	☐	255	0	☑	☑	Orange	165	255	☐

8

Table 8.1 lists the most common UI properties of the DataGrid.

TABLE 8.1 DataGrid User Interface Properties

Property	Description
AlternatingBackColor	Specifies the color for every other row to display (to allow the user to more easily distinguish rows).
BackColor	Specifies the background color of the grid.
BackgroundColor	Specifies the background color of the non-grid area.
BorderStyle	Indicates one of the BorderStyle enumeration values.
CaptionBackColor	Specifies the background color of the caption area.
CaptionFont	Specifies the font to use in the caption.
CaptionForeColor	Specifies the color of the font in the caption area.
CaptionText	Contains the text to display in the caption.
CaptionVisible	Indicates whether the caption is visible.
ColumnHeadersVisible	Indicates whether the column headers are visible.
FlatMode	Indicates whether the grid is displayed in flat mode (flat mode doesn't show visible lines between column and row headings).
ForeColor	Indicates the color of the font in the grid.
GridLineColor	Indicates the color of the gridlines.
GridLineStyle	Specifies one of the DataGridLineStyle enumeration values: None—No gridlines Solid—Solid gridlines
HeaderBackColor	Specifies the background color of the header.
HeaderFont	Specifies the font used in the header.
HeaderForeColor	Specifies the color of the font in the header.
LinkColor	Indicates the color of links used to navigate to child tables (more details on this property tomorrow).
LinkHoverColor	Indicates the color the links change to when the mouse cursor rests over them.

TABLE 8.1   continued

Property	Description
ParentRowsBackColor	Specifies the background color of parent rows.
ParentRowsForeColor	Specifies the font color of parent rows.
ParentRowsLabelStyle	Contains a DataGridParentRowsLabelStyle enumeration value:
	ColumnName—The name of the parent column
	TableName—The name of the parent table
	Both—Both names
	None—Neither name
ParentRowsVisible	Indicates whether parent rows are visible.
PreferredColumnWidth	Specifies the width of displayed columns.
PreferredRowHeight	Indicates the height of rows.
RowHeadersVisible	Indicates whether headers for rows are visible.
RowHeaderWidth	Indicates the width of row headers.
SelectionBackColor	Specifies the background color of a cell that is selected.
SelectionForeColor	Specifies the font color of a cell that is selected.

Taking a Sneak Peak at ADO.NET

Before you learn how to interact with the DataGrid control, you need to know about some more complex data structures. After all, arrays are great, but they're not exactly ideal for data storage or representation. For example, they aren't completely modifiable; you can change existing items in the array, but you can't easily take any out completely.

We're therefore going to take a sneak peak at some of the objects that are part of ADO.NET—specifically, the DataTable and its cohorts. Then, when you begin tomorrow's lesson, you'll have a head start.

A DataTable is a complete representation of data in a table. Think of it as a two-dimensional array with names. Look at Table 8.2, which provides name and handedness information.

TABLE 8.2   Sample Data

First Name	Last Name	Handedness
Walter	Saravia	right-handed
Eva	Payne	right-handed
Joel	Andres	left-handed

This table has three rows of data and three columns, named "First Name," "Last Name," and "Handedness," respectively. From this table, you can see that a column represents a type of information, and a row represents the actual data.

A `DataTable` is exactly the same. `DataRow` objects represent rows in the `DataTable`, and `DataColumn` objects represent the types of data. The `DataGrid`, then, is ideally suited for displaying the information in a `DataTable` because, as you'll recall from Figure 8.3, it displays data in a table format. Let's learn how to store data in a `DataTable`; you'll see that this procedure is very familiar.

You first need to create your `DataTable`, which you do just like you do with any other object:

```
//C#
DataTable objMyTable = new DataTable("My Table");
'VB.NET
dim objMyTable as New DataTable("My Table")
```

Here, the words in parentheses represent the name of the table—used for easier reference later. Next, you create `DataColumn` objects that represent each type of information you want to store and then add them to your `DataTable`. This process is just like adding controls to a form:

```
//create a column to hold integers
DataColumn ColumnA = new DataColumn();
ColumnA.DataType = System.Type.GetType("System.Int32");
ColumnA.ColumnName = "Column A";

//create a column to hold strings
DataColumn ColumnB = new DataColumn();
ColumnB.DataType = System.Type.GetType("System.String");
ColumnB.ColumnName = "Column B";

//add them to the datatable
objMyTable.Columns.Add(ColumnA);
objMyTable.Columns.Add(ColumnB);
```

Now, you have a complete, albeit empty, `DataTable` (that is, one with no data). This `DataTable` will hold two pieces of data for each row, or record: an integer and a string value. To add data, you simply add `DataRows`. The following code snippet shows a quick and easy way to enter data into the `DataTable` using a `for` loop:

```
DataRow myDataRow;
for (int i = 0; i <= 10; i++){
   myDataRow = objMyTable.NewRow();
   myDataRow["Column A"] = i;
   myDataRow["Column B"] = i.ToString();
   objMyTable.Rows.Add(myDataRow);
}
```

8

Note that you create a new `DataRow` by using the `NewRow` method of the already-existing `DataTable` object. By doing so, you ensure that your new row has all the proper columns and data types. You then fill those columns by referencing them by their names. Finally, you add the new row to the table, just as you did for the columns. After this code executes, you'll end up with the data in Table 8.3.

TABLE 8.3   Your New `DataTable`

Column A	Column B
0	"0"
1	"1"
2	"2"
3	"3"
4	"4"
5	"5"
6	"6"
7	"7"
8	"8"
9	"9"
10	"10"

Now you can just set the `DataGrid.DataSource` property to your new `DataTable`, and you'll end up with a table like the one in Figure 8.4.

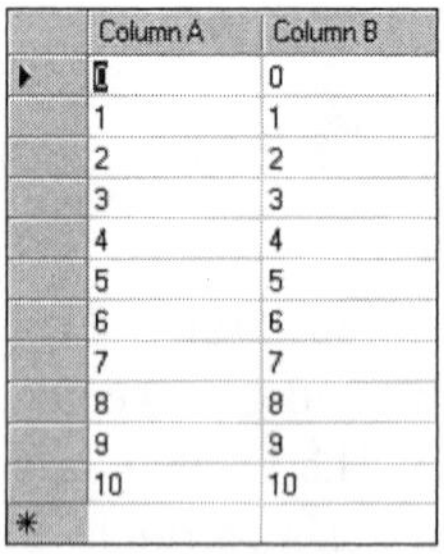

FIGURE 8.4

The `DataGrid` *shows your* `DataTable` *structure and data perfectly.*

The `DataTable`, `DataColumn`, and `DataRow` objects have many more interesting properties than the ones described here, but I'll save that discussion for tomorrow's lesson. For now, let's examine how to manipulate this data using a `DataGrid`.

Interacting with a `DataGrid`

If you played around with the previous example, you know that you can easily modify data; simply select the cell you want to edit and type new information. The `DataGrid` allows you to control how, and if, the cells can be edited, as well as their styles and formatting.

Through a series of style objects that you can apply to your `DataGrid`, you can change nearly every aspect of the `DataGrid`. Let's look at the `DataGridTableStyle` object first.

Creating a style is easy:

```
DataGridTableStyle dgStyle = new DataGridTableStyle();
dgStyle.MappingName = "My Table";
dgStyle.BackColor = Color.Blue;

dgData.TableStyles.Add(dgStyle);
```

The first line is obvious; it creates a new `DataGridTableStyle` object. The second line, `MappingName`, tells the `DataGrid` which table should have the styles applied to it. In this case, you use the `DataTable` name you created in the preceding section. Next, you set any of the properties you want and finally add the `DataGridTableStyle` object to the `DataGrid`.

Some of the properties you can customize are

- `AlternatingBackColor` and `BackColor`
- `HeaderBackColor` and `HeaderForeColor`
- `GridLineColor` and `GridLineStyle`
- `LinkColor`
- `ReadOnly` (indicates whether the `DataGrid` can be edited)

In short, the `DataGridTableStyle` has just about every property the `DataGrid` itself has. So why have both objects? The answer is because a `DataGrid` can be bound to more than one table at a time, as you'll see tomorrow. Therefore, you can have multiple styles—one for each table—without having to reformat the entire `DataGrid`. (This is why it's important to specify the `MappingName` as shown previously!)

The `DataGridColumnStyle` allows you to format each column (as well as add and remove each one). (Before you ask, there is no `DataGridRowStyle` object.) The `DataGridColumnStyle` object has a few different properties that apply to columns:

- `Alignment`—Indicates how text in the column should be aligned
- `HeaderText`—Specifies the text in the column header

- NullText—Indicates what should be displayed if the value for a particular cell is null (or Nothing in Visual Basic .NET)

- MappingName—Same as for the DataGridTableStyle object

- ReadOnly—Indicates whether the data in the specified column is read-only

- Width—Indicates the width of the column

These properties are all straightforward. To apply a DataGridColumnStyle, you must first create a type of DataGridTableStyle. You cannot create a DataGridColumnStyle object directly. Instead, use either DataGridBoolColumn (which displays check boxes in the cells) or DataGridTextBoxColumn (which displays text boxes—the default style), depending on your needs. (Each object has additional properties that you can customize; we'll get to them in a moment.) Then add your new column style to the GridColumnStyles property:

```
DataGridTableStyle dgTableStyle = new DataGridTableStyle();
//set some properties

DataGridTextBoxColumn dgColumnStyle = new DataGridTextBoxColumn();
//set some column properties

dgTableStyle.GridColumnStyles.Add(dgColumnStyle);
dgData.TableStyles.Add(dgTableStyle);
```

Note

If you create a DataGridTextBoxColumn or DataGridBoolColumn, it overrides some of the default values for each column. For instance, by default, the column headers display the mapping names. If you create a style with the DataGridTextBoxColumn or DataGridBoolColumn objects, the header text is overridden and ends up being blank. Use the HeaderText property in this case to set the headers.

Tip

With all these different object names and collections, keeping them straight is difficult. Try to think about the naming this way:

A DataGrid displays a table, and the *TableStyles* property defines the *style* for that *table*, using a DataGrid*TableStyle* object. In turn, a table displays *columns* in a *grid*, and the *GridColumnStyles* property defines the style for that column, using a DataGrid*ColumnStyle* object. In loose notation:

```
DataGrid.TableStyles = DataGridTableStyle
DataGridTableStyle.GridColumnStyle = DataGridColumnStyle
```

Let's continue and extend the color application developed earlier today by using a
`DataGrid` and the style objects. Listing 8.4 shows the basic structure of this application.

LISTING 8.4   The Enhanced Color Application

```
 1:  using System;
 2:  using System.Windows.Forms;
 3:  using System.Drawing;
 4:  using System.Data;
 5:
 6:  namespace TYWinforms.Day8 {
 7:     public class Listing84 : Form {
 8:        private DataGrid dgData = new DataGrid();
 9:        private DataTable objMyTable = new DataTable("Colors");
10:
11:        public Listing84() {
12:           DataColumn colName = new DataColumn();
13:           colName.DataType = System.Type.GetType("System.String");
14:           colName.ColumnName = "Color Name";
15:
16:           DataColumn colR = new DataColumn();
17:           colR.DataType = System.Type.GetType("System.Int32");
18:           colR.ColumnName = "Red";
19:
20:           DataColumn colG = new DataColumn();
21:           colG.DataType = System.Type.GetType("System.Int32");
22:           colG.ColumnName = "Green";
23:
24:           DataColumn colB = new DataColumn();
25:           colB.DataType = System.Type.GetType("System.Int32");
26:           colB.ColumnName = "Blue";
27:
28:           objMyTable.Columns.Add(colName);
29:           objMyTable.Columns.Add(colR);
30:           objMyTable.Columns.Add(colG);
31:           objMyTable.Columns.Add(colB);
32:
33:           DataRow myDataRow;
34:           myDataRow = objMyTable.NewRow();
35:           myDataRow["Color Name"] = Color.Blue.Name;
36:           myDataRow["Red"] = Color.Blue.R;
37:           myDataRow["Green"] = Color.Blue.G;
38:           myDataRow["Blue"] = Color.Blue.B;
39:           objMyTable.Rows.Add(myDataRow);
40:
41:           myDataRow = objMyTable.NewRow();
42:           myDataRow["Color Name"] = Color.Red.Name;
43:           myDataRow["Red"] = Color.Red.R;
44:           myDataRow["Green"] = Color.Red.G;
```

LISTING 8.4 continued

```
45:            myDataRow["Blue"] = Color.Red.B;
46:            objMyTable.Rows.Add(myDataRow);
47:
48:            myDataRow = objMyTable.NewRow();
49:            myDataRow["Color Name"] = Color.Green.Name;
50:            myDataRow["Red"] = Color.Green.R;
51:            myDataRow["Green"] = Color.Green.G;
52:            myDataRow["Blue"] = Color.Green.B;
53:            objMyTable.Rows.Add(myDataRow);
54:
55:            myDataRow = objMyTable.NewRow();
56:            myDataRow["Color Name"] = Color.PapayaWhip.Name;
57:            myDataRow["Red"] = Color.PapayaWhip.R;
58:            myDataRow["Green"] = Color.PapayaWhip.G;
59:            myDataRow["Blue"] = Color.PapayaWhip.B;
60:            objMyTable.Rows.Add(myDataRow);
61:
62:            dgData.DataSource = objMyTable;
63:            dgData.Dock = DockStyle.Fill;
64:
65:            this.Size = new Size(800,600);
66:            this.Controls.Add(dgData);
67:            this.Text = "Listing 8.4";
68:        }
69:
70:        public static void Main() {
71:            Application.Run(new Listing84());
72:        }
73:    }
74: }
```

ANALYSIS Lines 1–4 import the necessary namespaces. Don't forget System.Data! It contains the assorted DataTable objects. Next, you declare a DataGrid and DataTable on lines 8 and 9. On lines 12–26 you create new columns for your DataTable and then add them on lines 28–31.

Lines 33–60 add new rows to the table. Note that you refer to each column by its name assigned previously. Essentially, these lines are the identical code repeated four times, using different colors each time: Blue, Red, Green, and PapayaWhip (interesting name, I know).

If you execute this application, it simply displays the values in editable fields. Let's make it slightly more interesting by adding styles. Listing 8.5 shows the code that you should place in the constructor.

LISTING 8.5   The Styles for Your Color Application

```
 1:  DataGridTableStyle dgtStyle = new DataGridTableStyle();
 2:  dgtStyle.MappingName = "Colors";
 3:
 4:  DataGridTextBoxColumn dgcNameStyle = new DataGridTextBoxColumn();
 5:  dgcNameStyle.MappingName = "Color Name";
 6:  dgcNameStyle.HeaderText = "Color Name";
 7:
 8:  DataGridTextBoxColumn dgcRedStyle = new DataGridTextBoxColumn();
 9:  dgcRedStyle.MappingName = "Red";
10:  dgcRedStyle.ReadOnly = true;
11:  dgcRedStyle.HeaderText = "Red";
12:
13:  DataGridTextBoxColumn dgcGreenStyle = new DataGridTextBoxColumn();
14:  dgcGreenStyle.MappingName = "Green";
15:  dgcGreenStyle.ReadOnly = true;
16:  dgcGreenStyle.HeaderText = "Green";
17:
18:  DataGridTextBoxColumn dgcBlueStyle = new DataGridTextBoxColumn();
19:  dgcBlueStyle.MappingName = "Blue";
20:  dgcBlueStyle.ReadOnly = true;
21:  dgcBlueStyle.HeaderText = "Blue";
22:
23:  dgtStyle.GridColumnStyles.Add(dgcNameStyle);
24:  dgtStyle.GridColumnStyles.Add(dgcRedStyle);
25:  dgtStyle.GridColumnStyles.Add(dgcGreenStyle);
26:  dgtStyle.GridColumnStyles.Add(dgcBlueStyle);
27:
28:  dgData.TableStyles.Add(dgtStyle);
```

ANALYSIS   Listing 8.5 is easy to follow. You essentially set the header text for each column and set all but the "Color Name" column to read-only. This is done so that the user can modify only the first column—the color name. The application, however, is still boring. Let's add a method that will change the color of the DataGrid dynamically.

The CurrentCellChanged event fires whenever the user moves to a new cell in the grid. Let's monitor this event to apply color changes; when the user clicks on a cell, you'll change the color to the color specified by the cell. To do so, add the following delegate assignation to your constructor:

```
dgData.CurrentCellChanged += new EventHandler(this.HandleColor);
```

Then add the following method to your application:

```
public void HandleColor(Object Sender, EventArgs e) {
   if (Color.FromName(dgData[dgData.CurrentCell].
➥ToString()).IsKnownColor) {
```

```
       dgData.TableStyles[0].ForeColor =
➥Color.FromName(dgData[dgData.CurrentCell].ToString());
   }
}
```

This method is actually very simple, although it looks complex. Let's take it one step at a time. First, you need to evaluate whether the color in the cell is a valid color; because the cell is editable, the user could change the color to some invalid value. If you tried to modify the color using this invalid value, everything would turn white (the default color).

On the second line, you use an `if` statement. First, you retrieve the color specified in the cell by using the following command:

```
dgData[dgData.CurrentCell].ToString()
```

The `CurrentCell` property returns, naturally, the current cell in the grid (the one currently selected). This property returns a `DataGridCell` object, which has properties that can determine where in the `DataGrid` the cell resides. Unfortunately, it doesn't have any properties to tell you the contents of the cell. Therefore, you have to use the `DataGrid`'s items collection to retrieve the value and then convert it to a string for good measure. In Visual Basic .NET, your code would look like this:

```
dgData.Item(dgData.CurrentCell).ToString()
```

Next, you convert (or try to, anyway) that returned value into a `Color` object by using the `FromName` method. Finally, `IsKnownColor` returns a true or false value indicating whether the color is real. If it is, you move onto the next step:

```
dgData.TableStyles[0].ForeColor =
➥Color.FromName(dgData[dgData.CurrentCell].ToString());
```

The first part of this code is simple: You change the `ForeColor` property of the first `DataGridTableStyle` object in the `DataGrid`. The second part is exactly like the command in the previous `if` statement, except you leave off the `IsKnownColor` property. Now try executing this application. You should notice that the font color changes whenever you move to a new cell. You can even type in a new color, and it will change appropriately (assuming, of course, that what you type is a real color)! Figure 8.5 shows the output.

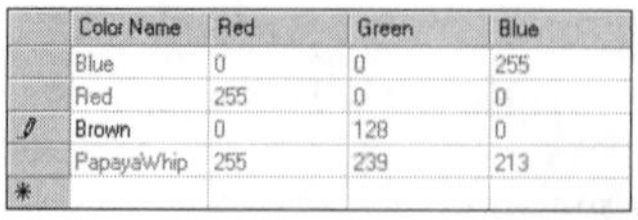

FIGURE 8.5

Your DataGrid *changes color.*

Color Name	Red	Green	Blue
Blue	0	0	255
Red	255	0	0
Brown	0	128	0
PapayaWhip	255	239	213

The `DataGridTextBoxColumn` and `DataGridBoolColumn` Classes

NEW TERM As you learned previously, you cannot create a `DataGridColumnStyle` object directly; you can create only instances of its derived classes, those derived from it (this type of class is known as an *abstract* class; a class from which you cannot create an instance is abstract). There are only two of these classes—`DataGridTextBoxColumn` and `DataGridBoolColumn`—and each has only a few interesting properties.

The `DataGridBoolColumn` displays a check box in the `DataGrid` for each row, indicating a true or false value. This column has `TrueValue` and `FalseValue` properties indicating the actual values of the column (whether true or false, or 1 or 0, and so on). Similarly, `NullValue` indicates the returned value when the bound data contains a null value. You use the `AllowNull` property to allow or disallow null values.

The `DataGridTextBoxColumn` displays a text box for each row in the column. One property of particular interest is `Format`, which specifies how the text in the column should be displayed. (Note that the formatting is applied only to the displayed value; the actual value does not change.) For instance, suppose you have a date value such as `"1/1/00"` bound to the `DataGrid`. You set the `Format` property to the string `"D"`, and it is output as `"Saturday, January 01, 2000"`. Table 8.4 lists the formatting strings and their descriptions.

TABLE 8.4 String and Datetime Formatting Codes

Strings	Description
c	Currency format. Indicates the string should be displayed as currency.
d	Decimal format. Indicates the string should be displayed as a decimal—for example, 45, 12345.
e	Exponential format. For example, 8.32e+12.
f	Fixed point format. By default, this format inserts two zeros to the right of a decimal point and any decimal values.
g	General. This string can be either decimal or exponential format. It returns the particular format that represents the given string in the least number of characters.
n	Number format. Similar to decimal format, but with commas and two decimal points—for example, 45,324.00.
p	Percent format.
r	Round-trip format. This format is used only when exact precision is important. For example, a `Double` value has 15 digits of precision, and when converting to a string, anything beyond 15 digits is dropped. Round-trip ensures that these values are not lost.
x	Hexadecimal format. The number "12345" would be "3036" in hexadecimal.

8

TABLE 8.4   continued

Dates	Description
d	Short date: `"1/28/02"`.
D	Long date: `"Monday, January 28, 2002"`.
t	Short time: `"12:31"`.
T	Long time: `"3:51:24 PM"`.
f	Combination of long date and short time: `"Monday, January 28, 2002 3:51"`.
F	Combination of long date and long time: `"Monday, January 28, 2002 3:51:24 PM"`.
g	Short date and short time: `"1/28/02 3:51"`.
G	Short date and long time: `"1/28/02 3:51:24 PM"`.
m	Month and day: `"January 28"`.
r	The RFC1123 pattern: `"Tue, 10 Apr 2001 15:51:24 GMT"`.
s	ISO 8601 datetime pattern: `"2001-04-10T15:51:24"`.
u	Universal datetime pattern: `"2001-04-10 15:51:24Z"`.
U	Universal datetime pattern: `"2001-04-10 15:51:24Z"`.
y	Year and month: `"January 2002"`.

Note   The string values in Table 8.4 are not case sensitive. Thus, `"c"` is the same as `"C"`. Dates, however, are case sensitive. Also, note that the outputs from date formatting strings vary by the culture settings on your computer.

You can suffix each formatting string with a number that indicates to how many digits the string should be carried out. For example, if you had the number `".12345"`, the `"p"` format would display the string as

```
12.35 %
```

In other words, it rounds to two decimal points. If you want to keep all the original values, add the number 3 after the `"p"` like this: `"p3"`. It would display the string as follows:

```
12.345 %
```

With the `"d"` format, zeros are added where necessary without changing the value of the number. With the number 12345, `"d6"` would display

```
012345
```

"f6" with the same value would display

```
12345.000000
```

Hit Testing

The last topic in this lesson covers the DataGrid's capability to determine what the user clicked—for example, which cell, which caption, and so on. This is known as *hit testing*. The HitTest method makes determining this information a snap.

To use hit testing, you must handle an event where the user clicks part of the DataGrid. Ideally, this is the MouseDown event, which uses a special delegate to return the x and y coordinates of the user's click. To assign a delegate to this event, use a line similar to the following:

```
dgData.MouseDown += new MouseEventHandler(this.HandleClick);
```

The signature of your HandleClick event would then look like this:

```
private void HandleClick(Object Sender, MouseEventArgs e) { }
```

Use the X and Y properties of the MouseEventArgs object to determine where, exactly, the user clicked and then the HitTest method to determine what part of the DataGrid those coordinates correspond to. The HitTest method returns a DataGrid.HitTestInfo object, which provides the necessary information. The following code snippet shows the HandleClick method using the HitTest method:

```
private void HandleClick(Object Sender, MouseEventArgs e) {
   DataGrid.HitTestInfo myInfo;
   myInfo = dgData.HitTest(e.X, e.Y);

   MessageBox.Show("Column: " + myInfo.Column.ToString());
   MessageBox.Show("Row: " + myInfo.Row.ToString());
   MessageBox.Show("Type: " + myInfo.Type.ToString());
}
```

The Type property indicates what part of the DataGrid was clicked. It can be any of these DataGrid.HitTestType enumeration values:

- Caption
- Cell
- ColumnHeader
- ColumnResize
- None
- ParentRows
- RowHeader
- RowResize

Note　These enumeration values don't actually return the associated objects (for example, `DataGrid.HitTestType.Cell` does not return a `DataGridCell` object). These values only indicate the type of object clicked.

Summary

Today you learned about databinding in Windows Forms, and along with this information, you learned several databinding controls, such as `DataGrid`. Databinding is a powerful and easy way to associated your UI to your data model.

To databind a control, you simply add a data source to its `DataBindings` property, specifying the data to bind:

```
MyControl.DataBindings.Add("Text", DataSource,
➥"optional data source name");
```

You can then use the `BindingContext.Position` property of that control to move through the associated data, one record at a time.

A large part of today's lesson covered the `DataGrid` control because it is so powerful and useful. This control allows you to easily display data in a grid format, and it can be editable or read-only. Simply set the `DataSource` property of this control to the data source to bind.

You can customize the appearance of the `DataGrid` by using various `DataGridTableStyle` and `DataGridColumnStyle` objects. The former object controls how the entire grid is displayed, whereas the latter controls the display for each column. Remember that you must have a `DataGridTableStyle` object before you can add any `DataGridColumnStyle` objects. Use these objects' `MappingName` property to indicate what member of the data they should display.

Tomorrow you'll learn how to incorporate databases into your applications.

Q&A

Q　**What if I don't want to display all the properties for a given object in a `DataGrid`?**

A　When you're using an array, there's not much you can do. If you must use an array, the best method is to create an array of only the properties you want to display.

With a `DataTable`, create `DataGridColumnStyles` for each column that you want displayed; those without associated styles simply won't be shown.

Tomorrow you'll learn about `DataSets` and `DataViews`—part of ADO.NET—so that you can customize the displayed columns.

Q Is there any way to customize an individual cell in a `DataGrid`?

A Unfortunately, no. If you need this type of control over the display, you should probably create your own UI and not rely on the `DataGrid`.

Workshop

This workshop will help reinforce the concepts covered in today's lesson. It is very helpful to understand fully the answers before moving on. Answers to the quiz questions and exercises are in Appendix A.

Quiz

1. Write a statement that will add a new databinding to a text box control named `"tbOne"`. Bind to the `Text` property the array `"arrOne"`.

2. Given the text box in question 1, is the following statement correct?

   `tbOne.BindingContext.Position += 1;`

3. True or False: You can bind data to a `Form` object.

4. What event is often used to call the `HitTest` method and why?

5. Given the number `"458.34e+04"`, what would the display be using the format string `"d3"`?

6. To which property of the `DataGrid` do you add `DataGridTableStyle` objects?

7. To which property of the `DataGrid` do you add `DataGridColumnStyle` objects?

8. Given a `DataTable` named `"dtData"`, with two columns `"ColA"` and `"ColB"`, create a new, empty, row.

9. Create the `"ColA"` column for the `DataTable` in question 8 as an integer type.

Exercise

Create an application using a `DataGrid` and `DataTable` that allows users to enter their checkbook register information, similar to Microsoft Money or Quicken. Do not allow the `DataGrid` to be manually edited; rather, provide other controls for the users to enter the information, which will then be displayed in the `DataGrid` upon submission. To keep this exercise simple, allow only withdrawals for now.

DAY 9

Using ADO.NET

Using databases is often a major component of nearly any application in today's world. Databases can store a wealth of information, from customer data for a multi-national corporation to guestbook visitors for a Web site. It follows that the interaction between an application and a database is often of utmost importance, as critical data may be on the line.

ADO.NET is a technology that allows your applications to communicate with virtually every type of database or data storage mechanism in existence, from Oracle to XML to plain text. With this powerful mechanism, you can display or retrieve data, edit and update it, or delete it all easily with a minimal requirement of resources. Today you'll learn to use ADO.NET and learn how it's a vast improvement over previous technologies.

Today you'll learn

- How to create databases in Access and SQL Server
- What the components of ADO.NET are
- How to bind data from a database to your application
- How to update a database
- How to read and write XML data

What Is ADO.NET?

Data is everywhere. From weather quotes to stock quotes, banking transactions to Web
site visits, even spy and surveillance equipment, they all generate data, and massive
amounts of it. What's needed is a powerful yet logical system for manipulating all that
data, without becoming lost in it.

Before the introduction of .NET, Windows applications often used ActiveX Data Objects
(ADO) to access and modify databases. ADO is a programming interface used to access
data. This method was efficient and fairly easy for developers to learn and implement.
ADO, however, suffered from a dated model for data access, with many limitations, such
as the inability to transmit data so that it was easily and universally accessible. Coupled
with the move from standard Structured Query Language (SQL) databases to more distributed types of data (such as Extensible Markup Language, or XML), Microsoft introduced ADO.NET—the next evolution of ADO.

ADO.NET, which is a major revision of ADO, enables Windows Forms applications to
present data in much more efficient and different ways. For example, it fully embraces
XML and can easily communicate with any XML-compliant application. ADO.NET
offers several exciting new features that will make your life as a developer much easier.
You should become familiar with ADO.NET because it's important for dynamic application development. Knowing its intricacies will save you many headaches down the road.

Figure 9.1 depicts the model of data access with ADO.NET. ADO.NET is completely
compatible with OLE DB-compliant data sources, such as SQL or Jet (Microsoft
Access's database engine).

FIGURE 9.1

*The relationship
between ADO.NET
and Windows Forms
applications.*

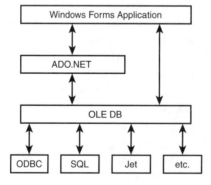

ADO.NET Versus ADO

Although Microsoft has touted ADO.NET as the next evolution of ADO, and although ADO.NET has some of the same objects, it's really very different from its predecessor. Whereas ADO was connection-based, ADO.NET relies on short, XML message-based interactions with data sources. This capability makes ADO.NET much more efficient for Internet-based applications.

A fundamental change from ADO to ADO.NET was the adoption of XML for data exchanges. ADO.NET is well acquainted with XML and uses it in all transactions, allowing ADO.NET to reach, exchange, and persist data stores much more easily than ADO. This capability also gives ADO.NET much better performance because XML data is easily converted to and from any type of data. It doesn't require the complex conversions that wasted processor time with classic ADO.

Another major change is the way ADO.NET interacts with databases. ADO requires "locking" of database resources and constant connections for its applications, but ADO.NET doesn't. ADO.NET is therefore much more scalable because users aren't in contention for database resources.

Table 9.1 summarizes the major changes from ADO to ADO.NET.

TABLE 9.1 Changes from ADO to ADO.NET

In ADO	In ADO.NET
Data represented by:	
Recordset, resembling a single table or query result	`DataSet`, which can contain multiple tables from any data source
Data access:	
Accesses rows in a recordset sequentially	Allows complete non-sequential access of data in `DataSet` through collection-based hierarchy
Relationships among multiple tables:	
Requires SQL `JOINs` and `UNIONs` to combine data from multiple tables into one recordset	Uses `DataRelation` objects, which can be used to navigate among related tables
Data sharing:	
Requires conversion of data sources	Uses XML, so no conversions are necessary

9

TABLE 9.1 continued

In ADO	In ADO.NET
Programmability:	
Uses a `Connection` object to transmit commands to a data source's underlying constructs	Uses strongly typed characteristics of XML; does not require use of data constructs; can reference everything by name
Scalability:	
Database locks and connections resulted in contention for data resources	No locks or lengthy active connections, so contentions are eliminated
Firewalls:	
Problematic because firewalls prohibit many types of requests	Not a problem because XML is completely firewall-proof

ADO.NET and XML

XML is a useful tool for data distribution. It's completely text-based, which means that it's easy for people to write and read, and it can be transported around the security measures put in place on the Internet.

XML stores data by providing a hierarchical representation of fields and their data. For instance, if you have a database named `Users` with the fields `Name`, `UserID`, and `Birthdate`, it would be represented in text form as

```
<Users>
<User>
   <Name />
   <UserID />
   <Birthdate />
<User>
</Users>
```

This basic structure is known as an XML *schema*. (Actually, it's a bit more complicated than that, but that discussion is beyond the scope of this book.) You can then use this schema to represent all the data in your tables:

```
<Users>
<User>
   <Name>Chris Payne</Name>
   <UserID>1</UserID>
   <Birthdate>June 27</Birthdate>
```

```
</User>
<User>
   <Name>Eva Payne</Name>
   <UserID>2</UserID>
   <Birthdate>July 15</Birthdate>
</User>
</Users>
...
...
```

This code can be read by anyone with a text editor (such as Notepad), whereas the corresponding database table can be read only by someone using that particular database application or converting it to another database application. XML is an efficient, implementation-independent way of storing and sending data, which is why it has become such a phenomenon on the Web. Thus, it's only logical for databases and their interfaces to adopt this method of communication. It makes life much easier for everyone. ADO.NET uses XML in all data exchanges and for internal representations. As soon as data comes out of a database, it's represented in XML and is sent wherever you need it to be. Because any application can easily convert XML, this approach ensures broad compatibility for your data.

The adoption of XML by ADO.NET is also a big step toward delivering applications as services across the Internet, which is the ideology behind the .NET Framework. This lesson just touches on the basics, but as you work with ADO.NET more and more, you'll see the benefits your applications will reap as you develop more distributed programs.

Creating a Database

For the purposes of this lesson, you'll find it helpful to have a database that you can use to test your example. Therefore, this section will describe how to create a database in both Access 2000 and SQL Server 2000—two of the most popular and readily available database systems.

 Note   After today's lesson, the rest of the book will focus on using SQL Server as the database system because it's more efficient and more likely to be used in a development environment. Luckily, though, you won't notice many differences either way, as you'll see in the next few sections.

Creating an Access Database

You'll use the database you build here in subsequent lessons, so let's design something useful. To start, create a user table for storing the following information:

- First name
- Last name
- Address
- City
- State
- ZIP Code
- Phone number

This type of typical user database can be applied to many different applications. To start your database in Access, run Access and select New from the File menu. When you see the dialog box in Figure 9.2, select Blank Access Database, name it TYWinForms.mdb, and save it in the c:\Winforms\data directory. (You can use any directory you choose; just be aware that the examples in this book will refer to this directory.)

FIGURE 9.2

You can create a new, blank database from this dialog box.

After clicking OK in the dialog box, you then should see the following options: Create table in Design view, Create table by using wizard, and Create table by entering data. Choose Design view and start entering your columns. Enter **FirstName** in the Field Name column and select Text in the Data Type column. Optionally, you can enter a description for this field, such as **User's first name**. Enter the other fields described in the previous list, and you should end up with a table similar to Figure 9.3.

Note

The options available may be different depending on the version of Access you're using.

FIGURE 9.3

You enter the field information for the table here.

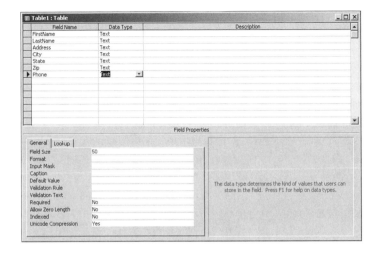

Finally, add one more column named UserID, which is your identity column. Assign it the data type Autonumber and right-click on the black arrow next to its name. Select Primary Key from the menu and notice how the key symbol appears next to the name. Next, simply save the table by choosing File, Save. Save the table with the name tblUsers. Finally, choose File, Close to close tblUsers.

Tip

If you want to define a primary key over more than one column, select each column by holding down the Ctrl key and right-click to select the primary key.

That's all there is to it! You can now add data simply by double-clicking on the tblUsers option that appears in the main window. Notice that when you input data, you don't need to enter a value for the UserID column. A number is inserted and incremented automatically, as shown in Figure 9.4.

Table 9.2 lists the various data types provided in Access 2000. Similar data types are present in all database systems, although the exact names may be different.

TABLE 9.2   Access 2000 Data Types

Data Type	Description
Autonumber	An automatically incremented integer used to uniquely identify rows in a table.
Currency	Used to store monetary data.

TABLE 9.2   continued

Data Type	Description
Date/Time	Used to store date and time values. Access 2000 can store dates between the years 100 and 9999.
Memo	Used to store up to 65,535 alphanumeric characters.
Number	Used to store numeric values.
Text	Used to store up to 255 alphanumeric characters.
Yes/No	Used for columns that can have only one of two values (similar to bit or Boolean types).

FIGURE 9.4

You can enter data into your new table.

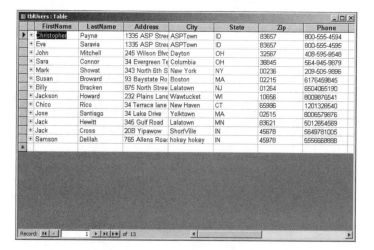

Creating a Database in SQL Server 2000

Creating a database is a bit more complicated in SQL Server 2000 than it is in Access, but the procedure is essentially the same. Access is appropriate for your individual needs, but typically, SQL Server is used for larger databases that require more security and stability.

Now let's create the tblUser database in Microsoft SQL Server 2000. Start by opening Enterprise Manager from the SQL Server 2000 menu group in your Start menu. If everything is set up properly, you should see a Windows Explorer-like navigation system, with Microsoft SQL Servers at the top and the name of your server a couple levels below. Expand the Databases folder, as shown in Figure 9.5, and select New Database from the Action menu.

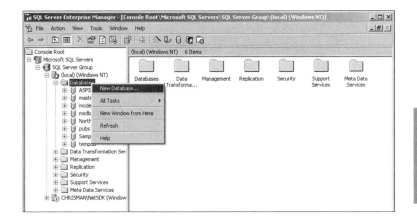

FIGURE 9.5

To create your database, expand the Databases folder and select New Database from the Action menu.

9

Enter the name **TYWinforms** in the dialog box that pops up. For now, simply accept the default options under the General tab and click OK. SQL Server will create the database and transaction log for you. You should now see TYWinforms under the Databases folder. Next, expand this tab and select the Tables node.

You'll see that SQL Server has already inserted quite a few tables for you. They are system tables used by SQL Server to keep track of the items you place in your database. Ignore these tables for now and select New Table from the Action menu. You then see a matrix similar to the one shown in Access. Enter the information as you did in Access, as shown in Figure 9.6, except this time use the varchar data type instead of Text because Text has a different meaning in SQL Server.

Notice that SQL Server provides many more data types than Access did. SQL Server is a more powerful application that allows developers to specify the database options with much greater granularity. With the UserID field selected, in the Columns panel below, select Yes for the Identity property (refer to Figure 9.6). Then right-click this field and select Set Primary Key. Next, save this table as tblUsers and close this design view by clicking the x (the close box) in the upper-right corner.

To enter data into your new table, right-click the table and select Open Table, Return All Rows to open a tabular data entry mechanism similar to that in Access. Enter a few names and addresses. (Don't enter anything in the UserID field, however.) Then click the exclamation point (Run) on the menu to autoincrement the UserIDs. Finally, close the new table by clicking x in the upper-right corner.

FIGURE 9.6

To create your table, enter field names and data types.

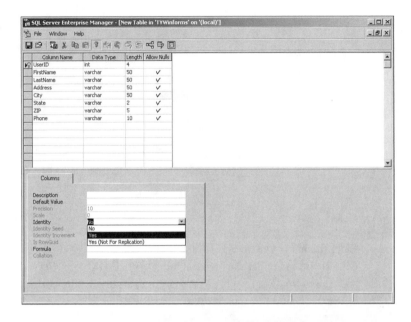

Using SQL to Query Databases

The Structured Query Language (SQL) is an industry-standard way to issue commands to a database. Applications such as Microsoft SQL Server, MS Access, and Oracle all use SQL to control data (although each has its own approach to the language). The basic capabilities of SQL are retrieving, editing, and deleting data, but in reality, it's a very powerful and intricate language, most of which we won't examine in this book. To work with ADO.NET, however, you'll need to have some familiarity with it, and the following section will introduce you. For more detailed information, try *Sams Teach Yourself SQL in 21 Days, Third Edition,* by Ryan K. Stephens and Ronald R. Pew (ISBN: 0-672-31674-9).

Just like any programming language such as Visual Basic .NET or C#, SQL has statements that are executed (unlike these languages, though, SQL does not need to be compiled). The four important statements that you'll need to know for the purposes of this lesson are SELECT, DELETE, INSERT, and UPDATE; luckily, they all follow similar syntaxes. The next few sections briefly cover each statement.

The SELECT Statement

SELECT is probably the most common SQL statement. Its basic purpose is to grab a set of data from a database table. The syntax for the SELECT statement is as follows:

```
SELECT selectlist
FROM tablename
[WHERE searchCondition]
[ORDER BY orderbyExpression [ASC | DESC ]}
```

The structure follows basic English patterns. *selectList* is generally a comma-delimited list of the columns you want to return. FirstName, LastName would return the values in those two columns, for instance. Additionally, you can use an asterisk to return all the columns from a particular table. *tablename* is the name of the table to grab the data from.

Here's a simple SELECT statement that you could use for the databases you've created:

```
SELECT * FROM tblUsers
```

This statement returns all the rows from all the columns in the tblUsers table, and you can do whatever you like with them.

The following statement is functionally identical to the one you just built:

```
SELECT UserID, FirstName, LastName, Address, City, State, ZIP,
Phone FROM tblUsers
```

Tip

You shouldn't use SELECT * because often it returns more information than you need. This can result in decreased performance. Instead, explicitly specify the columns you need to return. Doing so takes a bit longer when you're coding, but your code will enjoy performance benefits.

SELECT statements always return all the rows in the database (unless qualified with a WHERE clause, discussed next).

You can use a WHERE clause to specify additional criteria for the returned data. A WHERE clause can generally be any logical statement, similar to an if statement in regular programming languages. Here's an example:

```
SELECT * FROM tblUsers WHERE FirstName = 'Chris'
SELECT * FROM tblUsers WHERE City = 'ASP Town' AND LastName = 'Mitchell'
```

The first statement returns only records where the FirstName field value is Chris. The second statement returns only the records where City is ASP Town and the LastName field is equal to Mitchell.

To use wildcards for your SQL WHERE clause criteria, you can use the LIKE keyword followed by wildcard operators. Table 9.3 lists the operators the LIKE keyword accepts.

TABLE 9.3   Access LIKE Operator Wildcards

Operator	Translation
*	A string of zero or more characters (Note: In SQL Server, this wildcard is represented by %.)
_	Exactly one character
[]	A specific character in the given set

The following statements show how to use LIKE:

```
1  SELECT * FROM tblUsers WHERE FirstName LIKE '*s*'
2  SELECT * FROM tblUsers WHERE FirstName LIKE '_hris'
3  SELECT * FROM tblUsers WHERE FirstName LIKE '[abcd]hris'
```

The SQL statement on line 1 returns any rows where the first name contains an s somewhere in the value. The * operator works the same in SQL as it does in Windows, meaning zero or more characters. The SQL statement on line 2 returns any records where the first name contains any one letter, followed by the string "hris". With the given data, this statement returns only one record, but you get the point. Finally, the SQL statement on line 3 returns any records where the first name contains a string that begins with any of the letters a, b, c, or d, followed by the string "hris".

The ORDER BY clause specifies the order in which the data is returned, such as alphabetical order. If this clause is not used, you have no way of knowing in what order the database will return records. Even though they may have been entered alphabetically during data entry, that doesn't mean the records will be returned the same way. The ORDER BY clause enables you to specify which columns to order the data by and how. For example:

```
SELECT * FROM tblUsers
ORDER BY FirstName ASC
```

This statement returns all records sorted alphabetically by first name. Likewise, specifying DESC sort order instead of ASC returns reverse-alphabetic order. You can specify multiple columns delimited by commas in the ORDER BY clause as well, each with its own sort order. SQL uses the additional columns if the first one contains any duplicate data. Just don't specify any columns that aren't in the table!

You also can use SELECT statements to return data from more than one table at once. You use a comma-delimited list of table names for the *tablename* argument. Typically, you would have to relate the tables somehow, but that's beyond the scope of this chapter.

All the other SQL statements that you'll examine today follow the same basic form as the SELECT query. Consequently, we won't spend much time on the next three statements.

The INSERT Statement

Another common SQL statement is INSERT, which inserts new rows (new data) into a database table. Its basic syntax is as follows:

```
INSERT [INTO] tablename
[(column list)]
VALUES (DEFAULT | NULL | expression)
```

This straightforward statement is similar in syntax to SELECT. So, let's build an example using your user database:

```
INSERT INTO tblUsers (FirstName, LastName, Address, City,
➥State, Zip, Phone)
VALUES ('Chris', 'Payne', '135 ASP Street', 'ASPTown', 'FL',
➥'36844', '8006596598')
```

This statement inserts a new row with the field values specified in the VALUES clause. The data type you supply in VALUES must match the data type in the corresponding column, or you receive an error. Also, if you specify a column, you must specify a value, or you get another error.

The UPDATE Statement

The UPDATE statement updates existing rows in a database table. You can specify a WHERE clause with this statement to update only a subset of the values in a database table. The syntax is as follows:

```
UPDATE tablename
SET column name = (DEFAULT | NULL | expression)
[WHERE searchCondition]
```

If you leave off the WHERE clause, the specified column or columns are updated in every row in the database. Be very careful with this statement because you can easily ruin your data! Again, using the tblUser database table as an example, you use UPDATE as follows:

```
UPDATE tblUsers
SET Address = '136 ASP Street', City = 'ASPVille'
WHERE FirstName = 'Chris' AND LastName = 'Payne'
```

This statement changes the `Address` and `City` values for the record where the `FirstName` is `"Chris"` and the `LastName` is `"Payne"`, which currently is only one record. You can specify only the columns you need in the *column name* list. The `WHERE` clause is exactly the same as for the `SELECT` statement; you can use wildcards as well.

The DELETE Statement

The last SQL statement is `DELETE`, which deletes rows from a database. Let's look at the syntax:

```
DELETE FROM tablename
[WHERE searchCondition]
```

This one is relatively simple. The only thing to remember is the `WHERE` clause, which is very important. If you don't specify this clause, the `DELETE` statement deletes all the rows in the entire table—normally a disastrous occurrence. Again, the `WHERE` clause is exactly the same as for the `SELECT` statement. Here's an example:

```
DELETE FROM tblUsers
WHERE FirstName = 'Chris'
```

This statement deletes only records with the first name `"Chris"`.

Introduction to the DataSet

ADO.NET revolves around the `DataSet`. This object is a completely new concept that replaces the traditional recordset in ADO. The `DataSet` is a simple, memory-resident data store that provides a consistent programming model for accessing data, no matter what type of data it contains; think of it as a mini-database. Unlike a recordset, the `DataSet` contains complete sets of data, including constraints, relationships, and even multiple tables at once. The `DataSet` object model is shown in Figure 9.7.

When you establish a connection to the database, you hand it a box and tell the data store to fill it with some stuff. You can fill it with tables of data, your own data from else-where, other objects—any data you like. A `DataSet` is this box; the database gives you copies of all the data you ask for, and you can carry it around in the box without having to maintain a connection to the database.

Figure 9.7 includes a `DataTable` object, which represents a single database table. Recall this object from yesterday's lesson. (The `DataSet` maintains a collection of these tables in the `TablesCollection` object.) The `DataTable` completely represents the correspond-ing table, including its relationships and key constraints. It contains two other collec-tions, `Rows` and `Columns`, which represent the data and schema of the tables, respectively.

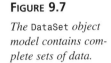

FIGURE 9.7

The DataSet *object model contains complete sets of data.*

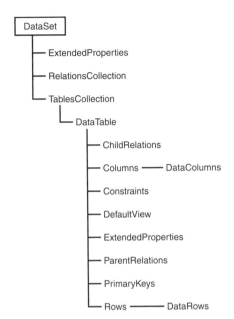

The RelationsCollection object allows you to navigate among tables based on the relationships defined on them. You no longer need to use complex joins and unions (the old way of relating tables) in your SQL queries because ADO.NET makes navigation much easier. The actual relationships are represented by DataRelation objects, which contain information on the two tables being joined, the primary and foreign key relationships, and the names of the relationships.

You also can add relationships using the DataRelation object. ADO.NET automatically enforces key constraints as well; it doesn't allow you to change one table in a way that would violate the relationship to the other table.

The ExtendedProperties object contains any additional information, such as usernames and passwords.

In sum, the DataSet is a versatile tool. It doesn't matter where the data came from or where it's going; it's completely separate from any data store. Therefore, you can use the DataSet as a standalone entity.

As mentioned earlier, the DataSet can contain multiple DataTables. Because you already know how to create DataTables, you already know how to create DataSets! Assuming you've already created a table and filled it with rows and columns, all you need to do is add it to the DataSet:

```
DataSet MyData = new DataSet("My data");
MyData.Tables.Add(Table);
```

This capability is interesting, but not very practical. After all, why would you manually create multiple `DataTables` to stick in a `DataSet`? When you start dealing with databases, though, this capability will become much more useful.

The ADO.NET Object Model

Now that you have your database set up and have some background information on ADO.NET, it's time to communicate with your databases. In the next few sections, you'll examine the objects within the ADO.NET framework, and you'll be happy to know that they're all simple.

To interact with data in your Windows Forms application, you follow these five general steps:

1. Create a database connection object.
2. Open the database connection.
3. Populate a `DataSet` with the desired data.
4. Optionally, set up a `DataView` object to display data.
5. Bind a control to the `DataSet` or `DataView`.

Because you examined the fifth step in detail yesterday, you'll concentrate on the first four today. In the next few sections, you'll examine each step outlined here.

 Note

You'll use two different types of objects. One set is for SQL Server exclusively (you can call it the SQL provider), and the other is for everything else (you can call it the OLE DB provider). The OLE DB provider works with SQL Server as well, but the SQL provider takes advantage of some special SQL Server characteristics that make it more efficient. You'll see that the different sets of objects are all prefixed by either `Sql` or `OleDB`. Most of the time, you can switch between the two by just changing the prefix on the object; all properties and methods are nearly identical. We'll focus on the SQL provider in this book.

Before we dig into the code, let's preview the ADO.NET controls we'll be using:

- `SqlConnection` object—This control represents a connection to a database.
- `SqlDataAdapter` object—This multipurpose tool will be used to communicate with a database after a connection is made (for example, to retrieve, insert, or update data).
- `SqlCommand` object—This control represents an individual command created by an `SqlDataAdapter`. The `SqlCommand` object contains information about the SQL statement you're trying to execute and is intimately associated with the `SqlDataAdapter`.
- `DataSet` — You already know what this one is—a disconnected representation of a database.

Steps 1 and 2 mentioned previously are associated with the `SqlConnection` object, whereas step 3 works with the `SqlDataAdapter` and `SqlCommand` objects. You'll be using all these objects in a moment.

Connecting to Your Database and Retrieving Data

NEW TERM The database connection is handled with the `SqlConnection` object (or `OleDbConnection` object—notice the prefixes). All you need to provide is a *connection string*—a string that tells .NET where the database is located, what type of database it is, what version it is, and so on. This connection string is generic, though, so after you create it the first time, you usually don't have to write it again.

Depending on the database you're using, however, the string varies. The following code snippet shows sample strings for both SQL Server and MS Access:

```
//SQL Server
"Initial Catalog=TYWinforms;Data Source=localhost;"

//Access, C#
"Provider=Microsoft.Jet.OLEDB.4.0;Data Source=" +
"C:\\winforms\\data\\TYWinforms.mdb;User ID=blah;Password=blah";

//Access, VB.NET
"Provider=Microsoft.Jet.OLEDB.4.0;Data Source=" & _
"C:\winforms\data\TYWinforms.mdb;User ID=blah;Password=blah"
```

Note   In C#, the backslash character (\) has special meaning, so you prefix it with another backslash to eliminate that special meaning and represent a literal character. Visual Basic .NET has no restrictions.

Next, you need to create an `SqlConnection` object with the connection string:

```
String strConn = "Initial Catalog=TYWinforms;Data
➥Source=localhost;";
SqlConnection objConn = new SqlConnection(strConn);
```

The next step is to populate a `DataSet` with the desired data. To do so, you need to write some SQL statements. Listing 9.1 shows a simple application that writes these statements and then displays the data in a `DataGrid`.

LISTING 9.1   Accessing a Database

```
 1:  using System;
 2:  using System.Windows.Forms;
 3:  using System.Drawing;
 4:  using System.Data;
 5:  using System.Data.SqlClient;
 6:
 7:  namespace TYWinforms.Day9 {
 8:      public class Listing91 : Form {
 9:          DataGrid dgData = new DataGrid();
10:          DataSet objDS = new DataSet();
11:
12:          public Listing91() {
13:              String strConn = "Initial Catalog=TYWinforms;Data
➥ Source=localhost;User ID=sa";
14:              SqlConnection objConn = new SqlConnection(strConn);
15:
16:              SqlDataAdapter objCmd = new SqlDataAdapter
➥ ("SELECT * FROM tblUsers", objConn);
17:              objCmd.Fill(objDS, "tblUsers");
18:
19:              dgData.DataSource = objDS;
20:              dgData.DataMember = "tblUsers";
21:              dgData.Dock = DockStyle.Fill;
22:
23:              this.Controls.Add(dgData);
24:          }
25:
26:          public static void Main() {
27:              Application.Run(new Listing91());
28:          }
29:      }
30:  }
```

Caution   You should change the `localhost` string on line 13 to match your installation of SQL Server. By default, `localhost` will work, but you should double-check in SQL Enterprise Manager.

Note

SQL Server can be configured to accept two kinds of login accounts: either Windows NT accounts (Windows Authentication) or SQL Server accounts (SQL Server Authentication) or both (Mixed Mode). `"sa"` is the SQL Server account for the system administrator. If your SQL Server is set up for Windows Authentication, you should use a connection string as follows and it will use your NT account to authenticate you:

```
"Initial Catalog=TYWinforms;Data Source=localhost;
➥Trusted_Connection=true;";
```

9

ANALYSIS   First, notice the addition of the `System.Data` and `System.Data.SqlClient` namespaces (the latter would be `System.Data.OleDb` if you were using the OLE DB provider). They are necessary for the various data connection objects. Then, on lines 13 and 14, you create the connection string and the `SqlConnection` object.

On line 16, you are introduced to the `SqlDataAdapter` object. This object is sort of a database multi-tool; it can execute SQL statements, return data, and fill `DataSets`. You use it here to execute a `SELECT` statement and then to populate the `DataGrid`. The constructor for this object takes two parameters: the first is the `SELECT` statement to execute (here you just retrieve all the records from the `tblUsers` table), and the second is the `SqlConnection` object, which informs the `SqlDataAdapter` where to look for the data. You'll learn more details about the `SqlDataAdapter` in a moment.

On line 17, you call the `Fill` method. This interesting method essentially executes the `SELECT` statement you passed in, creates a `DataTable` object whose rows are the results of the `SELECT statement`, and puts that `DataTable` in a `DataSet`. The two parameters to this method are the `DataSet` to place the returned results and the name of the created `DataTable`.

The rest of the code binds data to the `DataGrid`; it should look familiar from yesterday. You set the `DataSource` property to the newly populated `DataSet`, and the `DataMember` property to the `DataTable` in the `DataSet`. If you didn't specify the `DataMember`, the `DataGrid` would display the objects in the `DataSet` rather than the data (in other words, it would show `"tblUsers"` instead of the users in the table).

Adding database capabilities to your applications is simple, requiring five or six lines of code. Listing 9.1 produces the output shown in Figure 9.8.

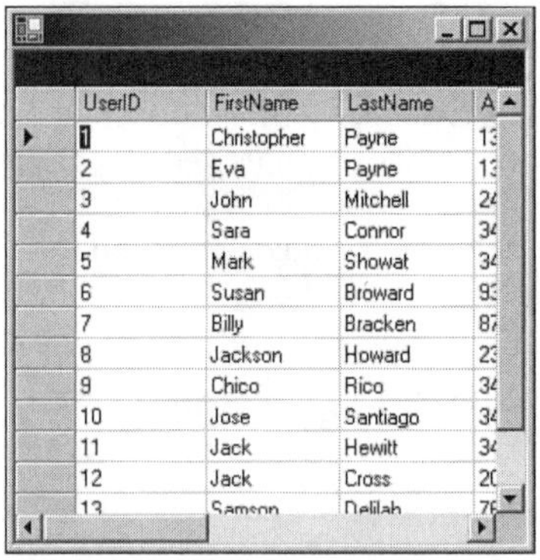

Figure 9.8

Your bound DataGrid *shows the information from the database.*

Editing Data

The SqlDataAdapter also allows you to edit data, using UPDATE, INSERT, and DELETE SQL statements. In fact, it has several properties just for these statements. They work a bit counterintuitively, so let's examine them closely.

The SqlDataAdapter has the UpdateCommand, InsertCommand, DeleteCommand, and SelectCommand properties. SelectCommand is populated in the constructor (line 16 of Listing 9.1) and executed when the Fill method is called. The rest are executed when the SqlDataAdapter's Update method (we'll discuss it in a moment) is called, but there's a catch.

These statements execute only if some data in the underlying DataSet has *already* changed. For example, assume you want to change all instances of the name Christopher in the user database to Chris. Theoretically, you could use an UpdateCommand property like the following:

```
objCmd.UpdateCommand = new SqlCommand
➥("Update tblUsers SET FirstName = 'Chris' WHERE
➥FirstName = 'Christopher');
objCmd.Update();
```

You create a new SqlCommand object (which you'll learn about in the next section), passing it the appropriate UPDATE statement, and then call the Update method to execute the statement. Ideally, this approach should update the DataSet first and then push the changes back to the database. However, it doesn't work as expected.

Essentially, this statement dictates how changes in the DataSet should be pushed to the database. The Update method checks the DataSet to see whether any values have changed. If none have changed, nothing happens. If some have changed, however, the SqlDataAdapter takes only those changed records, executes the SQL statement against them, and pushes the results to the database.

In the previous code snippet, if the user changed a record with the first name Christopher, that record in the database would be updated to read Chris instead, no matter what the user actually changed the value to (because the UPDATE statement says so). If the user edited a different record, one without the first name Christopher, nothing would happen at all (because the WHERE clause in the UPDATE statement excludes those records).

This method is cumbersome. If you want to change any data, you have to change it in the DataSet manually first and then construct an appropriate SQL statement that pushes those changes to the database. This is quite time consuming and prone to mistakes.

Luckily, though, ADO.NET is a bit smarter than that. It provides an object, the SqlCommandBuilder, that will create all these SQL statements for you automatically. Thus, when the user changes a field in the DataGrid, you don't need to worry about the SQL statements that are executed. You just call the Update method, and you're done. To use this object, add the following line after line 17 in Listing 9.1:

```
SqlCommandBuilder objBuilder = new SqlCommandBuilder(objCmd);
```

This line creates an SqlCommandBuilder object for the SqlDataAdapter you've already created. The command builder object is now a watchdog; it watches everything that happens to the data and quickly generates the appropriate SQL statements, without any work on your part.

Let's make the data in Listing 9.1 editable. First, add a delegate to the CurrentCellChanged event of the DataGrid so that you know when the user is finished modifying a cell:

```
dgData.CurrentCellChanged += new EventHandler(this.UpdateData);
```

Then add the event handler, which simply calls the Update method of the SqlDataAdapter:

```
public void Update(Object Sender, EventArgs e) {
   objCmd.Update(objDS, "tblUsers");
}
```

As long as you've already created the SqlCommandBuilder, this statement pushes any changes made to the DataSet (via the DataGrid) back to the database, effectively making them permanent changes. The first parameter is the DataSet in question, and the second parameter is the DataTable in the DataSet where changes have been made.

Recompile and execute this application. Any changes you make to the data are now automatically pushed back to the database. To test this, change some data and then close the application. You can then either reopen the application to see that the changes have stuck or open the database application (SQL Server or Access, for instance) directly to see the changes.

 Caution

This method of using an `SqlCommandBuilder` object works only if the data you've returned contains a primary key. You set the `UserID` field to the primary key when building the `tblUsers` table. Conversely, you can set the primary key in code by using your `DataTable` object:

```
DataColumn[] arrKeys = {myTable.Columns["Column A"]};
myTable.PrimaryKey = arrKeys;
```

The `PrimaryKey` property of the `DataTable` takes an array of `DataColumn` objects, which is why you create an array in this code snippet.

Also, the `SelectCommand` must first be populated with an SQL SELECT statement as well.

Your database application is now fully functional. You can display data, allow users to edit it, and then update the database when necessary. Let's look at another example, shown in Listing 9.2, before we move on. This time, you won't use a `DataGrid` control to display your data, but rather some text boxes that display one data record at a time. You'll provide buttons that allow users to navigate the data records and a "save" button that allows them to push changes to the database.

LISTING 9.2   A More Complex Database Application

```
 1:  using System;
 2:  using System.Windows.Forms;
 3:  using System.Drawing;
 4:  using System.Data;
 5:  using System.Data.SqlClient;
 6:
 7:  namespace TYWinforms.Day9 {
 8:      public class Listing92 : Form {
 9:          DataSet objDS = new DataSet("tblUsers");
10:          SqlDataAdapter objCmd;
11:
12:          TextBox tbFirstName = new TextBox();
13:          TextBox tbLastName = new TextBox();
14:          Label lblFirstName = new Label();
15:          Label lblLastName = new Label();
16:          Button btNext = new Button();
17:          Button btPrev = new Button();
18:          Button btSave = new Button();
19:
```

LISTING 9.2 continued

```
20:         public Listing92() {
21:             lblFirstName.Location = new Point(10,10);
22:             lblFirstName.Text = "First Name:";
23:             lblLastName.Location = new Point(10,35);
24:             lblLastName.Text = "Last Name:";
25:             tbFirstName.Location = new Point(75,10);
26:             tbLastName.Location = new Point(75,30);
27:
28:             btNext.Text = "Next";
29:             btNext.Location = new Point(150,75);
30:             btNext.Click += new EventHandler(this.MoveNext);
31:
32:             btPrev.Text = "Previous";
33:             btPrev.Location = new Point(10,75);
34:             btPrev.Click += new EventHandler(this.MovePrev);
35:
36:             btSave.Text = "Save";
37:             btSave.Location = new Point(75,125);
38:             btSave.Click += new EventHandler(this.Save);
39:
40:             String strConn = "Initial Catalog=TYWinforms;Data
➥Source=localhost;User ID=sa";
41:             SqlConnection objConn = new SqlConnection
➥ (strConn);
42:
43:             objCmd = new SqlDataAdapter("SELECT * FROM
➥tblUsers", objConn);
44:             objCmd.Fill(objDS, "tblUsers");
45:             SqlCommandBuilder objBuilder = new
➥SqlCommandBuilder(objCmd);
46:
47:             tbFirstName.DataBindings.Add("Text", objDS,
➥"tblUsers.FirstName");
48:             tbLastName.DataBindings.Add("Text", objDS,
➥"tblUsers.LastName");
49:
50:         this.Controls.Add(tbFirstName);
51:         this.Controls.Add(tbLastName);
52:         this.Controls.Add(lblFirstName);
53:         this.Controls.Add(lblLastName);
54:         this.Controls.Add(btNext);
55:         this.Controls.Add(btPrev);
56:         this.Controls.Add(btSave);
57:         }
58:
59:     private void Save(Object Sender, EventArgs e) {
60:             this.BindingContext[objDS, "tblUsers"].
➥EndCurrentEdit();
61:
```

9

LISTING 9.2   continued

```
62:            objCmd.Update(objDS, "tblUsers");
63:        }
64:
65:        private void MoveNext(Object Sender, EventArgs e) {
66:            this.BindingContext[objDS, "tblUsers"].
➡Position += 1;
67:        }
68:
69:        private void MovePrev(Object Sender, EventArgs e) {
70:            this.BindingContext[objDS, "tblUsers"].
➡Position -= 1;
71:        }
72:
73:        public static void Main() {
74:            Application.Run(new Listing92());
75:        }
76:    }
77:  }
```

ANALYSIS   Listing 9.2 has a lot of complex functionality, so let's move through it line by line. On lines 1–5, you import namespaces. Lines 9–18 set up the various objects and controls you'll be using in your application. Lines 21–38 set up various properties of the controls on the forms and assign a few delegates, which we'll examine in a moment.

Beginning on line 40, you create the database connection using the same standard connection string. On lines 43 and 44, you use an SqlDataAdapter object to retrieve records from the database and then fill a DataSet. On line 45, you create your SqlCommandBuilder object to ensure that SQL commands are automatically generated when changes are made.

Next, on lines 47 and 48, you bind pieces of the returned data to the TextBox controls using their DataBindings properties. Recall that the three parameters for the Add method are, respectively, the property of the TextBox to bind to, the data source object, and the field in the data source to bind. The values tblUsers.FirstName and tblUsers.LastName indicate the first and last name columns in the tblUsers table. If you were binding to a DataGrid, you could simply use "tblUsers" as the field name, but with TextBoxes you have to be more specific. After all, you don't want to bind more than one column to a single text box.

Let's move to the event handlers. Both the MoveNext and MovePrev methods simply change the Position property of the BindingContext to move back and forth between records (lines 66 and 70). Note that you're manipulating the BindingContext of the Form instead of each bound `TextBox` individually. When you manipulate the form, all bound controls on the form are also modified.

Finally, before we examine the `Save` method on line 59, let's see what happens with the application. When you run the application, you see the first and last name of the first record in the database, as shown in Figure 9.9. You can click the Next button to move to the next record, at which point the text in the `TextBox` controls change. The Previous button moves back a record.

FIGURE 9.9

You see the first and last name when you bind data to `TextBox` *controls.*

ANALYSIS Something peculiar happens behind the scenes when you edit items. Theoretically, when you modify the value in one of the text boxes, it updates the `DataSet` immediately, and then you can call the `Update` method of the `SqlDataAdapter` to push those changes to the database. What actually happens, however, is that the changes are not made to the `DataSet` until the `BindingContext` commits them. This can happen in a number of places (changing the `Position` property is one of them).

Now you have a problem. Suppose the user changes the value in the First Name text box and then clicks the Save button. Because the `BindingContext` has not had a chance to commit the changes, the `DataSet` hasn't changed yet, and the database won't either. You need some way to force the `BindingContext` to commit the changes so you can save the changes.

The `EndCurrentEdit` method, on line 60, does just this. It pushes any pending changes to the `DataSet` without having to modify the `Position` property. Then you can simply call the `Update` method, as shown on line 62. Now your application is complete.

Using Other ADO.NET Objects

So far, you've used the `SqlDataAdapter` and `DataSet` objects to manipulate your data sources. These objects are great, and they provide everything you need to data-enable your applications. Sometimes, however, they're less than ideal.

The `DataSet`, for example, can be a cumbersome object to use because it must maintain a complete mini-database of information, including table structures, constraints, keys, relationships, and so on. Sometimes you don't need all these extra capabilities, and because they consume resources, why use them?

To address this problem, ADO.NET introduces the `SqlDataReader` and `OleDbDataReader` objects. These objects don't maintain their own copies of the database; rather, they retrieve only one record at a time and must maintain a constant connection to the database (unlike the `DataSet`, which is a disconnected data store). The `DataReader` objects therefore are limited in their functionality; you can't, for example, move back and forth between records without incurring costs to re-retrieve data.

To use a `DataReader` object, you first have to use the `SqlCommand` and `OleDbCommand` objects. These two objects, which represent an SQL command executed on a database, may or may not return results. Although you may not know it, you've actually already used these objects. When you assign anything to the `UpdateCommand`, `SelectCommand`, `DeleteCommand`, or `InsertCommand` properties of the `SqlDataAdapter`, .NET creates various `SqlCommand` objects for you. These behind-the-scenes objects actually query your database and return results; the `SqlDataAdapter` just takes the credit for their hard work.

You can create an `SqlCommand` object in several ways. You can pass it an SQL statement to execute, an SQL statement and an `SqlConnection` object, or simply nothing at all, depending on your needs. Here's an example:

```
SqlCommand objCmd = new SqlCommand("SELECT * FROM tblUsers");
//or
SqlCommand objCmd = new SqlCommand("SELECT * FROM tblUsers",
➥objConn);
//or
SqlCommand objCmd = new SqlCommand();
```

If you don't provide one or more of these values during the instantiation of the object, you can do so with the `CommandText` and `Connection` properties.

When you have your `SqlCommand` object, you can execute the SQL command a few different ways. If your query doesn't return any data (for instance, a `DELETE` statement), you can use the `ExecuteNonQuery` method:

```
SqlCommand objCmd = new SqlCommand("DELETE FROM tblUsers",
➥objConn);
objCmd.ExecuteNonQuery();
```

If your query returns a single value, you can use the `ExecuteScalar` method. This method retrieves the first column of the first row in the returned results, as in this example:

```
SqlCommand objCmd = new SqlCommand("SELECT COUNT(*) FROM
➥tblUsers", objConn);
int intCount = (int)objCmd.ExecuteScalar();
```

If you want to return your data as XML, you can use the `ExecuteXmlReader` method, which returns an `XmlReader` object. We'll examine this method in the "Using XML with ADO.NET" section later today.

Finally, if you want to manipulate the data using an `SqlDataReader` object, you can use the `ExecuteReader` method:

```
SqlDataReader objReader;
SqlCommand objCmd = new SqlCommand("SELECT * FROM tblUsers",
➥objConn);
objReader = objCmd.ExecuteReader();
```

The simple application in Listing 9.3 uses an `SqlDataReader` to display the results from a database.

LISTING 9.3   Using an `SqlDataReader`

```
 1:  using System;
 2:  using System.Windows.Forms;
 3:  using System.Drawing;
 4:  using System.Data;
 5:  using System.Data.SqlClient;
 6:
 7:  namespace TYWinforms.Day9 {
 8:     public class Listing93 : Form {
 9:        Label lblData = new Label();
10:
11:        public Listing93() {
12:           lblData.Dock = DockStyle.Fill;
13:
14:           String strConn = "Initial Catalog=TYWinforms;Data
➥Source=localhost;User ID=sa";
15:           SqlConnection objConn = new SqlConnection(strConn);
16:           objConn.Open();
17:
18:           SqlDataReader objReader;
```

LISTING 9.3   continued

```
19:            SqlCommand objCmd = new SqlCommand("SELECT UserID,
➥FirstName FROM tblUsers", objConn);
20:            objReader = objCmd.ExecuteReader();
21:
22:            while (objReader.Read()) {
23:                lblData.Text += objReader.GetInt32(0) + ": " +
➥objReader.GetString(1) + "\n";
24:            }
25:
26:            objReader.Close();
27:            objConn.Close();
28:
29:            this.Controls.Add(lblData);
30:        }
31:
32:        public static void Main() {
33:            Application.Run(new Listing93());
34:        }
35:    }
36: }
```

ANALYSIS   On lines 14 and 15, you start off normally creating an SqlConnection object. On line 16, however, you have to open the connection using the Open method. When you use the SqlDataAdapter, this step isn't required, but the SqlDataReader needs an open connection to function. Lines 18–20 create an SqlDataReader object and an SqlCommand object with an SQL query and then call the ExecuteReader method to place the results of the query in the reader.

The Read method of the SqlDataReader moves to the next record in the resultset, until the end is reached, at which point it returns false. Therefore, you use a while loop on line 22 to loop through all the records in the reader; when you reach the end of the records, the while loop exits.

The SqlDataReader object has a series of Get methods that retrieve the values from the resultset. The exact method you use depends on the data type you're expecting. For example, the GetString method returns a string value, and GetInt32 returns an integer value. All these methods take a single parameter that indicates which field (or column) of the current record to return. On line 23, you retrieve the first and second column values for each record, which happen to be the UserID and FirstName fields from the tblUsers table.

After all the records have been traversed, make sure to close the reader and the SqlConnection objects by using their respective Close methods, as shown on lines 26 and 27.

Listing 9.3 produces the output shown in Figure 9.10.

FIGURE 9.10

*You can loop through
records with the
`SqlDataReader`
object.*

<table>
<tr><td>Do</td><td>Don't</td></tr>
<tr>
<td>Do use an <code>SqlDataReader</code> when you simply need to display data or don't need to manipulate it.</td>
<td>Don't use the <code>SqlDataReader</code> when you want to allow the user to modify data or when you need to perform more complex operations on it (such as manipulating table relationships). Use the <code>SqlDataAdapter</code> and <code>DataSet</code> instead.</td>
</tr>
</table>

Parameterized Queries and Stored Procedures

A stored procedure is a series of one or more SQL statements that is predefined outside your application. It resides in the database along with the tables. Often you'll want to use stored procedures for your database interactions. They are faster than regular SQL statements because they are compiled. They also make your application easier to maintain; when your data requirements change, updating the stored procedures is much easier than rewriting the queries inside your application and recompiling.

> **Note**
>
> In Access, stored procedures are known as *queries;* they use slightly different syntax than the ones in SQL Server. We'll focus on SQL Server stored procedures in this book.

To create a stored procedure in SQL Server, open Enterprise Manager and expand the list of databases until you see the Stored Procedures section under the TYWinforms database. Right-click and select New Stored Procedure. For now, keep it simple; type the following code into the window that pops up:

```
CREATE PROCEDURE qryGetUser
( @intUserID int )
 AS
SELECT * FROM tblUsers WHERE UserID = @intUserID
```

Your window should look like the one in Figure 9.11.

FIGURE 9.11

Use this window to create a stored procedure in SQL Server.

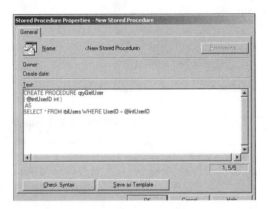

This query returns all the information for a specific user, as indicated by the user ID. The nifty part of this query is that the user ID can vary; the query accepts a parameter called `@intUserID` that your application must supply to retrieve the proper results. Let's see how to supply this parameter.

All parameters must be a part of an `SqlCommand` object (which means you can use either an `SqlDataAdapter` and `DataSet` or an `SqlDataReader` to retrieve your data). Using the `qryGetUser` stored procedure created earlier, the following code snippet creates an `SqlCommand` with the necessary parameters:

```
SqlCommand objQuery = new SqlCommand("qryGetUser", objConn);
objQuery.CommandType = CommandType.StoredProcedure;
objQuery.Parameters.Add("@intUserID", SqlDbType.Int, 4).
➥Value = 1;
```

The declaration of the `SqlCommand` object starts out as normal, except that instead of passing it the SQL statement to execute, you pass the name of the stored procedure. On the second line, you must set the `CommandType` property to the `StoredProcedure` value of the `CommandType` enumeration. Other values in this enumeration are `Text` (the default value, used when passing an SQL statement), and `TableDirect`, which simply returns a table's structure (this last value works only with the OLE DB provider).

Finally, you add a new parameter to the `Parameters` property of the `SqlCommand` object. The first parameter to the `Add` method is the name of the expected parameter in the stored procedure; it must be the same name used in the stored procedure. The second parameter indicates the type of data the parameter is; Table 9.4 lists the possible values of the `SqlDbType` enumeration. Finally, the third value indicates the size (this value was set when creating the table; it doesn't have to be exact). Then, using the `Value` property, you set the value that the stored procedure parameter should use. In this case, you end up returning the information for the user with the user ID of 1.

TABLE 9.4 `SqlDbType` Enumeration Values

SqlDbType *Value*	*Corresponding .NET Type*
BigInt	Int64
Binary	Array of type Byte
Bit	Boolean
Char	String
DateTime	DateTime
Decimal	Decimal
Float	Double
Image	Array of type Byte
Int	Int32
Money	Decimal
NChar	String
NText	String
NVarChar	String
Real	Single
SmallDateTime	DateTime
SmallInt	Int16
SmallMoney	Decimal
Text	String
Timestamp	DateTime
TinyInt	Byte
UniqueIdentifier	Guid
VarBinary	Array of type Byte
VarChar	String
Variant	Object

Now that you have your `SqlCommand` object with parameters, you can do with it as you like. For example, to return an `SqlDataReader`, use the following code:

```
SqlDataReader objReader;
objReader = objQuery.ExecuteReader();
```

If you want to populate a `DataSet`, use the following code:

```
DataSet objDS = new DataSet();
SqlDataAdapter objCmd = new SqlDataAdapter();
objCmd.SelectCommand = objQuery;
objCmd.Fill(objDS, "tblUsers");
```

In this latter code snippet, you simply assign the `SqlCommand` object you created to the `SelectCommand` property of the `SqlDataAdapter`. Depending on what the stored procedure actually does, you could have set any of the `UpdateCommand`, `InsertCommand`, or `DeleteCommand` properties instead.

Alternatively, with the `SqlDataAdapter`, you don't necessarily need to create a separate `SqlCommand` object. You can reference the necessary command from the `SelectCommand` property:

```
SqlDataAdapter objCmd = new SqlDataAdapter("qryGetUser",
➥objConn);
objCmd.SelectCommand.CommandType = CommandType.StoredProcedure;
objCmd.SelectCommand.Parameters.Add("@intUserID", SqlDbType.Int,
➥4).Value = 1;
```

The `DataView` Object

A `DataView` is a customized view of a `DataTable`. That means you can take an existing `DataTable` filled with data and filter it according to your needs. This capability provides you with much more flexibility than simply changing your `DataTable` because you don't have to keep requerying the database when you want filtered data. You also can bind the `DataView` to your Windows Forms controls.

Creating a `DataView` is easy; you simply tell it the table to customize:

```
DataView myView = new DataView(objDS.Tables["tblUsers"]);
```

You can then use the `RowFilter` property to filter the results; this property essentially acts like another WHERE clause for your SQL statement. For example, the following statement would cause only those records where the `FirstName` field contains the word `"Christopher"` to be displayed:

```
myView.RowFilter = "FirstName = 'Christopher'";
```

The Sort property of the DataView, which allows you to change the sorting order of the data, follows the same syntax as the ORDER BY clause in SQL statements:

```
myView.Sort = "FirstName ASC, LastName DESC";
```

The RowStateFilter property filters records depending on their current state, such as if they have been edited, are unchanged, have been added, and so on:

```
myView.RowStateFilter = DataViewRowState.Unchanged;
```

These values can be combined using the | operator (OR in Visual Basic .NET), similar to the Anchor property for controls. The possible values in the DataViewRowState enumeration are

- Added—Indicates that the row is new
- CurrentRows—Includes unchanged, new, and modified rows
- Deleted—Specifies a deleted row
- ModifiedCurrent—Indicates the current value of all rows after any row is modified
- ModifiedOriginal—Specifies the original values of all rows after any row is modified
- None—Specifies rows with no state
- OriginalRows—Specifies all original rows, including unchanged and deleted rows
- Unchanged—Specifies an unchanged row

Finally, you can control how the user interacts with the DataView by using the AllowDelete, AllowEdit, and AllowNew properties.

Note Because the DataView requires a DataTable object to work from, you cannot use a DataView with the SqlDataReader object. Instead, use the DataSet and SqlDataAdapter objects.

Using XML with ADO.NET

As mentioned earlier in the chapter, ADO.NET and XML are tightly integrated. ADO.NET uses XML in all its transactions, which makes it more versatile and efficient. Thus, you can easily go from ADO.NET's core object, the DataSet, to XML, and vice versa; in fact, you may smirk at just how easy this process is.

Most of the XML-related functions that you'll want to perform with ADO.NET can be accomplished with two methods: ReadXml and GetXml. The first loads XML from any XML-based object (such as a text file, a stream, XML document, and so on) and places the results in a DataSet. The second method, conversely, takes the data from a DataSet and returns a string containing the XML representing the data. It's that easy!

Let's look at an example. Listing 9.4 shows the XML snippet from the beginning of this chapter.

LISTING 9.4   Sample XML Data

```
 1:  <Users>
 2:  <User>
 3:     <Name>Chris Payne</Name>
 4:     <UserID>1</UserID>
 5:     <Birthdate>June 27</Birthdate>
 6:  </User>
 7:  <User>
 8:     <Name>Eva Payne</Name>
 9:     <UserID>2</UserID>
10:     <Birthdate>July 15</Birthdate>
11:  </User>
12:  </Users>
```

Save Listing 9.4 as Sample.xml in the c:\winforms\data directory. This XML essentially presents a database named Users, with a table named User. This table has three columns in it: Name (lines 3 and 8), UserID (lines 4 and 9), and Birthdate (lines 5 and 10). Next, Listing 9.5 shows a simple application that loads and binds the XML data.

LISTING 9.5   Binding XML Data with ADO.NET

```
 1:  using System;
 2:  using System.Windows.Forms;
 3:  using System.Drawing;
 4:  using System.Data;
 5:  using System.Data.SqlClient;
 6:
 7:  namespace TYWinforms.Day9 {
 8:     public class Listing95 : Form {
 9:        DataSet objDS = new DataSet();
10:
11:        TextBox tbName = new TextBox();
12:        TextBox tbBirthDate = new TextBox();
13:        Label lblName = new Label();
14:        Label lblBirthDate = new Label();
```

LISTING 9.5   continued

```
15:
16:         public Listing95() {
17:             lblName.Location = new Point(10,10);
18:             lblName.Text = "Name:";
19:             lblBirthDate.Location = new Point(10,35);
20:             lblBirthDate.Text = "Birth Date:";
21:             tbName.Location = new Point(75,10);
22:             tbBirthDate.Location = new Point(75,30);
23:
24:             objDS.ReadXml("c:\\winforms\\data\\sample.xml");
25:
26:             tbName.DataBindings.Add("Text", objDS,
➥"User.Name");
27:             tbBirthDate.DataBindings.Add("Text", objDS,
➥"User.Birthdate");
28:
29:             this.Controls.Add(tbName);
30:             this.Controls.Add(tbBirthDate);
31:             this.Controls.Add(lblName);
32:             this.Controls.Add(lblBirthDate);
33:         }
34:
35:         public static void Main() {
36:             Application.Run(new Listing95());
37:         }
38:     }
39:  }
```

ANALYSIS   Most of the code in Listing 9.5 simply initializes the user interface. The interesting part starts on line 24, where you use the ReadXml method to load a file. The parameter indicates the path to the XML file in question. Then, on lines 26 and 27, you bind the two TextBox controls, just like normal. Just make sure that the third parameter properly reflects the structure of the XML document. Listing 9.5 produces the output shown in Figure 9.12.

What happens when the data is updated? Can you call the Update method to write changes back to the XML document? Unfortunately, no. The only way to update the XML data source is to explicitly write an XML file, but luckily, this process is easy. First, create an XmlDataDocument object to retrieve the XML from the DataSet and then use the Save method of the XmlDataDocument object to write the file:

```
using System.Xml;
...
XmlDataDocument objXml = new XmlDataDocument(objDS);
objXml.Save("c:\\winforms\\data\\sample2.xml");
```

FIGURE 9.12

You can use the
application in Listing
9.5 to bind XML
data.

An `XmlDataDocument` object is the equivalent of the `SqlDataAdapter` in the world of XML. In fact, this object and the `DataSet` are related, so you can easily move from one to the other. The first line in the preceding code snippet instantiates a new `XmlDataDocument` object, passing it the `DataSet` in question. The `Save` method then writes the XML to the path specified.

The `XmlDataDocument` has quite a few other useful members that we won't discuss here. For a more complete reference, see the .NET Framework SDK documentation.

Summary

Because ADO.NET is a huge topic, many books have been dedicated solely to it. Thankfully, though, you can easily start using it. It adds tremendous capabilities to your applications, with just a little bit of extra code.

Today you learned quite a bit about databases, from creating them in both Access and SQL Server, to using parameterized stored procedures, to using XML. ADO.NET allows access to nearly any database system using a simple connection string that indicates where the data store is located, the permissions necessary to use it, and so on.

You also learned about SQL statements such as SELECT, INSERT, DELETE, and UPDATE. These statements allow you to retrieve and manipulate data from any database system that supports them (which is virtually every major commercial product out there nowadays). Each statement follows a similar syntax, so you can easily learn them all after you know one.

The `DataSet` is the central object of ADO.NET; it represents a complete mini-database, including tables, rows, constraints, and relationships. When the `DataSet` is coupled with the `SqlDataAdapter` or `OleDbDataAdapter` objects and databinding, you can easily present data to the user. The `SqlDataAdapter`'s `Update` method, when coupled with the `SqlCommandBuilder` object, allows you to send changes back to the database to make them permanent.

In addition to the `DataSet`, you learned about the `DataReader` objects, which are more efficient but have fewer capabilities. These objects can be populated using the `ExecuteReader` method of the `SqlCommand` object.

The `DataView` object allows you to customize the display of your `DataTable` objects efficiently, saving you the trouble of having to execute SQL statements over and over again when you need to filter data.

Finally, you learned how ADO.NET and the `DataSet` can load and manipulate XML data as well, using the `ReadXml` and `GetXml` methods. This data can be bound just like any other data, and changes can be written back to the XML files using the `Save` method of the `XmlDataDocument` object.

Tomorrow you'll look at creating multiple document interface applications, or applications with multiple user interface windows. These types of applications are everywhere you look, so it's a good idea to learn about them!

Q&A

Q Can I use the ADO recordset with ADO.NET and the `DataSet`?

A You bet! You can use the `Fill` method to fill a `DataSet` with data from a recordset, but not the other way around, due to limitations in ADO. This process requires importing the ADO type libraries into the .NET Framework. This topic is explained further on Day 14, "Using ActiveX."

Q Why are stored procedures more efficient than regular SQL statements? Should I *always* use stored procedures instead?

A Stored procedures are more efficient for two reasons. First, they are compiled, and compiled applications are always faster than their non-compiled counterparts. Second, SQL Server has what is known as an *execution plan*. After the first time a stored procedure is executed, SQL Server knows where exactly to look for the data and how best to retrieve it. This execution plan greatly increases the speed of query execution. The problem is that for regular queries, this execution plan isn't saved, and thus SQL Server must re-create it the next time the query is executed.

Whether you should always use stored procedures over regular queries is a subjective question. Some people say absolutely yes, whereas others disagree. The choice is really up to you, but there are a few guidelines to help you make the decision. In general, use a stored procedure if

- Your query is more than a very simple SELECT statement. (The more complex an SQL statement, the larger the performance impact, especially when an execution plan is unavailable.)

- You know that the query may change sometime in the future due to data model changes.

- The query is executed often, more than one or two times per use of the application.

- You're dealing with large sets of data.

Q Can I bind the data in an `SqlDataReader`?

A Unfortunately, no. Because the `SqlDataReader` can retrieve only one record at a time from the data source, you cannot bind it. This is the main reason you should stick with a `DataSet` if you need to allow the user to modify data.

Workshop

This workshop will help reinforce the concepts covered in today's lesson. It is very helpful to understand fully the answers before moving on. Answers to the quiz questions and exercises are in Appendix A.

Quiz

1. Write a `SELECT` statement that retrieves only those records from the `tblUsers` table where the `UserID` field is between 5 and 10.

2. What does the `SqlCommandBuilder` object require as a parameter to its constructor?

3. An `SqlCommandBuilder` will generate SQL commands automatically only if a primary key is present. Why?

4. True or False: Most of the time, you can simply change the prefix `Sql` to `OleDb` to use the objects in the OLE DB provider.

5. Is it enough to set the `DataSource` property of a `DataGrid` to a filled `DataSet`?

6. Given an `SqlCommand` object named `objCmd`, write a statement that adds a parameter named `"@BirthDate"` with a value of `"1/7/01"`.

7. What method causes changes to be pushed immediately to a `DataSet`?

Exercise

Create an application that allows a user to enter SQL statements in a text box. If the statement returns results, place them in a DataGrid and allow it to be editable. Don't worry if the query is entered in a proper format; error checking will be covered later in Day 21, "Debugging Your Windows Forms."

9

DAY 10

Creating MDI Applications

So far, you've created only single document interface (SDI) applications; that is, they have only one interface that the user interacts with. With a multiple document interface (MDI), the user can work with multiple copies of the same interface at the same time, which can often boost productivity. Many applications nowadays are MDI applications, including Microsoft Excel, Visual Studio, SQL Server Query Analyzer, and others (until version 2000, Microsoft Word used to be MDI as well).

Today you'll learn how to create MDI applications. Learning the basics is simple, but manipulating all these interfaces at once takes a bit of finesse.

Today you'll learn

- What MDI is and how it helps you
- How to create an Excel type interface
- How to handle menus and events for multiple documents at once
- How to make your MDI documents communicate with each other

Introduction to the Multiple Document Interface

The best way to learn what an MDI application means and represents is to use one. Figure 10.1 shows the MDI features of Microsoft Excel in action, and Figure 10.2 shows Adobe Photoshop.

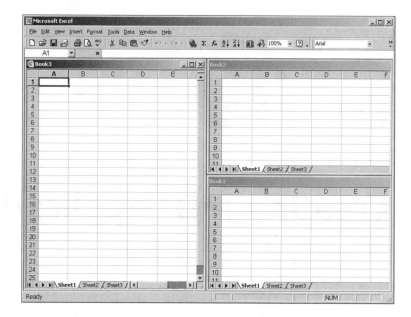

If Excel were an SDI application, you could work with only one document at a time; you could not have three documents open at once as shown in Figure 10.1. Each interface, or document, is self-contained and is independent from the others; anything you do in one doesn't affect the others. Each document can maintain its own set of data, objects, parameters, and so on.

An MDI application has several benefits over regular SDI applications. The first is obvious: increased productivity for your users. Theoretically, a user could get more work done with two windows open than with one; that's the whole theory behind a multitasking operating system. If it were more productive to use a single application or document at a time, the Windows operating system may have never evolved.

MDI applications are useful for data analysis programs, such as Excel. With more than one document open, and consequently more than one set of data to work with, users can more easily analyze and compare data. After all, how many times have you compared two charts or tables against each other? An MDI application is ideal for this situation.

FIGURE 10.2

Photoshop provides a different type of MDI.

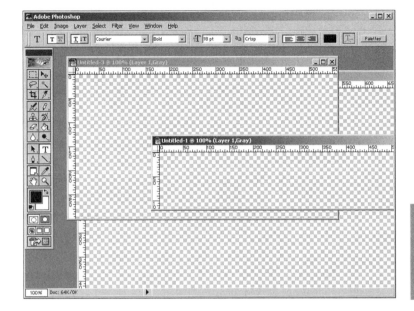

MDI applications also allow you to provide more useful information to a user. For example, consider Visual Studio. It has multiple windows that each provide different bits of information: One displays the properties of the current object, one displays the hierarchy of Windows Forms controls used on a form, and another one displays the code for the form. With multiple windows that each provide different facets of an application, a user can more easily get work done. (Such an application would be ideal, for instance, for a stock day trader!)

A single document in an MDI application can be maximized to cover up all other documents. In this way, it almost behaves as an SDI application; the menus even merge to reflect a single, open window. This flexibility allows the user to choose the type of environment she works in.

MDI applications have their drawbacks, however. Often most significant is usage of resources. The more documents you have open at once, the more computing resources you consume, which can adversely affect your application, as well as the rest of Windows. This is especially relevant in applications such as Photoshop, where each document can contain very large images, sometimes tens of megabytes in size.

Finally, some applications are just not suited for life as an MDI. The CD cataloging application you developed earlier in this book is one example. There is simply no reason for it to be an MDI. After all, you're working with only one CD collection; MDI may even serve to confuse users in this case. MDI introduces a level of complexity both to the end user and the developer that may be entirely avoidable.

Note

A distinction must be made between an MDI application and the multitasking environment of Windows. The former allows multiple interfaces to be contained in a single application. The latter allows multiple instances of the application to run at once, effectively providing multiple interfaces by brute force. For example, just because you have three Internet Explorer windows open at once doesn't mean Internet Explorer is an MDI.

MDI Menus

An interesting feature about MDI applications is the way they deal with menus. Traditional menus are mostly static; the available menus and options don't change (although Microsoft Office 2000 and later versions try to convince you they do). You have the same menu options no matter what you're doing in your application.

With MDI, each window can have its own set of menus. This feature allows you to perform certain actions on only the current document. Depending on what you're doing in the application, the menus may change.

The application as a whole can also have its own menus that can apply to all the documents. For example, you've probably seen a Window menu in most MDI applications. This menu often provides options to organize all the open documents, by cascading or tiling them, for instance.

When the different documents are selected, menu items may merge with each other so they don't show up more than once. This behavior is completely controllable, as you'll see later today.

Creating an MDI Application

To create an MDI application, you need, at a minimum, two things. First, you need a main, or parent, window to house all the other open documents. This parent should have very few user interface elements; most of them will be contained in the other documents. The parent is a class that inherits from the System.Windows.Forms.Form class just like all your other forms applications.

Second, you need a class that defines the child documents. This one also inherits from System.Windows.Forms.Form, but it should contain all the UI that is necessary for your application. As with custom dialog classes (see Day 7, "Working with Dialog Boxes"), you also don't need a Main method in the child document.

Let's look at a simple example of parent and child forms. First, Listing 10.1 shows the child document class.

LISTING 10.1   Your MDI Child

```
1:  using System;
2:  using System.Windows.Forms;
3:  using System.Drawing;
4:
5:  namespace TYWinforms.Day10 {
6:     public class Document : Form {
7:        private Button btClick = new Button();
8:
9:        public Document() {
10:           btClick.Text = "Close Me!";
11:           btClick.Location = new Point(100,100);
12:           btClick.Click += new EventHandler(this.Close);
13:
14:           this.Controls.Add(btClick);
15:        }
16:
17:        private void Close(Object Sender, EventArgs e) {
18:           this.Close();
19:        }
20:     }
21:  }
```

There's nothing special about the Document class in Listing 10.1; it looks just like every other Windows Forms application, except that it doesn't have a Main method. Notice the one control on the form (line 7), Button, that closes the form when clicked (line 18). Also, note the name of the class, Document. This information will be important in the MDI parent. Now let's look at the MDI parent, shown in Listing 10.2.

LISTING 10.2   The MDI Parent

```
1:  using System;
2:  using System.Windows.Forms;
3:  using System.Drawing;
4:
5:  namespace TYWinforms.Day10 {
6:     public class Listing102 : Form {
7:        public Listing102() {
8:           this.IsMdiContainer = true;
9:
10:          Document doc = new Document();
11:          doc.MdiParent = this;
```

LISTING 10.2 continued

```
12:         }
13:
14:         public static void Main() {
15:             Application.Run(new Listing102());
16:         }
17:     }
18: }
```

ANALYSIS The Listing102 class in Listing 10.2 is even simpler in terms of the number of code lines. Three lines here apply to MDI: lines 8, 10, and 11.

Line 8 uses the IsMdiContainer property to indicate that this form should be able to contain other, child, documents. This property is inherited from the System.Windows.Forms.Form object, so you can make any Windows Forms application an MDI just by setting this property to true.

Next, you create a new instance of the Document class created in Listing 10.1. On line 11, you tell this new object who its daddy is, so to speak. You set the MdiParent property to the current form, as indicated by the this (Me in Visual Basic .NET) keyword. This property is also inherited, so any Windows Forms application can also be the child of an MDI. When you compile and run this application, you end up with the form shown in Figure 10.3.

FIGURE 10.3

Your first MDI application should look like this.

You can see that you now have a parent form, which is simply a container for the child document. You can then manipulate the child document however you want—resize it, maximize or minimize it, and so on. If you click the button created in Listing 10.1, the child document will close, and you'll be left with the empty parent form.

You can use lines 10 and 11 over and over again to create new child documents. Often, you'll put this code in a menu item event handler so that the user can control when to add new documents. Let's add this functionality, as well as the ability to number the child documents. To do so, modify the constructor of Listing 10.1 slightly to look like the following code snippet:

```
public Document(String strName) {
   this.Text = strName;
   ...
```

This new constructor takes a string that is assigned to the caption of the form. In Listing 10.2, then, you need to add a variable that keeps track of the number of documents and the menu objects. Modify Listing 10.2 so that it looks like the following:

```
public class Listing102 : Form {
   private int intCounter = 0;
   private MainMenu mnuMain = new MainMenu();

   public Listing102() {
      MenuItem miFile = mnuMain.MenuItems.Add("&File");
      MenuItem miNew = miFile.MenuItems.Add("&New");
      miNew.Click += new EventHandler(this.HandleMenu);
      this.Menu = mnuMain;
      ...
```

The intCounter variable will be incremented every time the user opens a new document; this number will be an easy way to reference each new child document. The File menu is a standard menu with a New menu item that will cause a new document to open.

Next, move the old lines 10 and 11 from Listing 10.2 into a new method, the event handler for the New menu item, as shown in the following code snippet:

```
public void HandleMenu(Object Sender, EventArgs e) {
   intCounter++;

   Document doc = new Document("Document " + intCounter.ToString());
   doc.MdiParent = this;
   doc.Show();
}
```

This code takes advantage of the modified constructor of the Document class you made earlier. It passes a string to the new class that will become its title. Don't forget to call the Show method to display the new child document; this step wasn't necessary when this code was in the class's constructor, but it is otherwise. Now recompile this application and try the New menu item. Figure 10.4 shows the output with several child documents.

FIGURE 10.4

The user can control how many windows to open.

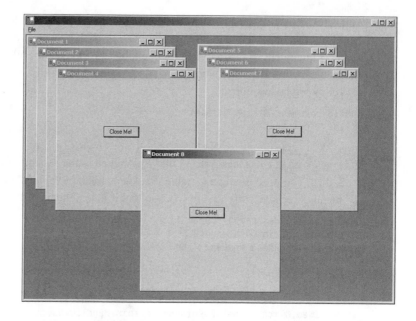

Theoretically, you could open new windows ad infinitum. If you ever wanted to limit the number of open windows, however, you could simply check the intCounter variable before creating a new document. If the number is above your threshold, don't create a new Document object.

Notice also that each new document has a user-friendly caption associated with it: Document 1, Document 2, and so on. When you maximize one of the child windows, the title, however, disappears. To remedy this situation, set a caption for the parent MDI form:

```
this.Text = "Listing 10.2";
```

Now when you maximize the windows, the parent's caption will change from "Listing 10.2" to reflect the appropriate child window: "Listing 10.2—Document 1," "Listing 10.2—Document 2," and so on. .NET handles much of the complexity involved with dealing with multiple child windows, but wait, there's more!

Menus are also handled automatically for you. If a child document has a menu associated with it, the menu bar of the parent form will change to reflect the current, or active, child document. Let's add a simple menu to the Document class to allow the user to change the background color of the form; we'll use the common ColorDialog dialog box for this application. First, add the menu, as shown in the following code snippet:

```
private MainMenu mnuMain = new MainMenu();
public Document(String strName) {
   MenuItem miFormat = mnuMain.MenuItems.Add("Format " +
➥strName);
   MenuItem miColor = miFormat.MenuItems.Add("&Color...");
   miColor.Click += new EventHandler(this.HandleMenu);
   this.Menu = mnuMain;
   ...
```

Note that the name of the menu is set to reflect the name of the child document. This naming convention will help you keep track of the active window. Next, add the event handler for the menu:

```
private void HandleMenu(Object Sender, EventArgs e) {
   ColorDialog dlgColor = new ColorDialog();

   if (dlgColor.ShowDialog() == DialogResult.OK) {
      this.BackColor = dlgColor.Color;
   }
}
```

Revisit Day 7 to refresh your memory on common dialog controls. Essentially, this method displays the ColorDialog control, and if the user selects a color and clicks the OK button, the background color of that particular child form changes.

Now when you run the application, notice first that the menu you added to the child document is displayed on the parent form's menu bar. Placing the menu here helps to avoid clutter. Second, notice that the menu caption changes when you click on different child documents, to reflect the active child. Then, when all child windows are closed, the new Format menu disappears.

Before we move on, let's examine one more common feature of MDI applications: window arrangement. Nearly all MDI applications have a standard Window menu that allows you to arrange the child windows in an easier-to-follow order within the parent window. These windows also usually contain a list of all the open child windows so that you can select one to quickly switch to it rather than wade through all the windows you have open trying to find a particular one.

Let's examine the different ways windows can be laid out:

- Cascading—Windows are placed on top of each other, with just enough offset to show the title bar of the window underneath.
- Tiled horizontally—Windows are arranged so that they don't overlap. The windows each take up the entire height of the parent form but divide the width of the window evenly among themselves.

10

- Tiled vertically—Similar to being tiled horizontally, but in this layout, the windows have a vertical orientation. Windows take up the entire width of the parent but divide the height among each other evenly.

These layouts are defined in the MdiLayout enumeration as MdiLayout.Cascade, MdiLayout.TileHorizontal, and MdiLayout.TileVertical. The LayoutMdi method of the Form object can use these values to arrange windows accordingly. Let's once again modify the application to take advantage of these layouts. Listing 10.3 shows the new version of Listing 10.2, complete with all the changes you've been making.

LISTING 10.3   The Completed MDI Parent Form

```
1:   using System;
2:   using System.Windows.Forms;
3:   using System.Drawing;
4:
5:   namespace TYWinforms.Day10 {
6:      public class Listing102 : Form {
7:         private int intCounter = 0;
8:         private MainMenu mnuMain = new MainMenu();
9:
10:        public Listing102() {
11:           MenuItem miFile = mnuMain.MenuItems.Add("&File");
12:           MenuItem miNew = miFile.MenuItems.Add("&New");
13:           MenuItem miWindow = mnuMain.MenuItems.Add
➥("&Window");
14:           miWindow.MenuItems.Add("Cascade", new
➥EventHandler(this.ArrangeWindows));
15:           miWindow.MenuItems.Add("Tile Horizontal",
➥new EventHandler(this.ArrangeWindows));
16:           miWindow.MenuItems.Add("Tile Vertical", new
➥EventHandler(this.ArrangeWindows));
17:
18:           miNew.Click += new EventHandler(this.HandleMenu);
19:           miWindow.MdiList = true;
20:
21:           this.IsMdiContainer = true;
22:           this.Menu = mnuMain;
23:           this.Size = new Size(800,600);
24:           this.Text = "Listing 10.2";
25:        }
26:
27:        private void ArrangeWindows(Object Sender,
➥EventArgs e) {
28:           MenuItem miTemp = (MenuItem)Sender;
29:
30:           switch (miTemp.Text) {
31:              case "Cascade":
```

LISTING 10.3 continued

```
32:                         this.LayoutMdi(MdiLayout.Cascade);
33:                         break;
34:                     case "Tile Horizontal":
35:                         this.LayoutMdi(MdiLayout.TileHorizontal);
36:                         break;
37:                     case "Tile Vertical":
38:                         this.LayoutMdi(MdiLayout.TileVertical);
39:                         break;
40:                 }
41:             }
42:
43:         private void HandleMenu(Object Sender,
➥EventArgs e) {
44:             intCounter++;
45:
46:             Document doc = new Document("Document " +
➥intCounter.ToString());
47:             doc.MdiParent = this;
48:             doc.Show();
49:         }
50:
51:         public static void Main() {
52:             Application.Run(new Listing102());
53:         }
54:     }
55: }
```

ANALYSIS Most of Listing 10.3 should look familiar. The new Window menu code is on lines 13–16. You first create the Window menu and then three submenu items for each of the window layout options. Notice that they all point to the same event handler, `ArrangeWindows`.

Next, on line 19, you set the `MdiList` property of the new Window menu to `true` to tell your application that this menu is intended to control child MDI windows. Essentially, this menu will automatically add and remove menu items that reflect the child documents you have open. When these dynamic menu items are clicked, the appropriate child window will gain focus for the user input.

Let's skip down to the `ArrangeWindows` method on line 27. You want to determine which window-layout menu item was clicked and arrange the children accordingly. First, you cast the `Sender` variable (which, as you may recall, represents the object that generated the event) to a `MenuItem` so that you can use the necessary properties and methods. The `switch` statement evaluates the caption of the `MenuItem` that was clicked and calls the `LayoutMdi` function supplying one of the `MdiLayout` enumeration values.

Now compile and execute this application. Note that when you add new documents, the Window menu changes dynamically to reflect the new windows. Try clicking the different layout options to test them. Figure 10.5 shows one example.

FIGURE 10.5

Horizontal tiling is only one of your layout options.

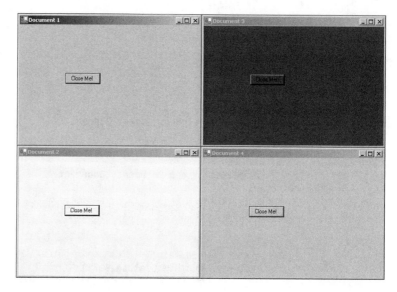

Creating Different Types of Child Windows

So far, you've created MDI applications that have multiple instances of the same child document. You are not, however, required to create your applications this way; each child document can be a completely different type of object, as long as they each inherit from the System.Windows.Forms.Form class. Let's build a useful example.

Many applications (such as Visual Studio) provide "toolbars" or "property windows" that you can move around onscreen. These windows are in addition to the main user interface, which is usually a place to type data, and they provide helpful functionality that may not be easily accessible otherwise.

Be aware, though, that often what you intend to do with a child MDI document may be better suited for a custom modeless dialog box. Each method has its advantages, so be sure to weigh your options before you commit to the complexity of MDI.

Do	**Don't**
Do use MDI and child documents when you don't want to clutter up the user's desktop and where the user can easily scroll to see otherwise hidden portions of child documents (for example, Microsoft Excel).	**Don't** use MDI when you need a window that can affect multiple child documents at once. One example is a window with buttons that can insert text into the active child automatically for the user. In this case, if you used an MDI child document, you couldn't insert the text into the active child because the active child would be the window with buttons; you would lose your reference to the intended target of this operation. The "Handling Children" section later today addresses this issue further.

10

Controlling the Specifics of MDI Forms

There's really not much to creating an MDI application. To create the bare minimum functionality, you have to add only a few lines of code (assuming you already have your child document class).

Under the surface, though, there's a bit more to controlling MDI applications than meets the eye. In the next few sections, you'll learn how to control those elements that most people take for granted, such as the combination of menu items.

Dealing with Menus

NEW TERM   Normally, when both the parent and child documents have associated menus, the parent's menu bar changes when that child is active. This is known as *menu merging*; the menus of the child and parent merge into one menu bar. When the different menus are unique, merging occurs without a hiccup, as you noticed earlier today. The process becomes more interesting, however, when you have duplicate menu items.

Let's see what happens in such a situation. Add the following code to the constructor of the Document class in Listing 10.1:

```
MenuItem miFile = mnuMain.MenuItems.Add("File");
```

Now both the parent and child forms have a File menu. Compile and run this application. When you open a new child document, you end up with the windows shown in Figure 10.6.

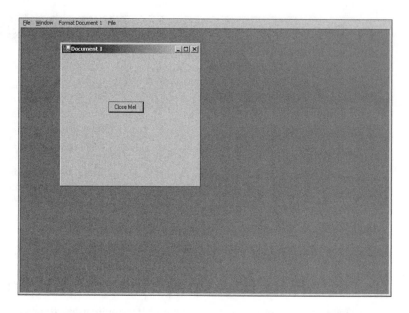

FIGURE 10.6

The application now has two File menus.

The menus of the parent and child windows merged, and now you have two File menus! This, obviously, is not what you want to happen. Somehow, you have to let the application know that the two File menus are the same menu and that their contents should be combined.

Thankfully, you have the MenuMerge enumeration to help you. Table 10.1 describes the values of this enumeration.

TABLE 10.1   MenuMerge Enumeration Values

Value	Description
Add	This is the default behavior. A child menu item will be added to the parent menu bar whether or not one already exists (this results in the "double File menu" problem).
MergeItems	All submenus of this MenuItem will be merged with those of the parent menu that have the same place in the menu.
Remove	This MenuItem will not be used in a merge; it will be dropped and not appear in the combined menu bar.
Replace	This MenuItem will replace any existing MenuItems with the same place in the menu. The child always takes precedence over the parent menu item. Use this value when you want to override the event handlers for a particular menu item.

For all except the `Remove` value to work, all `MenuItems` need to have a `MenuMerge` value assigned—meaning both parent and child forms. To assign it, add the following line to both Listing 10.1 and Listing 10.2:

```
miFile.MergeType = MenuMerge.MergeItems;
```

Now when you run the application and create a child document, only one File menu appears. Now, try adding the following line to Listing 10.1; it simply adds a submenu item to the child's File menu:

```
MenuItem miNew = miFile.MenuItems.Add("New");
```

Try running the application again. What happens when you create a child document? The File menus merge, but now you have two New menu items. To remedy this problem, you can either specify `MergeType = MenuMerge.Replace` in both listings, which would result in the child menu item replacing the parent menu item, or specify `MergeType = MenuMerge.Remove` in either listing.

10

> **Caution**
>
> The menu item that remains is the one in the class *opposite* the class you specify `MenuMerge.Remove` in. For example, if you specify `Remove` in the parent class, the child's menu item is the one to appear in the menu bar, and its functionality is executed when clicked.

Note that the whole merging issue applies to items that have the same place in the menu. For example, suppose you have a parent document menu with these items (in order from top to bottom): File, New, Save, Close. A corresponding child document menu has these items (again, in order from top to bottom): File, New, Close. The File and New menu items in both places should be handled according to the `MenuMerge` rules set out a moment ago. The menu items after that, however, run into a problem.

Imagine that you want the child's Close menu to override the parent's Close menu. So, you set `MergeType = MenuMerge.Remove` in the parent class and `MergeType = MenuMerge.Replace` in the child class. This technique should work, right?

Not exactly. The Close menu of the parent disappears as expected, but the parent's Save menu is now replaced with the child's Close menu, thereby throwing off the menu system and seriously confusing users.

Even though we both know that the Close menu of the parent should correspond to the Close menu of the child, the application doesn't. Rather, it can operate based only on the position of the menu item in the menu. Close in the parent is at position 3 (the numbering starts at zero), and Close in the child is at position 2. These two menu items will never cross each other's paths, so they can never merge with one another. Position 2 in the parent is occupied by the Save menu, so it is affected by the merge type of the child's Close menu.

There is a solution to this problem. The MergeOrder property of MenuItems can be used to dictate the order, and consequently the parent-child menu relation, that menu items appear in. In the preceding example, you can set both Close menu items to the same MergeOrder:

```
miClose.MergeOrder = 3;
```

Not only will the application know that these two menu items correspond to one another, but it will also place them in the ascending order of MergeOrder values. In other words, a menu item with a MergeOrder of 0 will be placed at the top of the menu, a MergeOrder of 1 will be placed next on the list, and so on. (Note, however, that the menu items won't be moved to the position dictated by MergeOrder until a merge occurs; therefore, initial position is still dictated by the order in which you add MenuItems to the menu.)

The actual MergeOrder value you set doesn't really matter; you could set the Close menu item's MergeOrder to 1000 if you wanted to. Windows Forms is smart enough that it won't put 999 empty menu items before the item in question (unless, of course, you tell it to put 999 empty spaces in). The MergeOrder is just a loose number that governs parent-child relationships and the ordering of merged items. A higher MergeOrder will always be placed lower in a menu than a lower MergeOrder.

Thus, it may not always be a good idea to number your MergeOrders sequentially—0 for the first item, 1 for the second, and so on. What if your child application has a menu item that you want to place between two menu items in the parent? In this case, spacing out your MergeOrders a bit will help, to give yourself room to expand. Figure 10.7 illustrates this concept.

Handling Children

Often you need to know the active MDI child. For instance, say you're performing a search on a RichTextBox or pasting text from another application. The ActiveMdiChild property of the parent form returns a Form object that corresponds to the child.

FIGURE 10.7

Exact MergeOrder *values are extraneous; only relative values matter.*

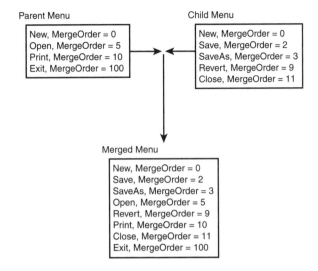

Parent Menu

```
New, MergeOrder = 0
Open, MergeOrder = 5
Print, MergeOrder = 10
Exit, MergeOrder = 100
```

Child Menu

```
New, MergeOrder = 0
Save, MergeOrder = 2
SaveAs, MergeOrder = 3
Revert, MergeOrder = 9
Close, MergeOrder = 11
```

Merged Menu

```
New, MergeOrder = 0
Save, MergeOrder = 2
SaveAs, MergeOrder = 3
Open, MergeOrder = 5
Revert, MergeOrder = 9
Print, MergeOrder = 10
Close, MergeOrder = 11
Exit, MergeOrder = 100
```

10

Let's add to your parent form a Color menu that presents a ColorDialog dialog box and changes the color of the active child. To do so, add the following code to Listing 10.2:

```
MenuItem miFormat = mnuMain.MenuItems.Add("Color");
MenuItem miColor = miFormat.MenuItems.Add("&Color...");
miColor.Click += new EventHandler(this.ChangeColor);
```

Now add the ChangeColor event handler:

```
private void ChangeColor(Object Sender, EventArgs e) {
    ColorDialog dlgColor = new ColorDialog();

    if (dlgColor.ShowDialog() == DialogResult.OK) {
        if (ActiveMdiChild != null) {
            ActiveMdiChild.BackColor = dlgColor.Color;
        }
    }
}
```

This method first creates and displays a ColorDialog dialog box, to allow the user to pick a color. Before you go on, you have to check whether the user has created any child windows in the application yet. If he hasn't, and you try to access the ActiveMdiChild property, you'll get an error. Finally, set the properties on the ActiveMdiChild just like you would for any other Form object.

You also can be alerted when a child is activated, or brought into focus by the user. The MdiChildActivate event does just this. Let's add to the parent form a status bar that tells the user which child is currently active. Add the following code to your parent form:

```
//outside the constructor
private StatusBar sbarMain = new StatusBar();

//inside the constructor
this.Controls.Add(sbarMain);
this.MdiChildActivate += new EventHandler(this.UpdateStatus);
```

Next, add the UpdateStatus method:

```
private void UpdateStatus(Object Sender, EventArgs e) {
    sbarMain.Text = ActiveMdiChild.Text + ": " +
➡ActiveMdiChild.BackColor.ToString();
}
```

Simple as that! Figure 10.8 shows an example.

FIGURE **10.8**

The MdiChildActivate
*event can alert you
when a child is
brought into focus.*

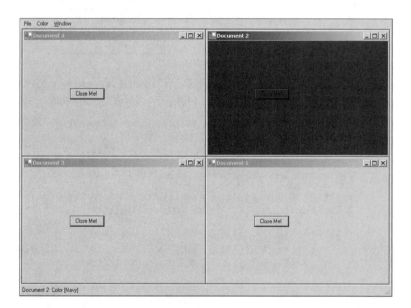

If you ever need to access a child document that is not the active child, you can use the
MdiChildren property, which returns an array of all the child forms, active or not.

Accessing Child Controls

You've seen that accessing child forms isn't very difficult. Accessing their controls, however, is a different issue. After all, you've been creating most of the controls with the
private modifier, so they should not be accessible from the parent form at all, right?

Thankfully, the answer is no. You can still access the controls contained on a child form
by using the Controls property of the child document. For example, look at the following code contained in a parent's constructor:

```
string strText;
Document doc = new Document("New Document");
doc.MdiParent = this;
strText = doc.Controls[0].Text;
```

This command retrieves the Text property of whatever the first control on the child form happens to be. Let's create a more realistic example.

Listing 10.4 shows a new parent application form that creates a new child form, which we'll get to in a moment. (The standard Window menus and event handlers have been left out of this code for brevity's sake.)

LISTING 10.4   An Intrusive Parent Control

```
1:   using System;
2:   using System.Windows.Forms;
3:   using System.Drawing;
4:
5:   namespace TYWinforms.Day10 {
6:       public class Listing104 : Form {
7:           private int intCounter = 0;
8:           private MainMenu mnuMain = new MainMenu();
9:
10:          public Listing104() {
11:              MenuItem miFile = mnuMain.MenuItems.Add("&File");
12:              MenuItem miNew = miFile.MenuItems.Add("&New");
13:              MenuItem miOpenIn = miFile.MenuItems.Add("Open
➥in new Window");
14:              miOpenIn.Enabled = false;
15:
16:              miFile.Popup += new EventHandler
➥ (this.EnableOpenIn);
17:              miNew.Click += new EventHandler(this.HandleMenu);
18:              miOpenIn.Click += new EventHandler(this.OpenIn);
19:              miWindow.MdiList = true;
20:
21:              this.IsMdiContainer = true;
22:              this.Menu = mnuMain;
23:              this.Size = new Size(800,600);
24:              this.Text = "Listing 10.3";
25:          }
26:
27:          private void EnableOpenIn(Object Sender,
➥EventArgs e) {
28:              if (this.ActiveMdiChild != null) {
29:                  if (((TextBox)ActiveMdiChild.Controls[0]).
➥SelectedText != "") {
30:                      mnuMain.MenuItems[0].MenuItems[1].
➥Enabled = true;
```

10

LISTING 10.4 continued

```
31:                } else {
32:                    mnuMain.MenuItems[0].MenuItems[1].
➥Enabled = false;
33:                }
34:            }
35:        }
36:
37:        private void OpenIn(Object Sender, EventArgs e) {
38:            if (ActiveMdiChild != null) {
39:                string strText = ((TextBox)ActiveMdiChild.
➥Controls[0]).SelectedText;
40:
41:                intCounter++;
42:                Document2 doc = new Document2("Document " +
➥intCounter.ToString());
43:                doc.MdiParent = this;
44:                doc.Controls[0].Text = strText;
45:                doc.Show();
46:            }
47:        }
48:
49:        private void HandleMenu(Object Sender,
➥EventArgs e) {
50:            intCounter++;
51:
52:            Document2 doc = new Document2("Document " +
➥intCounter.ToString());
53:            doc.MdiParent = this;
54:            doc.Show();
55:        }
56:
57:        public static void Main() {
58:            Application.Run(new Listing104());
59:        }
60:    }
61: }
```

ANALYSIS Listing 10.4 starts out as a standard MDI parent form. You have a File menu that allows the user to create new child documents, and its event handler is shown on line 49. This HandleMenu method is exactly the same as the HandleMenu method from Listing 10.2, but it creates an instance of a Document2 child document instead of Document. You'll see this new class in a moment; it's actually very simple.

You also have another menu item called "Open in new Window" on line 13. This menu item will take whatever text the user has selected in one child window, create a new child document, and place only that selected text in the new document. (By now, you should have guessed the new child class has at least a TextBox control.) When no child documents exist, however, you don't want the user to be able to choose this menu item. To control this aspect, you assign a delegate to the Popup event of the File menu (line 16), which fires whenever the user opens the menu.

Line 27 contains the event handler for the Popup event. From a conceptual point of view, you want to enable the "Open in" menu item only when a) a child document is active; and b) that child document has some selected text. The first if statement, then, on line 28 checks to see whether a child document is active. The second if is a bit more complicated.

Recall that you can access the controls contained on a child form by using the Controls property. While this is true, the Controls property returns only a Control object, so you need to cast it appropriately to whatever control you're expecting. In this case, you're expecting a TextBox control. Therefore, the if statement on line 29 retrieves the first control on the active child document, casts it as a TextBox, and then evaluates the SelectedText property to see whether any text has been selected. If none has been selected, the menu item should be disabled, as indicated by line 32. On the other hand, if some text is selected, enable the "Open in" menu item.

That's the first part of accessing the child document's controls. The next step is actually providing the "Open In" functionality, which is handled by the OpenIn method beginning on line 37. Again, you check to see whether a child document is active on line 38. Then, on line 39, you retrieve the SelectedText of the first control on the child document, again remembering to cast the object appropriately.

You then create a new child document just as you do when the user clicks the New menu item—increment the counter, create a new Document2 object, set its MdiParent to the current form, and call the Show method to display it. You perform one extra step here, though, as shown on line 44: You set the Text property of the first control on the new child document to the text retrieved from the last child document.

Finally, let's look at the new Document2 class, shown in Listing 10.5.

LISTING 10.5   The Document2 Class

```
1:  using System;
2:  using System.Windows.Forms;
3:  using System.Drawing;
4:
5:  namespace TYWinforms.Day10 {
6:     public class Document2 : Form {
7:        private TextBox tbText = new TextBox();
8:
9:        public Document2(String strName) {
```

LISTING 10.5   continued

```
10:              tbText.Dock = DockStyle.Fill;
11:              tbText.Multiline = true;
12:              tbText.HideSelection = false;
13:
14:              this.Text = strName;
15:              this.Controls.Add(tbText);
16:         }
17:      }
18:   }
```

ANALYSIS   Listing 10.5 shows a simple class that contains only a TextBox control. The
TextBox is set to fill the entire form on line 10, so the user can enter copious
amounts of text.

Compile and execute this application, and test the functionality by selecting some text
and clicking the "Open in" menu item. Figure 10.9 shows what your application should
look like.

FIGURE 10.9

*After you select some
text and click the Open
in menu item, your
selected text appears
in the new document
window.*

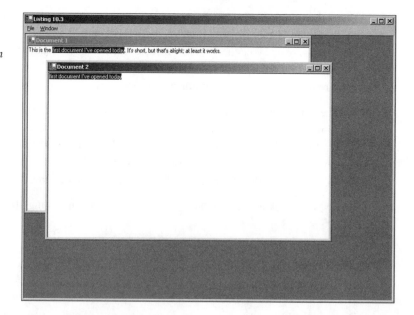

Summary

Multiple document interface applications are a useful take on the multitasking paradigm.
With more than one document open at a time in a single application, a user could theoretically accomplish twice as much work. Creating an MDI application is often more

efficient than requiring the user to open your application twice if she wants to have two documents open.

To create an MDI application, you need a parent form class and a child form class. They can be any classes that inherit from the Form object, and actually, any existing Windows Forms can be either MDI parents or children; there's no limitation.

MDI applications often have a Window menu, which allows the user to arrange the child windows in a more readable fashion. As you learned today, you can easily create a menu like this: Simply create the necessary menu items and call the LayoutMdi method with the appropriate MdiLayout enumeration value. You can also set the MdiList property of this menu to true to automatically list the child documents as menu items, allowing the user to easily choose which document to work with.

Menus are an interesting issue in MDI applications. Both child and parent documents can have associated menus, and problems sometimes arise when the two must merge. The MergeType and MergeOrder properties solve these problems, by allowing you to instruct the application which menus should merge and how.

To discover the current, or active, child in an MDI application, simply call the ActiveMdiChild property of the parent form. Similarly, the MdiChildActivate event fires when a child becomes active. You can access the controls contained on the children by using the Controls property of the child object; just remember to cast the returned value if necessary.

Tomorrow you'll learn how to work with input and output in Windows. This powerful topic opens many doors for your applications. You can, for instance, open and save documents, print them, and so on. Rest up, because tomorrow's lesson will be a long one.

Q&A

Q **When I have a certain number of windows (four or five, for instance), horizontal and vertical tiling both arrange the windows in the same fashion. Why?**

A The application tries to lay out the windows in a way that presents the most efficient use of space; it tries to display the largest size for each child window as it can. That's why, depending on the size of your screen, horizontal tiling will create a second column of windows when you have several open at once; after a certain point of dividing the height evenly, you can't see any part of each child except for its title bar.

The point at which a second column (or row, in the case of vertical tiling) is created may be the same for both horizontal and vertical tiling. In certain situations, there is simply one most efficient way to arrange windows, and both horizontal and vertical tiling use that one way.

Q How can I make my child windows dock to a corner or side of the parent document?

A Unfortunately, docking child windows isn't as easy as it seems. The `Dock` property doesn't work on `Form` objects like it does for other controls, so simply using a `DockStyle` value doesn't work, and it doesn't provide the "snapping" feature common in applications.

One method is to create an event handler for your child's `LocationChanged` event. When this event fires, you can evaluate the current position of the child window in question, and if it's in a certain range (say, 10 pixels from the left edge of the parent window), you can adjust the location and size to give the impression of docking and "snapping." A typical event handler would look like this:

```
private void SnapIt(Object Sender, EventArgs e) {
   Form frmTemp = (Form)Sender;

   if (frmTemp.Location.X < 10 & frmTemp.Location.Y < 10) {
      frmTemp.Location = new Point(0,0);
      frmTemp.Size = new Size(100,550);
   }
}
```

Note that this method doesn't actually dock the child window, but it provides a good alternative to doing so.

Q I've created a toolbar-type child window, but I can't move it outside the parent window's borders. In Photoshop and Visual Studio, I can. What gives?

A In these other applications, you're not actually dealing with MDI children. Rather, these toolbars are custom dialog classes, which can be moved wherever you please, and are not restricted to the boundaries of the parent window.

So, should you use one method over the other? The answer really depends on the type of application you're building. Also, if you don't want to clutter up the user's desktop, it's a good idea to create child MDI windows instead of custom dialogs.

Workshop

This workshop will help reinforce the concepts covered in today's lesson. It is very helpful to understand fully the answers before moving on. Answers to the quiz questions and exercises are in Appendix A.

Quiz

1. What property must you set on the MDI parent to make it an MDI application?

2. What property must you set on the MDI child to make it part of an MDI application?

3. What are the three values of the `MdiLayout` enumeration?

4. True or False: You must call the `Show` method to display an MDI child when it's created in the constructor of its parent.

5. The following code snippet does not cause the `tbText` `TextBox` control to fill the entire form:

```
TextBox tbText = new TextBox();
tbText.Dock = DockStyle.Fill;
```

Why not?

6. How do you find out whether an MDI child is active?

7. You've created three menu items in a child document, but they're not displayed properly in the parent document. Name three things to check to fix this problem.

8. True or False: The `MergeOrder` value must be incremental; you cannot skip orders.

Exercise

Create an MDI version of the "SQL statement execution" application from yesterday's exercise. Create a custom dialog box that displays a text box where the user can enter the query.

10

DAY 11

Working with Windows Input/Output

Working with input and output is an important part of working with any operating system. It's more than simply reading and writing files, as many would think. I/O involves printing, accessing the network, monitoring changes in a file system, and so on.

Today's lesson focuses on different aspects of I/O in .NET Windows Forms. You'll find that .NET has made much of the once-convoluted process easy, so you'll be saving documents in no time!

Today you'll learn

- What streams are and how to use them
- How to read and write to streams
- How to create an explorer-style interface
- How to manipulate text files
- The steps involved in printing a document

Introducing Streams

What is a file? From a user's point of view, a file is a piece of information on a computer's hard drive. It has a name, a directory path, and a file extension, and its properties, such as size, date created, and so on, can be easily measured. When a user creates a file, he makes the assumption that the file will not disappear; it will be written to the hard drive and won't be lost, barring some catastrophe.

To the programmer, a file is a bit different. You must think in terms of bits and bytes, so a file is a collection of 1s and 0s stored on the hard drive. For a particular collection of bits to make any sense, they have to be ordered in a particular way, and different file types each have their own schemas. Again, a file is always associated with a location, or directory structure, on the computer.

This mechanism is great for normal use and perfect when you're dealing with predetermined storage mechanisms. If you know exactly what files you're going to use, this bit-sequencing paradigm is ideal. It does have its shortcomings, however. Traditional file I/O deals only with file I/O; it can't handle any other type of storage mechanism. You have to supply the proper bit sequence and often the directory path for it to work correctly. Due to the nature of an operating system such as Windows, and the tendency of users to always do the unexpected, this type of system is prone to error.

NEW TERM   The .NET Framework introduces the *stream*. There is one main difference between a file and a stream: A stream can come from anywhere; it doesn't have to be stored on the hard drive like a file. It can come from memory, from a network, from a tape backup, and so on; the location is arbitrary, just like the data source for a `DataSet`. This location is called a stream's *backing store*. The most important point to remember about a stream is that it is simply some data that is independent of a source. In this way, the developer doesn't have to worry about the complexities of dealing with a particular data source.

The exact workings of a stream may be a bit confusing. It doesn't load the entire data source into memory, and it doesn't exactly "stream" the data source in the traditional Internet sense (like, for example, streaming video). Think of a stream, rather, as your personal concierge. It is the go-between from you to the associated data, and vice versa. Thus, your concierge can take data to the source and retrieve data from the source. He can bring you pieces of the source either in the order he comes across them or in any other manner you choose; you could, for example, tell him to retrieve a piece from the middle of the source. Figure 11.1 illustrates this delivery system.

FIGURE 11.1

A stream acts as a concierge to deliver information from you to the data source, and vice versa.

You can use four different types of streams, one for each type of source: FileStream, MemoryStream, NetworkStream, and CryptoStream, which links to cryptographic data (for security). In addition to these four types, the BufferedStream object connects solely to another stream. It provides buffering capability for those streams—but we're getting ahead of ourselves. Now you have four concierges to do different types of dirty work for you—similar to having one concierge to take out your trash, another to bring you food, and so on.

In addition, the streams can link to each other, in case one is not enough to do the job. For example, you can use a FileStream object to read data from a file and then a NetworkStream object to transmit that data over the network, without having to stop in the middle. Here again, you see that the original data source doesn't matter; a stream can link to almost anything.

This stream puzzle has one more piece: stream readers and writers.

Stream readers and writers help you interact with the contents of a stream. As their names imply, they read from and write to the stream, respectively.

Going back to the concierge analogy, you may find that your concierge doesn't speak the same language you do. Therefore, you need a translator, someone who will relay your instructions to the concierge and tell you what the foreign concierge has to say.

Why do you need readers and writers in .NET? Remember that a stream is simply a collection of bits and bytes. It doesn't have a mechanism to convey to you its contents; it's a non-speaking, non-hearing concierge. Therefore, you need something that knows about the type of information the stream is dealing with so that it can properly provide you the information you need.

Let's consider a real .NET situation. Suppose you have an XML file. To open and provide access to the contents of that file, you can use a FileStream. After you have the FileStream, however, you need to use an XmlReader object that can retrieve from the stream, translating it from 1s and 0s to XML content in the process. Alternatively, you could use a StringReader, which could read from the stream and produce a big string for you to examine. Obviously, the XmlReader is more suited in this case because it allows you to perform functionality specific to XML that the StringReader doesn't.

Figure 11.2 illustrates the chain of objects you need to interact with to deal with Windows I/O.

FIGURE **11.2**

Your stream can deliver from a data source, and a reader or writer can give you data in working format.

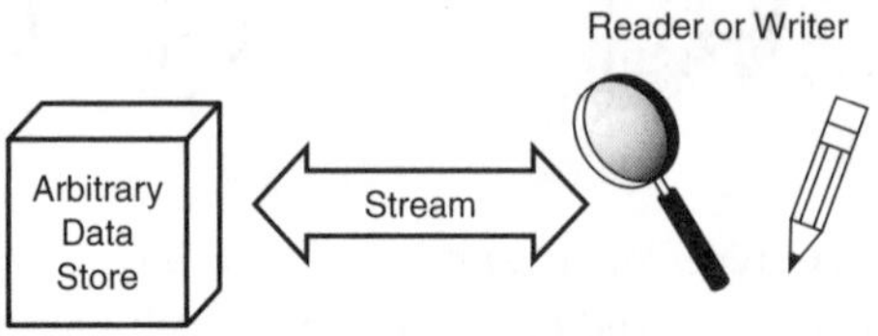

Using Files and Directories

Before you actually start reading from and writing to files, you need to know how to deal with these generic objects. Four .NET objects allow you to manipulate files and directories in an operating system: File, FileInfo, Directory, and DirectoryInfo.

The File and FileInfo objects are similar; they contain most of the same members. The difference, then, is that the File object is purely a static object. Recall that with static members you do not need an instance of the class to use them. Thus, you can use the File.Copy method to copy an arbitrary file from one location to another.

The FileInfo object applies to the current file instance only. The FileInfo.Copy method copies the *current* file. These same rules apply to the Directory and DirectoryInfo objects. Most of the time you'll use the associated Info objects in your applications because you'll be dealing with specific files and directories.

Let's look at an example. Listing 11.1 creates an explorer-style directory listing by looping through a directory and adding items to a TreeView control.

LISTING 11.1   Creating an Explorer-Style Listing

```
1:  using System;
2:  using System.Windows.Forms;
3:  using System.Drawing;
4:  using System.IO;
5:
6:  namespace TYWinforms.Day11 {
7:      public class Listing111 : Form {
8:          private TreeView tvFiles = new TreeView();
9:          private Label lblInfo = new Label();
10:
11:         public Listing111() {
12:             tvFiles.Dock = DockStyle.Left;
13:             tvFiles.Width = 150;
14:
```

LISTING 11.1   continued

```
15:                lblInfo.Size = new Size(100,100);
16:                lblInfo.Text = "Select a file or\ndirectory";
17:
18:                PopulateList("c:\\", tvFiles.Nodes.Add("c:\\"));
19:
20:                this.Controls.Add(tvFiles);
21:                this.Controls.Add(lblInfo);
22:            }
23:
24:        private void PopulateList(String strPath, TreeNode
➥currNode) {
25:                DirectoryInfo dir = new DirectoryInfo(strPath);
26:                TreeNode nodeSubDir;
27:
28:                foreach (DirectoryInfo d in dir.GetDirectories()) {
29:                    nodeSubDir = currNode.Nodes.Add(d.Name);
30:                    PopulateList(d.FullName, nodeSubDir);
31:                }
32:
33:                foreach (FileInfo f in dir.GetFiles("*.*")) {
34:                    currNode.Nodes.Add(f.Name);
35:                }
36:            }
37:
38:        public static void Main() {
39:            Application.Run(new Listing111());
40:        }
41:    }
42: }
```

ANALYSIS Listing 11.1 starts out normally—creating a `ListView` control, setting a few properties, and displaying the form. The `PopulateList` method, however, is something new.

NEW TERM The `PopulateList` method is known as a *recursive method* because it calls itself over and over again. Let's dissect. This method first retrieves information on the directory specified by the first parameter. The first time this method executes (as called from line 18), the directory is `C:`, or the root directory. Line 26 creates a temporary object we'll use in a moment.

The `DirectoryInfo` object on line 25 now contains a bunch of information about the current directory. Using the `GetDirectories` method, you can retrieve all the subdirectories, and using the `GetFiles` method, you can retrieve all the files contained within this directory. On line 28, using a `foreach` loop, you iterate through all the subdirectories in the current directory. Line 29 adds a new node to the `TreeView` using the name of each subdirectory. Let's skip line 30 for a moment.

11

Tip

> The `FullName` property of both the `DirectoryInfo` and `FileInfo` objects
> returns the name of the object, plus the entire path. Here's an example:
>
> `c:\inetpub\wwwroot\myfile.aspx`
>
> The `Name` property, on the other hand, returns only the name, excluding the
> path, as in this example:
>
> `myfile.aspx`

Line 33 is similar to what you just examined. For each file in the subdirectory, you simply add a new node to the `TreeView` with the name of the file.

Now, remember that the file system is hierarchical; you could have subdirectories of subdirectories of subdirectories ad infinitum. Without line 30, this method would list only the subdirectories and files of the root `C:` folder, and that's it; it doesn't go any deeper. You need a way to keep digging deeper and deeper through each subdirectory until you reach the end. Because you have no idea how deep this could be on a user's computer, you need a way to automatically determine the subdirectories.

The `PopulateList` method already does this job for you. If the current directory doesn't contain any subdirectories, lines 28–31 are simply not executed, and you move on. The same goes for lines 33–35. So, it makes sense to use this same method for the next level of subdirectories.

On line 30, you call the `PopulateList` method again, passing in the path of the current subdirectory and the current node in the tree. When this method executes this time, it grabs the information of the subdirectory, adds it under the current node, and loops through its subdirectories and files, just like always. If it encounters another subdirectory, the `PopulateList` method is called again for that subdirectory, and so on. In this way, you can easily loop through every directory and file on the hard drive without knowing ahead of time how deep to go. Recursion is very important for file I/O. Table 11.1 explains the process a bit more.

TABLE 11.1 The Recursion Process

Current Directory and Node	Subdirectories Left	Action
`C:\`	`ASPNET`, `Windows`	Loop through the first subdirectory in `C:\`
`C:\ASPNET`	None	List files in `C:\ASPNET` if available; move back to the parent directory
`C:\`	`Windows`	Loop through the second subdirectory in `C:\`
`C:\Windows`	`Wallpaper`, `System32`	Loop through the first subdirectory in `C:\Windows`

TABLE 11.1 continued

Current Directory and Node	Subdirectories Left	Action
C:\Windows\Wallpaper	None	List files in C:\Windows\Wallpaper if available; move back to the parent directory.
C:\Windows	System32	Loop through the second subdirectory in C:\Windows.
C:\Windows\System32	None	List files in C:\Windows\System32 if available; move back to the parent directory.
C:\Windows	None	List files in C:\Windows if available; move back to the parent directory.
C:\	None	List files in C:\ if available. Stop.

Figure 11.3 shows the output from this application. Note that looping through all the directories on your computer may take awhile (depending on your computer), so the application may not open immediately. One way to speed up this process is to dynamically build the tree structure during runtime, rather than all during initialization. In other words, iterate through a subdirectory and its files only when the user expands that node; this way, you have to do only one level at a time, and execution will speed up tremendously. I'll leave this task as an exercise for you.

FIGURE 11.3

Listing 11.1 creates this Explorer-like application.

11

You may receive an error when running the code in Listing 11.1 because you don't have the permissions to access the information on every directory and file. For now, try limiting the directories to be searched by changing the GetDirectories method on line 28 to search only for a particular directory. Here's an example:

```
.GetDirectories("windows*")
```

> This method causes the application to list only directories that have the word "windows" in their name. Most likely, this approach will circumvent your permission problem. You'll learn a better way of dodging this problem in Day 21, "Debugging Your Windows Forms."

Let's enhance this application a bit to get a better feel for dealing with file and directory objects. Add the following code to the constructor:

```
tvFiles.AfterSelect += new TreeViewEventHandler
➥(this.DisplayInfo);
```

Now when a user selects a node in the `TreeView`, you can display some extra information to her in the label on line 9 of Listing 11.1. Listing 11.2 shows the `DisplayInfo` method.

LISTING 11.2   Displaying Information to the User

```
1:   private void DisplayInfo(Object Sender,
➥TreeViewEventArgs e) {
2:       TreeNode tempNode = e.Node;
3:       String strFullName = tempNode.Text;
4:
5:       while (tempNode.Parent != null) {
6:           strFullName = tempNode.Parent.Text + "\\" +
➥strFullName;
7:           tempNode = tempNode.Parent;
8:       }
9:
10:      if (File.Exists(strFullName)) {
11:          FileInfo obj = new FileInfo(strFullName);
12:          lblInfo.Text = "Name: " + obj.Name;
13:          lblInfo.Text += "\nSize: " + obj.Length;
14:          lblInfo.Text += "\nAccessed: " +
➥obj.LastAccessTime.ToString();
15:      } else {
16:          DirectoryInfo obj = new DirectoryInfo(strFullName);
17:          lblInfo.Text = "Name: " + obj.Name;
18:          lblInfo.Text += "\nAttributes: " +
➥obj.Attributes.ToString();
19:          lblInfo.Text += "\nAccessed: " +
➥obj.LastAccessTime.ToString();
20:      }
21:  }
```

ANALYSIS   In Listing 11.2, the `TreeViewNodeEventArgs` object returns the particular `TreeNode` object that was clicked. You store this object in a variable on line 2 for easier access later. Then you retrieve the caption on line 3.

Next, you need to find the full path of whatever node was clicked so that you can accurately determine the file or directory to display information about. To find it, you use a while loop that checks the Parent property of the current node. If no parents exist (meaning this is the root directory), the Parent property will return null, and you'll know you have the complete path. In the loop, you simply append each parent's name to the string and move up a level.

The next bit of code determines the object you're dealing with, whether it's a file or a directory. The File.Exists method (remember that File is a static object) determines if the specified path points to a file. If it does, you display various information about the file in the label, as shown on lines 11–14. If the file doesn't exist, you know it's a directory instead, so you display different information on lines 16–19.

Now take another look at the application, shown in Figure 11.4.

FIGURE 11.4

You can provide feedback with your explorer.

11

Table 11.2 lists the members of the FileInfo object.

TABLE 11.2 FileInfo Properties

Property	Description
Attributes	Returns the attributes of the file. Can be one of the FileAttributes enumeration values: Archive, Compressed, Device, Directory, Encrypted, Hidden, Normal, NotContentIndexed, Offline, ReadOnly, ReparsePoint, SparseFile, System, Temporary
CreationTime	Specifies the date and time the file was created
Directory	Indicates a DirectoryInfo object representing this file's parent directory

TABLE 11.2   continued

Property	Description
DirectoryName	Contains a string representing the full path of the parent directory
Exists	Indicates whether this file is valid
Extension	Specifies the extension of this file
FullName	Indicates the name, including directory path, of this file
LastAccessTime	Indicates the date and time the file was last accessed
LastWriteTime	Indicates the date and time the file was last written to
Length	Specifies the size of the file
Name	Specifies the name of the file, not including the directory path

Method	Description
AppendText	Creates a StreamWriter that allows you to append text to the file
CopyTo	Copies the file to a new location
Create	Creates the file
CreateText	Creates the file and a StreamWriter that can write to the file
Delete	Deletes the file
MoveTo	Moves the file to a new location
Open	Opens the file with various privileges
OpenRead	Creates a read-only FileStream object for this file
OpenText	Creates a read/write FileStream object for this file

Table 11.3 lists the various members of the DirectoryInfo object. You can see that it shares quite a few properties with the FileInfo object.

TABLE 11.3   DirectoryInfo Members

Property	Description
Attributes	Returns the attributes of the directory. Can be one of the FileAttributes enumeration values: Archive, Compressed, Device, Directory, Encrypted, Hidden, Normal, NotContentIndexed, Offline, ReadOnly, ReparsePoint, SparseFile, System, Temporary
CreationTime	Indicates the date and time the directory was created
Exists	Indicates whether this directory is valid
Extension	Specifies the extension of this directory
FullName	Indicates the name, including directory path, of this directory

TABLE 11.3   continued

Property	Description
LastAccessTime	Indicates the date and time the directory was last accessed
LastWriteTime	Indicates the date and time the directory was last written to
Name	Specifies the name of the file, not including the directory path
Parent	Returns a `DirectoryInfo` object representing the parent of this directory
Root	Returns a `DirectoryInfo` object representing the root of this directory

Method	Description
Create	Creates the directory
CreateSubDirectory	Creates the directory and returns a `DirectoryInfo` object that represents the new directory
Delete	Deletes the directory
GetDirectories	Gets an array of `DirectoryInfo` objects representing all the subdirectories of the current one
GetFiles	Gets an array of `FileInfo` objects representing all the files in the current directory
GetFileSystemInfos	Gets an array of `FileSystemInfo` objects representing all the files and directories
MoveTo	Moves the file to a new location

Reading and Writing Files

Whether the file you want to manipulate is binary or plain text, the procedure for reading or writing remains the same: Attach a stream object of the necessary type and attach to that a reader or writer to access the data. In addition, all readers and writers share the same common members, so when you know how to use one, you can use them all.

Let's look at an example of writing a text file. Listing 11.3 shows a simple application that allows the user to enter a filename to create. This text file will be created with the text `"Hello World!"` inside it.

LISTING 11.3   Creating a File

```
1:  using System;
2:  using System.Windows.Forms;
3:  using System.Drawing;
4:  using System.IO;
5:
```

LISTING 11.3   continued

```
 6:   namespace TYWinforms.Day11 {
 7:       public class Listing112 : Form {
 8:           private Button btCreate = new Button();
 9:           private TextBox tbFileName = new TextBox();
10:
11:           public Listing112() {
12:               tbFileName.Location = new Point(25,100);
13:               tbFileName.Width = 150;
14:
15:               btCreate.Text = "Create!";
16:               btCreate.Location = new Point(200,100);
17:               btCreate.Click += new
➥EventHandler(this.CreateFile);
18:
19:               this.Text = "Listing 11.2";
20:               this.Controls.Add(btCreate);
21:               this.Controls.Add(tbFileName);
22:           }
23:
24:           public void CreateFile(Object Sender, EventArgs e) {
25:               String strFilename = tbFileName.Text;
26:
27:               if (!File.Exists(strFilename)) {
28:                   FileStream objFile = new
➥FileStream(strFilename, FileMode.CreateNew);
29:                   StreamWriter objWriter = new
➥StreamWriter(objFile);
30:
31:                   objWriter.WriteLine("Hello World!");
32:
33:                   objWriter.Close();
34:                   objFile.Close();
35:
36:                   MessageBox.Show("Done!");
37:               }
38:           }
39:
40:           public static void Main() {
41:               Application.Run(new Listing112());
42:           }
43:       }
44:   }
```

ANALYSIS   Let's skip over the constructor in Listing 11.3; it contains only one thing of interest, the delegate assignation on line 17. All the action is in the `CreateFile` method beginning on line 24. This code assumes that the user has entered some text into the text box. On line 27, you check to see whether the specified file already exists. If it does, you don't want to mess with it. If it doesn't, however, you're free to continue.

Line 28 creates a `FileStream` object to interact with the file. The constructor for `FileStream` takes a number of parameters. The first, obviously, is the path to the file in question. The second parameter is optional; here, it specifies the mode in which the file will be opened, and can be one of the following `FileMode` enumeration values:

- `Append`—Opens the file if it exists and moves to the end of the file. If it doesn't exist, a new file is created.
- `Create`—Creates a new file. If it already exists, the existing file is overwritten.
- `CreateNew`—Creates a new file. If it already exists, an error is raised.
- `Open`—Opens an existing file.
- `OpenOrCreate`—Opens the file if it exists. Otherwise, a new file is created.
- `Truncate`—Opens an existing file and erases all its existing content.

Here, you specify `FileMode.CreateNew` so that a new file will be created using the path supplied in the text box.

Now that you have a stream for your file, you need to create a writer to write data to it. Because you want to deal with plain text information, you create a `StreamWriter` on line 29. This object's constructor takes one parameter: the stream to attach the writer to.

The `WriteLine` method on line 31 simply writes the specified text to the stream (and therefore the file) and appends a new line to the end of the string. Conversely, the `Write` method doesn't append a new line character.

Finally, you must remember to call the `Close` methods for both the writer and stream so that the application knows you're done with them and can free up valuable resources. A message box is displayed on line 36 to alert the user the task is done.

Now compile and execute this application. Supply a valid path (for example, `c:\temp\blah.txt`) and click the Create button. Navigate to that path, and you'll notice a new text file with the words `"Hello World"` in it.

Let's go back a moment and look at the constructor for the stream object. This flexible constructor can take all sorts of parameters. For example, all the following lines are valid:

```
new FileStream(strFilename, FileMode.CreateNew);
new FileStream(strFilename, FileMode.Create, FileAccess.Read);
new FileStream(strFilename, FileMode.Create, FileAccess.Read,
➥FileShare.None);
new FileStream(strFilename, FileMode.Create, FileAccess.Read,
➥FileShare.None, 1024, true);
```

11

The first constructor you already know. The second constructor allows you to specify the functions the stream can perform on the file, using `FileAccess` enumeration values. These values can be `Read`, `ReadWrite`, or `Write`.

The third constructor adds another enumeration value to the list from `FileShare`. This value determines how other stream objects can access this file at the same time you do. Values can be `None`, `Read`, `ReadWrite`, or `Write`. A value of `FileShare.None` means that other streams will be denied access to this file while you're working on it.

Finally, the last constructor adds two more parameters. The first indicates the buffer size in bytes to use with the file. Setting a buffer can increase performance. The last parameter indicates whether the operations should be performed asynchronously; we'll cover that topic later today in the section titled "Creating Asynchronous I/O."

The creation of the stream object is the most complicated part of Listing 11.3. Using the writer is simple, with a choice of only two possible methods: `Write` or `WriteLine`.

Let's add a reader to this listing. To do so, modify the `if` block on line 27 of Listing 11.3 so that it includes an `else` statement like the following:

```
} else {
    FileStream objFile = new FileStream(strFilename,
➥FileMode.Open, FileAccess.Read);
    StreamReader objReader = new StreamReader(objFile);

    String strContents = objReader.ReadToEnd();

    objReader.Close();
    objFile.Close();

    MessageBox.Show(strContents);
}
```

In this case, you know the file exists. You create a `FileStream` object just like before, using the same path. This time, however, you create a `StreamReader` instead of a `StreamWriter`. The syntax is exactly the same.

Next, you call the `ReadToEnd` method of the reader to return the entire contents of the file. You then close the reader and stream, and display the contents of the file using a `MessageBox`.

Now execute the application again, specify the same file you did last time, and click the Create button. Now, instead of a `"Done!"` message popping up, a message pops up with the contents of the file you created. Modify the file manually and try again; the new contents show up in the message box. Figure 11.5 shows some sample output.

FIGURE 11.5

You can easily read and write text files using streams.

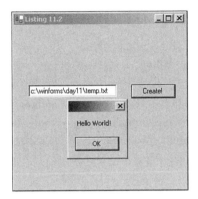

The `StreamReader` object has a few more methods for reading streams than the `StreamWriter` does for writing to them. You've already seen the `ReadToEnd` method, which returns the entire contents of a file. `ReadLine` returns one line of the file at a time, and `ReadBlock` reads a specified number of characters, starting at a specific point, and places the returned data in an array. For example, `ReadBlock(buffer, 0, 100)` reads from the first character to the 100th character, placing the results in the `char` array `buffer()`. If you encounter the end of the file before the 100th character, the method simply returns whatever is available.

The simple `Read` method reads a single character at a time from the stream. A pointer is moved to the next character each time you call this method, so the next character will be returned the next time you call `Read`. `Read` can also behave similarly to the `ReadBlock` method, if you pass in a `char` array and start and end values.

Finally, the `Peek` method is similar to `Read`; it retrieves the next character in the stream but does not move the pointer. This method is most often used to determine whether the stream in question has any more contents. If there are no more contents, `Peek` returns -1.

Many different types of readers and writers are available. Here, you've seen `StreamReader` and `StreamWriter`, which can read text information. Similarly, `StringReader` and `StringWriter` read and write to strings. `HttpWriter` can write output to a Web browser. In ASP.NET, you use `HtmlTextWriter` to render HTML to browsers as well. `BinaryReader` and `BinaryWriter` read and write binary data. Check out the .NET SDK Documentation, which contains more information on these readers and writers if you're curious. Remember, though, you already know how to use most of them because they are nearly identical to `StreamReader` and `StreamWriter`.

Reading and Writing Binary Data

The files you come across won't always be plain text; often, they contain binary data, which means you can't read them without a computer's help. For example, databases often come in binary format to save space and protect the contents from prying eyes.

Not to worry; .NET is fully capable of reading and writing binary data. And the great thing is that after the previous section, you already know how to do both! Let's jump right into an example application that reads and writes binary data, shown in Listing 11.4.

LISTING 11.4   Working in Binary

```
1:  Imports System
2:  Imports System.Windows.Forms
3:  Imports System.Drawing
4:  Imports System.IO
5:
6:  Namespace TYWinForms.Day11
7:
8:     Class Listing114 : Inherits Form
9:        private btWriteIt As New Button()
10:       private btReadIt As New Button()
11:       private nudHigh As New NumericUpDown()
12:       private nudLo As New NumericUpDown()
13:       private dtpDate As New DateTimePicker()
14:       private lblHigh As New Label()
15:       private lblLo As New Label()
16:
17:       Public Sub New()
18:          lblLo.Text = "Low Temp"
19:          lblLo.Location = new Point(10,10)
20:          nudLo.Location = new Point(110,10)
21:          nudLo.Minimum = -100
22:          nudLo.Maximum = 130
23:
24:          lblHigh.Text = "High Temp"
25:          lblHigh.Location = new Point(10,40)
26:          nudHigh.Location = new Point(110,40)
27:          nudHigh.Minimum = -100
28:          nudHigh.Maximum = 130
29:
30:      dtpDate.Location = new Point (10,80)
31:
32:          btWriteIt.Text = "Write it!"
33:          btWriteIt.Location = new Point(30,200)
34:          AddHandler btWriteIt.Click, new EventHandler
➥(AddressOf Me.WriteIt)
```

LISTING 11.4   continued

```
35:
36:            btReadIt.Text = "Read it!"
37:            btReadIt.Location = new Point(120,200)
38:            AddHandler btReadIt.Click, new EventHandler
➡ (AddressOf Me.ReadIt)
39:
40:            Me.Controls.Add(lblLo)
41:            Me.Controls.Add(nudLo)
42:            Me.Controls.Add(lblHigh)
43:      Me.Controls.Add(nudHigh)
44:            Me.Controls.Add(dtpDate)
45:            Me.Controls.Add(btWriteIt)
46:            Me.Controls.Add(btReadIt)
47:        End Sub
48:
49:        private sub WriteIt(Sender As Object, e As EventArgs)
50:            Dim objStream As New FileStream("c:\winforms\day11\records.dat",
➡FileMode.Create)
51:            Dim objWriter As New BinaryWriter(objStream)
52:
53:            objWriter.Write(CType(nudLo.Value, Short))
54:            objWriter.Write(CType(nudHigh.Value, Short))
55:            objWriter.Write(dtpDate.Value.ToString("d"))
56:
57:            objWriter.Close()
58:            objStream.Close()
59:        end sub
60:
61:        private sub ReadIt(Sender As Object, e As EventArgs)
62:            Dim strTemp As String
63:            Dim lo, hi as Short
64:
65:            if not File.Exists("c:\winforms\day11\records.dat") then
66:                MessageBox.Show("That file doesn't exist!")
67:                Return
68:            End If
69:
70:            Dim objStream = New FileStream("c:\winforms\day11\records.dat",
➡FileMode.Open, FileAccess.Read)
71:            Dim objReader As New BinaryReader(objStream)
72:
73:            lo = objReader.ReadInt16()
74:            hi = objReader.ReadInt16()
75:            strTemp = objReader.ReadString()
76:
77:            MessageBox.Show("High and low temperatures on " &
➡strTemp & " were " & hi.ToString() & " and " &
➡lo.ToString() )
78:
```

11

LISTING 11.4   continued

```
79:             objReader.Close()
80:             objStream.Close()
81:         end sub
82:
83:         Public Shared Sub Main()
84:             Application.Run(new Listing114())
85:         End Sub
86:     End Class
87: End Namespace
```

ANALYSIS   This program captures the high and low temperature for a day and writes those temperatures along with the date to a file. Along with buttons for writing and reading to the file we declare additional controls for entering the temperatures and the date on lines 9 through 15.

The controls are initialized and added to our form in the constructor in lines 18 through 46. The WriteIt and ReadIt methods on lines 49 and 61 respectively are the event handlers for our two buttons that create a new binary file, and read from the same file.

Starting with the WriteIt method, you have the creation of a new FileStream object on line 50. This is similar to what you had before. Line 51 also is similar, but you create a BinaryWriter instead of a StreamWriter as in Listing 11.3. Both of these writers, however, work the same.

On lines 53-55 you simply write the values from your controls to your file, in binary format. We use Ctype to convert the temperatures to a Short data type which requires less space and we use one of the DateTime formatting codes that we covered back in Day 8 to convert our date to the short (mm/dd/yyyy) format string. The BinaryWriter.Write method is overloaded for various data types so the calls on lines 53 and 54 invoke the version of the method that takes a Short while the call on line 55 invokes the String version of Write. Then on lines 57 and 58 you close your writer and stream objects. Before we go on with the code, let's see what happens when you run this application and click the "Write It" button.

Navigate to the c:\winforms\day11 directory after running the program, and you should see a new file named records.dat. Open this file using Notepad, and you'll see something like the following output:

??????????????????????????????????????

No, that's not an error with the outputting process. Notepad can only handle plain text files, so when it encounters the binary output you created in this file, it doesn't know what to do, and just displays garbage.

To prove that this isn't a trick, let's go back to the code in Listing 11.4. On line 65, in the `ReadIt` method, you check to make sure this file exists (and it should), and if not, the subroutine stops processing (line 67). On line 70, you create another `FileStream` object around the `records.dat` file, and a `BinaryReader` on line 71.

Since we know that we just wrote two `Shorts` followed by a `String` to output the data we will read two `Shorts` and then a `String` on lines 73-75 to read the data back in. Unlike the `BinaryWriter.Write` method which was overloaded for various data types (meaning it could take different data types as parameters), when reading binary data with the `BinaryReader` class we must call a different method based on the type of data we are trying to read. Since a `Short` in VB.NET is a 16-bit integer we use the `ReadInt16` method to read `Shorts` and we use the `ReadString` method to read in a string data type. Finally, you display the resulting text on line 77, and then close your reader and stream on lines 80-81.

When you run this application and click the `ReadIt` button, a message box pops up with something like the following:

```
High and low temperatures on 2/12/2002 were 65 and 34
```

Your binary reader has successfully translated back from binary into plain text.

When dealing with binary files, it's very important to know how the contents are structured, so you can read them out properly. Otherwise, the results may be unpredictable.

Serialization

NEW TERM   .NET also provides a method to *serialize* objects. Serialization is the process of storing the state of an object instance to a storage medium. In other words, when you serialize something, you are putting it into a format that can easily be saved to a hard drive or sent across the Internet. When an object is serialized, not only are the public and private members of the object stored but also metadata about the class itself. This way another program, perhaps on another machine, can read this data back in through a process known as deserialization and create an exact clone of the original object. It's almost like deconstructing a pizza into descriptions of its individual components, sending those over the phone, and having the person on the other end re-make the exact same pizza!

Like with so many things in .NET much of the difficult work is provided for us by the CLR, and therefore, serialization is quite easy to implement. The following example takes the same data that we wrote and read in Listing 11.4 but this time we turn that data into a class and let .NET's serialization take care of the writing and reading for us.

11

LISTING 11.5   Serializing Binary Data

```
1:   Imports System
2:   Imports System.Windows.Forms
3:   Imports System.Drawing
4:   Imports System.IO
5:   Imports System.Runtime.Serialization
6:   Imports System.Runtime.Serialization.Formatters.Binary
7:
8:   Namespace TYWinForms.Day11
9:
10:      <Serializable()> Class TempRec
11:         public loTemp as Short
12:         public hiTemp as Short
13:         public dateTemp as DateTime
14:      End Class
15:
16:      Class Listing115 : Inherits Form
17:         private btWriteIt As New Button()
18:         private btReadIt As New Button()
19:         private nudHigh As New NumericUpDown()
20:         private nudLo As New NumericUpDown()
21:         private dtpDate As New DateTimePicker()
22:         private lblHigh As New Label()
23:         private lblLo As New Label()
24:
25:         Public Sub New()
26:            lblLo.Text = "Low Temp"
27:            lblLo.Location = new Point(10,10)
28:            nudLo.Location = new Point(110,10)
29:            nudLo.Minimum = -100
30:            nudLo.Maximum = 130
31:
32:            lblHigh.Text = "High Temp"
33:            lblHigh.Location = new Point(10,40)
34:            nudHigh.Location = new Point(110,40)
35:            nudHigh.Minimum = -100
36:            nudHigh.Maximum = 130
37:
38:            dtpDate.Location = new Point (10,80)
39:
40:            btWriteIt.Text = "Write it!"
41:            btWriteIt.Location = new Point(30,200)
42:            AddHandler btWriteIt.Click, new EventHandler
➥(AddressOf Me.WriteIt)
43:
44:            btReadIt.Text = "Read it!"
45:            btReadIt.Location = new Point(120,200)
46:            AddHandler btReadIt.Click, new EventHandler
➥ (AddressOf Me.ReadIt)
47:
```

LISTING 11.5   continued

```
48:            Me.Controls.Add(lblLo)
49:            Me.Controls.Add(nudLo)
50:            Me.Controls.Add(lblHigh)
51:            Me.Controls.Add(nudHigh)
52:            Me.Controls.Add(dtpDate)
53:            Me.Controls.Add(btWriteIt)
54:            Me.Controls.Add(btReadIt)
55:        End Sub
56:
57:        private sub WriteIt(Sender As Object, e As EventArgs)
58:            Dim objStream As New FileStream("c:\winforms\day11\records.dat",
    ➥FileMode.Create)
59:            Dim objFormatter As New BinaryFormatter()
60:            Dim objTempREc As New TempRec()
61:
62:            objTempRec.loTemp = nudLo.Value
63:            objTempRec.hiTemp = nudHigh.Value
64:            objTempRec.dateTemp = dtpDate.Value
65:
66:            objFormatter.Serialize(objStream,objTempRec)
67:            objStream.Close()
68:        end sub
69:
70:        private sub ReadIt(Sender As Object, e As EventArgs)
71:
72:            if not File.Exists("c:\winforms\day11\records.dat") then
73:                MessageBox.Show("That file doesn't exist!")
74:                Return
75:            End If
76:
77:            Dim objStream = New FileStream("c:\winforms\day11\records.dat",
    ➥FileMode.Open, FileAccess.Read)
78:            Dim objFormatter As New BinaryFormatter()
79:            Dim objTempREc As New TempRec()
80:
81:            objTempRec = objFormatter.Deserialize(objStream)
82:
83:            MessageBox.Show("High and low temperatures on " &
    ➥objTempRec.dateTemp.ToString("d") & " were " &
    ➥objTempRec.hiTemp.ToString() & " and " &
    ➥objTempRec.loTemp.ToString() )
84:
85:            objStream.Close()
86:        end sub
87:
88:        Public Shared Sub Main()
89:            Application.Run(new Listing115())
90:        End Sub
91:    End Class
92: End Namespace
```

11

ANALYSIS On lines 5 and 6 we import the libraries we need to implement serialization. On line 10 we create a new class, `TempRec`, and give it the `Serializable` attribute. This attribute is what causes .NET to automatically provide the serialization functionality for our class. In C# the attribute would look as follows:

```
[Serializable] class TempRec
```

We've kept the class very simple with just three public fields to hold our data.

On line 59 in our `WriteIt` method we now declare an object of type `BinaryFormatter` where previously we had used `BinaryWriter`. On line 60 we declare an object of our `TempRec` type and initialize it in lines 62-63 using values from our controls. On line 66 we invoke the `Serialize` method of our `BinaryFormatter` object passing as parameters our `FileStream` object and our `TempRec` object. That's all there is to it—the `BinaryFormatter` object knows how to save the state of our object to the stream.

We prove that to ourselves in our `ReadIt` method where on lines 78 and 79 we again declare a `BinaryFormatter` object and a `TempRec` object. Then on line 81 we read our object back in from the file using the `Deserialize` method of the `BinaryFormatter`. On line 83 we output the results.

So what was the point of this exercise? It's to show you that in .NET, not only is data transferable, but your objects and classes are as well! Now, you can send the `records.dat` file to anyone and they will not only have the temperature data you stored, but also the class that contains the data.

When you learn about Web services in Day 15, "Using Web Services," you'll learn about another type of serialization known as XML serialization—where instead of translating your objects in binary data, they are transformed into XML.

For more information on serialization, check out the .NET Framework documentation.

Using the `RichTextBox` Control

Let's revisit the `RichTextBox` control from Day 6, "Enhancing Your Windows Forms with More Controls." You saw previously that this control enables the user to write text, just like a word processor. What you didn't see, however, is its capabilities to read and write files. Listing 11.6 is a simplification of Listing 6.9, which uses the `RichTextBox` control.

LISTING 11.6 The `RichTextBox` Control Again

```
1:  Imports System
2:  Imports System.Windows.Forms
3:  Imports System.Drawing
```

LISTING **11.6**   continued

```
 4:
 5:  Namespace TYWinForms.Day11
 6:
 7:     Public Class Listing116 : Inherits Form
 8:         private rtbText as New RichTextBox
 9:
10:         public sub New()
11:             rtbText.Dock = DockStyle.Fill
12:             rtbText.ScrollBars = RichTextBoxScrollBars.Both
13:
14:             Me.Text = "Listing 11.6"
15:             Me.Font = New Font("Times New Roman", 10)
16:             Me.Controls.Add(rtbText)
17:         end sub
18:
19:         public shared sub Main()
20:             Application.Run(new Listing116)
21:         end sub
22:     End Class
23:  End Namespace
```

11

You should already be familiar with the code in Listing 11.6, so we'll skip the analysis for now. The two methods you haven't previously seen are `LoadFile` and `SaveFile`. Let's examine the former first.

`LoadFile` takes the contents of either a file or a stream and places them in the `RichTextBox`, for the user to edit. For example, you can add the following code to the constructor of Listing 11.6 (remember to replace the path with the name of an actual file on your computer):

```
rtbText.LoadFile("c:\temp\happy.txt",
➥RichTextBoxStreamType.PlainText)
```

The first parameter is the file you created earlier today (it can be either a path or a stream—make sure you change this to a file that you have on your computer!), and the second parameter tells the `RichTextBox` control what type of file to expect. The possible values of the `RichTextBoxStreamType` enumeration are `PlainText`, `RichNoOleObjs` (a rich text file without OLE objects), `RichText`, `TextTextNoOleObjs` (a plain text file without OLE objects), and `UnicodePlainText`. (We'll discuss OLE objects on Day 14, "Using ActiveX.")

Figure 11.6 shows the new output of the application with the `LoadFile` method added.

FIGURE **11.6**

The LoadFile *method can load any text-based file into a* RichTextBox *control.*

The SaveFile method takes the exact same parameters and allows you to write or create a file.

Now you know that the RichTextBox control has I/O capabilities, and it's been right under your nose the whole time!

Using the `FileSystemWatcher` Object

If you ever need to monitor your computer for changes to files and directories, FileSystemWatcher is the object for you. It essentially sits there and waits, watching everything that happens on your system—acting somewhat like a security guard. When something happens, this object raises an event to which you can assign a delegate to perform any necessary functionality.

Let's say, using just what you know so far, you've developed an application that creates a directory listing, similar to Listing 11.1 from earlier today. If a user adds new files or deletes directories, the TreeView won't update to reflect the changes. Using the FileSystemWatcher object, however, you can alert the TreeView when such modifications have been made and add or delete nodes as necessary.

To set up a FileSystemWatcher, you need to specify which directories and files to watch, specify the types of changes you want to watch for, and then enable the object. The following code snippet does all three:

```
FileSystemWatcher objWatcher = new FileSystemWatcher();

//specify the path and files to watch
objWatcher.Path = "c:\";
objWatcher.Filter = "*.txt";
objWatcher.IncludeSubdirectories = true;
```

```
//specify the changes to watch for
objWatcher.NotifyFilter = NotifyFilters.LastWrite;

//enable the watcher
objWatcher.EnableRaisingEvents = true;
```

The first three properties are fairly self-explanatory. `Path` is simply the directory to watch, `Filter` is the type of file in that directory to watch (in this case, you're watching all text files, or files that end in the `.txt` extension), and `IncludeSubdirectories` indicates whether you want to watch subdirectories as well.

The next property, `NotifyFilter`, takes values from the `NotifyFilters` enumeration that can be combined using the | operator (`OR` in Visual Basic .NET). They can be any of the following values:

- `Attributes`—Indicates a change in the file or directory attributes has occurred.
- `CreationTime`—Indicates the creation time of a file or directory has been modified (in other words, it has been created).
- `DirectoryName`—Indicates the directory name has changed.
- `FileName`—Indicates the name of the file has changed.
- `LastAccess`—Indicates the file or directory has been accessed.
- `LastWrite`—Indicates the file has been written to.
- `Security`—Indicates the security properties of the file or directory have changed.
- `Size`—Indicates the size of the file or folder has changed.

Finally, you simply set `EnableRaisingEvents` to `true` to turn on the watcher.

The `FileSystemWatcher` has four events—`Changed`, `Created`, `Deleted`, and `Renamed`—to which you can assign delegates that each represent a type of manipulation. Let's create a simple example. Listing 11.7 creates an application that is meant to sit on your desktop. Any time something changes on the file system, this application will raise an alert.

LISTING 11.7   Watching Your Hard Drive

```
1:  using System;
2:  using System.Windows.Forms;
3:  using System.Drawing;
4:  using System.IO;
5:
6:  namespace TYWinforms.Day11 {
7:     public class Listing117 : Form {
8:        FileSystemWatcher objWatcher = new
➥FileSystemWatcher();
9:
```

LISTING 11.7 continued

```
10:        public Listing117() {
11:            objWatcher.Path = "c:\\temp";
12:            objWatcher.Filter = "*.*";
13:            objWatcher.IncludeSubdirectories = true;
14:            objWatcher.NotifyFilter =
➥NotifyFilters.CreationTime | NotifyFilters.LastWrite |
➥NotifyFilters.Size;
15:            objWatcher.EnableRaisingEvents = true;
16:
17:            objWatcher.Changed += new
➥FileSystemEventHandler(this.RaiseAlert);
18:            objWatcher.Created += new
➥FileSystemEventHandler(this.RaiseAlert);
19:            objWatcher.Deleted += new
➥FileSystemEventHandler(this.RaiseAlert);
20:
21:            this.Text = "Listing 11.7";
22:        }
23:
24:        private void RaiseAlert(Object Sender,
➥FileSystemEventArgs e) {
25:            MessageBox.Show("I see you!! You " +
➥e.ChangeType.ToString() + " " + e.Name);
26:        }
27:
28:        public static void Main() {
29:            Application.Run(new Listing117());
30:        }
31:    }
32: }
```

ANALYSIS   In Listing 11.7, lines 11–15 set up the FileSystemWatcher object as previously discussed. In this case, you watch the LastWrite, CreationTime, and Size properties for changes. Next, on lines 17–19, you set up the appropriate events to be triggered when one of the preceding properties changes. Note that these events use a delegate of type FileSystemEventHandler, which means you'll be using an event parameter of type FileSystemEventArgs in the event handler.

Line 24 contains this event handler. It simply pops up a message to the user when a change has been detected, taking advantage of a couple of properties of the FileSystemEventArgs object. ChangeType indicates the type of change that occurred. Values from the WatcherChangeTypes enumeration are valid: All (which encompasses all types of changes), Changed, Created, Deleted, or Renamed. The Name property indicates the directory or filename that was modified (alternatively, you could use the FullName property to return the entire directory path as well).

The `MessageBox.Show` method on line 25 provides a generic message to the user.

Compile and run this application, and modify the `happy.txt` file you created earlier (or whatever file you created before). The application should then alert you, as in Figure 11.7.

FIGURE 11.7

You're caught!

When you modify this file, you get two messages from the application, both saying `"Changed"`, because you changed two properties of the file: `Size` and `LastWrite`.

11

> **Tip**
> Remember to correlate your `NotifyFilter` types and the events that will be raised. For example, setting the `NotifyFilter` property to `NotifyFilters.FileName` does you no good if you don't watch the `Renamed` event.

Creating Asynchronous I/O

NEW TERM By default, all I/O operations you've performed so far have been *synchronous*. This means that your application can't do anything else until the I/O operation is complete. In other words, you can't display a message to the user at the same time you're reading or writing a file.

So far, the synchronous nature of the operations hasn't been an issue. All the I/O operations have been fairly quick, so you don't have to worry about the application waiting to continue other operations while the I/O operation is completed.

Sometimes, though, you simply can't wait for I/O to be complete. For example, say you're reading the entire contents of a very large file, or you have to wait on a slow network connection to provide you a stream. These processes can sometimes take extraordinarily long times. With synchronous operations, you simply have no choice but to make your application's users wait until the processes are done before they can continue with their work.

To combat these situations, .NET gives you the power of *asynchronous* operations. With asynchronous operation, your I/O processes occur separately from the rest of your application's execution so that your application doesn't have to wait on processes that may take forever. Imagine that all the operations that must occur in your application (initialization, control building, event handling, and so on) line up in a queue, waiting to be executed. With asynchronous operation, the most important processes in your line step out of the queue to do whatever they need to do and then come back when they're done.

Asynchronous operation is a complex topic, usually reserved for advanced users, so we won't cover it in detail here. Building an "async" application often involves a radical design shift from what you're used to, and in reality, it isn't used very often. For now, just know that streams, in addition to their normal read and write methods, have asynchronous versions of these methods as well. We'll revisit these operations on Day 19, "Creating Multithreaded Applications," when we talk about multithreading.

Printing in .NET

The last I/O topic we'll cover today is printing. Most of the people who have computers have printers as well, and they often like to print anything they possibly can, from screen shots of images to photos to text documents, so learning these concepts is important.

To print something, you must jump through a number of sometimes odd loops. The basic functionality revolves around the `PrintDocument` object and the `PrintPage` event. A `PrintDocument` is, unlike its name implies, not a document to be printed. Rather, it is the traffic cop that controls how a document is printed. It's there to start the process moving and to make sure the operation runs smoothly. Whenever you have something to be printed, the `PrintDocument` raises the `PrintPage` event and leaves it up to you to catch this event and actually print the document.

Before you learn how to do that, look at the basic setup first. Let's assume you'll allow the user to print the contents from the `RichTextBox` in Listing 11.6. (Note that we're using C# code in the following examples, so you'll have to convert from VB.NET to C# or vice versa to get these code snippets to work!) First, make sure to import the necessary namespaces:

```
using System.Drawing.Printing;
```

Then add a menu item so the user can print the document:

```
MainMenu mnuMain = new MainMenu();
MenuItem miFile = new MenuItem("File");
MenuItem miPrint = new MenuItem("Print");
miPrint.Click += new EventHandler(this.PrintClicked);

mnuMain.MenuItems.Add(miFile);
miFile.MenuItems.Add(miPrint);
```

In the event handler, PrintClicked, you can display the PrintDialog dialog box if you want to allow the user to configure print settings before actually printing (see Day 7, "Working with Dialog Boxes," for information on configuring print and page settings). For now, skip that step and just print the document. The event handler should look like the following code snippet:

```
private void PrintClicked(Object Sender, EventArgs e) {
    PrintDocument pd = new PrintDocument();
    pd.PrintPage += new PrintPageEventHandler
➡(this.pd_PrintPage);
    pd.Print();
}
```

Note these three lines of code: the creation of a PrintDocument, the assignation of a delegate to the PrintPage event, and the call to the Print command. You don't even have to tell it what to print yet. Once you create a pd_PrintPage method, you can compile and execute this application, and your printer will respond when you click the Print menu item. It just won't print anything yet; a blank document will be output.

Now, for each page that will be printed, the PrintPage event will be raised, and you'll actually print the document in this event handler. Let's look at the event handler in Listing 11.8.

LISTING 11.8   The PrintPage Event Handler

```
1:   private void pd_PrintPage(Object Sender,
➡PrintPageEventArgs e) {
2:       StringReader objReader = new StringReader(rtbText.Text);
3:
4:       Font fntPrint = this.Font;
5:       int count = 0;
6:       float yPos = 0;
7:       float lpp = e.MarginBounds.Height /
➡fntPrint.GetHeight(e.Graphics);
8:       float fltTopMargin = e.MarginBounds.Top;
9:       float fltLeftMargin = e.MarginBounds.Left;
10:      String strLine = null;
11:
```

11

LISTING 11.8 continued

```
12:     while (count < lpp && ((strLine = objReader.ReadLine())
➥!= null)) {
13:         yPos = fltTopMargin + (count * fntPrint.GetHeight
➥(e.Graphics));
14:
15:         e.Graphics.DrawString(strLine, fntPrint,
➥Brushes.Black, fltLeftMargin, yPos,
➥new StringFormat());
16:
17:         count++;
18:     }
19:
20:     if (strLine != null) {
21:         e.HasMorePages = true;
22:     } else {
23:         e.HasMorePages = false;
24:     }
25: }
```

ANALYSIS In Listing 11.8, first notice that this event handler requires a
PrintPageEventArgs object, which contains the necessary properties to use for
printing. Next, line 2 retrieves the text from the RichTextBox created earlier. You must
place the information you want to print in a stream or reader of some sort because they
are the only things that .NET can print.

Next comes some initialization. You need to know a few things about the page you're
printing on before you can print. Imagine the paper sitting in your printer as a canvas for
you to paint on. When you paint on this canvas, you need to know where to start, what
your boundaries are, how much you can fit on a single canvas, what paint to use, and
numerous other factors. This analogy works well because the printing functions of .NET
all lie in the System.Drawing namespace.

The only difference between printing a page with .NET and painting on a canvas is that
with the latter you can start painting anywhere you want and move around at random.
With printing, you must always start on the first line (even if nothing is there to print)
and move down line by line, one at a time. If you're familiar with the way printers work,
this process will make sense to you. The head on a printer moves horizontally across a
page, printing one line at time, and then moves back to the beginning to print the next
line, much like a typewriter. Therefore, you must approach the printing process in the
same way.

Line 4 retrieves the font that the printer will print with; in this case, you use the same
font that the RichTextBox uses, so the printed document will look the same as the

onscreen document. Line 5 initializes a variable you'll be using to loop through the lines in a document, but you'll learn more on that topic in a moment. Line 6 tells where vertically you want to start printing—the y coordinate. It is zero initially, and it doesn't account for the height of the margins—we'll address the margins later.

Caution

Be wary when retrieving the text to be printed; placement is very important. For example, in Listing 11.8, the text is retrieved in the `PagePrint` event handler. If the text you're printing is longer than one page, this event handler will execute again and re-retrieve the text. Your application will try to print the text from the beginning again, call a new `PagePrint` event because it's longer than one page, and execute all over again. This will cause your application to go into an infinite printing loop.

Instead, it's good practice to place the code on line 2 *outside* the `PagePrint` event handler method.

Line 7 determines the number of lines per page. Very simply, the number is determined by dividing the height of the page by the height of the font you're using. The height of the page is supplied by the `PrintPageEventArgs` object. Remember that you need to include the margins in your calculations, which is why line 7 determines the height on the `MarginBounds` property. The `Font` object has a `GetHeight` method, which determines the height of the current font you're using. Don't worry about the parameter for `GetHeight` yet.

Next, lines 8 and 9 determine the left and top margins, respectively. Finally, line 10 initializes a variable that you'll use in a moment.

Remember that printing involves moving one line at a time through the page. Therefore, you need to set up a loop to iterate through the lines in the reader you set up. The `while` loop on line 12 does just this. When it reaches the end of the page (as determined by the lines per page) or there is no more content to print, the loop exits. Note the shortcut syntax on line 12; you can assign a value to a variable directly in the `while` statement. You simply use `ReadLine` on the reader to return the current line to print.

Line 13 determines where, exactly, the current line should be printed on the page. You add the space for the margin and then figure out how many lines you've already written by multiplying your line increment by the height of the font you're using. Finally, you're ready to actually print the document, as shown on line 15.

.NET treats the page to be printed on as a canvas. To print a line, you call the `DrawString` method of the `Graphics` object associated with your printer. (When you read the GDI+ discussion on Day 13, "Creating Graphical Applications with GDI+," the graphics bit of this discussion will make much more sense.) DrawString takes six different parameters, in the following order:

- String—The string to be drawn on the page.
- Font—The font to use for printing the string.
- Brush—An object that tells the printer how to print the string (what color, whether solid or with a gradient, and so on). You'll learn more about this object on Day 13.
- X—The x coordinate to start printing from.
- Y—The y coordinate to start printing from.
- StringFormat—An object that formats the string to be printed (vertical or horizontal orientation, horizontal alignment).

Most of these parameters you already know, such as String and X and Y. For the ones you don't, Brush and StringFormat, you can just use generic values, as shown on line 15.

On line 17, you increment the counter that tells you which line is currently being printed. Table 11.4 walks you through the entire while loop on lines 12–18.

TABLE 11.4 The Print Process

Output File Line Number	X,Y Coordinates of Line	Line Contents (from happy.txt Created Earlier This Lesson)
1	0,TopMargin	Hello World!
2	0,TopMargin + line 1 height	This is more
3	0,TopMargin + line 1 height + line 2 height	text that I added here
4	0,TopMargin + height of lines 1,2,3	to test the application
5	0,TopMargin + height of lines 1,2,3,4	in Listing 11.3
6	0,TopMargin + height of lines 1,2,3,4,5	Null

Now let's look at the rest of the code from Listing 11.8:

```
20:    if (strLine != null) {
21:        e.HasMorePages = true;
22:    } else {
23:        e.HasMorePages = false;
24:    }
```

The PrintPageEventArgs object has a HasMorePages property, which indicates whether there are more pages to be printed. If there are, another PrintPage event is raised, and the entire print process starts over again. Unfortunately, the application cannot tell whether there are more pages to print; you have to figure that out yourself.

Thus, on line 20, you determine whether the last string read from the RichTextBox is null. If it is, it means there are no more lines to print, and you're done. At this point, you set HasMorePages to false. Otherwise, you have more text to print, and you need to print another page and raise PrintPage once again. In this case, you set HasMorePages to true (line 21).

Note that this bit of code comes after the while loop, which means the current page is completely printed up to the lines per page value (or the entire contents of the RichTextBox, whichever is shorter).

This process is a rather convoluted, so let's summarize:

1. Create a way for the user to print the document (that is, a menu item).
2. Create a PrintDocument object, assign an event handler to the PrintPage event, and call PrintDocument.Print.
3. In the PrintPage event handler, determine properties of the page, including lines per page, height of margins, and the font to use. Create a stream or reader object that contains the content to print.
4. Loop through the lines in the stream or reader until you reach the lines per page value, or the end of the reader. Set the starting y coordinate for printing for each line. Print the line by calling Graphics.DrawString from the PrintPageEventArgs object, passing in the necessary parameters.
5. Determine whether you have more content to print and set HasMorePages accordingly.

If you've allowed the user to change the page settings, you can simply assign the modified values to the PrintDocument, as in this example:

```
PageSettings objSettings = new PageSettings();
PrinterSettings objPrinter = new PrinterSettings();

//insert code here to customize settings (possibly through
// common dialog controls)

PrintDocument pd = new PrintDocument();
pd.DefaultPageSettings = objSettings;
pd.PrinterSettings = objPrinter;
```

When the PrintPage event is raised, the PrintPageEventArgs object will contain the new settings (such as margin changes and so on).

You also can cancel a print job by setting the `Cancel` property of the `PrintPageEventArgs` object to `true`.

Summary

I/O is often one of the more complex topics in any application-building exercise. In fact, before the introduction of .NET, you had to deal with hairy processes such as memory allocation for files before opening them and finding free file handles. Now you needn't worry about any of those tasks because .NET does most of the work for you.

Today you first learned about streams and their place in I/O. Any time you deal with I/O in .NET, you deal with streams, which are source-independent stores of information to which you can attach readers and writers to manipulate their contents. Even though there are many different types of streams, readers, and writers, they all work similarly.

To open a file, you simply create a stream around the file with the necessary `FileMode`, `FileAccess`, and `FileShare` enumeration values. The application can handle all the functionality needed to determine whether the file exists, if it should be overwritten or created, and so on. You then attach a reader or writer of the appropriate type (`StreamReader` and `StreamWriter` for most text files) and call one of these I/O methods: `Write`, `WriteLine`, `Read`, `ReadLine`, `ReadBlock`, `ReadToEnd`, and so on.

The `RichTextBox` object has built-in I/O functionality. You simply need to call the `LoadFile` and `SaveFile` methods to edit an existing document.

The `FileSystemWatcher` object is useful to monitor the changes going on in your file system. You can be alerted every time a file is created, modified, renamed, or otherwise changed, and then take appropriate action. Note, however, that this object should not be used for security purposes; much better objects are available for that task.

Finally, you learned how to print content. Printing is not an intuitive process. You create a `PrintDocument` object; call a `Print` method, which then raises events in which you must loop through the content to be printed; and then "draw" them on the paper. Luckily, though, after you learn how to print, you can use the same code almost anywhere; printing logic rarely changes.

Tomorrow you'll learn another way of enhancing your applications, and a very important way at that: the Internet. You can take advantage of the Internet from your applications in numerous ways, which you'll explore tomorrow.

Q&A

Q Can I use streams, writers, and readers, or a `RichTextBox` control to edit MS Word documents?

A Not exactly. Microsoft Word documents are not plain text; rather, they use a binary format exclusively developed by Microsoft. Not only does this format allow Microsoft to put custom functionality into Word documents, but it also ensures that only those who have Word (or a license for it) can edit Word documents.

You *can* use binary readers and writers to edit Word documents. Remember, though, that all files have a specific ordered format. Thus, if you don't know exactly how a Word document is structured, your attempts will be probably be in vain. Microsoft does give away the binary file format information to businesses interested in licensing Word, so if you run a company, good luck!

Q I've heard about isolated storage in .NET. What is that?

A Isolated storage is an interesting concept. Essentially, it means that every user of your application has his own dedicated repository for documents edited during the execution of the application. This repository is secure and protected by the operating system, so sensitive data can be stored in this location. You can also set quotas for the amount of information that can be stored in this location.

Isolated storage is not used very often in desktop applications. It is more common, however, in Internet applications, where many Internet users may access one computer.

For further discussion on isolated storage, check out *Sams Teach Yourself ASP.NET in 21 Days*.

11

Workshop

This workshop will help reinforce the concepts covered in today's lesson. It is very helpful to understand fully the answers before moving on. Answers to the quiz questions and exercises are in Appendix A.

Quiz

1. What is the difference between the `Read` and `Peek` methods?
2. What is a recursive function, and when is it useful?
3. What is the difference between synchronous and asynchronous operation?
4. To what namespace does the print functionality belong?

5. What are the four events of the `FileSystemWatcher` object?

6. What are the different `FileMode` enumeration values?

Exercise

Modify Listing 11.1 so that the `TreeView` control nodes are built dynamically whenever a user expands a node, instead of all at once during the initialization of the application. Also, add a custom printing function to print the visible contents of the tree view. (Tip: You need to collect the contents of the tree view in an appropriate variable to print.)

DAY **12**

Internet Enabling Your Forms

The Internet is an essential part of computing. What started as a response to cold-war tactics and moved into university research projects has now permeated the everyday life of nearly everyone in the civilized world. Therefore, it's only fair that you give the Internet adequate representation in your applications. Adding Internet capabilities, thanks to .NET, is a cinch.

Today you'll look at the various Internet protocols and how they are used in .NET. You'll see that you can easily perform several tasks, from making the simplest Web request to accessing secure servers, and you'll be building Web-capable applications in no time.

Today you'll learn

- What Internet and pluggable protocols are
- How the `WebRequest` object makes life easy
- What ASP.NET is
- How .NET integrates with Internet Explorer
- How to access secure Web sites

Internet Protocols

If you're familiar with the Internet—and who isn't nowadays?—you've probably heard of different Internet protocols, such as IP, FTP, HTTP, UDP, and TCP. They all are used in one way or another to make this magical thing called the Internet work.

The most familiar to most people is the Hypertext Transfer Protocol (HTTP). This protocol is used most often in Web browsers such as Netscape or Internet Explorer. You use it to retrieve Hypertext Markup Language (HTML) pages for display in your browser. Without it, the Internet would probably not be what you know it as today.

The File Transfer Protocol (FTP) is another fairly common one. FTP is used mainly to transfer files from one computer to another. It was designed in a way that makes it more efficient than HTTP at transferring large files.

Once upon a time, you needed to know all the ins and outs of these protocols to add Internet capabilities to your applications. Each protocol is different from the next, which compounds the problem if you want to use more than one protocol. As you'll see in the next section, .NET makes adding such capabilities simple for the developer. First, though, let's examine a bit more how the familiar Internet works.

Most Internet applications are based on the client/server model (sometimes known as the request/response model). In this paradigm, one computer acts as a store of information, known as the server, and another (possibly many) acts as a consumer of that information, known as the client. The client sends a request (via HTTP) to the server, and the server responds by sending the requested information back to the client (again, via HTTP—see Figure 12.1). In practical terms, you visit a Web site, acting as a client; your browser sends some HTTP request information to the server; and that Web site sends the page you requested. The overall concept is simple but efficient at what it does. Note that both the server and client can be arbitrary computers; your next-door neighbor could be running the server that you access.

FIGURE 12.1

In the client/server model, one computer stores information, and the other consumes that information.

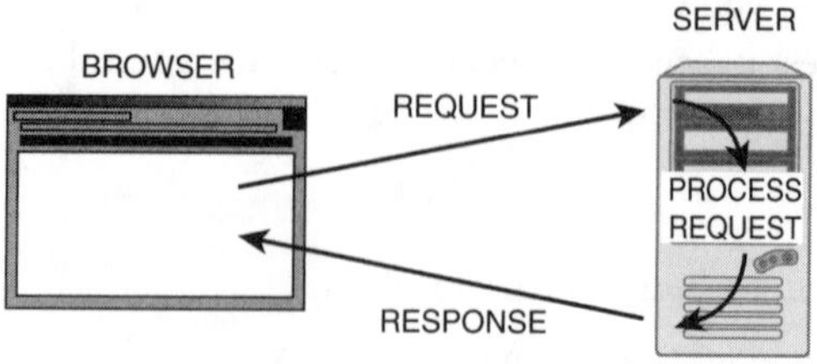

With millions of clients and servers connected to the Internet at any given time, the process of finding a particular server can be difficult. Therefore, the universal resource identifier (URI) system was developed; this system is key to .NET Internet capabilities. You've already seen URIs like this one before:

```
http://www.clpayne.com/default.asp?blah=bloh
```

Note   A uniform resource locator (URL) that most people are probably more familiar with is a form of URI that works with network protocols to find addresses.

The URI consists of four parts. The first, `http://`, specifies the protocol that should be used when requesting resources from the server. This part is known as the schema identifier. Don't worry; you don't need to remember this term.

The next part, `www.clpayne.com`, is the server name. It can be a user-friendly name as shown here—thanks in part to the domain naming system (DNS)—or simply an IP address such as 127.0.0.1. This server name is essentially the address of the server, just like you have an address for your home. The only difference is that this server name is supposed to be unique across the entire Internet (although conflicts do arise, but that's beside the point).

The next part, `/default.asp`, is the path identifier, which tells the server what specifically the client is requesting. In this case, it's an Active Server Page called `default.asp`. Often it's an HTML file such as `index.html`.

Finally, the fourth part is an optional query string. This string, `?blah=bloh`, is attached to the end of the path identifier via a question mark and specifies any additional parameters that the server may require for processing.

As you probably expected, these parts are represented by classes in the .NET Framework. We'll look at these classes next.

Pluggable Protocols

The most important Internet classes to .NET Windows Forms applications are `WebRequest` and `WebResponse`. `WebRequest` sends requests to a server using a URI, and `WebResponse` sends information back to the requesting client. The interesting aspect about these classes (and other .NET Internet classes) is that they work with any protocol, so you don't have to modify your application or write new code to use a new protocol.

`WebRequest` and `WebResponse` are like traffic cops, similar to the `SqlDataAdapter` class from Day 9, "Using ADO.NET." Recall that `SqlDataAdapter` created different `SqlCommand` objects depending on the type of SQL query you executed. When you use

12

WebRequest to request information from a server, it automatically detects the protocol that you're trying to use and creates the necessary helper object to process the request (for example, an HttpWebRequest object for HTTP requests).

 Because these helper objects can be dynamically switched out by a traffic object, they are known as *pluggable protocols*; .NET "plugs" in the appropriate class when necessary. Thus, you could build a Web browser-type application using only WebRequest. You don't need to worry about the type of address the user enters into your browser because WebRequest will dynamically adjust. This is the basis for .NET Internet applications—simplicity and ease for the developer, while maintaining power for the user.

Clients and Servers

As discussed earlier, a server is a repository of information, and a client is the user of that information. Because most of the Internet is based on clients and servers, they are typically the most common applications you'll try to develop. In the next few sections, we'll examine how to build clients that interact with servers; server applications are often reserved for ASP.NET.

> **Note**
>
> For some of the following examples, you'll need to have a Web server capable of receiving your requests. In some instances, a publicly available server, such as www.clpayne.com or www.Microsoft.com will work fine, but in others you'll need one that you can experiment on.
>
> Chances are, you already have a server running on your computer—Internet Information Server (IIS) by Microsoft. To test it, simply open a browser and type **http://localhost** into the address bar. If an error page comes up, you don't have a server running, so you need to install IIS. On the other hand, if a welcome page or a Web site pops up, you're ready to go.
>
> To install IIS, you need your Windows Installation CD. IIS is an optional component that you can install from the Add/Remove Programs control panel. Click Add/Remove Windows components in this applet, select the options for IIS, click Next, and then follow the directions to start using it.

Sending Requests with WebRequest

Sending a request is easy. At its simplest, only few new lines of code are required to start using it. So, let's jump right into Listing 12.1.

LISTING 12.1 Your First Internet Application

```
1:   using System;
2:   using System.Windows.Forms;
3:   using System.Drawing;
4:   using System.Net;
5:   using System.IO;
6:
7:   namespace TYWinforms.Day12 {
8:      public class Listing121 : Form {
9:         private RichTextBox rtbWeb = new RichTextBox();
10:
11:        public Listing121() {
12:           CallServer();
13:
14:           rtbWeb.Multiline = true;
15:           rtbWeb.Dock = DockStyle.Fill;
16:
17:           this.Text = "Listing 12.1";
18:           this.Size = new Size(800,600);
19:           this.Controls.Add(rtbWeb);
20:        }
21:
22:        private void CallServer() {
23:           WebRequest objRequest = WebRequest.Create
➥("http://www.clpayne.com");
24:           WebResponse objResponse = objRequest.
➥GetResponse();
25:
26:           StreamReader objReader = new
➥StreamReader(objResponse.GetResponseStream());
27:
28:           rtbWeb.Text = objReader.ReadToEnd();
29:
30:           objReader.Close();
31:           objResponse.Close();
32:        }
33:
34:        public static void Main() {
35:           Application.Run(new Listing121());
36:        }
37:     }
38:  }
```

ANALYSIS The first 20 lines of Listing 12.1 are fairly standard. On line 4, notice the use of the additional namespace `System.Net`, which contains all the Internet classes you need to use. The actual Internet request is made in the call to the custom `CallServer` method.

12

The first step to creating an Internet connection is to create a WebRequest object, as shown on line 23. The simplest way to create this object is to call the static Create method passing in the URI of the Internet resource you want to access. (This value is also available through the RequestUri property of the WebRequest class. Simply change the URI string to whatever you like and make sure you have an Internet connection.) Note that you haven't actually made a connection yet; you've just prepped for it.

On line 24, you actually make the connection. Using the WebRequest object you just created, you call GetResponse and store the result in a WebResponse object.

Next, you retrieve the server's response from the WebResponse object by calling GetResponseStream, which, as you can imagine, returns a stream object, just like any other stream. Line 26 attaches a reader to this stream so that you can access the contents.

On line 28, you read the contents of the stream using the reader and place the contents in the RichTextBox control. Don't forget to close both the reader and the WebRequest objects! Figure 12.2 shows the application after it processes the Web request.

FIGURE 12.2

You get these results from executing a Web request.

So, what do we have here? Figure 12.2 shows the content retrieved from the Web site www.clpayne.com. It's not a pretty Web page, but rather the HTML content from that Web page. You see the HTML content because this is what any application (even Internet Explorer) sees when it makes a request to a server. The actual presentation part is a separate piece of functionality.

Let's recap the steps involved:

1. Create a `WebRequest` object using `WebRequest.Create`.
2. Call `GetResponse` to open the connection.
3. Call `GetResponseStream` to retrieve the content, attaching a reader if necessary.
4. Close the Web objects (and stream reader if necessary).

Web interactions, just like other I/O operations, rely on streams. Streams are great for Web processing in particular, for a few reasons. First, with a stream, you don't have to download the entire resource before you can do something with it. You can read it *as it comes in* (much like you can watch streaming video before you download the whole thing). Also, recall that streams can access any type of data source, from HTML to XML. This makes retrieving any Web resource especially easy.

Using `WebRequest`, you also can post information to the Web server via a stream. Posting is a process by which a client can send additional, custom, information that isn't in the normal request message. This information can include form posts, for example. When you fill out a form online and click the submit button, you're actually posting a Web request to the server, so it can perform some processing with your data. (Conversely, the process you used earlier today is known as a "get" request.)

To test this application, let's first build a Web page that accepts form posts. Listing 12.2 shows a sample page.

LISTING 12.2 formpost.aspx

```
1:  <%@ Page Language="CS" %>
2:
3:  <script runat="server">
4:     public void Page_Load(Object Sender, EventArgs e) {
5:        if (Request.Form.Count == 0) {
6:           lblMessage.Text = "You didn't post anything!";
7:        } else {
8:           lblMessage.Text = "You posted: " +
➥Request.Form.ToString();
9:        }
10:    }
11: </script>
12:
13: <html><body>
14:    <ASP:Label id="lblMessage" runat="server"/>
15: </body></html>
```

12

ANALYSIS Save this file as `formpost.aspx` in your root Web directory (typically `c:\inet-pub\wwwroot` if you used the default installation settings for IIS). This file is a simple ASP.NET (Active Server Pages.NET) page, but as you can see, it's similar to a Windows Forms file (the beauty of .NET!).

> **Note** For the `formpost.aspx` page to work, you need to have the ASP.NET engine installed. The engine is an optional component of the .NET Framework.

We won't go into details of ASP.NET here, but let's briefly examine Listing 12.2. In ASP.NET, you have two types of code: server code and HTML code. The HTML portion of this file is contained on lines 13–15. The server code is just like any Visual Basic .NET or C# code you've already written, and it's contained in `<script>` tags, as shown on lines 3–11. This code is compiled just like Windows Forms applications and works in much the same way.

ASP.NET pages can have a method called `Page_Load` that executes as soon as the page is called from the browser, much like a constructor for a Windows Forms program when the application starts. Notice that the `Page_Load` method takes the same parameter list as many Windows Forms events because it is an event handler for the `Page.Load` event in ASP.NET, which is raised as the page is loaded.

ASP.NET has the `Request` object, which works similarly to the `WebRequest` object you've been using. The `Form` property is a collection of all the values that have been posted to the server; your form information would be here if you filled out a form online. If nothing has been posted, this collection is empty (the `Count` property is 0), and you display a message (you can think of this as the "sad message" for later reference) in the `Label` on line 14. The `Label` is just like a Windows Form `Label`, so this code should look familiar. On the other hand, if something is in the form post, you display a "happy message," which consists of `"You posted:"` and the posted value, as shown on line 8. `Request.Form.ToString` simply writes out everything that was posted.

Test the page by going to `http://localhost/formpost.aspx` in your browser. You should see the message `"You didn't post anything!"` because you haven't yet posted any data. We'll address that issue in a moment.

This section provided a brief overview of ASP.NET, but as you can see, it's not very complicated once you've learned Windows Forms. If you want to know more details, check out *Sams Teach Yourself ASP.NET in 21 Days* (ISBN: 0-672-32168-8), also by yours truly.

Now let's create the Windows Forms application that will post to this form. Listing 12.3 shows the code.

LISTING 12.3   Posting Data to Your ASP.NET Page

```
 1:  using System;
 2:  using System.Windows.Forms;
 3:  using System.Drawing;
 4:  using System.Net;
 5:  using System.IO;
 6:
 7:  namespace TYWinforms.Day12 {
 8:     public class Listing123 : Form {
 9:        private RichTextBox rtbWeb = new RichTextBox();
10:        private WebRequest objRequest;
11:         public Listing123() {
12:           rtbWeb.Dock = DockStyle.Fill;
13:
14:           objRequest = WebRequest.Create
➥("http://localhost/formpost.aspx");
15:
16:           PostData();
17:           GetData();
18:
19:           this.Text = "Listing 12.3";
20:           this.Controls.Add(rtbWeb);
21:        }
22:
23:        private void PostData() {
24:           objRequest.Method = "POST";
25:           objRequest.ContentLength = 23;
26:           objRequest.ContentType =
➥"application/x-www-form-urlencoded";
27:
28:           StreamWriter objWriter = new StreamWriter
➥ (objRequest.GetRequestStream());
29:           objWriter.Write("Hi this is a form post!");
30:           objWriter.Close();
31:        }
32:
33:        private void GetData() {
34:           WebResponse objResponse = objRequest.
➥GetResponse();
35:           StreamReader objReader = new StreamReader
➥ (objResponse.GetResponseStream());
36:
37:           rtbWeb.Text = objReader.ReadToEnd();
38:
```

LISTING 12.3   continued

```
39:              objReader.Close();
40:              objResponse.Close();
41:          }
42:
43:          public static void Main() {
44:              Application.Run(new Listing123());
45:          }
46:      }
47:  }
```

ANALYSIS   The application in Listing 12.3 posts some data to the `formpost.aspx` file from Listing 12.2 and displays the results in the `RichTextBox` declared on line 9. The constructor again is fairly simple, calling a `PostData` method to post the information to the server and `GetData` to retrieve the response. Notice the creation of the `WebRequest` object on line 14; it points to the `formpost.aspx` file you already created.

Let's look at `PostData` on line 23. To post data to the server, you must first tell it that you're going to do so by setting the `Method` property of the `WebRequest` object to `"POST"`, as shown on line 24. After the server receives this information, it knows to wait for data from the client. Next, on line 25, you set the length of the content you're going to send; in this case, it's the length of a string you're going to send. Note that setting the length is optional but generally a good idea. On line 26, you set the `ContentType` property of the `WebRequest` object. Setting this property is very important. The default value is `"text/html"`, which means that plain text formatted as HTML is being transferred. Posted data, however, isn't transferred as plain text, but rather is encoded in a special format. This format is specified on line 26 as `application/x-www-form-urlencoded`. If you don't set this value, the server won't recognize the posted data you send and will simply disregard it.

Now that you've prepared the server, it's time to start sending data. Remember that all I/O in .NET is performed via streams, and posting data is no exception. Thus, on line 28, you call the `GetRequestStream` function to return a writeable stream that will be sent to the server and then wrap a writer around it. On line 29, you call the `Write` method (just like you would for any writer object) to send your data to the server.

Tip

Note that the `ContentLength` property set on line 25 is the length of the string on line 29. Rather than manually count the characters on line 29, however, you could simply use the following:

`objRequest.ContentLength = "Hi this is a form post!".Length;`

Alternatively, you could store the data to send in a string variable and call its `Length` property.

Finally, just like when you're reading request information, you must close your writer, as shown on line 30.

The GetData method on lines 33–41 is virtually identical to the CallServer method in Listing 12.1. You call GetResponse to create a WebResponse object, then call the GetResponseStream method and create a reader, and finally call ReadToEnd. Both the reader and WebResponse objects are then closed on lines 39 and 40. The only difference between this method and CallServer from earlier is that here you've just posted data to the server, so you're expecting a tailored response from the server.

When you compile and run this application, you get results similar to those shown in Figure 12.3.

FIGURE **12.3**

*You get these results
after posting to the
server.*

In the figure, you can see that the returned content is HTML. The expected result is returned:

```
You posted: Hi+this+is+a+form+post!
```

Because the ASP.NET page received posted form data, it displayed the "happy message" with the data you submitted. Notice, however, the plus (+) sign between each word. Remember that posted data is in a special format; substituting pluses for spaces is just one of the formatting tricks required by posts.

The WebRequest is very flexible, allowing you to easily retrieve and send content to any server. Before the introduction of .NET, retrieving and posting data was much harder than simply writing to or reading from a stream. Table 12.1 shows the properties and some methods of the WebRequest object.

12

TABLE 12.1 WebRequest Members

Property	Description
ConnectionGroupName	This property is used for grouping connections (connection pools). Connection pools are used to enhance performance when multiple connections are required.
ContentLength	The length of the data being sent.
ContentType	The type and format of data being sent.
Credentials	Security credentials used to access Web resources. (You'll find more details on this property later today in "Internet Security.")
Headers	The collection of HTTP headers sent with a request.
Method	The protocol method for this request.
PreAuthenticate	Indicates whether authentication information should be sent to the server before being asked to do so.
Proxy	The proxy to use to access Web resources.
RequestUri	The URI of the request resource.
Timeout	The length of time allowed for the request to wait for a response from the server.
Method	**Description**
GetRequestStream	Returns a stream that can be used to send data to the server.
GetResponse	Returns a stream that contains the response of the server.

Processing Requests with WebResponse

The WebResponse class, as you've seen, processes the response from a server. This simple class doesn't contain many members. Table 12.2 shows the properties and methods of WebResponse.

TABLE 12.2 WebResponse Members

Property	Description
ContentLength	The length of the data being sent.
ContentType	The type and format of data being sent.
Headers	The collection of HTTP headers sent with a request.
ResponseUri	The URI of the response resource.
Method	**Description**
Close	Closes the response stream, in effect, closing the connection to the server.
GetResponseStream	Returns a stream that contains the response of the server.

Handling Protocol-Specific Classes

Previously, you learned that `WebRequest` and `WebResponse` create helper classes when dealing with Web interactions. Most of the time, `WebRequest` and `WebResponse` will be enough for whatever you need to do. You can, however, access the helper classes to provide additional functionality.

For example, suppose that for some reason you need to supply the type of application that is accessing the server—an Internet Explorer–compatible browser, for instance. This information is known as the user-agent. The `WebRequest` object doesn't directly allow you to supply the type, but its helper class, `HttpWebRequest`, which aids in HTTP processing, does:

```
((HttpWebRequest)objRequest).UserAgent = "Internet Explorer";
```

To access the `HttpWebRequest`-specific properties, you must cast the `WebRequest` variable appropriately, as shown in the preceding code snippet or as follows:

```
HttpWebRequest objHttpRequest = (HttpWebRequest)objRequest;
```

Table 12.3 shows the members of `HttpWebRequest`, in addition to those in Table 12.1.

TABLE 12.3   `HttpWebRequest` Members (Supplemental to Table 12.1)

Property	Description
Accept	Corresponds to the `Accept` HTTP header.
Address	Specifies the URI of the server that actually responds to the request (can be different than `Uri`).
AllowAutoRedirect	Indicates whether the request should allow redirects caused by the server.
AllowWriteStreamBuffering	Indicates whether the response stream should be buffered (often results in improved performance).
ClientCertificates	Returns client security certificates.
Connection	Corresponds to the `Connection` HTTP header.
ContinueDelegate	Identifies a delegate that can respond to an HTTP 100 message.
CookieContainer	Identifies the cookies associated with the request.
Expect	Corresponds to the `Expect` HTTP header.
HaveResponse	Indicates whether a response has been received from the server.
IfModifiedSince	Corresponds to the `If-Modified-Since` HTTP header.
KeepAlive	Indicates whether the request object should maintain a persistent connection to the server.
MaximumAutomaticRedirections	Specifies the maximum number of times the request object will allow itself to be redirected.

12

TABLE 12.3 continued

Property	Description
MediaType	Indicates the media type of the request.
Pipelined	Indicates whether requests should be pipelined to the server (works only if KeepAlive is set to true).
ProtocolVersion	Specifies the version of HTTP to use.
Referer	Corresponds to the Referer HTTP header.
SendChunked	Indicates whether data should be sent to the server in chunks or segments.
ServicePoint	Specifies the service point to use for the server.
TransferEncoding	Corresponds to the Transfer-encoding HTTP header.
UserAgent	Corresponds to the User-agent HTTP header.

For more information on the various HTTP headers, check out the World Wide Web Consortium's Web site (www.w3c.org).

Working with Internet Explorer

The .NET Framework allows your Windows Forms applications to work together with Internet Explorer. This can save you a lot of time that you used to spend rebuilding desktop applications for use on the Internet. For example, if you've built a useful Windows Forms application, anyone can access it over the Internet through IE (assuming that she has the correct permissions and the .NET Framework installed).

Let's reuse the calculator application you built in the exercise from Day 5, "Handling Events in Your Windows Forms." (If you didn't build this application, simply use any application you've already built.) Move this application into your root Web directory on your computer (c:\inetpub\wwwroot), open your browser, and then type the following:

```
http://localhost/application_name.exe
```

(Be sure to substitute your actual filename for *application_name.exe*.)

Your browser will call the application, which will run just like a normal Windows Forms application. Figure 12.4 shows the output.

Embedding Windows Forms Controls in Internet Explorer

You also can embed Windows Forms controls into IE by using the HTML <OBJECT> tag. Listing 12.4 shows a simple HTML page that embeds the TextBox control in the browser.

FIGURE 12.4

You can run your Windows Forms applications from the browser.

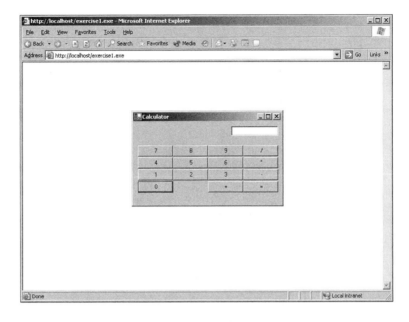

LISTING 12.4   Embedding Windows Forms Controls in Internet Explorer

```
1:  <html><body>
2:      <OBJECT id="MyControl"
➥classid="http:System.Windows.Forms.dll#
➥System.Windows.Forms.TextBox"
➥height=300 width=300 VIEWASTEXT>
3:          <param name="Text" value="Hi there!">
4:          <param name="Width" value="100">
5:          <param name="Height" value="100">
6:          <param name="Multiline" value="true">
7:      </OBJECT>
8:  </body></html>
```

12

ANALYSIS   If you aren't familiar with the <OBJECT> tag, it's really very simple to learn. The first parameter is id (on line 2), which is simply a user-friendly name you can use to refer to the control later in your code. In the second parameter, classid, the action takes place. To embed a .NET control, you need two things for the classid: the name and path of the assembly or executable that contains the control you want to embed. Then you need, separated from the path by a pound sign (#), the full namespace name of the control in question. Because you want to embed the TextBox control, you set the assembly path to System.Windows.Forms.dll, and the namespace name to System.Windows.Forms.TextBox.

> **Tip**
>
> The `System.Windows.Forms.dll` file is normally located in the
> `c:\winnt\Microsoft.NET\Framework\version` folder, but for convenience,
> you can place a copy in the `c:\inetpub\wwwroot` folder, which allows you to
> access it via the Web. If you don't move this DLL to the `wwwroot` folder, you
> may not see the text in the application.

Next, the `Height` and `Width` properties (lines 4 and 5) tell the browser how much screen
space the control should consume. Note that this does not necessarily mean that the control
will take up that much space, but rather these properties determine how much should
be reserved. `VIEWASTEXT` is a helper property that tells browsers how the control should
be rendered, should it not be compatible.

Each property of the control you want to embed can be exposed via a `PARAM` tag, as
shown on lines 3–6. Here, you expose the `Text`, `Width`, `Height`, and `Multiline` properties of the `TextBox` and set initial values for them as well. Also, note that you must close
the `OBJECT` tag, as shown on line 7.

Save this listing as an .HTML file and view it from your browser (take note of the previous tip). You should see something similar to Figure 12.5.

FIGURE 12.5

*Your `TextBox` control
is embedded in IE.*

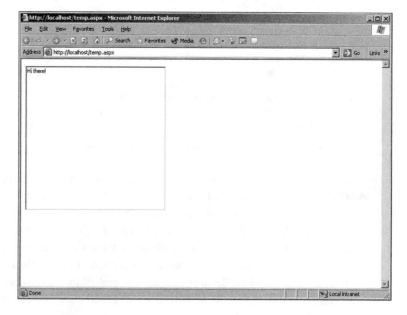

If you want, you can modify the exposed properties via JavaScript, as in this example:

```
function ChangeValues() {
   MyControl.Text = "I just changed the text!";
   MyControl.Width = "75";
}
```

You refer to the control with the `id` value you set earlier in Listing 12.4.

Of course, this example is contrived. Rather than embed such a Windows Forms control into IE, you could simply use a similar ASP.NET control—much easier and more efficient. But, if you've developed a custom control, using this technique would be a perfect way to expose it via the Web. (See Day 18, "Building Custom Windows Forms Controls," for more information on building custom controls.)

Internet Security

Internet security is a complex topic. This section won't cover security in detail—that's better suited for an ASP.NET book—but rather how Windows Forms applications deal with it.

Several forms of Internet security are in use today, and each serves different purposes. Secure Sockets Layer (SSL) is a protocol (similar to HTTP) that is used for transmitting data securely from a client to server. You've probably already used SSL on many credit-card processing Web sites such as www.amazon.com. You'll know these sites by noticing their URIs: They always start with HTTPS.

The `WebRequest` and `WebResponse` objects are completely compatible with SSL, and you don't need to do anything special to take advantage of it. Remember that these objects use pluggable protocols, so your application can already handle SSL.

Another type of security, which we'll focus on in a moment, is Internet authentication. Unlike SSL, which concentrates on sending data securely, authentication relies on verifying client security permissions before any data is even sent. This process assumes that once a user's identity is verified, he'll have permission to access all the necessary resources, and secure transmission will be handled by another means (such as SSL).

Security is an important issue for Web sites because they are more vulnerable to attacks than traditional desktop applications. Therefore, they often take extra security precautions to protect themselves. Luckily, Windows Forms is fully compliant with those measures, so you can access secure resources from your applications.

12

Authentication

Windows has three types of Internet authentication procedures. Each, as described previously, tries to verify a user's credentials before allowing her into the Web site; the site must make sure a user is who she says she is.

The first, and most common, is known as *basic authentication*. With this method, the Web site prompts the user for a username and password when accessed. If the supplied credentials match the server's secure user list, access is allowed. Figure 12.6 shows a typical basic-authentication protected site, as seen from Windows XP.

FIGURE 12.6

Basic authentication prompts you for username and password information.

The second method, known as *digest authentication*, is similar to basic; the Web site prompts the user for credentials. The only difference is that the credentials are sent to the server encrypted with digest mode, but unencrypted with basic.

The third method is *Integrated Windows Authentication* (also known as NTLM). This method is rather sneaky. It doesn't prompt the user for credentials, but the client's copy of Windows communicates with the server's copy behind the scenes to supply information. The credentials used are the ones you enter when you log in to your computer. This method is very secure, but both computers must be running the Windows operating system for it to work.

Permissions Classes

Windows Forms and the `WebRequest` method can work with all three types of authentication using one simple property: `WebRequest.Credentials`. This property takes a `NetworkCredential` object as a parameter:

```
WebRequest objRequest = WebRequest.Create
➥("http://localhost/secure");

objRequest.Credentials = new NetworkCredential
➥("Christopher Payne", "my password");
```

The constructor for the `NetworkCredential` object takes a username, password, and optional domain. Then you simply request the resource as you would normally. That's all there is to it! This method works with basic, digest, and NTLM methods. Alternatively, you could use

```
WebRequest objRequest = WebRequest.Create
➥("http://localhost/secure");

NetworkCredential objCredentials = new NetworkCredential();
objCredentials.UserName = "Christopher Payne";
objCredentials.Password = "My password";
objCredentials.Domain = "My Domain";

objRequest.Credentials = objCredentials;
```

Security can be a complex topic, but dealing with it through Windows Forms is easy.

Summary

Today you learned that Windows Forms uses pluggable protocols for its Web applications. Pluggable protocols are classes that deal with the various Internet protocols (HTTP, FTP, and so on) that can be dynamically replaced depending on the Internet resource requested. Thus, you have to write only one set of code to access any number of protocols.

The heart of pluggable protocols is the `WebRequest` and `WebResponse` classes. These two classes encapsulate all the functionality you need to access Web resources and perform the protocol handling for you. The general procedure for accessing Internet resources is to create a `WebRequest` object using the `WebRequest.Create` method with a supplied URI, call the `GetResponse` method, followed by the `GetResponseStream` to return the server's response, and finally to close the connection. Optionally, you can call `GetRequestStream` to write information to the server.

Windows Forms applications can work in different ways with Internet Explorer. You can simply call an application by using its URL or embed it in a Web page by using the `OBJECT` tag.

Finally, you learned that all authentication security issues are handled through the `WebRequest`'s `Credentials` property, which takes a `NetworkCredential` object that supplies username, password, and domain information to a server.

Tomorrow's lesson moves back to desktop-based applications. You'll learn about Windows Forms graphical capabilities with GDI+.

12

Q&A

Q How is an ASP.NET application different from an Internet-enabled .NET Windows application?

A ASP.NET applications are built especially for the Internet and can be accessed only through a server. ASP.NET was designed with the distributed nature of the Internet in mind, which makes it much more efficient than Windows Forms over the Internet. Therefore, you'll often want to build your server applications with ASP.NET instead of Windows Forms. That doesn't, however, stop you from building client applications in either paradigm.

Q Can I use asynchronous Web requests?

A Absolutely! Just like with regular I/O, the Web classes of Windows Forms have asynchronous access as well, and it is performed exactly the same way. Asynchronous operation, however, is beyond the scope of this book. See the .NET Framework documentation for more information.

Q What is a Web service?

A A Web service is the name of a broad category of Internet applications. The goal of Web services is to deliver applications (or pieces of those applications) across the Internet to a user's desktop invisibly. For example, one day, Microsoft Word may be a Web service. You'll still interact with it just as you do now on your desktop, but it won't actually be installed on your computer. You'll access it over the Internet, but without the hassles of dealing with a browser; the same Word interface will still be used.

Web services have both critics and fans who argue whether or not Web services are the future of Internet applications. Whatever your stance, it is true that Web services are a remarkable technology.

Workshop

This workshop will help reinforce the concepts covered in today's lesson. It is very helpful to understand fully the answers before moving on. Answers to the quiz questions and exercises are in Appendix A.

Quiz

1. True or False: To send POST information to the server, you use a WebResponse object.

2. What are the four parts of a URI?

3. What must the content type be to post form information?

4. What is the `HttpWebRequest` object?

5. What are the three types of Windows authentication?

Exercise

Create an application that examines a Web page (of your choosing), parses the images from that page (in HTML, images begin with `<img src="`), and displays all the images from that page, one at a time, in a `PictureBox` control. Use a button to cycle through the images. (Hint: Use the `Image.FromStream` method to retrieve an image from a stream.)

12

Creating Graphical Applications with GDI+

One of the most interesting features of Windows Forms is its graphical capabilities. With the Graphical Device Interface (GDI+), you can create all manner of graphical interfaces, from image editors to text modeling applications, or even something as simple as Microsoft Paint.

Today's lesson is all about GDI+: where it came from, how to find your way around it, and the neat tricks it can do for you. Graphical applications are often highly specialized, so you may not use the skills presented today very often, but they are very useful to know.

Today, you will learn

- Why we need a graphical device interface
- What the basic components of GDI+ are
- How to draw shapes and text on your forms
- How to manipulate and draw images
- How to create odd-shaped Windows Forms

Introduction to Graphics in Windows

Graphics in Windows covers a wide range of applications, from complex 3D games to the background image of your desktop. Nearly everything you do in Windows involves some sort of graphics.

Most people have at least heard about graphics or video cards for their computers. It is these pieces of hardware that take instructions from your computer, and send output to your monitors (in fact, your monitor plugs directly into the graphics card). The type, size, color depth, and so on of your display all depends on the video card you're using.

The traditional problem with graphics in any operating system is that you never know ahead of time what the video card's capabilities are. Due to the nature of modern PCs, where one can often switch components easily without making changes to the rest of the system, it is possible that no two computers are alike. This complicates the issue of handling graphics because your applications have to be able to deal with any number of video cards, and unfortunately, very few video cards do things similarly.

What is needed is a simple interface that developers may use to build graphical applications, regardless of the hardware in use. Originally, Microsoft developed the Graphical Device Interface (GDI) to handle this issue. GDI is a sort of translator for graphics hardware. You issue standard commands to GDI to perform graphics functionality, and GDI in turn speaks with your hardware. Luckily, GDI is multi-lingual; it is designed to communicate with nearly every type of video card on the market. This means that developers don't have to worry about the idiosyncrasies of each video card. Rather, you can concentrate only on dealing with GDI, and it will deal with the individual video cards.

 Note

GDI and GDI+ are used for the 2D graphics capabilities of Windows. The third dimension is a whole different issue, and requires different paradigms. DirectX and OpenGL are two of these paradigms that work similarly to GDI: they abstract the capabilities of the hardware for the developer.

GDI opened the door to a new world for developers. It became easy to create graphical applications. You could draw images or create text patterns; even printing was simplified. GDI encompassed every popular (and some not so popular) feature that was supported in video cards. If a user's particular video card didn't support a certain feature, it simply wasn't used; the user would never know the difference (unless, of course, he looked at his friend's computer that had a better video card).

The capabilities of video cards, however, are constantly evolving. New features such as alpha blending, texture mapping, splines, and per-pixel bump mapping and shading started to make 3D applications much more advanced than simple Windows 2D graphics. With each new version of Windows, a new version of GDI was released that tried to incorporate the latest features. However, the constant additions to GDI began to make it cumbersome. That, in addition to the move to .NET architecture, prompted Microsoft to revamp GDI into a new paradigm.

GDI+, then, is a redesigned, enhanced version of GDI. Not only does it contain support for all the latest graphical goodies, but it is fully .NET compliant, and, as you know from working with .NET, that simplifies development tasks. No longer is it necessary to obtain device contexts and handles (complex non-intuitive structures in GDI that were necessary for drawing). Now you simply deal with graphics classes and their members, just like any other class in Windows Forms.

Specifically, GDI+ is divided into three areas. The first, vector graphics, involves graphics primitives—things like lines, curves, and simple shapes. Vector graphics rely on a coordinate system; when the coordinates change, the graphics change.

The second area consists of images—things that cannot be represented by simple lines (such as the background for your desktop). To images, a coordinate system is meaningless; images simply get drawn without regard to x and y coordinates. Because vector graphics rely on coordinates, they are easier and more efficient than images to manipulate. For example, if you want to distort a line, you simply change the coordinates. If you want to distort an image, you need to manipulate the bits the image is composed of. Also, vector graphics can be arbitrarily distorted without losing quality because a coordinate is a coordinate. An image, however, will lose quality when reshaped or resized, because there is only so much data to begin with in an image; you can't add new details to an image without recapturing the image (that's why, for example, a photo becomes more "grainy" as you enlarge it—if you want to get a bigger photo, you have to retake it and tell the developer to enlarge it).

The third component is typography, or text. This deals with different fonts, font sizes, styles, and colors.

All three of these areas revolve around a few central GDI+ classes, and some basic concepts.

Brushes and Pens

Before you get started, there are a few terms you need to know. In GDI+, two of the most common concepts you'll come across are *pens* and *brushes*, which are similar to their real-life counterparts.

A Pen, essentially, is responsible for drawing a line. Think of a pen in real-life. You can have pens with different colored inks, different thicknesses (a fountain pen will draw a thicker line than a ball-point pen, for instance), and even different textures. In GDI+, a Pen is the same way. You can create a Pen that has all the characteristics you want, and then draw lines or text with it.

A Brush is responsible for filling the shapes drawn by a Pen with a specified color and texture. For example, you'd draw a circle with a Pen, but fill it with the color orange with a Brush. Brushes will affect some things you wouldn't normally consider as shapes, such as fonts. Brushes in GDI+ can even draw gradient colors, to make your objects more interesting.

The Graphics object is the central part of GDI+. Graphics contains all the methods and properties you need to draw lines and text and, as you saw in Day 11, "Working with Windows I/O," print pages. You'll become very familiar with the Graphics object as we move through today's lesson.

Rectangles and Regions

Two other important concepts are *rectangles* and *regions*. A Rectangle is simply a rectangular graphical object in .NET—nothing special about that. A Region represents the area inside the Rectangle. These two objects are often used to stipulate specific areas in which other graphics objects (such as images or lines) should be drawn—you almost never see these objects without a reference to some Graphics method.

There are two ways to create a rectangle: by specifying an upper-left corner starting point, and a Size value, or by specifying the X and Y coordinate for the upper-left corner and a width and height:

```
Rectangle objRect = new Rectangle(new Point(0,0),
➥new Size(100,100));
```

```
Rectangle objRect = new Rectangle(0, 0, 100, 100);
```

In the second constructor, the first two parameters are the X and Y coordinate of the starting point, and the last two coordinates are the width and height of the rectangle, respectively.

A Region is created by passing a Rectangle object to it:

```
Region objRegion = new Region(objRect);
```

Alternatively, you could specify an arbitrary shape with a GraphicsPath object, but we'll get to that in the "Drawing Shapes" section later today.

These two objects don't have very many useful methods by themselves, but are helpful when determining graphics boundaries, which is why you'll always see them with other graphics object.

Handling the `Paint` Event

The most important function of GDI+ is not to build complex drawing applications such as Photoshop, or even Windows Paint. It's much simpler than that. GDI+ is responsible for drawing the windows of every application you use. Every time a window needs to be drawn (such as during startup, maximizing, and so on), the `Paint` method is raised. Therefore, whenever you need to control how a Windows Form is drawn, you must provide an event handler for `Paint`.

Let's take a look at a simple example, shown in Listing 13.1. This listing draws some text on a Windows Form.

LISTING **13.1**   Drawing Text with the `Paint` Event

```
 1:  using System;
 2:  using System.Windows.Forms;
 3:  using System.Drawing;
 4:
 5:  namespace TYWinforms.Day13 {
 6:     public class Listing131 : Form {
 7:        public Listing131() {
 8:           this.Text = "Listing 13.1";
 9:           this.Paint += new PaintEventHandler(this.PaintMe);
10:        }
11:
12:     private void PaintMe(Object Sender, PaintEventArgs e) {
13:           Graphics objGraphics = e.Graphics;
14:           Brush brushText = new SolidBrush(Color.Black);
15:           Font fntText = new Font("Times New Roman", 24,
➥ FontStyle.Regular);
16:
17:           objGraphics.DrawString("I'm painting!", fntText,
➥brushText, new Point(50,100));
18:        }
19:
20:        public static void Main() {
21:           Application.Run(new Listing131());
22:        }
23:     }
24:  }
```

13

ANALYSIS The constructor for this class, on line 7, is very simple. It only sets the caption of the form, and assigns a delegate to the Paint method. Let's look at the PaintMe event handler beginning on line 12.

First, notice that the second parameter to this method is a PaintEventArgs object. This object contains a very important property, Graphics, that returns a Graphics object, which, as we discussed in the previous section, contains all the methods you need to draw lines, strings, font, and so on. Whenever you want to draw something, you need to have a Graphics object; GDI+ cannot function without it. So on line 13, you retrieve this Graphics object and assign it to a variable for easier use (in a moment we'll discuss another way to create a Graphics object).

On line 14, you set up a Brush object that will be used to draw the text. Note that you cannot use a Pen object to draw text. Then, on line 15, you set up a Font object that contains the typeface you'll use to draw text.

Finally, on line 17 you call the DrawString method of the Graphics object to draw the text I'm painting! on the form using the specified font and brush. The fourth parameter of DrawString specifies the location where the text should be drawn.

Figure 13.1 shows the output.

FIGURE 13.1

The string "I'm painting" will be drawn every time the Paint event is raised.

Alternatively, instead of adding a delegate for the Paint method, you can override the OnPaint method. Recall from Day 5 that every event has a corresponding OnEventName method. In this case, you can override the form's default OnPaint method by creating a new method called OnPaint. Your new OnPaint will override the form's default method to provide your custom drawing capabilities. Listing 13.2 performs the identical function as Listing 13.1, but uses the overridden method instead.

LISTING 13.2   Drawing a String with an Overridden `OnPaint`

```
 1:  using System;
 2:  using System.Windows.Forms;
 3:  using System.Drawing;
 4:  using System.Drawing.Drawing2D;
 5:
 6:  namespace TYWinforms.Day13 {
 7:     public class Listing132 : Form {
 8:        public Listing132() {
 9:           this.Text = "Listing 13.2";
10:        }
11:
12:        protected override void OnPaint(PaintEventArgs e) {
13:           Graphics objGraphics = e.Graphics;
14:           Brush brushText = new SolidBrush(Color.Black);
15:           Font fntText = new Font("Times New Roman", 24,
➥FontStyle.Regular);
16:
17:           objGraphics.DrawString("I'm painting!", fntText,
➥brushText, new Point(50,100));
18:        }
19:
20:        public static void Main() {
21:           Application.Run(new Listing132());
22:        }
23:     }
24:  }
```

ANALYSIS   This code is identical to Listing 13.1, except that the assignment of a delegate on line 10 is gone, and the painting method declaration on line 12 has changed. Note the keyword `override`, which specifies that the default `OnPaint` method should not be used. Overridden members cannot be `private`, so we mark this one as `protected`.

This method of overriding the `OnPaint` method is typically preferred over assigning `Paint` delegate simply because it hearkens back to the days of GDI, and therefore more developers are familiar with it. There are no performance advantages either way.

Although it is one of the most common methods, handling the `Paint` event is not the only way to retrieve a `Graphics` object for drawing. The `Form` object can also generate one for you with the `CreateGraphics` method:

```
Graphics objGraphics = this.CreateGraphics();
```

You can then use `objGraphics` to perform any drawing you need, and it doesn't need to be inside the `OnPaint` method.

13

Drawing Text

So what's the difference between drawing text using DrawString and simply creating a Label control? A Label is ideal when you know ahead of time where text should be placed and what it should say. DrawString, however, can be used to dynamically draw text wherever the user wants.

Let's look at an example. The code in Listing 13.3 allows the user to type text wherever the cursor is when he clicks his mouse.

LISTING 13.3   Drawing Text

```
1:   using System;
2:   using System.Windows.Forms;
3:   using System.Drawing;
4:   using System.Drawing.Text;
5:
6:   namespace TYWinforms.Day13 {
7:       public class Listing133 : Form {
8:           private bool blnIsWriting = false;
9:           private Point ptClick;
10:           private string strKey;
11:
12:           public Listing133() {
13:               this.Text = "Listing 13.3";
14:               this.MouseDown += new MouseEventHandler
➥(FormClicked);
15:               this.KeyPress += new KeyPressEventHandler
➥ (this.Type);
16:           }
17:
18:       private void Type(Object Sender, KeyPressEventArgs e) {
19:               if (blnIsWriting) {
20:                   strKey += e.KeyChar.ToString();
21:                   this.Invalidate();
22:               }
23:           }
24:
25:       private void FormClicked(Object Sender,
➥MouseEventArgs e) {
26:               blnIsWriting = !blnIsWriting;
27:
28:               if (blnIsWriting) {
29:                   this.Cursor = Cursors.IBeam; strKey = "";
30:               } else {
31:                   this.ResetCursor();
32:               }
33:               ptClick = new Point(e.X, e.Y);
```

LISTING 13.3   continued

```
34:        }
35:
36:        protected override void OnPaint(PaintEventArgs e) {
37:            Graphics objGraphics = e.Graphics;
38:            Brush brushText = new SolidBrush(Color.Black);
39:            Font fntText = new Font("Times New Roman", 1004,
➥FontStyle.Regular);
40:
41:            objGraphics.DrawString(strKey, fntText,
➥brushText, ptClick);
42:        }
43:
44:        public static void Main() {
45:            Application.Run(new Listing133());
46:        }
47:    }
48: }
```

ANALYSIS   On lines 8–10, you declare a few variables that will be used elsewhere in your application. blnIsWriting determines if the application is currently in a text-drawing state (in other words, it is waiting for keyboard input from the user). ptClick will represent the point where the user clicked the mouse cursor—this is where text will be drawn. Finally, strKey will hold the string to be written.

On lines 14 and 15 you declare event handlers for two events: MousePress, so that you can determine where the user wants text to be written, and KeyPress, so that you can determine what key the user has pressed to draw it on screen.

Let's look at the FormClicked event first, on line 25. The first thing this event does is set the blnIsWriting variable to its opposite value. In other words, if blnIsWriting is currently false (and the application is not waiting for keyboard input) then it is set to true, thereby enabling the text writing functionality. If blnIsWriting is currently true, it is set to false, and the writing functionality is disabled.

If blnIsWriting is true, then you change the cursor into the I-beam, and set strKey to nothing so any previously entered text isn't copied. On the other hand, if blnIsWriting is false, you reset the cursor to the default value using the ResetCursor method. Finally, on line 33, you grab the point on the form where the user clicked the mouse cursor.

Whenever the user types a letter from the keyboard, the Type method on line 18 executes. This method checks to see if we're in writing mode, and if so, appends the typed character to the strKey variable. To actually draw the string, remember that we need a Graphics object. So far, the only ways we've seen to retrieve a Graphics object are to

13

raise either the `Paint` or `PrintPage` event (see Day 11, "Working with Windows I/O," for details on `PrintPage`). The `Form.Refresh` method is an easy way to call `Paint`—it simply makes the form refresh itself. Let's move down to the overridden `OnPaint` method on line 36.

This method is similar to the `OnPaint` methods you've already seen. It creates a `Brush` and `Font`, and then calls `DrawString`. The new parameters here are `strKey`, which holds the characters the user has typed, and `ptClick`, which holds the position of the mouse click. Let's examine the process:

1. The application starts.
2. User clicks the mouse, enters typing mode. The mouse click position is stored in `ptClick`.
3. User types a character, which is appended to `strKey`, and `Refresh` is called.
4. Thanks to `Refresh`, `Paint` is raised and `OnPaint` executes, drawing `strKey` at the location specified by `ptClick`.
5. The user clicks the mouse again, leaves typing mode. Typing a character no longer does anything.

When you run the application, you can type whatever you like into the form. However, when you try to type more than one thing into the application at once, the previously entered text disappears. What's going on?

The key thing to note is the `OnPaint` method here. This method dictates everything that will be drawn on the screen when `Paint` is called (aside from the form itself, of course). At any given time, this method only knows about the current string to be drawn. Any previously drawn strings are forgotten and erased. If you'd like to keep the previously written strings, you'll either have to store them in some sort of array, or create `Labels` form them that will persist.

If you've ever looked very closely at the graphics on your computer, you may notice an effect known as *aliasing*. On pictures with curved or non-smooth edges, you may end up with "jaggies"—areas where there are visible breaks or sharp corners in a line, even though the edge is supposed to be smooth. This is due to the way computer monitors work; every monitor has a fixed number of pixels it can use to display an image. Because pixels on a monitor are rectangular in shape, they can't represent smooth curved edges very accurately, and the result is a stair-stepped effect known as *jaggies*. Figure 13.2 shows an extreme close-up of some text in Windows where aliasing is apparent.

Anti-aliasing, then, is the attempt of the video card to smooth out the jaggies by drawing adjacent pixels next to the jaggies in a lighter color. This gives the appearance of smoother edges, but can lead to a "blurry" effect in the image. Figure 13.3 shows an anti-aliased version of text in Figure 13.2.

Anti-aliasing can certainly make images and fonts look better, but can lead to a performance decrease, because the computer must do some extra work to calculate all of the adjacent pixels.

Fonts themselves (`.fnt` files) often provide hints on how best to anti-alias and render themselves—it only makes sense that the designers of the fonts would know best how to render them. With .NET, you can use these hints or ignore them completely when anti-aliasing. You can set the level of anti-aliasing you want to use for your fonts with the `Graphics.TextRenderingHint` property. `TextRenderingHint` takes a value from the `TextRenderingHint` enumeration:

- `AntiAlias`—Use the traditional anti-aliasing mechanism without hints from the font files.
- `AntiAliasGridFit`—Use the traditional anti-aliasing mechanism with hints from the font files.
- `ClearTypeGridFit`—Use a very sophisticated anti-aliasing mechanism designed specifically for LCD screens, with hints.
- `SingleBitPerPixel`—No anti-aliasing or hints will be used.

13

- `SingleBitPerPixelGridFit`—No anti-aliasing will be used, but hints will.

- `SystemDefault`—The `Graphics` object will use whatever anti-aliasing is recommended by the operating system.

For example, to use anti-aliasing while disregarding the hints from the font file, use the following code:

```
Graphics objGraphics = e.Graphics;
objGraphics.TextRenderingHint = TextRenderingHint.AntiAlias;
```

 Note   Note that the `TextRenderingHint` enumeration is contained in the `System.Drawing.Text` namespace, so be sure to import it if you need to use anti-aliasing.

Displaying Images

You've already seen a few examples of displaying images. .NET uses two main classes for pictures: `Image`, which works with a variety of image formats, and `Bitmap`, which extends `Image` and allows you to access individual pixels in the image.

The `Image` class doesn't have a constructor, so to create a new image you have to use one of its static methods, for example, `FromFile`, `FromStream`, or `FromHBitmap`:

```
Image objImage = Image.FromFile("c:\\My Pictures\\Smile.jpg");
```

`Bitmap`, on the other hand, does have constructors, so you can instantiate one in a number of different ways. For example:

```
Bitmap objBM = new Bitmap("c:\\My Pictures\\Smile.jpg");

Bitmap objBM = new Bitmap(Image.FromFile
➥("c:\\My Pictures\\Smile.jpg"));

Bitmap objBM = new Bitmap(Image.FromStream
➥(objResponse.GetResponseStream()));
```

Drawing images in .NET is easy; simply use the `DrawImage` method:

```
Image objImage = Image.FromFile("c:\\My Pictures\\Smile.jpg");
e.Graphics.DrawImage(objImage, 0, 0);
```

These code lines draw the `smile.jpg` image on the form at the coordinates 0, 0. It's that easy! The `DrawImage` method takes quite a few different parameters—too many to go over here—so be sure to check out the .NET Framework documentation if you need a particular method.

The DrawImage method also allows you to distort images using an array of Points (often useful for graphical artists). The syntax for the command is as follows:

```
DrawImage(image, points[], rectangle, GraphicsUnit);
```

The first parameter, *image*, is obviously the image to draw. The second parameter is an array of three point objects that determine the upper-left corner, upper-right corner, and lower-left corner of the image respectively. The third parameter is a rectangle object that specifies the original dimensions of the image—this is necessary so that GDI+ knows how to apply transformations.

The fourth parameter determines the units in which everything is measured. Most of the time, you'll simply use GraphicsUnit.Pixel. Other values include GraphicsUnit.Inch, GraphicsUnit.Millimeter, and GraphicsUnit.Point.

Listing 13.4 shows some sample code that loads an image, determines its boundaries, and scales the image.

LISTING 13.4   Manipulating Images

```
 1: private Image objImg;
 2: private Rectangle rectOriginal;
 3: private Point[] arrPoints = new Point[3];
 4: ...
 5: //in the constructor
 6: objImg = Image.FromFile("c:\\winforms\\day13\\sample.jpg");
 7: rectOriginal = new Rectangle(0, 0, objImg.Width,
➥objImg.Height);
 8:
 9: arrPoints[0].X = rectOriginal.X;
10: arrPoints[0].Y = rectOriginal.Y;
11: arrPoints[1].X = rectOriginal.Width;
12: arrPoints[1].Y = rectOriginal.Y;
13: arrPoints[2].X = rectOriginal.X;
14: arrPoints[2].Y = rectOriginal.Height;
15:
16: btClick.Click += new EventHandler(this.DistortImage);
17: ...
18: private void DistortImage(Object Sender, EventArgs e) {
19:     arrPoints[0].X = Convert.ToInt32(tbUpperLeftX.Text);
20:     arrPoints[0].Y = Convert.ToInt32(tbUpperLeftY.Text);
21:     arrPoints[1].X = Convert.ToInt32(tbUpperRightX.Text);
22:     arrPoints[1].Y = Convert.ToInt32(tbUpperRightY.Text);
23:     arrPoints[2].X = Convert.ToInt32(tbLowerLeftX.Text);
24:     arrPoints[2].Y = Convert.ToInt32(tbLowerLeftY.Text);
25:
26:     this.Refresh();
27: }
```

13

LISTING 13.4   continued

```
28:
29:   protected override void OnPaint(PaintEventArgs e) {
30:      Graphics objGraphics = e.Graphics;
31:
32:      objGraphics.DrawImage(objImg, arrPoints, rectOriginal,
➥GraphicsUnit.Pixel);
33:   }
34:   ...
35:   }
```

ANALYSIS   This application assumes that you've created six TextBox objects in which the user can enter coordinates for the Point array, and a Button that the user can click to apply the transformation.

On lines 1–3 you declare a few variables that will be used later. Then on line 6, you load the image using the Image.FromFile method (make sure this points to an actual image on your computer). On line 7, you create a Rectangle object based on the image's properties. This rectangle aids GDI+ in determining how to transform the image.

On lines 9–14 you initialize the Point objects in the arrPoints array. These points are used to determine where the upper-left, upper-right, and lower-left corners of the image should be drawn. Initially, they are set to the corners of the original rectangle.

In the DistortImage function, you retrieve values from various textboxes, place them in the transformation array, and then call Refresh, which raises the Paint method. On line 32, DrawImage is called, passing in the image, the transformation array, the original rectangle, and the units of measurement.

Figure 13.4 shows a sample application that uses this functionality, after a transformation has been applied.

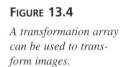

FIGURE 13.4

A transformation array can be used to transform images.

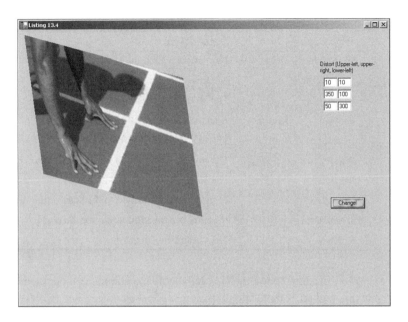

Drawing Shapes

The key to drawing shapes and lines in GDI+ is to know the capabilities of the Pen object. This object has numerous properties that can determine how your shapes are drawn. After that, you simply need to know the coordinates you plan to draw the shapes in. Let's look at the properties of the Pen object, shown in Table 13.1.

TABLE 13.1   Pen Properties

Property	Description
Alignment	The alignment for objects drawn with this Pen. In other words, if the pen's line is thick, this property determines to which edge of the line the drawing should be aligned.
Brush	The Brush to fill the contained space with.
Color	The color of the Pen.
CompoundArray	An array of custom dashes and spaces.
CustomEndCap	A custom shape that is attached to the end of the line (for example, an arrow head).
CustomStartCap	A custom shape that is attached to the beginning of the line.
DashCap	The shape that is attached to the start and end of dashes in a dashed line.

13

TABLE 13.1   continued

Property	Description
DashOffset	The distance from the start of a line to begin dashes.
DashPattern	An array of custom dashes.
DashStyle	The style of dashes to use.
EndCap	A shape that is attached to the end of the line.
LineJoin	The join style for two overlapping lines.
MiterLimit	The thickness of join on a mitered corner.
PenType	The style of line drawn with the Pen.
StartCap	A shape that is attached to the start of the line.
Transform	A geometric transformation for the pen.
Width	The width of the pen's line.

To learn how to use the Pen, let's look at a simple method, Graphics.DrawLine. This method takes three simple parameters: a Pen object, and two Points that determine the start and end points of the line. Listing 13.5 shows an example of different lines being drawn.

LISTING 13.5   Drawing Lines

```
1:  protected override void OnPaint(PaintEventArgs e) {
2:      Graphics objGraphics = e.Graphics;
3:
4:      Pen objPen = new Pen(Color.Black);
5:
6:      //simple black line
7:      objGraphics.DrawLine(objPen, new Point(10,700),
➥new Point(500,150));
8:
9:      //thicker line
10:     objPen.Color = Color.Red;
11:     objPen.Width = 10;
12:     objPen.Alignment = PenAlignment.Inset;
13:     objGraphics.DrawLine(objPen, new Point(50,200),
➥new Point(500,430));
14:
15:     //arrow
16:     objPen.Color = Color.Blue;
17:     objPen.EndCap = LineCap.DiamondAnchor;
18:     objPen.StartCap = LineCap.ArrowAnchor;
19:     objGraphics.DrawLine(objPen, new Point(600,10),
➥new Point(500,430));
20:
```

LISTING 13.5 continued

```
21:    //dashed line
22:    objPen.Color = Color.Green;
23:    objPen.EndCap = LineCap.NoAnchor;
24:    objPen.StartCap = LineCap.NoAnchor;
25:    objPen.DashStyle = DashStyle.DashDotDot;
26:    objGraphics.DrawLine(objPen, new Point(20,60),
➥new Point(300,600));
27:  }
```

ANALYSIS Line 4 starts by creating our new Pen object. The rest of the code draws a
sequence of lines: line 7 draws a simple black line; lines 10–13 draw a thicker
red line; lines 16–19 draw a thick blue line with an arrow head and tail; and lines 22–26
draw a dashed green arrow.

Figure 13.5 shows the output from Listing 13.5.

FIGURE 13.5

The output shows a variety of lines in various colors and widths, and a few other properties.

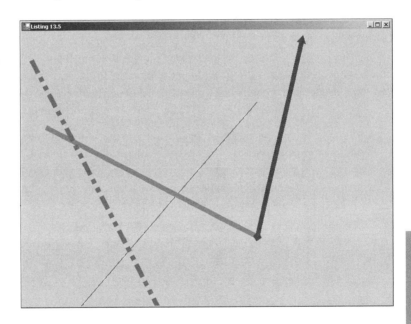

There are quite a few enumerations that are used with the Pen object. These are summarized in Table 13.2.

13

TABLE 13.2 Pen Enumerations and Their Properties and Values.

Enumeration	Pen *Property*	*Values*
PenAlignment	Alignment	Center, Inset, Left, Outset, Right
LineCap	DashCap, EndCap, StartCap	AnchorMask, ArrowAnchor, Custom, DiamondAnchor, Flat, NoAnchor, Round, RoundAnchor, Square, SquareAnchor, Triangle
DashStyle	DashStyle	Custom, Dash, DashDot, DashDotDot, Dot, Solid
LineJoin	LineJoin	Bevel, Miter, MiterClipped, Round
PenType	PenType	HatchFill, LinearGradient, PathGradient, SolidColor, TextureFill

To draw more advanced shapes than lines, you need to know about paths—specifically, the GraphicsPath object. GraphicsPath defines a set of lines or points that compose a single shape, such as a parallelogram.

There are two ways to define a path. You can either call StartFigure followed by a sequence of Add methods (we'll get to those in a moment) and the DrawPath method, or by declaring the points to be drawn in the GraphicsPath constructor itself. With the latter method, you must also specify the type of line to be drawn.

So let's examine what the GraphicsPath can do. More than just simple lines, GDI+ can draw ellipses, curves, arcs, beziers (complex paths calculated by mathematical formulas), pies, polygons, rectangles, and text. For each of these shapes, there is a corresponding Add method—AddLine, AddPolygon, AddBezier, and so on. Thus, you could draw a very interesting shape using the following code:

```
protected override void OnPaint(PaintEventArgs e) {
    Graphics objGraphics = e.Graphics;

    GraphicsPath objPath = new GraphicsPath();
    Pen objPen = new Pen(Color.Blue, 5);

    objPath.StartFigure();

    objPath.AddLine(new Point(10, 10), new Point(150, 10));
    objPath.AddArc(150, 10, 150, 50, 0, 10);
    objPath.AddCurve(new Point[] {new Point(150,150), new
➡Point(200,350), new Point(300,450)});
    objPath.AddBezier(new Point(300,450), new Point(500,100),
➡new Point(400,50), new Point(350,10));
    objPath.AddPie(350, 10, 150, 50, 0, 50);
```

```
    objPath.AddString("Hello World", new
➥FontFamily("Times New Roman"), Convert.ToInt32
➥ (FontStyle.Italic), 50, new Point(500,100),
➥new StringFormat());

    objPen.LineJoin = LineJoin.Round;

    objGraphics.DrawPath(objPen, objPath);
}
```

First, you call the `StartFigure` method to let GDI+ know that subsequent commands will draw to the form. Then follow a sequence of `Add` methods that add, in turn, a line, an arc, a curve, a bezier curve, a pie (actually, a slice of a pie), and a string. Each `Add` method takes a different set of arguments—we'll go over those in a second. Finally, you call the `DrawPath` method to draw the specified `GraphicsPath` object with the specified `Pen` object. What you end up with is shown in Figure 13.6.

FIGURE 13.6

Use a `GraphicsPath` *object to draw complex shapes.*

13

The `Add` methods can get quite complex, and it's difficult to remember all the different parameters. Table 13.3 summarizes them for you. Note, however, that all of the `Add` methods have multiple parameter lists and quite a few optional parameters, so this list is in no way a complete listing, but lists only the most common methods. All parameters are `Integer` types unless otherwise specified.

TABLE 13.3   The Add Methods and Their Parameters

Method	Parameter Types
AddArc	x position, y position, width, height, starting angle (Single data type), sweep angle (Single data type)
AddBezier	Starting point, first control point, second control point, end point (control points factor into mathematical equations to determine how the curves flows)
AddBeziers	An array of Beziers objects
AddClosedCurve	An array of Point objects that define the curve
AddCurve	An array of Point objects that define the curve
AddEllipse	x position, y position, width, height
AddLine	start point (Point object), end point (Point object)
AddLines	An array of Line objects
AddPath	A GraphicsPath object
AddPie sweep	x position, y position, width, height, starting angle (Single data type), angle (Single data type)
AddPolygon	An array of Point objects that define the polygon
AddRectangle	A Rectangle object
AddRectangles	An array of Rectangle objects
AddString	A string, a FontFamily object defining the font face, a FontStyle enumeration value that must be cast to an integer, the font size (Single data type), Point object that specifies the origin, StringFormat object that specifies the string characteristics

When you call the various Add methods in succession and you want lines to connect to each other, you must match the end point of one segment with the starting point of the next segment. This can occasionally be challenging, especially with curved lines (imagine the situation in 3 dimensions!).

Instead, you can declare all the lines to be drawn in the constructor of the GraphicsPath object:

```
GraphicsPath objPath = new GraphicsPath(
   new Point[] {
      new Point(40, 140), new Point(275, 200),
      new Point(105, 225), new Point(190, 300),
      new Point(50, 350), new Point(20, 180) },
   new byte[] { (byte)PathPointType.Start,
      (byte)PathPointType.Bezier, (byte)PathPointType.Bezier,
```

```
        (byte)PathPointType.Bezier, (byte)PathPointType.Line,
        (byte)PathPointType.Line }
);

objGraphics.DrawPath(objPen, objPath);
```

In this method, the first parameter to the constructor (although it may seem like the first six parameters) is an array of `Point` objects specifying each point in the path:

```
new Point[] { new Point(40, 140), new Point(275, 200),
    new Point(105, 225), new Point(190, 300), new
    Point(50, 350), new Point(20, 180) }
```

The second parameter (which looks like the next six parameters) specifies how the lines between those points should be drawn. All of these values are from the `PathPointType` enumeration, and must be cast as `byte` data types (don't ask why; GDI+ is funny that way):

```
new byte[] { (byte)PathPointType.Start,
    (byte)PathPointType.Bezier, (byte)PathPointType.Bezier,
    (byte)PathPointType.Bezier, (byte)PathPointType.Line,
    (byte)PathPointType.Line }
```

The `PathPointType` enumeration isn't as versatile as the `Add` methods discussed earlier. It only contains a few values: `Start`, which indicates that the point is the start of a line, and should not have a line drawn to it; `Bezier`, which indicates that the line between two points should be curved; `Line`, which indicates a straight line; and `DashMode`, which indicates the line should be dashed.

Figure 13.7 shows the output of our new `GraphicsPath` object.

The method you choose to draw your complex shapes is up to you; each has advantages. The series of `Add` methods may be a bit easier to use, is easier to read as well, and is more versatile. But you must remember the syntax for each type of `Add` method. On the other hand, the constructor method isn't as versatile, but you don't have to remember 1,000 different parameters and you don't have to mentally connect points and lines to each other—one point always leads to the next.

Drawing complex shapes is, as its name implies, a complex task, and not for the faint of heart. In most applications, you won't find a use for it, but it's there just in case. If you are building a Photoshop-like application, however, then you're in luck, most of the hard work (depending on your perspective) is already done for you.

13

Figure 13.7

*PathPointType enu-
meration values pro-
duce complex shapes.*

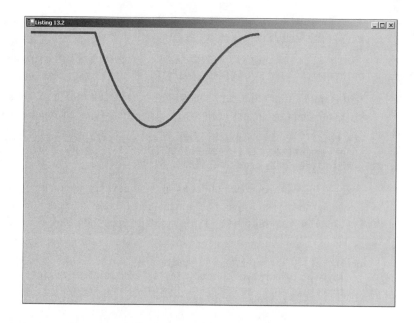

Filling Shapes

Now you know how to use the Pen object to draw shapes. To fill those shapes with colors, images, and gradients, you use the various Brush objects.

Remember, Brush objects don't have any methods, so they can't perform any functionality by themselves—brushes are simply tools for other objects to draw with. There are five
main types of brushes. The first, and most basic, is the SolidBrush. Very simply, it fills a
specified region with a solid color of your choice:

```
SolidBrush objBrush = new SolidBrush(Color.Black);
```

A HatchBrush fills a region with lines, to give the appearance of cross-hatched background. There are quite a few different styles of hatching you can use (56 in total), all
part of the HatchStyle enumeration. For example, HatchStyle.Cross draws a crisscross
pattern of horizontal and vertical lines, and HatchStyle.Horizontal simply fills the area
with horizontal lines. See the .NET Framework documentation for more choices.

The HatchBrush also has two different color properties: the first specifies the color of the
lines to draw with, and the second specifies the background color of the region. The following code snippet creates a blue region with black horizontal stripes:

```
HatchBrush objBrush = new HatchBrush(HatchStyle.Horizontal,
➥Color.Black, Color.Blue);
```

The next `LinearGradientBrush` and `PathGradientBrush` brushes deal with color gradients—regions that move gradually from one color to another. `LinearGradientBrush` specifies a linear gradient—that is, one that doesn't rely on complex mathematical formulas to calculate gradients; it simply moves from one color to the next. You can create a `LinearGradientBrush` by simply passing in two points (the start and end of the color gradient) and two colors (the start and end colors of the gradient):

```
LinearGradientBrush objBrush = new LinearGradientBrush(
➥new Point(0,0), new Point(100,100),
➥Color.White, Color.Black);
```

The `PathGradientBrush` is slightly more complex. It builds a gradient in a radial pattern; the color starts from the center and changes color as it moves away from the center. A `PathGradientBrush` can be created based upon a `GraphicsPath` object, or with an array of points as shown here:

```
PathGradientBrush objBrush = PathGradientBrush(new Point[]
➥{new Point(0,0), new Point(100,50), ...} );
```

You then set the center color:

```
objBrush.CenterColor = Color.White;
```

And finally an array of colors—one for each point you specified:

```
ObjBrush.SurroundColors = new Color[] { Color.Blue, Color.Red,
➥Color.Orange, ... } );
```

Figure 13.8 shows examples of both `LinearGradientBrush` and `PathGradientBrush` brushes.

FIGURE 13.8

`LinearGradientBrush` *(left) draws a simple color gradient (left);* `PathGradientBrush` *draws a radial gradient.*

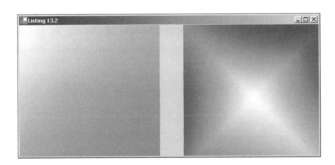

13

The final type of brush is the `TextureBrush`, which uses an image to fill the interior of a region. You create a `TextureBrush` by simply passing in an image:

```
TextureBrush objBrush = new TextureBrush(Image.FromFile
➥("c:\\temp\\sample.jpg"));
```

Now that you have your brushes, you can fill an area using one of a number of `Fill` methods: `FillClosedCurve`, `FillEllipse`, `FillPath`, `FillPie`, `FillPolygon`, `FillRectangle`, `FillRectangles`, and `FillRegion`. Like the series of `Add` methods we discussed earlier, each of these `Fill` methods has different parameter lists, but thankfully they're easier to deal with than the `Add` methods. Table 13.4 provides the parameter lists for these methods.

TABLE 13.4   The `Fill` Methods and Their Parameters

Method	Parameter Types
FillClosedCurve	A `Brush`, and an array of points that define the curve
FillEllipse	A `Brush`, and a `Rectangle` object that defines the four boundary points of the ellipse (left, top, right, and bottom apexes)
FillPath	A `Brush`, and a `GraphicsPath` object
FillPie	A `Brush`, a `Rectangle` that defines the four boundaries of the pie (much like the ellipse), a starting angle, and a sweep angle. (Note that the pie doesn't have to be a *complete* pie; it can be a slice.)
FillPolygon	A `Brush`, and an array of points that define the polygon
FillRectangle	A `Brush`, and either a `Rectangle` object or four integers that define a rectangle (upper-left x coordinate, upper-left y coordinate, width, and height)
FillRectangles	A `Brush`, and an array of `Rectangle` objects
FillRegion	A `Brush`, and a `Region` object

Listing 13.6 shows an example of using the `Fill` methods. When the user clicks and drags with the mouse cursor, a rectangle will be drawn showing the user's selection. When the mouse button is released, the selection area will be filled with a gradient.

LISTING 13.6   Filling Selections

```
 1:  using System;
 2:  using System.Windows.Forms;
 3:  using System.Drawing;
 4:  using System.Drawing.Drawing2D;
 5:
 6:  namespace TYWinforms.Day13 {
 7:     public class Listing136 : Form {
 8:        private Point ptStartClick;
 9:        private Point ptCurrentPos;
10:        private bool blnDrag = false;
11:        private bool blnFill = false;
```

LISTING **13.6** continued

```
12:        private GraphicsPath objPath;
13:        private PathGradientBrush objBrush;
14:        private Pen objPen = new Pen(Color.Black);
15:        private Rectangle rectSelect;
16:
17:        public Listing136() {
18:            this.Text = "Listing 13.6";
19:            this.Size = new Size(800,600);
20:        }
21:
22:        protected override void OnMouseDown(MouseEventArgs e) {
23:            blnDrag = true;
24:            ptStartClick = new Point(e.X, e.Y);
25:            ptCurrentPos = ptStartClick;
26:        }
27:
28:         protected override void OnMouseUp(MouseEventArgs e) {
29:            blnDrag = false;
30:            blnFill = true;
31:        }
32:
33:         protected override void OnMouseMove(MouseEventArgs e) {
34:            ptCurrentPos = new Point(e.X, e.Y);
35:
36:            if (blnDrag | blnFill) { this.Refresh(); }
37:        }
38:
39:         protected override void OnPaint(PaintEventArgs e) {
40:            if (blnDrag) {
41:                objPen.DashStyle = DashStyle.Dash;
42:
43:                if (ptCurrentPos.X < ptStartClick.X &
➥ptCurrentPos.Y < ptStartClick.Y) {
44:                    rectSelect = new Rectangle(ptCurrentPos.X,
➥ptCurrentPos.Y, ptStartClick.X - ptCurrentPos.X,
➥ptStartClick.Y - ptCurrentPos.Y);
45:                } else if (ptCurrentPos.X < ptStartClick.X
➥& ptCurrentPos.Y > ptStartClick.Y) {
46:                    rectSelect = new Rectangle(ptCurrentPos.X,
➥ptStartClick.Y, ptStartClick.X - ptCurrentPos.X,
➥ptCurrentPos.Y - ptStartClick.Y);
47:                } else if (ptCurrentPos.X > ptStartClick.X
➥& ptCurrentPos.Y < ptStartClick.Y) {
48:                    rectSelect = new Rectangle(ptStartClick.X,
➥ptCurrentPos.Y, ptCurrentPos.X - ptStartClick.X,
➥ptStartClick.Y - ptCurrentPos.Y);
49:                } else {
```

13

LISTING **13.6**   continued

```
50:                     rectSelect = new Rectangle(ptStartClick.X,
➥ptStartClick.Y, ptCurrentPos.X - ptStartClick.X,
➥ptCurrentPos.Y - ptStartClick.Y);
51:              }
52:              e.Graphics.DrawRectangle(objPen, rectSelect);
53:          }
54:
55:          if (blnFill && rectSelect.Width != 0 &&
➥rectSelect.Height != 0) {
56:              objPath = new GraphicsPath();
57:              objPath.AddRectangle(rectSelect);
58:              objBrush = new PathGradientBrush(objPath);
59:              objBrush.CenterColor = Color.White;
60:              objBrush.SurroundColors = new Color[]
➥{Color.Red, Color.Blue, Color.Orange, Color.Green};
61:
62:              e.Graphics.FillRectangle(objBrush, rectSelect);
63:              blnFill = false;
64:          }
65:
66:      }
67:
68:      public static void Main() {
69:          Application.Run(new Listing136());
70:      }
71:  }
72: }
```

ANALYSIS   This application may seem complex, but it's really not; there are just a lot of simple conditions that need to be met.

Let's skip down to line 22 where we override the OnMouseDown event. This code is identical to adding a delegate to the form's MouseDown event—we did the same thing earlier for the OnPaint event. The OnMouseUp and OnMouseMove events on lines 28 and 33 are similar.

When OnMouseDown executes, you know the user has just pressed the mouse button down, indicating that he is ready to start making a selection (we'll call this selection mode). Set the blnDrag variable to true, so that your other methods know that you're currently in selection mode, and then retrieve the starting point of the selection from the MouseEventArgs object. ptCurrentPos on line 25 is another Point object that we'll use in a moment.

In OnMouseUp, the user has just released the mouse button, signaling that he is done making a selection—selection mode is over. Set blnDrag to false. Once a selection has been made, you need to fill it with your gradient—in other words, you enter fill mode. Set the blnFill variable to true.

The OnMouseMove method executes every time the mouse moves. When this happens, you need to capture the new position of the mouse pointer, so that you can accurately determine the selected region.

The OnPaint method on line 39 is responsible for highlighting the selection the user has made, and for filling the selection with a gradient after the user leaves selection mode. If we are in selection mode, line 40 will evaluate to true, and lines 41–52 will execute. Let's examine why we need all of this obtuse-looking code.

Take a look at Figure 13.9. The user's first mouse click (and point at which the OnMouseDown method executes) is at the origin of the axes. From here, there are four places she can move the mouse: in to any of the four quadrants.

Figure 13.9

From the starting point, you can move in four different directions.

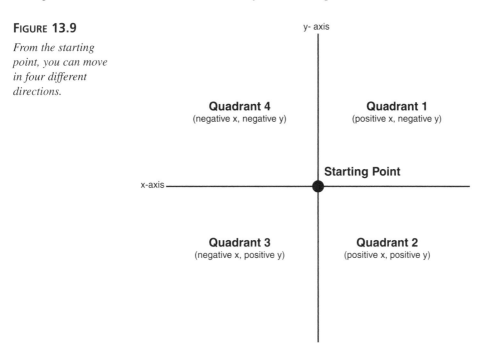

We need to build a region (we'll use a Rectangle here) from the user's selection, so we need to determine the corners of the selected area. The most common situation is to

> **Note**
>
> Remember that with Windows Forms, y values increase as you move down the form, which is why the y axis appears opposite of normal geometry.

move into quadrant 2. Here, the x value is positive, and the y value is negative. The upper-left corner is simply the starting point, the origin. The upper-right corner is the same as the starting y value, but a new, greater x value. The lower-right corner is a greater x and y value, and the lower-left corner is the same x value as the origin, but a greater y value. Follow so far? It helps to draw a small rectangle as shown on Figure 13.10.

FIGURE 13.10

The user drags the mouse down and to the right to make a selection.

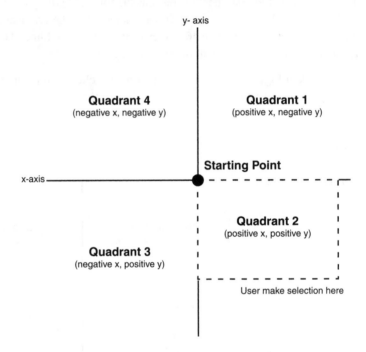

We only have two points to work from, however: the starting mouse click (the ptStartClick point created on line 24), and the current position of the mouse, which is updated every time the mouse moves (line 34). To determine the area enclosed by the selected region (remember, we're building a Rectangle), you have the

- Upper-left corner—Starting x value, starting y value
- Width of the Rectangle (as specified by the upper-right corner)—Current x value minus the original x value
- Height of the Rectangle—Current y value minus the starting y value

This works out fine when we're in quadrant 2 and current x and y values are *always* greater than the starting x and y values. In fact, this equation can be seen on line 50.

However, when we move into any one of the other quadrants, there is a possibility that the width and height equations in the preceding list may end up with a negative value—and Rectangles cannot be created with negative values. Thus, to properly create your non-negative Rectangle, you have to modify your equations a bit depending on the quadrant you're in.

The if statements on lines 43, 45, and 47 determine which quadrant the mouse cursor is in, in relation to the starting point (the final else on line 49 assumes you're in quadrant 2). The statements on 44, 46, and 48 then hold the different equations that apply to the quadrants. For example, in quadrant 4 (lines 43–44), the equations are as follows:

- Upper-left corner—Current x value, current y value
- Width of the Rectangle—Starting x value minus the current x value
- Height of the Rectangle—Starting y value minus the current y value minus

In other words, the width and height equations are opposite those of quadrant 2. You can figure out the other two quadrants on your own, so let's move on with the rest of the code.

Having correctly determined the Rectangle that represents the selected region, you call the DrawRectangle method on line 52, using a dashed-line Pen. Since this happens on every call to OnPaint (that is, every time the mouse moves) an outline is drawn wherever the user moves the mouse cursor, giving the impression that the area in question has been selected.

Once the user releases the mouse button, you leave selection mode and enter fill mode. The code on lines 55–64 takes over. To fill this area with a gradient, you use the PathGradientBrush. However, to create a PathGradientBrush you need the points that represent the four corners of your region. Rather than trying to deal with the Rectangle object directly, you create a GraphicsPath object from the Rectangle. Line 56 creates the GraphicsPath object, and line 57 adds the Rectangle to it. Now you can easily create the PathGradientBrush, as shown on line 58, and set the appropriate colors. Line 62 calls the FillRectangle method to fill the selected region, and line 63 effectively takes you out of fill mode.

To fully understand the way this application works, you need to build and play with it. Figure 13.11 shows the essence of the application.

13

FIGURE 13.11

When the user releases the mouse button, the selection, will be filled with a gradient.

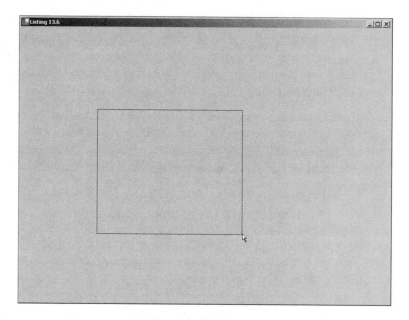

This application illustrates one of the most common tasks when dealing with GDI+: coordinating the OnPaint method with various user actions. Since OnPaint occurs so frequently, you have to make sure that you build this method properly, so it knows what it should be doing at any particular moment. This is typically done with Boolean variables—in Listing 13.6 they indicated selection and fill modes.

> **Caution**
>
> Be careful creating and instantiating variables when dealing with GDI+. Because the OnPaint method executes so many times during the course of an application, you can rapidly encounter unexpected problems. For example, if line 56 of Listing 13.6 were
>
> ```
> GraphicsPath objPath = new GraphicsPath();
> ```
>
> (in other words, you declared and instantiated a new objPath variable inside the OnPaint method every time OnPaint executed) the user's computer would unnecessarily waste memory. Essentially, you are creating a new GraphicsPath object instead of reusing an existing one, and that can quickly eat up memory. The effect may not be noticeable to the end-user because the CLR is good about cleaning up unused variables, but in some cases you can degrade performance.
>
> The moral of the story: declare your variables early, but only instantiate them when you need them, and reuse them when you can.

How to Make Your Shapes Persist

When you are running the application in Listing 13.6, notice that whatever you've previously drawn disappears once you start drawing a new rectangle. This is because there is a big limitation with the `Graphics` object: anything it draws remains onscreen only until the next time `OnPaint` is called.

As an analogy, imagine that you are carrying a painting. The painting is large, so you can only carry one at a time. You will hold this painting until someone gives you another painting, at which point you have to discard the first in order to take the second. `OnPaint` is the same way; it can only hold one method call's worth of drawing, and the next time `OnPaint` is called, it discards whatever it previously drew, to start drawing from scratch.

It may help to think about it this way: anything you draw on a form using the `Graphics` object does *not* become part of the form. It just sits on top of the form until `OnPaint` comes along again ands wipes the slate clean and starts over.

There is a sneaky way to get around the `OnPaint` limitation. By drawing on an image, you can be assured that your changes will not be lost, no matter how many times `OnPaint` is called. And you don't need a specific image for this to work; you can create a brand new image in your application that starts out as blank. For example:

```
Bitmap imgWorking = new Bitmap(800, 600,
➥PixelFormat.Format32bppArgb);
```

The first two parameters to the `Bitmap` constructor are the width and height. The third parameter is a `PixelFormat` enumeration value that determines the type of image to create. Here, you are creating a 32-bit image, with alpha transparency (see the .NET Framework documentation for a thorough discussion on this and other `PixelFormat` values).

Then, when you need to draw something on screen that needs to persist, draw it on this new image. You can obtain a `Graphics` object from the image using the following code:

```
Graphics objG = Graphics.FromImage(imgWorking);
```

`FromImage` is a static method of the `Graphics` object, so you can use this anywhere. Then, for instance, you could fill it with a white rectangle:

```
objG.FillRectangle(new SolidBrush(Color.White),
➥new Rectangle(0,0,800,600));
```

You simply have to make sure the image `imgWorking` is drawn on screen. This can be done in a number of different ways, from setting the image as the background image of the form, or by displaying it in the `OnPaint` method:

13

```
//setting the background image
this.BackgroundImage = imgWorking;

//using OnPaint
protected override void OnPaint(PaintEventArgs e) {
   e.Graphics.DrawImage(imgWorking, new Point(0,0));
}
```

Using these techniques, you can create a more fully-functional drawing application, but I leave this as an exercise for you.

Transforming Shapes

The Graphics object comes with three easy-to-use methods that allow you to transform the things you draw, from shapes to images. These are RotateTransform, ScaleTransform, and TranslateTransforms. The first method rotates things drawn by the Graphics object, the second scales them in size, and the third moves the object in a specified direction. Their usages are very simple:

```
e.Graphics.RotateTransform(angle) //angle is the number of
                                  //degrees to rotate
                                  // (Single data type)
e.Graphics.ScaleTransform(x, y)   // x and y are the
                                  // percentages to scale
                                  // in the x and y-directions
e.Graphics.TranslateTransform(x, y) // x and y are the
                                    // number of pixels to
                                    // move the drawings in the
                                    // x and y directions
```

The following code would draw a rectangle that is rotated by 30 degrees clockwise:

```
e.Graphics.RotateTransform(30);
e.Graphics.DrawRectangle(objPen, 0, 0, 200, 100);
```

When you call any of these transform methods, everything you subsequently draw is transformed accordingly. To return to normal drawing, call the ResetTransform method (note that items already drawn using the transform methods will not be un-transformed).

If you'd like to transform only specific objects, the GraphicsPath object is for you. GraphicsPath has a Transform method that allows you to do all of the previously mentioned transformations—but there's a catch. You need to use the Matrix object, which represents a 3×3 matrix of values. While Matrix does have a few user-friendly methods, to really tap its power you need to have paid attention in your linear algebra and matrix transformation classes. That said, we'll cover only the user-friendly methods here. (See the .NET Framework documentation under the Matrix object for more information on the complex stuff.)

To transform an object, you need to create a `GraphicsPath` object from the object you want to transform, create a new `Matrix` object, call the appropriate transformation method, and then call the `Transform` method of the `GrahpicsPath` object. For example:

```
//create object to be drawn as a path
GraphicsPath objPath = new GraphicsPath();
objPath.AddEllipse(0, 0, 140, 70);

//create Matrix object and call transformation methods
Matrix objMatrix = new Matrix();
objMatrix.Rotate(30);
objPath.Transform(objMatrix);

//call the appropriate Draw method
e.Graphics.DrawPath(objPen, objPath);
```

Table 13.5 lists the user-friendly methods of `Matrix`.

TABLE 13.5 Matrix Transformation Methods

Method	Description
Reset	Resets all transformations
Rotate	Rotates the object by a specified number of degrees
RotateAt	Rotates the object by a specified number of degrees, around a certain point. For example: `RotateAt(30, new PointF(0.0, 0.0));` (PointF is simply a floating-point version of Point)
Scale	Scales the object in x and y directions (functions like `Graphics.ScaleTransform`)
Shear	Applies a shear vector to the object (uses two `Single` data type parameters)
Translate	Functions like `Graphics.TranslateTransform`

Clipping Windows Forms

13

The last topic we'll cover today deals with `Regions`. The most common use for `Region` objects is to clip certain parts of a drawing. If you create a `Region` object, all drawing done outside that `Region` will be clipped—only the drawing inside is kept.

The most common way to create `Region` object is either with a `Rectangle`, or with a `GraphicsPath` object if you need to create more complex shaped regions.

Because clipping isn't a common situation in GDI+, we'll gloss over the topic. But a very interesting benefit of `Region` is that it allows you to create non-rectangular Windows Forms. You can have triangular or circular shaped applications if you want!

For example, add the following code to any of the applications you've written today:

```
Point[] polyPoints = {
    new Point(0, 0),
    new Point(300, 0),
    new Point(300, 75),
    new Point(150, 300),
    new Point(0, 75)
};
GraphicsPath objPath = new GraphicsPath();
objPath.AddPolygon(polyPoints);

this.Region = new Region(objPath);
```

You create a baseball-diamond–shaped polygon in the GraphicsPath, and then set the Region property of the current form to the new polygon. What you end up with is similar to what is shown in Figure 13.12.

FIGURE 13.12

Region can be used to make creative application windows.

Just because you can create odd-shaped windows doesn't mean you should—after all, windows are traditionally shaped as rectangles for a reason. However, this example gives you an idea of the power of Regions: anything outside of the diamond shaped polygon created in the preceding code snippet is simply not drawn. You can even interact with the applications behind those diamond-clipped areas if you want. Just be careful you don't clip out the title bar of the application, or you'll never be able to move it or close the application with the mouse!

Summary

One of the main goals of GDI+ is to simplify graphical development by providing the developer an abstract interface for dealing with different video hardware, while maintaining power and functionality. With GDI+, you can take advantage of the latest graphical trends such as anti-aliasing or texture mapping.

Today you learned about Pens and Brushes. Pen is used to draw lines, and Brush is used to fill enclosed regions with colors or textures. The most common region you'll deal with is the Rectangle object, which can represent anything from the Windows Form object to a highlighted selection.

Next you learned about the Paint event, which is raised every time the form needs to be redrawn. Because it is raised so often, this is the ideal place to put common drawing routines. Note, however, that depending on the structure of your application, things drawn during this event may not persist during the next call to Paint.

The only way to draw text (that is, without drawing custom shapes that look like text) is to use the DrawString method. You can determine the anti-aliasing quality of drawn text with the TextRenderingHint property of the Graphics object.

Drawing images, similarly, requires only the DrawImage method, which uses either an Image or Bitmap object. To transform images you can construct an array that consists of three Point objects that define, respectively, the transformed upper-left coordinate, upper-right coordinate, and lower-left coordinate.

Drawing shapes is probably the most complicated part of GDI+, simply because there are so many options—it may be difficult to remember the precise parameter list for a given drawing method.

In addition to the Draw methods, you have Add and Fill methods. The series of Add method is used to add various lines and shapes to a GraphicsPath object, while the Fill methods are used to fill enclosed regions with colors or textures.

Transforming shapes in GDI+ is done easily enough with the RotateTransform, ScaleTransform, and TranslateTransform methods. These three methods affect the Graphics object and everything it subsequently draws. If you want to transform only a particular object, you need to use the Matrix object and one of its transformation methods.

We're rapidly approaching the end of Week 2! Tomorrow you'll conclude your examination of useful, "helper" technologies by studying ActiveX, a scheme that allows different applications to talk to each other.

13

Q&A

Q Are there more advanced GDI+ capabilities?

A You bet! Aside from the advanced transformation capabilities with the Matrix object we discussed earlier, there are numerous capabilities that you typically only touch if you spend a lot of time with graphical editing software.

One interesting feature is the ability to create and edit *metafiles*. A metafile, represented by the `Metafile` object, allows you to record graphical commands (if you've used Photoshop's actions, metafiles are similar). If you notice that you are commonly performing the same task in your applications over and over again, you can save those actions to a metafile, and simply call the file instead of rewriting the code.

Another feature is the ability to recolor images. Just as you can use a `Matrix` to transform the size and shape of an object, you can use color matrices to manipulate the colors in an images. You can, for instance, turn a colored image into a black-and-white photo, or vice versa.

GDI+ has enough features to dedicate an entire book to the subject. Be sure to check out the .NET Framework documentation for more information.

Q How do I make transparent images and shapes?

A Making transparent shapes is easy—simply specify an *alpha* value for your color when creating your `Pen` or `Brush`. You can do this with the `FromArgb` method like so:

```
Pen objPen = new Pen(Color.FromArgb(128,0,0,0));
                    //a 50% black pen (50% see through)
```

Then just draw your shapes as normal. `FromArgb` takes four integer parameters, each ranging from 0 to 255: an alpha (transparency) value, and red, green, and blue values.

To make a transparent image, however, is more difficult. To do so, you'll need to learn about color matrices, which can be an entire chapter unto itself. You can also make only parts of an image transparent with the `ColorMatrix` object. Unfortunately, that's out of the scope of this book.

Workshop

This workshop helps reinforce the concepts we covered in today's lesson. It is very helpful to understand fully the answers before moving on. Answers can be found in Appendix A.

Quiz

1. What is the main object for GDI+?

2. What are the two ways to take advantage of the `Paint` event? Give a brief example of each.

3. Name five properties of the `Pen` object.

4. True or false: To draw a string, you use a `Pen`.

5. What, conceptually, is a `Matrix`?

6. What are the five types of `Brushes`?

7. What method must be called before you can call the `Add` methods to add shapes to a `GraphicsPath` object?

8. Are "jaggies" the result of aliasing, or anti-aliasing?

Exercise

Create a drawing application that allows the user to perform various drawing functions, including drawing with a pencil type cursor, filling rectangles, and erasing. Make sure the drawings persist! Use the common color dialog box to allow the user to choose the color of the `Pen` or filled rectangle. (Tip: make use of the `Graphics.FromImage` method.)

13

DAY **14**

Using ActiveX

As wonderful as the .NET Framework is, it's still a relatively new technology, which means that not many useful applications have been built from it. .NET, however, does allow you to access a wealth of applications built prior to .NET, so that you can incorporate already-built functionality into your applications.

The technology that enables this is ActiveX, a means by which different applications—both .NET and non-.NET—can speak to each other and share data. ActiveX has a long history and many developers are already familiar with it, so it adds tremendous possibilities for .NET.

Today's lesson covers everything you need to know about ActiveX to get going.

Today, you will learn

- How ActiveX and COM work together
- Where OLE automation fits into everything
- How to make a Web browser
- How to open Microsoft Word and Excel files in your own applications
- How to use ActiveX properly

Introduction to ActiveX

ActiveX is a term that is tossed about quite a bit in Windows programming. So what exactly is it? Simply put, it's a technology that allows one application to use the functionality of another. To understand how this works, you need to know a bit of history.

Way back when, Microsoft introduced a technology known as Object Linking and Embedding (OLE). OLE enabled users to include one type of document in another.

Figure 14.1 illustrates this concept. With OLE, you could embed a Microsoft Word document in your application without having to write any complex functionality. In this case, Word would be known as the hosted application, while the other would be known as the host. With ActiveX, any application could be a host or be hosted.

FIGURE 14.1

You could use Word's functionality in another application via OLE.

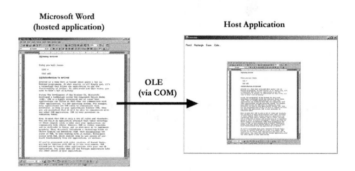

If you've programmed with older versions of Visual Basic, you may be familiar with OLE. OLE allowed you to insert other applications into your own VB application. You could then use the foreign application like any regular object.

Any exposed functionality of the hosted application was available to the host. You exposed functionality the same way you do with .NET, by using necessary keywords such as `Public` or `Protected`. A hosted application didn't have to expose everything, just the functionality it felt was necessary.

NEW TERM Then around 1993, Microsoft developed a technology called the *Component Object Model* (*COM*). COM is a highly structured set of rules that applications can follow in order to communicate with other applications, via the operating system. For example, many applications use COM rules to communicate with databases. As long as your application follows COM, you are guaranteed that it can communicate with any other COM application. COM is very prevalent in computing today. COM built upon the foundations laid by OLE and expanded on the simple linking and embedding to include a new technology, known as OLE Automation (similar to regular OLE, except OLE

Automation allows you to use one application from another, rather than simply embedding documents).

As time went on, technology changed, the Internet was introduced to the mass public, and OLE Automation underwent a name change (as well as minor technology changes) to ActiveX (apparently the name OLE Automation wasn't trendy enough). In other words, ActiveX is really a new name for an old technology. ActiveX works exactly the same as OLE Automation, so you can use it to embed one application in another.

ActiveX was, and still is, very popular because it allowed very different applications to communicate easily. One application could be written in C++ and another in Visual Basic, and as long as they followed the rules of COM, they could work together. Prior to .NET, different programming languages often required completely different programming paradigms, which further complicated communication issues, and in turn increased the importance of ActiveX.

With .NET, things have changed. Since all .NET applications use the same framework and work with the Common Language Runtime (CLR), they are automatically able to communicate with one another. ActiveX controls are no longer used in .NET—they have been replaced by the Windows Forms controls.

That doesn't mean that the millions of ActiveX applications developed prior to .NET are compatible with .NET, though, so .NET needed to support ActiveX in order to host ActiveX applications, and be hosted in them as well.

In the next section, we examine the technical requirements of building a .NET ActiveX host application, and take a look at a few common ActiveX applications.

Using ActiveX Controls

Windows Forms aren't exactly compatible with ActiveX. The only things you can put on a Windows Form are Windows Forms controls—that is, objects that derive from the `System.Windows.Forms.Control` class. An ActiveX application, therefore, cannot be placed directly on a Windows Form. Conversely, an ActiveX application can only be hosted in an ActiveX host, and Windows Forms can not.

You're in luck, however, because there is a workaround. It involves the `System.Windows.Forms.AxHost` class, a special class that provides the bridge between a Windows Form and an ActiveX application. `AxHost` is itself a Windows Forms control, so it can be placed on a Windows Form. But to an ActiveX application, `AxHost` appears to be an ActiveX host. It is essentially a container for ActiveX objects. Figure 14.2 shows the new programming model.

14

FIGURE 14.2

AxHost *wraps ActiveX applications up in the guise of a Windows Forms control for use with Windows Forms.*

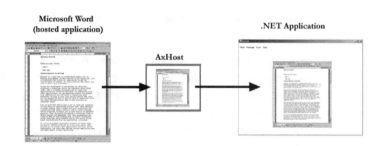

The AxHost control changes depending on the ActiveX application it contains. For example, if the latter has a property named Text, AxHost also has a property named Text. All functionality of the hosted application is added to the AxHost for use with your .NET application.

Before you can use AxHost, however, you have to perform an additional step, which involves the compiled source files associated with the hosted application. Recall that .NET applications are not compiled into executable code, but rather into MSIL. MSIL contains metadata that provides descriptive information to the CLR, which in turn executes the code (and provides other management features). Applications prior to .NET contain neither MSIL or metadata, which makes them incompatible with the CLR—not even the AxHost control can get around this.

Thus any ActiveX application you want to host must first be made compatible with .NET. Relax—you don't have to rewrite any code. .NET comes with a special tool, known as the ActiveX Importer tool (Aximp.exe), that automatically performs the necessary adjustments.

The tool doesn't actually alter the source code of an ActiveX application. It examines the code, discovers all of the functionality that ActiveX application has available, and then generates MSIL and metadata based upon that information. Exposed functionality of the ActiveX application is mapped to metadata, which in turn exposes itself to the .NET application.

NEW TERM This mapping is known as an ActiveX control *wrapper*. The wrapper sits on top of the existing files of the ActiveX application, and exposes the underlying functionality to .NET via compatible metadata. (The wrapper essentially *wraps up* the functionality in the application.)

Using Aximp.exe is simple. From the command line, type the following:

```
aximp ActiveXApplication
```

This generates the wrapped-up file of the same name as the original. `Aximp.exe` has a few optional parameters that we won't cover here because they involve security issues—something we haven't yet discussed. For more information, see the .NET Framework documentation.

> **Caution**
>
> Because `Aximp.exe` generates files of the same name as the originals, you may accidentally overwrite the original. Never call `Aximp.exe` from the same directory as the original file! Always call it from a different directory, or specify a value for the `/out` parameter, which allows you to specify a different output name:
>
> ```
> aximp SHDowVw.dll /out:Webbrowser.dll
> ```

The end result is a new, .NET-compatible Windows Forms control that inherits from `AxHost` and encapsulates the hosted application's functionality. You can now use this control just like any other in your Windows Forms applications. Let's take a look at a few examples.

Using the Web Browser ActiveX Control

The Web Browser ActiveX control provides virtually the same functionality as Internet Explorer. In fact, IE uses this ActiveX control itself to interact with the Web. This control allows you to access a Web page via the Internet, and display the results in your form.

Wait a minute. Didn't we already learn how to do that in Day 12, "Internet Enabling Your Forms"? What's the difference between the `WebRequest` object of that day and the Web Browser ActiveX control? Well, the biggest difference is that that ActiveX control actually parses the returned HTML and displays it as a Web page, just like IE. `WebRequest` simply returns the HTML, and doesn't display it as a Web page. The Web Browser ActiveX control is an easy way to display Web pages like a browser.

First, you need to find the compiled file that contains the functionality of this ActiveX control, and there's no easy way to do that, so I'll just tell you. The file is called `shdocvw.dll`, and is typically located in the `c:\winnt\system32` folder. From the `c:\winforms\day14` directory (recall that we've been creating a new directory for each day in this book), and execute the following command on the command prompt:

```
aximp c:\winnt\system32\shdocvw.dll
```

You should see the output shown in Figure 14.3.

14

FIGURE 14.3

Aximp.exe *generates*
two files from
shdocvw.dll.

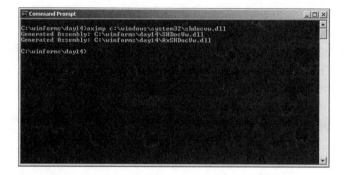

Two files—SHDocVw.dll and AxSHDocVw.dll—were generated because there were two exposed classes in the original shdocvw.dll file. For this example, you only need the latter. Aximp.exe places each of these classes in a namespace of the same name so you can reference them from your code.

Now let's use the new control in an application. Recall that you import .dll files using the using keyword (Imports in VB.NET). Listing 14.1 shows the code that creates a simple Web browser.

LISTING **14.1**   A Simple Web Browser Using ActiveX

```
1:  using System;
2:  using System.Windows.Forms;
3:  using System.Drawing;
4:  using AxSHDocVw;
5:
6:  namespace TYWinforms.Day14 {
7:      public class Listing141 : Form {
8:          private TextBox tbAddress = new TextBox();
9:          private Button btGo = new Button();
10:          private AxSHDocVw.AxWebBrowser objBrowser = new
    ➥AxSHDocVw.AxWebBrowser();
11:
12:          public Listing141() {
13:              tbAddress.Width = 650;
14:              tbAddress.Location = new Point(50,0);
15:              tbAddress.Text = "http://www.clpayne.com";
16:
17:              btGo.Size = new Size(50,20);
18:              btGo.Location = new Point(0,0);
19:              btGo.Text = "Go!";
20:              btGo.Click += new EventHandler(this.Go);
21:
22:              objBrowser.Size = new Size(800,550);
23:              objBrowser.Dock = DockStyle.Bottom;
24:
```

LISTING 14.1   continued

```
25:             this.Text = "Listing 14.1";
26:             this.Size = new Size(800,600);
27:             this.Controls.Add(objBrowser);
28:             this.Controls.Add(tbAddress);
29:             this.Controls.Add(btGo);
30:         }
31:
32:     private void Go(Object Sender, EventArgs e) {
33:         Object arg1 = 0; Object arg2 = ""; Object arg3
➥= ""; Object arg4 = "";
34:
35:         objBrowser.Navigate(tbAddress.Text, ref arg1,
➥ref arg2, ref arg3, ref arg4);
36:     }
37:
38:     public static void Main() {
39:         Application.Run(new Listing141());
40:     }
41:   }
42: }
```

ANALYSIS On line 4 notice that we import the newly created AxSHDocVw namespace, which contains the ActiveX Web browser control. This namespace contains all the necessary items we need to surf the Web. On line 10, we create the AxWebBrowser object, which we'll use to request and display Web pages. Lines 8 and 9 create a textbox and button that allow the user to enter a URL and browse to it. For now, set the URL to http://www.clpayne.com, as shown on line 15.

The only other interesting part of this listing is the Go method on lines 32–36. Line 33 creates a bunch of Object variables that I'll explain in a moment. Line 35 calls the Navigate method of the AxWebBrowser object, which performs the actual request, retrieval, and display of a Web page. The first parameter to this method is the URL to browse to, which is supplied from the tbAddress textbox. The next four parameters are references to the variables created on line 33. This code looks a bit odd because it isn't normal .NET syntax—it is required by the Web browser ActiveX control to function properly. We won't discuss it here (because it's not completely relevant and out-of-scope for this book)—just memorize the syntax if you want to use this ActiveX control another time.

14

Note

> In VB.NET, the last four parameters are not required, so you could simply use:
>
> `objBrowser.Navigate(tbAddress.Text)`
>
> Just one of the peculiarities of ActiveX.

When you compile this application, make sure to add a reference to the `AxSHDocVw.dll` file:

```
csc /t:winexe /r:system.dll /r:system.windows.forms.dll
➥/r:system.drawing.dll /r:axshdocvw.dll listing14.1.cs
```

Figure 14.4 shows the output after the Go button is clicked.

FIGURE 14.4

The Web page is displayed in the ActiveX control.

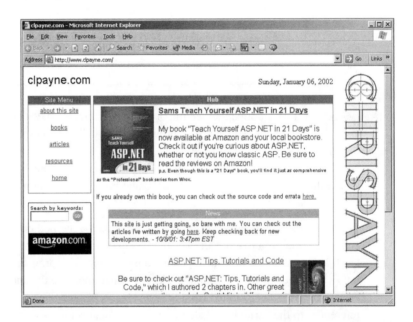

The most difficult part of this procedure was locating the proper `.dll` file and discovering the methods of the ActiveX control. After that, the code should look very familiar to you. Although there's no real new code here, you gain a lot of functionality from the ActiveX control.

> **Tip**
>
> When using ActiveX controls, it's often difficult to determine exactly what functionality is available to you. There are a few ways to do so. You can use the Object Browser in Visual Studio, or try to find the documentation for the ActiveX control in which you are interested. For Microsoft controls, try `Msdn.Microsoft.com`. Finally, you can try the Intermediate Language Disassembler Tool (`ildasm.exe`). This tool looks at the metadata from a .NET file and gives you information on the available methods, properties, events, and other members. For example,
>
> ```
> ildasm listing14.1.exe
> ```
>
> gives you information on the `Main` and `Go` methods and the parameters they require, and the `btGo`, `objBrowser`, and `tbAddress` variables. This tool only works for .NET files.

Using Microsoft Office Type Libraries

ActiveX can also be used to control applications such as Microsoft Word and Excel, although the process is a bit different than the previous one. Specifically, these applications don't expose themselves the way traditional ActiveX applications do, but that doesn't stop you from using them via the same mechanisms.

NEW TERM In computer programming, there is a special type of file called a *type library*. This file is built solely to be used by an application, and provides definitions for specific functionality (much like classes do in .NET). Each application in Microsoft Office has (at least) one type library file associated with it, which defines the classes and functions used by the application. Imagine a type library as the guts behind Word or Excel.

Even though the type library files each belong to a specific application, you can use the technologies behind ActiveX to use them in other applications. This means you can open or create Office documents in your own application. Complex functionality such as Microsoft's spell checker and grammar proofreader can also be used in this way.

Just like old `.dll` files, type libraries are not compatible with the .NET Framework, so you must make them so. This is done with the Type Library Importer Tool (`tlbimp.exe`), which works much the same way as the ActiveX Control Importer. For example:

```
tlbimp TypeLibraryName
```

The Type Library Importer creates a wrapper around the type library that contains the necessary metadata to work with the Common Language Runtime.

14

Note

> The following sections assumes you have Microsoft Office 2000 installed. Previous versions of Office may provide different results using this code. Regardless, you must have a version of Microsoft Office installed for the examples to work.

Using Word via ActiveX

Let's experiment with Word to see the capabilities we can "borrow." The type library associated with Word is called `msword9.olb` and is typically located in the `c:\Program Files\Microsoft Office\Office` directory. From the `c:\winforms\day14` directory, type the following command and press Enter:

`tlbimp "c:\Program Files\Microsoft Office\Office\msword9.olb"`

You should see the following output:

```
TlbImp - Type Library to .NET Assembly Converter Version
➥1.0.2914.16
Copyright (C) Microsoft Corp. 2001.  All rights reserved.

Type library imported to Word.dll
```

The newly created file `Word.dll` now contains all of the functionality you need to work with Word documents. Listing 14.2 shows an example application.

LISTING 14.2   Using Microsoft Word via ActiveX

```
1:  using System;
2:  using System.Windows.Forms;
3:  using System.Drawing;
4:  using Word;
5:
6:
7:  namespace TYWinforms.Day14 {
8:     public class Listing142 : Form {
9:        private Button btView = new Button();
10:        private Button btViewInWord = new Button();
11:        private RichTextBox rtbContent = new RichTextBox();
12:
13:        private Word.Application appWord;
14:        private Word.Document docWord;
15:        private Word._Document docWorking;
16:        private Word.Documents colDocs;
17:        private Word.Range objRange;
18:
19:
```

LISTING 14.2 continued

```
20:         private object missing = System.Reflection.
➥Missing.Value;
21:
22:         public Listing142() {
23:             btView.Text = "Click Here to Open a Word
➥Document";
24:             btView.Location = new Point(150,50);
25:             btView.Size = new Size(150,50);
26:             btView.Click += new EventHandler(this.OpenDoc);
27:
28:             btViewInWord.Text = "Click Here to Open a Word
➥Document in Word";
29:             btViewInWord.Location = new Point(350,50);
30:             btViewInWord.Size = new Size(150,50);
31:             btViewInWord.Click += new EventHandler(this.
➥OpenDocInWord);
32:
33:             rtbContent.Dock = DockStyle.Bottom;
34:             rtbContent.Size = new Size(800,400);
35:
36:             this.Text = "Listing 14.2";
37:             this.Size = new Size(800,600);
38:             this.Controls.Add(btView);
39:             this.Controls.Add(btViewInWord);
40:             this.Controls.Add(rtbContent);
41:         }
42:
43:         private void OpenDoc(Object Sender, EventArgs e) {
44:             OpenFileDialog dlgOpen = new OpenFileDialog();
45:
46:             if (dlgOpen.ShowDialog() == DialogResult.OK) {
47:                 InitializeWord(dlgOpen.FileName);
48:                 rtbContent.Text = objRange.Text;
49:                 CloseWord();
50:             }
51:         }
52:
53:         private void OpenDocInWord(Object Sender,
➥EventArgs e) {
54:             OpenFileDialog dlgOpen = new OpenFileDialog();
55:
56:             if (dlgOpen.ShowDialog() == DialogResult.OK) {
57:                 InitializeWord(dlgOpen.FileName);
58:                 appWord.Visible = true;
59:             }
60:         }
61:
62:         private void InitializeWord(string filename) {
63:             appWord = new Word.Application();
```

14

LISTING 14.2   continued

```
64:            colDocs = appWord.Documents;
65:
66:            object strFilename = (object) filename;
67:
68:            docWorking = (_Document)docWord;
69:            docWorking = colDocs.Open(ref strFilename,
➥ref missing, ref missing, ref missing, ref missing,
➥ref missing, ref missing, ref missing, ref missing,
➥ref missing, ref missing, ref missing);
70:            objRange = docWorking.Range(ref missing,
➥ref missing);
71:        }
72:
73:        private void CloseWord() {
74:            docWorking.Close(ref missing, ref missing,
➥ref missing);
75:            appWord.Quit(ref missing, ref missing,
➥ref missing);
76:        }
77:
78:        public static void Main()  {
79:            System.Windows.Forms.Application.Run
➥ (new Listing142());
80:        }
81:    }
82: }
```

ANALYSIS   This code is rather complex, so let's step through it slowly. First, the constructor on lines 22–41 is fairly standard; it sets up a few buttons and a RichTextBox to hold the contents of the Word documents we open. Note the event handlers for the different buttons: one is intended to open a Word document and place the contents in the RichTextBox control, and the other is intended to open a Word document in Word itself. We'll get to the implementation of these event handlers in a moment.

On line 4 you see a new namespace, Word. This namespace is the one created when you used the Type Library Importer tool. It contains all the Word objects you'll use in this application.

Lines 13–17 declare several important variables. The first, appWord, is of type Word.Application (from the Word namespace) and represents the actual Microsoft Word application. You must start the Word application before you can open any documents, so this variable is important. The second, docWord, represents a generic Word document. (Note that a Word application and a Word document are two different things; an application can be open without any open documents.)

Line 15 declares a variable `docWorking` that is a special type of variable, `_Document`. The underscore in front of the name is a convention from C and C++ that means this data type is a reference to a memory location. We don't need to get too deep into this data type because it isn't used in C# or VB.NET, except to reference older (pre-.NET) technology. For now, know that this variable is used to represent a specific Word document, rather than a generic one like the `docWord` variable.

Line 16 declares the `colDocs` variable, which represents a collection of Word documents. This is important because in Word, every document must belong to a collection, even if that collection is just one document. Finally, line 17 declares a `Word.Range` object, which represents a range of text in a document (similar to the ranges of the `RichTextBox` control).

Line 20 declares another special type of variable, an object with the value `Missing`. `Missing` is from the `System.Reflection` namespace, and is used generally to represent optional method parameters. You should have already come across many methods in the .NET Framework that have various optional parameters; if you don't want to specify one of the parameters, you simply leave it blank. Technology prior to .NET also had optional parameters. The problem is that optional parameters in .NET don't work well with optional parameters prior to .NET. Pre-.NET optional parameters become required in .NET. Often, however, you still don't want to specify a value for these parameters, so the `Missing` value is there to help you out. Just specify `Missing` for those parameters that you still want to be optional. You'll see some examples later in this code. Again, you typically see this type of variable only when working with older technologies.

Let's skip the event handlers for a moment and move down to the `InitializeWord` method on line 62. This method is responsible for setting up, starting, and retrieving a Word document. It takes a string parameter that specifies the Word file to open. On line 63 and 64 you instantiate the Word `Application` and `Documents` objects, just as you would any other object. Line 66 seemingly does something funny—it casts the filename passed in to `InitializeWord` to an `Object` data type. This is necessary for compatibility with older technology.

Line 68 instantiates the `docWorking` document. Recall that `docWorking` represents a specific Word document, while `docWord` represents the generic document. The interesting part, however, is that you cannot directly create a specific Word document (and therefore cannot directly instantiate `docWorking`). You have to create a generic document first, and then create the working document from that, which is why line 68 casts the generic document to a specific one and assigns it to the `docWorking` variable. This may seem kind of confusing, but don't worry, because this situation rarely occurs. It's just the way Microsoft Word was designed.

14

Line 69 is responsible for actually opening a Word document. It calls the Open method from the Documents collection object (remember that all Word documents must belong to a collection). The first parameter is the string representing the file to be opened. The next 11 parameters were all (at one time) optional, but because of the conversion to .NET, you must supply the Missing value. Again, note the keyword ref, which you saw in Listing 14.1 as well. This is required by older ActiveX technologies due to the conversion to .NET. Every call to a non-.NET method must use the ref keyword for each of its parameters.

Line 70 instantiates the objRange variable to contain the entire range of text in the document. Again, notice the ref keywords and Missing values.

The CloseWord method on lines 73–76 closes any open Word documents and shuts down the Word application with two, relatively simple methods. You first call the Close method on the docWorking object, to close any currently open documents. We replace the three optional parameters with Missing values once again. Line 75 closes the Word application by calling the Quit method and supplying the optional parameters.

Finally, let's go back to the event handlers on lines 43–51 and 53–60. These event handlers are similar in function. They both open an OpenFileDialog dialog to allow the user to choose a Word document to open. They then call the custom function InitializeWord (which initializes and opens the Word application and document). Since the OpenDoc method wants to display the text of the Word document in the RichTextBox control, it retrieves the content using the Text property of the Range object you set up earlier in InitializeWord. OpenDoc then calls the CloseWord method, to quit the Word application (after all, once you've retrieved the text from the document, there's no reason to leave the application running). OpenDocInWord doesn't bother with these last two steps and simply makes the Word application visible by setting the Visible property to true.

Compile and run this application (don't forget to reference the new Word.dll assembly). Open a document using the Click Here to Open a Word Document button. After choosing a document, you should see something similar to Figure 14.5, depending on the document you selected.

In Day 11, "Working with Windows Input/Output," I said that it would be difficult for you to manipulate Word documents because they are in a special file format. Well, why should you deal with that format when you can get Word to do it for you? Using ActiveX, you can make Word itself do all the hard work, and simply reap the benefits.

(Note that you lose special Word formatting when you do it this way. This is because the RichTextBox control that you place the text into doesn't have the same capabilities as Word.)

FIGURE 14.5

Your Word document should be displayed in the `RichTextBox` *control.*

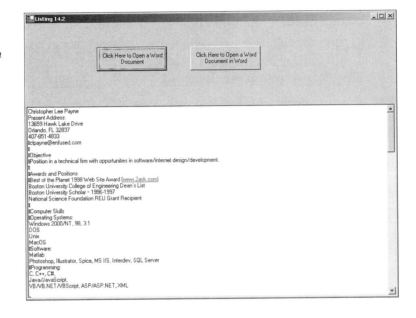

Try using the other button (Click Here to Open a Word Document in Word) to open a Word document inside Word. Word opens to display the document you selected, and you can edit it as normal. Figure 14.6 shows an example.

FIGURE 14.6

You can open and control Word from your own application using ActiveX.

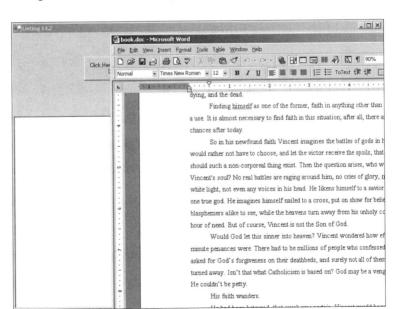

14

Using Excel via ActiveX

Excel works with a similar process to Word. The type library for Excel is `excel9.olb`, located in the same directory as Word's: `c:\Program Files\Microsoft Office\Office`. Import this library using the command:

```
tlbimp "c:\Program Files\Microsoft Office\Office\excel9.olb"
```

Listing 14.3 shows an example of using Excel to quickly sort the items in a `ComboBox` control. Note that this is just an example of using Excel via ActiveX—a similar process could be accomplished simply by using the `Sorted` property of the `ListBox`.

LISTING 14.3   Sorting via Excel and ActiveX

```
 1:  using System;
 2:  using System.Windows.Forms;
 3:  using System.Drawing;
 4:  using System.Reflection;
 5:  using Excel;
 6:
 7:  namespace TYWinforms.Day14 {
 8:      public class Listing143 : Form {
 9:          private System.Windows.Forms.Button btAdd = new
     ➥System.Windows.Forms.Button();
10:          private System.Windows.Forms.Button btSort = new
     ➥System.Windows.Forms.Button();
11:          private ComboBox cboUnsorted = new ComboBox();
12:          private System.Windows.Forms.ListBox lbSorted = new
     ➥System.Windows.Forms.ListBox();
13:
14:          private Excel.Application objApp;
15:          private Workbooks colWBooks;
16:          private _Workbook objWBook;
17:          private Sheets colSheets;
18:          private _Worksheet objSheet;
19:
20:          private object missing = Missing.Value;
21:
22:          public Listing143() {
23:             btAdd.Text = "Add";
24:             btAdd.Location = new System.Drawing.Point(210,50);
25:             btAdd.Click += new EventHandler(this.Add);
26:
27:             btSort.Text = "-> Sort It ->";
28:             btSort.Location = new System.Drawing.
     ➥Point(300,250);
29:             btSort.Size = new Size(150,50);
30:             btSort.Click += new EventHandler(this.Sort);
31:
```

LISTING 14.3   continued

```
32:            cboUnsorted.Location = new System.Drawing.
➥Point(50,50);
33:            cboUnsorted.Size = new Size(150,500);
34:            cboUnsorted.DropDownStyle = ComboBoxStyle.Simple;
35:
36:            lbSorted.Location = new System.Drawing.
➥Point(550,50);
37:            lbSorted.Size = new Size(150,500);
38:
39:            this.Text = "Listing 14.3";
40:            this.Size = new Size(800,600);
41:            this.Controls.Add(btSort);
42:            this.Controls.Add(btAdd);
43:            this.Controls.Add(cboUnsorted);
44:            this.Controls.Add(lbSorted);
45:        }
46:
47:        private void Add(Object Sender, EventArgs e) {
48:            cboUnsorted.Items.Add(cboUnsorted.Text);
49:            cboUnsorted.Text = "";
50:        }
51:
52:        private void Sort(Object Sender, EventArgs e) {
53:            lbSorted.Items.Clear();
54:            int intCount = cboUnsorted.Items.Count;
55:
56:            objApp = new Excel.Application();
57:            colWBooks = objApp.Workbooks;
58:            objWBook = colWBooks.Add(XlWBATemplate.
➥xlWBATWorksheet);
59:            colSheets = objWBook.Worksheets;
60:            objSheet = (_Worksheet) colSheets.get_Item(1);
61:
62:            Range objRange = objSheet.get_Range("A1",
➥Convert.ToChar(intCount+64).ToString() + "1");
63:
64:            String[] arrValues = new String[intCount];
65:            for (int i = 0; i < intCount; i++) {
66:                arrValues[i] = cboUnsorted.Items[i].
➥ToString();
67:            }
68:            objRange.Value2 = arrValues;
69:
70:            objRange.Sort(objSheet.Rows[1, Missing.Value],
➥XlSortOrder.xlAscending, Missing.Value, Missing.Value,
➥XlSortOrder.xlAscending, Missing.Value,
➥XlSortOrder.xlAscending, XlYesNoGuess.xlNo,
➥Missing.Value, Missing.Value,
➥XlSortOrientation.xlSortRows, XlSortMethod.xlStroke);
71:
```

14

LISTING 14.3   continued

```
72:             Object[,] arrSorted;
73:             arrSorted = (Object[,])objRange.Value2;
74:
75:             for (int i=arrSorted.GetLowerBound(0); i <=
➥arrSorted.GetUpperBound(0); i++) {
76:                 for (int j=arrSorted.GetLowerBound(1); j <=
➥arrSorted.GetUpperBound(1); j++) {
77:                     lbSorted.Items.Add(arrSorted[i,j]);
78:                 }
79:             }
80:
81:             cboUnsorted.Items.Clear();
82:             objWBook.Saved = true;
83:             objApp.Quit();
84:         }
85:
86:         public static void Main()  {
87:             System.Windows.Forms.Application.Run
➥ (new Listing143());
88:         }
89:     }
90:  }
```

ANALYSIS   This listing contains similar functionality to Listing 14.2, but let's cover it in detail. First, the constructor on lines 22–45 is fairly standard, and initializes a ComboBox, a ListBox, and a few Buttons. Note that we have to fully qualify the names of the controls with their namespace names because the Excel namespace has controls by the same name—the full namespace name distinguishes the ones we want. Lines 1–12 should also look familiar (remember to reference the newly created Excel namespace). Finally, the Add method on lines 47–50 is the event handler for the Add button, and it simply adds items to the ComboBox. We'll look at the event handler for the Sort button in a moment; it calls the Sort method, which does the bulk of the processing.

Let's examine the variables used next. On lines 14–18 you see various Excel types, which look similar to Word types. Excel's programming model is shown in Figure 14.7—it's a relatively deep hierarchy.

So, in order to enter any data into Excel, you need to drill all the way down to a Range object. Lines 14–18 declare all the objects in this hierarchy with the exception of Range, which we'll get to in a moment. Note the _WorkBook object on line 16; it is much like the _Document object from the example dealing with Word—it represents a specific object.

Line 20 again creates the Missing object that is used to represent optional parameters in method calls to Excel objects.

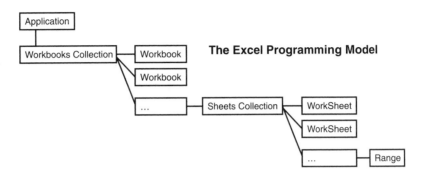

FIGURE 14.7

The Excel program-ming model relies on several collections and objects.

The Sort method beginning on line 52 is the method that actually creates the Excel objects and sorts the values entered into the ComboBox. This method's a bit complicated, so first examine the steps it takes:

1. Creates a new Excel application
2. Retrieves the empty workbooks collection from the application
3. Adds a new workbook to the workbooks collection
4. Retrieves the empty worksheets collection from the new workbook
5. Retrieves the first worksheet from the worksheets collection
6. Retrieves a range of cells
7. Creates an array of values from the items in the ComboBox, and puts it into the selected range
8. Sorts the values
9. Retrieves newly sorted values and adds them to the ListBox
10. Closes the Excel application

It's a fairly long process to sort the values, but most of the energy is spent initializing Excel. The first five steps are accomplished on lines 56–60; they are fairly self-explana-tory, so we'll move on.

Step 6 is performed on line 62. Just like you need to retrieve a range of text to work in a RichTextBox control or Word document, you need a range of cells in Excel. The range is retrieved using the get_Range method, but we have to perform a bit of magic to get it to work correctly. get_Range takes two parameters: the starting cell of the range, and the ending cell of the range. For simplicity's sake, the first cell is always A1, as shown on line 62. The ending cell, however, varies according to the number of items in the ComboBox, and since you can never know how many items the user is going to put in the list, you can't know ahead of time where your ending cell should be. Don't forget, each

14

cell in Excel must be referenced by both a letter and number—for example, A1 or C7 or Q33. Since we're going across columns, the number portion for the ending cell is always 1. Figure 14.8 shows this concept.

FIGURE 14.8

The ending cell is always in row 1, but in an unknown column.

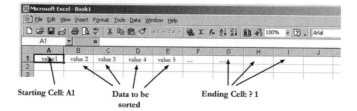

We have to transform the number of items in the ComboBox into a letter that can be used as a column reference, A, B, C, and so on. To do so, you need to know a bit about ASCII character references. Specifically, the number 65 is the same as the ASCII character capital A. 66 is capital B, and so forth. We take the number of items in the ComboBox and add 64 to it to arrive at the proper character number (for example, 1 item in the ComboBox plus 64 equals 65, the letter A), and then use the Convert.ToChar method to convert the number into the proper letter. Finally, we arrive at the ending cell for the range.

To insert the values in the ComboBox into the range of cells, you first need to put them in an array (lines 64–67). This is a simple for loop that adds items into the arrValues array. Line 68 then places them into the range by using the Value2 property.

Line 70 (step 7) is a long one, but very simple. The Sort method takes 12 parameters, but we only care about three of them. The first parameter is the data to sort. In this case, it's the first row in the worksheet. The Rows method takes two parameters, a row and column number, but since we don't care about columns in this example, the second value is Missing. The second parameter specifies how the ordering should take place, and can be either XlSortOrder.xlAscending or XlSortOrder.xlDescending. The next five parameters are used if you want to sort by additional values, but since we only have one row of data, default values are used as parameters. The eighth parameter indicates whether there are headers to the columns. The ninth and 10th parameters are irrelevant. The 11th parameter is another important one that specifies whether Excel is supposed to sort columns or rows. Normally this only matters if you have more than one row or column of data, but we specify xlSortRows to sort by rows all the same. The 12th parameter is also irrelevant.

After the values have been sorted, you need to retrieve them from Excel, and this is a bit more complex than it seems. One would think that since the Value2 property, which inserted values into the cells, accepted a single-dimension array, that it would return a single-dimension array. This isn't so. When used to retrieve values from cells, Value2 returns a two-dimensional array, which you assign to the 2D arrSorted array on line 73. To move the sorted values from the array to the ListBox, you have to make a double loop, as shown on lines 75–79.

Finally, you need to close the application (step 10). You can simply use the Quit method, shown on line 83, but Excel would prompt the users about whether they want to save the existing worksheet (recall that Excel is never visible from this application, so the users may get a bit confused at this message, especially if they thought you built the sorting mechanism yourself). To get around this, set the Saved property to true, which tells Excel that the worksheet has already been saved (even though it hasn't).

Compile this application (don't forget to make a reference to the new Excel namespace and assembly), and test it out to watch Excel sorting in action. Figure 14.9 shows an example.

FIGURE 14.9

Sesame Street characters are entered randomly in the ComboBox, *but sorted in the* ListBox.

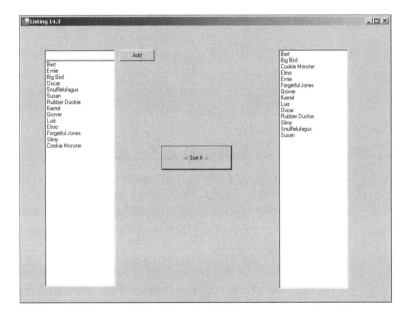

Because you may not be familiar with their inner workings, it sometimes may be a bit confusing working with the Office applications via ActiveX. A very helpful tool is the Object Browser in the Visual Basic Editor bundled with Microsoft Office. To access this tool, go to the Tools menu in any office application, select Macro and then Visual Basic Editor (if this option doesn't appear, it may mean you didn't install the VB Editor initially—simply insert the Office CD-ROM and select it from the menu). Once in the editor, select Object Browser from the View menu, or press F2.

14

The Object Browser (see Figure 14.10) lists all of the objects, methods, properties, and events that are available in each Office application. This is an invaluable tool for ActiveX applications.

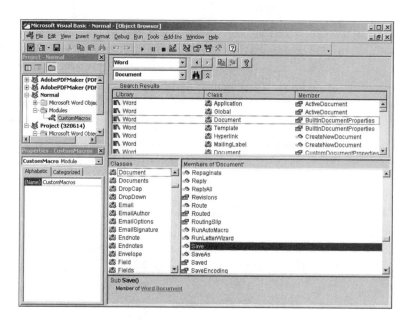

Creating .NET ActiveX Controls

Technically, ActiveX controls have been replaced in .NET by Windows Forms controls, so you can't actually create a .NET ActiveX control. You can, however, build your .NET applications so that they can be used as ActiveX controls by non-.NET applications. This is a relatively easy process, and there are only a few things you need to do that you may not be doing already.

The first thing is to design your application appropriately. Any functions or variables that you want an ActiveX application to have access to must be declared as `public`. This is nothing new; even a .NET class that needs to be accessed by other .NET classes must have `public` members.

For example, let's say you've created a calculator application that will be used by another application via ActiveX. You probably want the main calculation functions (add, subtract, and so on) to be available to the host application. These must be declared as `public`:

```
public int Add(int intA, int intB) {
    ...
}
```

On the other hand, you may not want the user to be able to access or modify the calculator's buttons, so you mark these as `private`:

```
private Button btnAdd = new Button();
```

The next thing you need to do is register your .NET application in the Windows registry. All ActiveX controls must be registered to function correctly, and although your .NET application isn't technically an ActiveX control, host applications treat it as such and, therefore, your application must act like one.

Registration is done using the Assembly Registration tool (`regasm.exe`). This tool reads the metadata from your application and adds the necessary entries to the registry so it can be used as an ActiveX control. The syntax is simple:

```
regasm AssemblyFilename
```

For example, you can register Listing 14.2 as an ActiveX control with the following command-line command:

```
regasm listing14.2.exe
```

You should see the following output:

```
RegAsm - .NET Assembly Registration Utility Version 1.0.2914.16
Copyright (C) Microsoft Corp. 2001.  All rights reserved.

Types registered successfully
```

That's all there is to it. Non-.NET applications can now access your application via ActiveX just like any other ActiveX control; there are no changes required to the way the host applications are built. So while you are basking in the glory that is .NET, writing your applications in a fully object-oriented way, you can allow those poor souls still stuck in old technology to use your applications via ActiveX.

Guidelines for Working with ActiveX

NEW TERM Because ActiveX is an older technology, there are some costs associated with using it. For example, a specific data type available in .NET technology may not be available in a pre-.NET technology, or vice versa (the `variant` data type in VB 6, for example, does not exist in VB.NET). When this happens, the CLR must translate one type into the other, a process known as *marshalling*. Marshalling takes extra processing time, and affects your applications more than you may think.

14

Also, due to limitations in technology, you lose a lot of flexibility when using ActiveX. For example, parameters that used to be optional must now always be supplied, whether or not you need them. This is where the `Missing` object comes into play; you must use it for those parameters you don't want to supply actual values for.

On a related note, it's sometimes difficult to figure out exactly what types you need to supply for ActiveX method parameters, even with documentation.

When you want to use an application via ActiveX, you can often find similar functionality already built into .NET. For example, prior to .NET, you may have used the `FileSystemObject` ActiveX control to perform file I/O operations. Now, you can use the classes you learned about in Day 11 to do the same thing.

Because of these and other details, you always want to double-check to see if the same functionality is already available in the .NET Framework, or if it wouldn't be too difficult to build it yourself. If you can at all avoid the penalties of dealing with ActiveX, do so.

Do	**Don't**
Do use ActiveX only when absolutely necessary, such as when the desired functionality is very complex, or you must rely on a proprietary technology to run your application (such as using Word to open Word documents).	**Don't** use ActiveX when the functionality you desire is simple, or is already available in a .NET Framework class. Do your research in the .NET documentation first!

Another issue that often complicates matters is the policy of licensing ActiveX controls. When an ActiveX control is licensed, it means that you can only use it if you have the proper licenses (which usually means purchasing them).

As an example, suppose you have Microsoft Office on your development computer, and you create the applications in Listings 14.2 and 14.3. Then you sell your product to a home user. If that user doesn't have Office, he can't use your applications. You can sometimes bundle the necessary ActiveX components with your application, but again, that requires extra licensing agreements, and typically costs big bucks.

To further complicate matters, there are often different types of licenses as well, for instance, production and development licenses, single-user licenses, single-processor licenses, and so on. You need to make sure everyone who uses your application has the same license. Some types of licenses can't be shared or transferred, which makes things even more interesting.

Note

As a developer, you can license your own controls so that people have to buy licenses from you. If you want to buy a license for someone else's control and use it in your own product, things get a bit more complicated. Different companies have different requirements and pricing schemes when you want to distribute their licenses. In these cases you must check with the control vendor.

If you like pain, you can delve further into the licensing issue by checking out the .NET Framework documentation. It explains how to properly obtain and use ActiveX licenses in your .NET applications, and even how to make licenses for your own .NET applications (which is helpful if you ever want to sell a product).

Summary

Today you learned about ActiveX: what it is, what it does for you, and some issues about using it. ActiveX can add greatly to the capabilities of your applications.

ActiveX, formerly known as OLE Automation, is a technology based on the Component Object Model, or COM. COM is a set of rules and specifications that govern how applications can talk to each other, regardless of the language or paradigm in which they were created.

Windows Forms are not exactly compatible with ActiveX; the only thing you can put on a Windows Form is a Windows Forms control. To use ActiveX applications or controls in your .NET applications, you must wrap the ActiveX control in the .NET AxHost class, which looks like a Windows Forms control to .NET, but like an ActiveX host to an ActiveX application. Luckily, you don't have to create this class yourself, because the ActiveX Importer tool does it for you by creating metadata for ActiveX controls.

In addition to the ActiveX Importer tool, there is the Type Library Importer, which enables you to use applications such as Microsoft Office or Excel as ActiveX controls.

To allow ActiveX applications to use your .NET applications, you only need to use the Assembly Registration tool to create registry entries from your metadata, and ensure that your methods and properties are properly declared (using public and private).

Tomorrow is the start of a new week, and a focus on a different aspect of Windows Forms. You'll begin learning about Web services, a major driving force behind the .NET revolution. Don't forget to check out the bonus application!

14

Q&A

Q **Is using ActiveX Controls on a Windows Form safe?**

A Because ActiveX is an older technology that is not fully compatible with .NET, there are certain assumptions you make when you use it in your applications. First, ActiveX controls cannot take advantage of the Common Language Runtime's built-in security features. Because of this, certain functionality in ActiveX controls may not be accessible in your .NET applications, and you cannot access them via Internet Explorer (see Day 12, "Internet Enabling Your Forms," for more information).

Additionally, ActiveX controls must be registered in a central repository to work correctly (specifically, in the Windows registry). This step also requires additional security precautions.

Finally, some ActiveX controls can simply not be imported into the .NET Framework. Trying to do so causes unpredictable results, ranging from memory leaks to crashed systems.

Q **Can I use any application in .NET via ActiveX?**

A Unfortunately, no. You'll note, however, that many applications can be used via ActiveX even though you'll never find any documentation that says so. Often times, the only thing that is required for applications to be used via ActiveX is that they have `public` members.

Some applications that were previously useable by ActiveX cannot be used in .NET at all, due to limitations in backward compatible technology.

The best thing to do is simply to try. You'll be surprised at how many of your favorites applications can be used via ActiveX, as long as you can find the appropriate `.dll` files.

Workshop

This workshop will help reinforce the concepts we've covered today. It is very helpful to understand fully the answers before moving on. Answers can be found in Appendix A.

Quiz

1. What are the executable files associated with the ActiveX Importer, Type Library Importer, and Assembly Registration tools we talked about today?

2. True or false? The ActiveX Importer tool modifies a `.dll`'s source code to comply with .NET.

3. True or false? It is better to use existing .NET technology than to use a similar ActiveX control.

4. What is marshalling?

5. What would the following code output?

```
MessageBox.Show(Convert.ToChar(88).ToString());
```

6. After you've created an Office application object, how do you make it visible to the user?

Exercise

Use the Intermediate Language Disassembler tool to examine the Web Browser ActiveX control (`AxSHDocVw.dll`), and then enhance Listing 14.1 to behave more like a true browser. Include Home, Stop, and Refresh buttons, and change the form's `Text` property to match the title of the Web page currently being viewed.

14

WEEK 2

In Review

Project 2: Extending the Word Processor

You've made it through 14 days of Windows Forms—hope you're still eager to learn because we're only 2/3 of the way through! In the past week you learned about many technologies that supplement Windows Forms and make your applications more powerful. These include databases, I/O, ActiveX, and the Internet. By now you're building fully functional, not to mention useful, applications at an intermediate level.

In this section, we're going to sum up the various technologies you learned over the past week and apply them to the word processor, NetWord, that you built at the end of Week 1. Specifically, you'll add I/O capabilities (so that your word processor can open and save documents), add a multiple document interface, and add printing capabilities.

Adding MDI

Before you get too far modifying the NetWord processor, let's convert it to an MDI application so the user can edit multiple documents at once. This section will encompass the largest amount of changes, though they are all pretty simple.

Recall from last time that we had one main class, `NetWord`, that contained a `RichTextBox` control for editing, and several menus. Because we're now going to transform the application into an MDI, we need to move things around a bit. First, create a copy of `NetWord` and rename it `Document`. This new class will represent each child window in the MDI, while NetWord will remain the main application window.

In the new Document class, first remove the Main method—you won't need it here. Then remove all references to the Open and Exit menus (the mniOpen and mniExit objects), which will be placed in the NetWord class. You can leave the other menu items, the context menu, the status bar, and pretty much all the other variables and methods.

For the remaining menu items, you'll need to specify MergeOrder values so they join properly with the menus in the NetWord class. Add the following code to the constructor:

```
mniSave.MergeOrder = 30;
mniFile.MenuItems[1].MergeOrder = 35;
mniPageSetup.MergeOrder = 40;
mniPrintPreview.MergeOrder = 45;
mniPrint.MergeOrder = 50;
```

In NetWord, there are more modifications you need to make. First, you'll need to remove all references to objects or variables that are particular to each document. Remove all references to the Save, Page Setup, Print Preview, Print, Edit, Copy, Paste, Cut, Find, Format, and Font menus. Leave, however, the Open and Exit menu items. Then remove all references to the RichTextBox control (rtbDocument). Remove the fntCurrent, fntColor, objPageSettings, and objPrinterSettings variables. All of these items are in the Document class, so you don't need them here.

Because users are going to be dealing with multiple windows at once, you'll want to add a Windows menu that lets them arrange the windows and choose a particular one. In the declarations section of NetWord, add the following code:

```
private MenuItem mniWindow = new MenuItem("Window");
private MenuItem mniWinC = new MenuItem("Cascade");
private MenuItem mniWinTH = new MenuItem("Tile Horizontal");
private MenuItem mniWinTV = new MenuItem("Tile Vertical");
```

In the constructor, add the following code:

```
mniWinC.Click += new EventHandler(this.WindowClicked);
mniWinTH.Click += new EventHandler(this.WindowClicked);
mniWinTV.Click += new EventHandler(this.WindowClicked);

mniWindow.MdiList = true;
mniWindow.MenuItems.Add(mniWinC);
mniWindow.MenuItems.Add(mniWinTH);
mniWindow.MenuItems.Add(mniWinTV);

mnuMain.MenuItems.Add(mniWindow);
```

Next, add the following method to the class:

```
private void WindowClicked(Object Sender, EventArgs e) {
    MenuItem miTemp = (MenuItem)Sender;

    switch (miTemp.Text) {
        case "Cascade":
            this.LayoutMdi(MdiLayout.Cascade);
            break;
        case "Tile Horizontal":
            this.LayoutMdi(MdiLayout.TileHorizontal);
            break;
        case "Tile Vertical":
            this.LayoutMdi(MdiLayout.TileVertical);
            break;
    }
}
```

Specify the proper `MergeOrder` values in the constructor:

```
mniNew.MergeOrder = 10;
mniOpen.MergeOrder = 20;
mniExit.MergeOrder = 99;
mniFile.MenuItems[2].MergeOrder = 98;
```

Recall that `MergeOrder` values don't have to be sequential—they are merged based on relative values.

You'll need a counter to keep track of all the child document windows floating about. Add the following in the declarations section:

```
private int intCounter = 0;
```

Finally, you need to tell `NetWord` that it is now an MDI parent, so add the following line in the constructor:

```
this.IsMdiContainer = true;
```

If all goes well, you can recompile the application with the following command:

```
csc /t:winexe /r:system.dll /r:system.drawing.dll
➥/r:system.windows.forms.dll Netword.cs
➥document.cs FindDialog.cs
```

Right now, there's no way to add child documents to the application (because the Open file menu doesn't do anything yet), but we'll remedy that in the next section.

Adding I/O

When we last left off, you had a rudimentary word processor that allowed the user to change fonts, cut, paste, copy, and search for specific text. You also had menus for opening and saving files, but they didn't have any event handlers—they didn't do anything.

Recall from Day 11, "Working with Windows Input/Output," that the `RichTextBox` control has built-in functions to open and save files. We'll take advantage of those here. However, because the `RichTextBox` can only open plain text and rich text files, we'll have to be careful.

The `NetWord` class should still have the `FileClicked` method to handle the Open menu item. Let's modify this slightly, as shown in Listing P2.1.

LISTING P2.1   Adding I/O Capabilities to the Open Menu

```
1:  private void FileClicked(Object Sender, EventArgs e) {
2:      MenuItem mniTemp = (MenuItem)Sender;
3:      Document doc;
4:
5:      switch (mniTemp.Text) {
6:         case "New":
7:            intCounter++;
8:
9:            doc = new Document("Document " + intCounter);
10:           doc.MdiParent = this;
11:           doc.Show();
12:           break;
13:        case "Open...":
14:
15:           dlgOpen.Filter = "All files (*.*)|*.* ";
16:
17:           if (dlgOpen.ShowDialog() == DialogResult.OK) {
18:              intCounter++;
19:
20:              doc = new Document(dlgOpen.FileName);
21:              doc.MdiParent = this;
22:
23:              FileInfo filTemp = new FileInfo
➥ (dlgOpen.FileName);
24:              if (filTemp.Extension == ".rtf") {
25:                 ((RichTextBox)doc.Controls[0]).
➥LoadFile(dlgOpen.FileName,
➥RichTextBoxStreamType.RichText);
26:              } else {
27:                 ((RichTextBox)doc.Controls[0]).
➥LoadFile(dlgOpen.FileName,
➥RichTextBoxStreamType.PlainText);
```

LISTING P2.1 continued

```
28:                }
29:
30:                doc.Show();
31:            }
32:            break;
33:        case "Exit":
33:            this.Close();
35:            break;
36:    }
37: }
```

ANALYSIS Most of this code should look familiar. The first new addition is line 3; we declare a variable of type Document (the new child MDI class created earlier) for use later in this method. The switch statement evaluates the menu item clicked, and because most of the menus have been removed, we're left with only the Open and Exit cases here.

Line 15 filters the available choices for our OpenFileDialog (see the project after Week 1 to find out where this is created) to allow any type of file. If the user selects a file, we need to increment the counter that keeps track of child documents. Line 18 does this.

Line 20 instantiates the new Document child, passing the filename in to the constructor. This means we're going to have to modify the constructor of the Document class to accept that filename. The declaration of the constructor in Document should be changed to

```
public Document(string strName) {
```

To display the name in the caption, use the following:

```
this.Text = strName;
```

Next, back in the NetWord class, we need to evaluate whether the file the user selected is a rich text document or a plain text document, or any other kind of document. To do so, we need to evaluate the file extension.

Line 23 creates a new FileInfo object (don't forget to import the System.IO namespace!) based on the selected file to do just this. If the extension is .rtf, we're dealing with a rich text file. Line 25 calls the LoadFile method of the RichTextBox control in the child document (see Day 10, "Creating MDI Applications," for more information on the specifics here), passing in the selected filename and a value from the RichTextBoxStreamType enumeration. Specifically, it passes the RichText value, which tells the RichTextBox to expect a rich text (.rtf) file.

On the other hand, if the selected file's extension is anything else, we pass RichTextBoxStreamType.PlainText to the LoadFile method.

Finally, the child document is shown on line 30. You can now open as many child documents as you want from any plain or rich text file.

To save documents, go to the Document class and modify the FileClicked method. Specifically, the Save case should now look like this:

```
case "Save":
   FileInfo filTemp = new FileInfo(this.Text);
   if (filTemp.Extension == ".txt") {
      rtbDocument.SaveFile(this.Text,
➥RichTextBoxStreamType.PlainText);
   } else {
      rtbDocument.SaveFile(this.Text,
➥RichTextBoxStreamType.RichText);
   }
   rtbDocument.Modified = false;
   break;
```

Like the Open menu command, the Save menu needs to evaluate the type of file we're dealing with and pass the appropriate RichTextBoxStreamType enumeration value in the SaveFile method. Set the Modified property of the RichTextBox to true to tell the application that all changes have been saved.

There's one more place the user can save the file. Recall that when the document is closed, if any changes have been made, a dialog asks the user whether he wants to save the changes. This is done in the DocumentClosing method, so we need to add some code here as well. However, you don't need to rewrite the previously described functionality. Instead, simply call the FileClicked method that passes in the appropriate parameters. The DocumentClosing method should look like Listing P2.2.

LISTING P2.2   Allowing the User to Save Before Closing

```
1:  private void DocumentClosing(Object Sender,
➥CancelEventArgs e) {
2:      if (rtbDocument.Modified) {
3:          DialogResult dr = MessageBox.Show("Do you want to
➥save the changes?", this.Name,
➥MessageBoxButtons.YesNoCancel);
4:
5:          if (dr == DialogResult.Yes) {
6:              FileClicked(mniSave, new EventArgs());
7:          } else if (dr == DialogResult.Cancel) {
8:              e.Cancel = true;
9:          }
```

```
10:      }
11:   }
```

The only modification is line 6. Now you call the `FileClicked` method passing in the `mniSave` menu and a new `EventArgs` object. That's all there is to it!

Adding Printing Capabilities

You may recall that printing in .NET is an unintuitive procedure: You use a `PrintDocument` object that raises a `PrintPage` event every time something needs to be printed. You must create an event handler for the `PrintPage` method that uses GDI+ to actually print the page.

The code to create the `PrintDocument` should be placed in the `Document.FileClicked` method, in the Print case section:

```
case "Print":
   PrintDialog dlgPrint = new PrintDialog();
   dlgPrint.PrinterSettings = new PrinterSettings();
   if (dlgPrint.ShowDialog() == DialogResult.OK) {
      objReader = new StringReader(rtbDocument.Text);

      PrintDocument pd = new PrintDocument();

      pd.DefaultPageSettings = objPageSettings;
      pd.PrintPage += new PrintPageEventHandler(this.PrintIt);
      pd.Print();
   }
   break;
```

Here you retrieve the text to be printed from your `RichTextBox` using a `StringReader` object. This object will be used in the actual routine to print the document. Remember to assign the `objPageSettings` object to the `PrintDocument`, assign a delegate, and call the `Print` method. Also, you need to define a new variable in your code declaration section for the new `StringReader` object, named `objReader`. The `PrintIt` method (the event handler for the `Print` event) should look like Listing P2.3.

LISTING P2.3   Printing a Page

```
1:   private void PrintIt(Object Sender, PrintPageEventArgs e) {
2:
3:
4:      Font fntPrint = this.Font;
```

LISTING P2.3   continued

```
5:      int count = 0;
6:      float yPos = 0;
7:      float lpp = e.MarginBounds.Height /
➥fntPrint.GetHeight(e.Graphics);
8:      float fltTopMargin = e.MarginBounds.Top;
9:      float fltLeftMargin = e.MarginBounds.Left;
10:     String strLine = null;
11:
12:     while (count < lpp && ((strLine = objReader.ReadLine())
➥!= null)) {
13:         yPos = fltTopMargin + (count * fntPrint.GetHeight
➥ (e.Graphics));
14:
15:         e.Graphics.DrawString(strLine, fntPrint,
➥Brushes.Black, fltLeftMargin, yPos, new
➥StringFormat());
16:
17:         count++;
18:     }
19:
20:     if (strLine != null) {
21:         e.HasMorePages = true;
22:     } else {
23:         e.HasMorePages = false;
24:     }
25:   }
```

This code is almost an exact copy from Listing 11.6, so we won't go over it completely
again. The only difference is that you are no longer creating your objReader object in
this listing; rather, you've moved it into the "Print" case in the previous code snippet.
This avoids the infinite page-printing loop described in Day 11. Your application now has
printing capabilities.

Figure P2.1 shows the newly enhanced application in action.

Note

In the project that follows Week 3, you will add advanced capabilities such
as custom Windows Forms controls. By the time you're finished, you'll have a
word processor that rivals many commercial ones!

FIGURE P2.1

The NetWord word processor application in action.

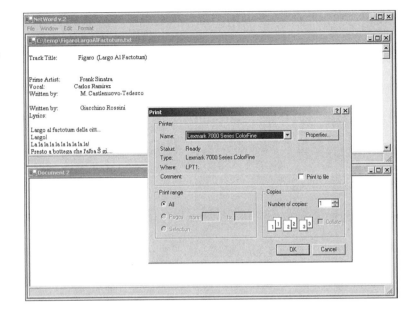

WEEK 3

At a Glance

Inside Windows Forms

Congratulations on making it to the third week in your journey through Windows Forms. By now, you are fast becoming an expert in the world of Windows Forms, and are ready to take on nearly any challenge.

The first two weeks were spent ramping you up from the basics. Week 1 introduced you to Windows Forms and taught you how to work with them. Week 2 introduced a few different .NET technologies that make your Windows Forms application much more useful and functional. In the coming week, we're going to get under the hood of Windows Forms and look at the technologies that drive Windows Forms, and how to get the most out of your applications.

Starting in Day 15, "Using Web Services," you'll learn about Web services, one of the biggest motivations for moving to .NET. Day 16, "Building Windows Services," teaches you about Windows services, which are completely different than Web services. Windows services allow you to tightly integrate your applications into the operating system.

You've already learned how to use most of the Windows Forms controls available in the .NET Framework, including `TextBoxes`, `ListBoxes`, and `Labels`. In Day 17, "Advanced Windows Forms Controls Techniques," along with the help of GDI+, you learn some advanced features of some controls, including how you can change their appearance and make

15

16

17

18

19

20

21

them do things that weren't possible before. In Day 18, "Building Custom Windows Forms Controls," you learn how to create your own custom Windows Forms controls that can greatly enhance your applications.

In Day 19, "Creating Multithreaded Applications," you learn how to make asynchronous method calls and squeeze the most performance possible out of your applications.

Day 20, "Configuring and Deploying Your Windows Forms," shows you how to deploy and configure your applications so they are ready for the prime time—that is, real customers and users. Finally, you'll wrap it up in Day 21, "Debugging and Profiling Your Windows Forms." Debugging is a critical part of building any application, and you'll learn the different methods to do so in Day 21. Profiling allows you to get into the "nitty-gritty" of performance tuning, to ensure that your applications run at optimum performance.

Let's get to work!

DAY 15

Using Web Services

Now that you have all the fundamentals of Windows Forms in place, you can begin learning about advanced technologies that greatly enhance Windows Forms. We'll start with Web services.

A Web service is an interesting beast, one that allows you to access and execute applications from anywhere on the Internet—you don't need to have an application installed on your computer to use it. Web services are a revolutionary way of thinking about traditional applications and, because they rely on tried and tested technologies and protocols, you can be sure that they will be around for a while.

Today you will learn

- What, exactly, is a Web service
- How to speak in SOAP
- How to easily access and integrate Web services
- Where to find those Web services

What Are Web Services?

Web services are often confusing to beginners in the .NET Framework. They seem to be the product of a Web site crossed with a desktop-based application—and still somehow don't quite resemble either. To fully understand Web services, you have to understand the technology behind them, and why they were developed in the first place. Let's take a quick trip back in time.

Before the Internet, there existed many lonesome computers and corporations. No computers were ever able to communicate with other ones (at least, not generally). A company would develop its own in-house applications, while the company next door could be doing the exact same thing, and neither would be aware of the other's applications. Additionally, the systems would often be so different that they could never share data.

Technologies like ActiveX had to be developed to allow differing systems to speak with one another, but even these were limited in scope. The applications had to be local—meaning they couldn't be spread over large distances—and platform dependent. COM and ActiveX were good ideas designed to attack a fundamental design flaw.

Then along came the Internet, which revolutionized the way everyone thought. Suddenly, two computers halfway around the world could communicate with each other easily over the Internet via standard protocols. Data could be shared like never before. New worlds were opened with the communication revolution.

Companies especially were scrambling. Development teams now had to think about globalization, and that meant incorporating the resources available over the Internet, and making desktop-bound applications Internet accessible. Entire new businesses sprang up just to attack these issues, and businesses that previously relied on mom-and-pop type establishments (such as craft shops) ventured into new territory.

The key driving force behind the Internet revolution was the development of a standard means of communication—specifically, HTTP, FTP, TCP, and so on. It didn't matter what kind of computer you used; as long as you had a phone line, you could use these standards to join in on the fun. Users could transcend their desktops and move into cyberspace with a few clicks.

In other words, the Internet offered the solution that had been evading companies large and small: standard platform independent communication protocols. These protocols helped communication jump a major hurdle, but companies still had no way to share their custom databases.

The next step toward Web services was the development of XML. XML allowed the transfer of large amounts of data over the Internet, using the same standard protocols that worked for other forms of communication. Because it relied on tried-and-true methods for communication, XML was instantly accepted and widely available.

Now we had mechanisms to transfer data (via XML), and the backbone communication protocols needed to transfer that data (via HTTP). There was, however, one component problem: Applications that control those messages and the data were still bound to desktops—sure, they could send XML via the Internet, but that remained the breadth of their capabilities.

Finally, we arrive at Web services. Web services fill in the gap, allowing applications to talk to each other over the Internet. How, you may ask? Via the same standard protocols that have been in use since the Internet revolution began. Using a special form of XML known as SOAP (which we'll discuss in the next section), Web services allow any application to create commands and send them over the Internet where a waiting application executes the commands and sends the results back. In other words, my computer could tell your computer to run an application and send any results back to me.

What does it mean to create a command? When you tell your computer to play a music CD, you are issuing a command. The operating system, in turn, is issuing a command (represented by bits and bytes) to the CD player, and it does what it's supposed to. Issuing commands over the Internet to a Web service is similar, although the commands are now represented in SOAP and XML rather than 1s and 0s.

Imagine, for example, that you don't have Microsoft Word installed on your desktop machine, but you need the functionality it provides. Microsoft, however, has a Word Web service on its computer halfway around the world. Your computer could connect to Microsoft's Word service and you could use all the functionality available in Word via the Web service just as if Word were on your computer. You would never have to buy Microsoft Word; you could rent it as a Web service for a small fee per month, just like you pay for AOL or MSN Internet service providers.

There are quite a few benefits to this paradigm. First, you don't ever have to install anything on your computer. This alone results in quite a few benefits, including less resource requirements on your part, less maintenance and troubleshooting, and the assurance that you're always using the latest version. Also, it costs you less (in the short term at least) to use the application. On Microsoft's side, this saves the company the trouble of dealing with installation problems on thousands or millions of different computers because it can maintain one copy of the Web service rather than a million copies of Word.

Because Web services rely on standard protocols, anyone can use them, from a home user to a corporation, and even Web sites! One application can even use multiple Web services. For example, suppose you're using a home-design application that enables you to design floor plans for your dream home. In construction, however. prices, materials, and requirements are always changing. Instead of the design application coming with all these rules itself (which would require constant updating), it can contact a few different Web services, such as a calculator service that figures out the amounts of the materials you're going to need, and a shopping Web service to check prices and place orders. The beautiful part is that the Web services integrate directly into the design application, and the user would never know the difference; to him it would appear as if the design application did everything itself. Figure 15.1 illustrates this example.

FIGURE 15.1

A home-design application (desktop-based) could utilize Web services invisibly to the user.

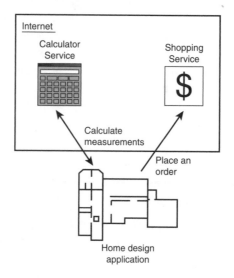

Another example is a stock-quoting service. From your favorite online broker (such as Etrade or Ameritrade) you place a stock quote request. With Web services, Etrade doesn't have to maintain and keep its own constantly updated database of prices. It could simply place a call to Web service that resides on the stock exchange's site that would return the price. You as the end user would never know how Etrade got its quotes. Figure 15.2 shows this flow chart.

While you know that Web services rely on XML and HTTP, there is a new protocol you need to know about: SOAP.

Figure 15.2

An online broker can rely on stock quoting Web services to provide features to end users.

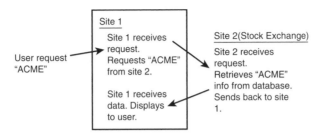

The Simple Object Access Protocol

New Term The *Simple Object Access Protocol*, or *SOAP*, essentially allows you to access objects over the Internet. (The simple in SOAP means that the protocol itself is simple, not that the objects you access are simple). It is a protocol that specifies how one application can send messages to another over the Internet. Although SOAP is itself a protocol, it relies on other protocols for its existence.

The language SOAP speaks is XML. In other words, every SOAP message (a command to another application) is actually written in XML; SOAP only provides a specific formatting style for that XML. Thus, if an application can understand XML, it can understand SOAP.

For transmission, SOAP relies on HTTP. HTTP allows SOAP messages to go anywhere plain text or HTML can, including around firewalls and other Internet security measures. If SOAP were to rely on any non-standard protocol for transmission, it would fail in its job.

We'll look at some examples of SOAP messages later today. For now, let's examine a few more protocols that come into play.

Other Protocols for Web Services

SOAP is not the only protocol Web services can use. HTTP offers a couple different means to transmit data: HTTP-Get and HTTP-Post. An HTTP-Get command is what you normally use to view Web pages. HTTP-Post is used to post data to servers (typically form data). Both of these mechanisms can be used to transfer Web service commands and data, but they have a few drawbacks.

Specifically, they cannot transfer anything more than very simple data or commands. In fact, the only data type that works with HTTP-Get or HTTP-Post is the string, so commands made to a Web service and the data that is returned must be very simple.

XML, on the other hand, was designed specifically to be able to represent many complex data types, and since SOAP relies on XML, it is much more versatile than either HTTP method.

Although we'll examine all three methods (SOAP, HTTP-Post, and HTTP-Get) today, we'll focus on SOAP because of the flexibility it offers.

Using ASP.NET to Build Web Services

Because accessing Web services is most like accessing Web pages, it is fitting that you can use ASP.NET to build them. Active Server Pages.NET is the latest version of Active Server Pages and is completely compatible with the .NET Framework. It is used to build Web sites and applications available over the Internet—dynamic Web sites. While we won't get into the specifics of ASP.NET here, you'll see that building ASP.NET pages is very much like building Windows Forms applications.

Let's take a look at some simple ASP.NET pages, so that you can understand better how a Web service works. Listing 15.1 shows a typical ASP.NET page. It simply prompts the user for information and then welcomes that user.

Note

In order to test the following examples, you'll need to have a Web server and ASP.NET installed. Internet Information Server is a Web server available with Windows 2000 or XP, and ASP.NET is an optional install from the free .NET Framework (http://www.microsoft.com/net).

For more information, see the .NET Framework documentation.

LISTING 15.1   A Simple ASP.NET Page

```
1:  <%@ Page Language="CS" %>
2:
3:  <script runat="server">
4:      public void Submit(Object Sender, EventArgs e) {
5:          lblMessage.Text = "Welcome " + tbName.Text +
6:              "!<br>It " +"is " +
7:              System.DateTime.Now.ToString();
8:      }
9:  </script>
10:
11:  <html><body>
12:      <form runat="server">
13:
14:          Please enter your name:<p>
```

LISTING 15.1   continued

```
15:         <ASP:TextBox id="tbName" runat="server" />
16:         <ASP:Button id="btSubmit" text="Submit"
17:             OnClick="Submit" runat="server" /><p>
18:         <ASP:Label id="lblMessage" runat="server"/>
19:     </form>
20: </body></html>
```

Save this file as Listing15.1.aspx in your c:\inetpub\wwwroot directory, and view it from your browser using the address http://localhost/listing15.1.aspx. After you enter your name and press the Submit button, you should see a screen similar to the one shown in Figure 15.3.

FIGURE 15.3

Here's example output from a simple ASP.NET page.

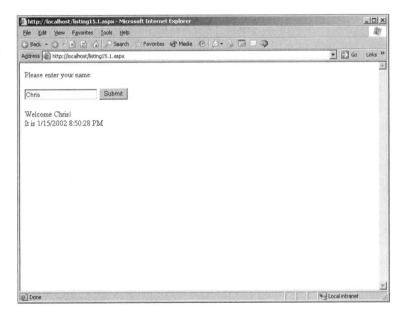

An ASP.NET page is divided into two main sections: the code declaration block (lines 3–9) and HTML (lines 11–20). The code declaration block is wrapped in script tags. As you can see, it looks just like typical Windows Forms code in C#. The Submit method is a simple event handler (complete with the standard event handler parameter list) that sets the text of a Label to a welcome message. Note the runat="server" on line 3; this is very important for ASP.NET pages—without it, the page wouldn't work properly.

The HTML section is mostly straight HTML, with a few ASP.NET specific tags, specifically, the ASP:TextBox on line 15, the ASP:Button on line 16, and the ASP:Label on line 18. These are ASP.NET controls, which are very much like the TextBox, Button, and Label controls in Windows Forms. They have all the same properties and events, so you are already familiar with them! (Again, note the runat="server" attributes on all these controls.)

Line 17 instructs the ASP.NET page to execute the Submit method when the Button control is clicked. (You must override the OnClick method instead of assigning a delegate to the event.)

This page is rendered in a user's Web browser as a regular Web page when he or she views, or requests, it. However, when she clicks the Submit button, the page uses an HTTP-Post operation to send information back to the server, where it executes like a Windows Forms application. When it's finished, it sends the output back to the user in the form of HTML.

A Web service functions very similarly to this page: a user (Web site, application, or actual human being) requests the Web service from a browser or application, but instead of returning HTML, the service sends XML. Then when the user decides to execute a method (akin to pushing the Submit button) the information is submitted to the server via SOAP (or HTTP-Get or HTTP-Post) and the results are sent back again as XML.

Web Methods

Let's look at a very simple Web service, an adding calculator, shown in Listing 15.2.

LISTING 15.2   A Simple Web Service

```
1:  <%@ WebService Language="CS" Class="Calculator" %>
2:
3:  using System.Web.Services;
4:
5:  public class Calculator : WebService {
6:     [WebMethod] public int Add(int intA, int intB) {
7:         return intA + intB;
8:     }
9:  }
```

Save this file as Listing15.2.asmx (all Web service files end in .asmx) in the c:\inetput\wwwroot directory.

ANALYSIS This file resembles a cross between an ASP.NET page and a Windows Forms application. The first line of a Web service file declares that it is a Web service,

15

the language it uses, and the main class of the service. Line 3 imports the
`System.Web.Services` namespace—another requirement. The `Calculator` class is shown
on line 5. (It derives from the `WebService` class instead of the `Form` class like regular
Windows Forms applications.)

Next is the most important part of the Web service: the Web method. A Web method is
actually just like any other method, except that it can be executed across the Internet. A
method is made into a Web method by adding the `[WebMethod]` attribute to the declaration, as shown on line 6 (use the syntax `<WebMethod()>` in VB.NET). You can have as
many Web methods in a single Web service as you want, but they all must have the
`[WebMethod]` attribute and be declared `public`. Those methods you don't want to be
exposed over the Internet should be declared as normal.

Take special note of the class and its method: `Calculator` and `Add`. Later today when
you begin incorporating Web services into your applications, you'll see these again.
Luckily, there are tools available in the .NET Framework that can remind you of these
member names in case you forget—but we're getting ahead of ourselves.

The function of this Web service is very simple. When the `Add` method is called, it
accepts two parameters, adds them, and returns the result, just like any regular method.
Remember, though, that this is a *Web method*, and can be accessed from anywhere across
the Internet. If Microsoft developed this adding Web service, you could access the application from the Microsoft Web site if you ever needed the capability to add numbers
(okay, so this situation would never arise in real life, but you get the point of Internet-accessible methods).

This `.asmx` file can be viewed through a browser, just like an ASP.NET page. This is
because ASP.NET is actually the engine that processes Web services and `.asmx` files.
ASP.NET comes built in with all the functionality necessary to initiate and respond to
Web requests, so it makes complete sense to bundle Web services with ASP.NET.

Web service files do not contain any UI elements. The UI is left completely up to the
client to implement—you only need to build the "behind-the-scenes" functionality.

Although this is a very simple method, you can imagine the possibilities. For example,
suppose this class was actually the `Word.Application` or `Word.Document` classes you
used in Day 14, "Using ActiveX." You could access any available Web methods of Word
over the Internet using this Web service!

The Service Description

If you already accessed the `Listing15.2.asmx` file from your browser, you're ahead of
the game. View it using the address `http://localhost/listing15.2.asmx`, and you
should the page shown in Figure 15.4.

FIGURE 15.4

Our application pro-vides the Web service description.

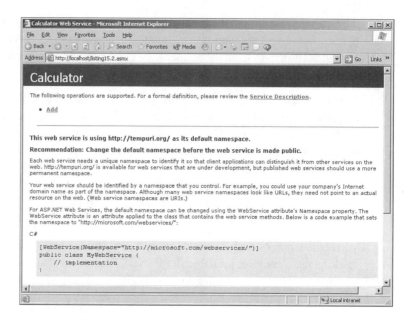

None of this text was in that .asmx file, but ASP.NET understands that it is a Web service and creates some additional output for you. The page shown in Figure 15.4 is a helpful description for those who want to use the Web service.

NEW TERM Click on the Service Description link near the top of the page, and you'll get the XML content that this Web service sends to prospective clients. It is used to tell clients exactly what this Web service is capable of, and what kind of data it expects and returns. This XML code is known as the *service description*, and is written in the Web Services Description Language (WSDL), which is really just a fancy way of format-ting XML.

If you are familiar with XML, you'll notice several interesting things as you glance through this code (if you aren't familiar with XML, don't worry about it—you'll under-stand it later today). Each of the Web service's methods (although there is only one cur-rently) is listed, as well as the input parameters it expects. There is also a section called AddResponse that details the response that the Web service will send when the Add method is executed. There are quite a few other sections in this XML that are all part of WSDL, but we needn't bother about them now. For more details, check out http://www.w3.org/TR/wsdl.

This WSDL service description comes into play later, when you use this Web service from a Windows Forms application.

Using Web Services with ASP.NET

Go back to the description page shown in Figure 15.4 and click the Add link near the top that will take you to a new page. Here, you can actually test the Web service out via `HTTP-Post`. Enter two values into the text boxes labeled intA and intB and click the Invoke button. You receive the following output:

```
<?xml version="1.0" encoding="utf-8" ?>
<int xmlns="http://tempuri.org/">8</int>
```

This is the XML content that would be sent back to the client of the Web service. This example is very simple, but the output can grow quite complex as XML can handle many different types of data, including ADO.NET `DataSets`!

So what if you don't know XML? That's not a problem, because you never have to deal with XML directly unless you want to. As you'll see in the next few sections, the .NET Framework can handle everything for you, so you only need to decide what Web service to use and then use it. All the communications are handled invisibly. It really does seem like you are using any other local class or object in your application, and that's one of the great benefits of Web services.

Before we move on, it's important to note that all of the transmissions so far (executing the Add method, viewing the WSDL description, receiving the XML output) have been executed over a standard protocol: HTTP. Even the SOAP methods (which you'll learn about in a few moments) travel over HTTP. Because HTTP is a standard that is available everywhere, it is ideal for all Web service transmissions.

Using Web Services in Your Applications

Using a Web service from a client Windows Forms application involves three steps: discovery, proxy, and implementation. Discovery is a process that is used to determine the capabilities of a Web service—you did some manual discovery by examining the WSDL description in the previous section. The second step is generating a proxy class to use the service, and the third step is actually implementing the service by sending commands to it from your application. Figure 15.5 illustrates these three interactions between a Web service and its client. The latter two steps we'll discuss in the next section, "Consuming Web Services." For now, let's take a closer look at discovery.

FIGURE 15.5

Interaction with a Web service involves discovery, examining the service description, and sending commands.

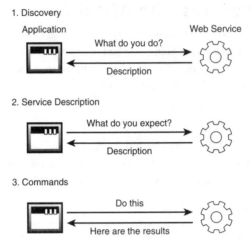

1. Discovery

2. Service Description

3. Commands

Discovery is the client's chance to get to know the Web service, so to speak. It is during this phase that you figure out what the Web service can do (in other words, the Web methods it has) and how to execute those methods. One method of discovery is accomplished by going to the service description, which you can find by tacking the string ?WSDL to the end of the URL of the service:

```
http://localhost/listing15.2.asmx?WSDL
```

While this is great to look at, it doesn't help your Windows Forms application much. What you need is an actual XML file that can be used by a prospective client application. This file can be generated using the Web Service Discovery Tool (disco.exe). To use this tool, you simply supply the URL of the Web service, and it does the rest. From the command line, enter the following command:

```
disco http://localhost/listing15.2.asmx
```

You should see the following output:

```
Microsoft (R) Web Services Discovery Utility
[Microsoft (R) .NET Framework, Version 1.0.3705.0]
Copyright (C) Microsoft Corporation 1998-2001. All rights
reserved.

Disco found documents at the following URLs:
http://localhost/listing15.2.asmx?wsdl
http://localhost/listing15.2.asmx?disco

The following files hold the content found at the
corresponding URLs:
   .\listing15.wsdl <- http://localhost/listing15.2.asmx?wsdl
   .\listing15.disco <- http://localhost/listing15.2.asmx?disco
The file .\results.discomap holds links to each of these files.
```

The Discovery tool created three files for you: `listing15.disco`, an XML document that provides links (URLs) to the Web service and its WSDL description; `listing15.wsdl`, a copy of the WSDL service description; and `results.discomap`, another XML file that simply provides links to the other two files. Now you have local copies of everything the service can do, and your applications can use these to properly use the Web service.

The discovery phase is an optional one, but most of the time you want to know what a Web service does before you use it. If you don't perform the discovery process, the next step, generating a proxy class, does it for you automatically.

NEW TERM Now that you have the service description, you're ready to begin *consuming* (a fancy term for using) the Web service. Let's look at the technical requirements.

To be able to send messages to the Web service, you must be able to access the service over the Internet, and send and receive HTTP messages. Additionally, you need to be able to read and write XML and SOAP messages. While you've seen that accessing the Internet isn't that difficult, you haven't yet learned how to write XML or SOAP, so we arrive at an impasse.

There is, however, a very easy solution. Rather than you building the functionality to access the Internet and writing XML data yourself, .NET comes with a tool that creates that functionality for you (I told you .NET was your friend). This tool, the WSDL utility (`wsdl.exe`) examines the service description (created in the last section) and generates a new class, known as the proxy class. The proxy class is often confusing to beginners, so let's examine its exact purpose.

Ideally, your application would access the Web service directly. Sending and receiving the XML messages and decoding them would be a non-issue, and integration would be very easy. Because, however, it isn't as easy as it sounds, the proxy class steps in for you. This class contains all the functionality needed to send HTTP messages, and translate SOAP and XML into properties that are easier to deal with. The proxy class also contains what, at first, seems like copies of the Web methods from the Web service. In fact, the names of the methods are identical, but if you look at the implementation of the methods, they are slightly different. This naming scheme is done to make working with the proxy class a painless process. Let's create a proxy class to make it more clear.

From the command prompt (in the same directory as the `.wsdl` file you generated earlier), use the WSDL utility to generate a proxy class using the following command:

```
wsdl /l:CS /n:TYWinforms.Day15 Listing15.wsdl
```

This command generates a proxy class in C# from the `.wsdl` file created in the discovery process. The class is created in the `TYWinforms.Day15` namespace. Table 15.1 lists the most common parameters used with the WSDL utility. For a more complete listing, type `wsdl /?` at the command line.

TABLE 15.1   Common WSDL Utility Parameters

Parameter	Description
/language	Specifies the language to generate the proxy class in. Can be abbreviated as /l.
/namespace	Specifies the namespace the proxy class should be generated in. Can be abbreviated as /n.
/nologo	Suppresses the Microsoft logo.
/out	The filename you want the proxy class to have.
/protocol	The protocol that the class should use to communicate with the Web service. Can be SOAP, HttpGet, or HttpPost.

You can pass either the `.wsdl` file or the actual online WSDL service description to the WSDL utility. The following command works exactly like the previous command:

```
wsdl /l:CS /n:TYWinforms.Day15
➡http://localhost/listing15.2.asmx?WSDL
```

When completed successfully, you'll see a new file, `Calculator.cs` (recall that the Web service class you created earlier was called `Calculator`), shown in Listing 15.3. (If it didn't complete successfully, verify that you've placed the `.asmx` file in the proper location and that your Web server is running.)

LISTING 15.3   The Proxy Calculator Class

```
 1:  //-----------------------------------------------------
 2:  // <autogenerated>
 3:  //      This code was generated by a tool.
 4:  //      Runtime Version: 1.0.3705.0
 5:  //
 6:  //      Changes to this file may cause incorrect behavior
 7:  //      and will be lost if the code is regenerated.
 8:  // </autogenerated>
 9:  //-----------------------------------------------------
10:
11:  //
12:  // This source code was auto-generated by wsdl,
13:  // Version=1.0.3705.0.
14:  namespace TYWinforms.Day15 {
15:      using System.Diagnostics;
16:      using System.Xml.Serialization;
17:      using System;
```

LISTING 15.3   continued

```
18:      using System.Web.Services.Protocols;
19:      using System.ComponentModel;
20:      using System.Web.Services;
21:
22:
23:        /// <remarks/>
24:        [System.Diagnostics.DebuggerStepThroughAttribute()]
25:        [System.ComponentModel.DesignerCategoryAttribute
➡("code")]
26:        [System.Web.Services.WebServiceBindingAttribute
➡ (Name="CalculatorSoap",
➡Namespace="http://tempuri.org/")]
27:        public class Calculator : System.Web.Services.
➡Protocols.SoapHttpClientProtocol {
28:
29:            /// <remarks/>
30:            public Calculator() {
31:                this.Url = "http://localhost/listing15.2.asmx";
32:            }
33:
34:            /// <remarks/>
35:            [System.Web.Services.Protocols.
➡SoapDocumentMethodAttribute("http://tempuri.org/Add",
➡RequestNamespace="http://tempuri.org/",
➡ResponseNamespace="http://tempuri.org/",
➡Use=System.Web.Services.Description.SoapBindingUse.
➡Literal, ParameterStyle=System.Web.Services.Protocols.
➡SoapParameterStyle.Wrapped)]
36:            public int Add(int intA, int intB) {
37:                object[] results = this.Invoke("Add",
➡new object[] {intA, intB});
38:                return ((int)(results[0]));
39:            }
40:
41:            /// <remarks/>
42:            public System.IAsyncResult BeginAdd(int intA,
➡int intB, System.AsyncCallback callback,
➡object asyncState) {
43:                return this.BeginInvoke("Add", new object[] {
44:                    intA, intB}, callback, asyncState);
45:            }
46:
47:            /// <remarks/>
48:            public int EndAdd(System.IAsyncResult
➡asyncResult) {
49:                object[] results = this.EndInvoke(asyncResult);
50:                return ((int)(results[0]));
51:            }
52:        }
53:    }
```

ANALYSIS   There's a lot of code in here that you haven't learned about, and we won't be going over that here. There are a few things you should examine about this class.

The constructor for this `Calculator` class is on lines 29–32. It derives from a `System.Web.Services.Protocols.SoapHttpClientProtocol` class. It is this parent class that contains the functionality to send and receive HTTP messages, and since `Calculator` inherits from it, it also inherits these functions. The URL of the Web service is also set as a property here. On lines 35–39 you see (after a long list of attributes) an `Add` method, which looks like the `Add` method you built in the Web service. The difference is that this `Add` doesn't perform the actual addition; rather, it calls the Web service's `Add` Web method over the Internet by using the `Invoke` method inherited from the `SoapHttpClientProtocol` class.

On lines 42 and 48 you see two methods, `BeginAdd` and `EndAdd`, that can be used to call the Web method asynchronously. We'll learn about asynchronous calls in Day 19, "Creating Multithreaded Applications," so we'll skip these methods for now.

Compile this class using the command:

```
csc /t:library /r:system.dll /r:system.web.dll Calculator.cs
```

You compile it as a library rather than a Windows executable because you can't use this proxy class by itself; it must be used from another application.

Now that you have a compiled class, you can use it just like any other object. Listing 15.4 shows a simple Windows Forms application that makes use of this class, and by proxy, the Web service.

LISTING 15.4   Consuming the Web Service

```
1:  using System;
2:  using System.Windows.Forms;
3:  using System.Drawing;
4:
5:  namespace TYWinforms.Day15 {
6:     public class Listing154 : Form {
7:        private Button btSubmit = new Button();
8:        private TextBox tbNumberA = new TextBox();
9:        private TextBox tbNumberB = new TextBox();
10:        private Label lblAdd = new Label();
11:
12:        public Listing154() {
13:           tbNumberA.Location = new Point(20,50);
14:           tbNumberB.Location = new Point(140,50);
15:
16:           lblAdd.Text = " + ";
```

15

LISTING 15.4   continued

```
17:             lblAdd.Location = new Point(120,50);
18:
19:             btSubmit.Text = "Add It!";
20:             btSubmit.Location = new Point(140,100);
21:             btSubmit.Click += new EventHandler
➥(this.CallService);
22:
23:             this.Text = "Listing 15.4";
24:             this.Controls.Add(tbNumberA);
25:             this.Controls.Add(tbNumberB);
26:             this.Controls.Add(lblAdd);
27:             this.Controls.Add(btSubmit);
28:         }
29:
30:         private void CallService(Object Sender,
➥EventArgs e) {
31:             Calculator objCalc = new Calculator();
32:             int intAnswer = objCalc.Add(
➥Convert.ToInt32(tbNumberA.Text),
➥Convert.ToInt32(tbNumberB.Text));
33:
34:             MessageBox.Show(intAnswer.ToString());
35:         }
36:
37:         public static void Main() {
38:             Application.Run(new Listing154());
39:         }
40:     }
41: }
```

ANALYSIS   Much of this listing is standard fare; the interface is set up in the constructor with a few TextBox controls, a Label, and a Button. The interesting part is in the CallService event handler beginning on line 30.

On line 31 you create a new instance of the Calculator proxy class. Then on line 32, you call the Add method, supplying the values from the two TextBoxes (don't forget to convert the string values to integers). On line 34, the output is shown in a MessageBox.

Compile this application with the following command:

```
csc /t:winexe /r:system.dll /r:system.windows.forms.dll
➥/r:system.drawing.dll /r:Calculator.dll
➥Listing15.4.cs
```

Figure 15.6 shows the output.

FIGURE 15.6

The result is actually returned from across the Internet.

So what happened here? Your application executed as normal. It created an instance of the proxy class, called one of its methods, and retrieved the results. To the class in Listing 15.4, this is no different than any other simple method call. All it knows is that the Calculator object returns a value—it doesn't care where the value comes from or how it comes to be.

The proxy class keeps its secrets; it encapsulates all the functionality that reaches over the Internet, sends a SOAP message, retrieves the response in XML, and translates it into a simple value that can be used by the application.

Now you see why we use a proxy class in the first place; it takes all the work out of using Web services. In fact, because the proxy class shares its name and its methods' names with the Web service, it's practically invisible. If you didn't know better, it would seem like you were interacting directly with the Web service, just as you would with any local object!

This may seem like a lot of work just to get this simple output, but all you really need to do is three steps: Use the wsdl.exe tool to generate the proxy, compile it, and build the Windows Forms application to access its Web methods. (And if someone does the first two steps for you, you only need to provide the implementation.) You don't need to know the output generated by the discovery and proxy generation steps—it's irrelevant unless you want to create your own proxies manually. Since the proxy hides all of the complex functionality, you can use just a few code lines in your Windows Forms application to do a lot of powerful work.

Using this simple paradigm, you can access a Web service from anywhere in the world. The service can receive commands and send results because they're transferred via XML and HTTP—two ubiquitous standards.

Finding Web Services

So now you know all about how to use a Web service in your applications. You've even built a simple one (and if you're adventurous, have built others using what you've learned here). It's rather pointless, however, to build and then consume your own Web services—you need to consume other people's services (after all, the point is to use functionality that you don't want to or can't build yourself).

To help you discover Web services, the Universal Description, Discovery, and Integration (UDDI) specification was developed—a set of rules that tell Web services and their clients how to look for each other. This specification allows companies or individuals to provide details on the services they offer, and even on the companies themselves.

UDDI is just a set of rules that is written in XML, which means UDDI information can be transmitted anywhere over the Internet. You can check out the actual specification at `http://www.uddi.org/schema/uddi_v2.xsd`.

The UDDI Web site (`www.uddi.org`), shown in Figure 15.7, provides a registry of services—a Web service search engine of sorts. You can register your business and its services so that other organizations can find you.

FIGURE 15.7

UDDI provides a searchable registry of Web services.

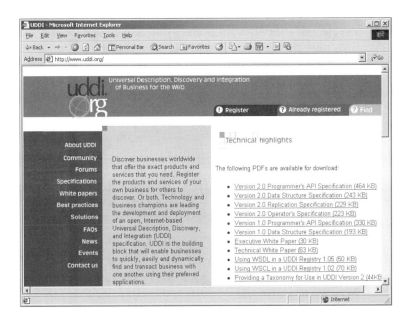

A search at the Web site results in a list of services that match your query. Each service provides a detailed listing of information, from who offers the service to how much it may cost (even Web service developers have to make a buck). There are a large number of Web services available, so chances are that you'll find one that meets your needs.

Because Web services can vary quite a bit from one implementation to another, browsing through the UDDI registry is a great way to familiarize yourself with what's out there. You'll see that some Web services disallow the discovery phase; some require special SOAP mechanisms to use; and others don't rely on SOAP at all. Try finding a few free ones and see if you can build a Windows Forms application to consume them.

Web Service Consumption Recommendations

How you consume a Web service depends on your situation. All of today's examples have used SOAP, which provides the richest methods for consuming services.

There's one drawback to using SOAP, however. As you may have noticed, encoding the commands and data in SOAP messages is rather complex. The messages sent back and forth are quite large because SOAP must send XML schema information.

Another method of consuming a Web Service is HTTP-Get. If you know the URL of the service and the method(s) and parameter(s) it expects, you can invoke the service's methods. For example, you can access the following URL to consume the Add method from the calculator service you created today by putting a forward slash and the method name after the URL, followed with the parameters in a query string:

```
http://localhost/Listing15.2.asmx/Add?intA=1&intB=2
```

When requested, this URL outputs the XML containing the output from the method. In this case, you see the following:

```
<?xml version="1.0"?>
<int xmlns="http://tempuri.org/">3</int>
```

You can also consume a service via an HTTP-Post operation. Simply set the action attribute of an HTML form to Add:

```
<form action="http://localhost/Listing15.2.asmx/Add">
```

This is the URL followed by a slash and the method name. When you submit the form, any parameters are posted to the service and the appropriate XML output is generated. Just remember that the form parameters must have the same names as the parameters expected by the service.

So which of these methods should you use? The choice is simple, really. If you don't require complex data, use the HTTP-Get or HTTP-Post methods. They send less data back and forth, resulting in better performance. When you require complex data to be sent back from the service, such as a `DataSet` or a class, use SOAP. The other two methods can't send this type of data.

Do	Don't
Do use SOAP when you think you'll need complex data or rich programmatic access to your service.	**Don't** use SOAP when bandwidth is a critical factor. Use `HTTP-Get` or `HTTP-Post` instead.

Summary

Web services are an interesting new technology, but once you grasp the basic concepts, they are very easy to implement. Web services provide you the key to delivering your applications over the Internet.

Web services are essentially applications that are available over the Internet. They evolved to fix the fundamental gaps left in intercomputing from older technologies like ActiveX and COM. Web services are based on HTTP and XML, so they rely on standard, universal protocols that everyone can use, regardless of their platform or operating system.

SOAP is the most common protocol used with Web services. It is a set of rules for formatting XML in a standard way that any Web service or Web service client can understand. Web services can also be used via `HTTP-Get` and `HTTP-Post`.

Web services are built using ASP.NET. The source code looks similar to ASP.NET pages and Windows Forms application, so they are easy to follow. They expose functionality by creating Web methods, which are like regular methods except that they can be accessed over the Internet.

To use a Web service, you perform three steps: discovery, proxy generation, and implementation. Discovery is an optional step where you can find out information on a Web service. Generating a proxy involves creating a class that encapsulates the functionality required to access a Web service over the Internet. Finally, implementation requires nothing more than using the proxy class in your application; something you're already quite familiar with.

The last protocol you learned about today was UDDI. This specification allows you to define and describe your Web service to perspective clients (in more user-friendly terms than a WSDL service description), and the UDDI Web site, `www.uddi.org`, provides a searchable UDDI database in which you can register your own services.

Tomorrow, we'll continue our look at advanced technologies and learn about Windows services, which are completely different from Web services.

Q&A

Q Are Web services secure?

A Because they rely on XML—plain text—they are not inherently secure. However, there are a few mechanisms you can use to secure them. ASP.NET has quite a few built in security capabilities, and you can use the same techniques you would use to secure a Web site to secure Web services. Additionally, SOAP has a subset of functionality known as SOAP headers, which can be used to secure Web services. For more information on Web service security, see the .NET Framework documentation, or check out *Sams Teach Yourself ASP.NET in 21 Days*.

Q What were all those attributes in Listing 15.3?

A Like a Web method needs the [WebMethod] attribute to work properly, the methods in a proxy class need some attributes as well. These attributes define additional information about a method that is helpful during execution, such as determining where required files are. For more information, see the documentation for C# and VB.NET bundled with the .NET Framework documentation.

Q I don't have a Web server. Is there any other way I can try creating Web services?

A You simply need a place that does have a Web server and supports the .NET Framework. www.Brinkster.com provides a free service that lets you upload and run Web sites based on ASP.NET and Web services. Build your Web services on your own machine and then upload them to Brinkster to test them out.

If you really want your own Web server, you can try out Microsoft's Personal Web server, which is a free download from www.Microsoft.com.

Workshop

This workshop helps reinforce the concepts we covered in today's lesson. It is very helpful to understand fully the answers before moving on. Answers can be found in Appendix A.

Quiz

1. What does SOAP stand for?

2. True or false? The disco.exe tool generates a copy of the WSDL service description locally.

3. What is a proxy class, and why use one?

4. Is anything wrong with the following code?

```
[WebMethod] private string HelloWorld() {
    return "Hello World!";
}
```

5. What file extensions are used for .NET Web service files?

6. Why do ASP.NET files look very similar to Windows Forms files?

Exercise

Create a Web service that converts values from one unit of measurement to another (from inches to centimeters, for example—and don't worry if you don't know the exact values; just make something up). Create a Windows Forms client that allows users to interact with the service.

DAY 16

Building Windows Services

Today you'll learn about a different aspect of .NET and Windows: Windows services. Windows services provide functionality that is integrated into your operating system, and works behind the scenes to ensure that everything else runs properly. Services have actually been around for quite awhile, so they are not new technology, but their application in .NET is.

With services you can maintain Web or FTP servers, keep tabs on security and application issues, or even run databases. These applications run without any user interaction.

Today, you will learn

- What Windows services are
- How you execute an application without an interface
- How to install applications
- How to control services with the SCM
- How to log information about your applications

What Are Windows Services?

Windows services are unlike any application you've developed so far. They are similar to Web services in that they can be accessed at any time, but the similarity stops there, so don't confuse Windows services with Web services.

When you build a normal Windows Forms application, the user receives an interface with which she can interact. The application must be started and stopped explicitly. With a Windows service, none of this is necessary. A Windows service runs as part of the operating system, essentially in the background, ready and waiting to be used at any time. And Windows services don't necessarily require any user input—they often do their own tasks while everything else is going on around them.

Why would you need a Windows service? If there's something that must be done on a continual basis or there's some event that might happen at any given time, a regular application isn't always the best solution, because the UI isn't always necessary and you don't want it clogging the user's desktop.

Windows comes with many preinstalled services that run in the background at every instant. In fact, a lot of the programs you are familiar with run as Windows services, including Internet Information Server (IIS), SQL Server, and even the print spooler that sends data to your printer. There are quite a few others as well that aren't as apparent. Go to Start, Control Panel, Administrative Tools, Services to view the list of Windows services running on your computer. Figure 16.1 shows a typical example on Windows XP.

FIGURE 16.1

A typical installation of Windows XP has more than 80 Windows services installed at any time.

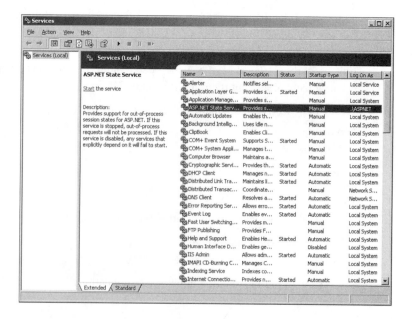

Most of these Windows services are running in the background while you do your work, to handle events that may arise. For instance, IIS sits there and waits until a Web request comes in from a client, and then does some processing to handle it. If there's not another request waiting when it finishes its processing, it goes idle again. All of these services ensure that your operating system keeps functioning the way it's supposed to, without bothering the user with unnecessary information or interfaces.

A Windows service can be configured to start as soon as your computer starts, when another application requests it, or at any other time you choose. It can be paused and restarted as well (Web developers are probably familiar with restarting the IIS service several hundred times).

16

When you create a Windows service, you can't just execute it and watch it run. You have to install it in the operating system and let it run as a Windows service. This makes it slightly more difficult to create one because you can't directly test it before execution.

So why are we studying Windows services when they aren't much like Windows Forms applications at all? For a few reasons. First, Windows services share the same framework as Windows Forms applications, so you'll see that building them is actually similar to building Windows Forms. This means you're learning a different aspect of the technology behind Windows Forms—.NET—and that's always a good thing. Second, Windows services are often useful to developers of traditional desktop applications. Many times, you'll find that you'll be called upon to develop an application that would be best done as a service, but often isn't. And finally, you'll learn about installers as part of Windows services, which are valuable tools for use with Windows Forms applications. Today's lesson shows you how you can easily apply your Windows Forms skills to another useful technology.

Building a Windows Service

Creating a Windows service is rather complex in terms of architecture, so let's step through it slowly. The first new class you need to know about is `System.ServiceProcess.ServiceBase`, which is the base class for all .NET Windows services. This class is like the `System.Windows.Forms.Application` class, of which the most common member is the `Run` method that's employed in every `Main` method you've used so far. It contains a generic set of properties that can define your Windows service, and a `Run` method that starts the service. The Windows services that you create will inherit from this class like Windows Forms classes inherit from `System.Windows.Forms.Form`:

```
public class MyFirstService : System.ServiceProcess.ServiceBase
```

We'll come back to the `ServiceBase` class in a moment.

Next, you need to know about the `System.ServiceProcess.ServiceProcessInstaller`, and `System.ServiceProcess.ServiceInstaller`, and `System.Configuration.` `Install.Installer` classes. These are the classes required to actually get your Windows service installed and running. Don't worry—their names make them sound worse than they really are, and there's really not much to them. `ServiceProcessInstaller` and `ServiceInstaller` are responsible for writing information about your service into the Windows registry, where all Windows services must be registered to work properly. `Installer` is the base class that is used to install any .NET application, and if you get further into developing installation procedures, you'll see this class quite often. For today, you'll only use it briefly to install your Windows service.

Finally, once your service is up and running, you'll be using the Service Control Manager (SCM) to control your Windows service. The SCM is a visual interface like any other application that can be used to manipulate Windows services. Although there is an analogous class in the .NET Framework (`System.ServiceProcess.` `ServiceController`), you'll use the SCM because it's easier.

Figure 16.2 shows a diagram of our architecture so far.

FIGURE 16.2

You create your Windows service from several different classes, and use the SCM to control it.

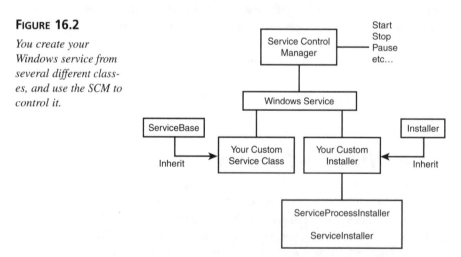

Now that you know how everything fits together, let's look a bit more at the `ServiceBase` class. This class has a number of events that you'll use to control your service, including `Start`, `Stop`, and `Pause`. (The next section shows you how to write your service so that these events provide you all the functionality you need.) Table 16.1 lists all of the properties of `ServiceBase`, and Table 16.2 lists the methods.

TABLE 16.1 ServiceBase Properties

Property	Description
AutoLog	Indicates if start, stop, and continue events should be reported in the built-in event log.
CanHandlePowerEvent	Indicates if the service can handle notifications of computer power status changes—in other words, whether the PowerEvent event is handled.
CanPauseAndContinue	Indicates whether the service can be paused and continued.
CanShutdown	Indicates whether the service should be notified when the system shuts down.
CanStop	Indicates whether the service can be stopped.
EventLog	An event log that you can write information to.
ServiceName	The name of the service in question.

TABLE 16.2 ServiceBase Methods

Method	Description
OnContinue	Executed when the service is started from a paused state from the SCM.
OnCustomCommand	Executes when the SCM issues a custom event to the service. (See the .NET Framework documentation for more information.)
OnPause	Executes when the service is paused.
OnPowerEvent	Executes when the power status changes.
OnShutdown	Executes when the computer shuts down.
OnStart	Executes when the service is started from a stopped state.
OnStop	Executes when the service is stopped.
Run	Provides the main starting point for the service.

Note

There are no publicly accessible non-inherited events for the ServiceBase class. Instead, you must override the corresponding OnEventName methods to perform your actions. I discuss this more in the next section.

Once you have your service and installer created and ready to go, you install them into the SCM. The SCM finds the executable file for your service, and executes it appropriately. The SCM should be the only one that accesses your service executable file directly.

Let's build a service to see how everything fits together.

Today we'll create a simple Windows service called `Day16Service` that monitors the computer it is running on. We'll use the `FileSystemWatcher` class you learned about from Day 11, "Working with Windows Input/Output," to determine when changes are made to the file system. When such an occurrence happens, we'll write a note in a special log known as the event log.

Caution

Remember that Windows services do not have user interfaces. They cannot interact directly with the user. Attempting to do so using traditional methods may result in problems. For example, if you use the `MessageBox.Show` method in your Windows service, the service will attempt to display a message box, but the user will never to see it. Your service will then sit forever waiting for the user to respond to the message box, which he cannot.

Listing 16.1 shows our simple `Day16Service` Windows service. Let's dive right in!

LISTING 16.1   A File System Watcher Service

```
1:  Imports System.ServiceProcess
2:  Imports System.IO
3:
4:  namespace TYWinforms.Day16
5:
6:      Public Class Day16Service : Inherits ServiceBase
7:          private objWatcher As New FileSystemWatcher
8:
9:          Public Sub New()
10:             objWatcher.Path = "c:\"
11:             objWatcher.IncludeSubdirectories = True
12:             objWatcher.NotifyFilter = (NotifyFilters.FileName
➡Or NotifyFilters.DirectoryName Or
➡NotifyFilters.LastWrite)
13:             objWatcher.EnableRaisingEvents = True
14:
15:             AddHandler objWatcher.Changed, new
➡FileSystemEventHandler(AddressOf Me.FileChanged)
16:             AddHandler objWatcher.Deleted, new
➡FileSystemEventHandler(AddressOf Me.FileDeleted)
17:             AddHandler objWatcher.Created, new
➡FileSystemEventHandler(AddressOf Me.FileCreated)
18:             AddHandler objWatcher.Renamed, new
➡RenamedEventHandler(AddressOf Me.FileRenamed)
19:
20:             Me.ServiceName = "TYWinforms Day 16 Service"
```

LISTING 16.1   continued

```
21:          End Sub
22:
23:          Shared Sub Main()
24:              ServiceBase.Run(New Day16Service())
25:          End Sub
26:
27:          Protected Overrides Sub OnStart(ByVal args()
➥As String)
28:              EventLog.WriteEntry("TYWinforms Day 16 Service
➥is starting")
29:          End Sub
30:
31:          Protected Sub FileChanged(Sender As Object, e As
➥FileSystemEventArgs)
32:              EventLog.WriteEntry(e.Name & " " &
➥e.ChangeType.ToString())
33:          End Sub
34:
35:          Public Sub FileCreated(Sender As Object, e As
➥FileSystemEventArgs)
36:              EventLog.WriteEntry(e.Name & " created at: " &
➥e.FullPath)
37:          End Sub
38:
39:          Public Sub FileDeleted(Sender As Object, e As
➥FileSystemEventArgs)
40:              EventLog.WriteEntry(e.Name & " deleted from: " &
➥e.FullPath)
41:          End Sub
42:
43:          Public Sub FileRenamed(Sender As Object, e As
➥RenamedEventArgs)
44:              EventLog.WriteEntry(e.OldName & " renamed to: " &
➥e.Name)
45:          End Sub
46:      End Class
47:  end namespace
```

ANALYSIS If you remember the FileSystemWatcher, this code should be very simple for you. The System.ServiceProcess namespace is imported on line 1 to make sure you have the proper classes available. Notice that your Windows service class, Day16Service, inherits from the ServiceBase class on line 6.

The constructor for Day16Service on lines 9–21 simply sets some properties of the FileSystemWatcher object, including the directory path to watch (c:\ in this case), the types of changes to watch for, and whether to include subdirectories. Lines 15–18 assign delegates to the various events of the FileSystemWatcher object, and the event handlers are on lines 31–45, but we'll get to those in a moment. On line 20, you set the name of the service that will be shown in the SCM as the user-friendly name.

On line 23 you have a typical Main method. However, instead of calling the System.Windows.Forms.Application.Run method to start the application, you call the Run method of the ServiceBase class. They both do essentially the same thing—load the application into memory. A Windows service, however, does not actually start until the SCM tells it to—otherwise the service just sits in memory waiting.

Since there are no public accessible events for the ServiceBase class, you must inherit the OnEventName methods to handle the events. On line 27 you override the OnStart event to handle the Start event. Initialization code for the service should still be placed in the constructor like in other applications and not here in the OnStart method. This method is mainly used to alert the system that the service has started, and not much else.

We call the WriteEntry method of the EventLog object to write the specified text into the system event log where it can be read later to provide information on how the service is running. We'll look at the event log later today.

Each of the next four methods does nearly the same thing as OnStart. The FileChanged, FileCreated, FileDeleted, and FileRenamed methods handle the FileSystemWatcher's event, and write appropriate entries into the event log.

Don't compile this application yet! You still need to create an installer. Listing 16.2 shows a very simple one to use for our simple service.

LISTING 16.2   Your Service Installer

```
1:  Imports System.ServiceProcess
2:  Imports System.ComponentModel
3:  Imports System.Configuration.Install
4:
5:  namespace TYWinforms.Day16
6:      <RunInstaller(True)> Public Class MyInstaller :
➥Inherits Installer
7:          Private objPInstaller As New ServiceProcessInstaller
8:          Private objInstaller As New ServiceInstaller
9:
10:         Public Sub New()
11:             objPInstaller.Account = ServiceAccount.LocalSystem
12:             objPInstaller.Password = Nothing
13:             objPInstaller.Username = Nothing
14:
15:             objInstaller.ServiceName =
➥"TYWinforms Day 16 Service"
```

Listing 16.2   continued

```
16:
17:               Installers.AddRange(New Installer()
➥{objPInstaller, objInstaller})
18:         End Sub
19:     End Class
20: End Namespace
```

Analysis   Once you know the classes involved, this listing is even easier than the last. We
need three namespaces for this class as shown on lines 1–3.

We create the installer class on line 6. First, notice that it inherits from the
`System.Configuration.Install.Installer` class—this is necessary for your class to be
considered an installer by the CLR. Second, it has an attribute in front of the class name.
Set to `true`, the `<RunInstaller>` attribute (`[RunInstaller]` in C#) simply tells the CLR
that this installer class should be used during the installation procedure.

Lines 7 and 8 create `ServiceProcessInstaller` and `ServiceInstaller` classes. Recall
that these classes are responsible for writing information about your Windows service
into the Windows registry so it can be properly used. To the developer, they each provide
different properties that will be used for the service.

Lines 11, 12, and 13 specify the account under which your Windows service will run.
This is very important. A typical Windows installation can have multiple users, and each
may have different permissions. For example, the files in one user's My Documents folder may not be viewable by another user. These types of permission are also used to
restrict the amount of control a user has over the operating system, so that an untrusted
or unknown user can't destroy the system.

For our Windows service, we'll allow it to run under the system account. This account
doesn't have many restrictions at all because it is the account your computer itself uses.
There are quite a few different types of accounts your service can use.

You specify the account your service should run under with the `Account`, `Username`, and
`Password` properties of the `ServiceProcessInstaller` class. The `Account` property uses
a value from the `ServiceAccount` enumeration:

- `LocalService`—An account that has extensive privileges and represents the computer itself.

- `LocalSystem`—Contains lesser permissions than `LocalService`, and represents an
  anonymous user.

- `NetworkService`—Even lesser permissions than `LocalSystem`, but represents the
  computer itself on a network.

- User—A specific user account. Values must be supplied for the
  ServiceProcessInstaller.Username and Password properties when User is used.

Typically you'll use the LocalSystem account for a service because you want it to run as
a system process. However, there are times when you might want to change the account.
For instance, if you want a service to run only when a user with appropriate permissions
logs on, then you can use the ServiceAccount.User value.

 Note   LocalService and NetworkService are only available on computers running
          Windows XP.

Because we are running under the LocalSystem account, we set the Username and
Password properties to Nothing (null in C#).

On line 15, you set the name the service installer will use. This must be the same name
as you set inside your service class (line 20 of Listing 16.1).

Finally, you tell the installer which installer is supposed to be executed. This may sound
funny at first, but a single installer file can actually have multiple installer classes. The
Installers.AddRange method can take an array of installer classes for this very purpose. On line 17, you specify which, specifically, of those installer classes should be run.
Simply create a new array of Installer objects containing the
ServiceProcessInstaller and ServiceInstaller objects that you've already initialized.

Now you're ready to go. Compile this application, making sure to include all the proper
assemblies:

```
vbc /t:winexe /r:system.dll /r:system.serviceprocess.dll
➥/r:system.configuration.install.dll
➥listing16.1.vb listing16.2.vb
```

Now you have an executable service, but you can't directly execute it. If you try, you'll
get the error message shown in Figure 16.3, along with an option to debug the service.

In the next section, we'll examine what you need to do to get your service installed and
running in Windows.

FIGURE 16.3

Your Windows service cannot be executed directly.

Getting Services to Play with Windows

If your Windows service compiled without any problems, then you theoretically have a working service. However, there's no way to test it unless you install it first. The .NET Framework provides a command line utility—the Installer Tool (`installutil.exe`)—to do this for you.

Navigate to the `c:\winforms\day16` directory (or wherever your newly compiled service application resides) and type the following command:

```
installutil listing16.1.exe
```

If all goes well, you'll see the following output:

```
Microsoft (R) .NET Framework Installation utility Version
1.0.3705.0
Copyright (C) Microsoft Corporation 1998-2001. All rights
reserved.

Running a transacted installation.

Beginning the Install phase of the installation.
See the contents of the log file for the c:\winforms\day16\
listing16.1.exe assembly's progress.
The file is located at c:\winforms\day16\listing16.1.InstallLog
Installing assembly 'c:\winforms\day16\listing16.1.exe'.
Affected parameters are:
    assemblypath = c:\winforms\day16\listing16.1.exe
    logfile = c:\winforms\day16\listing16.1.InstallLog
Installing service TYWinforms Day 16 Service...
Service TYWinforms Day 16 Service has been successfully
installed.
Creating EventLog source TYWinforms Day 16 Service in log
Application...

The Install phase completed successfully, and the Commit
phase is beginning.
See the contents of the log file for the c:\winforms\day16\
listing16.1.exe assembly's progress.
The file is located at c:\winforms\day16\listing16.1.InstallLog
Committing assembly 'c:\winforms\day16\listing16.1.exe'.
Affected parameters are:
    assemblypath = c:\winforms\day16\listing16.1.exe
    logfile = c:\winforms\day16\listing16.1.InstallLog
```

16

```
The Commit phase completed successfully.

The transacted install has completed.

C:\winforms\day16>
```

The Installer utility is very useful—it does things smartly and generates all sorts of outputs. Notice that the output describes a transacted installation. This means that should any part of the installation fail, the computer can return to the state before the installation began—and that means you won't be left with any half-installed programs that may ruin your system. This feature becomes more important as your applications become more complex, such as when you have more than one Windows service to install from a single file.

If your installation fails, you'll see the following output:

```
Microsoft (R) .NET Framework Installation utility Version
1.0.3705.0
Copyright (C) Microsoft Corporation 1998-2001. All rights
reserved.

Running a transacted installation.

Beginning the Install phase of the installation.
See the contents of the log file for the c:\winforms\day16\
listing16.1.exe assembly's progress.
The file is located at c:\winforms\day16\listing16.1.InstallLog
Installing assembly 'c:\winforms\day16\listing16.1.exe'.
Affected parameters are:
   assemblypath = c:\winforms\day16\listing16.1.exe
   logfile = c:\winforms\day16\listing16.1.InstallLog
Installing service TYWinforms Day 16 Service...
Creating EventLog source TYWinforms Day 16 Service in log
Application...

An exception occurred during the Install phase.
System.ComponentModel.Win32Exception: The specified service
already exists

The Rollback phase of the installation is beginning.
See the contents of the log file for the c:\winforms\day16\
listing16.1.exe assembly's progress.
The file is located at c:\winforms\day16\listing16.1.InstallLog
Rolling back assembly 'c:\winforms\day16\listing16.1.exe'.
Affected parameters are:
   assemblypath = c:\winforms\day16\listing16.1.exe
   logfile = c:\winforms\day16\listing16.1.InstallLog
Restoring event log to previous state for source TYWinforms
Day 16 Service.
```

```
The Rollback phase completed successfully.

The transacted install has completed.
The installation failed, and the rollback has been performed.
```

The error is described midway through the output, and the installation procedure rolls back to the state before installation began, ensuring that your computer continues to function properly.

Notice the Installer also generated a few output files: `installutil.InstallLog`, `listing16.1.InstallLog`, and `listing16.1.InstallState`. The first two files provide much of the same information as the `intallutil.exe` tool generated in its output. You can use these files to more easily diagnose any errors that occur. The last file is a SOAP message that can be used by a Web service to determine if the Windows service is properly installed. We won't cover it here, but you can glance through it and examine the XML used.

You should also know how to uninstall the service. This can also be done using the Installer utility:

```
installutil /u listing16.1.exe
```

The `/u` option instructs the utility to remove the Windows service from the SCM and delete the associated registry keys, keeping your machine free of rogue settings. If you need to modify your service's code at all, you should uninstall it before you recompile it, and then reinstall it so that you don't accidentally put your service or system into an unstable mode by introducing new settings.

Starting and Stopping Your Windows Service

Now you're ready to start your Windows service and ensure that it runs properly. Open up the Service Control Panel (Start, Control Panel, Administrative Tools, Services). Scroll down until you see your new service, which should be called TYWinforms Day 16 Service. Right-click the service and select Start. Figure 16.4 shows this process.

> **Tip**
>
> You can also start the service from the command line using the following command from the `c:\winforms\day16` directory:
>
> ```
> net start "TYWinforms Day 16 Service"
> ```

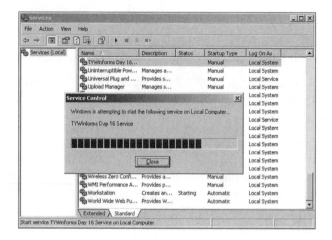

FIGURE 16.4

The SCM starts your Windows service.

The dialog that pops up gives you a progress meter indicating how the starting process is going. The Windows service has 30 seconds to properly start and get running, before the SCM thinks it is malfunctioning and terminates the process. If you do get an error message, you need to uninstall the service using the /u option of the Installer Utility, reexamine your source code and fix any errors you find. Then recompile and reinstall to try again.

If all goes well, your service should start up fairly quickly because it's not very complex. You can now right-click the service and select Stop to stop the Windows service from running. Had we set CanPauseAndContinue to true, you'd also be able to pause and continue the service as well. Like the pause and continue functions on a VCR, these two functions are used because they are faster than completely stopping and restarting the service.

Tip

> You can also stop the service from the command line using the following command from the c:\winforms\day16 directory:
>
> ```
> net stop "TYWinforms Day 16 Service"
> ```

Monitoring Your Services

Your Windows service is supposed to monitor the file system, but how do you know it's working? That's where the Event Log comes in. You can view the Event Log with the Event Viewer by going to Start, Control Panel, Administrative Tools, Event Viewer. Figure 16.5 shows the Event Viewer with a typical log.

FIGURE 16.5

The Event Log monitors your system and application events.

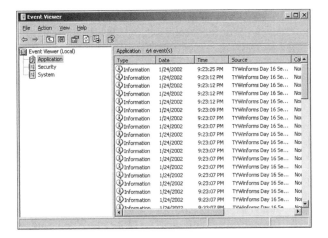

The Event Log is a central repository for information on the goings-on in your computer. Errors and warnings that your computer raises are frequently placed here (often you won't even know anything went wrong, so this is a good place to check). In the Event Viewer's left pane, you'll see three tabs by default: Application, Security, and System. Click on Application, and take a look at the resulting list in the right pane.

Most of the items in this list are generated from the File Watching service. Double-click on any item to see the details, as shown in Figure 16.6.

FIGURE 16.6

The description generated by your Windows service.

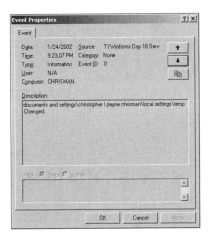

These details are the output that the Windows service created. In Figure 16.6 you can see that the `c:\documents and settings\christopher 1 payne.chrisman\` `local settings\temp` directory has changed. (Recall that you created this Windows service to monitor changes, renames, creations, and deletions for files and directories.) You'll also see some additional information, such as the time the message was generated, what Windows service generated it, the user it was running under, and so on.

Close the property window and go back to the Event Viewer. You can watch a number of files and directories changing—some that you wouldn't even know about unless you were watching them specifically. In fact, your event log will quickly fill up with messages from your file watcher service. For example, my computer had more than 60 messages in less than a minute, just by starting the service and editing a Word document.

Caution	Be careful that you don't let this Windows service run loose. It can be interesting to watch, but it will quickly fill up your Event Log, and the log only has a fixed amount of space. Once your log fills up, then your Windows service will begin to generate errors and begin performing unexpectedly. You can clear out your log by right-clicking on the appropriate left-hand tab and selecting Clear All Events.

Click on the System tab in the left pane of the Event Viewer. The right pane will show the messages and errors generated by your computer as it pertains to events other than those generated by applications. For example, you'll probably see a few messages here indicating that your Windows service was sent a start message (by the SCM), and was successfully started.

For all of your Windows Forms applications, and especially for Windows services, the Event Log can be a great benefit. Many times when you are stuck with an error you can't figure out, the Event Log will provide more detailed information that can help you solve the problem. For Windows services, which cannot have user interfaces, the Event Log is often the *only* place where you'll receive feedback. Don't be hesitant to take advantage of this useful tool, when debugging your applications, and just to see how your computer is functioning!

Interfaces for Windows Services

I said earlier that Windows services cannot have interfaces. While that is true, it doesn't mean you can't build an interface to interact with your service. To do this, you'll make use of the `ServiceController` class.

`ServiceController` does just what its name implies: it controls services. Using this class, you can start, stop, pause, and continue your Windows services, as well as determine their current status. In this way, you can build your own custom SCM.

`ServiceController` has two properties we're particularly interested in: `ServiceName` and `MachineName`. `ServiceName` is obviously the Windows service you want to control, and `MachineName` is the name of the computer the specified service is running on—this means you can control services running on different computers as long as they're on the same network as you are.

There are also methods to control your service, such as `Start`, `Stop`, and so on. Let's build a simple Windows Forms application to try this class out. Listing 16.3 shows the code.

16

LISTING 16.3 Your Custom SCM

```
1:   Imports System
2:   Imports System.Windows.Forms
3:   Imports System.Drawing
4:   Imports System.ServiceProcess
5:
6:   namespace TYWinforms.Day16
7:      public class Listing163 : Inherits Form
8:         private objController As New ServiceController
➥("TYWinforms Day 16 Service")
9:
10:          private btStart As New Button()
11:          private btStop As New Button()
12:          private tmrService As New Timer()
13:
14:          public sub New()
15:             objController.MachineName = "."
16:
17:             btStart.Location = new Point(20,75)
18:             btStart.Text = "Start"
19:             AddHandler btStart.Click, new EventHandler
➥ (AddressOf Me.StartService)
20:
21:             if objController.Status =
➥ServiceControllerStatus.Running then
22:                btStart.Enabled = false
23:             end if
24:
25:             btStop.Location = new Point(200,75)
26:             btStop.Text = "Stop"
27:             AddHandler btStop.Click, new EventHandler
➥ (AddressOf Me.StopService)
28:
29:             if objController.Status =
➥ServiceControllerStatus.Stopped then
30:                btStop.Enabled = false
31:             end if
```

LISTING 16.3 continued

```
32:
33:              tmrService.Interval = 1000
34:              tmrService.Enabled = true
35:              AddHandler tmrService.Tick, new EventHandler
➥ (AddressOf Me.CheckStatus)
36:
37:              Me.Text = objController.ServiceName & " " &
➥objController.Status.ToString()
38:
39:              Me.Controls.Add(btStart)
40:              Me.Controls.Add(btStop)
41:          end sub
42:
43:          private sub StartService(Sender As Object, e As
➥EventArgs)
44:              objController.Start()
45:              btStart.Enabled = false
46:              btStop.Enabled = true
47:
48:              ResetController()
49:
50:              Me.Text = objController.ServiceName & " " &
➥objController.Status.ToString()
51:          end sub
52:
53:          private sub StopService(Sender As Object, e As
➥EventArgs)
54:              objController.Stop()
55:              btStart.Enabled = true
56:              btStop.Enabled = false
57:
58:              ResetController()
59:
60:              Me.Text = objController.ServiceName & " " &
➥objController.Status.ToString()
61:          end sub
62:
63:          private sub CheckStatus(Sender As Object, e As
➥EventArgs)
64:              ResetController()
65:
66:              Me.Text = objController.ServiceName & " " &
➥objController.Status.ToString()
67:          end sub
68:
69:          private sub ResetController()
70:              objController = nothing
71:              objController = New ServiceController
➥ ("TYWinforms Day 16 Service")
```

LISTING **16.3**   continued

```
72:          end sub
73:
74:          public shared sub Main()
75:              Application.Run(new Listing163())
76:          end sub
77:       end class
78:  end namespace
```

ANALYSIS There's a lot of code here, but it's really very simple. Let's start on line 8. You create a new `ServiceController` class, passing in the name of the Windows service you want to control (the "TYWinforms Day 16 Service" from earlier today). Simple enough. Moving to the constructor, you set the `ServiceController.MachineName` property to `"."` on line 15, which means the local computer. This is the default value, but it's helpful to specify it anyway.

The next few lines initialize some buttons so that you can control your Windows service. Then on line 33 you initialize a `Timer` control (see Day 6, "Enhancing Your Windows Forms with More Controls," for more info on the `Timer`). The timer will keep an updated status of the service in question. Every second we'll check the status and keep the user informed—that's handled in the `CheckStatus` event handler on line 63, but we'll get there in a moment.

The status of a Windows service is represented by one of the values from the `ServiceControllerStatus` enumeration, as shown on lines 21 and 29. We check the status on these two lines to determine which, if any, of the start and stop buttons should be enabled. The `ServiceControllerStatus` values are

- `ContinuePending`
- `Paused`
- `PausePending`
- `Running`
- `StartPending`
- `Stopped`
- `StopPending`

Finally, on line 37, you set the caption of the form to the current status of the service. An interesting thing happens here, though. When you access the `ServiceController.Status` property, it returns only a snapshot of the service's status at the moment you *first* access `Status`. In other words, if your first call to `Status` returns

ServiceControllerStatus.Stopped, then all subsequent calls to Status will return the same, no matter what happens to the Windows service in between those calls. To get around this issue, you have to reinstantiate the ServiceController class each time you want to view the Status. (Note that this problem affects only Status; it doesn't affect any other property or method of ServiceController.) We do this in the ResetController method on line 69, which will be called whenever it is needed.

Let's look at the StartService and StopService methods on lines 43 and 53. These are nearly identical. They call the Start and Stop methods respectively, enable or disable the appropriate buttons, reinitialize the ServiceController, and then update the caption of the form. Remember that since we retrieved the Status property already in the constructor, the ServiceController must be reinitialized before you can view Status again.

Finally, the CheckStatus method on line 63 resets the ServiceController and simply updates the caption once again.

Compile this class (don't forget to reference the System.ServiceProcess.dll assembly) and execute it. Open the system SCM to verify that your application is indeed affecting the service. Notice the caption of the form changes as you click each button. Figure 16.7 shows a typical output.

FIGURE 16.7

Your custom SCM can control any Windows service.

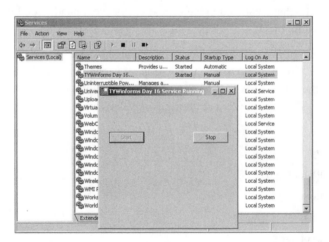

With some simple modifications, you can use this custom SCM to manage any Windows service you want. In fact, you can manage them all from this one application. The ServiceController.GetServices method retrieves an array of ServiceController objects that represents all of the Windows services currently installed on the system, running or otherwise. Quite nifty.

One thing that your custom SCM can do that the system SCM cannot is issue custom commands to your service beyond the regular start, stop, continue, and pause commands. Recall that the `ServiceBase` class has a method `OnCustomCommand` that you may override. The `ServiceController` class has a corresponding `ExecuteCommand` method for this purpose. Unfortunately, it's a bit limited in scope—this method can only take an integer for a parameter. In your service then, you retrieve this integer and use a `select case` statement to execute the proper functionality. For example, in your custom SCM do this:

```
objController.ExecuteCommand(128)
objController.ExecuteCommand(145)
```

In your corresponding service, create a method similar to the following:

```
Protected Overrides Sub OnCustomCommand(intCommand as integer)
    Select Case intCommand
        case 128
            'execute some command
        case 129
            'execute another command
        ...
        ...
        case 145
            'execute the 45th command
    End Select
End Sub
```

You can do nearly anything you want with this method within the range of a Windows service's abilities.

Caution The values for custom command parameters must be between the integers 128 and 256. Integers outside these values are reserved by the operating system, and attempts to use them will result in your service crashing.

Writing to Logs

The last thing we'll discuss today is using the `EventLog` class to write to custom event logs rather than to the Application, System, and Security ones we saw earlier.

Writing to a custom log is simple; you only have to modify a few lines of your service. First, you need to create a new `EventLog` object:

```
private objLog as New System.Diagnostics.EventLog()
```

Like the `ServiceController` class, you need to specify a `MachineName` for this class (although the default value is the local machine). You also need to specify a source, typically the application or Windows service that will write to the custom log. This source name is what appears in the event log as the generator of your events.

The source is also important in another way. All event logs must have an associated source; they cannot be written to without one. Therefore, every source has a single associated event log. An event log, however, can have multiple sources associated with it. By default, your service is associated with the built-in Application log. Since you want to write to a new log, you need to set the AutoLog property of the service to false to disassociate it from the Application log:

```
Me.AutoLog = false
```

What happens if this value is left as true? Your application continues writing to the Application log and your new log remains empty.

Before you set the source, you'll need to check if the source you want already exists—if it does, you'll receive an error. The EventLog class has a SourceExists property to determine this, and a CreateEventSource method to create a source if it doesn't exist:

```
If Not EventLog.SourceExists("MySource") Then
    EventLog.CreateEventSource("MySource", "MyNewLog")
End If
```

The first parameter of the CreateEventSource method is the source, which can be anything you like, and the second is the log to write to. This could be "Application", "Security", "System", or, as we have done here, a custom log with whatever name you like. Alternatively, you could specify a custom log file using the Log property:

```
objLog.Log = "MyNewLog"
```

Then you simply set the source of your event log:

```
objLog.Source = "MySource"
```

or:

```
objLog.Source = "TYWinforms Day 16 Service"
```

Now, everywhere else in your code that uses the EventLog.WriteEntry method must be changed to use the new EventLog object: objLog.WriteEntry. Everything else works the same. When your Windows service runs, it creates a new log;an actual file named MyNewLog.evt in the c:\winnt\system32\config directory. In the Event Viewer, you can add this new log file (choose Open Log File from the Action menu) so that you can view the contents, just like the default logs. Figure 16.8 shows the Event Viewer with the new log file.

FIGURE 16.8

You can create as many custom logs as you want, but don't go overboard!

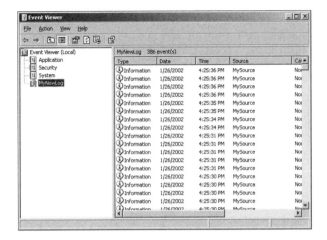

Summary

Today you learned about Windows services, another aspect of the .NET Framework. You also learned how to use your Windows Forms skills to tackle new problems. Windows services are an integral part of the Windows operating system, and now you can control them, log their actions, and build your own.

A Windows service is an application that runs in the background on your computer. It doesn't have user interfaces, and thus can't interact directly with the user, so its programming paradigm is a bit different than regular Windows Forms.

Services inherit from the `System.ServiceProcess.ServiceBase` class, which has all the necessary events and methods. To provide functionality for your service, you override the `OnStart`, `OnStop`, `OnPause`, and `OnContinue` methods. The `OnCustomCommand` method can also be overridden to perform custom functionality.

To install a service, you also need to work with the `ServiceInstaller` and `ServiceProcessInstaller` classes. These classes record information about your service into the registry, and allow the SCM to control it.

You can use the `ServiceController` class to control your service or any other service on the computer. This class can be used to start, stop, pause, and continue services, as well as perform custom actions and determine the status of a service. Use this class to build a custom SCM.

To write to a custom log, you need to create a new `EventLog` object and set its source accordingly. The `CreateEventSource` method establishes an application or Windows service as a viable source for writing information to a log. This method can also be used to create a new event log file for your source. The Event Viewer can be used to watch the events as they are added to your new log.

Tomorrow, we're going to go back to Windows Forms controls, and examine an aspect that we have so far left untouched. You'll see how some controls are more powerful than you previously thought.

Q&A

Q Can I write custom logs using the `File` and `Stream` objects?

A Absolutely, but often the custom event logs described earlier today are easier to use and will suffice. If, however, these logs don't provide you with enough functionality, you can use other methods to generate files as well.

Q How can I debug a service?

A To use a programmatic debugger, you need to attach it to your service during initialization. However, services often start up too quickly for you to do so. The trick is to introduce a delay in your service code that causes your service to be "put on hold" for a moment while you do what you need to do. For example, the following code placed anywhere in your code causes your service to wait 25 seconds before it executes the code after it:

```
System.Threading.Thread.Sleep(25000)
```

Be careful, however, that you don't make it wait for longer than 30 seconds, because the SCM will think the service is malfunctioning and interrupt it. Day 21, "Debugging Your Windows Forms," provides information on debuggers and attaching them.

Workshop

This workshop helps reinforce the concepts we covered in today's lesson. It is very helpful to understand fully the answers before moving on. Answers can be found in Appendix A.

Quiz

1. What namespace and assembly does the `ServiceBase` class belong to?

2. What namespaces and assemblies do the `ServiceProcessInstaller`, `ServiceInstaller`, and `Installer` classes belong to?

3. What attribute is necessary for an installer?

4. What are the four security accounts a service can run under?

5. Where are event log files stored?

6. What tool is used to install a service? To uninstall?

7. What command do you use to start a service from the command line?

8. Given the variable `objController` that is initialized to a valid `ServiceController`, is the following code valid?

```
dim strHello as String = "RunHelloMethod"
objController.ExecuteCommand(strHello)
```

9. What string do you use to specify the local machine?

Exercise

Create a file/folder back-up service. This service should back up the contents of the My Documents folder to another, separate directory at a certain time every day (for example, at 8 p.m.). For this example, the backup directory does not matter, and you don't need to worry about compressing files—just copy them. Write information to the Application event log when a backup is performed.

DAY 17

Advanced Windows Forms Controls Techniques

Today we go beyond the basics of Windows Forms controls and examine how you can customize them further. To do that, you need to understand who *owns* a control. The owner (by default, the developer) is responsible for drawing the control and creating its visual displays. We'll look at how you can take ownership of these controls and create your own custom displays.

The ListBox, ComboBox, TabControl, and MenuItem controls all are capable of changing owners and visual styles. The mechanism for doing so is the same for all them, but each technique varies slightly. Today we re-examine these four controls and see how much more customizable they are.

Today, you'll learn

- What it means to draw a control
- How to apply GDI+ to controls
- How to add images to your ListBoxes and ComboBoxes

- How to compare bit-wise values
- How to make menus appear highlighted

Reviewing Menus, `Listboxes`, `ComboBoxes`, and `TabControls`

We covered these controls fully in Days 4, "Adding Menus and Toolbars to Your Windows," and 6, "Enhancing Your Windows Forms with More Controls," but let's review them briefly to refresh your memory before we tackle today's advanced topics.

Menus are created with the `MainMenu` and `MenuItem` objects; `MainMenu` represents the menu bar in an application, and each menu and its submenus are `MenuItem`s. `MenuItem` controls function in a fairly standard way: a single `MenuItem` control represents a single menu choice in the application. These menu choices are always rendered in plain text, and can sometimes contain shortcut keys or modifiers.

While this is nice and functional, it doesn't provide much visual appeal. If you're going to have menus in your application, they're always going to look the same, no matter what they are used for. Figure 17.1 shows a typical menu.

FIGURE 17.1

Menus, by default, are bland controls.

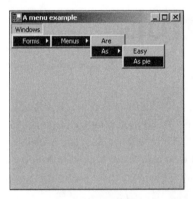

`Listboxes` and `ComboBoxes` are similar. They each contain items that are selectable. A selected item is highlighted in the default Windows highlight color, but that's all you can do. Again, the items must be represented as plain text.

If this were all there was to menus, `Listboxes`, and `ComboBoxes`, they'd be pretty stale and limited. Happily, though, there's more. Thanks to GDI+, you can circumvent the default behavior of these items and make them do whatever you want. This means these controls can display images, change colors, and anything else you can think of.

The TabControl is in a similar situation. The default behavior is to simply show a raised tab when one is selected, as shown in Figure 17.2. But we can be much more creative than that—we can make TabControls fun by overriding their default behavior and providing some more interesting effects.

FIGURE 17.2

Default tab controls can appear bo-o-ring.

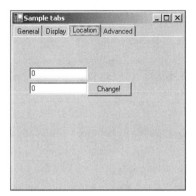

You actually have a lot of flexibility in the design and functionality of MenuItem, ListBox, ComboBox, and TabControl controls. Through careful manipulation of some properties and events, you'll see in the next few sections just how easy it is to create fancy controls that will leave your users in awe[el]well, maybe not in awe, but definitely wondering how you did it! (In case you're curious, these methods can be used to create the dynamic menus found in Microsoft Office 2000.)

Specifying DrawMode

The key to these enhancements for ListBoxes, ComboBoxes, and TabControls is the DrawMode property (menus use a slightly different paradigm, but we'll get to that later today in "Menus: A Case of Ownership"). DrawMode is a simple property that specifies who is responsible for drawing a particular control. By default, the operating system, Windows, will always be in control. It is Windows that makes your controls look as they do when they are selected, moused over, and so on. So you must wrest control from Windows to customize your ListBoxes, ComboBoxes, and TabControls.

DrawMode takes values from the DrawMode enumeration values shown in Table 17.1.

TABLE 17.1 DrawMode Enumeration Values

Value	Description
Normal	This is the default value. It specifies that the operating system is responsible for drawing your controls.
OwnerDrawFixed	Specifies that you will control the drawing of the controls, but that each item in the control (for example, items in a ListBox) will all be the same height.
OwnerDrawVariable	Like OwnerDrawFixed, but each item in the control can be of variable height. This is the most flexible method, but requires the most work on your part.

Given a ListBox, you can set the DrawMode property to OwnerDrawFixed and customize the display. Controls that have their DrawMode properties set to anything other than Normal are known as *owner-drawn controls*. In other words, you, the creator of these controls (at least in your application), are the owner of the controls, and thus responsible for drawing them. Try this in some code:

```
dim lbxItems As New ListBox()
...
'add items here
...
lbxItems.DrawMode = DrawMode.OwnerDrawFixed
```

If you compile an application using this code you'll quickly learn that something is missing. The items in the control simply won't display—the list box is invisible! That's because Windows has left the entire rendering of the control to you; nothing—borders, text, backgrounds—is drawn for you. For the operating system, it's an all-or-nothing proposition.

Fortunately, though, it's not that hard to draw controls once you've learned how to use GDI+ (see Day 13, "Creating Graphical Applications with GDI+," for a refresher). You must assign a delegate to the control's DrawItem event, and then use the necessary GDI+ calls to display the control. In C#, this looks like the following:

```
lbxItems.DrawItem += new DrawItemEventHandler(this.DrawMyBox);
```

The DrawItemEventHandler delegate means that you'll be using an event parameter of type DrawItemEventArgs for your event handler:

```
private void DrawMyBox(Object Sender, DrawItemEventArgs e)
```

DrawItemEventArgs is a very useful object; it contains quite a few useful members that will aid in drawing your control, including a Graphics object (which you'll recall is the central object of GDI+). Table 17.2 summarizes the properties of `DrawItemEventArgs`, and Table 17.3 lists its methods.

TABLE 17.2 `DrawItemEventArgs` Properties

Property	Description
BackColor	Retrieves the background color of the control to be rendered.
Bounds	Retrieves a `Rectangle` object that specifies the size and shape of the control to be rendered.
Font	Retrieves the font used in the control to be rendered.
ForeColor	The foreground color (in other words, font color) of the control to be rendered.
Graphics	A `Graphics` object that can be used to render the control.
Index	The index of the item to be rendered.
State	The current state of the control to be rendered.

TABLE 17.3 `DrawItemEventArgs` Methods

Method	Description
DrawBackground	Draws the background of the control if it is selected.
DrawFocusRectangle	Draws a rectangle that specifies the coordinates of the control's surface bounds. This rectangle is not visible.

In the next few sections, we'll look at putting the members listed in Tables 17.1–17.3 into action.

Enhancing the `ListBox` and `ComboBox`

One of a developer's most common customization desires for `ListBox` or `ComboBox` is to modify the colors for a list item. Using methods you learned earlier, you can customize only the whole list box—you can't customize a single row in a `ListBox` (see Listing 6.5 for an example).

With owner-drawn controls, you can customize each item.

There are two required steps to customize your controls:

1. Set the `DrawMode` property to something other than `Normal`.

2. Assign an event handler to the `DrawItem` event of that control, and use it to specify how the control should be drawn.

The first step is easy, but the second may require some thought. For example, a non–owner-drawn control can have several different faces (selected, deselected, mouse-overed, and so on). The face, or state, of the control is determined by the `DrawItemEventArgs.State` property. This property takes one of the `DrawItemState` enumeration values shown in Table 17.4.

TABLE 17.4   `DrawItemState` Enumeration Values

Value	Description
Checked	Indicates that the item is checked. (Only applies to `MenuItem` controls.)
ComboBoxEdit	The item to be drawn is the textbox portion of a `ComboBox` control.
Default	The default visual state.
Disabled	The item is disabled.
Focus	The item has the current focus.
Grayed	The item is grayed out. (Only applies to `MenuItem` controls.)
HotLight	The mouse pointer is currently over the item. In other words, the item is being hot-tracked.
Inactive	The item is inactive.
NoAccelerator	The item is displayed without a keyboard accelerator. (Only applies to `MenuItem` controls.)
NoFocusRect	The item is displayed without a visual cue that indicates it has focus. This is normally the case when the `DrawFocusRectangle` has not been called.
None	The item has no visual state.
Selected	The item is selected.

The values from `DrawItemState` can be combined bit-by-bit, so it's possible for a control to have more than one state. This requires a bit of manipulation in your code to determine if a control has a certain state.

Listing 17.1 shows how to manipulate these states.

LISTING 17.1   Customizing the `ListBox`

```
1:  using System;
2:  using System.Windows.Forms;
3:  using System.Drawing;
4:
5:  namespace TYWinForms.Day17 {
6:      public class Listing171 : Form {
```

LISTING **17.1** continued

```
7:        private ListBox lbxItems = new ListBox();
8:
9:        public Listing171() {
10:            lbxItems.Location = new Point(75,75);
11:
12:            lbxItems.Items.Add("Item 1");
13:            lbxItems.Items.Add("Item 2");
14:            lbxItems.Items.Add("Item 3");
15:            lbxItems.Items.Add("Item 4");
16:            lbxItems.Items.Add("Item 5");
17:
18:            lbxItems.DrawMode = DrawMode.OwnerDrawFixed;
19:            lbxItems.DrawItem += new DrawItemEventHandler
➥(this.DrawMyBox);
20:
21:            this.Text = "Listing 17.1";
22:            this.Controls.Add(lbxItems);
23:        }
24:
25:        public void DrawMyBox(Object Sender,
➥DrawItemEventArgs e) {
26:            e.DrawBackground();
27:
28:            if ((e.State & DrawItemState.Selected) ==
➥DrawItemState.Selected) {
29:                e.Graphics.FillRectangle(Brushes.Orange,
➥e.Bounds);
30:                e.Graphics.DrawString("Item " + e.Index +
➥" selected!", new Font("Arial",10), Brushes.Blue,
➥new Point(e.Bounds.X, e.Bounds.Y));
31:            } else {
32:                e.Graphics.DrawString("Item " + e.Index,
➥new Font("Arial",10), Brushes.Black, new Point
➥ (e.Bounds.X, e.Bounds.Y));
33:            }
34:        }
35:
36:        public static void Main() {
37:            Application.Run(new Listing171());
38:        }
39:    }
40:
41: }
```

ANALYSIS Let's start at the beginning. We declare the ListBox we'll be customizing on line 7. The constructor on lines 9–23 simply initializes the control with some default values. The most important part here is on lines 18 and 19. The DrawMode is set to

17

`OwnerDrawFixed` and a delegate is assigned to the `DrawItem` event, pointing to the `DrawMyBox` method on line 25.

Before we examine `DrawMyBox`, let's figure out the default execution process. Normally, as soon as your application is shown, Windows draws the form and all objects on the form. When you add items to the `ListBox` on lines 12–16, the `ListBox` is invalidated and must be redrawn (in other words, the `OnPaint` method is called for the `ListBox`). Windows examines each of the items in the `ListBox`, determines its state (selected, deselected, and so on), and draws the item appropriately (for example, a selected item will look different than a deselected item).

When `DrawMode` is anything other than `Normal`, `OnPaint` is still called, but no item in the `ListBox` is drawn. Thus, the event handler you specify for the `DrawItem` event is used to draw each individual item in the `ListBox`, rather than the entire `ListBox` itself. This is how you can color each item in the box separately instead of having to color the entire box.

Note the `DrawItemEventArgs` object on line 25; you'll use this object extensively. First, on line 26, you call the `DrawItemEventArgs.DrawBackground` method to draw the background of the control (which by default, is white). You generally call this method early in your drawing method, and always before any other drawing commands are issued! The background is always drawn over the top of whatever is already there.

Next, you need to determine the state of the item you're about to draw. This is done with the `DrawItemEventArgs.State` property, and a combination of `DrawItemState` enumeration values. Line 28 determines if the current item is selected by bit-wise combining a `DrawItemState` value and the `State` property, and comparing that to the `Selected` state. You must use this odd-looking code because of the way `DrawItemState`s are combined. For example, the following code would not work unless the only state currently on the control is the `Selected` state (which is seldom the case):

```
if (e.State == DrawItemState.Selected) {
```

The code on line 28 allows you to see if one particular state is on the control, rather than having to check for multiple states at once. In VB.NET, the same statement would look like the following:

```
if (e.State And DrawItemState.Selected) =
➥DrawItemState.Selected
```

Similarly, you could use the following to determine if the control current has the focus:

```
if ((e.State & DrawItemState.Focus) == DrawItemState.Focus) {
```

(Don't worry too much if you don't understand the concept of bit-wise addition. It isn't that important, and the syntax is easy to memorize. See the .NET Framework documentation if you're curious.)

Line 29 fills the rectangle occupied by the current item with an orange `Brush`. Remember that the `Bounds` property returns a `Rectangle` that covers the surface area of the item in question.

Line 30 uses the `DrawString` method to draw the text that is displayed in the control. In this case, it is the index of the item plus the word "selected!"

Line 32 handles all other states of the control. In these cases, you simply want to display the item text.

Figure 17.3 shows the output from Listing 17.1.

17

FIGURE 17.3

Your custom `ListBox` *control looks truly unique.*

You're on your way to making more interesting controls, but there's still more you can do. Using owner-drawn controls, you can add images to your `ListBoxes` and `ComboBoxes` and vary the height of each item.

When each item in the `ListBox` is created, a `MeasureItem` event is raised. If `DrawMode` is not `Normal`, you can use this event to size the items in the `ListBox`. Furthermore, if the `DrawMode` is set to `OwnerDrawVariable`, you can vary the height from one item to the next—something not possible with `Normal` or `OwnerDrawFixed` modes.

Note

> `MeasureItem` is raised every time an item in a `ListBox` is *created*, which is different than the `DrawItem` event, which is raised every time an item is *painted*. In other words, `MeasureItem` usually occurs once, while `DrawItem` can occur many times throughout an application's lifetime.
>
> Some developers don't understand why their items aren't resizing

> dynamically when they are painted (for example, when one is selected). This
> is because of the previous statement; MeasureItem is only raised once.

Take a look at Listing 17.2, which uses a ComboBox control to demonstrate variable
height items.

LISTING 17.2   A Variable-Height ComboBox

```
1:  using System;
2:  using System.Windows.Forms;
3:  using System.Drawing;
4:
5:  namespace TYWinForms.Day17 {
6:     public class Listing172 : Form {
7:        private ComboBox cboItems = new ComboBox();
8:        private Image[] arrImages;
9:
10:       public Listing172() {
11:          arrImages = new Image[] {
➥Image.FromFile("c:\\winforms\\day17\\icon1.bmp"),
➥Image.FromFile("c:\\winforms\\day17\\icon2.bmp"),
➥Image.FromFile("c:\\winforms\\day17\\icon3.bmp"),
➥Image.FromFile("c:\\winforms\\day17\\icon4.bmp"),
➥Image.FromFile("c:\\winforms\\day17\\icon5.bmp")};
12:
13:          cboItems.Location = new Point(50,25);
14:          cboItems.Size = new Size(200,200);
15:          cboItems.DropDownStyle = ComboBoxStyle.Simple;
16:
17:          cboItems.Items.Add("Item 1");
18:          cboItems.Items.Add("Item 2");
19:          cboItems.Items.Add("Item 3");
20:          cboItems.Items.Add("Item 4");
21:          cboItems.Items.Add("Item 5");
22:
23:          cboItems.DrawMode = DrawMode.OwnerDrawVariable;
24:          cboItems.DrawItem += new DrawItemEventHandler
➥ (this.DrawMyBox);
25:          cboItems.MeasureItem += new
➥MeasureItemEventHandler(this.MeasureIt);
26:
27:          this.Text = "Listing 17.2";
28:          this.Controls.Add(cboItems);
29:       }
30:
31:       public void MeasureIt(Object Sender,
➥MeasureItemEventArgs e) {
```

LISTING **17.2**   continued

```
32:              e.ItemHeight = (int)(arrImages[e.Index].
➥Height);
33:         }
34:
35:      public void DrawMyBox(Object Sender,
➥DrawItemEventArgs e) {
36:            e.DrawBackground();
37:
38:            if ((e.State & DrawItemState.Selected) ==
➥DrawItemState.Selected) {
39:               e.Graphics.FillRectangle(Brushes.Orange,
➥new Rectangle(e.Bounds.X, e.Bounds.Y, e.Bounds.Width,
➥e.Bounds.Height));
40:               e.Graphics.DrawString("Item " + e.Index +
➥" selected!", new Font("Arial",14), Brushes.White,
➥new Point(e.Bounds.X, e.Bounds.Y));
41:            } else {
42:               e.Graphics.DrawImage(arrImages[e.Index],
➥new Point(e.Bounds.X, e.Bounds.Y));
43:               e.Graphics.DrawString("Item " + e.Index,
➥new Font("Arial",10), Brushes.Black, new Point((int)
➥ (arrImages[e.Index].Width + 2), e.Bounds.Y));
44:            }
45:      }
46:
47:      public static void Main() {
48:         Application.Run(new Listing172());
49:      }
50:   }
51:
52:  }
```

ANALYSIS   The first new thing we come across is the creation of an array of images on lines 8 and 11. We'll use these images in our ComboBox in a moment (make sure to change the filenames to images you actually have!). Note that the order in which we add these images to the arrImages array is the same order in which we want them to appear in the ComboBox—this isn't necessary, but it is helpful later on.

The DrawMode is set to OwnerDrawVariable on line 23, and event handlers are assigned for the MeasureItem and DrawItem events on lines 24 and 25. Let's look at the MeasureIt event handler first.

MeasureIt, on lines 31-33, only does one thing: sets the height for the item that is being drawn. The MeasureItemEventArgs object has four simple members:

17

- Graphics—Returns a Graphics object used to draw
- Index—The index of the item currently being drawn
- ItemHeight—The height of the item to be drawn
- ItemWidth—The width of the item to be drawn

So on line 32 you set the ItemHeight property to specify how tall each item should be. Because we'll have images in the items, the height depends on those images, and you must retrieve the height of the image in the arrImages array with the same index as the item currently being drawn. We're using variable-sized images here, so each item should be a different height.

Now that the ComboBox knows how tall each item should be, the DrawMyBox method is called when the items need to be drawn. This DrawMyBox method is nearly identical to the one from Listing 17.1. The difference is that when drawing text in the items, you have to take into account the image, so the text must be moved over by the width of the image. Line 43 does just this adding 2 just for a good buffer. Don't forget to cast these values to integers.

Figure 17.4 shows the output from this application.

FIGURE 17.4

Your ComboBoxes can now contain images and items of variable height.

As you can see, once you know how to override a control's default drawing behavior, it's not difficult to create your own custom functionality, as long as you know the basics of GDI+. In the next section, we examine how to apply the DrawItemEventArgs object to make your TabControls more interactive.

Enhancing the TabControl

Customizing the TabControl control is similar to customizing ListBoxes or ComboBoxes, but there are a few differences. First, you cannot draw different-sized tabs in a

`TabControl`; all of the tabs must be the same size. Thus, trying to set the `DrawMode` to `OwnerDrawVariable` would result in an error.

Second, `TabControls` cannot be hot-tracked in your custom drawing code. In other words, you can't determine when the user's mouse is over a tab, which means you can't react to that state.

Because of these limitations, developers often settle for the default implementation of the `TabControl`. However, you should look at how customization with `TabControl` works before you make that judgment. Listing 17.3 shows an example.

LISTING 17.3 Customizing a `TabControl`

```
1:  Imports System
2:  Imports System.Windows.Forms
3:  Imports System.Drawing
4:
5:  namespace TYWinForms.Day17
6:
7:     public class Listing173 : Inherits Form
8:        private tcMain As New TabControl()
9:        private tpGeneral As New TabPage("General")
10:       private tpDisplay As New TabPage("Display")
11:       private tpLocation As New TabPage("Location")
12:       private tpAdvanced As New TabPage("Advanced")
13:
14:       public sub New()
15:          Me.Text = "Listing 17.3"
16:          Me.Width = 600
17:          Me.Controls.Add(tcMain)
18:
19:          tcMain.Width = Me.Width
20:          tcMain.Height = Me.Height
21:          tcMain.TabPages.Add(tpGeneral)
22:          tcMain.TabPages.Add(tpDisplay)
23:          tcMain.TabPages.Add(tpLocation)
24:          tcMain.TabPages.Add(tpAdvanced)
25:
26:          tcMain.ItemSize = new Size(75,20)
27:          tcMain.SizeMode = TabSizeMode.Fixed
28:          tcMain.DrawMode = TabDrawMode.OwnerDrawFixed
29:          AddHandler tcMain.DrawItem, new
➥DrawItemEventHandler(AddressOf Me.DrawTab)
30:       end sub
31:
32:       private sub DrawTab(Sender As Object, e As
➥DrawItemEventArgs)
33:          if (e.State And DrawItemState.Selected) =
➥DrawItemState.Selected then
```

17

LISTING 17.3   continued

```
34:              e.Graphics.DrawRectangle(Pens.Purple,
➥tcMain.GetTabRect(e.Index))
35:              e.Graphics.DrawString(tcMain.TabPages
➥ (e.Index).Text, new Font("Arial",10), Brushes.Red,
➥RectangleF.op_implicit(tcMain.GetTabRect(e.Index)))
36:          else
37:              e.Graphics.DrawString(tcMain.TabPages
➥ (e.Index).Text, new Font("Arial",10), Brushes.Black,
➥RectangleF.op_implicit(tcMain.GetTabRect(e.Index)))
38:          end if
39:       end sub
40:
41:       public shared sub Main()
42:          Application.Run(new Listing173())
43:       end sub
44:    end class
45:  end namespace
```

ANALYSIS   If you remember the TabControl from Day 6, you know that a single TabControl consists of one or more TabPages that represent each tab. The TabControl and TabPages are created on lines 8–12, and are assembled on lines 21–24.

Even though you can't size each tab individually, you can change all their sizes at once. This is done on line 26. But, by default, a tab cannot change its width. To override this behavior and allow the change in width, you need to set the SizeMode property to TabSizeMode.Fixed, as shown on line 27. The other values of the TabSizeMode enumeration are Normal (the default value) and FillToRight. The latter value only applies when there is more than one row of tabs, and enlarges the tabs so that they fill the width of the TabControl.

The last step in the constructor is to set the DrawMode to OwnerDrawFixed and assign an event handler for the DrawItem event. Notice that the TabControl doesn't use the DrawMode enumeration like the other controls you've looked at today. Rather, it uses a TabDrawMode enumeration, which contains the same values as DrawMode, minus the OwnerDrawVariable value.

After studying the ListBox and ComboBox earlier today, the DrawTab method on line 32 should look familiar to you. If the current tab is selected (line 33), you draw a colored rectangle around the tab (line 34) and display the text in a red color (line 35). There are a few interesting things happening in lines 34 and 35.

First, notice that you use the GetTabRect method of the TabControl. This method returns the visible portion of a particular tab—the current tab as specified by

`DrawItemEventArgs.Index` in this case. Normally, you'd use the `DrawItemEventArgs.Bounds` property to return the proper rectangle. The reason we don't here is because the `Bounds` property returns the entire surface area of a tab, including *nonvisible* portions. Because we don't want to draw on invisible areas, we call `GetTabRect` instead, which returns the proper rectangle.

> **Tip**
>
> If you want to make a selected tab appear to pop out from the others (in other words, the bottom tab line disappears), draw a rectangle using the color `LightGray`:
>
> `e.Graphics.DrawRectangle(Pens.LightGray,`
>
> ➥`tcMain.GetTabRect(e.Index))`

17

Line 35 does the same for the `DrawString` method. Here, we call `GetTabRect` to define the bounds for which the tab's text caption will be drawn. Any text outside these bounds won't be shown, and the text won't be cut off midcharacter. If you used `DrawItemEventArgs.Bounds` here, the text would run off of the edge of the tab.

There's another curious method here: `RectangleF.op_implicit`. The `DrawString` method can only take a `RectangleF` object (which is just like a `Rectangle` object but can contain fractional sizes). Because `GetTabRect` returns a regular `Rectangle` object, you need to use the static `op_implicit` method of the `RectangleF` object to convert between the two.

Line 37 simply displays the default tab view with black Arial text and no outlines.

Figure 17.5 shows the output.

FIGURE 17.5

You can change the font and background colors in a customized `TabControl`.

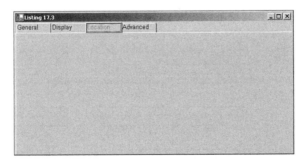

Unfortunately, besides changing the background color, font face, and font color, there's not much else you can do with `TabControls`. However, you certainly can customize your controls with the functionality that is available.

Menus: A Case of Ownership

The basic procedure for drawing customized menus is essentially the same as it is for other controls, but a few properties are different. And since each item in a menu is actually a separate MenuItem control, you'll need to have a whole slew of DrawItem event handlers—not to mention MeasureItem event handlers—if you want each menu item to behave differently.

The main difference between menus and other controls is the way you turn custom drawing on. Instead of setting the DrawMode property for menus to OwnerDrawFixed or OwnerDrawVariable as you do with other controls, you set the MenuItem's OwnerDraw property to true:

```
private MenuItem miCustom = new MenuItem();
miCustom.OwnerDraw = true;
```

The effect is the same—that is, setting OwnerDraw to true allows you to customize the drawing procedure for each method; it lets the owner of the control (you) specify how the control should be drawn. The distinction is made because MenuItems do not derive from the same place as other controls. For example, the parent-hierarchy of a ListBox is shown in the left-hand side of Figure 17.6. Specifically, ListBoxes and other controls derive (directly or indirectly) from the System.Windows.Forms.Control class. MenuItems don't, so in the strictest sense they are not Windows Forms controls. Therefore, the mechanism behind customized drawing is a bit different for MenuItems.

FIGURE 17.6

MenuItems *don't inherit from the same place as other controls.*

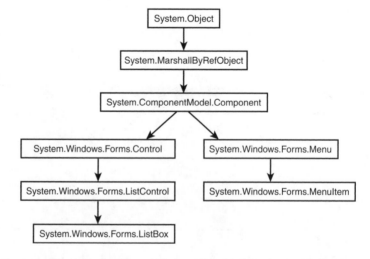

Enough theory; let's get right into an example. Listing 17.4 shows the first part of the code for a customized menu application.

LISTING 17.4   Initializing Your Customized Menus

```
 1:  using System;
 2:  using System.Windows.Forms;
 3:  using System.Drawing;
 4:
 5:  namespace TYWinForms.Day17 {
 6:
 7:     public class Listing174 : Form {
 8:        private MainMenu mnuCustom = new MainMenu();
 9:        private MenuItem miCustom = new MenuItem();
10:        private MenuItem miRed = new MenuItem();
11:        private MenuItem miBlue = new MenuItem();
12:        private MenuItem miOrange = new MenuItem();
13:        private MenuItem miGreen = new MenuItem();
14:
15:        public Listing174() {
16:           this.Text = "Listing 17.4";
17:           this.Menu = mnuCustom;
18:
19:           miCustom = mnuCustom.MenuItems.Add("Custom Menu");
20:           miRed = miCustom.MenuItems.Add("Red");
21:           miBlue = miCustom.MenuItems.Add("Blue");
22:           miOrange = miCustom.MenuItems.Add("Orange");
23:           miGreen = miCustom.MenuItems.Add("Green");
24:
25:           miCustom.OwnerDraw = true;
26:           miCustom.DrawItem += new DrawItemEventHandler
➥(this.DrawTopLevel);
27:           miCustom.MeasureItem += new
➥MeasureItemEventHandler(this.MeasureItem);
28:
29:           miRed.OwnerDraw = true;
30:           miRed.DrawItem += new DrawItemEventHandler
➥ (this.DrawItem);
31:           miRed.MeasureItem += new MeasureItemEventHandler
➥ (this.MeasureItem);
32:
33:           miBlue.OwnerDraw = true;
34:           miBlue.DrawItem += new DrawItemEventHandler
➥ (this.DrawItem);
35:           miBlue.MeasureItem += new MeasureItemEventHandler
➥ (this.MeasureItem);
36:
37:           miOrange.OwnerDraw = true;
38:           miOrange.DrawItem += new DrawItemEventHandler
➥ (this.DrawItem);
39:           miOrange.MeasureItem += new
➥MeasureItemEventHandler(this.MeasureItem);
40:
41:           miGreen.OwnerDraw = true;
```

17

LISTING 17.4 continued

```
42:            miGreen.DrawItem += new DrawItemEventHandler
➥ (this.DrawItem);
43:            miGreen.MeasureItem += new
➥MeasureItemEventHandler(this.MeasureItem);
44:        }
```

ANALYSIS This code is fairly simple. On lines 8–13 you create five MenuItem controls and a MainMenu. Lines 19–23 add each submenu to its appropriate parent—mnuCustom or miCustom in this case.

Lines 25–43 do the same thing for each of the different MenuItems: set the OwnerDraw property to true and assign delegates for the DrawItem and MeasureItem events. Note that all of the delegates point to the MeasureItem event handler, and all but the miCustom MenuItems point to the DrawItem event handler. We want to draw the miCustom menu a bit differently because it is a top-level menu. Listing 17.5 shows the code for these event-handling methods.

LISTING 17.5 The Methods for Measuring and Drawing Menus

```
45:        private void MeasureItem(Object Sender,
➥MeasureItemEventArgs e) {
46:            SizeF stringSize = e.Graphics.MeasureString
➥ (((MenuItem)Sender).Text, this.Font);
47:
48:            e.ItemHeight = (int)stringSize.Height + 6;
49:            e.ItemWidth = (int)stringSize.Width + 10;
50:        }
51:
52:        private void DrawTopLevel(Object Sender,
➥DrawItemEventArgs e) {
53:            if (((e.State & DrawItemState.HotLight) ==
➥DrawItemState.HotLight) |
➥ (e.State & DrawItemState.Selected) ==
➥DrawItemState.Selected) {
54:                e.Graphics.DrawString(((MenuItem)Sender).Text,
➥new Font("Times New Roman",12), Brushes.Blue,
➥new Point(e.Bounds.X, e.Bounds.Y));
55:            } else {
56:                e.Graphics.DrawString(((MenuItem)Sender).Text,
➥new Font("Times New Roman",12), Brushes.Black,
➥new Point(e.Bounds.X, e.Bounds.Y));
57:            }
58:        }
59:
60:        private void DrawItem(Object Sender,
➥DrawItemEventArgs e) {
```

LISTING 17.5   continued

```
61:             e.Graphics.FillRectangle(Brushes.WhiteSmoke,
➥new Rectangle(e.Bounds.X, e.Bounds.Y, e.Bounds.Width,
➥e.Bounds.Height));
62:
63:             if (((e.State & DrawItemState.HotLight) ==
➥DrawItemState.HotLight) |
➥ (e.State & DrawItemState.Selected) ==
➥DrawItemState.Selected) {
64:                 e.Graphics.FillRectangle(Brushes.LightGray,
➥new Rectangle(e.Bounds.X, e.Bounds.Y, e.Bounds.Width,
➥e.Bounds.Height));
65:                 e.Graphics.DrawString(((MenuItem)Sender).Text,
➥new Font("Times New Roman",12), Brushes.Blue,
➥new Point(e.Bounds.X, e.Bounds.Y));
66:             } else {
67:                 e.Graphics.DrawString(((MenuItem)Sender).Text,
➥new Font("Times New Roman",12), Brushes.Black,
➥new Point(e.Bounds.X, e.Bounds.Y));
68:             }
69:         }
70:
71:     public static void Main() {
72:         Application.Run(new Listing174());
73:     }
74:     }
75:
76:  }
```

ANALYSIS   There are a lot of long lines in that code, but the functionality is simple. Let's start with the MeasureItem method on line 45.

As you saw in Listing 17.4, this method is responsible for measuring each of the MenuItems to ensure that they are drawn at the correct size. This method is very important for customized menus, because without it, your menus would remain at the default size, and would likely cut off anything you wanted to display in them.

First, the Graphics.MeasureString method is called to measure the size of the string to be drawn. We determine this string from the Text property of the item that called this method. For example, line 46 would measure the size of the string "Custom Menu" when the miCustom object is being measured. The height and width of the menu are then set to the values returned from MeasureString plus a few pixels for a gutter on each side of the MenuItem (lines 48 and 49).

Let's move to the DrawTopLevel method on line 52. There are two cases we're interested in: when the menu is being hot-tracked (when the mouse cursor is over the menu) and when the menu item is selected (in other words, when the menu is dropped down and showing its submenus). Both of these cases should result in the menu item being highlighted. In all other cases, you should just draw the MenuItem normally.

So on line 53 you determine the cases. Remember that when checking the DrawItemState values, you have to bit-wise combine them (see the analysis of Listing 17.1 earlier today for a recap). Line 53 checks to see whether the state of the menu is HotLight *or* Selected (remember that the | operator in C# means "or"). If either of these cases is satisfied, line 54 draws the text from the menu using the Times New Roman font in a blue brush. If neither case is satisfied, line 56 draws the text in a black brush.

The DrawItem method on line 60 does the same thing as DrawTopLevel, with two additional steps. First, on line 61, you fill the background of the menu item with a WhiteSmoke brush (just for some variety). The same two cases as before are evaluated on line 63. Then line 64 fills the background of the menu with a LightGray brush, and line 65 draws the text in blue again. These last two steps add some extra pizzazz to your menus. Finally, if none of the cases match, line 67 draws the menus normally.

Combine Listing 17.4 and 17.5 into one file and compile it. Figure 17.7 shows the output from the customized menus application.

FIGURE 17.7

Menus with pizzazz.

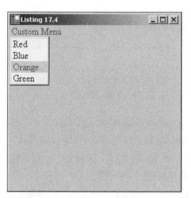

Notice that when you highlight a menu item, its background color changes as well as the text color. This behavior also happens on regular Windows-drawn menus, but the colors you've chosen here bring an extra spark to your menus. Also note that had you not evaluated the DrawItemState.Selected case for the miCustom menu, its font would not remain blue after you click it to open the submenus.

You can, of course, get a lot fancier with your menus. For instance, you can show any keyboard shortcuts in the menus, or draw images next to the text to provide more visual information.

Summary

Today's lesson focused on creating customized controls, and you learned how to use GDI+ to create visual effects and add interactivity.

The basic procedure to create customized visual effects is to set the DrawMode property to a value from the DrawMode enumeration, and then assign a delegate for the DrawItem event. In your event handler for DrawItem, you use GDI+ methods to draw strings, images, background colors, and whatever else you like. Everything you learned from Day 13, "Creating Graphical Applications with GDI+," is valid.

Use the State property of the DrawItemEventArgs object and the DrawItemState enumeration to determine the current visual state your control is in. For example, the hot-tracked, selected, or default states. These values must be combined bit-wise to check for each case.

Menus are slightly different because you use the OwnerDraw property instead of the DrawMode property, but the procedure is still the same: assign a delegate to the DrawItem event.

Now that you know the basics of drawing controls, we'll examine how to create them from scratch tomorrow.

Q&A

Q Are the MenuItem, ListBox, ComboBox, and TabControl the only controls I can customize?

A Aside from custom controls, yes. You'll see tomorrow how you can create a control from scratch to do whatever you want.

Q I'm setting an event handler for the DrawItem event, but it's not working. What's going on?

A For the DrawItem event to be raised in the first place, you must set the DrawMode property to either OwnerDrawFixed or OwnerDrawVariable, or OwnerDraw to true for menus. If the default values are used for these properties, the DrawItem event is never raised, and your event handler does no good.

17

Q **How can I make dynamic menus like Office 2000, where seldom-used menus disappear and reappear?**

A Using the methods learned today, you can't. Again, this is something you can do with custom controls, which you'll examine tomorrow.

If you are adventurous, you may have tried doing this already by setting a menu's `Visible` property to `false` initially, and then setting it to `true` at the appropriate time after the menu pops up. If you've tried this, then you know, unfortunately, it doesn't work; instead, the menus just disappear altogether, leaving a strange box behind. This doesn't work because the `MeasureItem` and `DrawItem` events must be raised *before* a menu pops up. If you try to execute these methods afterward (by setting the `Visible` property to `true`) the menu gets confused because it doesn't know what it should do with the other items in the menu, and it errors out. You need to override the default behavior of menu "pop-ups" for this to work, but again, that will have to wait until tomorrow.

Workshop

This workshop helps reinforce the concepts we covered today. It is very helpful to understand fully the answers before moving on. Answers can be found in Appendix A.

Quiz

1. Name four of the values from the `DrawItemState` enumeration.
2. What is the difference between the `DrawMode` and the `TabDrawMode` enumerations?
3. When is the `MeasureItem` event raised?
4. True or false? Tabs in a `TabControl` can be different sizes.
5. Why would you call the `GetTabRect` method?
6. How are `MenuItems` different than other controls?
7. What must you do to change the size of the tabs in a `TabControl`?

Exercise

Create an application that allows users to customize the appearance of a menu. Use customized `ComboBoxes` to let them choose colors for the menus.

DAY **18**

Building Custom Windows Forms Controls

Until now, you've been stuck with the built-in Windows Forms control that you learned about in Week 1. While these controls cover a wide range of capabilities, they don't always meet your needs. The .NET Framework, however, allows you to easily create controls that do.

Because all of the controls in the .NET Framework rely on a common framework and base class, it is simple to extend them or create new ones. Today you'll learn what that base is, and how you can use it to create custom functionality. You'll also see how to tweak existing controls so that they are more functional, without having to rewrite them completely.

Today you will learn

- What the `Control` class is
- How to make use of events in your custom controls
- How to build controls to smartly interact with users
- How the `UserControl` class is similar to a Windows Form

Why Create Custom Controls?

Custom controls address two issues in the .NET Framework:

- Extensibility
- Encapsulation and reusability

First, let's talk about extensibility. There may be times as you develop your Windows Forms applications that the existing Windows Forms controls don't fulfill your needs. For example, have you ever wanted to make dynamic menus like those in Microsoft Office? Or perhaps make the text on a Button directly editable? Or make something that doesn't resemble any of the Windows Forms controls, such as a clock?

None of these tasks can be accomplished with the built-in set of Windows Forms controls. That doesn't mean that the existing controls aren't doing their jobs well. It just means that the developers at Microsoft who built the default controls couldn't anticipate every task you would like to perform, or type of control that you would need. The possibilities are endless, so there must be a way to extend the existing controls.

Reusability is another issue with any application. Some tasks can be accomplished with clever manipulation of a combination of controls. You could, for example, create a clock by using a Timer control and a Label. It gets tedious, however, to create this functionality, handle the necessary events, set the display properties, and so on, every time you need a clock.

One thing we've learned from the .NET Framework is that encapsulation is good. When you encapsulate functionality in a class or object, you (or its implementers) don't have to worry about the complexity of the object. You can just implement it (or in this case, add it to your Windows Form), without worrying about how the object does things internally. Additionally, when something is encapsulated, it can easily be used over and over again in different applications. Since the code for that object is encapsulated and doesn't rely on the parent application, it can be used anywhere.

So, why do we need to be able to create custom controls? To extend the .NET Framework as we see fit, and encapsulate custom functionality in a neat, handy object that can be used over and over again.

This description fits just about any custom class you create. What makes Windows Forms controls so special? Remember that a Windows Form can only contain Windows Forms controls (and ActiveX objects wrapped in the AxHost class). You can create as many custom classes as you want, but unless it qualifies as a control you won't be able to use it on your Windows Forms.

In the rest of today's lesson, you're going to learn how to make controls for any purpose, and adapt existing controls to suit all your Windows Forms desires.

Creating Custom Controls

As you might guess, a Windows Forms control, by definition, is any object that inherits directly or indirectly from the `System.Windows.Forms.Control` class. This class represents a component that has a visual interface. It provides a lot of the functionality you need for displaying controls on a form; we'll examine this class more in the next section.

You already know how to derive from other classes, and the `Control` class is no different. There are only a few more steps you need to accomplish before you have a full-blown custom control:

1. Create a class that inherits from the `Control` class.

2. Define properties, methods, and events for your class.

3. Override the `OnPaint` method to draw your custom control.

4. Compile and then use your custom class.

The next few sections discuss the first three steps, as well as how to add some extra functionality to your custom controls. We'll save step 4 for the end of today's lesson, because you already know how to do it!

A Review of Windows Forms Controls Architecture

So let's review the `Control` class, which will quickly become your friend as we move through today's lesson. `Control` is the root for nearly all of the Windows Forms controls you've been using. Many of the members you've been using for your controls such as the `Size` and `Location` properties are inherited from `Control`. Figure 18.1 shows the class architecture surrounding `Control`. Notice that even the `Form` class is derived from `Control`.

Note   Figure 18.1 doesn't represent all of the Windows Forms controls—just those that derive from the `Control` class. Controls like `MenuItems` and `TreeNodes` don't share the same hierarchy as the other controls, so they aren't shown here.

FIGURE 18.1

The Windows Forms control component hierarchy.

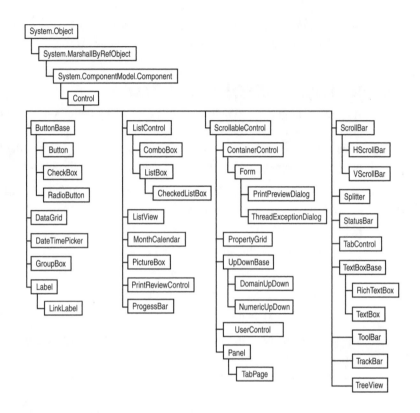

All of the controls that have `Control` at their base share the same members. We'll use this to our advantage when designing custom controls; you won't have to build any of this inherited functionality because it's already there.

Let's examine the order-of-execution for a typical application. The first thing that is executed is always the `Main` method, which typically has only one line:

```
Application.Run(new ClassName());
```

Two things happen from this one line. First, the constructor of your Windows Forms class is called. Here is where you initialize variables, Windows Forms controls, and so on. After the constructor executes, the `Run` method causes your `Form` to display onscreen.

NEW TERM The first time your form displays on screen, the Common Language Runtime creates a *handle* for it. A handle is simply a reference to a location in graphics memory, or, in other words, a location on your computer monitor. This location is used by the CLR behind-the-scenes to ensure that your form is displaying properly. This is key: your form does *not* have a handle until it is first displayed. After your form displays, the space it occupies on your monitor is known as the *client area* (this is represented in .NET by a `Rectangle` object).

Now let's look at a control inside that form—for example, a `TextBox`. Your form's constructor is likely where you initialize your `TextBox`. Like a form, the first thing that is executed is the `TextBox`'s constructor (at this point, the `TextBox` is still invisible). Controls have handles too, and like a form, the handle is not created until the control is shown for the first time. This is important: until your control is shown for the first time, it does not have a handle.

(Technically, if your control did not have a handle, it wouldn't have a location set aside in memory or on your screen. In practical terms, this means that your control wouldn't know how it is going to be displayed. Sure, it may have `Size` and `Location` values specified, but having these numbers and translating them to pixels on your monitor are two different things. So without a handle, and consequently, a location on your monitor, your control wouldn't know how big it is going to be, where it is going to be located, and so on.)

When your `TextBox` control is finally displayed and a handle is created, the space it occupies is its client area. Note that this client area is different (and usually smaller) than the form's client area. Every time the `TextBox` raises the `Paint` event, it uses its client area to mark its borders. In other words, the `TextBox` won't and can't be shown outside of its client area. The `Paint` event depends on the client area, and in turn, the handle, to function properly. Figure 18.2 shows the flow chart.

18

FIGURE 18.2

A form cannot be displayed until a handle is created, and a handle is not created until immediately before the form displays.

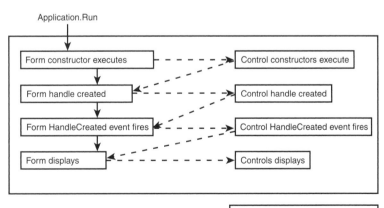

When designing custom controls it is a must to know your client area. And therefore, it is a must to have a handle. Most of the time, you won't do anything directly with the handle, but there must be one for your control to paint properly. You can determine when a handle is created with the HandleCreated event—but we're getting ahead of ourselves. We'll examine this and other special events later today.

So here's your basic custom control:

```
public class MyControl : Control {
    ...
}
```

So far, the only requirement is that it inherits from the Control class. Let's examine how to fill that control up with members to make it more useful.

Properties, Methods, and Events

For the purposes of this lesson, we'll develop an "eye" control. This control will essentially represent a human eye (or the best representation of one we can make) on your form, and will contain properties, methods, and events that can be used to follow the cursor around onscreen.

What properties do we need? For starters, you'll have iris color, "bloodshotedness," and the current position of the pupil. At first attempt, our custom class looks like Listing 18.1.

LISTING **18.1**   The Framework for the Eye

```
 1: using System;
 2: using System.Windows.Forms;
 3: using System.Drawing;
 4:
 5: namespace TYWinforms.Day18 {
 6:    public class EyeControl : Control {
 7:       public Point PupilPosition;
 8:       public Color IrisColor;
 9:       public int BloodShotedness;
10:
11:       public EyeControl() {
12:          ...
13:       }
14:    }
15: }
```

NEW TERM   This basic framework for properties works, but it's not very functional. For example, if the person who uses this control changes the IrisColor property, she'll have to wait until the control paints itself again before the color changes, and there's no telling when that could happen. What you want to do is to force the color to change and the drawing to update as soon as the property is changed. To do this, you use the *property declaration syntax*. This syntax, which is part of most programming languages, allows you to execute code in addition to setting or getting a property value. If you've worked with Visual Basic or C# before, you're likely familiar with this syntax already. It follows in C# as such:

```
public type name {
    get {
        //code to execute and retrieve property
    }
    set {
        //code to execute and set property
    }
}
```

And in VB.NET:

```
Public Property name As type
    Get
        'code to execute and retrieve property
    End Get
    Set
        'code to execute and set property
    End Set
End Property
```

Using this syntax, you can execute a method any time your property is set or retrieved with the syntax `YourControl.Property`. It will make more sense when you see it in working code, as in Listing 18.2.

LISTING 18.2   Better Eye Properties

```
 1:  using System;
 2:  using System.Windows.Forms;
 3:  using System.Drawing;
 4:
 5:  namespace TYWinforms.Day18 {
 6:     public class EyeControl : Control {
 7:        private Point ptPosition;
 8:        private Color clrIris;
 9:        private int intBlood;
10:
11:        public Point PupilPosition {
12:           get { return ptPosition; }
13:           set {
14:              ptPosition = value;
```

18

LISTING 18.2   continued

```
15:                    Invalidate();
16:                }
17:            }
18:
19:        public Color IrisColor {
20:            get { return clrIris; }
21:            set {
22:                clrIris = value;
23:                Invalidate();
24:            }
25:        }
26:
27:        public int BloodShotedness {
28:            get { return intBlood; }
29:            set {
30:                intBlood = value;
31:                Invalidate();
32:            }
33:        }
34:
35:        public EyeControl() {
36:            ...
37:        }
38:    }
39: }
```

ANALYSIS   On lines 7–9, you create three private variables that will represent the properties iris color, bloodshotedness, and pupil position. It is important to note that these variables are internal, and cannot be accessed directly by a user. The public properties you declare using the property declaration syntax will reference these internal variables.

The first public property is PupilPosition on line 11. It follows the get/set syntax. When a get is called (in other words, when the user executes something like Point mypoint = EyeControl.PupilPosition), you simply return the value stored in the ptPosition internal variable (line 12). If the user sets the value of the property (using something like EyeControl.PupilPosition = new Point(30,30)) then you set the ptPosition internal variable to value, which represents the incoming value.

Finally, since you want the control to redraw itself immediately upon setting of this value (so the user can see that the position has indeed changed), you call the Invalidate method. This method causes the Paint event to fire—we'll look at that in the next section.

Next, we need to update the position of the eyeball every time the mouse cursor moves. Logically, this would seem like a perfect candidate for the MouseMove event, but there is a limitation here. The MouseMove event only fires when the mouse cursor moves directly over the top of the control. In other words, the eyeball would only move when the cursor passes directly over it. We don't want this; rather, we want the eye to follow the cursor no matter where it is onscreen.

To solve this problem we use a Timer control. When the Timer's event goes off, we update the position of the eyeball. So in your control's constructor, create a Timer and set its Interval property to something appropriately small (such as 100 milliseconds), and assign an event handler:

```
objTimer.Interval = 100;
objTimer.Elapsed += new System.Timers.ElapsedEventHandler
➡(this.Update);
objTimer.Enabled = true;
...
private void Update(Object Sender,
➡System.Timers.ElapsedEventArgs e) {
   ptPosition = Cursor.Position;

   Invalidate();
}
```

The Cursor class represents the current mouse cursor, and the static Position property returns a point that describes the current location. Retrieve this value and store it in your internal ptPosition variable. Once again, you need to call the Invalidate method to make sure the eyeball updates onscreen.

18

> **Note**
>
> In this example we're using the System.Timers.Timer class rather than the System.Windows.Forms.Timer class that you used earlier. You can use either here, but the former was designed to be more accurate, which suits our purposes better. Note that instead of the Tick event and an EventHandler delegate, you must watch the Elapsed event and use an ElapsedEventHandler.

We want to alert the user every time the eyeball moves as well (whether she cares or not; it's good design practice). This means our eyeball control needs a custom event as well.

> **Tip**
>
> Need a quick refresher on creating custom events? Look back at Day 5, "Handling Events in Your Windows Forms."

We'll call our event `EyeMoved`, and declare it as follows:

```
private EventHandler onEyeMoved;
...
public event EventHandler EyeMoved {
   add { onEyeMoved += value; }
   remove { onEyeMoved -= value; }
}
```

Recall that before you create an event, you must create a delegate using the on*EventName* syntax. The first line does just that. Then, using syntax similar to the property declarations, you create the event. The `add` and `remove` sections work similarly to the `get` and `set` for properties. When the user assigns an event handler to the `EyeMoved` event, such as

```
objEye.EyeMoved += new EventHandler(this.Whatever)
```

the `add` section adds that method to the `onEyeMoved` delegate. If a user decides to remove that event handler from the `EyeMoved` event, the `remove` section executes.

Next, we need to create a method that executes the delegate:

```
protected virtual void OnEyeMoved(EventArgs e) {
   if (onEyeMoved != null) {
      onEyeMoved(this, e);
   }
}
```

This method simply checks to see if an event handler has been assigned to the `onEyeMoved` delegate, and if so, executes it. (Remember that C# is case-sensitive, so `onEyeMoved` is different than `OnEyeMoved`!) In VB.NET, this code would look like the following:

```
Protected Overridable Sub OnEyeMoved(e As EventArgs)
   RaiseEvent EyeMoved(Me, e)
End Sub
```

Now let's look at how to draw the eyeball.

Drawing Your Control

Drawing the eye is actually more complicated than it sounds. You could simply call the `FillEllipse` method three times (once for the outer, white portion of the eye, once for the iris, and once for the pupil), but that doesn't take into account the mouse cursor position. We need to somehow translate the mouse cursor coordinates to the eyeball position.

Also, our eyeball will be round, but remember that all drawing in Windows Forms is usually done with squares and rectangles. If we draw the iris and pupil to follow the mouse cursor, it may move outside of the ellipse of the outer eye, and that would look really funny (see Figure 18.3). Therefore, we need to only draw inside the outer eye.

FIGURE 18.3

Oooh...spooky eye.

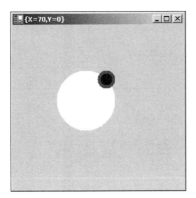

Finally, don't forget that we need to somehow incorporate the "bloodshotedness." The higher the bloodshotedness, the more red the eye should be. These three issues add up to some complicated tasks, but we can handle them!

Drawing Inside `Regions`

Let's tackle the second problem—drawing inside the outer eye—first. Recall from Day 13 that you can use `Region` objects to "clip" drawings. In other words, anything you try to draw outside of a specified `Region` won't be shown. We'll need a `Region` object that represents the outer eye, and then make sure we only draw inside it. The easiest way to create your `Region` object is from a `GraphicsPath` object; `GraphicsPath` has an `AddEllipse` method, which is exactly the shape we want to clip for.

First, create your `GraphicsPath` and `Region` objects:

```
private GraphicsPath pthClip = new GraphicsPath();
private Region regClip;
```

Then add an ellipse to your path:

```
pthClip.AddEllipse(ClientRectangle);
regClip = new Region(pthClip);
```

`ClientRectangle` (a property inherited from the base `Control` class) is a `Rectangle` object that specifies the client area we spoke about before; it is governed by the `Size` property.

But wait a second. Didn't we say that the client area isn't created until the control is displayed and the handle created? If that is so, then we'll need to wait until the handle is created before we can add an ellipse to the path and create our `Region`. This is where the `HandleCreated` event comes in. In your control's constructor, add the following code:

```
this.HandleCreated += new EventHandler(this.SetBounds);
```

18

Then, create the `SetBounds` method and place your `Region`-creation code in there:

```
private void SetBounds(Object Sender, EventArgs e) {
   pthClip.AddEllipse(ClientRectangle);
   regClip = new Region(pthClip);
}
```

Your `Region` is now properly initialized. We can create the beginning of your `OnPaint` method like so:

```
protected override void OnPaint(PaintEventArgs e) {
   e.Graphics.Clip = regClip;
   ...
}
```

Now anything you draw using this `Graphics` object will be constrained to the inside of the outer eye.

There's one more catch we have to watch for. Remember we said that the `ClientRectangle` is governed by the `Size` property. But what if the user doesn't set it in her code? Then the `ClientRectangle` will be nothing, and your control won't display on screen. You need to initialize the `Size` property, and thus the `ClientRectangle`, in your constructor, just in case:

```
this.Size = new Size(100,100);
```

Changing Brush Colors

Next let's examine how to get the eye to be bloodshot. We'll keep things simple, and just color the outer eye red as necessary. The degree of redness will be determined by the `Bloodshotedness` property. Recall that the internal variable `intBlood` is an integer, however, and you can't specify a red color (or any color, for that matter) from a single integer. Therefore, you'll have to transform this integer into a percentage-of-redness value. For example, when the user writes the following code, your eye should be 100% red:

```
objEye.BloodShotedness = 100;
```

Similarly, the following would make it 50% red:

```
objEye.BloodShotedness = 50;
```

To perform this calculation, you need to know a bit about color. Most people know that colors are composed of three primary ingredients: red, green, and blue (typically abbreviated as RGB). The actual color of an object is determined by the mix of these components. For a typical palette, these component values can range from 0 to 255. So a color with RGB values of 255, 255, and 255 will be white; 0, 0, and 0 will be black; 0, 255, 0 will be pure green, and so on. To get our percentage of redness, you'll need to decrease the concentrations of the green and blue values equally. Now we're ready to create the `Bloodshotedness` property. It should look like the following:

```
public int BloodShotedness {
   get { return intBlood; }
   set {
      intBlood = value;
      clrBlood = Color.FromArgb(255,
➥255 - (int)(255 * (intBlood / 100.0)),
➥255 - (int)(255 * (intBlood / 100.0)));
      Invalidate();
   }
}
```

We've declared a new private `Color` object called `clrBlood` that will be used to draw with. The `FromArgb` method allows you to create a color based on the RGB components. Since our eye will range in color from pure white to pure red, the R component in our color should always be 255. The green and blue values will need to decrease as the bloodshotedness increases.

Here's the math: the `intBlood` property is supposed to represent a percentage value, so you divide it by 100 to get the percent:

```
intBlood / 100.0
```

(We specify 100.0 instead of 100 because we need the result to be a floating-point value instead of a rounded-down integer.) Next, you need to determine what percentage of the result is of 255, the max color value:

```
255 * (intBlood / 100.0)
```

For example, if the `intBlood` value was 50, the first calculation would give us .5 (which equals 50%), and the second calculation would give us 127.5. This equates to half, which is what we want.

Finally, you subtract this value from the max color value, 255. The result is that now the green and blue values decrease by a percentage of 255 when the bloodshotedness increases. Figure 18.4 shows a very bloodshot eye.

So we can now add a new line to the `OnPaint` method that uses your new `Color` object to fill the interior of your eye:

```
protected override void OnPaint(PaintEventArgs e) {
   e.Graphics.Clip = regClip;
   e.Graphics.FillEllipse(new SolidBrush(clrBlood),
➥ClientRectangle);
   ...
}
```

18

Figure 18.4

A very mad eye.

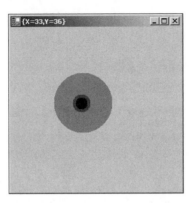

We need to translate mouse coordinates into eyeball position. In the next section, you'll see how to do this using some math tricks.

Translating Coordinates

How can we transform the mouse coordinates into the eye position? This one's a bit complicated. We'll use the Update method, which was the event handler for the Timer's Elapsed event. A few pages back we saw that it looked like this:

```
private void Update(Object Sender,
➥System.Timers.ElapsedEventArgs e) {
    ptPosition = Cursor.Position;

    Invalidate();
}
```

What happens if we leave it like this and try to draw the eye using ptPosition? The mouse cursor obviously has a larger range of movement than the control has dimensions. In other words, a typical screen would measure 800 pixels wide by 600 pixels high. This means the cursor can move from (0,0) to (799,599). Our control, by default, is only 100 by 100. We need to scale the upper range down to our control's size, and if you guessed "by using percentages," you guessed right.

We need to divide the monitor's width and height by our control's width and height, which will give us the proper range of values. This is done with the following code in the Update method:

```
ptPosition = Cursor.Position;

ptPosition.X /= (Screen.PrimaryScreen.Bounds.Width /
➥ClientRectangle.Width);
```

The Screen class represents a monitor, and the PrimaryScreen property represents the monitor currently in use. Bounds returns a rectangle representing the monitor. You divide this width by the width of our control (specified by the ClientRectangle).

What happens here? If the user's mouse cursor is currently at the point (800,0), then this formula gives 800 divided by 100 = 80. Likewise, a cursor position of (0,0) translates to 0 divided by 100 = 0. Both of these X-coordinate values—and everything in between—fit perfectly into the width of our 100 by 100 control.

Note — This formula certainly isn't precise, and the resulting eye may not move *exactly* with the cursor, but the approximation is close enough for our needs.

The same thing is done for the Y coordinates:

```
ptPosition.Y /= (Screen.PrimaryScreen.Bounds.Height /
➥ClientRectangle.Height);
```

There's one more catch (isn't there always?). Remember that a drawing's upper-left corner is placed at the Point value. In this situation, if the ptPosition.X value happens to be 0, we're fine. But what if it is 100, the width of our control? The eye will be drawn *outside* the eye (but since we have our clipping Region set, it simply won't be drawn at all). We need to take into account the width of the eye, and move the X and Y coordinates back accordingly, to make sure it isn't drawn outside the boundaries. We do this by comparing the X and Y coordinates with the ClientRectangle:

```
if (ptPosition.X > ClientRectangle.Width-30) {
    ptPosition.X = ClientRectangle.Width-30;
}

if (ptPosition.Y > ClientRectangle.Height-30) {
    ptPosition.Y = ClientRectangle.Height-30;
}
```

This code essentially says that if the position is greater than the width of our control *minus the width of the eye*, set the position to the width of the control *minus the width of the eye*. This way, the eye never goes past the edge.

Finally, remember that we wanted to raise our custom event every time the eye position moved. The last step is to call the OnEyeMoved method (note the capital O) to raise the event, and then call the Invalidate method:

```
OnEyeMoved(EventArgs.Empty);
Invalidate();
```

18

Our OnPaint method now looks like this:

```
protected override void OnPaint(PaintEventArgs e) {
    e.Graphics.Clip = regClip;
    e.Graphics.FillEllipse(new SolidBrush(clrBlood), ClientRectangle);

    e.Graphics.FillEllipse(new SolidBrush(clrIris),
➥new Rectangle(ptPosition.X, ptPosition.Y, 30, 30));
    e.Graphics.FillEllipse(Brushes.Black,
➥new Rectangle(ptPosition.X+5, ptPosition.Y+5, 20, 20));
}
```

You have two new ellipses here. The first represents the iris, and is drawn using the clrIris Color (that can be set by the user) and modified ptPosition point values. The second ellipse represents the pupil and is drawn inside the iris using a Black brush. Let's put it all together.

Putting It All Together

There were a lot of little pieces with this custom control. Let's recap.

First, you created your properties using the property declaration syntax. Then you used a Timer to update the position of the eyeball every tenth of a second. You created a custom delegate and event to be raised when the eye is moved.

Next you created your clipping Region (after some careful examination of handles). The bloodshotedness was specified using a custom RGB color. Finally, you transformed the mouse coordinates to more appropriate control coordinates. Take a deep breath—Listing 18.3 shows the entire code.

LISTING **18.3**   Your Custom Eyeball

```
1:   using System;
2:   using System.Windows.Forms;
3:   using System.Drawing;
4:   using System.Drawing.Drawing2D;
5:
6:   namespace TYWinforms.Day18.Controls {
7:       public class EyeControl : Control {
8:           private Point ptPosition;
9:           private Color clrIris;
10:          private int intBlood;
11:          private Color clrBlood;
12:          private System.Timers.Timer objTimer = new
➥System.Timers.Timer();
13:          private EventHandler onEyeMoved;
14:          private GraphicsPath pthClip = new GraphicsPath();
15:          private Region regClip;
```

LISTING 18.3 continued

```
16:
17:        public Point PupilPosition {
18:            get { return ptPosition; }
19:            set {
20:                ptPosition = value;
21:                Invalidate();
22:            }
23:        }
24:
25:        public Color IrisColor {
26:            get { return clrIris; }
27:            set {
28:                clrIris = value;
29:                Invalidate();
30:            }
31:        }
32:
33:        public int BloodShotedness {
34:            get { return intBlood; }
35:            set {
36:                intBlood = value;
37:                clrBlood = Color.FromArgb(255,
➡255 - (int)(255*(intBlood/100.0)),
➡255 - (int)(255*(intBlood/100.0)));
38:                Invalidate();
39:            }
40:        }
41:
42:        public EyeControl() {
43:            ptPosition = new Point(0,0);
44:            intBlood = 0;
45:            clrBlood = Color.White;
46:            clrIris = Color.Blue;
47:
48:            objTimer.Interval = 100;
49:            objTimer.Elapsed += new
➡System.Timers.ElapsedEventHandler(this.Update);
50:            objTimer.Enabled = true;
51:
52:            this.Size = new Size(100,100);
53:            this.HandleCreated += new EventHandler
➡ (this.SetBounds);
54:        }
55:
56:        public event EventHandler EyeMoved {
57:            add { onEyeMoved += value; }
58:            remove { onEyeMoved -= value; }
59:        }
60:
```

LISTING 18.3 continued

```
61:         private void SetBounds(Object Sender, EventArgs e) {
62:             pthClip.AddEllipse(ClientRectangle);
63:             regClip = new Region(pthClip);
64:         }
65:
66:         private void Update(Object Sender,
➥System.Timers.ElapsedEventArgs e) {
67:             ptPosition = Cursor.Position;
68:
69:             ptPosition.X /= (Screen.PrimaryScreen.Bounds.Width
➥ / ClientRectangle.Width);
70:             ptPosition.Y /= (Screen.PrimaryScreen.Bounds.Height
➥ / ClientRectangle.Height);
71:
72:             if (ptPosition.X > ClientRectangle.Width-30) {
73:                 ptPosition.X = ClientRectangle.Width-30;
74:             }
75:
76:             if (ptPosition.Y > ClientRectangle.Height-30) {
77:                 ptPosition.Y = ClientRectangle.Height-30;
78:             }
79:
80:             OnEyeMoved(EventArgs.Empty);
81:             Invalidate();
82:         }
83:
84:         protected virtual void OnEyeMoved(EventArgs e) {
85:             if (onEyeMoved != null) {
86:                 onEyeMoved(this, e);
87:             }
88:         }
89:
90:         protected override void OnPaint(PaintEventArgs e) {
91:             e.Graphics.Clip = regClip;
92:             e.Graphics.FillEllipse(new SolidBrush(clrBlood),
➥ClientRectangle);
93:
94:             e.Graphics.FillEllipse(new SolidBrush(clrIris),
➥new Rectangle(ptPosition.X, ptPosition.Y, 30, 30));
95:             e.Graphics.FillEllipse(Brushes.Black, new
➥Rectangle(ptPosition.X+5, ptPosition.Y+5, 20, 20));
96:         }
97:     }
98: }
```

ANALYSIS Let's take one more tour of the code. All of the internal private variables are declared on lines 8–15, including the clipping region, colors used by bloodshot-edness and iris, and event delegate.

Lines 17–40 are the public properties—the properties that users can set from their code. PupilPosition and IrisColor are simple, but the Bloodshotedness property uses a bit of math to transform a percentage value into an actual color. Each of these properties calls the Invalidate method to redraw the eye.

Line 42 starts the constructor. The internal variables are all initialized (including the Size property), and the timer is set up and started. Event handlers are specified for the timer and HandleCreated events.

The custom EyeMoved event is declared on lines 56–59. This code is similar to the property declaration syntax, and simply assigns or removes an event handler from your delegate.

The event handler for the HandleCreated event, SetBounds, is on lines 61–64. Here, after your control has received a handle, you initialize the clipping region.

The Update method on line 66 is the event handler for the Timer control. It starts by retrieving the current position of the mouse cursor, and then translates that to coordinates that fit inside your control. The series of if statements on lines 72–78 ensures that the iris and pupil are never drawn on the outside of the control by taking into account the width and height of the iris. Line 80 calls the OnEyeMoved method, which simply raises the EyeMoved event.

On line 84 you declare the OnEyeMoved event, whose sole responsibility is to raise the EyeMoved event.

Finally, the overridden OnPaint method on line 90 draws the outer eye, the iris, and the pupil, taking into account the various properties set earlier in the code. These include the redness of the outer eye, the color of the iris, and the translated position of the iris and pupil.

Whew! But you're not quite done—you need to put your control to use in an application. We'll tackle that in the next section.

The control we developed here was relatively complex. In contrast, the simplest custom control can consist of only an overridden OnPaint method. To get something really useful, though, you need to incorporate properties and events.

This control could be made more useful as well. For example, you could change the shape of the iris and pupil depending on the position of the cursor, so that it appears foreshortened and more 3D. Or you could add a blink or stare method, where the eye would stop following the cursor until called to start again. Once you know the basics of creating custom controls, the only limit to the functionality you can add is your imagination.

18

Using Custom Controls in Windows Forms

Now that you have your custom control, compile it into an assembly with the following command:

```
csc /t:library /r:system.dll /r:system.windows.forms.dll
➥/r:system.drawing.dll listing18.3.cs
```

The last step is to create a regular Windows Forms application that uses your control. Remember, all the hard work is done already. You can use your custom control in any application just as you would use a TextBox, or ComboBox. Listing 18.4 shows an example.

LISTING 18.4   Putting Your Eye to Use

```
1:  using System;
2:  using System.Windows.Forms;
3:  using System.Drawing;
4:  using TYWinforms.Day18.Controls;
5:
6:  namespace TYWinforms.Day18 {
7:     public class Listing184 : Form {
8:        private EyeControl objEye = new EyeControl();
9:
10:       public Listing184() {
11:          objEye.EyeMoved += new EventHandler(this.Go);
12:          objEye.Location = new Point(75,75);
13:          objEye.BloodShotedness = 0;
14:
15:          this.Controls.Add(objEye);
16:          this.Text = "Listing 18.4";
17:       }
18:
19:       private void Go(Object Sender, EventArgs e) {
20:          this.Text = objEye.PupilPosition.ToString();
21:       }
22:
23:       public static void Main() {
24:          Application.Run(new Listing184());
25:       }
26:    }
27:  }
```

ANALYSIS Your eye control is created on line 8. Its properties are initialized on lines 12 and 13, and an event handler is assigned on line 11. The Go method on lines 19–21 simply updates the caption of the application with the PupilPosition property of your control.

Figure 18.5 shows an example of the output.

FIGURE 18.5

Private eye...watching you.

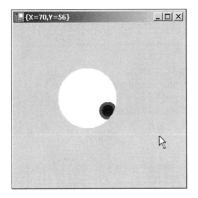

Creating Custom Controls from Existing Controls

Sometimes you don't need the flexibility of creating a control from scratch. Perhaps most of the functionality you need is already encapsulated in another, existing control, but you need just "a little bit extra." In these cases, you have two options: you can enhance an existing control or create a new control by combining existing ones. The first method is known as simply extending a control, and the latter is known as a composite, or user control.

Let's take a look at these two methods. Don't worry—neither method is as complex as creating a control from scratch!

Extending Existing Controls

I mentioned earlier today that one control that is often desired is a Button where the text is directly editable by the keyboard. In other words, a user could simply type characters, and the text in the Button would change in response. For this situation, you don't need to create a completely new control—after all, the complexity of drawing a button is already done for you. Why reinvent the wheel?

To add the editable-text functionality, you simply create a new class that inherits from the existing Button class, rather than from the Control class directly. Listing 18.5 shows the code you need.

18

LISTING 18.5   A Custom Button

```
1:  using System;
2:  using System.Windows.Forms;
3:  using System.Drawing;
4:  using System.Drawing.Drawing2D;
5:
6:  namespace TYWinforms.Day18.Controls {
7:     public class CustomButton : Button {
8:        private String strText;
9:        private Boolean blnEdit = false;
10:
11:        protected override void OnMouseDown
➥ (MouseEventArgs e) {
12:           if (e.Button == MouseButtons.Right) {
13:              blnEdit = !blnEdit;
14:              strText = "";
15:           } else {
16:              base.OnMouseDown(e);
17:           }
18:        }
19:
20:        protected override void OnKeyPress
➥(KeyPressEventArgs e) {
21:           if (blnEdit) {
22:              strText += e.KeyChar;
23:              this.Text = strText;
24:           }
25:        }
26:     }
27:  }
```

ANALYSIS   We need two things here: a variable that can tell us whether or not we're in "edit" mode, and a string to contain the characters the user will type. These variables are declared on lines 8 and 9.

When the user right-clicks the button, we want to override the default behavior and go into edit mode. This is easy enough: line 11 overrides the OnMouseDown method. We use the MouseEventArgs parameter to determine which mouse key was pressed. If it was the right mouse button, you flip the blnEdit Boolean on line 13 and clear the text currently in the button on line 14. Otherwise, you simply perform the default behavior by calling base.OnMouseDown(e). Initially, blnEdit is false, meaning that the edit mode is turned off. The code on line 13 sets blnEdit to true the first time the button is clicked, and back to false when the button is clicked again.

We also need to be able to retrieve keyboard input. This is normally done with the KeyPress event, and this case is no different. We override the default OnKeyPress method on line 20, and if edit mode is on, we catch the key press, accumulate it in the `strText` string, and then display it in the button using the `Text` property.

In this case, we don't even need to override the `OnPaint` method. When you set the `Text` property to a value (as on line 23), the control automatically raises the `Paint` method and displays whatever is specified in `Text`, which is exactly what we want.

Figure 18.6 shows example output after the user has entered some text.

FIGURE **18.6**

The user can enter text directly into the `Button`.

Creating User Controls

Creating a new control by combining other controls is even easier than extending an existing control, because you don't need to create or override any `OnPaint` methods. This type of control, composed of two or more other controls, is known as a composite control, or more often, a user control.

A user control is another level of encapsulation in the .NET Framework. If you have a set of controls that you often use together—a registration form, for instance—then it makes sense to combine those controls into one so that you can hide the complexity of creating them individually. Since this type of task always does the same thing, you can easily wrap up the functionality in a custom control.

Think of a user control as a Windows Form that you can use in other Windows Forms. The user control is essentially a piece of UI that is more complex than a single Windows Form control. Listing 18.6 shows a simple example of a user control combining two `TextBoxes` and a `Button`.

LISTING 18.6   A Registration User Control

```
1:  Imports System
2:  Imports System.Drawing
3:  Imports System.Windows.Forms
4:
5:  namespace TYWinforms.Day18.Controls
6:     public class LoginForm : Inherits UserControl
7:        private lblUsername As New Label()
8:        private lblPassword As New Label()
9:        private tbUsername As New TextBox()
10:        private tbPassword As New TextBox()
11:        private btSubmit As New Button()
12:
13:        public sub New()
14:           lblUsername.Text = "Username: "
15:           lblUsername.Width = 70
16:           lblUsername.Location = new Point(10,10)
17:
18:           lblPassword.Text = "Password: "
19:           lblPassword.Width = 70
20:           lblPassword.Location = new Point(10,40)
21:
22:           tbUsername.Location = new Point(80,10)
23:           tbPassword.Location = new Point(80,40)
24:
25:           btSubmit.Text = "Submit"
26:           btSubmit.Location = new Point(50,70)
27:           AddHandler btSubmit.Click, new EventHandler
➡(AddressOf Me.Register)
28:
29:           Me.BackColor = Color.Beige
30:           Me.Size = new Size(190,100)
31:           Me.Controls.Add(lblUsername)
32:           Me.Controls.Add(lblPassword)
33:           Me.Controls.Add(tbUsername)
34:           Me.Controls.Add(tbPassword)
35:           Me.Controls.Add(btSubmit)
36:        end sub
37:
38:        private sub Register(Sender As Object,
➡e As EventArgs)
39:           MessageBox.Show(tbUsername.Text &
➡" has registered!")
40:        end sub
41:     end class
42:  end namespace
```

ANALYSIS At first glance, this listing looks exactly like a regular Windows Forms application, without a Main method. It creates a few controls on lines 7–11, initializes them in the constructor on lines 14–27, sets some general properties for the class on lines 29–36, and has an event handler for the Button.Click event on lines 38–40. This control is exactly like a Windows Forms class...almost.

Notice line 6. Instead of inheriting from the Form class, we inherit from UserControl. The UserControl class behaves both like a Form and a Control. It can contain other controls like a Form, but is itself a control that can be placed on a Form. Thus, if you know how to make Windows Forms classes, you can make user controls.

Compile this as an assembly with the following command:

```
vbc /t:library /r:system.dll /r:system.drawing.dll
➥/r:system.windows.forms.dll listing18.6.vb
```

Listing 18.7 shows a very simple application that uses this user control.

LISTING 18.7 Using the User Control

```
1:  using System;
2:  using System.Windows.Forms;
3:  using System.Drawing;
4:  using TYWinforms.Day18.Controls;
5:
6:  namespace TYWinforms.Day18 {
7:     public class Listing187 : Form {
8:        private LoginForm objFrm = new LoginForm();
9:
10:       public Listing187() {
11:          objFrm.Location = new Point(75,75);
12:
13:          this.Controls.Add(objFrm);
14:       }
15:
16:       public static void Main() {
17:          Application.Run(new Listing187());
18:       }
19:    }
20:  }
```

Again, there's nothing out of the ordinary here. Listing 18.7 is just another run-of-the-mill Windows Forms application that happens to use your LoginForm user control.

But wait a second. Listing 18.7 is in C#, but Listing 18.6 is in VB.NET. Here's another great thing about user controls and encapsulation. The controls you create (user controls

or otherwise) don't have to be in the same language as the containing application! This is
the CLR at work—enabling cross-language components to work together. Figure 18.7
shows the output from Listing 18.7.

FIGURE 18.7

*A user control encap-
sulates the complexity
of its component con-
trols.*

All of the controls we declared in Listing 18.6 were private. This is generally a good idea
for user controls because you don't want the end-user messing with the internal workings
of your control. After all, that's why you encapsulated them as a user control in the first
place.

That doesn't mean, however, that you can't create custom properties, methods, or events
just like the custom controls earlier today. In fact, often times it is necessary. With
Listing 18.6, for example, instead of handling the Click method internally, the user control could have created a custom event that passed the Click event to the containing
application. That way, the creator of the application could determine exactly what should
happen when the end-user clicks the Submit button—enter data into a database, for
example.

To do this in Listing 18.6, you'd only need to add the following code:

```
public event Registered(Sender As Object,
➡username as String, password as String)

Protected Sub OnRegistered()
    RaiseEvent Registered(Me, tbUsername.Text, tbPassword.Text)
End Sub
```

Declare your event (Registered, in this case) with the parameters you want to pass to
the containing application, and then create the corresponding OnEventName method that
raises the event. VB.NET handles everything else for you (in C#, you would have to create a custom event handler class that takes the three parameters used here, but VB.NET

does it for you—see Day 5, "Handling Events in Your Windows Forms," for more information).

To take advantage of your event, add the following code to the constructor in Listing 18.7:

```
objFrm.Registered += new LoginForm.RegisteredEventHandler
➥(this.RegisterMe);
```

Then create the `RegisterMe` method:

```
private void RegisterMe (Object Sender, String username,
➥String password) {
   MessageBox.Show ("Registered " + username);
}
```

User controls allow you to create custom interfaces and pass those to other developers without worrying that they'll mess around with your code and change your hard work—especially if you are a C# coder and the other developers code in VB.NET!

Summary

We covered a lot of material today, but it went by fairly quickly. You learned about three behind-the-scenes ways to enhance your applications: build custom controls, extend existing controls, and create user controls.

The base class for any control is the `Control` class. If you need to create your own controls, be sure to derive from `Control`. `Control` comes pre-filled with many properties, methods, and events that you can take advantage of, but you can easily create your own if none of the built-ins suits your needs.

We learned in the custom control you developed today that creating custom functionality is often more difficult than you first think. The eyeball control had a lot of little issues that needed to be addressed to form the whole. With careful planning, however, you shouldn't come across any unexpected problems.

To extend an existing control, you simply need to inherit from it instead of from the `Control` class directly. Since all controls inherit from `Control`, you are still inheriting from it as well, although indirectly. If you want to maintain the existing control's visual display, make sure that you call the `base.OnPaint` method.

Finally, user controls act just like Windows Forms classes. The only difference is that you inherit from the `UserControl` class instead of `Form`, which allows your user controls to be placed on `Form`s.

18

Today's lesson highlighted a number of key concepts of the .NET Framework, namely encapsulation, extensibility, and reusability. Being able to create your own controls from other controls or from scratch is an excellent way to create unique applications.

Tomorrow you'll examine creating multithreaded applications—a powerful, though complex, technique for increasing your applications' performance.

Q&A

Q Can I be notified when one of my control's properties change? For example, when the `PupilPosition` property is updated by the user?

A Yes, you can. When a property changes in your control, the `PropertyChanged` event is raised. You can attach an event handler to this event, or override the `OnPropertyChanged` method to perform some custom code when a property changes.

The corresponding `PropertyChangedEventArgs` object has a property named `PropertyName`, that tells you what property has changed.

Workshop

This workshop helps reinforce the concepts covered today. It is very helpful to understand fully the answers before moving on. Answers can be found in Appendix A.

Quiz

1. What are the four steps of creating a custom control?
2. What method must you call to redraw your control?
3. Write an example of a public property in C# using the property declaration syntax.
4. Write an example of a public property in VB.NET using the property declaration syntax.
5. Which happens first: a handle is created, or your control is displayed on screen. Why?
6. True or false? You can inherit from a `RichTextBox` control.
7. Name three benefits of creating user controls.

Exercise

Create a thermostat custom control that displays the current temperature in a mercury-style thermometer. Remember to not allow the temperature to go above the maximum or below 0. Implement it in a Windows Form application and provide buttons for the user to turn the temperature up and down. (Of course, this will all be made up since you can't determine the actual temperature, but you get the point.)

18

WEEK 3

DAY 19

Creating Multithreaded Applications

Threading is a complex topic that's often left for advanced treatments. However, it is a useful tool that can greatly enhance the performance and usability of your Windows Forms applications and, therefore, should be given adequate treatment here.

A thread is the basic unit to which a computer executes instructions. Having multiple threads allows you to take advantage of the speed of your CPU and the parallel nature of your operating system to execute things quickly and efficiently. In high-level terms, you can practically double your performance by doubling your threads.

Today you'll learn exactly what threads are, and what it means to execute more than one at a time. By the end of today, you'll have conquered the stigma that is often associated with multithreaded applications.

Today you will learn

- What exactly a thread is, and what it means to your CPU
- How threads work in Windows
- How to create new threads and manage them
- What cross-thread call marshalling is
- How to take advantage of thread pools
- How to safely communicate between multiple threads with synchronization
- How to create a fully multithreaded application

Introduction to Multithreading

Before you learn about multithreading, you need to know about plain-old regular threading and processes, and how they work with your operating system. Threading and processes are the operating system's way of dividing tasks up so they can be accomplished more efficiently. A process is an operating system's way of separating applications from each other; a single application typically represents a single process. A thread is a single "line of execution." A single thread is responsible for handling all commands from a single task. In technical terms, a thread is the basic execution unit to which an operating system allocates resources. Typically, a single thread is created per process.

Suppose, for example, that you are the owner of a new restaurant that's just getting off the ground. Right now, you are the only employee. When a customer comes in, you are the only person available to do everything that needs to be done, including cooking the food, mixing drinks, serving, and cleaning up. You must finish one task before you can start another. This certainly isn't the best way to do things. Both you and your customers suffer because you're spreading yourself too thin.

In computer terms, this would be a single-threaded environment. There is one thread (you) to do all the tasks that are required. Go back a decade and recall a classic single-threaded operating system: DOS. In DOS, you could only have one application running at any given time because DOS only had one thread to devote to its tasks; one thread that can execute things one at a time. When a thread is executing a task, the whole system has to halt and wait for it to finish, before the user can do anything again. In short, DOS was a one process OS with one thread for the process.

Let's imagine the CPU in this situation. The CPU can only process one thing at a time (this is generally true even today). When you do something in an application—for instance, click a button—the operating system receives your input, translates it into something the computer can understand (bits and bytes), and sends the command to the CPU. If the CPU has other things it needs to do first, the new command must wait in line. As the CPU processes one command, it spits out the result, and moves onto the next command, until there are no more. When the CPU isn't doing anything, it is said to be in an idle state.

Fast forward to today. CPUs have become so powerful that they can process commands faster than they can come in. CPUs once measured in megahertz or slower (1 million cycles per second), are now measured in gigahertz (1 *billion* cycles per second). Any particular command can take from 1 to 5 cycles (or more, depending on the complexity of the command), so this translates to roughly anywhere from 200 million to 1 billion commands *per second*.

(This is a vast simplification of CPUs, and one button click does not necessarily translate into one CPU command (nor does it even translate to 100 CPU commands). The CPU has a lot things to do other than waiting for your clicks, so it can't really do 200 million things per second.)

Obviously, you can't issue 200 million commands per second to the CPU. The single-threaded environment was developed when CPU speed was limited so that commands issued in this way would occupy the CPU completely.

Enter multithreading. Modern operating systems have more than a single thread to accomplish tasks. In fact, Windows can have hundreds of threads going at once, and creates new ones as necessary.

Let's go back to the restaurant. Now your client base is growing larger, and you can't handle everything yourself, so you hire four more workers: a cook, a waiter, a busboy, and a concierge. Now you can do four things at once (five if you count yourself), satisfying a lot more customers in the process. More employees would make things even easier for you (see Figure 19.1).

19

FIGURE 19.1

A multithreaded environment provides many "waiters" that can accomplish tasks for you.

A Single-threaded Environment

A Multithreaded Environment

NEW TERM When you start an application such as Microsoft Word, a new process is created. A new thread is also created to handle all of the execution tasks for that process; it is allocated to handle all of Word's commands. Meanwhile, the OS is still running independent of this new thread, keeping your computer running properly. You are free to do what you need to do. If you start another application, such as Photoshop, another process and thread are created and handle that application. Now, two threads are running simultaneously: the Word thread and the Photoshop thread. You can easily switch between the two threads because they run independently of one another. This is very important: threads do not mess with other threads. If they do, some unpredictable results occur—we'll discuss this situation in the next section, "Problems with Threading."

Once again, let's look at the CPU. Before, it was executing one command at a time so quickly that you couldn't keep up. Now, the CPU is still executing commands one at a time, but because you have multiple processes (and threads) running at once, the CPU is constantly kept busy. Each thread can issue its own commands to the CPU. In the two-thread situation described previously, the CPU has two data feeds that fill the queue with commands waiting to be executed. But since the CPU executes commands so quickly, even these two feeds are not enough to bog it down, and it executes commands and spits out results very quickly. This is why it appears that you can run multiple things at once on your computer, although the CPU is actually only doing one thing at a time.

So now you know about multithreaded operating systems and how the CPU handles them. But wait, it gets better! The threading doesn't have to stop with single threads—in other words, just like the OS can have multiple processes, each process can have multiple threads.

The focus of today's lesson isn't the multithreaded operating system, but multithreaded *applications*. A single application can have multiple threads devoted to it, increasing the application's efficiency. After all, if the CPU has time to spare, why not send it more commands?

In Microsoft Word, for example, you can have one thread devoted to processing user input from the keyboard and displaying it on screen. You could have another thread, working in the background, archiving files. Normally, you'd have to stop writing while the archiving is taking place, but with multithreading capabilities, Word can have one thread devoted to each task, and you never have to stop working! Figure 19.2 illustrates this concept.

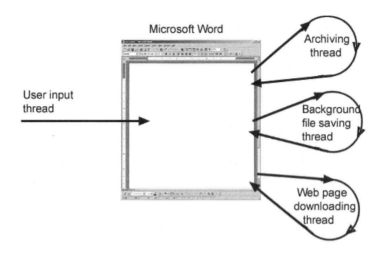

FIGURE 19.2

With multiple threads, a single application can accomplish many things at once.

A more common example deals with the Internet. Web sites are getting more and more complex, and sometimes take quite a bit of time to download, no matter what kind of connection speed you have. Unfortunately, your Web browser, which represents a single process, can't do anything but wait while the Web pages download; this is an unavoidable situation. If you introduce a multithreaded browser, however, you can download from multiple sites at once, and assuming you have enough bandwidth in your connection, you can get two Web pages for the price (which, here, is time) of one! It still takes the same amount of time to download a single page, but in that same amount of time, you could download 2, 3, or even 10 pages at once.

Let's go back to the restaurant analogy one last time. Each of your employees runs his own "application." The waiter runs a waiting program, the busboy runs a cleaning program, and so on. Suppose you hire one more waiter, busboy, and concierge. Now you have two waiters running the waiting program. Just as having more people to run your restaurant is more efficient than having one, having more people to wait on tables is equally more efficient, as long as there is room enough in your restaurant.

So let's recap. A thread is a line of execution, a unit that is responsible for executing commands for a single application. A multithreaded operating system is one that can have multiple threads running at once, one to handle each application or process that is currently executing. And a multithreaded application has multiple threads assigned to it, to perform multiple tasks within the application at once.

Now that you know the benefits of multithreading, let's look at a few drawbacks.

19

Problems with Threading

The first drawback that comes to mind is obviously lack of resources. Specifically, the more threads you have, the more resources you're going to use. And your computer isn't an infinite well of resources; you have to work within the boundaries of the CPU, the memory, and so on.

Adding a second thread to a particular task does not necessarily mean a two-fold increase in performance, unfortunately. The performance gain versus resource usage may not be a one-to-one mapping. This is because the computer requires resources just to maintain each thread. Therefore, when you create a new thread, you not only need resources to perform the tasks required of the thread, but also some additional overhead resources just to make sure the thread is working properly. In addition, when the CPU switches between threads, it has to "remember" the state of each thread, so that it knows where to pick up again when it comes back to that thread. All of these requirements may eat more in resources than your thread gives back in performance.

Another problem deals with thread communication. It's often necessary for one thread to talk with another, especially when both of those threads belong to the same application. Because threads are isolated from one another, and each has its own set of resources, this can be an issue. Threads have to perform special procedures to ensure that their data is safe enough to travel across thread borders into another thread's territory. This can eat up performance as well.

An even bigger issue is when two or more threads need to share the same set of data. Suppose you have two Microsoft Word threads running at once, accessing the same file. What happens when one thread modifies the file? The data contained in the other thread is no longer valid, and must be updated. And if the two threads try to work on the same file at the exact same time, you'll end up with problems, and your application may crash.

Because of this, threads can "lock" their resources. In other words, when a thread is using a particular resource, it lets all other threads know not to try using the same resource. These locks also eat up resources and decrease performance, but they are necessary. Other threads should obey locks, but aren't required to do so.

Using threads isn't all bad, however, as you know from the previous section. Creating multithreading applications requires some careful planning, and can often provide more benefits than drawbacks.

Do	**Don't**
Do consider multithreading when you are able to take the precautions necessary to avoid the issues described previously, when it is necessary to provide fast responses in your applications, or to give your user greater control while other tasks are going on.	**Don't** use multithreading when you don't know ahead of time how resource intensive your applications will be, or how resource-limited your target system is.

Using Threading Objects

The most important threading class used in the .NET Framework is the `System.Threading.Thread` class (those Microsoft guys sure are sticklers for the obvious). The `Thread` class represents a single thread currently running in the operating system, and has a number of properties and methods that can give you information on what's currently happening with that thread. We'll examine it further in a moment.

When you start your application, a new `Thread` is created (or taken from a thread pool) and assigned to that application. That thread remains responsible for executing the application's tasks for the lifetime of the application. This thread is known as the main thread because it is always the central thread in your application, no matter how many additional ones you create.

Working with a `Thread` object is a bit different than anything we've covered so far. We'll wait for a full discussion until the next section, but for now, you should know that a thread must have something to execute; there must be some code for the thread to process, or it won't do anything. This is kind of like specifying an event handler for a Windows Forms control. The main thread in your application has the `Main` method to keep it occupied (which, in turn, calls the constructor of your application, and so on).

19

`Thread` is the most important class we'll cover today, but it has quite a few helpers. `ThreadPool` is used to implement thread pooling—the process of sharing threads among applications. The `Timer` thread object is similar to the `System.Windows.Forms.Timer` class you've worked with. It allows you to execute a particular task on another thread at a specified interval. `Monitor` enables you to lock your resources to protect them from other threads.

We'll cover all of these classes in today's lesson, but first, let's look at exactly how to work with a thread.

Creating a Multithreaded Application

Before you build a fully multithreaded application, let's examine some properties of a single-threaded one first. Specifically, we'll take a look at what a normal thread looks like. Then, beginning with Listing 19.2, you'll start to add more threads.

Recall that when you start your Windows Forms application, a thread, known as the main thread, is created and assigned to your application. If it stops, your application stops. If it pauses, your application pauses. Thus, it is helpful to think of this thread as intimately tied to your application. Listing 19.1 shows a simple application that examines this main thread.

LISTING **19.1**   Examining a Thread

```
1:  using System;
2:  using System.Windows.Forms;
3:  using System.Drawing;
4:  using System.Threading;
5:
6:  namespace TYWinforms.Day19 {
7:     public class Listing191 : Form {
8:        private Label lblInfo = new Label();
9:
10:       public Listing191() {
11:          lblInfo.Size = new Size(300,300);
12:          lblInfo.Location = new Point(10,10);
13:
14:          Thread thdCurrent = Thread.CurrentThread;
15:          lblInfo.Text = "Is alive: " + thdCurrent.
➥IsAlive.ToString() + "\n";
16:          lblInfo.Text += "Is background: " + thdCurrent.
➥IsBackground.ToString() + "\n";
17:          lblInfo.Text += "Priority: " + thdCurrent.
➥Priority.ToString() + "\n";
18:          lblInfo.Text += "Thread state: " + thdCurrent.
➥ThreadState.ToString() + "\n";
19:
20:          this.Text = "Listing 19.1";
21:          this.Controls.Add(lblInfo);
22:       }
23:
24:       public static void Main() {
25:          Application.Run(new Listing191());
26:       }
27:    }
28: }
```

ANALYSIS This application creates a simple `Label` and displays a few properties of the main thread. On line 14 you retrieve a reference to the main thread. A new `Thread` object is created called `thdCurrent`, and the main thread is retrieved by using the static `CurrentThread` method of the `Thread` class. Lines 15–18 then display the properties of that thread.

`IsAlive`, on line 15, indicates if the thread is currently executing. Naturally, we'd expect the main thread to be running if your application is running, so this property should return `true`.

`IsBackground` on line 16 indicates if this thread is running in the background of your operating system. The difference between a background and foreground thread is that the latter is not necessary to keep an application running. In other words, a background thread executes things that are not necessary for the execution of your application (such as the spell-checker in Word). On the other hand, your application must have a foreground thread to keep running. Again, since the main thread represents your application itself, it must be a foreground thread, and `IsBackground` will return `false`.

A thread also has a priority assigned to it. This priority tells the operating system how much CPU time it should receive relative to other threads. For example, a thread that must accomplish its task quickly should have a high priority, causing the CPU to devote most of its time to it. The `Priority` property can be used to set or retrieve this value, and it uses a value from the `ThreadPriority` enumeration:

- `Highest`—Threads with the highest priority
- `AboveNormal`—Threads with second-highest priority
- `Normal`—Typical threads
- `BelowNormal`—The fourth highest priority, immediately below `Normal`
- `Lowest`—Threads with this priority will execute after all others

By default, threads are assigned the `Normal` priority, and our main thread is no different.

Finally, the `ThreadState` property on line 18 indicates the state a thread is currently in (similar to the `ServiceControllerStatus` property you learned about in Day 16, "Building Windows Services"). This property is dictated by values from the `ThreadState` enumeration:

- `Aborted`—The thread is stopped
- `AbortRequested`—The thread is still running, but a command has been sent to stop the thread
- `Background`—The thread is a background thread

19

- `Running`—The thread is currently executing
- `Stopped`—The thread is stopped (similar to `Aborted`)
- `StopRequested`—The thread has been issued a stop command (this value can only be used by the .NET Framework internally)
- `Suspended`—The thread is paused
- `SuspendRequested`—The thread has been issued a command to suspend
- `Unstarted`—The thread has been created but has not yet been started
- `WaitSleepJoin`—The thread is blocked, and therefore inaccessible, until a specified condition is met (which we'll examine in a moment)

You can guess that our main thread is most likely in the `Running` state after our application starts.

Figure 19.3 shows the output from Listing 19.1.

FIGURE 19.3

The properties for a typical main thread.

To create a new thread you need something for the thread to execute—in other words, a method. Think of this method as the event handler for the thread; as soon as a thread starts, this method is executed. The association between the method and the thread is handled with a `ThreadStart` delegate. For example,

```
Thread thdNewThread = new Thread(new ThreadStart(MyMethod));
```

`MyMethod` is the method that our new thread will execute once it starts running. The `ThreadStart` delegate is just like any other delegate that points an event to a method. If the `Thread` class had a `Start` event, the preceding line could be written as follows:

```
Thread thdNewThread = new Thread();
thdNewThread.Start += new ThreadStart(this.MyMethod);
```

Alas, the Thread class doesn't have a Start event that you can assign an event handler to, so the preceding two statements must be combined into one, as shown in the preceding single line of code.

To start executing the thread, call the Start method:

```
thdNewThread.Start();
```

The thread will not do anything until you call Start.

Now that you're familiar with a few basic properties of threads, let's look at a simple multithreaded application. Listing 19.2 shows an application that creates a new thread. This application demonstrates the idiosyncrasies of dealing with multiple threads in Windows Forms.

LISTING 19.2 Thread Order-of-Execution

```
 1:  using System;
 2:  using System.Windows.Forms;
 3:  using System.Drawing;
 4:  using System.Threading;
 5:
 6:  namespace TYWinforms.Day19 {
 7:     public class Listing192 : Form {
 8:        private Label lblInfo = new Label();
 9:        private Button btStart = new Button();
10:
11:        public Listing192() {
12:           lblInfo.Size = new Size(300,100);
13:           lblInfo.Location = new Point(10,75);
14:
15:           btStart.Location = new Point(100,10);
16:           btStart.Text = "Start!";
17:           btStart.Click += new EventHandler(this.StartIt);
18:
19:           Thread.CurrentThread.Name = "Main thread";
20:
21:           this.Text = "Listing 19.2";
22:           this.Controls.Add(lblInfo);
23:           this.Controls.Add(btStart);
24:        }
25:
26:        private void StartIt(Object Sender, EventArgs e) {
27:           lblInfo.Text = "Thread 2 started from " +
➥Thread.CurrentThread.Name + "...\n";
28:
29:           Thread thdTest = new Thread(new
➥ThreadStart(DoIt));
30:           thdTest.Name = "Thread 2";
```

LISTING 19.2   continued

```
31:
32:            thdTest.Start();
33:            lblInfo.Text += Thread.CurrentThread.Name +
➥" sleeping...\n";
34:            Thread.Sleep(2000);
35:            lblInfo.Text += Thread.CurrentThread.Name +
➥" waking...\n";
36:            thdTest.Join();
37:
38:            lblInfo.Text += "Thread 2 ended...\n";
39:        }
40:
41:        private void DoIt() {
42:            Thread.Sleep(1000);
43:            MessageBox.Show(Thread.CurrentThread.Name);
44:            lblInfo.Text += "Hello from " +
➥Thread.CurrentThread.Name + "\n";
45:        }
46:
47:        public static void Main() {
48:            Application.Run(new Listing192());
49:        }
50:    }
51: }
```

ANALYSIS   The constructor on lines 11–24 sets up a Label and Button control. The Button will be used to create a new thread. The main thread's Name property is set on line 19 to "Main Thread." This will help us refer to the main thread later.

Let's look at the Button's event handler, StartIt, on line 26. This method is rather complex, so for now, we'll just examine the syntax; we'll get to the actual functionality in a moment. The first thing this method does is write some text to our label. On line 29, a new Thread is created that will execute the DoIt method. Its name is set on line 30, and it is started on line 32.

Some more text is displayed in the label, and the Sleep method is called. This method pauses the current thread for the specified amount of time (in milliseconds). Some text is written to the label again on line 35, then the mysterious Join method is called on line 36, and finally, some more text is displayed on line 38. Join causes the current thread to wait until another thread is finished doing whatever it's supposed to do. For example, on line 36, the main thread will wait until thread 2 is finished processing, and then it will resume its own execution. Because you call Join on line 36, the main thread must wait until thread 2 finishes its duties. In this case, it must wait until a MessageBox is shown and closed before it can continue.

The DoIt method on line 41 is rather simple; it makes the current thread sleep for one second, displays a MessageBox, and then displays some text.

When you run this application and click the button, you get the following output in the label:

```
(1 second passes)
(MessageBox displays with text "Thread 2")
(application waits until MessageBox is closed)
Thread 2 started from Main Thread...
Main thread sleeping...
Main thread waking...
Hello from Thread 2
Thread 2 ended...
```

Okay, so what happened here? Theoretically, the order of execution is displayed in Figure 19.4.

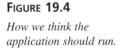

FIGURE **19.4**

How we think the application should run.

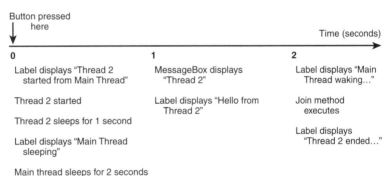

If the flow chart in Figure 19.4 were correct, we would expect the following output:

```
Thread 2 started from Main Thread...
Main thread sleeping...
(1 second passes)
(MessageBox displays with text "Thread 2")
Hello from Thread 2
(1 second passes)
Main thread waking...
Thread 2 ended...
```

NEW TERM You can see, however, that this is not what really happened. What's going on? The key is to know that Windows Forms controls are not thread-safe; in other words, because the controls cannot safely communicate across threads, they only respond to the thread that created them, and no others. Here, only the main thread can access the Label control. When another thread wants to access the Label, it must issue a command to the main thread, known as *marshalling a command*. The main thread then executes those marshaled commands as it sees fit (which is usually once it gets a free moment). This is why the text written to the label in the DoIt method is displayed *after* things that come after it in the timeline.

But wait. The MessageBox displayed at the right time—one second into execution. Why is this? Because the MessageBox was not created in the main thread. Its owner is thread 2, and therefore it doesn't have to place any marshalled commands to the main thread and wait for them to be executed.

This issue brings up one of the most complex problems when dealing with multiple threads: trying to access objects created on one thread from multiple threads. Unfortunately, there's not much you can do to skirt around this problem. All Windows Forms controls are not thread-safe, so anytime a thread (aside from the creation thread) needs to access a control, the command must be marshalled, and will be subject to the main thread's execution discretion, even if you set the Priority property of the second thread to Highest.

Note

If you are familiar with threading technology prior to .NET, then the preceding description should remind you of the single-threaded apartment model (STA). Simply put, this model groups objects that share resource requirements, but limits that group (called an apartment) to the use of only one thread. The multiple-threaded apartment model (MTA), on the other hand, allows multiple threads per apartment. One of the requirements of STA is that objects can only be used on the thread that created them; all other threads must marshal calls to those objects.

.NET does not use apartments for grouping objects, but the technology is still there for backward compatibility.

So you've learned that it's usually not a good idea to manipulate your controls from more than one thread at a time. That still leaves a great deal of functionality for your new threads, and a classic example is a file system search application.

Take a look at the Search utility in Windows (go to Start Menu, Search), for example. When you enter in some keywords to search for and click the Search button, the utility searches through your hard drive looking for files with your keywords. The user interface remains responsive, though. If this were a single-threaded utility, the UI would freeze up while it waited for the search to complete. Thanks to multiple threads, you can enter new keywords or cancel the search while it is still going on.

Another example is the automatic spell checker in Word. While you are typing in your latest novel, Word is silently checking your spelling in the background, so it can automatically detect a misspelled word as soon as you type it, without slowing down or freezing the user interface while you work. Again, this is due to the magic of multiple threads.

In the next few sections, you'll learn some more advanced threading techniques, but first, let's recap the lessons from this section.

Creating and using a thread is as simple as creating a new Thread object, and supplying it with a ThreadStart delegate that points to a method. When the Start method is called for that new thread, it begins execution with that method, and from there, it can call any other method as necessary.

Perhaps the most important thing to note is that Windows Forms controls are not thread-safe. This essentially means that your controls will not be very responsive to threads other than the main thread; plan your usage of threads and controls carefully.

Synchronizing Threads in Your Application

Synchronization is the process of making sure that all of your threads know who currently has the right-of-way. When you synchronize something in real life, you make sure everyone involved is on the same page as you are. For example, when you synchronize your watch with your friends', everyone sets the time to the same value. The same goes for thread synchronization; during synchronization, all threads take note of the current state of affairs (with specific regard to code and data access).

This definition is still kind of fuzzy. What does it mean to synchronize code or data access? Suppose you and two of your friends bought a car together to share. However, only one of you can actually drive at a time; the others must wait their turns. Thus, you and your friends must synchronize your driving times. When you jump in the driver's seat first, you are telling your friends you were there first and they must wait. When you're done driving, then you let them know, and they can take their turns.

You could look at this in two different ways. In one case, you are synchronizing the "methods" used to drive your car. In the other, you are synchronizing the car itself. In other words, code synchronization versus data synchronization. This will make more sense later on.

With threading, the objective is to execute some code or access some data or object. Three threads (symbolizing you and your two friends) are competing to execute the same piece of code. Without synchronization, all three threads would try to "get in the driver's seat" at the same time, and your results would be unpredictable. A third of the time the

19

first thread would be running, with the other two threads competing for the rest of the time, and you wouldn't be able to tell who's currently running. (Imagine you and your friends trying to all cram into the driver's seat at once.)

Even worse is when that particular piece of code is accessing or modifying some variables that your application depends on (the car, in this case). Each thread will try to keep those variables to itself, but won't be able to, which could result in a lot of confusion, and possibly cause your application (or car) to crash (see Figure 19.5). If each of your friends tried to keep the car to himself, it would certainly crash.

FIGURE 19.5

Without synchronization, multiple threads may try to access the same objects at the same time, resulting in a traffic jam.

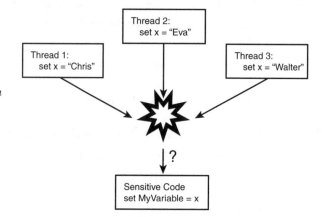

When you synchronize your threads, you are essentially telling all the threads to "wait your turn." The first thread that reaches the code in question will place a "lock" on the code, and all other threads must obey it. Until the lock is released, only the thread that set the lock can execute that code. Now, you can have predictable results because you always know who is in charge. The traffic accident in Figure 19.5 is avoided, and your situation looks like Figure 19.6 instead.

Beginners to threading often get synchronization and cross-thread command marshalling (discussed in the previous section) confused. With synchronization, you are dealing with a *piece of code* that is being executed, or an object that is being accessed, all within a single thread. With command marshalling, you are trying to access an *object* or *variable* across multiple threads. While the piece of code in question may be trying to access a particular object, that object may still be subject to command marshalling; synchronization and marshalling are two separate procedures. Don't assume that you can combat the problems discussed with command marshalling by placing locks on an object—it won't work, and actually doesn't really make sense.

FIGURE 19.6

FIGURE 19.6

With synchronization, only one thread is allowed in at a time, and all others are locked out.

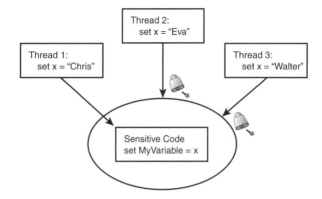

Before you examine how to synchronize your threads (beginning in Listing 19.4), let's take a quick look at an example without synchronization. Listing 19.3 creates three different threads that try to display some text in a label, with rather interesting results.

LISTING 19.3 Threading Without Synchronization

```
1:  using System;
2:  using System.Windows.Forms;
3:  using System.Drawing;
4:  using System.Threading;
5:
6:  namespace TYWinforms.Day19 {
7:     public class Listing193 : Form {
8:        private Label lblInfo = new Label();
9:        private Button btStart = new Button();
10:
11:        public Listing193() {
12:           lblInfo.Size = new Size(300,100);
13:           lblInfo.Location = new Point(10,75);
14:
15:           btStart.Location = new Point(100,10);
16:           btStart.Text = "Start!";
17:           btStart.Click += new EventHandler(this.StartIt);
18:
19:           this.Text = "Listing 19.3";
20:           this.Controls.Add(lblInfo);
21:           this.Controls.Add(btStart);
22:        }
23:
24:        private void StartIt(Object Sender, EventArgs e) {
25:           lblInfo.Text = "";
26:           Thread thdTest1 = new Thread(new
➥ThreadStart(DoIt));
27:           thdTest1.Name = "Thread 1";
```

LISTING 19.3   continued

```
28:            thdTest1.Start();
29:
30:            Thread thdTest2 = new Thread(new
➥ThreadStart(DoIt));
31:            thdTest2.Name = "Thread 2";
32:            thdTest2.Start();
33:
34:            Thread thdTest3 = new Thread(new
➥ThreadStart(DoIt));
35:            thdTest3.Name = "Thread 3";
36:            thdTest3.Start();
37:        }
38:
39:      private void DoIt() {
40:            lblInfo.Text += Thread.CurrentThread.Name +
➥" started...\n";
41:            Thread.Sleep(100);
42:            lblInfo.Text += Thread.CurrentThread.Name +
➥" ending...\n";
43:        }
44:
45:      public static void Main() {
46:            Application.Run(new Listing193());
47:        }
48:    }
49: }
```

ANALYSIS This listing is similar to Listing 19.2. A label and button are created in the constructor on lines 11–22, and the button's event handler, StartIt, begins on line 24.

Line 26 creates a new thread and points it to the DoIt method. The name of the thread is set to "Thread 1" on line 27, and then it is started. Lines 30–32 and 34–36 repeat the process with two new threads, named "Thread 2" and "Thread 3."

The DoIt method on line 39 is simple: it displays some text in the label, waits for one-tenth of a second, and displays some more text in the label.

Now, when this application is executed, the results will be unpredictable. If you click the button several times, you'll get different output each time. You can never tell which thread will write text to the label at any given time. Figure 19.7 shows a typical example.

FIGURE 19.7

The order in which text is output is unpredictable.

Ideally, we'd like to know who is going to spit out text at a given time, and more specifically, we'd like one thread to complete all of its processing before the next thread starts. This is a task for synchronization.

The solution is to place a lock on the code on lines 40–42. When the first thread reaches the code, it will place a lock, and the second two threads must wait in a queue (in the order they arrived at the block) until the lock is released. That way, each thread will have time to completely execute the code in question without worrying about what the other threads are trying to do.

There are quite a few different ways to synchronize your threads in .NET, but we'll only discuss the most prevalent one here, which involves the Monitor class. This class is very interesting because it doesn't have any properties or events, and you can't create it explicitly. Rather, it only contains six static methods that are used to synchronize your threads. These methods are listed in Table 19.1.

TABLE 19.1 Monitor Methods

Method	Description
Enter	Acquires a lock on an object. If the lock is already taken, the thread waits until it becomes available.
Exit	Releases the lock on an object.
Pulse	Alerts a waiting thread to a change in the locked state. In other words, Pulse lets another thread that has called Wait know that it doesn't have to wait much longer.
PulseAll	Alerts all waiting threads to a change in the locked state.
TryEnter	Attempts to acquire a lock on an object, but if it is already taken, the thread will not wait, and this method will return false.

TABLE 19.1 continued

Method	Description
Wait	Causes the holder of the lock to release the lock and go back into the queue to wait to reacquire the lock. Used when one thread depends on the execution of another.

The simplest way to put a lock on your code is to use the Enter and Exit methods on the code in question (the rest of the methods in Table 19.1 are more advanced and are out of the scope of this chapter). For example, change the DoIt method in Listing 19.3 to read as follows:

```
private void DoIt() {
   Monitor.Enter(this);

   lblInfo.Text += Thread.CurrentThread.Name + " started...\n";
   Thread.Sleep(100);
   lblInfo.Text += Thread.CurrentThread.Name + " ending...\n";

   Monitor.Exit(this);
}
```

We've added two new lines: Monitor.Enter(this) and Monitor.Exit(this). Now, when you execute the application, you'll get the same results, every time, as shown in Figure 19.8 (depending on your system, threads two and three may arrive in different orders, but they will always have their lines of execution grouped).

FIGURE 19.8

Each thread's execution is now grouped together.

The Enter and Exit methods take as a parameter the object you want to place the lock on. In other words, even though the lock is protecting a batch of code, it must still be placed on an actual object. Most of the time, the variable this (or Me in VB.NET) will suffice. You can, however, place the lock solely on the object that you intend to access or modify. For example,

```
Monitor.Enter(lblInfo);
```

> **Note**
>
> Both C# and VB.NET have their own syntax for placing locks as well. C# has the `lock` keyword:
>
> ```
> lock(this) {
>     ...
> }
> ```
>
> And VB.NET has the SyncLock keyword:
>
> ```
> SyncLock (Me)
>     ...
> End SyncLock
> ```
>
> Both of these methods work exactly the same as using the `Monitor` class. In fact, they rely on the `Monitor` class to function. The different syntax is used to make migration for developers of previous versions of these languages easier.

Let's look at a slightly more realistic example of multithreading and synchronization. Listing 19.4 shows the basis for a Web site searching application. The user can enter search terms even while a search is going on. The results from each search will display in a common label.

19

LISTING 19.4   A VB.NET Multithreaded, Synchronized Searching Application

```
1:  Imports System
2:  Imports System.Windows.Forms
3:  Imports System.Drawing
4:  Imports System.Threading
5:
6:  namespace TYWinforms.Day19
7:     public class Listing194 : Inherits Form
8:        private lblInfo As new Label()
9:        private tbSearch As new TextBox()
10:       private btStart As new Button()
11:       private intCounter As integer
12:
13:       public sub New()
14:          intCounter = 0
15:
16:          lblInfo.Size = new Size(300,100)
```

LISTING 19.4   continued

```
17:              lblInfo.Location = new Point(10,75)
18:
19:              tbSearch.Location = new Point(10,10)
20:
21:              btStart.Location = new Point(120,10)
22:              btStart.Text = "Search!"
23:              AddHandler btStart.Click, new EventHandler
➥(AddressOf StartIt)
24:
25:              Me.Text = "Listing 19.4"
26:              Me.Controls.Add(lblInfo)
27:              Me.Controls.Add(btStart)
28:              Me.Controls.Add(tbSearch)
29:          End Sub
30:
31:          private sub StartIt(Sender As Object, e As
➥EventArgs)
32:              intCounter += 1
33:
34:              dim thdSearch As New Thread(new ThreadStart
➥ (AddressOf Search))
35:              thdSearch.Name = "Search " & intCounter
36:              thdSearch.Start()
37:          End Sub
38:
39:          private sub Search()
40:              'Perform search
41:              Thread.Sleep(2000)
42:
43:              Monitor.Enter(Me)
44:
45:              dim rnd As new Random()
46:              dim i as integer
47:              for i = 0 to 4
48:                  lblInfo.Text += Thread.CurrentThread.Name &
➥": " & rnd.Next & Microsoft.VisualBasic.vbCrLf
49:              next i
50:
51:              Monitor.Exit(Me)
52:          End Sub
53:
54:          public shared sub Main()
55:              Application.Run(new Listing194())
56:          End Sub
57:      End Class
58:  End Namespace
```

ANALYSIS The basic layout of this listing is the same as Listings 19.2 and 19.3. You have a label, button, and textbox for the user interface. The button's `Click` event handler is the `StartIt` method, on line 31.

In `StartIt`, you increment a counter that tells the user how many searches have been performed (line 32), and create a new thread with a name based on that counter (lines 34–35). Each time the Search button is clicked, a new thread is created and started on the `Search` method beginning on line 39.

We haven't actually built the search mechanism here (I'll leave that as homework for you) but we put the thread to sleep for two seconds on line 41 to simulate the search. Note that this command is outside of any locked code. If this code were placed inside of a lock, then each search would have to wait until the previous search is finished before it could start searching. This defeats the purpose of a multithreaded searching application because we want the searches to occur in parallel, thus speeding up the responsiveness of the application.

Lines 43–51 execute after the search is complete, and simply display a message in the label indicating how many results were returned. Because you could potentially have many threads modifying the label at once (and because you want search results to be grouped together), we place this code in a lock using the `Monitor.Enter` method. To simulate the number of results returned, a random number is generated from the `Random` class and displayed in the label.

Finally, the `Exit` method is called on line 51. If we hadn't used the locking mechanisms here, we couldn't be sure that the results from each search would be grouped together.

Figure 19.9 shows an example output.

19

FIGURE 19.9

A multithreaded searching application needs to lock the label that displays the results.

There are two other common methods to lock your code besides using `Monitor`. The first involves a class called `Mutex`, which works similarly to the `Monitor` class, but doesn't offer as much functionality. Synchronization with `Mutex` involves passing a particular `Mutex` object back and forth between threads; the thread that currently has the `Mutex` is the only one allowed to execute a piece of code.

The second method deals with the `ReaderWriterLock` class. This class uses two different kinds of locks depending on what your application needs to do. It offers a single-writer/multiple-reader lock, which means only one thread can modify locked objects, but all others can still access them (as long as they don't try to modify the objects). This may increase performance, depending on your situation.

For more information on these types of locks, see the .NET Framework documentation.

Using Thread Pooling

A thread pool is simply a bunch of threads idling around together, and *thread pooling* is the process of taking advantage of those threads.

On a multithreaded operating system, it is a fact that most of a thread's time is spent doing nothing; each thread is most often just waiting around waiting to acquire locks or waiting for an event to occur. During this idle time, the processor is essentially going to waste; the operating system still has to devote resources to maintaining the thread, but because the thread isn't doing anything, it isn't gaining any performance for your application. Technically, thread pooling allows the operating system to control the threads. If a thread becomes idle and the processor is left with nothing to do, the OS will allow another thread to take the first's place, to keep the processor busy.

Thread pooling is something that happens normally in your OS. You can take advantage of it in your applications so that you, as the developer, are no longer required to manage threads individually; in other words, creating, maintaining, and destroying threads are handled by the OS. You just tell the OS what piece of code needs to be executed with a thread, and the OS handles the process of assigning a particular thread and getting rid of that thread when it is done. The OS does this very efficiently.

To handle this in your applications, you use the `ThreadPool` class, and it's even easier than it sounds. Using the static `QueueUserWorkItem` method, you can tell the system you need a thread to execute a particular task. The system will handle all assignation and execution of threads, so you don't have to worry about it yourself. When the thread is finished processing, it can alert your main thread accordingly.

The difference between using a `ThreadPool` and regular `Thread` objects is that the `Thread` class gives you more flexibility. You can, for example, name your threads and identify them individually with Thread. With ThreadPool, you can't do anything directly with specific threads, but it is generally more efficient at thread maintenance.

Before we look at an example, we need to know about the WaitCallBack delegate, a helper for the ThreadPool class. WaitCallBack is similar to the ThreadStart delegate; it points a thread to a method to execute. The only difference is that the method pointed to by WaitCallBack must take an object as a parameter. This object can be used to represent a particular thread, among other things; we'll discuss this more later.

Listing 19.5 shows a simple example of using the ThreadPool class.

LISTING 19.5   Using ThreadPool

```
1:  Imports System
2:  Imports System.Windows.Forms
3:  Imports System.Drawing
4:  Imports System.Threading
5:
6:  namespace TYWinforms.Day19
7:     public class Listing195 : Inherits Form
8:        private lblInfo As new Label()
9:        private btStart As new Button()
10:
11:       public sub New()
12:          lblInfo.Size = new Size(300,200)
13:          lblInfo.Location = new Point(10,75)
14:
15:          btStart.Location = new Point(100,10)
16:          btStart.Text = "Start!"
17:          AddHandler btStart.Click, new EventHandler
➡(AddressOf StartIt)
18:
19:          Me.Text = "Listing 19.5"
20:          Me.Controls.Add(lblInfo)
21:          Me.Controls.Add(btStart)
22:       End Sub
23:
24:       private sub StartIt(Sender As Object,
➡e As EventArgs)
25:          dim i as integer
26:
27:          for i = 0 to 10
28:             ThreadPool.QueueUserWorkItem(new WaitCallBack
➡ (AddressOf DoIt))
29:          next i
30:       End Sub
31:
32:       private sub DoIt(state As Object)
```

19

LISTING 19.5   continued

```
33:            lblInfo.Text += "Hello from the thread pool!" &
➥Microsoft.VisualBasic.vbCrLf
34:        End Sub
35:
36:        public shared sub Main()
37:            Application.Run(new Listing195())
38:        End Sub
39:    End Class
40:  End Namespace
```

ANALYSIS By now, this listing should be getting familiar. It is using the same framework as all the other listings in today's lesson. The only difference is in the `StartIt` on line 24 and `DoIt` method on line 32.

In the `StartIt` method you create a simple loop. This loop calls the `QueueUserWorkItem` method 11 times, each time passing a `WaitCallBack` delegate that points to the `DoIt` method. The result is that the `ThreadPool` object grabs 11 threads that each executes the `DoIt` method as efficiently as possible.

The `DoIt` method simply writes a message to the label (line 33).

Figure 19.10 shows the output from this listing.

FIGURE 19.10

*Each thread is queued
and handled by*
`ThreadPool.`

Each thread handled by the `ThreadPool` class is started, maintained, stopped, and destroyed (if necessary) automatically. With the `ThreadPool` class, you can replace lines 32–36 of Listing 19.4 with one line:

```
ThreadPool.QueueUserWorkItem(new WaitCallBack(AddressOf Search))
```

And your application will execute more efficiently. The synchronization techniques you learned earlier still apply when using the ThreadPool class, so you don't have to do anything additional.

So what about that parameter to the DoIt method on line 32 of Listing 19.5? This parameter can be used for nearly anything you want—it's a generic object that is passed to "help" your threads. To specify an actual value for it, you need to modify the call to QueueUserWorkItem slightly. We'll examine two uses for this object.

First, this object can be used to identify a particular thread. For example, modify line 28 to read as follows:

```
ThreadPool.QueueUserWorkItem(new WaitCallBack(AddressOf DoIt),
➥i.ToString())
```

We are passing an additional parameter to the QueueUserWorkItem method, and since the DoIt method expects an Object data type, we can pass whatever we want here (because all types in .NET derive from Object). i is the loop counter variable we used to create 11 different threads, so this new line passes a string representation of the current thread's number in the queue.

Now modify line 33 slightly:

```
lblInfo.Text += "Hello from thread " & state.ToString() &
➥Microsoft.VisualBasic.vbCrLf
```

The value you passed in the QueueUserWorkItem method call is passed into the state parameter of the DoIt method. Here we just call the ToString method once more to convert the Object to a string, and output a string particular for each thread. The output with these changes will be

```
Hello from thread 0
Hello from thread 1
Hello from thread 2
Hello from thread 3
Hello from thread 4
Hello from thread 5
Hello from thread 6
Hello from thread 7
Hello from thread 8
Hello from thread 9
Hello from thread 10
```

You now have a rudimentary way of identifying each thread.

The second use for the state parameter is to notify other threads when one thread has finished executing. This is done through the help of the AutoResetEvent class. AutoResetEvent provides methods to cause one thread to wait on another, until a flag is

19

set. Imagine `AutoResetEvent` as a toaster. The waiting thread must wait until the toast pops up before it can continue.

Listing 19.6 shows an example.

LISTING 19.6   Alerting Threads in a Thread Pool

```
1:  Imports System
2:  Imports System.Windows.Forms
3:  Imports System.Drawing
4:  Imports System.Threading
5:
6:  namespace TYWinforms.Day19
7:     public class Listing196 : Inherits Form
8:         private lblInfo As new Label()
9:         private btStart As new Button()
10:        private objAREvent As new AutoResetEvent(false)
11:        private intCounter As Integer = 10
12:
13:        public sub New()
14:            lblInfo.Size = new Size(300,200)
15:            lblInfo.Location = new Point(10,75)
16:
17:            btStart.Location = new Point(100,10)
18:            btStart.Text = "Start!"
19:            AddHandler btStart.Click, new EventHandler
➡ (AddressOf StartIt)
20:
21:            Me.Text = "Listing 19.6"
22:            Me.Controls.Add(lblInfo)
23:            Me.Controls.Add(btStart)
24:        End Sub
25:
26:        private sub StartIt(Sender As Object,
➡e As EventArgs)
27:            dim i as integer
28:
29:            for i = 0 to 10
30:                ThreadPool.QueueUserWorkItem(new WaitCallBack
➡(AddressOf DoIt), objAREvent)
31:            next i
32:
33:            objAREvent.WaitOne()
34:            lblInfo.Text += "Done!"
35:        End Sub
36:
37:        private sub DoIt(state As Object)
38:            Thread.Sleep(2000)
39:            lblInfo.Text += "Working..." &
➡Microsoft.VisualBasic.vbCrLf
```

LISTING 19.6 continued

```
40:
41:              if intCounter = 0 then
42:                  CType(state, AutoResetEvent).Set()
43:              else
44:                  Monitor.Enter(Me)
45:                  intCounter = intCounter - 1
46:                  Monitor.Exit(Me)
47:              end if
48:          End Sub
49:
50:          public shared sub Main()
51:              Application.Run(new Listing196())
52:          End Sub
53:      End Class
54:  End Namespace
```

ANALYSIS One final time we'll look at this framework. On lines 10 and 11 we create two new variables: an `AutoResetEvent` object and a counter that indicates how many threads we're going to create in this application. The parameter to the `AutoResetEvent` constructor indicates the initial state of the object; passing `false` means that it is not yet ready (the toast has not yet popped up).

The next change from Listing 19.5 is on line 30. Now we're passing the newly created `AutoResetEvent` object to the `QueueUserWorkItem` method. The `DoIt` method, on line 37, can access this `AutoResetEvent` object through its `state` parameter.

On line 33 we call the `WaitOne` method of the `AutoResetEvent` object. This causes the main thread to wait until the `AutoResetEvent` object tells it that it can continue (when the toast pops). The signal is made by calling the `Set` method of the `AutoResetEvent` object (which we'll see in the next paragraph). We want to wait until all other threads have finished executing before we continue the main thread. The `StartIt` method displays some text in the label indicating that all execution has finished.

Line 38 puts the thread to sleep for two seconds, and some text is displayed in the label on line 39. Lines 41–47 contain the interesting bit. When all threads are done, we want to call the `Set` method of the `AutoResetEvent` object. The number of threads currently running is indicated by the `intCounter` variable. If there are threads still running (in other words, `intCounter` is greater than `0`), then we need to decrement `intCounter` each time a thread finishes its task. Don't forget to use synchronization here; more than one thread accesses the `intCounter` variable, so you need to use some locks (line 44) to make sure only one thread accesses `intCounter` at a time. When we finally reach the last thread, we call the `Set` method, and the main thread will pick up from line 34.

19

(Remember that this application is still subject to command marshalling because the label in use is not thread-safe. Thus, no output will be shown in the label until *all* of the threads have finished executing.)

Figure 19.11 shows the output of Listing 19.6.

FIGURE 19.11

The AutoResetEvent *class can be used to signal the main thread when all other threads have finished execution.*

ThreadPool provides an easy and efficient way to use multiple threads in your application by taking advantage of idling threads. You can use the ThreadPool.GetMaxThreads method to see how many threads you can execute at once (in other words, how many threads are currently available for immediate use). ThreadPool.GetAvailableThreads indicates the number of additional threads you can queue until you run out of idling threads. After this number is reached, queued items will just wait until another thread becomes available.

Unless you need the flexibility of working with individual Thread objects, I recommend using the ThreadPool object.

Do	Don't
Do use a ThreadPool object when you need to execute small blocks of code with multiple threads efficiently.	**Don't** use ThreadPool when you need to modify individual threads (such as setting priorities or names) or when your threads need to execute a very long and complex piece of code. In these cases, it's more efficient to handle the Threads yourself.

> **Creating Multithreaded Controls**
>
> Creating a multithreaded control is just as easy as creating a multithreaded application. Simply create a new class that inherits from the `Control` class as normal, and then follow the guidelines for using threads described in today's lesson. Your controls can be made much more responsive when using multiple threads. For example, you could encapsulate the multithreading searching application discussed earlier today as a custom control. Applications that use that control need not worry about the multithread issues because they're all encapsulated in the control itself.
>
> Creating multithreaded controls, however, does not mean you can somehow get around the cross-thread marshalling limitations. Unfortunately, anything that derives from the `Control` class will be limited to a single thread when used in an application. All other threads must still marshal calls to the creation thread.
>
> In short, if you know how to create custom controls and use multiple threads, you know how to create multithreaded controls.

Summary

We covered a lot of very complex topics today. Multithreading is usually reserved for only the most advanced users, but with .NET and your knowledge of Windows Forms, multithreading is made easy.

A thread is the basic unit of execution in an operating system. The OS devotes resources to executing and maintaining threads, and the CPU divides its time between multiple threads to run your applications. Because the CPU is so fast, it appears that you are running multiple applications at once, even though the CPU is actually only doing one thing at a time.

Threading in .NET revolves mostly around the `Thread` class. With this class, you can create new threads, assign priorities and names, start and stop threads, and on and on. A thread must be given a piece of code to execute, and this is done using the `ThreadStart` delegate.

Synchronization is the process of making sure only one thread is executing a particular piece of code at a time. You typically use synchronization when the piece of code in question is sensitive; that is, when it accesses or modifies objects that the application relies upon. You lock your objects for synchronization using the `Monitor` class and its `Enter` and `Exit` methods.

The `ThreadPool` class takes advantage of the way threads work to accomplish multithreading tasks more efficiently. Its main method is `QueueUserWorkItem`, which uses a `WaitCallBack` delegate to send a thread on its way. You can use an `AutoResetEvent` class to signal threads when one has accomplished its task.

19

We're rapidly approaching the end of our three weeks! There are only a couple more important topics to cover. Tomorrow, you'll learn how to configure and deploy your applications, and on our last day you'll learn about debugging and error-handling techniques.

Q&A

Q How does threading work with multiprocessor systems?

A When your computer has multiple processors, the processors do not share threads; rather, each processor receives a percentage of the total number of threads, and works only on those. The exact implementation depends on your platform.

Q What is a thread-static variable?

A Thread-static variables are similar to regular static variables. The latter represents a variable or property that applies to a class in general, rather than to a particular instance of a class. Thread-static variables similarly apply to all threads, rather than a particular instance of a thread.

When you use a thread-static variable, each thread that accesses that variable will receive its own copy. That is, if one thread modifies the variable, it will not affect the variable in other threads. Thread-static variables are useful when you know that a particular variable should be unique for each thread. Using thread-static variables is more efficient than creating new local variables for each thread.

You can declare a thread-static variable simply by prefacing the declaration with the ThreadStatic attribute:

```
[ThreadStatic] int intValue;          //C#
```

```
<ThreadStatic()> dim intValue as integer    'VB.NET
```

Workshop

This workshop will help reinforce the concepts we covered in today. It is very helpful to understand fully the answers before moving on. Answers can be found in Appendix A.

Quiz

1. Infer three tasks in Microsoft Word that may be multithreaded.

2. What does it mean to be non–thread-safe?

3. Why can the ThreadPool class execute tasks more efficiently?

4. True or false? The Monitor.Enter method must be passed the this variable.

5. Is the following code correct?

```
Monitor.Enter(this)
for i = 0 to 10
    lblInfo.Text += "hi!"
next i
```

6. Which of the following is correct?

```
1.   ThreadPool.QueueUserWorkItem(new ThreadStart(this.Go));

2.   ThreadPool.QueueWorkUserItem(new WaitCallBack(this.Go));

3.   ThreadPool.QueueUserWorkItem(new WaitCallBack(this.Go));
```

7. What is `ThreadStart`?

8. True or false? A `Thread` begins execution as soon as you have specified a `ThreadStart` delegate.

9. What is the default `ThreadState` and `ThreadPriority` value for a newly started thread?

Exercise

Create a multithreaded file searching application. This application should allow a user to enter in a filename and press a Search button, upon which a new thread will be created to search through the file system recursively for a file with that name. Display the results in a `ListBox`. (Check out Day 11, "Working with Windows Input/Output" for more information on a directory searching algorithm.)

19

DAY 20

Configuring and Deploying Your Windows Forms

The last steps in building your application are configuring and deploying it. Configuration entails making sure that all the proper settings are used, that version numbers are correct, and so on. Deployment is getting your application to the user's computer.

Today's lesson will cover configuring and deploying in detail. As you'll see, neither is complex, and deployment is actually very simple. You'll be introduced to quite a few new technologies that help you with configuration and deployment.

In addition, we'll look at localization and accessibility—two steps that are often overlooked. Localizing your application means making it work with different cultures and languages. Accessibility is providing disabled users with aids that help them use your application.

It's time to get rolling on one of your last topics!

Today, you will learn

- What `.config` and `.resources` files are
- How to use the `ResourceManager` class
- How to separate your application logic from the user interface aspects in your code
- The different settings that are available for your applications in the .NET Framework
- Where to install your application on a user's computer

Introduction to .NET Configuration

When most people think of configuring an application, they think of superficial features. Using Microsoft Word as an example, people think of configuration as setting the correct fonts and styles, numbering, tables, and so on. Configuring might also entail setting up your page margins and your print settings. These are all things that a user must accomplish; you can't, for example, know ahead of time when you're building the application what type of printer the user will have. Therefore, this task is left for the user.

That doesn't mean, however, that the developer doesn't have to worry about configuration issues. The developer should prepare for quite a few things ahead of time so that the application runs properly. Two examples of these prepare-ahead items are security and version information. It is often necessary to bundle your application with default configuration information.

Prior to .NET, two popular methods were available for supplying configuration information. The first was to use the Windows registry, a central repository for data that is required by the operating system. This registry contained information about every program on the computer, in addition to user and OS data. When an application was installed for the first time, it would write information to the registry, which would then be referenced every time the application was executed (see Figure 20.1). If necessary, changes could be written back to the registry to modify the application's settings.

This method had a couple of problems. First, the registry is rather difficult to edit. It contains an abundance of information that is organized in a sometimes non-intuitive manner, and you can forget about requiring users to modify their own registry settings. More often than not, users end up messing up their own computers because critical information is stored in the same place as non-critical application data.

Additionally, if any of the settings needed to be changed, or if new settings needed to be added, you had to modify the application and recompile it, which is not always an easy task, especially if you don't have developers on hand.

FIGURE 20.1

The Registry Editor (regedit.exe) shows all the information in the Windows registry (a configuration for Word 2000 is shown).

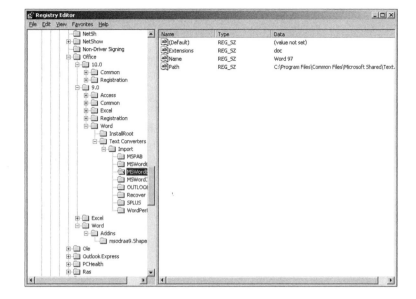

Another popular method was to use configuration files. In Windows, these most often ended with the extension .ini. These .ini files made up for a lot of problems that were associated with the registry; mainly, .ini files were easy to read and modify. An application would come bundled with an .ini file (or sometimes several) that would contain settings used by the application. For example, Listing 20.1 shows a typical .ini file bundled with Adobe Photoshop.

LISTING 20.1   Photoshop Configuration Information

```
 1:  [Startup]
 2:  AppName=Adobe Photoshop 6.0
 3:  FreeDiskSpace=2441
 4:  EnableLangDlg=Y
 5:
 6:  [ISUPDATE]
 7:  UpdateURL=http://
 8:
 9:  [AdobePI]
10:  ProductName=Photoshop
11:  ProductType=Retail
12:  ProductVersion=6.0
13:  ProductLanguage=Not Applicable
14:  PIVersion=1.0
15:  PIValue=1869701
```

20

Information such as the application's name, version, and language are contained in the `.ini` file. This information is used to configure Photoshop properly each time it starts up.

.NET takes the `.ini` file concept one step further and makes all configuration files XML files. Now, not only are the configuration settings easy to read, but they are in a standard format that makes it easy for applications to read and write data. .NET configuration files always end in the `.config` extension. The actual name of the configuration file must match that of the application you are configuring. For example, if your application were `Listing20.1.exe`, your configuration file would be `Listing20.1.exe.config`. As you've learned through the past 19 days, applications are not required to have configuration files (more on this in a moment). Listing 20.2 shows a typical file.

LISTING 20.2   A Typical `.config` File

```
1:   <configuration>
2:       <configSections>
3:           <section name="sampleSection"
4:               type="System.Configuration.
➥SingleTagSectionHandler" />
5:       </configSections>
6:
7:       <sampleSection setting1="Value1" setting2="value two"
8:           setting3="third value" />
9:   </configuration>
```

Don't worry about the syntax for now—you'll learn all about it soon enough. For now, all you need to know is that .NET defines several XML elements in the `.config` file. In addition, you can easily create your own custom ones so that your application can retrieve any settings it needs.

The .NET Framework has a configuration file. Typically located in the `c:\winnt\Microsoft.NET\Framework\version\CONFIG` directory, it is appropriately called `machine.config` because it contains settings that your entire computer uses.

Interestingly enough, if you don't specify individual settings for your application, your application will inherit them from `machine.config` (which is why each of your applications doesn't need a `.config` file). This `machine.config` file contains information such as what classes handle security issues, what files are associated with the ASP.NET engine, what default language and culture the user has specified on his computer, how debugging should be handled, and so on. Because `machine.config` needs to contain settings for every aspect of the .NET Framework, the file is quite large. (By default, it is more than 750 lines in length.) As such, this book doesn't cover `machine.config` in detail, but feel free to take a look at it—if you dare. You'll see a lot of familiar configuration information that you probably took for granted.

Configuring Your Applications

Before you start building .config files, you first need to build an application to configure. Listing 20.3 shows a basic framework for an application with an About menu.

LISTING 20.3   An Application Ready to Configure

```
 1:   using System;
 2:   using System.Windows.Forms;
 3:   using System.Drawing;
 4:
 5:   namespace TYWinforms.Day20 {
 6:       public class Listing203 : Form {
 7:           private MainMenu mnuMain = new MainMenu();
 8:           private MenuItem miHelp = new MenuItem("Help");
 9:           private MenuItem miAbout = new MenuItem("About");
10:
11:           public Listing203() {
12:               mnuMain.MenuItems.Add(miHelp);
13:               miHelp.MenuItems.Add(miAbout);
14:
15:               miAbout.Click += new EventHandler(this.ShowAbout);
16:
17:               this.Text = "My Configurable App";
18:               this.Menu = mnuMain;
19:           }
20:
21:           private void ShowAbout(Object Sender, EventArgs e) {
22:               MessageBox.Show
➥("TYWinforms Listing 20.3 Example");
23:           }
24:
25:           public static void Main() {
26:               Application.Run(new Listing203());
27:           }
28:       }
29:   }
```

20

ANALYSIS This listing is pretty simple. It has only three controls: two MenuItems and a MainMenu. The About menu item has an event handler that simply displays a MessageBox with a nice description of the application.

Assuming that you saved this listing as Listing20.3.cs, after compiling this application, you'll end up with a file named Listing20.3.exe. The configuration file for this application should then be named Listing20.3.exe.config. The configuration file must be placed in the same directory as the executable file; therefore, if your application was in the `c:\winforms\day20` directory, the `Listing20.3.exe.config` file must be placed in the same directory.

> **Note**
>
> If you are familiar with ASP.NET configuration, then Windows Forms configuration should be a breeze; the two configurations use the same paradigm, but they are different in four ways:
>
> 1. Configuration files are not named `Web.config`, but rather `application_name.exe.config`.
> 2. Windows Forms configuration files must be placed in the same directory as the application. .NET will not look in other directories, and `bin` directory support is not available.
> 3. The `<location>` configuration element is not used in Windows Forms.
> 4. In ASP.NET, changes to the `.config` files were automatically applied to the application. In Windows Forms, the application must be restarted before changes will take effect.

Now let's look at the `.config` file.

Configuration Sections

The most basic `.config` file looks like the following:

```
<configuration>
</configuration>
```

In other words, the only required XML tag is the `<configuration>` element. All other settings are placed inside `<configuration>`, in their own elements. For example, `<appSettings>` is another common configuration element. You could add this element to make the previous code snippet like the following:

```
<configuration>
   <appSettings>
      <add key="AppName" value="Listing 20.3"/>
   </appSettings>
</configuration>
```

You need to take a couple of precautions when you create these `.config` files. First, remember that these files are in XML, which means that they require strict XML syntax. Every open tag needs a closing tag:

```
<whatever> ... </whatever>
 — or —
<whatever/>
```

Second, all the sections in the `.config` files must be camel-cased. In other words, the first letter of the first word in the section name is lowercase, and all subsequent words are uppercase (unless separated by a period). For example:

```
<appSettings> ... </appSettings>
<webRequestModules />
<globalization> ... </globalization>
<system.diagnostics />
```

Although these rules are simple, they often trip up beginners. Just take note of these, and if your configuration files seem to crash your application, double check the casing.

Table 20.1 shows all of the configuration sections that are available with Windows Forms.

TABLE 20.1 Windows Forms Configuration Sections

Section	Description
`<application>`	Contains information on remote objects that your application consumes and exposes.
`<appSettings>`	Can be used to contain custom application settings.
`<authenticationModules>`	Specifies the modules used to authenticate Internet requests.
`<channels>`	Contains channels that the application uses to communicate with remote objects.
`<channelSinkProviders>`	Contains templates for handling events from remote object channels.
`<configSections>`	Defines the sections in a configuration file as well as the modules and assemblies that process those sections.
`<connectionManagement>`	Specifies the maximum allowed number of Internet connections.
`<debug>`	Specifies whether all the classes that are contained in your `.config` file should be loaded when your application starts (to help validate the `.config` file).
`<defaultProxy>`	Specifies the proxy server to be used for HTTP requests to the Internet.
`<mscorlib>`	Contains cryptography information.
`<runtime>`	Contains information on assemblies and garbage collection.
`<startup>`	Contains information on the version of the .NET Framework that should be used for your application.

20

TABLE 20.1 continued

Section	Description
`<system.diagnostics>`	Specifies that information should be written to files when tracing is enabled (more on tracing tomorrow).
`<system.net>`	Serves as a container for the `<authenticationModules>`, `<defaultProxy>`, `<connectionManagement>`, and `<webRequestModules>` sections.
`<system.runtime.remoting>`	Serves as a container for the `<application>`, `<channels>`, `<channelSinkProviders>`, and `<debug>` sections.
`<system.windows.forms>`	Specifies how to debug Windows Forms applications.
`<webRequestModules>`	Specifies modules that are used to make Internet requests.

The rest of this section discusses the most common predefined configuration elements.

Note Whenever you make a change to the configuration file, you must restart the application for the changes to take effect.

`<configSections>`

We'll cover the `<configSections>` section first because it is one of the more important ones. As mentioned in Table 20.1, this section lists the various other configuration sections and how they should be handled. Therefore, for every subsequent section that is discussed, you'll find an entry for it in the `<configSections>` section in your `machine.config` file. For example:

```
<configuration>

   <configSections>
      <section name="runtime" type="System.Configuration.
➥IgnoreSectionHandler, System, Version=1.0.3300.0,
➥Culture=neutral, PublicKeyToken=b77a5c561934e089"
➥allowLocation="false"/>
      <section name="mscorlib" type="System.Configuration.
➥IgnoreSectionHandler, System, Version=1.0.3300.0,
➥Culture=neutral, PublicKeyToken=b77a5c561934e089"
➥allowLocation="false"/>
   </configSections>
</configuration>
```

That's a lot of confusing code, but luckily, it's not necessary to understand it thoroughly. Essentially, the `name` attribute of each section that is defined here defines that section's name. The `type` attribute indicates the class that will be used to handle all aspects of that section—such as reading from and writing to—followed by the assembly where the class is located, the version of that assembly, and some supplemental information.

If you ever need to retrieve values from a particular section, you'll look in the `<configSections>` element to determine what type of class to expect to return your values. For example, the `IgnoreSectionHandler` class doesn't return any information; sections that users shouldn't modify use this class. Similarly, the `<appSettings>` section uses a class of type `NameValueFileSectionHandler`, which returns a group of key/value pairs representing your application's information.

`<configSections>` is really only useful on two occasions: when you need to know how to handle a particular section, and when you need to define your own sections. To do the latter, you need only to specify the name of the new custom section and the class that will handle it. (You can ignore most of the information that was presented in the previous code snippet.)

For example, the following code snippet creates a new section called "myApplication" that will return key/value pairs of information from your `.config` file:

```
<configuration>
   <configSections>
      <section name="myApplication"
         type="System.Configuration.SingleTagSectionHandler" />
   </configSections>
```

Your new section would follow as this:

```
   <myApplication setting1="Value1" />
</configuration>
```

Don't worry about the classes such as `SingleTagSectionHandler` that have been specified here. You never use them directly, and your choice of which to use when creating your own sections is often insignificant. Today's later section "Retrieving Configuration Values" discusses the classes you might need to know.

You can also create your own custom classes to handle your configuration sections. This requires creating a class that implements the `IConfigurationSectionHandler` interface, and can read XML from your `.config` files. This is beyond the scope of this book, but you can find further information in the .NET Framework documentation and Quick Start examples.

`<appSettings>`

The `<appSettings>` section is the most common found with Windows Forms application. Essentially, it is a custom configuration area that you can use to store whatever information you like. You've already seen an example:

20

```
<configuration>
   <appSettings>
      <add key="AppName" value="Listing 20.3"/>
   </appSettings>
</configuration>
```

The configuration data in `<appSettings>` is arranged in key/value pairs. Using the `add` element, you can create as many new key/value pairs as necessary, and they will easily be accessible from your application (more on that in the "Retrieving Configuration Values" section later today).

The preceding code snippet defined a new key named `AppName` with a value of `Listing 20.3`. As you can guess, this setting specifies the name of our application. You can easily add another element to indicate the version of the application:

```
...
   <add key="Version" value="1.0"/>
...
```

There's not much else to this section, so it's a good time to move on.

`<startup>`

If you need to specify that your Windows Forms application must use a specific version of the .NET Framework, you can do it in the `<startup>` section. Because the only version of the .NET Framework out right now is version 1.0, `<startup>` doesn't have much use. However, as Microsoft starts releasing new versions, this section becomes more handy.

For example, suppose that .NET version 2.0 came out and had many new features. You've designed your application to work with version 2.0, and as such, it contains features that aren't in version 1.0. You can use this section to specify that your application can only be run when version 2.0 is present. If the user tries to run your application without having version 2.0 installed, the application simply won't load and displays an error message.

The syntax for this section is as follows:

```
<startup>
   <requiredRuntime version="version" safemode="safemode" />
</startup>
```

The only two things you need to worry about are the *version* and *safemode* placeholders. *version* holds, obviously, the version of the .NET Framework to use. It must be in the format v*x.x.x.x*, where each x value is a number from 0 to 65,535. *safemode* can either be true or false; it indicates whether the Common Language Runtime should search the Windows registry for the proper version to use.

For example:

```
<configuration>
   <startup>
      <requiredRuntime version="v1.0.0.0" safemode="false" />
   </startup>
</configuration>
```

Note that `version` and `safemode` are not both required. If you do specify a `version` number and true for `safemode`, then the version you specify must match the one that is returned from the registry, or you will receive an error.

`<system.windows.forms>`

Even though it might seem like this section would have a lot of configuration information, it only specifies one thing: what should handle errors encountered in your application. Take a quick look at the syntax before examining what this means:

```
<system.windows.forms jitDebugging="value" />
```

Recall from Day 1, "Getting Started with .NET Windows Forms," that the .NET Framework uses a just-in-time (JIT) compiler to compile your applications into machine code from the Microsoft Intermediate Language (MSIL) when your application executes. In other words, the application is compiled just in time for the application to execute. A JIT debugger works similarly. It steps in "just in time" to help you fix your application when an error arises.

When you encounter an error in your Windows Forms applications, you have two options. The first is to simply do nothing. By default, in Windows Forms, you get an error box like the one shown in Figure 20.2.

FIGURE 20.2

The default error-handler in Windows Forms.

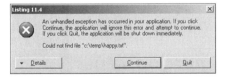

20

The dialog box shown in Figure 20.2 provides a bit of information on what caused the error, but it doesn't let you do anything about it. You can either continue with the application as if nothing happened, or quit, essentially ignoring the error.

The second option is to use a JIT debugger to fix your application. A JIT debugger allows you to fix an error in the application (assuming you still have the source code) so that the error doesn't happen again. By default, Windows Forms has disallowed a JIT debugger from "jumping in" to fix your application. That's where the `<system.windows.forms>` configuration section steps in.

If you set *value* to true in the previous code snippet, then the box shown in Figure 20.2 won't appear, and you'll get something like Figure 20.3 instead. In this case, you get a choice of JIT debuggers to use to fix an error.

FIGURE 20.3

Enabling JIT debugging allows you to use a JIT debugger to fix your errors.

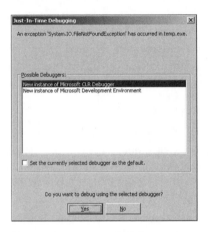

Tomorrow's lesson covers debugging more thoroughly. You can move to the next section now.

Note

For the `<system.windows.forms>` configuration section to work, you first need to compile your application with debugging enabled. This is done by specifying the `/debug` option when you compile your code:

```
vbc /t:winexe /r:system.dll /debug MyListing.vb
```

A new file with the extension `.pdb` will be created. This file contains special information about your application that can be used in debuggers.

Retrieving Configuration Values

After you've created and set up your `.config` file, it's pretty simple to access those configuration values from your application with the `ConfigurationSettings` class. This class only has two members, and both are covered here.

The first is the `GetConfig` method. You use this method by specifying a configuration section that you want to retrieve. For example, the following code snippet returns the information that is contained in the `<system.windows.forms>` section:

```
ConfigurationSettings.GetConfig("system.windows.forms")
```

Note

The ConfigurationSettings class is contained in the System.Configuration namespace, so be sure to import it if you use ConfigurationSettings.

The previous statement returns an object of type System.Windows.Forms.ConfigData, which isn't very useful, unfortunately.

It is because of the fact that most configuration sections return objects that you can't really use that the <appSettings> section came to be. This section returns an easy-to-use object, which leads into the second member of the ConfigurationSettings class.

The AppSettings property returns, appropriately, the settings that are contained in the <appSettings> section of your .config file. Rather than using GetConfig and having to cast the return object appropriately, AppSettings presents all of the data to you in a ready-to-use format.

Create a .config file for the application created from Listing 20.3 (listing20.3.exe) and name it listing20.3.exe.config. Add to it the code shown in Listing 20.4.

LISTING 20.4 The .config File for Listing 20.3

```
1:   <configuration>
2:      <appSettings>
3:         <add key="AppName" value="Listing 20.3" />
4:         <add key="Version" value="1.0" />
5:         <add key="Description" value="A sample application
➥for testing configuration files." />
6:      </appSettings>
7:   </configuration>
```

Now change line 17 of Listing 20.3 to read this:

```
this.Text = ConfigurationSettings.AppSettings["AppName"] +
➥" version " + ConfigurationSettings.
➥AppSettings["Version"];
```

This code retrieves the "AppName" and "Version" information from your .config file and displays it in the caption of the application. Change line 22 to read this:

```
MessageBox.Show(ConfigurationSettings.
➥AppSettings["Description"]);
```

This displays the "Description" setting in your About box. Recompile the application (don't forget to import the System.Configuration namespace!) and click the About menu. You should see something similar to Figure 20.4.

20

FIGURE 20.4

Your configuration data can be displayed in your application.

That's all there is to it! Use the AppSettings property to specify inside brackets (parentheses in VB.NET) the setting in which you're interested and you're ready to rock.

Localizing Your Application

NEW TERM *Localization* is the process of converting certain aspects of your application into culture-specific versions depending on your audience, such as displaying French text instead of English when your application is used in France. Windows maintains a particular user's culture and language choice, and your applications can detect this choice and adjust themselves accordingly.

Localization might sound like a complex process, but it's not. The .NET Framework makes it easy for you to change the culture for your application. The only part left up to you is to actually translate the information from one language to another (not always a trivial task, but one that is way out of the scope of this book).

NEW TERM The most common items that need translating are text and graphics images. In terms of localization, these items are called *resources*, and they can be stored separately from your application. (Note though, that all the resources you've been using the past 20 days have been embedded in the application code.) Therefore, when you localize your application, all you really need to do is translate your resources appropriately. .NET can handle the rest.

Localizing your application is a four-step process:

1. Create the resource files that you'll need for the different cultures of your application in plain text.
2. Convert the resource files into .resource files.

3. Compile your resource files into an assembly and place the assemblies in the appropriate directories.

4. Access the resource files from your application.

The first step is the easiest. Open Notepad and enter the text from Listing 20.5.

LISTING 20.5 English Resources

```
1:  Caption = TYWinforms Day 20 Application
2:  WelcomeMessage = Welcome to localization techniques!
3:  GoodbyeMessage = Leaving so soon?
```

Save this listing as `Day20.txt`. There's very little to this, or any resource file. Simply create a property to be used in your application, and set a value. In this case, `Caption`, `WelcomeMessage`, and `GoodbyeMessage` properties have been created with appropriate text to display at various points in the application.

Now you will create another resource, this time in Spanish, shown in Listing 20.6.

LISTING 20.6 Spanish Resources

```
1:  Caption = TYWinforms Applicacion Dia 20
2:  WelcomeMessage = ¡Bienvenidos a tecnicas de localizacion!
3:  GoodbyeMessage = Ya se va?
```

Save this file as `Day20.es-ES.txt`. You need to note a couple of things about this listing. First, the name of the file is `Day20.es-ES.txt`. The root part of the filename is the same as for Listing 20.5—that is, "Day20." The "es" is the code for the Spanish culture. Similarly, "fr" is French, and "zh" is Chinese. Note that some codes also have subcultures. "es-GT" is Guatemalan Spanish, "fr-MC" is French in Monaco, and "zh-HK" is Chinese in Hong Kong. "es-ES" is Spanish in Spain. This culture code was omitted from Listing 20.5 because it is in the default culture—English in this case. If English isn't set as your default, its culture code is "en." It is important to name your files with the appropriate code. You'll learn why in a moment. For a complete listing of the culture codes, check out the .NET Framework documentation under the `CultureInfo` class.

Note that the property names have stayed the same. This makes it easy for developers to refer to them in code. The only part that needs to change is the actual text value.

Now that you have the resource files, you need to compile them into something that the .NET Framework can use. This is a two-step process. The first step is to use the

20

Resource Generator tool (`resgen.exe`) to turn your `.txt` files into `.resources` files. The syntax is simple:

```
resgen txt_File resource_file
```

In this case, you would have two commands:

```
resgen Day20.txt Day20.resources
resgen Day20.es-ES.txt Day20.es-ES.resources
```

You should see output similar to the following:

```
Read in 3 resources from 'Day20.txt'
Writing resource file...  Done.

Read in 3 resources from 'Day20.es-ES.txt'
Writing resource file...  Done.
```

> **Caution**
>
> If you are using Visual Studio.NET (VS.NET) to localize your applications, be aware that the resource files that VS.NET creates automatically are *not* compatible with the ones that the `resgen.exe` tool creates. After you start using one method, you cannot switch to the other without starting over.

The next step is to compile these `.resources` files into an assembly. The recommended way of doing so is to embed your default resource files (for English, in this case) into your executable application and compile all other resource files (Spanish, in this case) into separate assemblies, called *satellite assemblies*. This way, when you need to add a new resource to your application, you don't need to mess with the executable file at all—just create a new resource and place it in an assembly in the appropriate directory with your application.

To embed a resource into your executable, you use your normal command prompt command (`csc` for C# and `vbc` for VB.NET) along with the `/resource` parameter.

To create satellite assemblies from your non-default `.resources` files, use the Assembly Linker Tool (`al.exe`). The syntax for this tool is as follows:

```
al /t:library /embed:filename /culture:culture /out:out_file
```

The first parameter, *filename*, is the `.resources` file you want to compile. In this case, *filename* will be `Day20.es-ES.resources`. The second parameter, *culture*, specifies the culture of the particular resource file you are compiling. This is important because you can have only one resource file per assembly, and each assembly must have the same name (more on that in a moment). Therefore, the only way that the .NET Framework can identify which assembly goes with which culture is to use this *culture* property. The last parameter, *out_file*, is the filename of the compiled assembly (a .dll file). In this case, you should use the following command:

```
al /t:library /embed:Day20.es-ES.resources /culture:es-ES
➡/out:Day20.resources.dll
```

You'll end up with a file named Day20.resources.dll that contains your Spanish resources. You still have the Day20.resources file that contains your English resources to deal with.

This discussion will detour for a moment so you can examine the filenames. It is important in .NET localization that all your filenames match. For example, your two resource files have the same root: Day20. Your satellite assembly also shares the same root, and in a moment you'll see that your executable application must again share the Day20 root. .NET depends on this naming structure to locate the proper resources when called upon.

In addition, you have to create the proper directory structure for your resources. For every non-default satellite assembly you have, you should create a new directory with the culture name. For example, in this case, you have a resource file for the es-ES culture. Therefore, you create a directory in your application's folder named es-ES, and place your compiled resource assembly into it. Figure 20.5 shows a typical directory structure.

FIGURE 20.5

Your compiled resource files should be placed in their own culture directories.

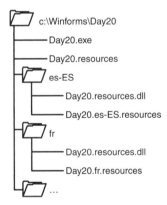

20

When your application is called upon to change cultures, it will look in each culture directory for the appropriate resource assembly. If one isn't available, then the default resources are used. If you have a folder that specifies the culture but not the subculture, then the application will use the parent culture instead. For example, if you've created a satellite assembly and directory for only plain Spanish (es), but the user's culture is es-ES, then the application will use the es resources. This is known as *resource fallback*.

Now you just need an application to use your resources. Listing 20.7 shows a simple application that reads from your compiled resource assembly file.

LISTING 20.7   Your First Culture-Aware Application

```
1:  using System;
2:  using System.Windows.Forms;
3:  using System.Drawing;
4:  using System.Resources;
5:  using System.Reflection;
6:  using System.Threading;
7:  using System.Globalization;
8:  using System.ComponentModel;
9:
10:  namespace TYWinforms.Day20 {
11:      public class Listing207 : Form {
12:          private ResourceManager rsmDay20;
13:          private Label lblMessage = new Label();
14:
15:          public Listing207() {
16:              rsmDay20 = new ResourceManager("Day20",
➥this.GetType().Assembly);
17:
18:              lblMessage.Text = rsmDay20.
➥GetString("WelcomeMessage");
19:              lblMessage.Size = new Size(300,100);
20:
21:              this.Text = rsmDay20.GetString("Caption");
22:              this.Controls.Add(lblMessage);
23:              this.Closing += new CancelEventHandler
➥ (this.CloseMe);
24:          }
25:
26:          private void CloseMe(Object Sender,
➥CancelEventArgs e) {
27:              MessageBox.Show(rsmDay20.GetString
➥ ("GoodbyeMessage"));
28:          }
29:
30:          public static void Main() {
31:              Application.Run(new Listing207());
32:          }
33:      }
34:  }
```

ANALYSIS   Save this listing as Day20.cs. (Remember that the filename must match your resource filenames.) On lines 1–8, you see quite a few additional namespaces imported. These namespaces are necessary for localization and a few other things in the code.

On line 12, you create a new `ResourceManager` class, which is the key for interacting with resources. `ResourceManager` has various methods that can load resource files and retrieve the data contained within. On line 16, you instantiate this `ResourceManager`. The constructor takes two parameters. The first specifies the root name of the resources you're trying to use. (Now you see why all the files need to have the same root.) The second parameter is the main assembly for your resources. Most of the time, this assembly is simply your main executable file. `this.GetType().Assembly` returns the assembly that contains your `Listing207` class.

On line 18, you see the first retrieval of a resource. Instead of setting the `Text` of the label to some static text, you use the `GetString` method of the `ResourceManager` class and specify the property of the resource file you want to retrieve. Recall from Listings 20.5 and 20.6 that you had the `Caption`, `WelcomeMessage`, and `GoodbyeMessage` properties. The second of these is used on line 18 to set the text contained in the label.

The `Caption` property is used on line 21, again by calling the `GetString` method from your `ResourceManager` object. You want to display a message to the user when he closes the application, so you attach an event handler to the `Closing` event.

The `CloseMe` method on line 26 displays a message box with the `GoodbyeMessage` property.

Don't forget that you still have the default resource file, `Day20.resources`. You must embed it into the compiled version of Listing 20.7. To do so, use the following command to compile your application:

```
csc /t:winexe /r:system.dll /r:system.drawing.dll
➥/r:system.windows.forms.dll /res:Day20.resources
➥Day20.cs
```

The only new thing with this command is the `/res` parameter (short for `/resource`). It specifies the default resource file that should be embedded along with the executable. Now, assuming your culture is English, you'll see the output shown in Figure 20.6 when you try to close the application. The values that are shown in the caption, label, and message box are all pulled from the default resource file.

If you want to test your application in a different culture, you have two options: Take your application to a different country and install it on a machine there, or use the `CultureInfo` class. Although it might be fun to travel to Spain, stick with the `CultureInfo` class.

20

Figure 20.6

*Your localized applica-
tion behaves as normal
in the default culture.*

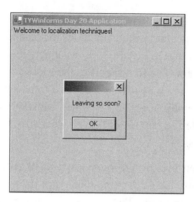

The main thread in your application (see Day 19, "Creating Multithreaded Applications,"
for information on threads) has a `CurrentUICulture` property that determines what culture, and therefore what resources, the application should use. The `CultureInfo` class
can be used to specify a specific culture. To test the Spanish application, add the following code between lines 15 and 16:

```
Thread.CurrentThread.CurrentUICulture = new
➥CultureInfo("es-ES");
```

This code sets the `CurrentUICulture` property of the main thread to `es-ES` using the
`CultureInfo` class. Recompile your application (don't forget to use the `/res` parameter
to embed the default resource file), and you should end up with Figure 20.7. All the
resources have been converted to Spanish.

Figure 20.7

*Your application is
now multilingual!*

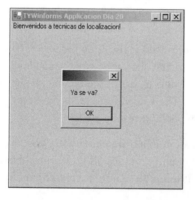

When you change the culture using the `CultureInfo` class, your application looks to see
if an `es-ES` subdirectory exists in the executable's directory. If this directory exists, the
application retrieves the resources from there. If the directory isn't there, your application falls back to the default culture, English.

When you need to translate your application into a new language, you simply create a new `.resources` file, compile it into a satellite assembly, and place it in the appropriate subdirectory of your application. In essence, repeat steps 1–3 in the list presented at the beginning of this section. You don't need to recompile your application (unless, of course, you want to test it using different `CultureInfo` objects), which makes it easy to localize your application.

It is often recommended that you place all items in your application that can be localized into resource files, even if you don't plan to ship your application to different countries. This way, whenever some wording or an image in your application needs to change, you can do so just by modifying your resource files, instead of recompiling your entire application.

Handling Accessibility

Often, you will need to tune your application for people with disabilities or difficulties using computers. Microsoft Active Accessibility (MSAA) is a technology designed to make it easy for you to incorporate features that will aid this segment of your application's audience.

Thankfully, each Windows Forms control already implements MSAA by default; every control contains several properties that apply specifically to MSAA. Certain applications, known as accessibility client applications, use these properties to help disabled users, often in the form of visual cues or spoken descriptions. Table 20.2 discusses these properties.

TABLE 20.2 Accessibility Properties

Property	Description
AccessibilityObject	Returns an `AccessibleObject` object that describes the accessibility of the control in question.
AccessibleDefaultActionDescription	Describes the action that a control in question will perform.
AccessibleDescription	Gets or sets description that is used by accessibility client applications.
AccessibleName	Indicates the name of the control as seen by accessibility clients.
AccessibleRole	Indicates the type of the control in question, such as a dialog or `MenuItem`.
IsAccessible	Indicates whether the control in question is compliant with accessibility clients.

20

You can see the different accessibility clients that are built into Windows by going to Start, Programs, Accessories, Accessibility.

The Easy Part: Deployment

Deployment is by far the easiest topic in today's lesson. *Deployment* means installing your application on users' computers. Because applications in the .NET Framework are completely self contained, all that is required to deploy is copying files.

Recall from Day 1 that each compiled .NET application contains metadata that provides the computer all the information needed to run that application. It's not necessary to write entries into the registry, put files into the Windows directory, or any other such thing that was required prior to .NET.

That said, you can use a few techniques to deploy your applications. The first, as mentioned previously, is to simply copy files to the target computer. For the applications that were developed today, that would mean copying the `.exe` files, creating any necessary culture subdirectories, and placing the appropriate satellite assemblies in them. That's all there is to it! This copying can be done in a number of ways, from the File Transfer Protocol (FTP) to XCOPY.

Another method is to use the Windows Installer application. This program packages all the necessary files for your applications and creates a file with the extension `.msi`. Windows can use the `.msi` file to install your application (much like the familiar `setup.exe` program included with many older applications). The Windows Installer also puts entries into the Add/Remove Programs control panel to easily delete applications from your hard drive.

A third method is to compress your application files into a single `.CAB` file, known as a cabinet file. *Cabinet files* are simply compressed versions of your files that can be extracted as necessary.

For more information on Windows Installer and packaging files with cabinet files, check out Microsoft's site at the following URL:

`http://www.microsoft.com/msdownload/platformsdk/sdkupdate/psdkredist.htm`

 Note

The preceding URL may require you to download an ActiveX control that will be used to help identify any supporting components you need for the Windows Installer. You don't need to download it, but it may help the procedure.

Summary

Configuration and deployment are typically the last steps to perform when building your applications. Therefore, it is appropriate that they are covered near the end of the book, after you've already learned how to build the applications.

Windows Forms application configuration is typically handled with `.config` XML files. These files hold settings that your application can use, including an indication of which version of the .NET Framework to use and how to provide debugging support.

To retrieve these settings from within your application, you use the `ConfigurationSettings` class and either the `AppSettings` property, which returns values from the `<appSettings>` configuration element, or the `GetConfig` method to return any other section of the `.config` file.

Localizing your application means translating its resources into different languages and cultures. This involves creating `.resources` files and satellite assemblies for each new culture that you want to support. The naming scheme for localized application is important: All files must have the same root name. You can use the `ResourceManager` class to retrieve values that are contained in the resource files, thereby completely disassociating your application logic from the UI presentation.

Microsoft Active Accessibility is built into all Windows Forms controls. It helps users who have difficulties use your application by providing them with visual and aural cues to help them navigate around their computer. This is supported in each control by a few special properties.

Finally, *deployment* is the process of delivering your application to a user or users. The only requirement here is to simply copy the files in question. The .NET Framework and the Common Language Runtime handle everything else for you.

Tomorrow, your last lesson, will cover debugging techniques in Windows Forms. Debugging is often a trial and error process, but with the tools that you'll learn about tomorrow, you'll make it an exact science.

20

Q&A

Q How do I create resource files from images?

A Unfortunately, this is more difficult than creating resource files from plain text. You need to convert your images into appropriately formatted XML before you can compile them into assemblies.

The .NET Framework QuickStart package comes with a tool called `ResXGen.exe`. It uses the following syntax:

```
ResXGen /i:filename /o:resource_name /n:name
```

where `filename` specifies the image file (for example, a `.gif` or `.jpg` file), `resource_name` specifies the resource file to be generated (which must end in the extension `.resx`), and `name` is the property name for your resource, much like "Caption" or "GoodbyeMessage" that were specified earlier today.

For more information on `ResXGen`, check out the .NET Framework documentation.

Q Before .NET, I could store user-specific information in the registry. In other words, for a single application, there could be different settings depending on the current user. Can I do this in .NET?

A Not directly with `.config` files. You can, however, still keep information in the Windows registry using the `Registry` class. This class provides information on data contained in the registry, and allows you to write to it as well.

Q I can't figure out what properties a particular configuration section handler has, or what type of data it returns. Help!

A The Intermediate Disassembler tool (`ildasm.exe`) is a useful tool for examining the contents of any .NET assembly (`.dll` or `.exe` files). This tool provides a visual interface that details all the members that are available in any particular assembly. By examining the contents of the class in which you are interested, you can determine what types the object returns and what methods and properties it supports. This tool is often a good substitute for the .NET Framework documentation.

Workshop

This workshop will help reinforce the concepts that were covered in today's lesson. It is helpful to understand the answers fully before moving on. Answers can be found in Appendix A, "Answers to Quiz Questions and Exercises."

Quiz

1. What is one advantage of `.config` files over `.ini` files?
2. What does the `al.exe` tool do?
3. Which two parameters does the `resgen` tool expect?
4. True or false: A configuration file for an application that is named `MyApp.exe` should be called `MyApp.config`.

5. True or false: When you are translating resource files, you must translate the property names as well as their values.

6. What is the base element for all `.config` files?

7. For what purpose is the `<system.windows.forms>` configuration element used?

8. What is camel-casing, and where is it required?

9. Write a simple `.config` file that has an `<appSettings>` section. This section should contain one element, `Color`, with the value `Black`.

Exercises

1. Incorporate three more locales in the example from Listing 20.6: French (from France), Danish, and Greek. Don't worry about translating the actual phrases—just tweak the phrases to indicate the current culture. (See the .NET Framework documentation under the `CultureInfo` class for the culture codes for these languages.)

2. Create a `.config` file to specify the culture to use in your application from Exercise 1. This way, you won't have to modify your source code and recompile your application every time you want to test a new culture. (Hint: Use the `<appSettings>` section.)

20

DAY 21

Debugging and Profiling Your Windows Forms

Welcome to your last day in *Sams Teach Yourself .NET Windows Forms in 21 Days*! Today's lesson covers the last, but certainly not least, topics that are important to building Windows Forms applications: debugging and profiling. *Debugging* is the process of weeding out any errors in your applications, whether you know about them or not. *Profiling* is a technique to optimize your applications for performance by watching how they perform normally.

These two topics have been grouped together because they involve similar processes. Both topics involve attaching to a running application so you can see what, exactly, is going on under the hood as a user interacts with the application.

Today you will learn

- The benefits of using `try-catch` blocks in your code
- How to create program database files for debugging
- How JIT debugging works

- Aspects of the CLR Debugger and its command-line companion, CorDbg
- How to use the Process class

Debugging in Windows Forms

You've no doubt stumbled upon errors while building your Windows Forms applications. Errors are a part of everyday life as a developer, so you must learn to deal with them. Often, the process of eliminating your errors (debugging) is a time-consuming, tedious task that involves pouring over your code line by line, and often character by character. With the .NET Framework, fixing your errors is much easier.

You can debug your applications in several ways. This section examines ways that you can zero in on your errors while writing your code. Subsequent sections look at a couple of tools that the .NET Framework provides to help you fix your errors after you've created your application.

NEW TERM   Before you learn how to debug, though, it's a good idea to take a quick look at the debugging framework that .NET provides. When an error occurs in your application (assuming it has already compiled fine), the Common Language Runtime raises an *exception*, which is just a fancy word for an error. When an error arises, the CLR *throws* an exception. .NET has an Exception class (and many other classes that derive from Exception) that is used to represent any error that arises in your application.

This is a good thing because now your errors are actual objects with which you can fiddle. Because each error is an object, you can retrieve its properties, call methods on it, and even create your own errors. You can imagine that debugging in Windows Forms involves finding these Exception classes and handling them appropriately.

The rest of this section examines one of the easiest ways to handle Exception classes: by using the try-catch syntax of the .NET Framework.

It is easy to conceptualize the nature of tries and catches in .NET. The *try* portion means that you are *trying*, or tentatively executing, a piece of code. When you use a try code block, the CLR becomes more careful when executing code. Without try code blocks, the CLR executes everything it comes across without care; if a piece of code doesn't work, then too bad; an exception is thrown and the CLR can't stop its momentum, so your application crashes in a blaze of glory. (Okay, so maybe it's not that grandiose.)

With try blocks, however, the CLR takes caution when executing code. This isn't to say that it executes code more slowly, but now, when an exception is thrown, the CLR is aware of it and can prevent a crash.

This leads into the second part of the equation: a `catch` block. Literally, this block catches any exceptions that are thrown. In a `catch` block, you can manipulate and correct any exceptions that occur. Coupled with the `try` block, you can now discretely handle errors when they arise, rather than upsetting the user by causing the application to crash.

The syntax for a `try`-`catch` block is simple:

```
try {
    //sensitive code
} catch (Exception e) {
    //code to handle the exception
}
```

Or, in VB.NET:

```
Try
    'sensitive code
Catch e as Exception
    'code to handle the exception
End Try
```

"Sensitive code" represents any piece of code that might throw an exception or that you don't think will work correctly. This can be quite a number of things, from initializing a variable, to using the I/O capabilities of .NET to open a file that isn't necessarily there.

The `catch` statement, as mentioned earlier, catches a particular `Exception`. The previous two code snippets have caught an object of type `Exception`. You can substitute any other classes that derive from `Exception`, such as `ArithmeticException` or `IOException`. Each particular exception class represents a certain type of error and can have any number of subexceptions that narrow the error even further. For example, when you try to access a file that isn't there, the exception that is thrown is `IOException`, which is derived from `SystemException`, which in turn is derived from `Exception` (see Figure 21.1).

Because the .NET Exception framework is hierarchical, you can use a `catch` block for a parent exception and also catch all exceptions that derive from that parent. In the two previous code snippets, you are actually catching any type of exception because the `Exception` class is the granddaddy of them all. This means that you can have multiple `catch` blocks per `try` block, in case you need to handle different types of exceptions. For example:

```
try {
    //sensitive code
} catch (IOException e) {
    //handle an I/O exception
} catch (SystemException e) {
    //handle any System exception, including IOException and
```

21

```
        //its brothers
    } catch (Exception e) {
        //handle all exceptions, including System Exceptions
    }
```

FIGURE 21.1

*The exception hierarchy in the .NET Framework is quite complex (*System. SystemException *even has sub-sub-, and sub-sub-sub-exceptions, which aren't shown here).*

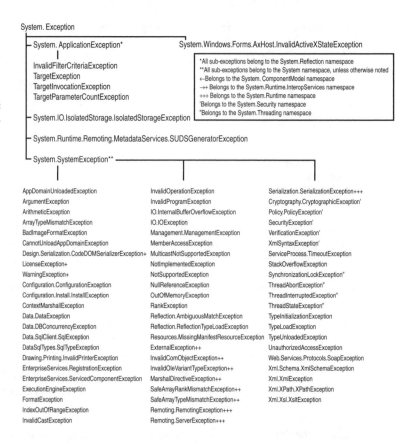

Make sure that if you use multiple `catch` blocks, you go in most specific to least specific order. In other words, code that handles a specific error should come before code that handles a generic error, like `Exception`. Otherwise, because only one `catch` block will be executed, your generic handler will always execute before any others.

It's time for an example. Listing 21.1 shows a simple application that tries to open a text file and display its contents in a `RichTextBox` control.

LISTING 21.1 A Simple IO Application

```
 1: Imports System
 2: Imports System.Windows.Forms
 3: Imports System.Drawing
 4:
 5: Namespace TYWinForms.Day21
 6:
 7:    Public Class Listing211 : Inherits Form
 8:        private rtbText as New RichTextBox
 9:        private btPush as new Button()
10:
11:        public sub New()
12:            rtbText.Height = 225
13:            rtbText.Dock = DockStyle.Bottom
14:            rtbText.ScrollBars = RichTextBoxScrollBars.Both
15:
16:            btPush.Location = new Point(100,10)
17:            btPush.Text = "Open It!"
18:            AddHandler btPush.Click, new EventHandler(
➥AddressOf Me.OpenFile)
19:
20:            Me.Text = "Listing 21.1"
21:            Me.Controls.Add(rtbText)
22:            Me.Controls.Add(btPush)
23:        end sub
24:
25:        private sub OpenFile(Sender As Object, e As
➥EventArgs)
26:            rtbText.LoadFile("c:\temp\happy.txt",
➥RichTextBoxStreamType.PlainText)
27:        end sub
28:
29:        public shared sub Main()
30:            Application.Run(new Listing211)
31:        end sub
32:    End Class
33: End Namespace
```

ANALYSIS This listing should look fairly familiar if you've covered Day 11, "Working with Windows Input/Output." On lines 8 and 9, a `RichTextBox` and `Button` control are created. They are initialized on lines 12–18; the button's `Click` event has an event handler on line 25 that uses the `LoadFile` method of the `RichTextBox` control to open the `c:\temp\happy.txt` file and display it to the user. However, if you execute this application as is, and the `c:\temp\happy.txt` file does not exist, you get the error shown in Figure 21.2 if you don't have debuggers installed, or the error in Figure 21.3 if you do.

21

FIGURE 21.2

The default exception-handling routine allows you to continue and ignore the error or to quit the application.

FIGURE 21.3

If you have a JIT debugger installed, you can debug the application. Note the type of exception that is raised.

If you were the user of this application, you would be pretty frustrated if you were presented with either Figure 21.2 or 21.3. You need to handle the error so that the user is presented with a more user-friendly error message, if one at all. Modify the OpenFile method on line 25 of Listing 21.1 so it looks like the following code snippet:

```
private sub OpenFile(Sender As Object, e As EventArgs)
   Try
      rtbText.LoadFile("c:\temp\happy.txt",
➥RichTextBoxStreamType.PlainText)
   Catch ex As Exception
      MessageBox.Show("That file does not exist!")
   End Try
end sub
```

Now, when the user pushes the button and the file doesn't exist, she is presented with Figure 21.4.

When the user clicks the OK button, the application continues on as if the error were never raised—in other words, as if the OpenFile method never executed. A message box is displayed inside the Catch block, but you could do nearly anything you wanted. For example, you could modify the text to ask the user if she would like to create the file if it doesn't exist, and do so using the I/O capabilities of .NET.

FIGURE 21.4

Using a try-catch *block enables you to create a much more user-friendly message.*

The try-catch block has an additional, optional part: the finally statement. This statement's syntax follows the catch statement. finally is used to execute code that needs to be run, regardless of whether the code in a try block works.

For example, the following code snippet creates an array of strings and tries to create a FileInfo object from each string. If the file exists, then a message box is display showing its length. If the file does not exist, then a user-friendly message is shown. A message box is shown indicating the number of strings processed regardless of whether a FileInfo object is created.

```
int i = 0;
FileInfo tmpFile;
String[] arrFileStrings = new String[] {"c:\\temp\\happy.txt",
➡"c:\\winforms\\day21\\listing21.1.vb"};
foreach (String strName in arrFileStrings) {
   try {
      tmpFile = new FileInfo(strName);
      MessageBox.Show("Length of " + strName + ": " +
➡tmpFile.Length.ToString());
   } catch (Exception ex) {
      MessageBox.Show(strName + " is not a valid file!");
   } finally {
      i++;
      MessageBox.Show(i.ToString() + " files processed");
   }
}
```

All exception classes have a few useful properties that provide additional information about the error in question. Table 21.1 describes the properties of the Exception class, which are inherited by all sub-exception classes.

TABLE 21.1 Exception Properties

Property	Description
HelpLink	Returns an optional file that is associated with the exception in question. It must be in a URL format. For example: `file://C:/TYWinforms/Day21/help.html#ErrorNum42`
InnerException	When one exception throws another, this property provides a reference to the originating exception.
Message	The user-friendly message that describes the exception.
Source	The name of the application or object that generated the exception.
StackTrace	A string representation of all frames on the call stack at the time the exception was raised. In other words, this property tells you all the methods that were currently executing. (Remember that one method often calls another, so you can trace back to the root method of the problem.)
TargetSite	Returns the method that raised the exception.

Instead of waiting for an error to occur in your application, you can create your own error at any time by using the throw statement. Simply create a new exception of the type you need, and you can sabotage your own application:

```
throw(new Exception());
```

Why would anyone want to throw an error that the application explicitly created? This would happen for a number of different reasons, the most common of which occurs when you create your own custom Windows Forms controls. When you create custom functionality, you might want an error to be thrown where one normally isn't. The throw keyword is perfect for this purpose. You can specify the Message and InnerException properties for new exceptions that you create, which the handling application can use as you've done with the built-in exceptions.

In general, you should use a try-catch block whenever you are executing code that cannot be guaranteed to execute properly, such as database calls, file I/O calls, network calls, and operations that depend on a specific user input.

Throughout this book, the try-catch blocks are omitted in most places that they should be, but now that you know how to use this syntax, don't hesitate to use them!

Do	**Don't**
Do use `try-catch` blocks anywhere the code cannot be guaranteed to execute properly.	**Don't** depend on `try-catch` blocks to validate user input. For example, if you present the user with a textbox to enter a number, verify that the input is indeed a number before you execute code that depends on that number. Don't try to execute such code and hope the `try-catch` block handles it properly.

JIT Debugging

Just-in-time debugging, as mentioned earlier, is the process of debugging your application while it is running, as soon as an error occurs. Whereas `try-catch` blocks were designed to fix errors before a user sees them, JIT debugging is designed to alert the user to these errors so that they can be fixed. In this case, however, the user is the developer (because she typically is the only one who can fix the errors).

NEW TERM When you run an application, the computer executes compiled code. This code executes instructions, creates variables along the way, assigns values to the variables, and destroys them as well. Recall that all of these variables are stored in memory. *Attaching a debugger* means that another application, a JIT debugger, is watching the memory that the first application used. The debugger can interpret the instructions and memory that the application used and let the developer know, in readable terms, what is going on.

Because the JIT debugger can't know the internals of the application while it's running (because it can't access the source code in the application), it needs some help to provide debugging information. This is done with the help of a program database file (`.pdb`) that contains debugging information such as the methods and variables in the program.

Creating a `.pdb` file is easy; simply add the `/debug` parameter to your command-line compilers. For example, for the VB.NET compiler, use this:

```
vbc /t:winexe /r:system.dll,... /debug temp.vb
```

With this command, a new file named `temp.pdb` is created. When a JIT debugger tries to debug your application—`temp.exe` in this case—it uses the contents of the `.pdb` file to aid in processing.

21

There's one more step to enabling JIT debugging. Recall from yesterday the `.config` file and the `<system.windows.forms>` configuration element. You need to enable JIT debugging in this element as well. For example, your `.config` file for the `temp.exe` application could look like this:

```
<configuration>
   <system.windows.forms jitDebugging="true"/>
</configuration>
```

Now you will learn about all the different .NET tools that are available for debugging.

Using the `DbgClr` Tool

The Common Language Runtime Debugger, or `DbgClr`, is an application that allows you to attach to a process and watch and control the execution of your application. This application is typically located in the `c:\Program Files\Microsoft.NET\FrameworkSDK\GuiDebug` directory and is called `DbgClr.exe`. You can either attach this debugger to an already running application or start a new application from within the debugger. In this case, you start from scratch and open the debugger by running the `DbgClr.exe` file. You should see something similar to Figure 21.5.

FIGURE 21.5

The Common Language Runtime Debugger interface looks similar to Visual Studio.NET.

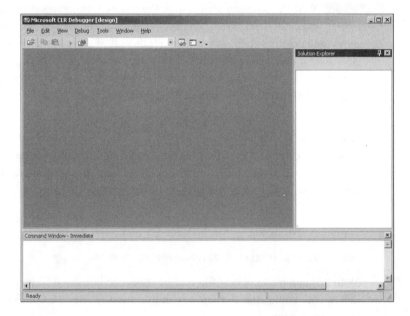

After you open the debugger, then debugging the applications is a three-step process:

1. Open the application you want to debug, or attach it to the already running application.

2. Set breakpoints.

3. Use the debugger's tools to manipulate your application.

Assuming that you've saved Listing 21.1 as listing21.1.vb, open it from the CLR Debugger by going to the File menu, Open, File, and choosing your file. You should see the source code in the CLR debugger. The file appears in the Solution Explorer on the right side of the screen. When you start debugging, you can use this file to follow along during the execution process. To start the debugging process, select Program to Debug from the Debug menu, and enter the name of your executable file (c:\winforms\day21\listing21.1.exe). Now the debugger knows what application is associated with the source code you opened. Press F5 to start your application, or go to the Debug menu and select Start. Your application appears as normal, and the CLR Debugger is ready for use.

Conversely, if you've already started your application, go to the Tools menu in the CLR Debugger and select Debug Processes. A listing appears, similar to Figure 21.6. Choose your application from the list and click the Attach button. Your application will appear in the Debugged Processes Window (XXX in Figure 21.6); click the Break button to stop execution and view the code. Attaching to a running application is useful when you don't have the source code available (although you won't be able to modify the application without the source code).

FIGURE 21.6

Attach the debugger to your running application by clicking Attach.

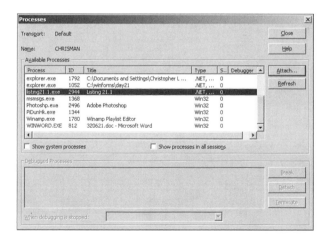

A new window, Output, is now available in the CLR Debugger. This window shows you what modules are loaded for your application, which can help you determine the dependencies the application may have.

21

Caution When you attach to any process with a debugger, that application is usually frozen (meaning it will be unusable by users) and any unsaved information might be lost. Make sure that when you attach to the process, you are not running serious applications.

NEW TERM A *breakpoint* is a place in the code where execution halts—it is essentially paused. Breakpoints are useful for debugging specific lines in your code. For example, if you knew a line was causing errors in your application, you could set a breakpoint immediately before it and then use the debugger to analyze the instructions and variables.

To set a breakpoint, click the left column next to the source code of your file. A red dot should appear, meaning that the execution halts at this line. Hold your mouse cursor over the breakpoint to see exactly where it will occur, as shown in Figure 21.7.

FIGURE 21.7

Setting a breakpoint in your code causes execution to halt temporarily at the specified line.

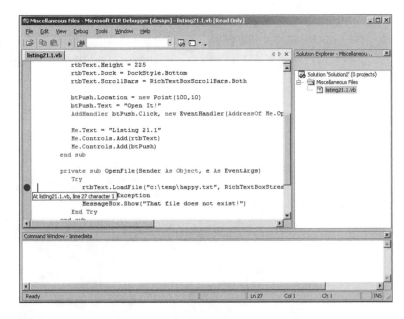

Now you can interact with your application as normal. If you haven't set any breakpoints, or there are no errors in your application, the code will execute so fast you won't be able to see anything happen. While this is a good indication that your application is running properly, it doesn't help you in the debugging process at all. We need to examine our application, so click the Stop button in the debugger or press Shift+F5), and set a breakpoint at the beginning on the `OpenFile` method on line 25 of Listing 21.1. Now press F5 again.

Your application starts up just as normal, but as soon as you click the button, the application halts and your debugger takes over. The Output window (lower right corner) changes to display the current files and assemblies that are loaded. This lets you know all of the modules that are affected by your application.

The Locals window (lower left corner—you may have to click the Locals tab to view it) appears displaying all the current variables in the application and their values. Use the Locals window to determine if your variables are being set properly. For example, if you can't figure out why the caption for your application isn't displaying properly, look in the Locals window under `this` (`Me` in VB.NET), `System.Windows.Forms.Form`, `WindowText`, and check the value there. If it isn't what you expected, then you know something went wrong prior to that breakpoint. You can even change the values in the Locals window, although any changes you make won't be permanent; you'll lose them as soon as you stop debugging. This information can help you fix problems as they occur in your application.

> **Note**
>
> The CLR Debugger cannot be used as an editor. In other words, you won't be able to use the CLR Debugger to modify your source code. Instead, you have to use Notepad or your favorite editor to modify your code as necessary.

When your application is stopped at a breakpoint, open the Command window (lower right corner, or select Windows, Immediate from the Debug menu). This window allows you to execute commands from your application just as if they were in the source code. For example, in the Command window type `MessageBox.Show("Hi from the Command Window")`, and press Enter. The debugger executes the command from your application and a message box pops up. You can execute virtually any command from this window.

Next, open the Watch window (from the Debug, Windows menu) and type a variable name that is used in your page (such as `rtbText`) and press Enter. You can now watch this variable as you move through your application, and see if it is ever assigned a proper value. If you type `Me` into the Watch window, you'll be able to see all of the variables that belong to `Me`.

These two windows are great for examining information about your application at any given instant. These alone can help you fix a lot of problems, but sometimes you need to see the application in action, rather than in a frozen state.

21

At the top of the CLR Debugger window are buttons that allow you to control the execution of your application in real-time, such as moving to the next line of execution, and stopping debugging altogether. Next to the yellow Show Next Statement arrow are three buttons: Step Into, Step Over, and Step Out. These three buttons allow you to navigate through your application's execution. For example, if you've set your breakpoint on a method, clicking the Step Over button stops execution at every statement in the method. This is helpful if you need to see every line being executed, but can be a bit tedious, especially if you have lots of code. Note that if you come across a method invocation, the debugger doesn't take you to that method, but simply "steps over" it. Step Into is similar to Step Over, except that it allows you to branch into different sections of code (such as other methods) if the logic requires it. Click the Step Out button and the application executes the current method without stopping until it reaches the beginning of the next method. In other words, Step Out enables you to skip entire methods in your code if you know they function correctly.

To the left of the Step buttons are controls that look like a VCR's buttons: Continue, Pause, Stop, and Restart. These buttons do exactly what they imply, allowing you to control the debug process as a whole.

Debugging compiled applications can often be a pain because you cannot stop execution without losing information or watch variables in real-time. This makes it difficult to track down where an error is occurring, especially if your application is complex. The CLR Debugger provides all of the preceding capabilities for Windows Forms applications, making debugging a snap.

Using the `CorDbg` Tool

`CorDbg.exe` is essentially the command-line version of the `DbgClr.exe` JIT debugger. It functions the same way, but instead of using a visual interface, you must issue commands via the command prompt. Because of this, `CorDbg.exe` is a bit more difficult to use than `DbgClr.exe`; therefore, it's not covered in detail here (besides, you already know the capabilities of `DbClr.exe`).

To start the `CorDbg` tool without starting an application first, simply type `CorDbg` at the command line. Then type the command:

```
run application name
```

Make sure that the application you want to debug is in the same directory that you typed the command from. Using `listing21.1.exe`, you should see something similar to Figure 21.8.

Your application is now started and paused at the Main method. To move to the next line of execution, type the command si. You move step-by-step through your application, which can be a tedious process. You can use the next command to move to the next line in your source code, which can sometimes be different from moving to the next line of execution (as with the si command). As you move through the application, you often see strange output such as the following:

```
(cordbg) next

[0044] call        dword ptr ds:[02FF17B8h]
(cordbg) next

[004a] mov         ecx,ebx
(cordbg) next

[004c] call        dword ptr ds:[02FF2C18h]
```

These commands show you what is happening in memory as your application is running. dword ptr is a special instruction that points to a location in your computer memory. Most of the time, you won't care about this information, but it's there if you need to dig into low-level execution processes.

For more information on the oodles of commands that are available with the CorDbg.exe tool, see the .NET Framework documentation.

Profiling Your Applications

NEW TERM   *Profiling* is the process of watching an application and examining the resources it consumes. Profiling is useful when you need to fine-tune the performance of your applications because you can see where bottlenecks occur and which pieces of your code take a long time to execute. With this information, you can restructure or rewrite your code to gain performance—something that is always a good change.

21

Unfortunately, no built-in tool is available to profile your applications. However, the good news is that you can easily build your own, thanks to the `Process` class. Recall from the discussion on threads on Day 19 that a process represents a running application on your computer. Threads work for processes, and processes are displayed in the Windows Task Manager (see Figure 21.9).

FIGURE 21.9

The Windows Task Manager shows all the currently running processes.

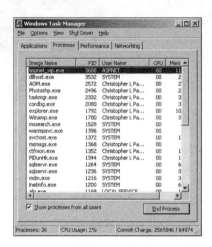

The `Process` class can be used to examine any one of these running processes, and it provides information such as the amount of memory that the application uses, the percent of CPU time, the start and end times of a particular method, and so on. Therefore, not only can you see how well your application is performing, but you can also compare it to other processes on your computer.

Now you will look at an example application. Listing 21.2 uses the `Process` class to display statistics about the current application to the user.

LISTING 21.2   Watching Processes

```
1:  using System;
2:  using System.Windows.Forms;
3:  using System.Drawing;
4:
5:  using System.Diagnostics;
6:
7:  namespace TYWinforms.Day21 {
8:     public class Listing212 : Form {
9:        private Label lblProcessor = new Label();
10:        private Label lblMemory = new Label();
11:        private Label lblTotProcessor = new Label();
```

LISTING 21.2   continued

```
12:        private Process objProcess = new Process();
13:        private System.Windows.Forms.Timer tmrProcess = new
➥System.Windows.Forms.Timer();
14:
15:        public Listing212() {
16:            lblProcessor.Size = new Size(250,20);
17:            lblProcessor.Location = new Point(10,10);
18:
19:            lblMemory.Size = new Size(250,20);
20:            lblMemory.Location = new Point(10,30);
21:
22:            lblTotProcessor.Size = new Size(250,20);
23:            lblTotProcessor.Location = new Point(10,50);
24:
25:            tmrProcess.Tick += new EventHandler(this.Update);
26:            tmrProcess.Interval = 500;
27:            tmrProcess.Start();
28:
29:            objProcess = Process.GetCurrentProcess();
30:
31:            this.Text = ".NET Profiler";
32:            this.Controls.Add(lblProcessor);
33:            this.Controls.Add(lblMemory);
34:            this.Controls.Add(lblTotProcessor);
35:        }
36:
37:        private void Update(Object Sender, EventArgs e) {
38:            objProcess.Refresh();
39:            lblMemory.Text = "Memory: " +
➥objProcess.PrivateMemorySize.ToString();
40:            lblProcessor.Text = "Private Processor Time: " +
➥objProcess.PrivilegedProcessorTime.ToString();
41:            lblTotProcessor.Text = "Total Processor Time: " +
➥objProcess.TotalProcessorTime.ToString();
42:        }
43:
44:        public static void Main() {
45:            Application.Run(new Listing212());
46:        }
47:    }
48: }
```

ANALYSIS   First, you need to import the proper namespaces. On line 5, you import the
System.Diagnostics namespace, which contains the Process class. On lines
9–13, you create a few controls, including your Process object and a Timer. (You'll see
why in a moment.) Note that your new Process object isn't watching any processes yet;
currently, it's not doing anything. That will be fixed on line 29.

21

In the constructor, on lines 16–23, you initialize the various `Label` controls that you have created. Each of these labels displays one aspect about the process you want to watch. The `Timer` is set to go off every half second (line 26) so that you can keep updating the labels; otherwise, you wouldn't get accurate statistics. The `Tick` event handler is the `Update` method on line 37, but you'll get there in a second.

On line 29, you call the `GetCurrentProcess` method of the `Process` class. Like the name infers, this line makes your new `Process` object watch the process that represents this application. In other words, you'll be watching statistics on the application that is created by Listing 21.2.

Although watching the current application's process is a nice feature, it's not always possible or useful. Therefore, the `Process` class has a few other methods that you can use to watch processes that other applications create. `GetProcessById` retrieves a process by the operating system's identifier. (If you don't see the process ID (PID) in Task Manager, click on the View menu, select Columns, and choose PID.) This method is great if you know the PID of the process you want to watch, but that isn't always possible. `GetProcesses` returns all the processes that are currently running on the system, which allows you to watch statistics for multiple applications at once. Finally, `GetProcessesByName` returns an array of `Processes` that match a specified name. This name is typically the name of your executable application, minus the `.exe` ending. For example, if you were running `listing21.1.exe`, you could watch its process with the following command:

```
objProcess = Process.GetProcessesByName("listing21.1")[0];
```

Remember that this method returns an array, so you must specify which item in the array you want to watch. Most of the time, only one item exists in the array, so specifying `[0]` (or `(0)` in VB.NET) works fine. Note that the process must be running, or you will receive an error. (Here's the perfect place for a `try-catch` block that you learned about earlier today.)

Now move down to the `Update` method. When you initially display one of the properties from the `Process` class, you are retrieving a snapshot of that property. In other words, the properties do not update themselves. Therefore, you must call the `Process.Refresh` method to retrieve updated values, as shown on line 38. Finally, lines 39–41 display various properties about the currently running process. (You'll examine these more in a moment.) Figure 21.10 shows the output after running this application for a few seconds.

FIGURE 21.10

You can watch the dynamically updating resource statistics for your application.

> .NET Profiler
>
> Private Processor Time: 00:00:00.1602304
> Memory: 9859072
> Total Processor Time: 00:00:00.2904176

The `Process` class provides quite a few pieces of information about a particular application, from the amount of time that your CPU must devote to it to the caption on the currently open window. Table 21.2 lists all the useful properties of `Process`—there's quite a few of them.

TABLE 21.2 Process-Related Properties of `Process`

Property	Description
`BasePriority`	Returns the priority of the current process. (See Day 19 for more information on priorities.)
`ExitCode`	An integer that an application returns when it closes. Zero typically means that the application exited normally; other values might mean errors. (See your application's documentation for more information.)
`ExitTime`	Indicates the time that the associated process stopped.
`Handle`	Returns the handle that is associated with a process.
`HandleCount`	Returns the number of handles that are associated with a process.
`HasExited`	Indicates if the process has stopped.
`Id`	Indicates the process identifier (PID) value.
`MachineName`	Indicates the name of the machine on which the process is currently running.
`MainModule`	Returns a `ProcessModule` object that represents the module that started your application (typically an `.exe` or `.dll` file).

21

TABLE 21.2 continued

Property	Description
MainWindowHandle	Indicates the handle of the process's primary window.
MainWindowTitle	Indicates the caption of the process's primary window.
MaxWorkingSet	Indicates the maximum amount of memory that will be reserved for a given process.
MinWorkingSet	Indicates the minimum amount of memory that will be reserved for a given process. In other words, the amount of memory that your application uses will never go below this amount.
Modules	Returns an array of ProcessModule objects that your application has loaded (for example, .exe and .dll files).
NonpagedSystemMemorySize	Indicates the amount of memory that is allocated to the process that cannot be written to the virtual memory paging file (see your operating system documentation for information on virtual memory and page files).
PagedMemorySize	Indicates the amount of memory that is allocated to the process that can be written to the virtual memory paging file.
PagedSystemMemorySize	Indicates the amount of system memory that is allocated to the process that can be written to the virtual memory paging file.
PeakPagedMemorySize	Indicates the maximum amount of memory that can be written to the virtual memory page file that has been allocated to your process.
PeakVirtualMemorySize	Indicates the maximum amount of virtual memory that your process has requested.
PeakWorkingSet	Indicates the maximum amount of memory that the process has requested at one time.
PriorityBoostEnabled	Indicates whether the process should temporarily be given a higher priority (and therefore executed faster) when its main window has the focus.
PriorityClass	A PriorityClass object that represents the type of priority that a process has (such as Normal or High).

TABLE 21.2 continued

Property	Description
PrivateMemorySize	Indicates the amount of memory that is allocated to the current process that cannot be shared by other applications.
PrivilegedProcessorTime	Indicates the amount of time that the CPU has spent running code for a process inside the operating system core.
ProcessName	The name of the current process.
ProcessorAffinity	Indicates the CPUs on which a process can run in a multi-processor system.
Responding	Indicates whether the user interface of the current process is responding to user input (in other words, if the program is hanging).
StandardError	Gets a StreamReader object to read error output from the application.
StandardInput	Gets a StreamWriter object that can be used to send input to the process.
StandardOutput	Gets a StreamReader object to read standard output from the application.
StartInfo	Information that is associated with the process when it is started (for example, the name of the executable file that launched the process).
StartTime	The time that the process was started.
Threads	The Thread objects that are associated with the current process.
TotalProcessorTime	Indicates the total amount of time that the CPU has spent executing this process (the sum of the UserProcessorTime and PrivilegedProcessorTime values).
UserProcessorTime	Indicates the amount of time that the CPU has spent executing code inside the application that is represented by this process.
VirtualMemorySize	Indicates the current size of the current process's virtual memory.
WorkingSet	Indicates the associated process's current memory usage.

21

With all these different properties, it's often difficult to figure out which ones to use to profile your applications. It really depends on the type of application you are building. For example, if you're dealing with a database-accessing program, you might want to watch the various memory properties. A high `PrivateMemorySize` value might mean that you are storing a lot of database information in memory, which is not necessarily a bad thing. A high `VirtualMemorySize` means that a lot of information that should be in memory is stored on disk, which can adversely affect performance. Perhaps you are retrieving too much data from the database at one time and some is being stored as virtual memory. One possible solution is to retrieve smaller bits of data as a time.

If you are designing an application with complex calculations, watch the various processor time properties. For example, a 3D graphical computer-aided design (CAD) application must perform many complex linear algebra calculations that eat up processor time. You can monitor the `UserProcessorTime` property to see just how intensive your calculations are. In addition, you can watch the effects that adding more threads to your application has.

Summary

Debugging and profiling are two steps in application development that, unfortunately, are often overlooked. Both are necessary to ensure that your application performs stably and efficiently. With the .NET Framework, these two steps are easy.

You first learned about the `try-catch` block to handle errors that you can't always predict. Such errors can be generated from code that deals with I/O, or code that depends on specific user input. You can, after all, never predict what a user is going to do.

Just-in-time (JIT) debugging is the process of attaching a debugger to your application as it runs so that you can watch the process of execution. The CLR Debugger and `CorDbg` are two JIT Debuggers that allow you to see everything that happens in your application, from executing code to references to memory locations.

Finally, profiling is the process of watching the resources that an application consumes as it executes. By examining the amount of memory that your application consumes and the amount of time that the CPU takes to execute it, you can see if and how your application needs to be optimized.

You've finally reached the end of your 21 days. I hope you've enjoyed your journey through Windows Forms. Don't forget to check out the final Bonus Project, "Completing Your Word Processor," to recap everything you've learned the past three weeks!

Q&A

Q Can I use the Windows Performance Monitor (`perfmon.exe`) to examine my applications?

A You bet! Open the Performance Monitor and click the plus button (Add) to add information about your running application to the window. For the Performance Object option, choose .NET CLR Memory. The Select Counters from List list box lists various aspects you can watch. In the Selected Instance from list box, you should see your application. Select it and click Add to monitor that aspect of your application.

If this default behavior doesn't provide you with enough information, you can create a custom Performance Monitor using the `PerformanceCounter` class. This class allows you to define aspects of your application that you want to follow, known as counters. For more information, see the .NET Framework documentation.

Workshop

This workshop will help reinforce the concepts covered in today's lesson. It is helpful to understand the answers fully before moving on. Answers can be found in Appendix A, "Answers to Quiz Questions and Exercises."

Quiz

1. True or false? A `catch` block that specifies an exception of type `IOException` will also catch exceptions of type `SystemException`.

2. Is the following code correct?
```
Process[] objProcess = Process.GetProcessesByName
➥("listing21.2.exe ");
```

3. How do you create a program database file?

4. What is a breakpoint?

5. Name three properties of the `Exception` class.

6. How can you raise your own errors?

Exercise

Create an application that is similar to the Windows Task Manager. This application should let the user choose any running process from a list box. The process's properties, `Id`, `MainModule`, `PrivateMemorySize`, `TotalProcessorTime`, and number of running threads should display in labels. Don't forget to use `try-catch` blocks!

21

WEEK 3

In Review

Project 3: Completing Your Word Processor

This is it, the end of the line. Through the last 21 Days
you've learned all of the major topics that deal with Windows
Forms, from the basic building blocks to complex data
access. In the last week specifically you learned multithreading, localization, Web services, Windows services, deployment, and debugging—all ingredients in building a full fea-
tured advanced application.

In this final week-in-review section, we're going to build on
the NetWord application you created in the previous two
week in reviews. Last time, you turned it into an MDI application and created a Document class that represents each child
document in the parent window. Now we'll expand a bit on
that and make the functionality more Microsoft Word-like by
creating a custom Windows Forms control.

In this lesson you'll see a lot of the engineering it takes to get
an application to come together.

Creating a New Page Class

Before we get too far, let's take a look at the code from last
time. We have the NetWord.cs file, which will remain
unchanged (for discussion on this code, see "Week 1 in
Review: Creating a Word Processor"). NetWord.cs is the
main entry point of the application. Then we have the
FindDialog.cs file, which contains a custom dialog box control that allows the user to search for text in the document.

Finally, there is the `Document.cs` file, which contains the main portion of the user interface, a `RichTextBox` that the users enter their documents into. This class also has menus to provide standard functionality, and utilizes the `FindDialog` class for searching.

So far, the application works very similar to Notepad. It presents a single point of data entry that simply grows larger as the user enters more text. This is in contrast to Microsoft Word, where documents are represented by actual pages. In Word you can divide your text into logical bundles that you can manipulate—printing, searching, setting margins, and so on.

We're going to implement similar functionality by creating a new `Page` class to replace the existing document interface. This class will extend the `RichTextBox` control and provide some functionality that isn't built in—functionality that will be useful in our application. Listing P3.1 shows the code for the new `Page` class.

LISTING P3.1   The Page Class

```
1:  using System;
2:  using System.Drawing;
3:  using System.Windows.Forms;
4:  using System.Drawing.Printing;
5:
6:  namespace TYWinforms.P3 {
7:      public class Page : RichTextBox {
8:          public int PageNumber;
9:          private int intCharIndex;
10:          private int intLineIndex;
11:          public event EventHandler Filled;
12:
13:          private PageSettings objPageSettings;
14:
15:          public int CharIndex {
16:             get { return intCharIndex; }
17:          }
18:
19:          public int LineIndex {
20:             get { return intLineIndex; }
21:          }
22:
23:          public Page(Form frmParent, PageSettings
    ➥objPageSettings, int intPageNumber) {
24:             intCharIndex = 1;
25:             intLineIndex = 1;
26:             PageNumber = intPageNumber;
27:             int intWidth = (int)(.96 * (objPageSettings.
    ➥Bounds.Width - (objPageSettings.Margins.Left +
    ➥objPageSettings.Margins.Right)));
```

LISTING P3.1 continued

```
28:            int intHeight = (int)(.96 * (objPageSettings.
➥Bounds.Height - (objPageSettings.Margins.Top +
➥objPageSettings.Margins.Bottom)));
29:
30:            this.Parent = frmParent;
31:            this.ScrollBars = RichTextBoxScrollBars.None;
32:            this.Font = frmParent.Font;
33:            this.objPageSettings = objPageSettings;
34:            this.RightMargin = objPageSettings.Bounds.Width -
➥ (int)(.96 * (objPageSettings.Margins.Left +
➥objPageSettings.Margins.Right));
35:            this.Size = new Size(intWidth,intHeight);
36:        }
37:
38:        public void SetFont(Font fnt, Color clr) {
39:            this.SelectionFont = fnt;
40:            this.SelectionColor = clr;
41:        }
42:
43:        protected virtual void OnFilled(EventArgs e) {
44:            Filled(this, e);
45:        }
46:
47:        public void UpdatePageSettings(PageSettings
➥objPageSettings) {
48:            this.objPageSettings = objPageSettings;
49:
50:            this.RightMargin = objPageSettings.Bounds.Width -
➥ (int)(.96 * (objPageSettings.Margins.Left +
➥objPageSettings.Margins.Right));
51:        }
52:
53:        protected override void OnSelectionChanged(EventArgs e) {
54:            intLineIndex = this.GetLineFromCharIndex
➥ (this.SelectionStart) + 1;
55:
56:            int i = this.SelectionStart;
57:            while (this.GetPositionFromCharIndex(i).X > 1) {
58:                --i;
59:            }
60:
61:            intCharIndex = SelectionStart - i + 1;
62:
63:            if (this.GetPositionFromCharIndex
➥ (this.SelectionStart).Y + (this.SelectionFont.GetHeight()*2) >=
➥this.ClientSize.Height) {
64:                OnFilled(new EventArgs());
65:            }
66:
```

LISTING P3.1   continued

```
67:            base.OnSelectionChanged(e);
68:        }
69:    }
70: }
```

ANALYSIS   On line 7 you see the declaration of our `Page` class, which derives from the
`RichTextBox` class. Recall from Day 18, "Building Custom Windows Forms
Controls," that this allows us to create a new control based upon the derived one. This is
ideal because we don't want to have to re-create the control entirely.

Lines 8–21 show various properties we'll use in our application. On line 11 we create a
custom event called `Filled`. This event will fire whenever a page's boundaries are passed
(by entering too much text or by scrolling through the page, for example). The containing control can use this event to determine when a new page needs to be added.

We want to make available the `CharIndex` and `LineIndex` properties (lines 15 and 19) so
that the containing control (which will be the `Document` class) can access these variables.
You'll see how they become important a little later. Note the use of the property declaration syntax.

The constructor beginning on line 23 takes a few properties. The first, `frmParent` represents the containing control. `objPageSettings` represents the settings specified by the
container control (for example, margins, paper size, and page orientation). The final
property, `intPageNumber` represents the number of the page in the containing control—
for example, if the application contains more than one page, this property can be used to
identify the current page. The class that creates an instance of this `Page` class must supply all three parameters when creating new pages.

Lines 24–35 instantiate various properties of the control. Of particular interest are the
`RightMargin` property on line 34. `RightMargin` is a property of the `RichTextBox` class
that specifies how much text can fit on one line—in other words, the right edge of the
textbox. This is determined by examining the `objPageSettings` variable that was passed
in; you subtract the margins from the total page width to get the proper value.

The `SetFont` method on line 38 is used by the containing object to set the fonts used in
this new `Page` class. You'll see it in use later when we examine the revamped `Document`
class.

On line 43 we create the `OnFilled` method, which simply raises the `Filled` event you
learned about earlier. (See Day 5, "Handling Events in Your Windows Forms," for a
recap on why we need an `OnFilled` method.)

The `UpdatePageSettings` method on line 47 should be executed every time the page settings change. Since the page settings are not contained in the `Page` class (they are contained in the `Document` class), this method needs to be called with the new page settings object. The `RightMargin` member is updated to the new settings similar to the way it was initialized in the constructor.

`OnSelectionChanged` on line 53 is the final method in the `Page` class. This functionality used to be in the `Document` class, but we've moved it here for more logical flow. Essentially, this method updates the `intLineIndex` and `intCharIndex` values to whatever the current position in the control is. The container control can then use the `LineIndex` and `CharIndex` public properties to display the current location of the cursor. (See Week 2 in Review, "Project 2: Extending the Word Processor," for more information on this functionality.)

The only difference in this method is the bit on lines 63–65. We need a way in the `Page` class to let the containing object know when we've filled up a page (remember that each `Page` object represents one printed page). The check on line 63 does just this; it uses the `GetPositionFromCharIndex` method to determine what the `Y` coordinate of the current character is. If this value is sufficiently large (compared to the height of the control), it means the control is full and a new `Page` should be created. (Note the addition of the font height to the `Y` coordinate on line 63; this is because the `Y` coordinate returns the position of the *top* of the text, and we need to find the *bottom*, to see if we've reached the bottom of the control.) The `OnFilled` method raises our custom `Filled` event to let the containing control know the page is full.

Save this listing as `Page.cs`, and compile it using the following command:

```
csc /t:library /r:system.dll /r:system.windows.forms.dll
/r:system.drawing.dll Page.cs
```

Now you're ready to modify your `Document` class to use the new `Page` class instead of the regular `RichTextBox` control. Listing P3.2 shows the code for `Document.cs` in its entirety. There's a lot of code here, but much of it hasn't changed, so we won't examine it completely here. Again, see Week 2 in Review for more details.

LISTING P3.2   The Revised `Document` Class

```
1:  using System;
2:  using System.Windows.Forms;
3:  using System.IO;
4:  using System.Drawing;
5:  using System.Drawing.Printing;
6:  using System.ComponentModel;
7:  using System.Collections;
8:
```

LISTING P3.2   continued

```
9:   namespace TYWinforms.P3 {
10:      public class Document : Form {
11:          public ArrayList arrPages = new ArrayList();
12:          public int intCurrentPage;
13:
14:          private Panel pnlView = new Panel();
15:          private ContextMenu cmnuDocument = new ContextMenu();
16:          private StatusBar sbarMain = new StatusBar();
17:          private StatusBarPanel spnlLine = new
➥StatusBarPanel();
18:          private VScrollBar scrlbar = new VScrollBar();
19:
20:          private MainMenu mnuMain = new MainMenu();
21:
22:          private MenuItem mniFile = new MenuItem("File");
23:          private MenuItem mniSave = new MenuItem("Save");
24:          private MenuItem mniPageSetup = new MenuItem
➥ ("Page Setup...");
25:          private MenuItem mniPrintPreview = new MenuItem
➥ ("Print Preview");
26:          private MenuItem mniPrint = new MenuItem("Print...");
27:          private MenuItem mniEdit = new MenuItem("Edit");
28:          private MenuItem mniUndo = new MenuItem("Undo");
29:          private MenuItem mniCut = new MenuItem("Cut");
30:          private MenuItem mniCopy = new MenuItem("Copy");
31:          private MenuItem mniPaste = new MenuItem("Paste");
32:          private MenuItem mniFind = new MenuItem("Find...");
33:          private MenuItem mniFormat = new MenuItem("Format");
34:          private MenuItem mniFont = new MenuItem("Font...");
35:
36:          private Font fntCurrent = new Font
➥ ("Times New Roman", 10);
37:          private Color fntColor = Color.Black;
38:          private FontDialog dlgFont = new FontDialog();
39:          private PageSetupDialog dlgPageSetup = new
➥PageSetupDialog();
40:
41:          private PageSettings objPageSettings = new
➥PageSettings();
42:          private PrinterSettings objPrintSettings = new
➥PrinterSettings();
43:          private StringReader objReader;
44:
45:          public Document(string strName) {
46:              mniSave.Click += new EventHandler(this.
➥FileClicked);
47:              mniPageSetup.Click += new EventHandler(this.
➥FileClicked);
48:              mniPrintPreview.Click += new EventHandler(this.
➥FileClicked);
```

LISTING P3.2 continued

```
49:            mniPrint.Click += new EventHandler(this.
➥FileClicked);
50:
51:            mnuMain.MenuItems.Add(mniFile);
52:
53:            mniFile.MergeType = MenuMerge.MergeItems;
54:            mniFile.MenuItems.Add(mniSave);
55:            mniFile.MenuItems.Add("-");
56:            mniFile.MenuItems.Add(mniPageSetup);
57:            mniFile.MenuItems.Add(mniPrintPreview);
58:            mniFile.MenuItems.Add(mniPrint);
59:
60:            mniFile.MergeOrder = 1;
61:            mniEdit.MergeOrder = 2;
62:            mniFormat.MergeOrder = 3;
63:            mniSave.MergeOrder = 30;
64:            mniFile.MenuItems[1].MergeOrder = 35;
65:            mniPageSetup.MergeOrder = 40;
66:            mniPrintPreview.MergeOrder = 45;
67:            mniPrint.MergeOrder = 50;
68:
69:            sbarMain.ShowPanels = true;
70:            sbarMain.Font = new Font("Arial", 10);
71:            sbarMain.Panels.Add(spnlLine);
72:            spnlLine.AutoSize = StatusBarPanelAutoSize.Spring;
73:            spnlLine.Alignment = HorizontalAlignment.Right;
74:
75:            mniUndo.Click += new EventHandler(this.
➥EditClicked);
76:            mniCut.Click += new EventHandler(this.
➥EditClicked);
77:            mniCopy.Click += new EventHandler(this.
➥EditClicked);
78:            mniPaste.Click += new EventHandler(this.
➥EditClicked);
79:            mniFind.Click += new EventHandler(this.
➥EditClicked);
80:
81:            mniFont.Click += new EventHandler(this.
➥FormatClicked);
82:
83:            mnuMain.MenuItems.Add(mniEdit);
84:            mnuMain.MenuItems.Add(mniFormat);
85:
86:            mniUndo.ShowShortcut = true;
87:            mniCut.ShowShortcut = true;
88:            mniCopy.ShowShortcut = true;
89:            mniPaste.ShowShortcut = true;
90:            mniFind.ShowShortcut = true;
91:
```

LISTING P3.2 continued

```
92:            mniEdit.MenuItems.Add(mniUndo);
93:            mniEdit.MenuItems.Add("-");
94:            mniEdit.MenuItems.Add(mniCut);
95:            mniEdit.MenuItems.Add(mniCopy);
96:            mniEdit.MenuItems.Add(mniPaste);
97:            mniEdit.MenuItems.Add("-");
98:            mniEdit.MenuItems.Add(mniFind);
99:
100:           mniFormat.MenuItems.Add(mniFont);
101:
102:           cmnuDocument.MenuItems.Add(mniCut.CloneMenu());
103:           cmnuDocument.MenuItems.Add(mniCopy.CloneMenu());
104:           cmnuDocument.MenuItems.Add(mniPaste.CloneMenu());
105:           cmnuDocument.MenuItems.Add("-");
106:           cmnuDocument.MenuItems.Add(mniFont.CloneMenu());
107:           cmnuDocument.Popup += new EventHandler
➥(this.HandleContext);
108:           pnlView.ContextMenu = cmnuDocument;
109:
110:           scrlbar.Dock = DockStyle.Right;
111:           scrlbar.Scroll += new ScrollEventHandler
➥(this.ScrollView);
112:           scrlbar.Maximum = 10;
113:
114:           this.Text = strName;
115:           this.Font = new Font("Courier New", 12);
116:           this.Size = new Size(800, 900);
117:           this.Name = "NetWord";
118:           this.WindowState = FormWindowState.Maximized;
119:           this.Menu = mnuMain;
120:           this.Closing += new CancelEventHandler
➥(this.DocumentClosing);
121:
122:           pnlView.AutoScroll = false;
123:           pnlView.BackColor = Color.DarkGray;
124:           pnlView.Width = this.Width - 16;
125:           pnlView.Height = this.Height - 50;
126:           pnlView.Location = new Point(0,0);
127:           pnlView.Font = fntCurrent;
128:
129:           this.Controls.Add(scrlbar);
130:           this.Controls.Add(sbarMain);
131:           this.Controls.Add(pnlView);
132:           AddPage();
133:       }
134:
135:     private void ScrollView(Object Sender,
➥ScrollEventArgs e) {
136:           pnlView.Top = 0 - (e.NewValue * 30);
```

```
137:          }
138:
139:      private void DocumentCreated(Object Sender,
➥EventArgs e) {
140:          AddPage();
141:      }
142:
143:      private void AddPage() {
144:          int intHeight;
145:
146:          intHeight = objPageSettings.Bounds.Height -
➥ (int)(.96 * (objPageSettings.Margins.Top +
➥objPageSettings.Margins.Bottom));
147:
148:          Page objPage = new Page(this,objPageSettings,
➥arrPages.Count+1);
149:          pnlView.Height = (arrPages.Count+1) * intHeight;
150:          pnlView.Controls.Add(objPage);
151:          scrlbar.Maximum = (30 * arrPages.Count+1) + 15;
152:
153:          objPage.Location = new Point(50,intHeight *
➥arrPages.Count + 5);
154:          objPage.Filled += new EventHandler
➥ (this.PageFilled);
155:          objPage.Enter += new EventHandler
➥ (this.PageGotFocus);
156:          objPage.SelectionChanged += new EventHandler
➥ (this.UpdateStatus);
157:
158:          arrPages.Add(objPage);
159:          objPage.Focus();
160:      }
161:
162:      private void PageFilled(Object Sender,
➥EventArgs e) {
163:          if (intCurrentPage == arrPages.Count) {
164:              AddPage();
165:          } else {
166:              ((Page)arrPages[intCurrentPage]).Focus();
167:          }
168:      }
169:
170:      private void PageGotFocus(Object Sender,
➥EventArgs e) {
171:          intCurrentPage = ((Page)Sender).PageNumber;
172:      }
173:
174:      private void UpdateStatus(Object Sender,
➥EventArgs e) {
```

LISTING P3.2   continued

```
175:            Page tmpPage = (Page)arrPages[intCurrentPage-1];
176:
177:            spnlLine.Text = "Page " + intCurrentPage.
➥ToString() + "  Line " + tmpPage.LineIndex.ToString() +
➥" Char " + tmpPage.CharIndex.ToString();
178:        }
179:
180:    private void HandleContext(Object Sender,
➥EventArgs e) {
181:        if (((Page)arrPages[intCurrentPage-1]).
➥SelectionLength == 0) {
182:            cmnuDocument.MenuItems[0].Enabled = false;
183:            cmnuDocument.MenuItems[1].Enabled = false;
184:        } else {
185:            cmnuDocument.MenuItems[0].Enabled = true;
186:            cmnuDocument.MenuItems[1].Enabled = true;
187:        }
188:    }
189:
190:    private void FileClicked(Object Sender,
➥EventArgs e) {
191:        MenuItem mniTemp = (MenuItem)Sender;
192:        PrintDocument pd;
193:        String strText;
194:
195:        switch (mniTemp.Text) {
196:            case "Save":
197:                FileInfo filTemp = new FileInfo(this.Text);
198:                if (filTemp.Extension == ".rtf") {
199:                    ((Page)arrPages[intCurrentPage-1]).
➥SaveFile(this.Text, RichTextBoxStreamType.RichText);
200:                } else {
201:                    ((Page)arrPages[intCurrentPage-1]).
➥SaveFile(this.Text, RichTextBoxStreamType.PlainText);
202:                }
203:                ((Page)arrPages[intCurrentPage-1]).
➥Modified = false;
204:                break;
205:            case "Page Setup...":
206:                dlgPageSetup.PageSettings = objPageSettings;
207:                dlgPageSetup.ShowDialog();
208:
209:                foreach (Page tmpPage in arrPages) {
210:                    tmpPage.UpdatePageSettings
➥ (objPageSettings);
211:                }
212:
213:                break;
214:            case "Print Preview":
```

LISTING P3.2   continued

```
215:                    strText = "";
216:
217:                    foreach (Page tmpPage in arrPages) {
218:                        strText += tmpPage.Text;
219:                    }
220:
221:                    objReader = new StringReader(strText);
222:
223:                    pd = new PrintDocument();
224:                    pd.DefaultPageSettings = objPageSettings;
225:                    pd.PrintPage += new PrintPageEventHandler
➥ (this.PrintIt);
226:
227:                    PrintPreviewDialog dlgPrintPreview = new
➥PrintPreviewDialog();
228:                    dlgPrintPreview.Document = pd;
229:
230:                    dlgPrintPreview.ShowDialog();
231:                    break;
232:                case "Print...":
233:                    PrintDialog dlgPrint = new PrintDialog();
234:                    dlgPrint.PrinterSettings = new
➥PrinterSettings();
235:                    if (dlgPrint.ShowDialog() ==
➥DialogResult.OK) {
236:                        strText = "";
237:
238:                        foreach (Page tmpPage in arrPages) {
239:                            strText += tmpPage.Text;
240:                        }
241:
242:                        objReader = new StringReader(strText);
243:
244:                        pd = new PrintDocument();
245:
246:                        pd.DefaultPageSettings =
➥objPageSettings;
247:                        pd.PrintPage += new PrintPageEventHandler
➥ (this.PrintIt);
248:                        pd.Print();
249:                    }
250:                    break;
251:                case "Exit":
252:                    this.Close();
253:                    break;
254:            }
255:        }
256:
257:        private void PrintIt(Object Sender,
➥PrintPageEventArgs e) {
```

LISTING P3.2   continued

```
258:            Font fntPrint = this.Font;
259:            int count = 0;
260:            float yPos = 0;
261:            float lpp = e.MarginBounds.Height /
➥fntPrint.GetHeight(e.Graphics);
262:            float fltTopMargin = e.MarginBounds.Top;
263:            float fltLeftMargin = e.MarginBounds.Left;
264:            String strLine = null;
265:
266:            while (count < lpp && ((strLine = objReader.
➥ReadLine()) != null)) {
267:                yPos = fltTopMargin + (count * fntPrint.
➥GetHeight(e.Graphics));
268:
269:                e.Graphics.DrawString(strLine, fntPrint,
➥Brushes.Black, fltLeftMargin, yPos, new StringFormat());
270:
271:                count++;
272:            }
273:
274:            if (strLine != null) {
275:                e.HasMorePages = true;
276:            } else {
277:                e.HasMorePages = false;
278:            }
279:        }
280:
281:        private void EditClicked(Object Sender,
➥EventArgs e) {
282:            MenuItem mniTemp = (MenuItem)Sender;
283:            Page tmpPage = (Page)arrPages[intCurrentPage-1];
284:
285:            switch (mniTemp.Text) {
286:                case "Undo":
287:                    tmpPage.Undo();
288:                    break;
289:                case "Cut":
290:                    if (tmpPage.SelectedRtf != "") {
291:                        tmpPage.Cut();
292:                    }
293:                    break;
294:                case "Copy":
295:                    if (tmpPage.SelectedRtf != "") {
296:                        tmpPage.Copy();
297:                    }
298:                    break;
299:                case "Paste":
300:                    tmpPage.Paste();
301:                    break;
302:                case "Find...":
```

LISTING P3.2 continued

```
303:                        FindDialog dlgFind = new FindDialog(this);
304:                        dlgFind.Show();
305:                        break;
306:                }
307:        }
308:
309:        private void FormatClicked(Object Sender,
➥EventArgs e) {
310:                MenuItem mniTemp = (MenuItem)Sender;
311:
312:                switch (mniTemp.Text) {
313:                    case "Font...":
314:                        dlgFont.ShowColor = true;
315:                        dlgFont.Font = this.Font;
316:                        if (dlgFont.ShowDialog() ==
➥DialogResult.OK) {
317:                                fntCurrent = dlgFont.Font;
318:                                fntColor = dlgFont.Color;
319:                                this.Font = fntCurrent;
320:                                this.ForeColor = fntColor;
321:                                ((Page)arrPages[intCurrentPage - 1]).
➥SetFont(fntCurrent, fntColor);
322:                        }
323:                        break;
324:                }
325:        }
326:
327:        private void DocumentClosing(Object Sender,
➥CancelEventArgs e) {
328:                if (((Page)arrPages[intCurrentPage-1]).
➥Modified) {
329:                        DialogResult dr = MessageBox.Show("Do you
➥want to save the changes?", this.Name,
➥MessageBoxButtons.YesNoCancel);
330:
331:                        if (dr == DialogResult.Yes) {
332:                            FileClicked(mniSave, new EventArgs());
333:                        } else if (dr == DialogResult.Cancel) {
334:                            e.Cancel = true;
335:                        }
336:                }
337:        }
338:    }
339: }
```

ANALYSIS The first thing to note is that all references to the RichTextBox control are eliminated here. Instead, we point to our new Page class.

We need a mechanism to store individual pages in this document. This is done with an ArrayList object, declared on line 11 (and the ArrayList's containing namespace, System.Collections is imported on line 7). When we create a new Page object, we'll add it to this array. Whenever we need to access the current page, we'll use this array and the intCurrentPage variable (which you'll see more of in a moment).

The next change comes on line 14, where we create a new Panel control. This panel will hold each new page as we create it. Its properties are initialized in the Document constructor. Line 18 creates a new VScrollBar object that we'll use to scroll through the document. Recall that the Panel control has an AutoScroll property that can provide scroll bars for us, but it has some drawbacks. For example, when you move from one Page to the next in the Panel and AutoScroll is set to true, the Page objects will scroll around way too much—it is hard to keep track of where you were working. So we implement custom scroll bars to give us exactly the functionality we need. The VScrollBar is initialized on lines 110–112, and its event handler, ScrollView, is on line 135. This method simply shifts our panel control around appropriately by a scaled amount.

The last part of the constructor calls the AddPage method (line 132). AddPage contains some of the most important new functionality. It creates a new Page object (line 148— notice the passing of the necessary variables). Line 153 determines the placement of the new Page within our Panel control. It simply counts the number of existing Page objects and sets the top coordinate accordingly. On lines 154–156, event handlers are assigned to the Filled, Enter, and SelectionChanged events. We also add the newly created Page object to the arrPages array and the Panel control, and give it focus. The Panel's size must be changed to accommodate the new Page (line 149), and the VScrollBar's Maximum property is changed as well (line 151). To make sense of this, think of the scroll bar in Microsoft Word; as you add new pages, the scroll box keeps shrinking (or in other words, the maximum value keeps increasing).

Recall that the Filled event is our custom event that fires whenever the page's boundaries are passed. Filled's event handler, PageFilled on line 162, either adds a new page (if the page the user is currently on is the last page in the document), or gives focus to the next page in the document. Note the use of the arrPages and intCurrentPage variables on line 166.

The event handler for the Enter event, PageGotFocus, is on line 170. It simply updates the intCurrentPage variable. The event handler for the SelectionChanged event, UpdateStatus, is on line 174. Recall from Week 2 in Review that this method performed the functionality that is now in the Page class's OnTextChanged method. So instead, we can simply access the Page's properties as shown on line 177. Again, note the use of the arrPages and intCurrentPage variables on line 175.

The rest of the code, on lines 180–339, has changed only slightly. All references to the RichTextBox control are replaced with references to a Page object. The Print Preview and Print cases on lines 214 and 232 have changed to cycle through all of the Page objects in our document, collecting each's text before passing that to our StringReader object on lines 221 and 242. The FormatClicked method on line 309 now references the new Page.SetFont method we created in Listing P3.1. Finally, the call to the FindDialog class on line 303 has changed slightly to pass in a new variable in the constructor. I'll explain this in the next few paragraphs.

There's one last change we need to make: the FindDialog class must be modified to search through each of the Page objects in our document, rather than a single RichTextBox as before. There are two specific changes we need to make to accommodate this functionality: modify the constructor of FindDialog to reference the Document class instead of its RichTextBox; and modify the Find, Replace, and Replace All methods to search through each Page object.

First, modify the constructor to begin as follows:

```
private Document docParent;

public FindDialog(Form frmDocument): base() {
    docParent = (Document)frmDocument;
    ...
```

Now the docParent variable holds a reference to our main Document class, which, in turn, holds a reference to all of the Page objects. Next, Listing P3.3 shows the modifications to the ButtonClicked event handler, which is responsible for the actual Find and Replace functionality.

LISTING P3.3 Finding and Replacing in Page Objects

```
 1:  private void ButtonClicked(Object Sender, EventArgs e) {
 2:      Button btTemp = (Button)Sender;
 3:      int intLocation;
 4:      int intCount = 0;
 5:
 6:      switch (btTemp.Text) {
 7:        case "Find":
 8:            for (int i = docParent.intCurrentPage-1;
➥i < docParent.arrPages.Count; i++) {
 9:
10:                rtbDoc = (RichTextBox)docParent.arrPages[i];
11:
12:                if (i != docParent.intCurrentPage-1) {
13:                    rtbDoc.Focus();
14:                    rtbDoc.SelectionStart = 0;
```

```
15:                    }
16:
17:                    intLocation = rtbDoc.Find(tbFind.Text,
➥rtbDoc.SelectionStart + rtbDoc.SelectionLength,
➥RichTextBoxFinds.None);
18:                    if (intLocation != -1) {
19:                        rtbDoc.SelectionStart = intLocation;
20:                        rtbDoc.SelectionLength =
➥tbFind.Text.Length;
21:                        rtbDoc.Focus();
22:                        break;
23:                    }
24:                }
25:            break;
26:        case "Replace":
27:            for (int i = docParent.intCurrentPage-1;
➥i < docParent.arrPages.Count; i++) {
28:
29:                rtbDoc = (RichTextBox)docParent.arrPages[i];
30:
31:                if (i != docParent.intCurrentPage-1) {
32:                    rtbDoc.Focus();
33:                    rtbDoc.SelectionStart = 0;
34:                }
35:
36:                intLocation = rtbDoc.Find(tbFind.Text,
➥rtbDoc.SelectionStart + rtbDoc.SelectionLength,
➥RichTextBoxFinds.None);
37:                if (intLocation != -1) {
38:                    rtbDoc.SelectionStart = intLocation;
39:                    rtbDoc.SelectionLength = tbFind.Text.Length;
40:                    rtbDoc.SelectedText = tbReplace.Text;
41:                    rtbDoc.SelectionStart = intLocation;
42:                    rtbDoc.SelectionLength =
➥tbReplace.Text.Length;
43:                }
44:            }
45:            break;
46:        case "Replace All":
47:            for (int i = 0; i < docParent.arrPages.Count;
➥i++) {
48:
49:                rtbDoc = (RichTextBox)docParent.arrPages[i];
50:
51:                if (i != docParent.intCurrentPage-1) {
52:                    rtbDoc.Focus();
53:                    rtbDoc.SelectionStart = 0;
54:                }
55:
```

LISTING P3.3 continued

```
56:                 intLocation = rtbDoc.Find(tbFind.Text);
57:                 while (intLocation != -1) {
58:                     rtbDoc.SelectionStart = intLocation;
59:                     rtbDoc.SelectionLength =
➥tbFind.Text.Length;
60:                     rtbDoc.SelectedText = tbReplace.Text;
61:                     intCount += 1;
62:                     intLocation = rtbDoc.Find(tbFind.Text,
➥rtbDoc.SelectionStart + rtbDoc.SelectionLength,
➥RichTextBoxFinds.None);
63:                 }
64:             }
65:             MessageBox.Show(intCount.ToString() +
➥" occurrences replaced","Find");
66:             break;
67:         case "Cancel":
68:             this.Close();
69:             break;
70:     }
71: }
```

ANALYSIS Most of this functionality has not changed. There is actually only one new bit of code that is used in three different places. On line 8 we have a `for` loop that iterates through each of the `Page` objects in the `Document.arrPages` collection. Each `Page` object is temporarily assigned to the `rtbDoc` variable on line 10. This temporary variable is then used like it was last time, to search for text.

There is one interesting thing to note, however. You cannot search a `RichTextBox` unless it has the input focus. So on lines 12–15 you give each `Page` object the focus if it doesn't already have it.

This code is repeated in the Replace case beginning on line 27, and the Replace All case beginning on line 47.

Compile the revised `Document` and `FindDialog` classes (as well as the rest of the application) with the following command:

```
csc /t:winexe /r:system.dll /r:system.drawing.dll
/r:system.windows.forms.dll /r:Page.dll
NetWord.cs FindDialog.cs Document.cs
```

This command is just like the others you've used in the previous Weeks in Review sections. Call the C# compiler referencing the necessary assemblies and your source code files. (Note the reference to the `Page.dll` file.)

That's all there is to it! Figure P3.1 shows the output of this application after creating a few pages.

FIGURE P3.1

Your NetWord application now behaves very similarly to Microsoft Word.

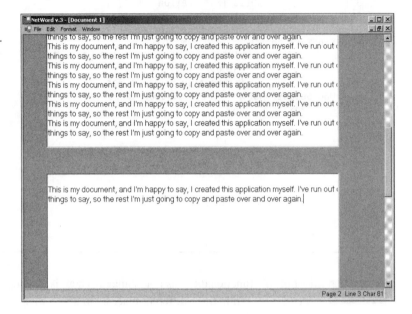

Play around with the application. Note that when you hit the end of a page, a new one is automatically created and your cursor position is moved. You can print out documents (and preview them) and they will appear exactly as they do in the application (that is, one page in the application will equal one printed page). Congratulations on building a complete word processor!

Where to Go from Here

Although you now have a complete Word processing application, there are quite a few things that can be done to NetWord to make it more efficient and functional.

First, the process of moving from page to page isn't exactly as it is in Word. Specifically, you cannot move up or down from one page to the next page without explicitly clicking on that page (in Word you can simply press the up or down arrow). This would be an easy issue to remedy.

The paging process currently works for new documents, but if you open an existing file, it won't automatically paginate that file. Similarly, you may have noticed that the pagination works when entering normal content, but if you copy large amounts of text, that text won't be paginated correctly. Instead, it is appended to the bottom of the current page, which simply grows to accommodate the new text. Also, you can't currently delete pages.

In its current implementation, NetWord can only work with plain text and rich text files. However, using your knowledge of serialization (Day 11, "Working with Windows Input/Output"), you can create your own file types. That way a document can be saved with its pages (in Page objects) intact, saving you the process described previously of having to repaginate documents when you open them. Using ActiveX from Day 14, you could even use NetWord to open Word documents!

Finally, NetWord could offer much more functionality in terms of document editing—for example, the ability to center or right-align text; modify line spacing; add bullets and numbered lists, and so on. All of this functionality is already in the RichTextBox control, so adding it to NetWord involves simply providing the user interface for doing so.

While some of this functionality is simple to implement, others may take quite a bit of ingenuity and engineering. With the skills you've gained over the last 21 days, however, I have no doubt that you can accomplish it all.

Note

The purpose of the bonus projects is to approach an application at every stage of development. After this lesson you should feel pretty confident in your abilities to build Windows applications, and we hope that you don't feel too timid to attack any new project. Along with the knowledge you've gained about the .NET Framework, you have become quite a proficient developer.

Thanks for spending the last 21 days with us!

APPENDIX **A**

Answers to Quiz Questions and Exercises

Answers for Day 1

Quiz

1. True or false: Windows Forms is Win32 programming.

   True. We won't be doing any Win16 programming in this book.

2. True or false: Metadata contains information about the environment in which an application was built.

   True.

3. How does MSIL allow cross-platform operation?

   MSIL is platform independent language, so it can be transferred to any operating system easily. A JIT compiler is then used to translate the MSIL into the native machine's language—a more efficient process than recompiling or rewriting your application for every platform that needs to be supported.

4. What is the next evolution of ActiveX Data Objects called?

   ADO.NET.

5. True or false: You can create Windows Forms applications with any text editor you're comfortable with.

   True, as long as the files are saved as plain text.

6. What is a Windows Forms control?

   A Windows Forms control is an object that provides an interface to the user, often capable of interaction.

7. What does the Imports statement do?

   It enables your application to use the objects in another namespace, or collection of objects.

Exercise

What would the following code do when compiled and executed?

```
1:  Imports System
2:  Imports System.Windows.Forms
3:
4:  Public Class MyApp : Inherits Form
5:
6:      Public Shared Sub Main()
7:          Application.Run(New MyApp)
8:      End Sub
9:
10:     Public Sub New()
11:         Me.Height = 100
12:         Me.Width = 50
13:     End Sub
14:
15:  End Class
```

It creates a Windows Form and changes its size to 100 by 50 pixels.

Answers for Day 2

Quiz

1. What is the base class that all other classes inherit from?

   The Object class.

2. What does the Shared or static keyword do?

These keywords indicate that a member is a fundamental part of class that is common across all instances of the class. For example, while different car instances may have different colors, they could all share the same metal type.

3. True or false: You can extend existing namespaces with your own classes.

   True.

4. True or false: The `Main` method will execute every time a new instance of your class is created.

   False. The `Main` method only executes once—when your application is started.

5. Why is the following code not sufficient? What else must be used?

   ```
   dim MyObject as Button
   ```

   It is not sufficient because you are only declaring a variable of type `Button`; you are not assigning a value to the variable, which must be done before it can be used. To use this variable, you must use the `New` keyword:

   ```
   dim MyObject as New Button
   ```

   or

   ```
   dim MyObject as Button = New Button
   ```

6. What is wrong with the following compilation command? (Hint: there may be more than one thing wrong with it.)

   ```
   csc /type:windowsexe /r:system.dll /r:system.drawing.dll
   /r:system.drawing.text.dll filename.vb
   ```

   There is no type `windowsexe`. Use `winexe` instead. There is no `system.drawing.text.dll` assembly; the `system.drawing.text` namespace is contained in the `system.drawing.dll` assembly. Finally, this line uses the C# compiler to compile a VB.NET file, as indicated by the extension on the source code file.

7. Infer the meaning of the following properties:

   `Button.CanSelect`—Indicates if the button can be selected by the user.

   `Button.Cursor`—Indicates the mouse cursor icon that is used when the cursor is over the button.

   `Form.AllowDrop`—Indicates if this form can handle drag-and-drop processing.

   `Form.Visible`—Is the form visible to the user?

8. Name three differences in semantics between C# and VB.NET.

   Variables types go before a variable name in C#.

   Semicolons must be used at the end of each line.

   C# is case-sensitive.

9. True or false: Every class must have a constructor.

This is a trick question. It is true that every class must have a constructor, but you do not have to explicitly create one yourself. The CLR creates one automatically for you if one is not present.

Exercise

Expand on the calculator example from today's lesson. Add additional buttons to perform the other arithmetic operations: subtraction, multiplication, and division. Try building the application in both C# and VB.NET. Also enhance the UI with liberal use of Labels.

The code in C#:

```
1:using System;
2:using System.Windows.Forms;
3:using System.Drawing;
4:
5:namespace TYWinforms.Day2 {
6:
7:    public class Calculator : Form {
8:        private Button btnAdd;
9:        private Button btnSubtract;
10:        private Button btnMultiply;
11:        private Button btnDivide;
12:        private TextBox tbNumber1;
13:        private TextBox tbNumber2;
14:        private Label lblAnswer;
15:        private Label lblNum1;
16:        private Label lblNum2;
17:
18:        public static void Main() {
19:            Application.Run(new Calculator());
20:        }
21:
22:        public Calculator() {
23:            this.btnAdd = new Button();
24:            this.btnSubtract = new Button();
25:            this.btnMultiply = new Button();
26:            this.btnDivide = new Button();
27:            this.tbNumber1 = new TextBox();
28:            this.tbNumber2 = new TextBox();
29:            this.lblAnswer = new Label();
30:            this.lblNum1 = new Label();
31:            this.lblNum2 = new Label();
32:
33:            this.Width = 325;
34:            this.Height = 150;
35:            this.Text = "My Calculator";
36:
```

```
37:          tbNumber1.Location = new Point(100,0);
38:          tbNumber2.Location = new Point(100,25);
39:
40:          btnAdd.Location = new Point(0,75);
41:          btnAdd.Text = "+";
42:          btnAdd.Click += new EventHandler(this.Add);
43:
44:          btnSubtract.Location = new Point(75,75);
45:          btnSubtract.Text = "-";
46:          btnSubtract.Click += new EventHandler(this.Subtract);
47:
48:          btnMultiply.Location = new Point(150,75);
49:          btnMultiply.Text = "*";
50:          btnMultiply.Click += new EventHandler(this.Multiply);
51:
52:          btnDivide.Location = new Point(225,75);
53:          btnDivide.Text = "/";
54:          btnDivide.Click += new EventHandler(this.Divide);
55:
56:          lblNum1.Text = "Enter number 1:";
57:          lblNum1.Location = new Point(0,0);
58:
59:          lblNum2.Text = "Enter number 2:";
60:          lblNum2.Location = new Point(0,25);
61:
62:          lblAnswer.Location = new Point(0,55);
63:
64:          this.Controls.Add(btnAdd);
65:          this.Controls.Add(btnSubtract);
66:          this.Controls.Add(btnMultiply);
67:          this.Controls.Add(btnDivide);
68:          this.Controls.Add(tbNumber1);
69:          this.Controls.Add(tbNumber2);
70:          this.Controls.Add(lblAnswer);
71:          this.Controls.Add(lblNum1);
72:          this.Controls.Add(lblNum2);
73:      }
74:
75:      public void Add(object Sender, EventArgs e) {
76:          lblAnswer.Text = Convert.ToString(Convert.ToInt32
➥(tbNumber1.Text) +
77:              Convert.ToInt32(tbNumber2.Text));
78:      }
79:
80:      public void Subtract(object Sender, EventArgs e) {
81:          lblAnswer.Text = Convert.ToString(Convert.ToInt32
➥(tbNumber1.Text) -
82:              Convert.ToInt32(tbNumber2.Text));
83:      }
84:
```

A

```
85:      public void Multiply(object Sender, EventArgs e) {
86:          lblAnswer.Text = Convert.ToString(Convert.ToInt32
➥(tbNumber1.Text) *
87:              Convert.ToInt32(tbNumber2.Text));
88:      }
89:
90:      public void Divide(object Sender, EventArgs e) {
91:          lblAnswer.Text = Convert.ToString(Convert.ToInt32
➥(tbNumber1.Text) /
92:              Convert.ToInt32(tbNumber2.Text));
93:      }
94:  }
95:}
```

The code in VB.NET:

```
1:Imports System
2:Imports System.Windows.Forms
3:Imports System.Drawing
4:
5:namespace TYWinforms.Day2
6:
7:   Public class Calculator : Inherits Form
8:      private WithEvents btnAdd as Button
9:      private WithEvents btnSubtract as Button
10:      private WithEvents btnMultiply as Button
11:      private WithEvents btnDivide as Button
12:      private tbNumber1 as TextBox
13:      private tbNumber2 as TextBox
14:      private lblAnswer as Label
15:      private lblNum1 as Label
16:      private lblNum2 aS Label
17:
18:      Public shared Sub Main()
19:          Application.Run(new Calculator)
20:      End Sub
21:
22:      Public Sub New()
23:          Me.btnAdd = new Button()
24:          Me.btnSubtract = new Button()
25:          Me.btnMultiply = new Button()
26:          Me.btnDivide = new Button()
27:          Me.tbNumber1 = new TextBox()
28:          Me.tbNumber2 = new TextBox()
29:          Me.lblAnswer = new Label()
30:          Me.lblNum1 = new Label()
31:          Me.lblNum2 = new Label()
32:
33:          Me.Width = 325
34:          Me.Height = 150
35:          Me.Text = "My Calculator"
```

A

```
36:
37:          tbNumber1.Location = new Point(100,0)
38:          tbNumber2.Location = new Point(100,25)
39:
40:          btnAdd.Location = new Point(0,75)
41:          btnAdd.Text = "+"
42:          AddHandler btnAdd.Click, new EventHandler
➡ (AddressOf Add)
43:
44:
45:          btnSubtract.Location = new Point(75,75)
46:          btnSubtract.Text = "-"
47:          AddHandler btnSubtract.Click, new EventHandler
➡(AddressOf Subtract)
48:
49:          btnMultiply.Location = new Point(150,75)
50:          btnMultiply.Text = "*"
51:          AddHandler btnMultiply.Click, new EventHandler
➡ (AddressOf Multiply)
52:
53:          btnDivide.Location = new Point(225,75)
54:          btnDivide.Text = "/"
55:          AddHandler btnDivide.Click, new EventHandler
➡ (AddressOf Divide)
56:
57:          lblNum1.Text = "Enter number 1:"
58:          lblNum1.Location = new Point(0,0)
59:
60:          lblNum2.Text = "Enter number 2:"
61:          lblNum2.Location = new Point(0,25)
62:
63:          lblAnswer.Location = new Point(0,55)
64:
65:        Me.Controls.Add(btnAdd)
66:        Me.Controls.Add(btnSubtract)
67:        Me.Controls.Add(btnMultiply)
68:        Me.Controls.Add(btnDivide)
69:        Me.Controls.Add(tbNumber1)
70:        Me.Controls.Add(tbNumber2)
71:        Me.Controls.Add(lblAnswer)
72:        Me.Controls.Add(lblNum1)
73:        Me.Controls.Add(lblNum2)
74:      End Sub
75:
76:      Public Sub Add(ByVal Sender as Object, ByVal e as EventArgs)
77:          lblAnswer.Text = CStr(Cint(tbNumber1.Text) +
➡Cint(tbNumber2.Text))
78:      End Sub
79:
80:      Public Sub Subtract(ByVal Sender as Object, ByVal e as EventArgs)
81:          lblAnswer.Text = CStr(Cint(tbNumber1.Text) -
```

```
➥Cint(tbNumber2.Text))
82:        End Sub
83:
84:        Public Sub Multiply(ByVal Sender as Object, ByVal e as EventArgs)
85:            lblAnswer.Text = CStr(Cint(tbNumber1.Text) *
➥Cint(tbNumber2.Text))
86:        End Sub
87:
88:        Public Sub Divide(ByVal Sender as Object, ByVal e as EventArgs)
89:            lblAnswer.Text = CStr(Cint(tbNumber1.Text) /
➥Cint(tbNumber2.Text))
90:        End Sub
91:    End Class
92:End Namespace
```

Answers for Day 3

Quiz

1. What would the following statement return if placed after line 9?

   ```
   Console.Write(this.ToString());
   ```

   MyForm, Text: Hello World!

2. What would the following code return if placed after line 9?

   ```
   Label lblTemp = new Label();
   Console.Write(lblTemp.Equals(this.lblMessage).ToString());
   ```

   False.

3. What would the following code return if placed after line 9?

   ```
   Label lblTemp = new Label();
   Console.Write(Object.ReferenceEquals(lblTemp, this.lblMessage)
   ➥.ToString());
   ```

   False.

4. True or false: The KeyPress event takes a handler of type KeyEventHandler.

   False. The KeyPress events take a KeyPressEventHandler.

5. What are the five properties of the MouseEventArgs object?

   Button, Clicks, Delta, X, and Y.

6. Write a single statement in VB.NET that will set the width of a form to 1/3 of the height of the screen.

   ```
   Me.Width = Screen.GetWorkingArea(Me).Height / 3
   ```

7. What property controls which button will be activated when the user presses the Escape key?

   `CancelButton`.

8. What is the default `FormBorderStyle`?

   `Sizable`.

9. Which three events use the two-event for a single action paradigm?

   `Closed`, `InputLanguageChanged`, and `Validated`.

Exercises

1. Build an application, in C#, that monitors all six of the mouse events. Display a message in a label when each of the events occurs.

```
1:  using System;
2:  using System.Windows.Forms;
3:  using System.Drawing;
4:  using System.ComponentModel;
5:
6:  namespace TYWinForms.Day3 {
7:
8:      public class Exercise1 : Form {
9:          private Label lblMessage = new Label();
10:
11:         public Exercise1() {
12:             lblMessage.Width = this.Width;
13:             lblMessage.Height = this.Height;
14:
15:             this.Text = "Mouse events Example";
16:             this.Width = 800;
17:             this.Height = 600;
18:             this.MouseEnter += new EventHandler(this.
    ➥MouseEntered);
19:             this.MouseHover += new EventHandler(this.
    ➥MouseHovered);
20:             this.MouseLeave += new EventHandler(this.
    ➥MouseLeft);
21:             this.MouseMove += new MouseEventHandler(this.
    ➥MouseMoved);
22:             this.MouseDown += new MouseEventHandler(this.
    ➥MouseClicked);
23:             this.MouseUp += new MouseEventHandler(this.
    ➥MouseReleased);
24:
25:             this.Controls.Add(lblMessage);
26:         }
27:
```

```
28:         public void MouseEntered(Object Sender,
➥EventArgs e) {
29:             lblMessage.Text += "Mouse entered\r\n";
30:         }
31:
32:         public void MouseHovered(Object Sender,
➥EventArgs e) {
33:             lblMessage.Text += "Mouse hovered\r\n";
34:         }
35:
36:         public void MouseLeft(Object Sender, EventArgs e) {
37:             lblMessage.Text += "Mouse left\r\n";
38:         }
39:
40:         public void MouseMoved(Object Sender,
➥MouseEventArgs e) {
41:             lblMessage.Text += "Mouse moved: x=" + e.X +
➥", y=" + e.Y + "\r\n";
42:         }
43:
44:         public void MouseClicked(Object Sender,
➥MouseEventArgs e) {
45:             lblMessage.Text += "Button clicked: " +
➥e.Button + "\r\n";
46:         }
47:
48:         public void MouseReleased(Object Sender,
➥MouseEventArgs e) {
49:             lblMessage.Text += "Button released: x=" + e.X +
➥", y=" + e.Y + "\r\n";
50:         }
51:
52:         public static void Main() {
53:             Application.Run(new Exercise1());
54:         }
55:     }
56: }
```

2. Build an application in VB.NET that allows users to customize the Text, Height, Width, and Opacity properties by entering values in a TextBox, and pressing a Submit Button.

The code for the application is as follows:

```
1: Imports System
2: Imports System.Windows.Forms
3: Imports System.Drawing
4: Imports System.ComponentModel
5:
6: Namespace TYWinForms.Day3
7:
```

A

```
8:      public class Exercise2 : Inherits Form
9:          private btSubmit as new Button
10:         private tbText as new TextBox
11:         private tbHeight as new TextBox
12:         private tbWidth as new TextBox
13:         private tbOpacity as new TextBox
14:         private lblText as new Label
15:         private lblHeight as new Label
16:         private lblWidth as new Label
17:         private lblOpacity as new Label
18:
19:         public sub New()
20:             Me.Text = "Event Example"
21:             Me.Width = 800
22:             Me.Height = 600
23:
24:             btSubmit.Location = new Point(50, 150)
25:             btSubmit.Text = "Submit"
26:             AddHandler btSubmit.Click, AddressOf Me.HandleIt
27:
28:             lblText.Location = new Point(25,25)
29:             lblText.Text = "Text:"
30:             tbText.Location = new Point(75,25)
31:             tbText.Text = Me.Text
32:
33:             lblHeight.Location = new Point(25,50)
34:             lblHeight.Text = "Height:"
35:             tbHeight.Location = new Point(75,50)
36:             tbHeight.Text = Me.Height
37:
38:             lblWidth.Location = new Point(25,75)
39:             lblWidth.Text = "Width:"
40:             tbWidth.Location = new Point(75,75)
41:             tbWidth.Text = Me.Width
42:
43:             lblOpacity.Location = new Point(25,100)
44:             lblOpacity.Text = "Opacity:"
45:             tbOpacity.Location = new Point(75,100)
46:             tbOpacity.Text = Me.Opacity
47:
48:             Me.Controls.Add(btSubmit)
49:             Me.Controls.Add(tbText)
50:             Me.Controls.Add(tbHeight)
51:             Me.Controls.Add(tbWidth)
52:             Me.Controls.Add(tbOpacity)
53:             Me.Controls.Add(lblText)
54:             Me.Controls.Add(lblHeight)
55:             Me.Controls.Add(lblWidth)
56:             Me.Controls.Add(lblOpacity)
57:         end sub
58:
```

```
59:        public sub HandleIt(Sender as Object, e as EventArgs)
60:            Me.Text = tbText.Text
61:            Me.Height = CInt(tbHeight.Text)
62:            Me.Width = CInt(tbWidth.Text)
63:            Me.Opacity = CInt(tbOpacity.Text)
64:        end sub
65:
66:    end class
67:
68:
69:    public class StartForm
70:        public shared sub Main()
71:            Application.Run(new Exercise2)
72:        end sub
73:    end class
74:
75: End Namespace
```

Answers for Day 4

Quiz

1. True or false? All controls, including the `Form` object, inherit from the `Control` class.

   True.

2. What object must be associated to toolbars to display images in the tool bar buttons?

   The `ImageList` object.

3. What are the three optional parameters for a `MenuItem` constructor, and what are their types?

   The first parameter is string representing the menu item's caption (or `Text` property). The second parameter specifies the event handler that should execute when the menu item is clicked; it is an `EventHandler` object. The third parameter is a `ShortCut` enumeration value that specifies the keyboard shortcut that can be used to access the menu item.

4. What character is used to provide a keyboard shortcut for a letter in menu item's caption?

   The ampersand (&).

5. Write a line of code in C# that instructs a `ToolBarButton` control named `myFirstButton` to use the fourth image in the associated `ImageList`.

   `myFirstButton.ImageIndex = 3;`

6. True or false? The event that is used to handle toolbar button clicks is called `Click`.

   False. The event is called `ButtonClick`, and belongs to the `ToolBar` object.

7. What are the default values for a scroll bar's `Minimum`, `Maximum`, `SmallChange`, and `LargeChange` properties?

   Respectively: 0, 100, 1, and 10.

Exercise

Create an application in VB.NET that uses a personalized menu like those introduced with Microsoft Office 2000 and Windows 2000. These menus display only the most recently used menu items, hiding others, and allow users to click an arrow to display the seldom-used choices. Your application should provide a menu that has hidden items. When a particular menu item is clicked, the hidden items should be displayed. Don't worry about adding event handlers for every menu item.

Your menu can be rather simple—it doesn't need to remember which items the user chooses most often, and it won't display hidden menu items simply by hovering over the menu. Finally, once the user clicks on the "more" button, she will have to reopen the menu to see the newly discovered items. (You'll see how to perform some more advanced functionality when you learn about GDI+ in Day 13, "Creating Graphical Applications with GDI+.")

The code for the application is as follows:

```
1:   Imports System
2:   Imports System.Windows.Forms
3:
4:   Namespace TYWinForms.Day4
5:
6:      public class Exercise1 : Inherits Form
7:         private mnuFile as new MainMenu
8:         private miFile as new MenuItem("File")
9:         private miOpen as new MenuItem("Open...")
10:         private miClose as new MenuItem("Close")
11:         private miPrintPreview as new
➥MenuItem("Print Preview")
12:         private miPrint as new MenuItem("Print...")
13:         private miProperties as new MenuItem("Properties")
14:         private miSendTo as new MenuItem("Send To...")
15:         private miExit as new MenuItem("Exit")
16:         private WithEvents miMore as new
➥MenuItem("More items...")
17:
18:         public event PopUp as EventHandler
19:
```

```
20:        public sub New()
21:            Me.Text = "Exercise 1"
22:            Me.Menu = mnuFile
23:
24:            CreateMenus()
25:
26:        End Sub
27:
28:        public sub CreateMenus()
29:            mnuFile.MenuItems.Add(miFile)
30:
31:            miFile.MenuItems.Add(miOpen)
32:            miFile.MenuItems.Add(miClose)
33:            miFile.MenuItems.Add("-")
34:            miFile.MenuItems.Add(miPrintPreview)
35:            miFile.MenuItems.Add(miPrint)
36:            miFile.MenuItems.Add("-")
37:            miFile.MenuItems.Add(miSendTo)
38:            miFile.MenuItems.Add(miProperties)
39:            miFile.MenuItems.Add("-")
40:            miFile.MenuItems.Add(miExit)
41:            miFile.MenuItems.Add("-")
42:            miFile.MenuItems.Add(miMore)
43:
44:            miPrintPreview.Visible = false
45:            miProperties.Visible = false
46:            miSendTo.Visible = false
47:            miFile.MenuItems(5).Visible = false
48:
49:            AddHandler miMore.Click, new
➥EventHandler(AddressOf Me.ShowMenu)
50:        end sub
51:
52:        public sub ShowMenu(Sender as Object, e as
➥EventArgs)
53:            miPrintPreview.Visible = true
54:            miProperties.Visible = true
55:            miSendTo.Visible = true
56:            miFile.MenuItems(5).Visible = true
57:
58:            miFile.MenuItems(10).Visible = false
59:            miMore.Visible = false
60:        end sub
61:
62:        public Shared Sub Main()
63:            Application.Run(new Exercise1)
64:        end sub
65:    end class
66:
67: End Namespace
```

Answers for Day 5

Quiz

1. What is the standard event handler signature?

```
public sub HandlerName(Object as Sender, e as EventArgs)
```

2. Create an event named ShowText in C# that uses the KeyPressEventHandler delegate.

```
public event KeyPressEventHandler ShowText;
```

3. Create a custom delegate that uses the KeyPressEventArgs object.

```
public delegate void CustomEventHandler(Object Sender,
➡KeyPressEventArgs e);
```

4. True or false: To compare object types, you use the equals (=) operator.

False. The equals operator is only for simple data types. Use the is operator for objects.

5. Which of the following statements is incorrect?

```
AddHandler btOne.Click, new EventHandler(AddressOf btOne_Click)
public sub MyEventHandler(Sender as Object, e as EventArgs)
➡Handles btTemp.Click

AddHandler btOne.Click += new EventHandler(AddressOf btOne.Click)
```

The third statement is wrong—it tries to combine both VB.NET and C# syntax.

6. Why should the properties of a custom EventArgs object be readonly?

The event handler—the method that receives the custom EventArgs object—should not be able to modify these properties. They should be generated by the event to provide supplemental information to the handler.

7. Is the following code snippet correct? What, if anything, needs to be changed?

```
public virtual void OnMyEvent(EventArgs e) {
    MyEvent(this, e);
}
```

First, the access modifier needs to be changed from public to protected; only the class this method is contained in should be able to execute it, and public will allow any class to do so. Second, there should be a check to see if a delegate has been assigned:

```
if (MyEvent != null) {
    MyEvent(this, e);
}
```

8. Where must custom events and delegates be declared (in what part of your code)?

An event must be declared inside the class that will raise the event, but outside any method declarations. A delegate can be declared either outside or inside of a class.

Exercise

Create a calculator application in C# like the Windows calculator. It should have numeric buttons that display numbers when pushed, and operator buttons that perform calculations when clicked. Use one event handler for all numeric buttons, and one handler for all operator buttons. (Hint: use hidden controls—controls with their `Visible` property set to `false`—to store temporary variables.)

```
1:  using System;
2:  using System.Windows.Forms;
3:  using System.Drawing;
4:
5:  namespace TYWinforms.Day5 {
6:
7:      public class Calculator : Form {
8:          private TextBox tbNumber = new TextBox();
9:          private TextBox tbHiddenNumber = new TextBox();
10:         private TextBox tbHiddenOperator = new TextBox();
11:         private TextBox tbHiddenAnswer = new TextBox();
12:
13:         private Button btZero = new Button();
14:         private Button btOne = new Button();
15:         private Button btTwo = new Button();
16:         private Button btThree = new Button();
17:         private Button btFour = new Button();
18:         private Button btFive = new Button();
19:         private Button btSix = new Button();
20:         private Button btSeven = new Button();
21:         private Button btEight = new Button();
22:         private Button btNine = new Button();
23:
24:         private Button btAdd = new Button();
25:         private Button btSubtract = new Button();
26:         private Button btMultiply = new Button();
27:         private Button btDivide = new Button();
28:         private Button btEquals = new Button();
29:
30:         public Calculator() {
31:             tbNumber.Location = new Point(210,10);
32:             tbNumber.Width = 100;
33:
34:             tbHiddenNumber.Visible = false;
35:             tbHiddenOperator.Visible = false;
36:             tbHiddenAnswer.Visible = false;
37:
```

A

```
38:            btZero.Text = "0";
39:            btZero.Location = new Point(10,125);
40:            btZero.Click += new EventHandler(this.NumberClick);
41:
42:            btOne.Text = "1";
43:            btOne.Location = new Point(10,100);
44:            btOne.Click += new EventHandler(this.NumberClick);
45:
46:            btTwo.Text = "2";
47:            btTwo.Location = new Point(85,100);
48:            btTwo.Click += new EventHandler(this.NumberClick);
49:
50:            btThree.Text = "3";
51:            btThree.Location = new Point(160,100);
52:            btThree.Click += new EventHandler(this.
➥NumberClick);
53:
54:            btFour.Text = "4";
55:            btFour.Location = new Point(10,75);
56:            btFour.Click += new EventHandler(this.
➥NumberClick);
57:
58:            btFive.Text = "5";
59:            btFive.Location = new Point(85,75);
60:            btFive.Click += new EventHandler(this.
➥NumberClick);
61:
62:            btSix.Text = "6";
63:            btSix.Location = new Point(160,75);
64:            btSix.Click += new EventHandler(this.NumberClick);
65:
66:            btSeven.Text = "7";
67:            btSeven.Location = new Point(10,50);
68:            btSeven.Click += new EventHandler(this.
➥NumberClick);
69:
70:            btEight.Text = "8";
71:            btEight.Location = new Point(85,50);
72:            btEight.Click += new EventHandler(this.
➥NumberClick);
73:
74:            btNine.Text = "9";
75:            btNine.Location = new Point(160,50);
76:            btNine.Click += new EventHandler(this.
➥NumberClick);
77:
78:            btAdd.Text = "+";
79:            btAdd.Location = new Point(160,125);
80:            btAdd.Click += new EventHandler(this.
➥OperatorClick);
81:
```

```
82:            btSubtract.Text = "-";
83:            btSubtract.Location = new Point(235,100);
84:            btSubtract.Click += new EventHandler(this.
➥OperatorClick);
85:
86:            btMultiply.Text = "*";
87:            btMultiply.Location = new Point(235,75);
88:            btMultiply.Click += new EventHandler(this.
➥OperatorClick);
89:
90:            btDivide.Text = "/";
91:            btDivide.Location = new Point(235,50);
92:            btDivide.Click += new EventHandler(this.
➥OperatorClick);
93:
94:            btEquals.Text = "=";
95:            btEquals.Location = new Point(235,125);
96:            btEquals.Click += new EventHandler(this.
➥OperatorClick);
97:
98:
99:            this.Text = "Calculator";
100:           this.Width = 325;
101:           this.Height = 200;
102:           this.Controls.Add(btZero);
103:           this.Controls.Add(btOne);
104:           this.Controls.Add(btTwo);
105:           this.Controls.Add(btThree);
106:           this.Controls.Add(btFour);
107:           this.Controls.Add(btFive);
108:           this.Controls.Add(btSix);
109:           this.Controls.Add(btSeven);
110:           this.Controls.Add(btEight);
111:           this.Controls.Add(btNine);
112:           this.Controls.Add(btAdd);
113:           this.Controls.Add(btSubtract);
114:           this.Controls.Add(btMultiply);
115:           this.Controls.Add(btDivide);
116:           this.Controls.Add(btEquals);
117:           this.Controls.Add(tbNumber);
118:           this.Controls.Add(tbHiddenOperator);
119:           this.Controls.Add(tbHiddenNumber);
120:           this.Controls.Add(tbHiddenAnswer);
121:       }
122:
123:       public void NumberClick(Object Sender,
➥EventArgs e) {
124:           if (tbNumber.Text != "" & tbNumber.Text != "0"
➥& tbHiddenAnswer.Text != "1") {
125:               tbNumber.Text += ((Button)Sender).Text;
126:           } else {
```

```
127:                    tbNumber.Text = ((Button)Sender).Text;
128:                    tbHiddenAnswer.Text = "";
129:                }
130:            }
131:
132:        public void OperatorClick(Object Sender,
➥EventArgs e) {
133:                int intAnswer = 0;
134:
135:                if (tbNumber.Text != "" & ((Button)Sender).Text
➥!= "=") {
136:                    tbHiddenNumber.Text = tbNumber.Text;
137:                    tbHiddenOperator.Text = ((Button)Sender).
➥Text;
138:                    tbNumber.Text = "0";
139:                } else if (tbNumber.Text != "" &
➥ ((Button)Sender).Text == "=") {
140:                    switch(tbHiddenOperator.Text) {
141:                        case "+":
142:                            intAnswer = Convert.ToInt32
➥ (tbHiddenNumber.Text) + Convert.ToInt32(tbNumber.Text);
143:                            break;
144:                        case "-":
145:                            intAnswer = Convert.ToInt32
➥ (tbHiddenNumber.Text) - Convert.ToInt32(tbNumber.Text);
146:                            break;
147:                        case "*":
148:                            intAnswer = Convert.ToInt32
➥ (tbHiddenNumber.Text) * Convert.ToInt32(tbNumber.Text);
149:                            break;
150:                        case "/":
151:                            intAnswer = Convert.ToInt32
➥ (tbHiddenNumber.Text) / Convert.ToInt32(tbNumber.Text);
152:                            break;
153:                    }
154:                    tbNumber.Text = intAnswer.ToString();
155:                    tbHiddenAnswer.Text = "1";
156:                    tbHiddenNumber.Text = "";
157:                    tbHiddenOperator.Text = "";
158:                }
159:            }
160:
161:        public static void Main() {
162:            Application.Run(new Calculator());
163:        }
164:    }
165: }
```

Answers for Day 6

Quiz

1. How are `RadioButton` selections limited?

   The user can only select one radio button per container control.

2. What does the following custom date/time string mean?

   `"hh:MM:yy-dddd"`

   Two-digit hour, followed by a colon and the two-digit month, followed by a colon and the two-digit year, followed by a dash and the full day-of-week name.

3. What object is associated with the `TreeView` control?

   The `TreeNode` object, which is used to represent each node in the tree.

4. For a `Button` control named `btHappy`, set properties that will cause it to expand vertically when its container form is resized.

   `btHappy.Anchor = AnchorStyles.Top Or AnchorStyles.Bottom`

5. Name ten members that are shared by every control discussed today.

   The `Anchor`, `Dock`, `BackColor`, `Location`, `Font`, and `Text` properties, the `GetType` and `Refresh` methods, and the `Click` and `Resize` events, among many others.

6. What are the five members of the `Timer` control discussed today?

   `Enabled`, `Interval`, `Tick`, `Start`, and `Stop`.

7. How do you add "tabs" to the `TabControl` control? Describe in words and with a line of code.

   Use `TabPage` objects to add more tabs to a `TabControl`. For example, given a `TabControl` named `MyTabControl`:

   `MyTabControl.TabPages.Add(new TabPage("Label text"));`

8. What two methods should you execute when you plan on adding many items to a `ComboBox` control using the `Add` method? Given what you know about Windows Forms controls, what other controls (discussed today) do you think also have these methods?

   The `BeginUpdate` method is used to prevent the control from updating its display until the `EndUpdate` method is called. In addition to the `ComboBox`, the `ListBox` and `TreeView` controls are also able to use these methods.

9. True or false: The `PictureBox` control can only display bitmap (BMP) and GIF images.

   False. The `PictureBox` can display these, and many other formats including JPG and icon (ICO) files.

Exercise

Create an application in C# that allows users to insert and view their CD collections. They must be able to enter new artists/albums/songs, and view them using a hierarchical list. (Don't worry about saving the input just now—we'll learn how to do that in Day 9, "Using ADO.NET.")

Remember to make sure that albums are only added to artists, and songs are only added to albums.

```
1:  using System;
2:  using System.Windows.Forms;
3:  using System.Drawing;
4:
5:  namespace TYWinForms.Day6 {
6:
7:      public class CDCatalog : Form {
8:          private TreeView tvList = new TreeView();
9:          private TextBox tbName = new TextBox();
10:         private Button btArtist = new Button();
11:         private Button btAlbum = new Button();
12:         private Button btSong = new Button();
13:
14:         public CDCatalog() {
15:             tvList.Location = new Point(10,10);
16:             tvList.Size = new Size(200,550);
17:             tvList.LabelEdit = true;
18:
19:             tbName.Location = new Point(250,10);
20:             tbName.Width = 150;
21:
22:             btArtist.Location = new Point(225,40);
23:             btArtist.Text = "Add Artist";
24:             btArtist.Click += new EventHandler
➡(this.AddArtist);
25:
26:             btAlbum.Location = new Point(300,40);
27:             btAlbum.Text = "Add Album";
28:             btAlbum.Click += new EventHandler(this.AddAlbum);
29:
30:             btSong.Location = new Point(375,40);
31:             btSong.Text = "Add Song";
32:             btSong.Click += new EventHandler(this.AddSong);
33:
34:             this.Text = "CD Catalog";
35:             this.Size = new Size(800,600);
36:             this.Controls.Add(tvList);
37:             this.Controls.Add(tbName);
38:             this.Controls.Add(btArtist);
39:             this.Controls.Add(btAlbum);
```

```
40:              this.Controls.Add(btSong);
41:          }
42:
43:      public void AddArtist(Object Sender, EventArgs e) {
44:          if (tbName.Text == "") {
45:              MessageBox.Show("You forgot to enter a name");
46:              return;
47:          }
48:
49:          tvList.Nodes.Add(new TreeNode(tbName.Text));
50:          tbName.Text = "";
51:      }
52:
53:      public void AddAlbum(Object Sender, EventArgs e) {
54:          if (tbName.Text == "") {
55:              MessageBox.Show("You forgot to enter a name");
56:              return;
57:          }
58:
59:          if (tvList.SelectedNode != null &
➥tvList.Nodes.Contains(tvList.SelectedNode)) {
60:                  tvList.SelectedNode.Nodes.Add(new TreeNode
➥ (tbName.Text));
61:              tbName.Text = "";
62:              tvList.ExpandAll();
63:          } else {
64:              MessageBox.Show("You must first select an
➥artist");
65:          }
66:      }
67:
68:      public void AddSong(Object Sender, EventArgs e) {
69:          if (tbName.Text == "") {
70:              MessageBox.Show("You forgot to enter a name");
71:              return;
72:          }
73:
74:          if (tvList.SelectedNode != null &
➥tvList.Nodes.Contains(tvList.SelectedNode.Parent)) {
75:                  tvList.SelectedNode.Nodes.Add(new TreeNode
➥ (tbName.Text));
76:              tbName.Text = "";
77:              tvList.ExpandAll();
78:          } else {
79:              MessageBox.Show("You must first select an
➥album");
80:          }
81:      }
82:
83:      public static void Main() {
84:          Application.Run(new CDCatalog());
```

```
85:        }
86:      }
87:  }
```

Answers for Day 7

Quiz

1. True or false: Any `Form` object can be a dialog box.

   True.

2. How do you make a dialog modal? Modeless?

   Call the `ShowDialog` method. Call the `Show` method.

3. True or false: You can directly instantiate a `MessageBox` object.

   False. You can only access the static `Show` method of this object.

4. What are the seven parameters that the `MessageBox.Show` method can take? (Just list their types and a short description.)

   - `Iwin32Window` —The window to display the dialog in front of
   - `String`—The text to display in the box
   - `String`—The caption of the window
   - `MessageBoxButtons`—The buttons that should appear in the dialog
   - `MessageBoxIcon`—The icon to appear
   - `MessageBoxDefaultButton`—The button that should be pre-selected
   - `MessageBoxOptions`—Various non-related properties

5. Assigning a `DialogResult` value in your custom dialog class does what two things for you?

   It returns a `DialogResult` value to the parent form, and automatically closes the dialog box when the user selects a button (you don't need to call the `Hide` method).

6. Is the following code snippet correct? If not, what's wrong with it?
```
public property IsClicked as string
    Get
        return blnClicked
end property
```

   If only the `Get` statement is used, the property must be marked as `readonly`. Also, the `End Get` statement is missing.

7. What two members are common to almost all common dialog controls? Name the exception(s).

    `ShowHelp` and `Reset`. These members are part of all the common dialog controls except the `PrintPreviewDialog` control.

8. Write a filter string for an `OpenFileDialog` control that displays: `.txt` files, `.gif` files, and all files.

    ```
    "Text files (*.txt)|*.txt|GIF Images (*.gif)|*.gif|
    All files (*.*)|*.*"
    ```

9. Name the main properties (that is, the properties you are most interested in when the user makes a selection) for the `OpenFileDialog`, `SaveFileDialog`, `ColorDialog`, and `FontDialog` controls.

    Respectively, `Filename`, `Filename`, `Color`, and `Font`.

Exercise

Create a fully-featured application in C#, using menus, that uses all of the common dialog controls. Also, use a modeless dialog to display context related help information. When a user moves from one menu item to another, the content in this dialog should change. (Hint: Use the MenuItem.Select event to determine which menu item the mouse is currently over.)

```
1:  using System;
2:  using System.Windows.Forms;
3:  using System.Drawing;
4:  using System.Drawing.Printing;
5:
6:  namespace TYWinforms.Day7 {
7:     public class Exercise1 : Form {
8:        PageSettings objPageSettings = new PageSettings();
9:        MainMenu mnuMain = new MainMenu();
10:        MenuItem mniFile = new MenuItem("File");
11:        MenuItem mniOpen = new MenuItem("Open");
12:        MenuItem mniSave = new MenuItem("Save");
13:        MenuItem mniPageSetup = new MenuItem("Page Setup");
14:        MenuItem mniPrintPreview = new MenuItem
➥("Print Preview");
15:        MenuItem mniPrint = new MenuItem("Print");
16:        MenuItem mniEdit = new MenuItem("Edit");
17:        MenuItem mniFont = new MenuItem("Font");
18:        MenuItem mniColor = new MenuItem("Color");
19:
20:        HelpDialog dlgHelp = new HelpDialog();
21:
22:        public Exercise1() {
23:           mnuMain.MenuItems.Add(mniFile);
```

```
24:          mnuMain.MenuItems.Add(mniEdit);
25:
26:          mniFile.MenuItems.Add(mniOpen);
27:          mniFile.MenuItems.Add(mniSave);
28:          mniFile.MenuItems.Add("-");
29:          mniFile.MenuItems.Add(mniPageSetup);
30:          mniFile.MenuItems.Add(mniPrintPreview);
31:          mniFile.MenuItems.Add(mniPrint);
32:
33:          mniEdit.MenuItems.Add(mniFont);
34:          mniEdit.MenuItems.Add(mniColor);
35:
36:          mniOpen.Click += new EventHandler(this.
➥FileMenuClick);
37:          mniSave.Click += new EventHandler(this.
➥FileMenuClick);
38:          mniPageSetup.Click += new EventHandler(this.
➥FileMenuClick);
39:          mniPrintPreview.Click += new EventHandler(this.
➥FileMenuClick);
40:          mniPrint.Click += new EventHandler(this.
➥FileMenuClick);
41:          mniFont.Click += new EventHandler(this.
➥EditMenuClick);
42:          mniColor.Click += new EventHandler(this.
➥EditMenuClick);
43:
44:          mniOpen.Select += new EventHandler(this.
➥DisplayHelp);
45:          mniSave.Select += new EventHandler(this.
➥DisplayHelp);
46:          mniPageSetup.Select += new EventHandler(this.
➥DisplayHelp);
47:          mniPrintPreview.Select += new EventHandler(this.
➥DisplayHelp);
48:          mniPrint.Select += new EventHandler(this.
➥DisplayHelp);
49:          mniFont.Select += new EventHandler(this.
➥DisplayHelp);
50:          mniColor.Select += new EventHandler(this.
➥DisplayHelp);
51:
52:          this.Menu = mnuMain;
53:          this.Text = "Exercise 1";
54:       }
55:
56:      public void FileMenuClick(Object Sender,
➥EventArgs e) {
57:          MenuItem mniTemp = (MenuItem)Sender;
58:
```

```
59:            switch (mniTemp.Text) {
60:               case "Open":
61:                   OpenFileDialog dlgOpen = new
➥OpenFileDialog();
62:                   if (dlgOpen.ShowDialog() ==
➥DialogResult.OK) {
63:                       //open file
64:                   }
65:                   break;
66:               case "Save":
67:                   SaveFileDialog dlgSave = new
➥SaveFileDialog();
68:                   if (dlgSave.ShowDialog() ==
➥DialogResult.OK) {
69:                       //save file
70:                   }
71:                   break;
72:               case "Page Setup":
73:                   PageSetupDialog dlgPageSetup = new
➥PageSetupDialog();
74:                   dlgPageSetup.PageSettings =
➥objPageSettings;
75:                   dlgPageSetup.ShowDialog();
76:                   break;
77:               case "Print Preview":
78:                   PrintPreviewDialog dlgPrintPreview =
➥new PrintPreviewDialog();
79:                   dlgPrintPreview.Document = new
➥PrintDocument();
80:                   dlgPrintPreview.ShowDialog();
81:                   break;
82:               case "Print":
83:                   PrintDialog dlgPrint = new PrintDialog();
84:                   dlgPrint.PrinterSettings = new
➥PrinterSettings();
85:                   if (dlgPrint.ShowDialog() ==
➥DialogResult.OK) {
86:                       //print
87:                   }
88:                   break;
89:           }
90:       }
91:
92:       public void EditMenuClick(Object Sender,
➥EventArgs e) {
93:           MenuItem mniTemp = (MenuItem)Sender;
94:
95:           switch (mniTemp.Text) {
96:               case "Font":
97:                   FontDialog dlgFont = new FontDialog();
```

```
98:                      if (dlgFont.ShowDialog() ==
➥DialogResult.OK) {
99:                          this.Font = dlgFont.Font;
100:                      }
101:                      break;
102:                  case "Color":
103:                      ColorDialog dlgColor = new ColorDialog();
104:                      if (dlgColor.ShowDialog() ==
➥DialogResult.OK) {
105:                          this.BackColor = dlgColor.Color;
106:                      }
107:                      break;
108:              }
109:          }
110:
111:          public void DisplayHelp(Object Sender,
➥EventArgs e) {
112:          MenuItem mniTemp = (MenuItem)Sender;
113:
114:          if (!dlgHelp.Visible) { dlgHelp.Show(); }
115:
116:          switch (mniTemp.Text) {
117:              case "Open":
118:                  dlgHelp.HelpText = "Open a file";
119:                  break;
120:              case "Save":
121:                  dlgHelp.HelpText = "Save this file";
122:                  break;
123:              case "Page Setup":
124:                  dlgHelp.HelpText = "Change page
➥settings";
125:                  break;
126:              case "Print Preview":
127:                  dlgHelp.HelpText = "Preview the
➥document before printing";
128:                  break;
129:              case "Print":
130:                  dlgHelp.HelpText = "Print the
➥current document";
131:                  break;
132:              case "Font":
133:                  dlgHelp.HelpText = "Change the
➥current font face, color, size, etc";
134:                  break;
135:              case "Color":
136:                  dlgHelp.HelpText = "Change the
➥background color of the application";
137:                  break;
138:              }
139:          }
140:
```

```
141:        public static void Main() {
142:            Application.Run(new Exercise1());
143:        }
144:    }
145:
146:    public class HelpDialog : Form {
147:        private Label lblMessage = new Label();
148:
149:        public String HelpText {
150:            get { return lblMessage.Text; }
151:            set { lblMessage.Text = value; }
152:        }
153:
154:        public HelpDialog() {
155:            lblMessage.Size = new Size(100,100);
156:            lblMessage.Text = "Help screen";
157:
158:            this.Controls.Add(lblMessage);
159:            this.BackColor = Color.Yellow;
160:            this.Size = new Size(100,100);
161:            this.FormBorderStyle = FormBorderStyle.
➥FixedToolWindow;
162:        }
163:    }
164: }
```

Answers for Day 8

Quiz

1. Write a statement that will add a new databinding to a text box control named
   "tbOne". Bind to the Text property the array "arrOne".

   ```
   tbOne.DataBindings.Add("Text", arrOne, "");
   ```

2. Given the text box in question 1, is the following statement correct?

   ```
   tbOne.BindingContext.Position += 1;
   ```

   No, you must specify the particular binding context to increment:

   ```
   tbOne.BindingContext[arrOne].Position += 1;
   ```

3. True or False: You can bind data to a Form object.

   True. Binding data like this is often an easy way to associate your application with
   data.

4. What event is often used to call the HitTest method and why?

   The MouseDown event is often used to call the HitTest method because it returns
   specific coordinates of the user's click.

5. Given the number "458.34e+04", what would the display be using the format string "d3"?

    This is a trick question; the display would be "4583400". If you specify a precision value in the format string with fewer digits than in the original value, the precision is ignored.

6. To which property of the DataGrid do you add DataGridTableStyle objects?

    The TableStyles property.

7. To which property of the DataGrid do you add DataGridColumnStyle objects?

    Another trick question. You don't add DataGridColumnStyle objects to a DataGrid, you add them to the GridColumnStyles property of the DataGridTableStyle object.

8. Given a DataTable named "dtData", with two columns "ColA" and "ColB", create a new, empty, row.

```
DataRow myRow;
myRow = dtData.NewRow();
dtData.Rows.Add(myRow);
```

9. Create the "ColA" column for the DataTable in question 8 as an integer type.

```
DataColumn colA = new DataColumn();
colA.DataType = System.Type.GetType("System.Int32");
colA.ColumnName = "ColA";
dtData.Columns.Add(colA);
```

Exercise

Create an application using a DataGrid and DataTable that allows users to enter their checkbook register information, similar to Microsoft Money or Quicken. Do not allow the DataGrid to be manually edited; rather, provide other controls for the user to enter the information, which will then be displayed in the DataGrid upon submission. To keep this exercise simple, allow only withdrawals for now.

```
1:  using System;
2:  using System.Windows.Forms;
3:  using System.Drawing;
4:  using System.Data;
5:
6:  namespace TYWinforms.Day8 {
7:      public class Exercise1 : Form {
8:          private DataGrid dgMoney = new DataGrid();
9:          private DataTable dtMoney = new DataTable("Money");
10:
11:         private Panel pnlAdd = new Panel();
12:         private TextBox tbNum = new TextBox();
```

```
13:        private TextBox tbDate = new TextBox();
14:        private TextBox tbPayee = new TextBox();
15:        private TextBox tbAmount = new TextBox();
16:        private Label lblNum = new Label();
17:        private Label lblDate = new Label();
18:        private Label lblPayee = new Label();
19:        private Label lblAmount = new Label();
20:        private Button btSubmit = new Button();
21:
22:        public Exercise1() {
23:            //create columns
24:            DataColumn colNum = new DataColumn();
25:            colNum.DataType = System.Type.GetType
➥("System.Int32");
26:            colNum.ColumnName = "Check Number";
27:            dtMoney.Columns.Add(colNum);
28:
29:            DataColumn colAmount = new DataColumn();
30:            colAmount.DataType = System.Type.GetType
➥ ("System.Double");
31:            colAmount.ColumnName = "Amount";
32:            dtMoney.Columns.Add(colAmount);
33:
34:            DataColumn colPayee = new DataColumn();
35:            colPayee.DataType = System.Type.GetType
➥ ("System.String");
36:            colPayee.ColumnName = "Payee";
37:            dtMoney.Columns.Add(colPayee);
38:
39:            DataColumn colDate = new DataColumn();
40:            colDate.DataType = System.Type.GetType
➥ ("System.DateTime");
41:            colDate.ColumnName = "Date";
42:            dtMoney.Columns.Add(colDate);
43:
44:            //create styles
45:            DataGridTableStyle dgtStyle = new
➥DataGridTableStyle();
46:            dgtStyle.MappingName = "Money";
47:
48:            DataGridTextBoxColumn dgcStyle = new
➥DataGridTextBoxColumn();
49:            dgcStyle.MappingName = "Check Number";
50:            dgcStyle.ReadOnly = true;
51:            dgcStyle.HeaderText = "Check No.";
52:            dgcStyle.Width = 100;
53:            dgtStyle.GridColumnStyles.Add(dgcStyle);
54:
55:            dgcStyle = new DataGridTextBoxColumn();
56:            dgcStyle.MappingName = "Date";
57:            dgcStyle.ReadOnly = true;
```

```
58:          dgcStyle.HeaderText = "Date";
59:          dgcStyle.Width = 100;
60:          dgtStyle.GridColumnStyles.Add(dgcStyle);
61:
62:          dgcStyle = new DataGridTextBoxColumn();
63:          dgcStyle.MappingName = "Payee";
64:          dgcStyle.ReadOnly = true;
65:          dgcStyle.HeaderText = "Payee";
66:          dgcStyle.Width = 452;
67:          dgtStyle.GridColumnStyles.Add(dgcStyle);
68:
69:          dgcStyle = new DataGridTextBoxColumn();
70:          dgcStyle.MappingName = "Amount";
71:          dgcStyle.ReadOnly = true;
72:          dgcStyle.HeaderText = "Amount";
73:          dgcStyle.Width = 100;
74:          dgcStyle.Format = "c";
75:          dgtStyle.GridColumnStyles.Add(dgcStyle);
76:
77:          //create add form
78:          lblNum.Text = "Check No.";
79:          lblNum.Location = new Point(10,250);
80:          tbNum.Location = new Point(75,245);
81:
82:          lblDate.Text = "Date";
83:          lblDate.Location = new Point(600,250);
84:          tbDate.Location = new Point(675,245);
85:
86:          lblPayee.Text = "Pay To:";
87:          lblPayee.Location = new Point(10,280);
88:          tbPayee.Location = new Point(75,275);
89:          tbPayee.Width = 400;
90:
91:          lblAmount.Text = "Amount";
92:          lblAmount.Location = new Point(600,280);
93:          tbAmount.Location = new Point(675,275);
94:
95:          btSubmit.Text = "Enter";
96:          btSubmit.Location = new Point(675,310);
97:          btSubmit.Click += new EventHandler
➥ (this.AddRecord);
98:
99:          pnlAdd.Size = new Size(800,500);
100:          pnlAdd.Dock = DockStyle.Bottom;
101:          pnlAdd.BackColor = Color.Tan;
102:          pnlAdd.Controls.Add(tbNum);
103:          pnlAdd.Controls.Add(tbDate);
104:          pnlAdd.Controls.Add(tbPayee);
105:          pnlAdd.Controls.Add(tbAmount);
106:          pnlAdd.Controls.Add(lblNum);
107:          pnlAdd.Controls.Add(lblDate);
```

```
108:            pnlAdd.Controls.Add(lblPayee);
109:            pnlAdd.Controls.Add(lblAmount);
110:            pnlAdd.Controls.Add(btSubmit);
111:
112:            dgMoney.Dock = DockStyle.Top;
113:            dgMoney.Size = new Size(800,300);
114:            dgMoney.CaptionText = "Checkbook Register";
115:            dgMoney.BackgroundColor = Color.White;
116:            dgMoney.TableStyles.Add(dgtStyle);
117:            dgMoney.DataSource = dtMoney;
118:
119:            this.Size = new Size(800,600);
120:            this.Text = ".NET Check Book Register";
121:            this.Controls.Add(dgMoney);
122:            this.Controls.Add(pnlAdd);
123:        }
124:
125:    private void AddRecord(Object Sender,
➥EventArgs e) {
126:            if (tbPayee.Text == "" | tbAmount.Text == "") {
127:            MessageBox.Show("You forgot to enter a
➥payee or amount.","Check Register");
128:        } else {
129:            DataRow newRow = dtMoney.NewRow();
130:
131:            newRow[0] = Convert.ToInt32(tbNum.Text);
132:            newRow[1] = Convert.ToDouble(tbAmount.Text);
133:            newRow[2] = tbPayee.Text;
134:            newRow[3] = Convert.ToDateTime(tbDate.Text);
135:
136:            dtMoney.Rows.Add(newRow);
137:
138:            tbNum.Text = "";
139:            tbDate.Text = "";
140:            tbAmount.Text = "";
141:            tbPayee.Text = "";
142:        }
143:        }
144:
145:    public static void Main() {
146:        Application.Run(new Exercise1());
147:        }
148:    }
149:    }
```

Answers for Day 9

Quiz

1. Write a SELECT statement that retrieves only those records from the tblUsers table where the UserID field is between 5 and 10.

   You can write this statement in two different ways:

   ```
   SELECT * FROM tblUsers WHERE UserID < 11 and UserID > 4
   ```

   Or

   ```
   SELECT * FROM tblUsers WHERE UserID BETWEEN 5 AND 10
   ```

2. What does the SqlCommandBuilder object require as a parameter to its constructor?

   The SqlCommandBuilder object requires an instance of an SqlDataAdapter object.

3. An SqlCommandBuilder will generate SQL commands automatically only if a primary key is present. Why?

   The commands that are generated must have a WHERE clause that limits the records changed to only the proper ones. Using a primary key is one way to ensure that you're modifying the correct record. For example, the following statement *might* modify more than one record:

   ```
   DELETE FROM tblUsers WHERE LastName = 'Payne'
   ```

   Rather, you want to make sure that only one record is affected, so the primary key, which must be unique for every record, ensures this. The following command *will* delete only one record, guaranteed:

   ```
   DELETE FROM tblUsers WHERE UserID = 1
   ```

4. True or False: Most of the time, you can simply change the prefix Sql to OleDb to use the objects in the OLE DB provider.

   True. For example, SqlDataAdapter becomes OleDbDataAdapter, SqlConnection becomes OleDbConnection, and so on.

5. Is it enough to set the DataSource property of a DataGrid to a filled DataSet?

   No. You also need to set the DataMember property to the DataTable that contains the information to display.

6. Given an SqlCommand object named objCmd, write a statement that adds a parameter named "@BirthDate" with a value of "1/7/01".

   You can write this statement in two ways:

   ```
   objCmd.Parameters.Add("@BirthDate", SqlDbType.VarChar, 10)
   ➥.Value = "1/7/01";
   ```

   Or

```
objCmd.Parameters.Add("@BirthDate", SqlDbType.DateTime, 10)
➥.Value = "1/7/01";
```

7. What method causes changes to be pushed immediately to a `DataSet`?

The `EndCurrentEdit` method of the `BindingContext` causes changes to be pushed immediately to a `DataSet`.

Exercise

Create an application that allows a user to enter SQL statements in a text box. If the statement returns results, place them in a DataGrid and allow it to be editable. Don't worry if the query is entered in a proper format; error checking will be covered in a future lesson.

```
1:  using System;
2:  using System.Windows.Forms;
3:  using System.Drawing;
4:  using System.Data;
5:  using System.Data.SqlClient;
6:
7:  namespace TYWinforms.Day9 {
8:      public class Exercise1 : Form {
9:          private DataGrid dgData = new DataGrid();
10:         private TextBox tbCommand = new TextBox();
11:         private Button btExecute = new Button();
12:         private DataSet objDS = new DataSet();
13:         private String strConn;
14:
15:         public Exercise1() {
16:             strConn = "Initial Catalog=TYWinforms;Data
➥Source=localhost;User ID=sa";
17:
18:             tbCommand.Location = new Point(150,75);
19:             tbCommand.Multiline = true;
20:             tbCommand.Height = 50;
21:             tbCommand.Width = 300;
22:
23:             btExecute.Location = new Point(475,75);
24:             btExecute.Text = "Execute!";
25:             btExecute.Click += new EventHandler
➥ (this.Execute);
26:
27:             dgData.Dock = DockStyle.Bottom;
28:             dgData.Size = new Size(800,400);
29:             dgData.Enabled = false;
30:             dgData.CurrentCellChanged += new
➥EventHandler(this.UpdateData);
31:
```

```
32:             this.Size = new Size(800,600);
33:             this.Text = "Exercise 1";
34:             this.Controls.Add(dgData);
35:             this.Controls.Add(tbCommand);
36:             this.Controls.Add(btExecute);
37:         }
38:
39:     private void Execute(Object Sender,
➥EventArgs e) {
40:         if (tbCommand.Text != "") {
41:             SqlConnection objConn = new
➥SqlConnection(strConn);
42:
43:             SqlDataAdapter objCmd = new
➥SqlDataAdapter(tbCommand.Text, objConn);
44:             objDS.Clear();
45:             int intRows = objCmd.Fill(objDS, "Query");
46:
47:             if (intRows > 0) {
48:                 dgData.ResetBindings();
49:                 dgData.DataSource = objDS;
50:                 dgData.DataMember = "Query";
51:                 dgData.Enabled = true;
52:             } else {
53:                 dgData.Enabled = false;
54:             }
55:         }
56:     }
57:
58:     public void UpdateData(Object Sender,
➥EventArgs e) {
59:         SqlConnection objConn = new
➥SqlConnection(strConn);
60:         SqlDataAdapter objCmd = new
➥SqlDataAdapter(tbCommand.Text, objConn);
61:         SqlCommandBuilder objBuilder =
➥new SqlCommandBuilder(objCmd);
62:
63:         objCmd.Update(objDS, "Query");
64:     }
65:
66:     public static void Main() {
67:         Application.Run(new Exercise1());
68:     }
69:   }
70: }
```

Answers for Day 10

Quiz

1. What property must you set on the MDI parent to make it an MDI application?

   Set `IsMdiContainer` to `true`.

2. What property must you set on the MDI child to make it part of an MDI application?

   Set the `MdiParent` property of the child to the parent form. This must happen in the parent form itself.

3. What are the three values of the `MdiLayout` enumeration?

   `MidLayout.Cascade`, `MdiLayout.TileHorizontal`, and `MdiLayout.TileVertical`.

4. True or False: You must call the `Show` method to display an MDI child when it's created in the constructor of its parent.

   False. You need to call the `Show` method only when the child document is created outside the constructor.

5. The following code snippet does not cause the `tbText` TextBox control to fill the entire form:

   ```
   TextBox tbText = new TextBox();
   tbText.Dock = DockStyle.Fill;
   ```

   Why not?

   For a `TextBox` to increase in height more than the default value, you must also set the `Multiline` property to `true`:

   ```
   tbText.Multiline = true;
   ```

6. How do you find out whether an active MDI child is active?

   Evaluate the `ActiveMdiChild` property and see whether it evaluates to `null` (`Nothing` in Visual Basic.NET).

7. You've created three menu items in a child document, but they're not displayed properly in the parent document. Name three things to check to fix this problem.

   If you're using any `MenuMerge` value other than `Remove`, make sure that the menu items are assigned in both parent and child classes.

   Make sure the `MergeOrder` values line up (that is, the menus that should combine/merge/replace have equal `MergeOrders`).

   Double-check that you're using the proper `MenuMerge` values. For example, you may accidentally use `Remove` in the child class, thinking that it would remove the parent's menu item, when in reality it removes the child item.

8. True or False: The MergeOrder value must be incremental; you cannot skip orders.

False. The actual value of MergeOrder does not matter when you're arranging menu items; only relative values matter.

Exercise

Create an MDI version of the "SQL statement execution" application from yesterday's exercise. Create a custom dialog box that displays a text box where the user can enter the query.

Exercise1.cs:

```
1:  using System;
2:  using System.Windows.Forms;
3:  using System.Drawing;
4:
5:  namespace TYWinforms.Day10 {
6:      public class Exercise1 : Form {
7:          private MainMenu mnuMain = new MainMenu();
8:          private int intCounter = 0;
9:
10:         public Exercise1() {
11:             MenuItem miQuery = mnuMain.MenuItems.Add
➥("Query");
12:             MenuItem miNew = miQuery.MenuItems.Add("New");
13:             miNew.Click += new EventHandler(this.HandleMenu);
14:
15:             MenuItem miWindow = mnuMain.MenuItems.Add
➥ ("&Window");
16:             miWindow.MenuItems.Add("Cascade", new
➥EventHandler(this.ArrangeWindows));
17:             miWindow.MenuItems.Add("Tile Horizontal",
➥new EventHandler(this.ArrangeWindows));
18:             miWindow.MenuItems.Add("Tile Vertical",
➥new EventHandler(this.ArrangeWindows));
19:             miWindow.MdiList = true;
20:
21:             QueryDialog dlgQuery = new QueryDialog();
22:             this.AddOwnedForm(dlgQuery);
23:             dlgQuery.TopMost = true;
24:             dlgQuery.Show();
25:
26:             this.Size = new Size(800,600);
27:             this.Text = "Exercise 1";
28:             this.Menu = mnuMain;
29:             this.IsMdiContainer = true;
30:         }
31:
```

```
32:          private void ArrangeWindows(Object Sender,
➥EventArgs e) {
33:            MenuItem miTemp = (MenuItem)Sender;
34:
35:            switch (miTemp.Text) {
36:              case "Cascade":
37:                  this.LayoutMdi(MdiLayout.Cascade);
38:                  break;
39:              case "Tile Horizontal":
40:                  this.LayoutMdi(MdiLayout.TileHorizontal);
41:                  break;
42:              case "Tile Vertical":
43:                  this.LayoutMdi(MdiLayout.TileVertical);
44:                  break;
45:            }
46:          }
47:
48:          private void HandleMenu(Object Sender,
➥EventArgs e) {
49:            intCounter++;
50:
51:            DataDocument doc = new DataDocument
➥ ("Query Results " + intCounter.ToString());
52:            doc.MdiParent = this;
53:            doc.Show();
54:          }
55:
56:          public static void Main() {
57:              Application.Run(new Exercise1());
58:          }
59:      }
60:  }
```

QueryDialog.cs:

```
1:  using System;
2:  using System.Windows.Forms;
3:  using System.Drawing;
4:
5:  namespace TYWinforms.Day10 {
6:     public class QueryDialog : Form {
7:         private TextBox tbCommand = new TextBox();
8:         private Button btExecute = new Button();
9:
10:        public QueryDialog() {
11:            tbCommand.Location = new Point(10,10);
12:            tbCommand.Multiline = true;
13:            tbCommand.Height = 50;
14:            tbCommand.Width = 250;
15:
16:            btExecute.Location = new Point(10,75);
```

```
17:            btExecute.Text = "Execute!";
18:            btExecute.Click += new EventHandler
➥(this.Execute);
19:
20:            this.Size = new Size(300,150);
21:            this.Text = "Query Executor";
22:            this.Controls.Add(tbCommand);
23:            this.Controls.Add(btExecute);
24:        }
25:
26:        private void Execute(Object Sender, EventArgs e) {
27:            if (tbCommand.Text != "") {
28:                if (this.Owner.ActiveMdiChild != null) {
29:
30:                    ((DataDocument)this.Owner.ActiveMdiChild).
➥Execute(tbCommand.Text);
31:                }
32:            }
33:        }
34:    }
35: }
```

DataDocument.cs:

```
1: using System;
2: using System.Windows.Forms;
3: using System.Drawing;
4: using System.Data;
5: using System.Data.SqlClient;
6:
7: namespace TYWinforms.Day10 {
8:    public class DataDocument : Form {
9:        private DataGrid dgData = new DataGrid();
10:        private DataSet objDS = new DataSet();
11:        private String strConn;
12:        private String strQuery;
13:
14:        public DataDocument(string strName) {
15:            strConn = "Initial Catalog=TYWinforms;Data
➥Source=localhost;User ID=sa";
16:
17:            dgData.Dock = DockStyle.Fill;
18:            dgData.Enabled = false;
19:            dgData.CurrentCellChanged += new
➥EventHandler(this.UpdateData);
20:
21:            this.WindowState = FormWindowState.Maximized;
22:            this.Text = strName;
23:            this.Controls.Add(dgData);
24:        }
25:
```

```
26:         public void Execute(string strQuery) {
27:             this.strQuery = strQuery;
28:
29:             SqlConnection objConn = new
➥SqlConnection(strConn);
30:
31:             SqlDataAdapter objCmd = new
➥SqlDataAdapter(strQuery, objConn);
32:             objDS.Clear();
33:             int intRows = objCmd.Fill(objDS, "Query");
34:
35:             if (intRows > 0) {
36:                 dgData.ResetBindings();
37:                 dgData.DataSource = objDS;
38:                 dgData.DataMember = "Query";
39:                 dgData.Enabled = true;
40:             } else {
41:                 dgData.Enabled = false;
42:             }
43:         }
44:
45:         public void UpdateData(Object Sender, EventArgs e) {
46:             SqlConnection objConn = new
➥SqlConnection(strConn);
47:             SqlDataAdapter objCmd = new
➥SqlDataAdapter(strQuery, objConn);
48:             SqlCommandBuilder objBuilder = new
➥SqlCommandBuilder(objCmd);
49:
50:             objCmd.Update(objDS, "Query");
51:         }
52:     }
53: }
```

Answers for Day 11

Quiz

1. What is the difference between the Read and Peek methods?

   Both the Read and Peek methods return the next character from a stream, but Peek does not move the pointer in the stream. Thus, subsequent calls to Peek will always return the same character, whereas calls to Read will move the pointer and return subsequent characters.

2. What is a recursive function, and when is it useful?

   A recursive function is one that calls itself over and over again. You use such as function when you don't know ahead of time how many times something must be executed—for example, with a directory structure.

3. What is the difference between synchronous and asynchronous operation?

Synchronous operation requires everything to execute in turn. Asynchronous operation allows execution to split into different branches that execute at the same time, thereby saving you time.

4. To what namespace does the print functionality belong?

`System.Drawing.Printing`.

5. What are the four events of the `FileSystemWatcher` object?

`Created`, `Changed`, `Renamed`, and `Deleted`.

6. What are the different `FileMode` enumeration values?

`Append`, `Create`, `CreateNew`, `Open`, `OpenOrCreate`, and `Truncate`.

Exercise

Modify Listing 11.1 so that the TreeView control nodes are built dynamically whenever a user expands a node, instead of all at once during the initialization of the application. Also, add a custom printing function to print the visible contents of the tree view. (Tip: You need to collect the contents of the tree view in an appropriate variable to print.)

```
1:  using System;
2:  using System.Windows.Forms;
3:  using System.Drawing;
4:  using System.IO;
5:  using System.Drawing.Printing;
6:
7:  namespace TYWinforms.Day11 {
8:      public class Exercise1 : Form {
9:          private TreeView tvFiles = new TreeView();
10:          private Label lblInfo = new Label();
11:          private MainMenu mnuMain = new MainMenu();
12:          private String strList = "";
13:          private StringReader objPrintReader;
14:
15:          public Exercise1() {
16:              tvFiles.Dock = DockStyle.Left;
17:              tvFiles.Width = 200;
18:              tvFiles.AfterSelect += new TreeViewEventHandler
➡(this.DisplayInfo);
19:              tvFiles.BeforeExpand += new
➡TreeViewCancelEventHandler(this.ExpandThread);
20:
21:              lblInfo.Size = new Size(150,150);
22:              lblInfo.Location = new Point(210,10);
23:              lblInfo.Text = "Select a file or\ndirectory";
24:
25:              PopulateList("c:\\", tvFiles.Nodes.Add("c:\\"));
```

```
26:
27:            MenuItem miFile = new MenuItem("File");
28:            MenuItem miPrint = new MenuItem("Print");
29:            miPrint.Click += new EventHandler
➥ (this.PrintClicked);
30:
31:            mnuMain.MenuItems.Add(miFile);
32:            miFile.MenuItems.Add(miPrint);
33:
34:            this.Menu = mnuMain;
35:            this.Text = "Exercise 1";
36:            this.Size = new Size(800,600);
37:            this.Controls.Add(tvFiles);
38:            this.Controls.Add(lblInfo);
39:        }
40:
41:        private void PopulateList(String strPath,
➥TreeNode currNode) {
42:            DirectoryInfo dir = new DirectoryInfo(strPath);
43:            TreeNode nodeSubDir;
44:
45:            foreach (DirectoryInfo d in
➥dir.GetDirectories()) {
46:                nodeSubDir = currNode.Nodes.Add(d.Name);
47:                nodeSubDir.Nodes.Add("");
48:            }
49:
50:            foreach (FileInfo f in dir.GetFiles("*.*")) {
51:                currNode.Nodes.Add(f.Name);
52:            }
53:        }
54:
55:        private void ExpandThread(Object Sender,
➥TreeViewCancelEventArgs e) {
56:            if (e.Node.Nodes[0].Text == "") {
57:                TreeNode tempNode = e.Node;
58:                String strFullName = e.Node.Text;
59:
60:                while (tempNode.Parent != null) {
61:                    strFullName = tempNode.Parent.Text + "\\" +
➥strFullName;
62:                    tempNode = tempNode.Parent;
63:                }
64:
65:                e.Node.Nodes[0].Remove();
66:                PopulateList(strFullName, e.Node);
67:            }
68:        }
69:
70:        private void DisplayInfo(Object Sender,
```

```
➥TreeViewEventArgs e) {
71:             TreeNode tempNode = e.Node;
72:             String strFullName = tempNode.Text;
73:
74:             while (tempNode.Parent != null) {
75:                 strFullName = tempNode.Parent.Text + "\\" +
➥strFullName;
76:                 tempNode = tempNode.Parent;
77:             }
78:
79:             if (File.Exists(strFullName)) {
80:                 FileInfo obj = new FileInfo(strFullName);
81:                 lblInfo.Text = "Name: " + obj.Name;
82:                 lblInfo.Text += "\nSize: " + obj.Length;
83:                 lblInfo.Text += "\nAccessed: " +
➥obj.LastAccessTime.ToString();
84:             } else {
85:                 DirectoryInfo obj = new DirectoryInfo
➥ (strFullName);
86:                 lblInfo.Text = "Name: " + obj.Name;
87:                 lblInfo.Text += "\nAttributes: " +
➥obj.Attributes.ToString();
88:                 lblInfo.Text += "\nAccessed: " +
➥obj.LastAccessTime.ToString();
89:             }
90:         }
91:
92:         private void PrintClicked(Object Sender,
➥EventArgs e) {
93:             //Assemble string of nodes
94:             strList = "";
95:             TreeNode nodeTemp = tvFiles.TopNode;
96:
97:             for (int i = 0; i < tvFiles.GetNodeCount(true);
➥i++) {
98:                 /*pad the string with spaces for easier
99:                   reading */
100:                strList += "".PadRight(GetLevel(nodeTemp)*2) +
➥nodeTemp.Text + "\n";
101:
102:                nodeTemp = nodeTemp.NextVisibleNode;
103:                if (nodeTemp == null) break;
104:
105:                nodeTemp.EnsureVisible();
106:             }
107:
108:             PrintDocument pd = new PrintDocument();
109:             pd.PrintPage += new PrintPageEventHandler
➥ (this.pd_PrintPage);
110:             objPrintReader = new StringReader(strList);
```

```
111:          pd.Print();
112:      }
113:
114:      /* Returns an integer indicating how many levels
➡deep
115:         the specified node is in the treeview */
116:      private int GetLevel(TreeNode objNode) {
117:          int intLevel = 0;
118:          TreeNode nodeTemp = objNode;
119:
120:          while (nodeTemp.Parent != null) {
121:              intLevel++;
122:              nodeTemp = nodeTemp.Parent;
123:          }
124:
125:          return intLevel;
126:      }
127:
128:      private void pd_PrintPage(Object Sender,
➡PrintPageEventArgs e) {
129:          Font fntPrint = this.Font;
130:          int count = 0;
131:          float yPos = 0;
132:          float lpp = e.MarginBounds.Height /
➡fntPrint.GetHeight(e.Graphics);
133:          float fltTopMargin = e.MarginBounds.Top;
134:          float fltLeftMargin = e.MarginBounds.Left;
135:          String strLine = null;
136:
137:          while (count < lpp && ((strLine = objPrintReader.
➡ReadLine()) != null)) {
138:              yPos = fltTopMargin + (count *
➡fntPrint.GetHeight(e.Graphics));
139:
140:              e.Graphics.DrawString(strLine, fntPrint,
➡Brushes.Black, fltLeftMargin, yPos,
➡new StringFormat());
141:
142:              count++;
143:          }
144:
145:          if (strLine != null) {
146:              e.HasMorePages = true;
147:          } else {
148:              e.HasMorePages = false;
149:          }
150:      }
151:
152:      public static void Main() {
153:          Application.Run(new Exercise1());
154:      }
```

```
155:    }
156: }
```

Answers for Day 12

Quiz

1. True or False: To send POST information to the server, you use a WebResponse object.

   False. You use a WebRequest method and call GetRequestStream to send POST data.

2. What are the four parts of a URI?

   The protocol, the server name, the directory path, and an optional query string.

3. What must the content type be to post form information?

   application/x-www-form-urlencoded

4. What is the HttpWebRequest object?

   The HttpWebRequest object, which is a helper to the WebRequest object, provides more fine-grained control over an HTTP request. You can cast your WebRequest object into an HttpWebRequest to set custom HTTP headers and other HTTP settings.

5. What are the three types of Windows authentication?

   Basic, digest, and Integrated Windows Authentication.

Exercise

Create an application that examines a Web page (of your choosing), parses the images from that page (in HTML, images begin with <img src="), and displays all the images from that page, one at a time, in a PictureBox control. Use a button to cycle through the images. (Hint: Use the Image.FromStream method to retrieve an image from a stream.)

```
1:  using System;
2:  using System.Windows.Forms;
3:  using System.Drawing;
4:  using System.Net;
5:  using System.IO;
6:
7:  namespace TYWinforms.Day12 {
8:     public class Exercise1 : Form {
9:        private Uri URL;
10:       private PictureBox pbImages = new PictureBox();
11:       private Button btNext = new Button();
```

```
12:         private Image[] arrImages;
13:         private int intCurrentImage;
14:         private String strHTML;
15:
16:         public Exercise1() {
17:             btNext.Text = "Next";
18:             btNext.Dock = DockStyle.Bottom;
19:             btNext.Click += new EventHandler(this.NextImage);
20:
21:             pbImages.Dock = DockStyle.Fill;
22:
23:             URL = new Uri("http://www.clpayne.com");
24:
25:             CallServer();
26:
27:             int intCounter = 0;
28:             int intIndex = strHTML.IndexOf("<img src=\"");
29:             while (intIndex != -1) {
30:                 intCounter++;
31:                 intIndex = strHTML.IndexOf("<img src=\"",
➥intIndex+1);
32:
33:                 if (intIndex == -1) break;
34:             }
35:
36:             arrImages = new Image[intCounter];
37:
38:             if (strHTML != "") {
39:                 intCounter = 0;
40:                 intIndex = strHTML.IndexOf("<img src=\"");
41:                 string strTemp;
42:
43:                 while (intIndex != -1) {
44:                     strTemp = strHTML.Substring(intIndex+10,
➥strHTML.IndexOf("\"", intIndex + 11) - intIndex-10);
45:
46:                     arrImages[intCounter] = GetImage(strTemp);
47:
48:                     intIndex = strHTML.IndexOf("<img src=\"",
➥intIndex+1);
49:                     intCounter++;
50:                 }
51:             }
52:
53:             pbImages.Image = arrImages[0];
54:             intCurrentImage = 0;
55:
56:             this.Text = "Exercise 1";
57:             this.Controls.Add(pbImages);
58:             this.Controls.Add(btNext);
59:         }
```

```
60:
61:        private void NextImage(Object Sender, EventArgs e) {
62:            if (intCurrentImage == arrImages.Length - 1) {
63:                intCurrentImage = 0;
64:            } else {
65:                intCurrentImage++;
66:            }
67:
68:            pbImages.Image = arrImages[intCurrentImage];
69:        }
70:
71:        private Image GetImage(String strImageUrl) {
72:            Image imgTemp;
73:            try {
74:                WebRequest objRequest = WebRequest.Create
➥ ("http://" + URL.Host + strImageUrl);
75:                WebResponse objResponse = objRequest.
➥GetResponse();
76:
77:                imgTemp = Image.FromStream(objResponse.
➥GetResponseStream());
78:
79:                objResponse.Close();
80:
81:                return imgTemp;
82:            } Catch (Exception e) {
83:                return null;
84:            }
85:        }
86:
87:        private void CallServer() {
88:            WebRequest objRequest = WebRequest.Create(URL);
89:            WebResponse objResponse = objRequest.
➥GetResponse();
90:
91:            StreamReader objReader = new StreamReader
➥ (objResponse.GetResponseStream());
92:
93:            strHTML = objReader.ReadToEnd();
94:
95:            objReader.Close();
96:            objResponse.Close();
97:        }
98:
99:        public static void Main() {
100:            Application.Run(new Exercise1());
101:        }
102:    }
103: }
```

Answers for Day 13

Quiz

1. What is the main object for GDI+?

   The `Graphics` object.

2. What are the two ways to take advantage of the `Paint` event? Give a brief example of each.

   To assign a delegate to the `Paint` event:

   ```
   this.Paint = new PaintEventHandler(this.Method);
   ```

   Or to override the `OnPaint` method:

   ```
   protected override void OnPain(PaintEventArgs e) { ... }
   ```

3. Name five properties of the `Pen` object.

   The 17 properties of the `Pen` object are: `Alignment`, `Brush`, `Color`, `CompoundArray`, `CustomEndCap`, `CustomStartCap`, `DashCap`, `DashOffset`, `DashPattern`, `DashStyle`, `EndCap`, `LineJoin`, `MiterLimit`, `PenType`, `StartCap`, `Transform`, and `Width`.

4. True or false: To draw a string, you use a `Pen`.

   False. You use a `Brush` object.

5. What, conceptually, is a `Matrix`?

   A `Matrix` is a 3×3 grid of data, often used to transform shapes and colors.

6. What are the five types of `Brushes`?

   `SolidBrush`, `HatchBrush`, `LinearGradientBrush`, `PathGradientBrush`, and `TextureBrush`.

7. What method must be called before you can call the `Add` methods to add shapes to a `GraphicsPath` object?

   `StartFigure`.

8. Are "jaggies" the result of aliasing, or anti-aliasing?

   Aliasing. Anti-aliasing tries to smooth the jaggies out by adding additional pixels.

Exercise

Create a drawing application that allows the user to perform various drawing functions, including drawing with a pencil type cursor, filling rectangles, and erasing. Make sure the drawings persist. Use the common color dialog box to allow the user to choose the color of the pen or filled rectangle. (Tip: make use of the `Graphics.FromImage` method.)

```
1:  using System;
2:  using System.Windows.Forms;
3:  using System.Drawing;
4:  using System.Drawing.Drawing2D;
5:  using System.Drawing.Imaging;
6:
7:  namespace TYWinforms.Day13 {
8:      public class Exercise : Form {
9:          private ToolBar tlbStandard = new ToolBar();
10:         private string strFunction;
11:         private Point ptStartClick;
12:         private Point ptCurrentPos;
13:         private bool blnDrag = false;
14:         private bool blnFill = false;
15:         private SolidBrush objBrush;
16:         private Pen objPen = new Pen(Color.Black);
17:         private Rectangle rectSelect;
18:         private Color currColor = Color.Black;
19:         private Bitmap imgWorking;
20:         private Graphics objG;
21:
22:         public Exercise() {
23:             imgWorking = new Bitmap(800,600,
➥PixelFormat.Format32bppArgb);
24:             objG = Graphics.FromImage(imgWorking);
25:             objG.FillRectangle(new SolidBrush(Color.White),
➥new Rectangle(0,0,800,600));
26:
27:             ToolBarButton tbbPen = new ToolBarButton();
28:             tbbPen.Text = "Pencil";
29:
30:             ToolBarButton tbbRect = new ToolBarButton();
31:             tbbRect.Text = "Rectangle";
32:
33:             ToolBarButton tbbErase = new ToolBarButton();
34:             tbbErase.Text = "Erase";
35:
36:             ToolBarButton tbbColor = new ToolBarButton();
37:             tbbColor.Text = "Color...";
38:
39:             tlbStandard.Buttons.Add(tbbPen);
40:             tlbStandard.Buttons.Add(tbbRect);
41:             tlbStandard.Buttons.Add(tbbErase);
42:             tlbStandard.Buttons.Add(tbbColor);
43:             tlbStandard.Appearance = ToolBarAppearance.Flat;
44:
45:             tlbStandard.ButtonClick += new
➥ToolBarButtonClickEventHandler(this.MyToolBarHandler);
46:
47:             this.BackgroundImage = imgWorking;
48:             this.Text = "Exercise";
```

```
49:            this.Size = new Size(800,600);
50:            this.Controls.Add(tlbStandard);
51:        }
52:
53:        private void MyToolBarHandler(Object Sender,
➥ToolBarButtonClickEventArgs e) {
54:            if (e.Button.Text == "Color...") {
55:                ColorDialog dlgColor = new ColorDialog();
56:
57:              if (dlgColor.ShowDialog() == DialogResult.OK) {
58:                  currColor = dlgColor.Color;
59:              }
60:            } else {
61:                strFunction = e.Button.Text;
62:                tlbStandard.Buttons[0].Pushed = false;
63:                tlbStandard.Buttons[1].Pushed = false;
64:                tlbStandard.Buttons[2].Pushed = false;
65:                e.Button.Pushed = true;
66:            }
67:
68:        }
69:
70:        protected override void OnMouseDown
➥ (MouseEventArgs e) {
71:            blnDrag = true;
72:            ptStartClick = new Point(e.X, e.Y);
73:            ptCurrentPos = ptStartClick;
74:        }
75:
76:        protected override void OnMouseUp
➥ (MouseEventArgs e) {
77:            blnDrag = false;
78:            blnFill = true;
79:
80:            DrawIt(objG);
81:        }
82:
83:        protected override void OnMouseMove
➥ (MouseEventArgs e) {
84:            ptCurrentPos = new Point(e.X, e.Y);
85:
86:            if (blnDrag | blnFill) {
87:                DrawIt(objG);
88:            }
89:        }
90:
91:        private void DrawIt(Graphics objGraphics) {
92:
93:            switch(strFunction) {
94:                case "Pencil":
95:                    objPen.Color = currColor;
```

A

```
96:                   objPen.Width = 2;
97:
98:               if (blnDrag) {
99:                   objGraphics.DrawLine(objPen,
➡ptStartClick, ptCurrentPos);
100:                     ptStartClick = ptCurrentPos;
101:                     this.Invalidate();
102:               }
103:               break;
104:           case "Rectangle":
105:               if (blnDrag) {
106:                   if (ptCurrentPos.X < ptStartClick.X
➡& ptCurrentPos.Y < ptStartClick.Y) {
107:                       rectSelect = new Rectangle
➡ (ptCurrentPos.X, ptCurrentPos.Y, ptStartClick.X -
➡ptCurrentPos.X, ptStartClick.Y - ptCurrentPos.Y);
108:                   } else if (ptCurrentPos.X <
➡ptStartClick.X & ptCurrentPos.Y > ptStartClick.Y) {
109:                       rectSelect = new Rectangle
➡ (ptCurrentPos.X, ptStartClick.Y, ptStartClick.X -
➡ptCurrentPos.X, ptCurrentPos.Y - ptStartClick.Y);
110:                   } else if (ptCurrentPos.X >
➡ptStartClick.X & ptCurrentPos.Y < ptStartClick.Y) {
111:                       rectSelect = new Rectangle
➡ (ptStartClick.X, ptCurrentPos.Y, ptCurrentPos.X -
➡ptStartClick.X, ptStartClick.Y - ptCurrentPos.Y);
112:                   } else {
113:                       rectSelect = new Rectangle
➡ (ptStartClick.X, ptStartClick.Y, ptCurrentPos.X -
➡ptStartClick.X, ptCurrentPos.Y - ptStartClick.Y);
114:                   }
115:               }
116:
117:               if (blnFill) {
118:                   objBrush = new SolidBrush(currColor);
119:
120:                   objGraphics.FillRectangle(objBrush,
➡rectSelect);
121:                   this.Invalidate();
122:                   blnFill = false;
123:               }
124:               break;
125:           case "Erase":
126:               objPen.Color = Color.White;
127:               objPen.Width = 5;
128:
129:               if (blnDrag) {
130:                   objGraphics.DrawLine(objPen,
➡ptStartClick, ptCurrentPos);
131:                   ptStartClick = ptCurrentPos;
132:                   this.Invalidate();
```

```
133:                          }
134:                          break;
135:                  }
136:             }
137:
138:          public static void Main() {
139:             Application.Run(new Exercise());
140:          }
141:      }
142:  }
```

Answers for Day 14

Quiz

1. What are the executable files associated with the ActiveX Importer, Type Library Importer, and Assembly Registration tools we talked about today?

   ActiveX Importer tool—Aximp.exe

   Type Library Importer—tlbimp.exe

   Assembly Registration tool—regasm.exe

2. True or false? The ActiveX Importer tool modifies a .dll's source code to comply with .NET.

   False. The original .dll is not modified, a wrapper is simply created around it.

3. True or false? It is better to use existing .NET technology than to use a similar ActiveX control.

   True.

4. What is marshalling?

   Marshalling is the process of coercing one data type to another when moving from one technology to another.

5. What would the following code output?

   `MessageBox.Show(Convert.ToChar(88).ToString());`

   The letter X will be shown.

6. After you've created an Office application object, how do you make it visible to the user?

   Set the object's visible property to true. For example:

   ```
   Excel.Application objApp = new Excel.Application();
   objApp.Visible = true;
   ```

Exercise

Use the Intermediate Language Disassembler tool to examine the Web Browser ActiveX control (AxSHDocVw.dll), and then enhance Listing 14.1 to behave more like a true browser. Include Home, Stop, and Refresh buttons, and change the form's Text property to match the title of the Web page currently being viewed.

```
1:  using System;
2:  using System.Windows.Forms;
3:  using System.Drawing;
4:  using AxSHDocVw;
5:
6:  namespace TYWinforms.Day14 {
7:      public class Exercise : Form {
8:          private StatusBar sbrMain = new StatusBar();
9:          private StatusBarPanel sbpStatus;
10:         private TextBox tbAddress = new TextBox();
11:         private Button btGo = new Button();
12:         private Button btStop = new Button();
13:         private Button btRefresh = new Button();
14:         private Button btHome = new Button();
15:
16:         private AxSHDocVw.AxWebBrowser objBrowser = new
➥AxSHDocVw.AxWebBrowser();
17:         private object arg1 = 0;
18:         private object arg2 = "";
19:         private object arg3 = "";
20:         private object arg4 = "";
21:
22:         public Exercise() {
23:             sbpStatus = sbrMain.Panels.Add("");
24:             sbpStatus.AutoSize =
➥StatusBarPanelAutoSize.Spring;
25:             sbrMain.ShowPanels = true;
26:
27:             btStop.Size = new Size(55,30);
28:             btStop.Location = new Point(0,0);
29:             btStop.Text = "Stop";
30:             btStop.Click += new EventHandler(this.Stop);
31:             btStop.FlatStyle = FlatStyle.Popup;
32:
33:             btRefresh.Size = new Size(55,30);
34:             btRefresh.Location = new Point(54,0);
35:             btRefresh.Text = "Refresh";
36:             btRefresh.Click += new EventHandler(this.Refresh);
37:             btRefresh.FlatStyle = FlatStyle.Popup;
38:
39:             btHome.Size = new Size(55,30);
40:             btHome.Location = new Point(108,0);
41:             btHome.Text = "Home";
```

```
42:            btHome.Click += new EventHandler(this.GoHome);
43:            btHome.FlatStyle = FlatStyle.Popup;
44:
45:            btGo.Size = new Size(50,20);
46:            btGo.Location = new Point(0,33);
47:            btGo.Text = "Go!";
48:            btGo.Click += new EventHandler(this.Go);
49:
50:            tbAddress.Width = 750;
51:            tbAddress.Location = new Point(50,33);
52:            tbAddress.Anchor = AnchorStyles.Top |
➥AnchorStyles.Left | AnchorStyles.Right;
53:
54:            objBrowser.Size = new Size(800,498);
55:            objBrowser.Location = new Point(0,55);
56:            objBrowser.Anchor = AnchorStyles.Top |
➥AnchorStyles.Bottom | AnchorStyles.Left |
➥AnchorStyles.Right;
57:
58:            //TitleChange occurs when the title of the
➥Web browser changes
59:            objBrowser.TitleChange += new
➥DWebBrowserEvents2_TitleChangeEventHandler(this.ChangeTitle);
60:
61:            //NavigateComplete2 occurs after a web page has
➥fully downloaded
62:            objBrowser.NavigateComplete2 += new
➥DWebBrowserEvents2_NavigateComplete2EventHandler
➥ (this.UpdateAddress);
63:
64:            //Occurs when the status bar of the browser
➥updates
65:            objBrowser.StatusTextChange += new
➥ DWebBrowserEvents2_StatusTextChangeEventHandler
➥ (this.UpdateStatus);
66:
67:            //occurs when the control has been created
➥in the form
68:            objBrowser.HandleCreated += new EventHandler
➥ (this.GoHome);
69:
70:        this.Text = ".NET Browser";
71:        this.Size = new Size(800,600);
72:        this.Controls.Add(objBrowser);
73:        this.Controls.Add(tbAddress);
74:        this.Controls.Add(btGo);
75:        this.Controls.Add(btStop);
76:        this.Controls.Add(btRefresh);
```

```
77:              this.Controls.Add(btHome);
78:              this.Controls.Add(sbrMain);
79:          }
80:
81:        private void Go(Object Sender, EventArgs e) {
82:            //Navigate goes to the specified URL
83:            objBrowser.Navigate(tbAddress.Text, ref arg1,
➥ref arg2, ref arg3, ref arg4);
84:          }
85:
86:        private void Stop(Object Sender, EventArgs e) {
87:            //Stops navigation
88:            objBrowser.Stop();
89:          }
90:
91:        private void Refresh(Object Sender, EventArgs e) {
92:            //refreshes the browser window
93:            objBrowser.Refresh();
94:          }
95:
96:        private void GoHome(Object Sender, EventArgs e) {
97:            //goes to the default home page specified
➥by the user
98:            objBrowser.GoHome();
99:          }
100:
101:         private void ChangeTitle(Object Sender,
➥DWebBrowserEvents2_TitleChangeEvent e) {
102:            this.Text = e.text;
103:          }
104:
105:         private void UpdateAddress(Object Sender,
➥DWebBrowserEvents2_NavigateComplete2Event e) {
106:            tbAddress.Text = e.uRL.ToString();
107:          }
108:
109:         private void UpdateStatus(Object Sender,
➥DWebBrowserEvents2_StatusTextChangeEvent e) {
110:            sbpStatus.Text = e.text;
111:          }
112:
113:         public static void Main() {
114:            Application.Run(new Exercise());
115:          }
116:      }
117: }
```

Answers for Day 15

Quiz

1. What does SOAP stand for?

   The Simple Object Access Protocol.

2. True or false? The `disco.exe` tool generates a copy of the WSDL service description locally.

   True.

3. What is a proxy class, and why use one?

   A proxy class is a class that encapsulates all the functionality required to speak with a Web service, from sending HTTP messages to generating SOAP. You use them to greatly simplify your development.

4. Is anything wrong with the following code?

   ```
   [WebMethod] private string HelloWorld() {
       return "Hello World!";
   }
   ```

   Yes. The `HelloWorld` method must be declared as `public` for it to work properly as a Web method.

5. What file extensions are used for .NET Web service files?

   `.asmx`

6. Why do ASP.NET files look very similar to Windows Forms files?

   Because they both are part of the .NET Framework, hence, the .NET in the name. The .NET Framework allows any application, Web or otherwise, to use the same standard objects and syntax, thereby simplifying development.

Exercise

Create a Web service that converts values from one unit of measurement to another (from inches to centimeters, for example—and don't worry if you don't know the exact values; just make something up). Create a Windows Forms client that allows users to interact with the service.

`ConvertUnits.asmx:`

```
1:  <%@ WebService Language="C#" Class="ConvertUnits" %>
2:
3:  using System;
4:  using System.Web.Services;
5:
```

A

```
6:  public class ConvertUnits : WebService {
7:
8:      [WebMethod]public double Convert(Double dblValue,
➡String strFrom, String strTo) {
9:          switch(strTo) {
10:             case "mm":
11:                 return ConvertTo(dblValue/1, strFrom);
12:                 break;
13:             case "cm":
14:                 return ConvertTo(dblValue/10, strFrom);
15:                 break;
16:             case "in":
17:                 return ConvertTo(dblValue/25.4, strFrom);
18:                 break;
19:             case "ft":
20:                 return ConvertTo(dblValue/304.8, strFrom);
21:                 break;
22:             case "m":
23:                 return ConvertTo(dblValue/1000, strFrom);
24:                 break;
25:             case "yd":
26:                 return ConvertTo(dblValue/914.4, strFrom);
27:                 break;
28:             case "mi":
29:                 return ConvertTo(dblValue/1609344, strFrom);
30:                 break;
31:             case "km":
32:                 return ConvertTo(dblValue/1000000, strFrom);
33:                 break;
34:             default:
35:                 return 0.0;
36:                 break;
37:         }
38:     }
39:
40:     private double ConvertTo(double dblValue,
➡String strFrom) {
41:         switch(strFrom) {
42:             case "mm":
43:                 return dblValue * 1;
44:                 break;
45:             case "cm":
46:                 return dblValue * 10;
47:                 break;
48:             case "in":
49:                 return dblValue * 25.4;
50:                 break;
51:             case "ft":
52:                 return dblValue * 304.8;
53:                 break;
54:             case "m":
```

```
55:              return dblValue * 1000;
56:              break;
57:          case "yd":
58:              return dblValue * 914.4;
59:              break;
60:          case "mi":
61:              return dblValue * 1609344;
62:              break;
63:          case "km":
64:              return dblValue * 1000000;
65:              break;
66:          default:
67:              return 0.0;
68:              break;
69:        }
70:      }
71:
72:  }
```

Exercise.cs:

```
1:  using System;
2:  using System.Windows.Forms;
3:  using System.Drawing;
4:
5:  namespace TYWinforms.Day15.Clients {
6:      public class Exercise : Form {
7:          private ComboBox cboToUnit = new ComboBox();
8:          private ComboBox cboFromUnit = new ComboBox();
9:          private TextBox tbValue = new TextBox();
10:         private Label lblTo = new Label();
11:         private Label lblFrom = new Label();
12:         private Label lblAnswer = new Label();
13:         private Button btConvert = new Button();
14:
15:         public Exercise() {
16:             btConvert.Location = new Point(20,90);
17:             btConvert.Text = "Convert";
18:             btConvert.Click += new EventHandler
➥(this.ConvertIt);
19:
20:             lblAnswer.Location = new Point(125,90);
21:             lblAnswer.Size = new Size(200,20);
22:             lblTo.Location = new Point(250,35);
23:             lblTo.Text = "To:";
24:             lblFrom.Location = new Point(125,35);
25:             lblFrom.Text = "From:";
26:
27:             tbValue.Location = new Point(20,50);
28:
```

A

```
29:             cboFromUnit.Location = new Point(125,50);
30:             cboFromUnit.Items.Add("mm");
31:             cboFromUnit.Items.Add("cm");
32:             cboFromUnit.Items.Add("m");
33:             cboFromUnit.Items.Add("km");
34:             cboFromUnit.Items.Add("in");
35:             cboFromUnit.Items.Add("ft");
36:             cboFromUnit.Items.Add("yd");
37:             cboFromUnit.Items.Add("mi");
38:
39:             cboToUnit.Location = new Point(250,50);
40:             cboToUnit.Items.Add("mm");
41:             cboToUnit.Items.Add("cm");
42:             cboToUnit.Items.Add("m");
43:             cboToUnit.Items.Add("km");
44:             cboToUnit.Items.Add("in");
45:             cboToUnit.Items.Add("ft");
46:             cboToUnit.Items.Add("yd");
47:             cboToUnit.Items.Add("mi");
48:
49:             this.Text = "Enter a value and choose the units";
50:             this.Size = new Size(400,200);
51:             this.Controls.Add(cboToUnit);
52:             this.Controls.Add(cboFromUnit);
53:             this.Controls.Add(tbValue);
54:             this.Controls.Add(lblTo);
55:             this.Controls.Add(lblFrom);
56:             this.Controls.Add(lblAnswer);
57:             this.Controls.Add(btConvert);
58:         }
59:
60:        private void ConvertIt(Object Sender, EventArgs e) {
61:             string strAnswer;
62:             ConvertUnits objConvert = new ConvertUnits();
63:             if (tbValue.Text != "") {
64:                 strAnswer = objConvert.Convert
➥ (Convert.ToDouble(tbValue.Text),
➥cboFromUnit.SelectedItem.ToString(),
➥cboToUnit.SelectedItem.ToString()).ToString();
65:
66:                 lblAnswer.Text = strAnswer + " " +
➥cboToUnit.SelectedItem.ToString();
67:             }
68:         }
69:
70:        public static void Main() {
71:             Application.Run(new Exercise());
72:         }
73:     }
74:  }
```

Answers for Day 16

Quiz

1. What namespace and assembly does the `ServiceBase` class belong to?

   `System.ServiceProcess` and `System.ServiceProcess.dll`

2. What namespaces and assemblies do the `ServiceProcessInstaller`, `ServiceInstaller`, and `Installer` classes belong to?

   The first two belong to `System.ServiceProcess` and `System.ServiceProcess.dll`, and the third belongs to `System.Configuration.Install` and `System.Configuration.Install.dll`.

3. What attribute is necessary for an installer?

   `<RunInstaller(true)>`

4. What are the four security accounts a service can run under?

   `User`, `LocalSystem`, `LocalService`, and `NetworkService`.

5. Where are event log files stored?

   Typically in the `c:\winnt\system32\config` folder.

6. What tool is used to install a service? To uninstall?

   The Install Utility: `installutil.exe`. To uninstall, use the same utility, with the `/u` option. For example:

   ```
   installutil listing16.1.exe
   ```

   or:

   ```
   installutil /u listing16.1.exe
   ```

7. What command do you use to start a service from the command line?

   Use `net start "`*service name*`"` to start a service, and `net stop "`*service name*`"` to stop one.

8. Given the variable `objController` that is initialized to a valid `ServiceController`, is the following code valid?

   ```
   dim strHello as String = "RunHelloMethod"
   objController.ExecuteCommand(strHello)
   ```

   No. The `ExecuteCommand` method can only take integers as a parameter.

9. What string do you use to specify the local machine?

   `"."`

Exercise

Create a file/folder back-up service. This service should back up the contents of the My Documents folder to another, separate directory at a certain time every day (for example, at 8 p.m.). For this example, the backup directory does not matter, and you don't need to worry about compressing files—just copy them. Write information to the Application event log when a backup is performed.

Exercise.vb:

```
1:  Imports System
2:  Imports System.ServiceProcess
3:  Imports System.IO
4:  Imports System.Timers
5:
6:  namespace TYWinforms.Day16
7:
8:      Public Class BackUpper : Inherits ServiceBase
9:          private tmrTimer As New Timer()
10:         private strTo As String = "c:\temp\mybackups"
11:         private strFrom As String = "C:\Documents and
➥Settings\Christopher L Payne.CHRISMAN\My Documents"
12:
13:         Public Sub New()
14:             tmrTimer.Interval = 10000
15:             AddHandler tmrTimer.Elapsed, new
➥ElapsedEventHandler(AddressOf Me.BackUpNow)
16:
17:             Me.ServiceName = "TYWinforms Backup Service"
18:         End Sub
19:
20:         Shared Sub Main()
21:             ServiceBase.Run(New BackUpper())
22:         End Sub
23:
24:         Protected Overrides Sub OnStart(ByVal args() As
➥String)
25:             Dim dir As New DirectoryInfo(strTo)
26:
27:             if not dir.Exists then
28:                 dir.Create()
29:             end if
30:
31:             tmrTimer.Enabled = true
32:         End Sub
33:
34:         private sub BackUpNow(Sender As Object, e as
➥ElapsedEventArgs)
35:             BackItUp(strFrom)
36:         end sub
37:
```

```
38:         private sub BackItUp(strLocalFrom As String)
39:            Dim dirFrom As New DirectoryInfo(strLocalFrom)
40:            Dim d As DirectoryInfo
41:            Dim dirTo As DirectoryInfo
42:            Dim f as FileInfo
43:
44:            ' Uncomment the below code to do a recursive
➥backup
45:            'for each d in dirFrom.GetDirectories()
46:            '    dirTo = New DirectoryInfo(d.FullName.
➥Replace(strFrom,strTo))
47:            '    if not dirTo.Exists then
48:            '        dirTo.Create()
49:            '    end if
50:
51:            '    BackItUp(d.FullName)
52:            'next
53:
54:            for each f in dirFrom.GetFiles("*.*")
55:                f.CopyTo(f.FullName.Replace(strFrom,strTo),
➥true)
56:            next
57:
58:            EventLog.WriteEntry("Contents of " &
➥strLocalFrom & " backed up")
59:
60:         end sub
61:
62:    End Class
63: end namespace
```

Exercise_Installer.vb:

```
1:  Imports System.ServiceProcess
2:  Imports System.ComponentModel
3:  Imports System.Configuration.Install
4:
5:  namespace TYWinforms.Day16
6:     <RunInstaller(True)> Public Class MyInstaller :
➥Inherits Installer
7:        Private objPInstaller As New ServiceProcessInstaller
8:        Private objInstaller As New ServiceInstaller
9:
10:        Public Sub New()
11:            objPInstaller.Account = ServiceAccount.
➥LocalSystem
12:            objPInstaller.Password = Nothing
13:            objPInstaller.Username = Nothing
14:
15:            objInstaller.ServiceName = "TYWinforms Backup
➥Service"
```

```
16:
17:            Installers.AddRange(New Installer()
➥{objPInstaller, objInstaller})
18:        End Sub
19:    End Class
20:  End Namespace
```

Answers for Day 17

Quiz

1. Name four of the values from the `DrawItemState` enumeration.

   The values are `Checked`, `ComboBoxEdit`, `Default`, `Disabled`, `Focus`, `Grayed`, `HotLight`, `Inactive`, `NoAccelerator`, `NoFocusRect`, `None`, and `Selected`.

2. What is the difference between the `DrawMode` and the `TabDrawMode` enumerations?

   The `TabDrawMode` enumeration is missing the `OwnerDrawVariable` value.

3. When is the `MeasureItem` event raised?

   The first time a control is created.

4. True or false? Tabs in a `TabControl` can be different sizes.

   False. All tabs must be the same size.

5. Why would you call the `GetTabRect` method?

   For `TabControls`, you use `GetTabRect` to return a `Rectangle` object that represents the display area of a tab. The `Bounds` property of the `DrawItemEventArgs` object returns the entire surface area of a tab, whether it is visible or not.

6. How are `MenuItems` different than other controls?

   Regular controls derive from the `System.Windows.Forms.Control` class. `MenuItems` do not.

7. What must you do to change the size of the tabs in a `TabControl`?

   Set the `SizeMode` property to `TabSizeMode.Fixed`.

Exercise

Create an application that allows users to customize the appearance of a menu. Use customized `ComboBoxes` to let them choose colors for the menus.

```
1:  using System;
2:  using System.Windows.Forms;
3:  using System.Drawing;
4:
5:  namespace TYWinForms.Day17 {
6:
```

```
7:    public class Exercise : Form {
8:        private MainMenu mnuCustom = new MainMenu();
9:        private MenuItem miCustom = new MenuItem();
10:       private MenuItem miOne = new MenuItem();
11:       private MenuItem miTwo = new MenuItem();
12:       private MenuItem miThree = new MenuItem();
13:       private MenuItem miFour = new MenuItem();
14:
15:       private Label lblHighlight = new Label();
16:       private Label lblActiveText = new Label();
17:       private Label lblBackground = new Label();
18:       private Label lblRegText = new Label();
19:
20:       private ComboBox cboHighlight = new ComboBox();
21:       private ComboBox cboActiveText = new ComboBox();
22:       private ComboBox cboBackground = new ComboBox();
23:       private ComboBox cboRegText = new ComboBox();
24:
25:       private Brush brsHighlight;
26:       private Brush brsActiveText;
27:       private Brush brsBackground;
28:       private Brush brsRegText;
29:
30:     private SolidBrush[] arrBrushes = new SolidBrush[10];
31:
32:       public Exercise() {
33:           arrBrushes[0] = (SolidBrush)Brushes.White;
34:           arrBrushes[1] = (SolidBrush)Brushes.Red;
35:           arrBrushes[2] = (SolidBrush)Brushes.Green;
36:           arrBrushes[3] = (SolidBrush)Brushes.Blue;
37:           arrBrushes[4] = (SolidBrush)Brushes.LightGray;
38:           arrBrushes[5] = (SolidBrush)Brushes.Orange;
39:           arrBrushes[6] = (SolidBrush)Brushes.Yellow;
40:           arrBrushes[7] = (SolidBrush)Brushes.Black;
41:           arrBrushes[8] = (SolidBrush)Brushes.
➥BlanchedAlmond;
42:           arrBrushes[9] = (SolidBrush)Brushes.DarkSalmon;
43:
44:           brsHighlight = Brushes.Blue;
45:           brsActiveText = Brushes.White;
46:           brsBackground = Brushes.LightGray;
47:           brsRegText = Brushes.Black;
48:
49:         miCustom = mnuCustom.MenuItems.Add("Custom Menu");
50:         miOne = miCustom.MenuItems.Add("Item 1");
51:         miTwo = miCustom.MenuItems.Add("Item 2");
52:         miThree = miCustom.MenuItems.Add("Item 3");
53:         miFour = miCustom.MenuItems.Add("Item 4");
54:
55:         miCustom.OwnerDraw = true;
```

A

```
56:          miCustom.DrawItem += new DrawItemEventHandler
➥ (this.DrawTopLevel);
57:          miCustom.MeasureItem += new
➥MeasureItemEventHandler(this.MeasureItem);
58:
59:          miOne.OwnerDraw = true;
60:          miOne.DrawItem += new DrawItemEventHandler
➥ (this.DrawItem);
61:          miOne.MeasureItem += new
➥MeasureItemEventHandler(this.MeasureItem);
62:
63:          miTwo.OwnerDraw = true;
64:          miTwo.DrawItem += new DrawItemEventHandler
➥ (this.DrawItem);
65:          miTwo.MeasureItem += new
➥MeasureItemEventHandler(this.MeasureItem);
66:
67:          miThree.OwnerDraw = true;
68:          miThree.DrawItem += new DrawItemEventHandler
➥ (this.DrawItem);
69:          miThree.MeasureItem += new
➥MeasureItemEventHandler(this.MeasureItem);
70:
71:          miFour.OwnerDraw = true;
72:          miFour.DrawItem += new DrawItemEventHandler
➥ (this.DrawItem);
73:          miFour.MeasureItem += new
➥MeasureItemEventHandler(this.MeasureItem);
74:
75:          lblHighlight.Text = "Highlight color:";
76:          lblHighlight.Width = 80;
77:          lblHighlight.Location = new Point(0,10);
78:
79:          lblActiveText.Text = "Active Text color:";
80:          lblActiveText.Size = new Size(80,30);
81:          lblActiveText.Location = new Point(0,50);
82:
83:          lblBackground.Text = "Background color:";
84:          lblBackground.Size = new Size(80,30);
85:          lblBackground.Location = new Point(0,90);
86:
87:          lblRegText.Text = "Regular Text color:";
88:          lblRegText.Size = new Size(80,30);
89:          lblRegText.Location = new Point(0,130);
90:
91:          cboHighlight.DataSource = arrBrushes.Clone();
92:          cboHighlight.Location = new Point(90,10);
93:          cboHighlight.Width = 200;
94:          cboHighlight.DisplayMember = "Color";
95:          cboHighlight.DrawMode = DrawMode.OwnerDrawFixed;
```

```
96:          cboHighlight.DrawItem += new
➥DrawItemEventHandler(this.DrawBox);
97:          cboHighlight.SelectedValueChanged += new
➥EventHandler(this.ChangeHighLightColor);
98:
99:          cboActiveText.DataSource = arrBrushes.Clone();
100:         cboActiveText.Location = new Point(90,50);
101:         cboActiveText.Width = 200;
102:         cboActiveText.DisplayMember = "Color";
103:         cboActiveText.DrawMode = DrawMode.OwnerDrawFixed;
104:         cboActiveText.DrawItem += new
➥DrawItemEventHandler(this.DrawBox);
105:         cboActiveText.SelectedValueChanged += new
➥EventHandler(this.ChangeActiveTextColor);
106:
107:         cboBackground.DataSource = arrBrushes.Clone();
108:         cboBackground.Location = new Point(90,90);
109:         cboBackground.Width = 200;
110:         cboBackground.DisplayMember = "Color";
111:         cboBackground.DrawMode = DrawMode.OwnerDrawFixed;
112:         cboBackground.DrawItem += new
➥DrawItemEventHandler(this.DrawBox);
113:         cboBackground.SelectedValueChanged += new
➥EventHandler(this.ChangeBackgroundColor);
114:
115:         cboRegText.DataSource = arrBrushes.Clone();
116:         cboRegText.Location = new Point(90,130);
117:         cboRegText.Width = 200;
118:         cboRegText.DisplayMember = "Color";
119:         cboRegText.DrawMode = DrawMode.OwnerDrawFixed;
120:         cboRegText.DrawItem += new
➥DrawItemEventHandler(this.DrawBox);
121:         cboRegText.SelectedValueChanged += new
➥EventHandler(this.ChangeRegTextColor);
122:
123:         this.Text = "Exercise";
124:         this.Menu = mnuCustom;
125:         this.Controls.Add(lblHighlight);
126:         this.Controls.Add(lblActiveText);
127:         this.Controls.Add(lblBackground);
128:         this.Controls.Add(lblRegText);
129:         this.Controls.Add(cboHighlight);
130:         this.Controls.Add(cboActiveText);
131:         this.Controls.Add(cboBackground);
132:         this.Controls.Add(cboRegText);
133:      }
134:
135:      private void DrawBox(Object Sender,
➥DrawItemEventArgs e) {
136:         e.DrawBackground();
137:
```

```
138:            if ((e.State & DrawItemState.Selected) ==
➥DrawItemState.Selected) {
139:                e.Graphics.FillRectangle(arrBrushes[e.Index],
➥new Rectangle(e.Bounds.X, e.Bounds.Y, e.Bounds.Width,
➥e.Bounds.Height));
140:                e.Graphics.DrawString(((SolidBrush)
➥cboHighlight.Items[e.Index]).Color.Name,
➥new Font("Arial",10), ((SolidBrush)cboHighlight.
➥Items[9-e.Index]), new Point(e.Bounds.X, e.Bounds.Y));
141:            } else {
142:                e.Graphics.DrawString(((SolidBrush)
➥cboHighlight.Items[e.Index]).Color.Name,
➥new Font("Arial",10), ((SolidBrush)cboHighlight.
➥Items[e.Index]), new Point(e.Bounds.X, e.Bounds.Y));
143:            }
144:        }
145:
146:        private void ChangeHighLightColor(Object Sender,
➥EventArgs e) {
147:            brsHighlight = (SolidBrush)((ComboBox)Sender).
➥SelectedValue;
148:        }
149:
150:        private void ChangeActiveTextColor(Object Sender,
➥EventArgs e) {
151:            brsActiveText = (SolidBrush)((ComboBox)Sender).
➥SelectedValue;
152:        }
153:
154:        private void ChangeBackgroundColor(Object Sender,
➥EventArgs e) {
155:            brsBackground = (SolidBrush)((ComboBox)Sender).
➥SelectedValue;
156:        }
157:
158:        private void ChangeRegTextColor(Object Sender,
➥EventArgs e) {
159:            brsRegText = (SolidBrush)((ComboBox)Sender).
➥SelectedValue;
160:        }
161:
162:        private void MeasureItem(Object Sender,
➥MeasureItemEventArgs e) {
163:            SizeF stringSize = e.Graphics.MeasureString
➥ (((MenuItem)Sender).Text, this.Font);
164:
165:            e.ItemHeight = (int)stringSize.Height + 6;
166:            e.ItemWidth = (int)stringSize.Width + 10;
167:        }
168:
```

```
169:        private void DrawTopLevel(Object Sender,
➥DrawItemEventArgs e) {
170:            if (((e.State & DrawItemState.HotLight) ==
➥DrawItemState.HotLight) |
➥ (e.State & DrawItemState.Selected) ==
➥DrawItemState.Selected) {
171:                e.Graphics.DrawString(((MenuItem)Sender).
➥Text, new Font("Times New Roman",12), Brushes.Blue,
➥new Point(e.Bounds.X, e.Bounds.Y));
172:            } else {
173:                e.Graphics.DrawString(((MenuItem)Sender).
➥Text, new Font("Times New Roman",12), Brushes.Black,
➥new Point(e.Bounds.X, e.Bounds.Y));
174:            }
175:        }
176:
177:        private void DrawItem(Object Sender,
➥DrawItemEventArgs e) {
178:            e.Graphics.FillRectangle(brsBackground,
➥new Rectangle(e.Bounds.X, e.Bounds.Y,
➥e.Bounds.Width, e.Bounds.Height));
179:
180:            if (((e.State & DrawItemState.HotLight) ==
➥DrawItemState.HotLight) |
➥ (e.State & DrawItemState.Selected) ==
DrawItemState.Selected) {
181:                e.Graphics.FillRectangle(brsHighlight,
➥new Rectangle(e.Bounds.X, e.Bounds.Y,
➥e.Bounds.Width, e.Bounds.Height));
182:                e.Graphics.DrawString(((MenuItem)Sender).
➥Text, new Font("Times New Roman",12), brsActiveText,
➥new Point(e.Bounds.X, e.Bounds.Y));
183:            } else {
184:                e.Graphics.DrawString(((MenuItem)Sender).
➥Text, new Font("Times New Roman",12), brsRegText,
➥new Point(e.Bounds.X, e.Bounds.Y));
185:            }
186:        }
187:
188:        public static void Main() {
189:            Application.Run(new Exercise());
190:        }
191:    }
192:
193: }
```

Answers for Day 18

A

Quiz

1. What are the four steps of creating a custom control?

    1. Create a class that inherits from the `Control` class.

    2. Define properties, methods, and events for your class.

    3. Override the `OnPaint` method to draw your custom control.

    4. Compile, and then use your custom class.

2. What method must you call to redraw your control?

    ```
    Invalidate()
    ```

3. Write an example of a public property in C# using the property declaration syntax.

    ```csharp
    public String Text {
       get { return strText; }
       set {
          strText = value;
          Invalidate();
       }
    }
    ```

4. Write an example of a public property in VB.NET using the property declaration syntax.

    ```vbnet
    Public Property Text As String
       Get
          Return strText
       End Get
       Set
          strText = value
          Invalidate()
       End Set
    End Property
    ```

5. Which happens first: a handle is created, or your control is displayed on screen. Why?

    The handle is always created first. A control does not have a client area on screen, and thus cannot be drawn until a handle is created.

6. True or false? You can inherit from a `RichTextBox` control.

    True. How else would you extend it?

7. Name three benefits of creating user controls.

    Encapsulation, reusability, and extensibility.

Exercise

Create a thermostat custom control that displays the current temperature in a mercury-style thermometer. Remember to not allow the temperature to go above the maximum or below 0. Implement it in a Windows Form application and provide buttons for the user to turn the temperature up and down. (Of course, this will all be made up since you can't determine the actual temperature, but you get the point.)

The `Thermostat` control:

```
1:  using System;
2:  using System.Drawing;
3:  using System.Windows.Forms;
4:
5:  namespace TYWinforms.Day18.Controls {
6:      public class Thermostat : Control {
7:          private int intTemp;
8:          private int intMaxTemp;
9:
10:         public int Temperature {
11:             get { return intTemp; }
12:             set {
13:                 intTemp = value;
14:                 Invalidate();
15:             }
16:         }
17:
18:         public Thermostat() {
19:             intTemp = 10;
20:             intMaxTemp = 120;
21:
22:             this.Size = new Size(50,150);
23:         }
24:
25:         protected override void OnPaint(PaintEventArgs e) {
26:             e.Graphics.DrawEllipse(Pens.Black, new
    ➥Rectangle(10,120,30,30));
27:             e.Graphics.DrawRectangle(Pens.Black, new
    ➥Rectangle(15,10,20,120));
28:
29:             if (intTemp <= intMaxTemp & intTemp >= 0) {
30:                 e.Graphics.FillEllipse(Brushes.Red, new
    ➥Rectangle(10,120,30,30));
31:                 e.Graphics.FillRectangle(Brushes.Red, new
    ➥Rectangle(15,120 - intTemp + 10,20,intTemp));
32:                 e.Graphics.DrawString(intTemp.ToString() +
    ➥"°", new Font("Arial",15), Brushes.White,
    ➥new Point(9,126));
33:             } else if (intTemp < 0) {
```

A

```
34:                e.Graphics.FillEllipse(Brushes.Blue,
➡new Rectangle(10,120,30,30));
35:                e.Graphics.DrawString("BROKE!", new
➡Font("Arial",10), Brushes.White, new Point(0,126));
36:             } else {
37:                e.Graphics.FillEllipse(Brushes.Red, new
➡Rectangle(10,120,30,30));
38:                e.Graphics.FillRectangle(Brushes.Red, new
➡Rectangle(15,10,20,120));
39:                e.Graphics.DrawString("BROKE!", new
➡Font("Arial",10), Brushes.White, new Point(0,126));
40:             }
41:          }
42:       }
43:    }
```

The containing application:

```
1:   using System;
2:   using System.Windows.Forms;
3:   using System.Drawing;
4:   using TYWinforms.Day18.Controls;
5:
6:   namespace TYWinforms.Day18 {
7:      public class ExerciseContainer : Form {
8:         private Thermostat objStat = new Thermostat();
9:         private Button btUp = new Button();
10:         private Button btDown = new Button();
11:
12:         public ExerciseContainer() {
13:            btUp.Text = "Up";
14:            btUp.Location = new Point(30,30);
15:            btUp.Click += new EventHandler(this.TurnItUp);
16:
17:            btDown.Text = "Down";
18:            btDown.Location = new Point(30,70);
19:            btDown.Click += new EventHandler
➡(this.TurnItDown);
20:
21:            objStat.Location = new Point(125,10);
22:
23:            this.Text = "Thermostat Control";
24:            this.Controls.Add(objStat);
25:            this.Controls.Add(btUp);
26:            this.Controls.Add(btDown);
27:         }
28:
29:         private void TurnItUp(Object sender, EventArgs e) {
30:            objStat.Temperature += 1;
31:         }
32:
```

```
33:        private void TurnItDown(Object sender,
⮑EventArgs e) {
34:            objStat.Temperature -= 1;
35:        }
36:
37:        public static void Main() {
38:            Application.Run(new ExerciseContainer());
39:        }
40:    }
41: }
```

Answers for Day 19

Quiz

1. Infer three tasks in Microsoft Word that may be multithreaded.

   The background-saving mechanism, spell-checking, printing, pagination, and macros are a few.

2. What does it mean to be non–thread-safe?

   You cannot safely use a non–thread-safe object from more than a single thread. Any thread aside from the object's creation thread must marshal calls to the creation thread.

3. Why can the ThreadPool class execute tasks more efficiently?

   It relies on the fact that most of a thread's time is spent idling, waiting for events or for locks.

4. True or false? The Monitor.Enter method must be passed the this variable.

   False. You can pass any object you want into the Monitor.Enter method.

5. Is the following code correct?

   ```
   Monitor.Enter(this)
   for i = 0 to 10
       lblInfo.Text += "hi!"
   next i
   ```

   No. It doesn't call Monitor.Exit, and it used this instead of Me (the code is in VB.NET).

6. Which of the following is correct?

   1. ThreadPool.QueueUserWorkItem(new ThreadStart(this.Go));

   2. ThreadPool.QueueWorkUserItem(new WaitCallBack(this.Go));

   3. ThreadPool.QueueUserWorkItem(new WaitCallBack(this.Go));

   The third line is correct.

7. What is `ThreadStart`?

`ThreadStart` is a delegate that points a new `Thread` object to a method to execute.

8. True or false? A `Thread` begins execution as soon as you have specified a `ThreadStart` delegate.

False. A `Thread` does not start execution until you call its `Start` method.

9. What is the default `ThreadState` and `ThreadPriority` value for a newly started thread?

`ThreadState.Running` and `ThreadPriority.Normal` respectively.

Exercise

Create a multithreaded file searching application. This application should allow a user to enter in a filename and press a "Search" button, upon which a new thread will be created that searches through the file system recursively for a file with that name. Display the results in a `ListBox`. (Check out Day 11, "Working with Windows Input/Output," for more information on a directory searching algorithm.)

```
1:  using System;
2:  using System.Drawing;
3:  using System.Windows.Forms;
4:  using System.Threading;
5:  using System.IO;
6:
7:  namespace TYWinforms.Day19 {
8:      public class Exercise : Form {
9:          private ListBox lbxResults = new ListBox();
10:         private TextBox tbSearch = new TextBox();
11:         private Button btSearch = new Button();
12:         private Label lblStatus = new Label();
13:
14:         private bool blnSearching;
15:         private Thread thdSearch;
16:
17:         public Exercise() {
18:             blnSearching = false;
19:
20:             btSearch.Location = new Point(125,10);
21:             btSearch.Text = "Search!";
22:             btSearch.Click += new EventHandler
➥(this.BeginSearch);
23:
24:             tbSearch.Location = new Point(10,10);
25:             lblStatus.Location = new Point(10,50);
26:
27:             lbxResults.Location = new Point(250,10);
```

```
28:                lbxResults.Size = new Size(525,590);
29:
30:                this.Size = new Size(800,600);
31:                this.Text = "Exercise";
32:                this.Controls.Add(lbxResults);
33:                this.Controls.Add(tbSearch);
34:                this.Controls.Add(btSearch);
35:                this.Controls.Add(lblStatus);
36:            }
37:
38:        public void BeginSearch(Object Sender, EventArgs e){
39:            if (blnSearching) { return; }
40:
41:            lblStatus.Text = "Searching...";
42:            btSearch.Enabled = false;
43:            thdSearch = new Thread(new ThreadStart
➡ (ThreadSearch));
44:            blnSearching = true;
45:            thdSearch.Start();
46:        }
47:
48:        private void RecurseDirectory(string strSearchPath){
49:            string strDirectory = Path.GetDirectoryName
➡ (strSearchPath);
50:            string strSearch = Path.GetFileName
➡ (strSearchPath);
51:
52:            if (strDirectory == null || strSearch == null) {
53:                return;
54:            }
55:
56:            string[] arrFiles;
57:
58:            try {
59:                arrFiles = Directory.GetFiles(strDirectory,
➡strSearch);
60:            } catch (Exception e) {
61:                return;
62:            }
63:
64:            for (int i = 0; i < arrFiles.Length; i++) {
65:                lbxResults.Items.Add(arrFiles[i]);
66:            }
67:
68:            string[] arrDirectories = Directory.
➡GetDirectories(strDirectory);
69:            foreach(string d in arrDirectories) {
70:                RecurseDirectory(Path.Combine(d, strSearch));
71:            }
72:        }
73:
```

```
74:        private void ThreadSearch() {
75:            string strSearch = tbSearch.Text;
76:            if (Path.GetPathRoot(strSearch) == "") {
77:                strSearch = "c:\\" + strSearch;
78:            }
79:
80:            RecurseDirectory(strSearch);
81:            btSearch.Enabled = true;
82:            blnSearching = false;
83:            lblStatus.Text = "Done";
84:        }
85:
86:        private static void Main() {
87:            Application.Run(new Exercise());
88:        }
89:    }
90: }
```

Answers for Day 20

Quiz

1. What is one advantage of .config files over .ini files?

   .config files are in XML, an industry standard, which makes them more universally accepted.

2. What does the al.exe tool do?

   al.exe is the Assembly Linker tool that allows you to compile your files into assemblies, which is especially useful for resource files.

3. Which two parameters does the resgen tool expect?

   The resgen tool expects the name of the input, the plaintext resource file, and the name of the output, .resources file.

4. True or false: A configuration file for an application that is named MyApp.exe should be called MyApp.config.

   False. The correct name of the configuration file is MyApp.exe.config.

5. True or false: When you are translating resource files, you must translate the property names as well as their values.

   False. Property names should not be translated. If they were, your application would not be able to access them properly.

6. What is the base element for all .config files?

   <configuration> is the base element for all .config files.

7. For what purpose is the `<system.windows.forms>` configuration element used?

   The `<system.windows.forms>` element provides a way to enable JIT debugging.

8. What is camel-casing, and where is it required?

   Camel-casing is used in `.config` XML files. Camel-cased means that the first word in a multi-word combination is lowercase, whereas all subsequent words' initial characters are uppercase. Single words are all lowercase. For example:

   ```
   iAmCamelCased
   yippee
   goHome
   ```

9. Write a simple `.config` file that has an `<appSettings>` section. This section should contain one element, `Color`, with the value `Black`.

   ```
   <configuration>
     <appSettings>
       <add key="Color" value="Black"/>
     </appSettings>
   </configuration>
   ```

Exercises

1. Incorporate three more locales in the example from Listing 20.6: French (from France), Danish, and Greek. Don't worry about translating the actual phrases—just tweak the phrases to indicate the current culture. (See the .NET Framework documentation under the `CultureInfo` class for the culture codes for these languages.)

   Download the answer for this exercise from the Sams Publishing Web site. You'll notice several directories contained in the solution: `/da`, `/el`, and `/fr-FR`. Each directory contains the `.txt` file with the localization resources (for example, `Day20.fr-FR.txt`), a `.resources` file that is generated from the `.txt` file using `resgen.exe`, and a `.dll` file that represents the compiled satellite assembly. There is very little code to write; just create the `.txt` files, compile them using the commands discussed earlier today, and place them in the necessary directories.

2. Create a `.config` file to specify the culture to use in your application from Exercise 1. This way, you won't have to modify your source code and recompile your application every time you want to test a new culture. (Hint: Use the `<appSettings>` section.)

   The solution is simply your new `.config` file, also available from the Sams Publishing Web site. Your application should use the `ConfigurationSettings.AppSettings` property to retrieve the localization settings.

Answers for Day 21

Quiz

1. True or false? A `catch` block that specifies an exception of type `IOException` will also catch exceptions of type `SystemException`.

   False. It is the other way around; exceptions of type `SystemException` will catch types of `IOException`.

2. Is the following code correct?
   ```
   Process[] objProcess = Process.GetProcessesByName
   ➥("listing21.2.exe ");
   ```

   No. When specifying processes by name, you must leave the extension `.exe` off the process name.

3. How do you create a program database file?

   Compile your application using the `/debug` parameter to the compiler.

4. What is a breakpoint?

   A breakpoint is a predetermined place in your code where execution will halt for debugging purposes.

5. Name three properties of the `Exception` class.

   The properties of `Exception` are `HelpLink`, `InnerException`, `Message`, `Source`, `StackTrace`, and `TargetSite`.

6. How can you raise your own errors?

   Use the `throw` keyword, specifying a particular type of `Exception` object.

Exercise

Create an application that is similar to the Windows Task Manager. This application should let the user choose any running process from a list box. The process's properties, `Id`, `MainModule`, `PrivateMemorySize`, `TotalProcessorTime`, and number of running threads should display in labels. Don't forget to use `try-catch` blocks!

```
1:  using System;
2:  using System.Windows.Forms;
3:  using System.Drawing;
4:  using System.Diagnostics;
5:
6:  namespace TYWinforms.Day21 {
7:     public class Exercise : Form {
8:        private ListBox lbxProcesses = new ListBox();
9:
```

```
10:          private Label lblCaptionId = new Label();
11:          private Label lblCaptionModule = new Label();
12:          private Label lblCaptionProcessor = new Label();
13:          private Label lblCaptionMemory = new Label();
14:          private Label lblCaptionThreadCount = new Label();
15:
16:          private Label lblId = new Label();
17:          private TextBox tbModule = new TextBox();
18:          private Label lblProcessor = new Label();
19:          private Label lblMemory = new Label();
20:          private Label lblThreadCount = new Label();
21:
22:          private System.Windows.Forms.Timer tmrProcess =
➥new System.Windows.Forms.Timer();
23:
24:          public Exercise() {
25:              lbxProcesses.Location = new Point(10,10);
26:              lbxProcesses.Width = 280;
27:              lbxProcesses.DisplayMember = "ProcessName";
28:              lbxProcesses.SelectedIndexChanged += new
➥EventHandler(this.StartWatch);
29:
30:              foreach (Process tmpProcess in
➥Process.GetProcesses()) {
31:                  lbxProcesses.Items.Add(tmpProcess);
32:              }
33:
34:              lblCaptionId.Location = new Point(10,120);
35:              lblCaptionId.Text = "PID:";
36:              lblCaptionModule.Location = new Point(10,150);
37:              lblCaptionModule.Text = "Modules:";
38:              lblCaptionProcessor.Location = new Point(10,180);
39:              lblCaptionProcessor.Text = "Processor Time:";
40:              lblCaptionMemory.Location = new Point(10,210);
41:              lblCaptionMemory.Text = "Memory:";
42:              lblCaptionThreadCount.Location =
➥new Point(10,240);
43:              lblCaptionThreadCount.Text = "Thread Count:";
44:
45:              lblId.Location = new Point(110,120);
46:              lblId.Width = 150;
47:              tbModule.Location = new Point(110,150);
48:              tbModule.Multiline = true;
49:              tbModule.Size = new Size(500,25);
50:              tbModule.ReadOnly = true;
51:              tbModule.ScrollBars = ScrollBars.Vertical;
52:              lblProcessor.Location = new Point(110,180);
53:              lblProcessor.Width = 150;
54:              lblMemory.Location = new Point(110,210);
55:              lblMemory.Width = 150;
56:              lblThreadCount.Location = new Point(110,240);
```

```
57:             lblThreadCount.Width = 150;
58:
59:             tmrProcess.Tick += new EventHandler(this.Update);
60:             tmrProcess.Interval = 500;
61:
62:             this.Text = ".NET Profiler";
63:             this.Width = 640;
64:             this.Controls.Add(lblCaptionId);
65:             this.Controls.Add(lblCaptionModule);
66:             this.Controls.Add(lblCaptionProcessor);
67:             this.Controls.Add(lblCaptionMemory);
68:             this.Controls.Add(lblCaptionThreadCount);
69:             this.Controls.Add(lbxProcesses);
70:             this.Controls.Add(lblId);
71:             this.Controls.Add(tbModule);
72:             this.Controls.Add(lblProcessor);
73:             this.Controls.Add(lblMemory);
74:             this.Controls.Add(lblThreadCount);
75:         }
76:
77:         private void StartWatch(Object Sender, EventArgs e){
78:             //put things that don't change here
79:             try {
80:                 Process tmpProcess =
➥ (Process)lbxProcesses.SelectedItem;
81:
82:                 tbModule.Text = "";
83:                 foreach (ProcessModule tmpModule in
➥tmpProcess.Modules) {
84:                     tbModule.Text += tmpModule.ModuleName + " ";
85:                 }
86:                 lblId.Text = tmpProcess.Id.ToString();
87:
88:                 tmrProcess.Start();
89:             } catch (Exception ex) {
90:                 MessageBox.Show("That process is unwatchable");
91:             }
92:         }
93:
94:         private void Update(Object Sender, EventArgs e) {
95:             try {
96:                 Process tmpProcess =
➥ (Process)lbxProcesses.SelectedItem;
97:
98:                 tmpProcess.Refresh();
99:                 lblMemory.Text = tmpProcess.PrivateMemorySize.
➥ToString();
100:                lblProcessor.Text = tmpProcess.
➥TotalProcessorTime.ToString();
101:                lblThreadCount.Text = tmpProcess.Threads.
➥Count.ToString();
```

```
102:                } catch (Exception ex) {
103:                    //do nothing
104:                }
105:            }
106:
107:            public static void Main() {
108:                Application.Run(new Exercise());
109:            }
110:        }
111:    }
```

APPENDIX **B**

Windows Forms Controls

This appendix covers the properties and methods for every Windows Forms control. It also covers some controls that are not technically Windows Forms controls, but that provide aid for them.

The `Control` Class

All of the controls in this appendix (except where noted) inherit the properties described in Table B.1 from the `System.Windows.Forms.Control` class. The `Control` class is the most important to remember, because it is responsible for all other controls.

TABLE B.1 Properties of the `Control` Class Inherited by All Controls

Property	Description
`AccessibilityObject`	Returns the `AccessibleObject` object for the control
`AccessibleDefaultActionDescription`	The string used to describe the default action of a control
`AccessibleDescription`	The description of the control used by accessibility clients

TABLE B.1   continued

Property	Description
AccessibleName	The name of the control used by accessibility clients
AccessibleRole	The role (or type) of the control; uses values from the AccessibleRole enumeration
AllowDrop	Indicates whether the control can accept drag-and-drop data
AllowDropAnchor	Indicates the edges of the control that are anchored to the containing control
AccessibleRoleBackColor	The background color of the control
BackgroundImage	The image to be displayed in the background of the control
BindingContext	The BindingContext of the control (used for data binding)
Bottom	The distance between the bottom edge of the control and the top edge of its containing control
Bounds	A Rectangle representing the size and location of the control
CanFocus	Indicates whether the control can receive focus
CanSelect	Indicates whether the control can be selected
Capture	Indicates whether the control has captured the mouse
CausesValidation	Indicates whether the control should perform any validation routines when it receives focus
ClientRectangle	A Rectangle representing the client area of the control (not necessarily the same as Bounds)
ClientSize	The height and width of the client area of the control
CompanyName	The name of the company or creator of the control or its containing application
ContainsFocus	Indicates whether the control, or one of its child controls, contains the current focus
ContextMenu	A ContextMenu object associated with this control
Controls	Returns a ControlCollection object that represents all of the child controls for the specified control
Created	Indicates whether the control has been created
Cursor	Indicates the type of mouse cursor used when the mouse pointer is over the control

TABLE B.1 continued

Property	Description
DataBindings	Retrieves the data bindings for the control
DefaultBackColor	The default background color of a control
DefaultFont	The default font of a control
DefaultForeColor	The default foreground color (typically the font color) of a control
DisplayRectangle	A Rectangle object that represents the display area of the control
Disposing	Indicates whether the control is currently being disposed of
Dock	Indicates which edge of its container the control is docked to
Enabled	Indicates whether the control can respond to user input
Focused	Indicates whether the control has input focus
Font	The font used in the control
ForeColor	The foreground color (typically the font color) of the control
Handle	Gets the window handle the control is bound to
HasChildren	Indicates whether the control has any child controls
Height	The height of the control
ImeMode	The input method editor mode of the control (allows you to enter foreign characters and symbols using a standard keyboard)
InvokeRequired	Indicates that the caller of this control cannot interact with it directly because it resides on a different thread (in other words, an Invoke method call is required)
IsAccessible	Indicates whether the control is visible to accessibility clients
IsDisposed	Indicates whether the control has been disposed of
IsHandleCreated	Indicates whether the control's handle has been created (typically when the control is displayed onscreen)
Left	The left edge of the control in pixels, relative to the left edge of the containing control
Location	A Point object that specifies the upper-left corner of the control, relative to the upper-left corner of its containing control

B

TABLE B.1 continued

Property	Description
ModifierKeys	Indicates which, if any, of the modifier keys (Shift, Ctrl, or Alt) are pressed when the control is activated
MouseButtons	Indicates which of the mouse buttons is pressed when the control is activated
MousePosition	Indicates the position of the mouse cursor
Name	The name of the control
Parent	Gets the control's parent in the UI hierarchy
ProductName	The product name of the assembly containing the control
ProductVersion	The version of the assembly containing the control
RecreatingHandle	Indicates whether the control is currently recreating its handle
Region	The window region associated with the control
Right	The distance between the right edge of the control and the left edge of its containing control
RightToLeft	Indicates whether the control is to accept right-to-left languages
Site	Specifies the site information for the control
Size	A Size object that specifies the height and width of the control
TabIndex	The tab order of this control in its containing control
TabStop	Indicates whether users can give this control focus by pressing the Tab key
Tag	The object that contains data about this control
Text	The text associated with this control (often has different significance with different controls)
Top	The y coordinate of the control's top edge in pixels
TopLevelControl	Indicates the topmost containing control of the current control
Visible	Specifies whether the control should render on the page
Width	The width of the control in pixels

Table B.2 lists the methods shared by all controls, inherited from the Control object.

TABLE B.2   Methods of the `Control` Class Inherited by All Controls

Method	Description
BeginInvoke	Executes a delegate asynchronously
BringToFront	Brings the control to the front of the z-order in its parent control
Contains	Indicates whether the current control contains the specified control
CreateControl	Forces the creation of the control
CreateGraphics	Creates a `Graphics` object based on the control
DoDragDrop	Begins a drag-and-drop operation
EndInvoke	Retrieves the return value of the asynchronous operation started by `BeginInvoke`
FindForm	Retrieves the form that the control is on
Focus	Sets input focus to the control
FromChildHandle	Retrieves the control that contains the specified handle
FromHandle	Retrieves the control from the specified handle
GetChildAtPoint	Retrieves the child control that is located at the specified `Point`
GetContainerControl	Returns the control's containing control
GetNextControl	Retrieves the next control in the containing control's tab order
Hide	Conceals the control from the user (note that this does not necessarily disable the control's functionality)
Invalidate	Forces the control to redraw a specific region
Invoke	Executes a delegate on the control's creation thread
IsMnemonic	Determines whether the specified character is the mnemonic character associated with the control
PerformLayout	Forces the control to apply layout logic to its child controls
PointToClient	Converts the specified screen point into client coordinates
PointToScreen	Converts the specified client point into screen coordinates
PreProcessMessage	Causes the control to preprocess input messages before they are dispatched to the default functionality
RectangleToClient	Computes the size and location of the screen rectangle in client coordinates
RectangleToScreen	Computes the size and location of the client rectangle in screen coordinates
Refresh	Forces the control to redraw itself and any child controls
ResetBackColor	Resets the `BackColor` property to its default value
ResetBindings	Resets the `DataBindings` property to its default value

TABLE B.2   continued

Method	Description
ResetCursor	Resets the Cursor property to its default value
ResetFont	Resets the Font property to its default value
ResetForeColor	Resets the ForeColor property to its default value
ResetImeMode	Resets the ImeMode property to its default value
ResetRightToLeft	Resets the RightToLeft property to its default value
ResetText	Resets the Text property to its default value
ResumeLayout	Resumes normal layout logic after a call to SuspendLayout
Scale	Scales the control and any child controls
Select	Activates a control
SelectNextControl	Activates the next control in the containing control's tab order
SendToBack	Sends the control to the back of the z-order
SetBounds	Sets the bounds of the control
Show	Displays the control to the user
SuspendLayout	Temporarily suspends layout logic for the control; resumes with the ResumeLayout method
ToString	Returns a string representing the control
Update	Causes the control to redraw invalidated regions in its client area

Table B.3 lists the events shared by all Windows Forms controls, inherited from the Control object.

TABLE B.3   Events of the Control Class Inherited by All Controls

Event	Description
BackColorChanged	Occurs when the BackColor property changes
BackgroundImageChanged	Occurs when the BackgroundImage property changes
BindingContextChanged	Occurs when the BindingContext property changes
CausesValidationChanged	Occurs when the CausesValidation property changes
ChangeUICues	Occurs when the focus or keyboard UI cues change
Click	Occurs when the control is clicked
ContextMenuChanged	Occurs when the ContextMenu property changes
ControlAdded	Occurs when a control is added to this control's Controls collection
ControlRemoved	Occurs when a control is removed from this control's Controls collection

TABLE B.3 continued

Event	Description
CursorChanged	Occurs when the Cursor property changes
DockChanged	Occurs when the Dock property changes
DoubleClick	Occurs when the control is double-clicked
DragDrop	Occurs when a drag-and-drop operation is completed
DragEnter	Occurs when an object is dragged into the control's bounds
DragLeave	Occurs when an object is dragged out of the control's bounds
DragOver	Occurs when an object is dragged over the control
EnabledChanged	Occurs when the Enabled property changes
Enter	Occurs when the control is entered
FontChanged	Occurs when the Font property changes
ForeColorChanged	Occurs when the ForeColor property changes
GiveFeedback	Occurs during a drag operation
GotFocus	Occurs when the control receives input focus
HandleCreated	Occurs after a handle is created for the control
HandleDestroyed	Occurs when the control's handle is being destroyed
HelpRequested	Occurs when the user requests help for a control
ImeModeChanged	Occurs when the ImeMode property changes
Invalidated	Occurs when a control's UI requires redrawing
KeyDown	Occurs when a key is pressed while the control has the focus
KeyPress	Occurs immediately after the KeyDown event
KeyUp	Occurs immediately after the KeyUp event
Layout	Occurs when a control should reposition its child controls
Leave	Occurs when the control loses input focus
LocationChanged	Occurs when the Location property changes
LostFocus	Occurs when the control loses focus
MouseDown	Occurs when a mouse button is pressed over the control
MouseEnter	Occurs when the mouse pointer enters the control
MouseHover	Occurs when the mouse pointer hovers over the control
MouseLeave	Occurs when the mouse pointer moves out of the control
MouseMove	Occurs when the mouse pointer is moved over the control
MouseUp	Occurs when the mouse pointer is over a control and a mouse button is released (note that the mouse button does not necessarily have to be pressed over the button)

B

TABLE B.3 continued

Event	Description
MouseWheel	Occurs when the mouse wheel moves when the control has focus
Move	Occurs when the control is moved
Paint	Occurs when the control is redrawn
ParentChanged	Occurs when the `Parent` property changes
QueryAccessibilityHelp	Occurs when the `AccessibleObject` property is providing help to accessibility clients
QueryContinueDrag	Occurs during a drag-and-drop operation and allows the drag source to determine whether the drag-and-drop operation should be canceled
Resize	Occurs when the control is resized
RightToLeftChanged	Occurs when the `RightToLeft` property changes
SizeChanged	Occurs when the `Size` property changes
StyleChanged	Occurs when the control's style changes
SystemColorsChanged	Occurs when the system colors change
TabIndexChanged	Occurs when the `TabIndex` property changes
TabStopChanged	Occurs when the `TabStop` property changes
TextChanged	Occurs when the `Text` property changes
Validated	Occurs when the control is finished validating
Validating	Occurs when the control starts to validate
VisibleChanged	Occurs when the `Visible` property changes

The `Button`, `CheckBox`, and `RadioButton` Controls

Table B.4 lists the properties of the `ButtonBase` class, which are inherited by the `Button`, `CheckBox`, and `RadioButton` controls.

TABLE B.4 `ButtonBase` Control Properties

Property	Description
FlatStyle	Indicates the flat style appearance of the control; uses values from the `FlatStyle` enumeration
Image	The image that is displayed in the control

TABLE B.4 Continued

Property	Description
ImageAlign	The alignment of the image displayed by the control
ImageIndex	The image list index of the image currently displayed on the control
ImageList	An ImageList object that contains an array of images associated with the control
TextAlign	The alignment of the text displayed in the control

Button

The Button control represents a clickable button on a Windows Form. Table B.5 lists the property and method of the Button class.

TABLE B.5 Button Class Property and Method

Property	Description
DialogResult	A value that is returned to the containing control when the button is clicked
Method	Description
PerformClick	Generates a Click event for the button

CheckBox

CheckBox represents a box that can be checked or unchecked. Table B.6 lists the properties and events of the CheckBox class.

TABLE B.6 CheckBox Properties and Events

Property	Description
Appearance	Uses a value from the Appearance enumeration to determine the appearance of the CheckBox
AutoCheck	Indicates whether the CheckBox's appearance changes when clicked
CheckAlign	Gets or sets a value indicating the horizontal and vertical alignment of check boxes in a CheckBox
Checked	Indicates whether the CheckBox is checked
CheckState	Indicates the check state of the control, from the CheckState enumeration
ThreeState	Indicates whether the CheckBox will allow three states instead of two

B

TABLE B.6   continued

Event	Description
AppearanceChanged	Occurs when the Appearance property changes
CheckedChanged	Occurs when the Checked property changes
CheckStateChanged	Occurs when the CheckState property changes

RadioButton

The RadioButton represents a box that can be selected. RadioButtons are typically grouped together to allow the user the ability to select one choice from many. Table B.7 lists the properties, method, and events of the RadioButton control.

TABLE B.7   Properties, Method, and Events of the RadioButton Control

Property	Description
Appearance	Uses a value from the Appearance enumeration to determine the appearance of the control
AutoCheck	Indicates whether the control's appearance changes when clicked
CheckAlign	Gets or sets a value indicating the horizontal and vertical alignment of check boxes in a RadioButton
Checked	Indicates whether the CheckBox is checked
Method	**Description**
PerformClick	Generates a Click event for the control
Event	**Description**
AppearanceChanged	Occurs when the Appearance property changes
CheckedChanged	Occurs when the Checked property changes

The ComboBox, ListBox, and CheckedListBox Controls

The ListControl class is the parent of the ComboBox, ListBox, and CheckedListBox controls. All members in ListControl are inherited by these three controls. Table B.8 lists the properties, method, and events of ListControl.

TABLE B.8 Properties, Method, and Events of `ListControl`

Property	Description
DataSource	The data source for this control
DisplayMember	A string that represents which property of the data source you wish to display in the control
SelectedIndex	The zero-based index of the currently selected item in the control
SelectedValue	The value of the member property specified by the `ValueMember` property
ValueMember	A string that specifies the property of the data source from which to draw the value

Method	Description
GetItemText	Returns the text representation of the selected item

Event	Description
DataSourceChanged	Occurs when the `DataSource` property changes
DisplayMemberChanged	Occurs when the `DisplayMember` property changes
SelectedValueChanged	Occurs when the `SelectedValue` property changes
ValueMemberChanged	Occurs when the `ValueMember` property changes

ComboBox

The `ComboBox` control represents a combination of a `ListBox` and a `TextBox` control. It allows the user to select from a list of items and enter or modify displayed text. Table B.9 lists the properties, methods, and events of the `ComboBox` control.

TABLE B.9 Properties, Methods, and Events of `ComboBox`

Property	Description
DrawMode	Indicates whether your code or the operating system will draw the items in the control; uses values from the `DrawMode` enumeration
DropDownStyle	The style of the control; uses values from the `ComboBoxStyle` enumeration
DropDownWidth	The width of the drop-down portion of this control
DroppedDown	Indicates whether the control is displaying its drop-down portion
IntegralHeight	Indicates whether the control should resize to avoid showing partial items
ItemHeight	Indicates the height of an item in the control
Items	A collection of items in the control

TABLE B.9   continued

Property	Description
MaxDropDownItems	The maximum number of items to be shown in the drop-down portion of the control
MaxLength	The maximum number of characters that can fit in the text box portion of the control
PreferredHeight	The preferred height of the control
SelectedIndex	The zero-based index of the currently selected item
SelectedItem	The currently selected item
SelectedText	The text that is selected in the text box portion of the control
SelectionLength	The number of selected characters in the text box portion of the control
SelectionStart	The index of the starting character of the selected text in the text box portion of the control
Sorted	Indicates whether items in the control should be sorted

Method	Description
BeginUpdate	Prevents the control from redrawing itself each time a new item is added until EndUpdate is called
EndUpdate	Resumes drawing for the control after BeginUpdate has been called
FindString	Finds the first item in the control that starts with the specified string
FindStringExact	Finds the first item in the control that exactly matches the specified string
GetItemHeight	Returns the height of an item in the control
Select	Selects a range of text
SelectAll	Selects all of the text in the text box portion of the control

Event	Description
DrawItem	Occurs when a visual aspect of an owner-drawn control changes
DropDown	Occurs when the drop-down portion of the control is shown
DropDownStyleChanged	Occurs when the DropDownStyle property changes
MeasureItem	Occurs each time an owner-drawn control needs to display an item
SelectedIndexChanged	Occurs when the SelectedIndex property changes
SelectionChangeCommitted	Occurs when the selected item has changed and the change has been committed

ListBox

The ListBox represents a list of selectable items. Table B.10 lists the properties, methods, and events of the ListBox control.

TABLE B.10 Properties, Methods, and Events of the ListBox Control

Property	Description
ColumnWidth	The width of columns in a multicolumn ListBox
DrawMode	Indicates whether your code or the operating system will draw the items in the control; uses values from the DrawMode enumeration
HorizontalExtent	The width to which the horizontal scrollbar can scroll
HorizontalScrollbar	Indicates whether a horizontal scrollbar should be shown in the control
IntegralHeight	Indicates whether the control should resize to avoid showing partial items
ItemHeight	Indicates the height of an item in the control
Items	A collection of items in the control
MultiColumn	Indicates whether the control should create as many columns as necessary to avoid having to scroll vertically through items
PreferredHeight	The preferred height of the control
ScrollAlwaysVisible	Indicates whether a vertical scrollbar is shown at all times
SelectedIndex	The zero-based index of the currently selected item
SelectedIndices	A collection that contains the indices of selected items in the control
SelectedItem	The currently selected item
SelectedItems	A collection of selected items
SelectionMode	Indicates how items may be selected in the control; uses values from the SelectionMode enumeration
Sorted	Indicates whether items in the control should be sorted
TopIndex	Gets the index of the first item in the control
UseTabStops	Indicates whether the control can display Tab characters in each item in the list
Method	*Description*
BeginUpdate	Prevents the control from redrawing itself each time a new item is added until EndUpdate is called
ClearSelected	Deselects all items in the control
EndUpdate	Resumes drawing for the control after BeginUpdate has been called
FindString	Finds the first item in the control that starts with the specified string

B

TABLE B.10   continued

Method	Description
FindStringExact	Finds the first item in the control that exactly matches the specified string
GetItemHeight	Returns the height of an item in the control
GetItemRectangle	Returns the bounding rectangle for an item in the control
GetSelected	Indicates whether the specified item is selected
IndexFromPoint	Returns the zero-based index of the item nearest the specified Point
SetSelected	Selects or clears the selection for a specified item in the control

Event	Description
DrawItem	Occurs when a visual aspect of an owner-drawn control changes
MeasureItem	Occurs each time an owner-drawn control needs to display an item
SelectedIndexChanged	Occurs when the SelectedIndex property changes

CheckedListBox

The CheckedListBox control represents a ListBox control that has check boxes next to each item in the list. The CheckedListBox's direct parent is the ListBox control, so it inherits all of that control's members, in addition to those in ListControl. Table B.11 lists the properties, methods, and event of the CheckedListBox control.

TABLE B.11   Properties, Methods, and Event of CheckedListBox

Property	Description
CheckedIndices	The indices of all checked items in this control
CheckedItems	A collection of the checked items in this control
CheckOnClick	Indicates whether the check box for an item should be checked when the item is clicked
ThreeDCheckBoxes	Indicates whether the check boxes should be displayed with a 3-D feel

Method	Description
GetItemChecked	Indicates whether the specified item is checked
GetItemCheckState	Returns a value indicating the current state of the check box for an item
SetItemChecked	Checks the item at the specified index
SetItemCheckState	Sets the check state of the item at the specified index

Event	Description
ItemCheck	Occurs when an item is checked

Common Dialog Controls

Common dialog controls represent dialog boxes that provide standard operating system functionality such as opening or saving files and selecting fonts. Each common dialog derives from the System.Windows.Forms.CommonDialog class, whose methods and event are shown in Table B.12.

TABLE B.12 Methods and Event of CommonDialog

Method	Description
Reset	Resets the properties of the control to their default values
ShowDialog	Displays the dialog box
Event	Description
HelpRequest	Occurs when the user clicks the Help button on a common dialog control

ColorDialog

The ColorDialog control is a dialog that allows the user to choose from a palette of colors along with controls that allow users to define custom colors. Table B.13 lists the properties of the ColorDialog control.

TABLE B.13 Properties of ColorDialog

Property	Description
AllowFullOpen	Indicates whether the user can use the dialog to define custom colors
AnyColor	Indicates whether the dialog displays all available colors in the dialog window
Color	The color selected by the user
CustomColors	Gets or sets the custom colors shown in the dialog
FullOpen	Indicates whether the controls used to define custom colors are displayed when the dialog is opened
ShowHelp	Indicates whether the Help button is displayed in the dialog
SolidColorOnly	Indicates whether the dialog will restrict users to selecting only solid colors

File Dialogs

The two file common dialog controls (OpenFileDialog and SaveFileDialog) are similar. They both derive from the FileDialog class, shown in Table B.14.

TABLE B.14 Properties and Event of `FileDialog`

Property	Description
AddExtension	Indicates whether the dialog should automatically add an extension to a file if the user omits one
CheckFileExists	Indicates whether the dialog should verify that a user-specified file exists
CheckPathExists	Indicates whether the dialog should verify that a user-specified directory exists
DefaultExt	The default extension to use for filenames
DereferenceLinks	Indicates whether the dialog should follow shortcut files (.lnk files) or not
FileName	Gets or sets a string containing the filename selected in the dialog
FileNames	The filenames of all selected files in the dialog
Filter	The filter string that determines what types of file extensions the user can view
FilterIndex	The index of the currently selected filter
InitialDirectory	The starting directory of the dialog
RestoreDirectory	Indicates whether the dialog should restore the original directory after closing if the user has changed it
ShowHelp	Indicates whether the Help button is displayed in the dialog
Title	The title of the dialog box
ValidateNames	Indicates whether the dialog will only accept valid Win32 filenames
Event	**Description**
FileOk	Occurs when the user clicks the Open or Save button

OpenFileDialog

`OpenFileDialog` allows the user to select a file to open. Table B.15 lists the properties and method of the `OpenFileDialog` control.

TABLE B.15 Properties and Method of `OpenFileDialog`

Property	Description
MultiSelect	Indicates whether the user can select multiple files
ReadOnlyChecked	Indicates whether the read-only box is checked
ShowReadOnly	Indicates whether the read-only box should be shown

TABLE B.15   continued

Method	Description
OpenFile	Opens the file selected by the user with read-only permissions

SaveFileDialog

SaveFileDialog allows the user to save a file by selecting an existing file to overwrite or by typing in a new filename. Table B.16 lists the properties and method of the SaveFileDialog control.

TABLE B.16   Properties and Method of SaveFileDialog

Property	Description
CreatePrompt	Indicates whether the dialog should prompt the user to create a file if it doesn't already exist
OverwritePrompt	Indicates whether the dialog should prompt the user to overwrite a file if it already exists
Method	**Description**
OpenFile	Opens the file selected by the user with read-only permissions

FontDialog

FontDialog allows the user to select a font and its properties (size, weight, and so on) to use for an application. Table B.17 lists the properties and event of the FontDialog control.

TABLE B.17   Properties and Event of FontDialog

Property	Description
AllowScriptChange	Indicates whether the user can change the default script to display a different character set
AllowSimulations	Indicates whether the dialog allows GDI font simulations
AllowVectorFonts	Indicates whether the dialog allows vector font selections
AllowVerticalFonts	Indicates whether the dialog allows vertical fonts
Color	Indicates the font's color
FixedPitchOnly	Indicates whether the dialog allows only fixed-pitch fonts
Font	The selected font
FontMustExist	Indicates whether the dialog raises an error when the selected font does not exist

TABLE B.17 continued

Property	Description
MaxSize	The maximum font size a user can select
MinSize	The minimum font size a user can select
ScriptsOnly	Indicates whether the dialog allows non-OEM and symbol character sets
ShowApply	Indicates whether the dialog has an Apply button
ShowColor	Indicates whether the dialog allows the user to select a font color
ShowEffects	Indicates whether the dialog allows the user to select effects such as strikethrough, underline, and color
ShowHelp	Indicates whether the Help button is displayed in the dialog
Event	Description
Apply	Occurs when the Apply button is clicked

PageSetupDialog

PageSetupDialog allows the user to define page-specific properties such as margins and paper source. Table B.18 lists the properties of the PageSetupDialog control.

TABLE B.18 Properties of PageSetupDialog

Property	Description
AllowMargins	Indicates whether the dialog allows the user to modify margin values
AllowOrientation	Indicates whether the dialog allows the user to select paper orientation (landscape or portrait)
AllowPaper	Indicates whether the dialog allows the user to select paper size and source
AllowPrinter	Indicates whether the dialog should show the Printer button
Document	Indicates the PrintDocument object to retrieve page settings from
MinMargins	The minimum margins a user is allowed to specify, in hundredths of an inch
PageSettings	The PageSettings object to modify
PrinterSettings	The printer settings for use when the user clicks the Printer button
ShowHelp	Indicates whether the Help button is displayed in the dialog
ShowNetwork	Indicates whether the dialog should display the Network button

PrintDialog

PrintDialog allows the user to print a document. Table B.19 lists the properties of the PrintDialog control.

TABLE B.19 Properties of PrintDialog

Property	Description
AllowPrintToFile	Indicates whether the Print to File check box should be shown
AllowSelection	Indicates whether the From...To...Page option button is enabled
AllowSomePages	Indicates whether the Pages option button is enabled
Document	Indicates the PrintDocument object to retrieve page settings from
PrinterSettings	The printer settings to retrieve settings from
PrintToFile	Indicates whether the Print to File check box is checked
ShowHelp	Indicates whether the Help button is displayed in the dialog
ShowNetwork	Indicates whether the dialog should display the Network button

Menus

Menus represent groups of commands that can be executed by bringing up a menu-type listing. These include regular application menus and context-sensitive menus. All the controls in this section derive from the System.Windows.Forms.Menu class, shown in Table B.20.

TABLE B.20 Properties and Methods of Menu

Property	Description
Handle	The handle for a given menu
IsParent	Indicates whether this menu has any submenus
MdiListItem	Indicates whether this menu is to be used to display the windows from an MDI application
MenuItems	A collection of the submenus contained in this menu
Method	*Description*
GetContextMenu	Retrieves the ContextMenu that this Menu belongs to
GetMainMenu	Gets the MainMenu control this menu belongs to
MergeMenu	Merges the MenuItems of a specified menu with the current menu

ContextMenu

A context menu represents a menu that is context-sensitive. These menus typically appear when the user right-clicks the mouse over an object. Table B.21 lists the method and event of the ContextMenu control.

TABLE B.21   Method and Event of ContextMenu

Method	Description
Show	Displays the menu at the specified position
SourceControl	Retrieves the control that contains the shortcut menu.
Event	Description
Popup	Occurs immediately before a context menu is displayed

MainMenu

The MainMenu control represents the top-level menu structure for a form. It does not actually display a menu itself, but contains MenuItem controls that do. Table B.22 lists the methods of the MainMenu control.

TABLE B.22   Methods of MainMenu

Method	Description
CloneMenu	Creates a copy of the MainMenu object
GetForm	Retrieves the Form object for this menu item

MenuItem

A MenuItem represents the actual user interface for a menu; it is the visible portion of the menu that the user can interact with. Table B.23 lists the properties, methods, and events of the MenuItem control.

TABLE B.23   Properties, Methods, and Events of MenuItem

Property	Description
BarBreak	Indicates whether a menu should be displayed on a new line (in a containing MenuItem object) or in a new column (in a ContextMenu object)
Break	Indicates whether a menu should be displayed on a new line (in a containing MenuItem object) or in a new column (in a ContextMenu object)

TABLE B.23 continued

Property	Description
Checked	Indicates whether a check mark appears next to the menu item
DefaultItem	Indicates whether this menu is the default menu
Enabled	Indicates whether the menu allows user interaction
Index	The position of this menu in its parent menu
MdiList	Indicates whether this menu is to be used to display the windows from an MDI application
MergeOrder	A value indicating the position of this menu item in relation to others when it is merged with another menu
MergeType	Indicates the behavior of this menu item in relation to others when merged with another menu; uses values from the MenuMerge enumeration
Mnemonic	The mnemonic character that is associated with this menu
OwnerDraw	Indicates whether the owner or the operating system draws the menu item
Parent	Retrieves the parent menu of the current menu item
RadioCheck	Indicates whether the menu item displays a radio button instead of a check mark
Shortcut	The shortcut key associated with this menu item; uses values from the ShortCut enumeration
ShowShortcut	Indicates whether the menu item should display the associated shortcut key next to the menu caption
Text	The caption of the menu item
Visible	Indicates whether the menu item is visible to the user

Method	Description
CloneMenu	Creates a copy of the menu item
PerformClick	Raises a Click event for the menu item
PerformSelect	Raises a Select event for the menu item

Event	Description
DrawItem	Occurs when a menu item needs to be drawn and the OwnerDraw property is set to true
MeasureItem	Occurs when a menu item needs to be measured before it is drawn and the OwnerDraw property is set to true
Popup	Occurs before a menu item is shown
Select	Occurs when the user places the mouse cursor over a menu item

B

DataGrid

This control represents an editable table of information. Table B.24 lists the properties, methods, and events of the `DataGrid` control.

TABLE B.24   Properties, Methods, and Events of `DataGrid`

Property	Description
AllowNavigation	Indicates whether navigation to child tables and data sets is allowed
AllowSorting	Indicates whether the user can re-sort the data by clicking on a column header
AlternatingBackColor	The background color of alternating rows
BackColor	The background color of the grid
BackgroundColor	The background color of the non-row areas of the grid
BorderStyle	The border style of the grid; uses a `BorderStyle` enumeration value
CaptionBackColor	The background color of the caption area
CaptionFont	The font used in the caption area
CaptionForeColor	The foreground color of the caption area
CaptionText	The text displayed in the caption area
CaptionVisible	Indicates whether the caption area is visible
ColumnHeadersVisible	Indicates whether the headers of each column are visible
CurrentCell	Gets or sets the cell that has the focus
CurrentRowIndex	The index of the selected row
DataMember	Gets the specific list in the `DataSource` property that should be displayed in the grid
DataSource	The data source that the grid should display
FirstVisibleColumn	The index of the first visible column in the grid
FlatMode	Indicates whether the grid should display in 3-D or flat
GridLineColor	The color of the grid lines
GridLineStyle	The style of the grid lines; uses values from the `DataGridLineStyle` enumeration
HeaderBackColor	The background color of all row and column headers
HeaderFont	The font used in all row and column headers
HeaderForeColor	The foreground color of all row and column headers
Item	The value of a specified cell

TABLE B.24 continued

Property	Description
LinkColor	The color of the text you can click to navigate to child tables
LinkHoverColor	The color a link changes to when the mouse cursor is placed over it
ParentRowsBackColor	The background color of parent rows
ParentRowsForeColor	The foreground color of parent rows
ParentRowsLabelStyle	The way parent rows are displayed; uses values from the DataGridParentRowsLabelStyle enumeration
ParentRowsVisible	Indicates whether rows of the parent table should be visible
PreferredColumnWidth	The default width of columns in pixels
PreferredRowHeight	The default height of each row
ReadOnly	Indicates whether the data displayed in the grid is editable
RowHeadersVisible	Indicates whether the row headers are visible
RowHeaderWidth	The width of the row headers.
SelectionBackColor	The background color of selected rows
SelectionForeColor	The foreground color of selected rows
TableStyles	A collection of DataGridTableStyle objects that define the style for the grid
VisibleColumnCount	The number of visible columns
VisibleRowCount	The number of visible rows

Method	Description
BeginEdit	Attempts to put the grid in a state where editing is allowed
BeginInit	Starts the initialization of the grid
Collapse	Collapses all child table relations
EndEdit	Stops the edit-mode called by BeginEdit
EndInit	Ends initialization of the grid
Expand	Displays child relations for any or all rows
GetCellBounds	A Rectangle object that specifies the four corners of a given cell
GetCurrentCellBounds	A Rectangle object that specifies the four corners of the selected cell
HitTest	Returns information about the grid at the specified Point
IsExpanded	Indicates whether a row's node is expanded
IsSelected	Indicates whether a row is selected
NavigateBack	Navigates back to the table that was previously shown in the grid

B

TABLE B.24 continued

Method	Description
NavigateTo	Navigates to the specified table
ResetAlternatingBackColor	Resets the AlternatingBackColor property to its default value
ResetGridLineColor	Resets the GridLineColor property to its default value
ResetHeaderBackColor	Resets the HeaderBackColor property to its default value
ResetHeaderFont	Resets the HeaderFont property to its default value
ResetHeaderForeColor	Resets the HeaderForeColor property to its default value
ResetLinkColor	Resets the LinkColor property to its default value
ResetSelectionBackColor	Resets the SelectionBackColor property to its default value
ResetSelectionForeColor	Resets the SelectionForeColor property to its default value
Select	Selects a specified row
SetDataBinding	Sets the DataSource and DataMember properties
UnSelect	Deselects a specified row

Event	Description
AllowNavigationChanged	Occurs when the AllowNavigation property changes
BackButtonClick	Occurs when the Back button on a child table is clicked
BackgroundColorChanged	Occurs when the BackgroundColor property changes
BorderStyleChanged	Occurs when the BorderStyle property changes
CaptionVisibleChanged	Occurs when the CaptionVisible property changes
CurrentCellChanged	Occurs when the CurrentCell property changes.
DataSourceChanged	Occurs when the DataSource property changes
FlatModeChanged	Occurs when the FlatMode property changes
Navigate	Occurs when the user navigates to a different table in the grid
ParentRowsLabelStyleChanged	Occurs when the ParentRowsLabelStyle property changes
ParentRowsVisibleChanged	Occurs when the ParentRowsVisible property changes
ReadOnlyChanged	Occurs when the ReadOnly property changes
Scroll	Occurs when the user scrolls the grid
ShowParentDetailsButtonClick	Occurs when the Show Parent Details button is clicked

DateTimePicker

The DateTimePicker control represents a Windows calendar and time control that can be used to set or choose date and time information. Table B.25 describes properties and events of the DateTimePicker control.

TABLE B.25   Properties and Events of `DateTimePicker`

Property	Description
CalendarFont	The font used in the calendar
CalendarForeColor	The foreground color of the calendar
CalendarMonthBackground	The background color of the calendar month
CalendarTitleBackColor	The background color of the title of the calendar
CalendarTitleForeColor	The foreground color of the title of the calendar
CalendarTrailingForeColor	The foreground color of the calendar's trailing dates
Checked	Indicates whether the `Value` property is set to a valid date and the displayed value is updateable
CustomFormat	The custom date-time format string
DropDownAlign	The alignment of the drop-down calendar on the control; uses a value from the `LeftRightAlignment` enumeration
Format	The format of the displayed date and time
MaxDate	The maximum date and time that can be selected from this control
MinDate	The minimum date and time that can be selected from this control
PreferredHeight	The preferred height of the control
ShowCheckBox	Indicates whether a check box is displayed to the left of the date
ShowUpDown	Indicates whether an up-down control is used to adjust the date and time
Value	The date-time value of the control
Event	**Description**
CloseUp	Occurs when the drop-down calendar is closed
DropDown	Occurs when the drop-down calendar is shown
FormatChanged	Occurs when the `Format` property changes
ValueChanged	Occurs when the `Value` property changes

Scrollable Controls

Scrollable controls are a special type of control that provides default scrolling capabilities when the contents of the control are too large to fit in one screen. Examples include the `Form` and `Panel` controls. All of the scrollable controls inherit values from the `System.Windows.Forms.ScrollableControl` class, shown in Table B.26.

TABLE B.26   Properties and Method of `ScrollableControl`

Property	Description
AutoScroll	Indicates whether the control will allow the user to scroll to child controls placed outside the borders of the container using scrollbars
AutoScrollMargin	The size of the auto-scrollbars margin
AutoScrollMinSize	The minimum size of the auto-scroll
AutoScrollPosition	The location of the auto-scrollbar
DockPadding	The padding for all edges of the container control
Method	**Description**
SetAutoScrollMargin	Sets the size of the auto-scroll margin

In addition, the `Form`, `PropertyGrid`, `PrintPreviewDialog`, `DomainUpDown`, and `NumericUpDown` controls all share properties from the `System.Windows.Forms.ContainerControl` class, shown in Table B.27. `ContainerControl` inherits from `ScrollableControl`.

TABLE B.27   Properties and Method of `ContainerControl`

Property	Description
ActiveControl	The active control in the container
ParentForm	The parent container of the control
Method	**Description**
Validate	Validates the last invalidated control, including all of its parent controls but excluding the current control

Finally, the `DomainUpDown` and `NumericUpDown` controls inherit from the `System.Windows.Forms.UpDownBase` control shown in Table B.28, in addition to the `ScrollableControl` and `ContainerControl` classes.

TABLE B.28   Properties and Methods of `UpDownBase`

Property	Description
BorderStyle	The border style for the control; uses values from the `BorderStyle` enumeration
InterceptArrowKeys	Indicates whether the user can use the up arrow and down arrow keys to select values
PreferredHeight	The preferred height of the control

TABLE B.28   continued

Property	Description
ReadOnly	Indicates whether the value of the control can be changed
TextAlign	The alignment of the text in the control; uses values from the HorizontalAlignment enumeration
UpDownAlign	The alignment of the Up and Down buttons on the control; uses values from the LeftRightAlignment enumeration

Method	Description
DownButton	Handles the pressing of the Down button
Select	Selects a range of text in the control
UpButton	Handles the pressing of the Up button

DomainUpDown

This control represents an up-down control that displays strings. This class inherits directly from the UpDownBase class, and indirectly from ContainerControl and ScrollableControl. Table B.29 shows the properties of this control.

TABLE B.29   Properties of DomainUpDown

Property	Description
Items	A collection of objects assigned to this control
SelectedIndex	The zero-based index of the currently selected item in the control
SelectedItem	The currently selected item in the control
Sorted	Indicates whether the items in the control are sorted
Wrap	Indicates whether the control will move to the first item if the user scrolls past the last item, or to the last item if the user scrolls before the first item

Form

This container represents a window in your application (typically the main container in your application). This class inherits directly from the ContainerControl and indirectly from ScrollableControl. Table B.30 lists the properties, methods, and events of this control.

TABLE B.30 Properties, Methods, and Events of Form

Property	Description
AcceptButton	The button that is associated with the Enter key
ActiveForm	Gets the currently active form for this application
ActiveMdiChild	The currently active MDI child window
AutoScale	Indicates whether the form automatically adjusts its size to accommodate different font sizes
AutoScaleBaseSize	The base size used for auto-scaling
CancelButton	The button that is associated with the Esc key
ClientSize	The size of the client area of the form
ControlBox	Indicates whether the control box is displayed in the form
DesktopBounds	The size and location of the form on the client desktop
DesktopLocation	The location of the form on the client desktop
DialogResult	The value the form returns when closed; uses a value from the DialogResult enumeration
FormBorderStyle	Indicates the type of border on the form; uses a value from the FormBorderStyle enumeration
HelpButton	Indicates whether a Help button should be displayed on the form
Icon	The icon associated with the form; if it is the top-level form, this icon will be used to represent your application
IsMdiChild	Indicates whether the form is an MDI child
IsMdiContainer	Indicates whether the form can contain MDI children
KeyPreview	Indicates whether the form will receive keyboard events before the control that has the focus
MaximizeBox	Indicates whether the Maximize button will appear
MaximumSize	Indicates the maximum size to which the user can resize the form
MdiChildren	Gets an array of forms representing the MDI children of this form
MdiParent	Gets or sets the MDI parent for this form
Menu	The MainMenu associated with this form
MergedMenu	The merged menu for the form
MinimizeBox	Indicates whether the Minimize button will be shown on the form
MinimumSize	The minimum size the form can be resized to
Modal	Indicates the modality of the form (in other words, whether it will allow the user to switch focus from this form to another)
Opacity	The opacity of the form

TABLE B.30 continued

Property	Description
OwnedForms	An array of Form objects that represent all forms owned by the current form
Owner	Gets or sets the form that is the owner of the current form
ShowInTaskbar	Indicates whether the form will be shown in the Windows taskbar
SizeGripStyle	Determines the type of grips the user can use to resize the form; uses values from the SizeGripStyle enumeration
StartPosition	The starting position of the form
TopLevel	Indicates whether the form should be displayed as a top-level window
TopMost	Indicates whether the form is the top most in your application
TransparencyKey	The color that will represent the transparent areas of the form
WindowState	The state of the form; uses values from the FormWindowState enumeration

Method	Description
Activate	Activates the form and gives it focus
AddOwnedForm	Adds a form to the current form
Close	Closes the form
LayoutMdi	Arranges the MDI child forms in the parent; uses values from the MdiLayout enumeration
RemovedOwnedForm	Removes an owned form from the current form
SetDesktopBounds	Sets the bounds of the form on the client desktop
SetDesktopLocation	Sets the location of the form on the client desktop
ShowDialog	Shows the form as a modal dialog box

Event	Description
Activated	Occurs when the form is activated
Closed	Occurs when the form is closed
Closing	Occurs immediately before the form is closed
Deactivate	Occurs when the form loses focus
InputLanguageChanged	Occurs when the input language of the form changes
InputLanguageChanging	Occurs immediately before the input language of the form changes
Load	Occurs when the form is displayed for the first time
MaximizedBoundsChanged	Occurs when the MaximizedBounds property changes
MaximumSizeChanged	Occurs when the MaximumSize property changes

B

TABLE B.30 continued

Event	Description
MdiChildActivate	Occurs when an MDI child form is activated or closed
MenuComplete	Occurs when the menu of the form loses focus
MenuStart	Occurs when the menu of the form gains focus
MinimumSizeChanged	Occurs when the MinimumSize property changes

NumericUpDown

NumericUpDown represents a Windows up-down control that displays numeric values. This class inherits directly from the UpDownBase class, and indirectly from ContainerControl and ScrollableControl. Table B.31 lists the properties and event of this control.

TABLE B.31 Properties and Event of NumericUpDown

Property	Description
DecimalPlaces	The number of decimal places to show in the control
Hexadecimal	Indicates whether the control should display hexadecimal values
Increment	The value to increment or decrement the control's value when the up or down keys are pressed
Maximum	The maximum value for the control
Minimum	The minimum value for the control
ThousandsSeparator	Indicates whether a separator should be shown for thousands
Value	The current value shown in the control
Event	**Description**
ValueChanged	Occurs when the Value property changes

Panel

This control represents a panel that can contain other controls, but must itself be contained in another control. This class inherits directly from ScrollableControl. Table B.32 lists the lone property of this control.

TABLE B.32 Property of `Panel`

Property	Description
BorderStyle	The type of border around the control; uses values from the `BorderStyle` enumeration

PrintPreviewDialog

This control shows a preview of a document to be printed. Although it is a common dialog box, it does not follow the same inheritance path as the other common dialogs. Rather, it inherits directly from the `Form` class. Table B.33 lists the properties of this control.

TABLE B.33 Properties of `PrintPreviewDialog`

Property	Description
Document	The `PrintDocument` to preview
PrintPreviewControl	Returns the `PrintPreviewControl` contained in this control
UseAntiAlias	Indicates whether the preview should antialias the text to present a smoother-looking preview

PropertyGrid

This control provides an interface for browsing properties of an object. It inherits directly from `ContainerControl` and indirectly from `ScrollableControl`. Table B.34 lists the properties, methods, and events of this control.

TABLE B.34 Properties, Methods, and Events of `PropertyGrid`

Property	Description
BrowsableAttributes	An `AttributeCollection` that contains the attributes of the object to browse
CanShowCommands	Indicates whether commands can be shown for the object to browse
CommandsBackColor	The background color of the commands pane
CommandsForeColor	The foreground color of the commands pane
CommandsVisible	Indicates whether the commands pane is visible
CommandsVisibleIfAvailable	Indicates whether the commands pane is visible for the objects that expose commands
ContextMenuDefaultLocation	The default location for the context menu

TABLE B.34 continued

Property	Description
HelpBackColor	The background color of the Help region
HelpForeColor	The foreground color of the Help region
HelpVisible	Indicates whether the Help region is visible
LargeButtons	Indicates whether the control should display in larger-than-standard buttons
LineColor	The color of the grid and border lines
PropertySort	The type of sorting used by the control; uses values from the PropertySort enumeration
PropertyTabs	A collection of the property tabs for this control
SelectedGridItem	The currently selected item
SelectedObject	The object for which this control displays properties
SelectedObjects	The currently selected objects
SelectedTab	The currently selected property tab
ToolbarVisible	Indicates whether the toolbar is visible
ViewBackColor	The background color of the grid
ViewForeColor	The foreground color of the grid

Method	Description
CollapseAllGridItems	Collapses all categories in the grid
ExpandAllGridItems	Expands all categories in the grid
RefreshTabs	Refreshes the property tabs of the grid

Event	Description
PropertySortChanged	Occurs when the sort mode changes
PropertyTabChanged	Occurs when a property tab changes
PropertyValueChanged	Occurs when a property value changes
SelectedGridItemChanged	Occurs when the selected item changes
SelectedObjectsChanged	Occurs when the SelectedObjects property changes

TabPage

This control is nearly identical to the Panel control, except that it can only be used inside a TabControl control and represents a particular tab. TabPage derives directly from Panel. Table B.35 lists the properties and events of this control.

TABLE B.35 Properties of `TabPage`

Property	Description
ImageIndex	The index of the image to display on the tab; see the `ImageList` property of `TabControl` for more information
ToolTipText	The ToolTip text for this control

ErrorProvider

`ErrorProvider` provides a means of displaying a user interface to the user to describe an error associated with a control. It does not, however, derive from `Control`. Table B.36 lists the properties and methods of this control.

TABLE B.36 Properties and Methods of `ErrorProvider`

Property	Description
BlinkRate	The rate at which the error icon flashes
BlinkStyle	The style in which the error icon flashes; uses values from the `ErrorBlinkStyle` enumeration
ContainerControl	The parent control for this control
DataMember	The data table to monitor
DataSource	The data set to monitor
Icon	The icon to display in the control

Method	Description
BindToDataAndErrors	Provides a way to set both the `DataMember` and `DataSource` properties
CanExtend	Indicates whether the control can be extended
GetError	The error description for a specified control
GetIconAlignment	Indicates where the icon should be placed relative to the text in the control; uses values from the `ErrorIconAlignment` enumeration
GetIconPadding	The extra space to display around the error icon
SetError	Sets the error description string for a specified control
SetIconAlignment	Used to set where the icon should be placed relative to the text in the control; uses values from the `ErrorIconAlignment` enumeration
SetIconPadding	Sets the extra space to display around the error icon
UpdateBinding	Updates the bindings in the `DataSource`, `DataMember`, and error description text

GroupBox

This control represents a grouped section (or box) of other controls. Table B.37 lists the property of this control.

TABLE B.37   Property of GroupBox

Property	Description
FlatStyle	The 3-D appearance of the control; uses values from the FlatStyle enumeration

Scrollbars

Scrollbars are controls that can be used to navigate around another control. While some controls have built-in scrollbars, you can use the controls in this section to add scrollbars to any control. All controls in this section derive from the base ScrollBar class, shown in Table B.38, which in turn inherits directly from Control.

TABLE B.38   Properties and Events of ScrollBar

Property	Description
LargeChange	The value to be added or subtracted from the Value property when the scroll box is moved a great distance (typically when the user clicks the scrollbar above or below the scroll box)
Maximum	The maximum value of the Value property
Minimum	The minimum value of the Value property
SmallChange	The value to be added or subtracted from the Value property when the scroll box is moved a short distance (typically when the user clicks the arrows on the scrollbar, or directly moves the scroll box)
Value	A numeric value that represents the current position of the scroll box
Event	**Description**
Scroll	Occurs when the scroll box has been moved
ValueChanged	Occurs when the Value property has changed

HScrollBar

This control represents a horizontal scrollbar on a control. It derives directly from the ScrollBar class and does not contain any noninherited properties, methods, or events.

VScrollBar

This control represents a vertical scrollbar on a control. It derives directly from the ScrollBar class and does not contain any noninherited properties, methods, or events.

ImageList

The ImageList control represents a collection of Image objects that can be assigned to another control. It does not derive from the Control class. Table B.39 lists the properties, method, and event of this control.

TABLE B.39 Properties, Method, and Event of ImageList

Property	Description
ColorDepth	The color depth of the images in the list
Handle	The handle of this control
HandleCreated	Indicates whether the handle for this control has been created
Images	An ImageCollection object representing the images in the list
ImageSize	The size of the images in the list
ImageStream	The handle to the ImageListStreamer associated with this list
TransparentColor	The color in the images to be treated as transparent
Method	**Description**
Draw	Draws the specified image
Event	**Description**
RecreateHandle	Occurs when the handle is recreated

Label Controls

Labels represent a way to display static text to the user. There are two label controls in the .NET Framework: Label and LinkLabel. Table B.40 lists the properties and events of the Label control.

TABLE B.40 Properties and Events of Label

Property	Description
AutoSize	Indicates whether the control should automatically adjust its size based on the size of the font contained within
BorderStyle	The border style to use for the control; uses values from the BorderStyle enumeration

B

TABLE B.40   continued

Property	Description
FlatStyle	The 3-D appearance of the control; uses values from the FlatStyle enumeration
Image	The image that is displayed on this control
ImageAlign	The alignment of the image displayed with the Image property; uses a value from the ContentAlignment enumeration
ImageIndex	The index of the image to display; see the ImageList property
ImageList	The ImageList that is associated with this control
PreferredHeight	The preferred height of the control
PreferredWidth	The preferred width of the control
TextAlign	Indicates the alignment of the text in the control; uses values from the ContentAlignment enumeration
UseMnemonic	Indicates whether the control interprets an ampersand character to be an access key prefix
Event	**Description**
AutoSizeChanged	Occurs when the AutoSize property changes
TextAlignChanged	Occurs when the TextAlign property changes

The LinkLabel control is similar to the Label control, except that it can display hyperlinks. It derives directly from the Label class. Table B.41 lists the properties and event of this control.

TABLE B.41   Properties and Event of the LinkLabel Control

Property	Description
ActiveLinkColor	The color of an active link
DisabledLinkColor	The color of a disabled link
LinkArea	The range of text in the control to treat as a link
LinkBehavior	The behavior of the link; uses values from the LinkBehavior enumeration
LinkColor	The color of a regular link
Links	A collection of links contained within this control
LinkVisited	Indicates whether a particular link should be displayed as if it were already clicked
VisitedLinkColor	The color of an already visited link
Event	**Description**
LinkClicked	Occurs when a link in the control is clicked

ListView

This control displays a collection of items that can be displayed in four different manners, similar to Windows Explorer. Table B.42 lists the properties, methods, and events of this control.

TABLE B.42 Properties, Methods, and Events of `ListView`

Property	Description
Activation	The type of action a user must take to activate an item; uses a value from the `ItemActivation` enumeration
Alignment	The alignment of items in the control; uses values from the `ListViewAlignment` enumeration
AllowColumnReorder	Indicates whether the user can reorder columns in the control by dragging the column headers to new positions
AutoArrange	Indicates whether the items are automatically arranged
BorderStyle	The border style for the control; uses values from the `BorderStyle` enumeration
CheckBoxes	Indicates whether check boxes should appear next to each item in the control
CheckedIndices	The zero-based indices of the currently checked items in the control
CheckedItems	The currently checked items in the control
Columns	The collection of all columns that appear in the control
FocusedItem	The item that currently has the input focus
FullRowSelect	Indicates whether clicking an item will select all of its subitems
GridLines	Indicates whether grid lines should be drawn
HeaderStyle	The style of column headers; uses values from the `ColumnHeaderStyle` enumeration
HideSelection	Indicates whether the selected item in the control remains highlighted even when the control loses focus
HoverSelection	Indicates whether an item is automatically selected when the mouse pointer hovers over the item
Items	The collection of all items in the list
LabelEdit	Indicates whether the user can edit the labels of each item in the control
LabelWrap	Indicates whether labels should wrap when items are displayed as icons
LargeImageList	The `ImageList` control to use when displaying items as large icons

TABLE B.42   continued

Property	Description
ListViewItemSorter	The sorting comparer for the control
MultiSelect	Indicates whether multiple items can be selected at once
Scrollable	Indicates whether scrollbars are automatically added as necessary
SelectedIndices	The zero-based indices of the selected items in the control
SelectedItems	The currently selected items in the control
SmallImageList	The ImageList control to use when displaying items as small icons
Sorting	The sort order for items in the control; uses values from the SortOrder enumeration
StateImageList	The ImageList control associated with application-defined states in the control
TopItem	The first visible item in the control
View	Indicates how items should be displayed in the control; uses values from the View enumeration

Method	Description
ArrangeIcons	Arranges items in the control when they are displayed as icons
BeginUpdate	Prevents the control from redrawing itself each time a new item is added until EndUpdate is called
Clear	Removes all items and columns from the control
EndUpdate	Resumes drawing for the control after BeginUpdate has been called
EnsureVisible	Ensures that the currently selected item is visible in the control by scrolling the control
GetItemAt	Retrieves the item as the specified location
GetItemRect	Returns the bounding Rectangle for a specified item
Sort	Sorts the items in the control

Event	Description
AfterLabelEdit	Occurs after an item's label is edited by the user
BeforeLabelEdit	Occurs before an item's label is edited by the user
ColumnClick	Occurs when the user clicks on a column header
ItemActivate	Occurs when an item is activated
ItemCheck	Occurs when an item is checked or unchecked
ItemDrag	Occurs when the user begins dragging an item
SelectedIndexChanged	Occurs when the index of the selected item changes

PictureBox

This control displays an image. Table B.43 lists the properties and event of this control.

TABLE B.43 Properties and Event of `PictureBox`

Property	Description
BorderStyle	The border style for the control; uses values from the `BorderStyle` enumeration
Image	The image to display in the control
SizeMode	Indicates how the image should be displayed; uses values from the `PictureBoxSizeMode` enumeration
Event	Description
SizeModeChanged	Occurs when the `SizeMode` property changes

PrintDocument

This control represents a document that is sent to the printer to print. It does not inherit from the `Control` class. Table B.44 lists the properties, method, and events of this control.

TABLE B.44 Properties, Method, and Events of `PrintDocument`

Property	Description
DefaultPageSettings	The `PageSettings` object that provides the defaults for all printed pages
DocumentName	The name of the document to be printed
PrintController	The print controller that guides the printing process
PrinterSettings	The `PrinterSettings` object that represents the printer to be used for printing
Method	Description
Print	Starts the document's printing process
Event	Description
BeginPrint	Occurs when the `Print` method is called but before any pages are printed
EndPrint	Occurs when the last page of the document has been printed
PrintPage	Occurs each time a page needs to be printed
QueryPageSettings	Occurs immediately before each `PrintPage` event

PrintPreviewControl

This control represents the actual previewing part of the `PrintPreviewDialog`. Note that this control can be used by itself outside of a `PrintPreviewDialog`. Table B.45 lists the properties and method of this control.

TABLE B.45   Properties and Method of the `PrintPreviewControl` Control

Property	Description
AutoZoom	Indicates whether resizing the control or changing the number of pages displayed automatically adjusts the `Zoom` property
Columns	The number of preview pages displayed horizontally in the control
Document	The `PrintDocument` to be previewed
Rows	The number of preview pages displayed vertically in the control
StartPage	The page number of the upper-left page displayed in the control
UseAntiAlias	Indicates whether the control should antialias the preview display to show a smoother image
Zoom	Indicates how large the previewed pages should be in the control
Method	*Description*
InvalidatePreview	Refreshes the view of the preview
StartPageChanged	Occurs when the `StartPage` property changes.

ProgressBar

This control represents a Windows progress bar. Table B.46 lists the properties and methods of this server control.

TABLE B.46   Properties and Methods of `ProgressBar`

Property	Description
Maximum	The maximum value or range of the control
Minimum	The minimum value or range of the control
Step	The amount by which the progress bar location should increase when the `PerformStep` method is called
Value	The current position of the progress bar
Method	*Description*
Increment	Advances the position of the progress bar by the specified amount
PerformStep	Advances the position of the progress bar by the amount in the `Step` property

Text Box Controls

There are two text box controls in the .NET Framework: `TextBox` and `RichTextBox`. Both of these controls inherit from the `TextBoxBase` class shown in Table B.47, which in turn inherits from `Control`.

TABLE B.47 Properties, Methods, and Events of `TextBoxBase`

Property	Description
AcceptsTab	Indicates whether pressing the Tab key displays a tab character in the control rather than forcing a move to the next control
AutoSize	Indicates whether the control should automatically adjust its size when the Font property changes
BorderStyle	The border style of the control; uses values from the BorderStyle enumeration
CanUndo	Indicates whether the user can undo a previous operation
HideSelection	Indicates whether highlighted text should remain highlighted when the control loses focus
Lines	An array of strings representing the lines in the control
MaxLength	The maximum number of characters that can be entered into the control
Modified	Indicates whether the control has been modified since the contents were first set
Multiline	Indicates whether the control can contain multiple lines of text
PreferredHeight	The preferred height of the control
ReadOnly	Indicates whether the contents of the control are editable
SelectedText	Gets or sets the currently selected text in the control
SelectionLength	The number of selected characters in the control
SelectionStart	The zero-based index of the character where the selection starts
TextLength	The length of text in the control
WordWrap	Indicates whether a multiline text box should automatically wrap lines that are too long to display

Method	Description
AppendText	Appends text to the end of the control
Clear	Removes all text from the control
ClearUndo	Clears information about the most recent operation in the undo buffer

TABLE B.47   continsued

Method	Description
Copy	Copies the current selection to the Clipboard
Cut	Removes the current selection from the control and places it in the Clipboard
Paste	Inserts the contents of the Clipboard into the current location in the control
ScrollToCaret	Scrolls the contents of the control to the cursor location
Select	Selects some text within the control
SelectAll	Selects all of the text within the control
Undo	Reverses the last operation performed in the control

Event	Description
AcceptsTabChanged	Occurs when the AcceptsTab property changes
AutoSizeChanged	Occurs when the AutoSize property changes
BorderStyleChanged	Occurs when the BorderStyle property changes
Click	Occurs when the control is clicked
HideSelectionChanged	Occurs when the HideSelection property changes
ModifiedChanged	Occurs when the Modified property changes
MultilineChanged	Occurs when the Multiline property changes
ReadOnlyChanged	Occurs when the ReadOnly property changes

RichTextBox

This control represents a text box that contains Rich Text formatting characters. Table B.48 lists the properties, methods, and events of this control.

TABLE B.48   Properties, Methods, and Events of RichTextBox

Property	Description
AutoWordSelection	Indicates whether an entire word should be automatically selected when one of its characters is selected
BulletIndent	The number of pixels a bullet should be indented in the control
CanRedo	Indicates whether there are operations that can be reapplied
DetectUrls	Indicates whether the control should automatically format a URL when it is typed in the control
RedoActionName	The name of the most recent operation that can be reapplied in the control

TABLE B.48 continued

Property	Description
RightMargin	The right edge of the editable portion of the control; determines how many characters can fit on one line
Rtf	The text contained in the control, including all Rich Text formatting codes
ScrollBars	Indicates how scrollbars should be shown in the control; uses values from the RichTextScrollBars enumeration
SelectedRtf	The currently selected text in the control, including the Rich Text formatting codes
SelectionAlignment	The alignment to apply to the currently selected text; uses values from the HorizontalAlignment enumeration
SelectionBullet	Indicates whether a bullet is applied to the current selection
SelectionCharOffset	Indicates whether the selected text should appear as baseline, superscript, or subscript
SelectionColor	The color of highlighted text
SelectionFont	The font of the currently selected text
SelectionHangingIndent	The distance between the left edge of the first line of text in the selected paragraph and the left edge of subsequent lines in the same paragraph
SelectionIndent	The distance in pixels that the current selection should be indented
SelectionProtected	Indicates whether the current selection is protected; when such text is edited, the Protected event will be raised
SelectionRightIndent	The distance in pixels between the right edge of the control and the right edge of the currently selected text
SelectionTabs	The tab stop positions in the control
SelectionType	The type of the current selection; uses values from the RichTextBoxSelectionTypes enumeration
ShowSelectionMargin	Indicates whether a left margin that allows the user to select multiple lines at once should be shown
UndoActionName	The name of the most recent operation that can be undone
ZoomFactor	The zoom level of the control

Method	Description
CanPaste	Indicates whether you can paste content from the Clipboard into the current position in the control
Find	Searches for text in the control
GetCharFromPosition	Retrieves the character that is closest to the specified Point

TABLE B.48   continued

Method	Description
GetCharIndexFromPosition	Retrieves the zero-based character index that is closest to the specified `Point`
GetLineFromCharIndex	Retrieves the line that the specified character index is on
LoadFile	Loads the contents of a file into the control
Redo	Reapplies the last operation performed in the control
SaveFile	Saves the contents of the control to a file

Event	Description
ContentsResized	Occurs when the contents of the control are resized
HScroll	Occurs when the user scrolls horizontally through the control
ImeChange	Occurs when the user switches input methods on Asian versions of Windows
LinkClicked	Occurs when the user clicks a hyperlink in the control
Protected	Occurs when the user tries to edit a selection marked with the `Protected` property
SelectionChanged	Occurs when the current selection in the control changes
VScroll	Occurs when the user scrolls vertically through the control

TextBox

This control represents a simple text box that can contain text, but no formatting. Table B.49 lists the properties and event of this control.

TABLE B.49   Properties and Event of `TextBox`

Property	Description
AcceptsReturn	Indicates whether pressing the Enter key adds a new line to the control rather than activating the default button of the containing form
CharacterCasing	Indicates whether the control modifies the casing of characters as they are entered; uses values from the `CharacterCasing` enumeration
PasswordChar	The character that should be used to mask typed characters of a password
ScrollBars	Indicates whether scrollbars should be displayed in a multiline text box; uses values from the `ScrollBars` enumeration
TextAlign	The alignment of text in the control; uses values from the `HorizontalAlignment` enumeration

TABLE B.49   continued

Event	Description
TextAlignChanged	Occurs when the TextAlign property changes

Status Bar Controls

The StatusBar control represents a status bar in a Windows application. It can contain StatusBarPanel controls that display data. Table B.50 lists the properties and events of this control.

TABLE B.50   Properties and Events of StatusBar

Property	Description
Panels	A collection of the StatuBarPanels in this control
ShowPanels	Indicates whether this control should display contained StatusBarPanels
SizingGrip	Indicates whether a sizing grip is displayed in the lower-right corner of the status bar
Event	Description
DrawItem	Occurs when a visual aspect of an owner-drawn control changes
PanelClick	Occurs when the user clicks one of this control's contained StatusBarPanel controls

Table B.51 lists the properties of the StatusBarPanel control. This control does not inherit from the Control class.

TABLE B.51   Properties of StatusBarPanel

Property	Description
Alignment	The alignment of the contents within the panel; uses values from the HorizontalAlignment enumeration
AutoSize	Indicates whether the control should automatically adjust its size based on the size of the containing StatusBar control; uses values from the StatusBarPanelAutoSize enumeration
BorderStyle	The border style for this control; uses values from the BorderStyle enumeration
Icon	The icon to display within the control

TABLE B.51   continued

Property	Description
MinWidth	The minimum width of the panel with the containing StatusBar control
Parent	The parent StatusBar control
Style	The style of this control; uses values from the StatusBarPanel enumeration
Text	The text to display in the control
ToolTipText	The text to display as a ToolTip for this control
Width	The width of the control within the containing StatusBar control

TabControl

A TabControl represents the structure for a tabbed panel view in an application. It contains TabPage controls that represent each individual tab. Table B.52 lists the properties, method, and event of the TabControl control.

TABLE B.52   Properties, Method, and Event of TabControl

Property	Description
Alignment	The alignment of tabs in the control; uses values from the TabAlignment enumeration
Appearance	The style of the tab control; uses values from the TabAppearance enumeration
DrawMode	Indicates how tabs are drawn within the control; uses values from the TabDrawMode enumeration
HotTrack	Indicates whether the tabs change appearance when the mouse cursor is moved over them
ImageList	An ImageList control that contains images to use for each tab
ItemSize	The size of the control's tabs
Multiline	Indicates whether tabs should appear on multiple lines
Padding	The space in pixels around each item on a TabPage
RowCount	The number of rows of tabs in the tab control
SelectedIndex	The zero-based index of the currently selected tab
SelectedTab	The currently selected TabPage object
ShowToolTips	Indicates whether ToolTips should be shown for a tab when the mouse cursor passes over it

TABLE B.52 continued

Property	Description
SizeMode	The way in which tabs are sized; uses values from the TabSizeMode property
TabCount	The number of tabs in this control
TabPages	A collection of the TabPage controls in this control
Method	*Description*
GetTabRect	Returns the bounding rectangle for the specified tab
Event	*Description*
DrawItem	Occurs when the tabs are drawn and the DrawMode property is set to OwnerDrawFixed

B

Timer

Timer represents a timer that raises events at a specified time interval. This control does not inherit from Control. Table B.53 lists the properties, methods, and event of this control.

TABLE B.53 Properties, Methods, and Event of Timer

Property	Description
Enabled	Indicates whether the timer is currently running
Interval	The time interval at which the timer should raise the Tick event
Method	*Description*
Start	Starts the timer
Stop	Stops the timer
Event	*Description*
Tick	Occurs when the specified timer interval has elapsed

Toolbar Controls

This control represents the structure of a Windows toolbar. It can contain ToolBarButton controls that represent the actual buttons on the toolbar. Table B.54 lists the properties and events of this control.

TABLE B.54   Properties and Events of `ToolBar`

Property	Description
Appearance	The style of the toolbar; uses values from the `ToolBarAppearance` enumeration
AutoSize	Indicates whether the toolbar should automatically adjust its size based on the buttons it contains
BorderStyle	The style of the border for this control uses values from the `BorderStyle` enumeration
Buttons	The collection of `ToolBarButtons` on this control
ButtonSize	The size of the buttons in this control
Divider	Indicates whether the toolbar displays a divider
DropDownArrows	Indicates whether drop-down style buttons on the toolbar should display drop-down arrows
ImageList	The `ImageList` control that is used to associate images with this toolbar
ImageSize	The size of the images in the associated `ImageList` control
ShowToolTips	Indicates whether ToolTips should be shown for each `ToolBarButton`
TextAlign	The alignment of text in each button relative to the image in the button
Wrappable	Indicates whether the toolbar buttons form a new line in order to show all available toolbar buttons
Event	Description
ButtonClick	Occurs when a `ToolBarButton` in this control is clicked
ButtonDropDown	Occurs when a drop-down style `ToolBarButton` is clicked

The `ToolBarButton` control represents the buttons on a `ToolBar`, and does not inherit from the `Control` class. Table B.55 lists properties of this control.

TABLE B.55   Properties of `ToolBarButton`

Property	Description
DropDownMenu	The `Menu`-derived control that should be shown as the drop-down menu for this button
Enabled	Indicates whether the button allows user interaction
ImageIndex	The index of the image in the containing `ToolBar`'s `ImageList` property

TABLE B.55 continued

Property	Description
Parent	The containing `ToolBar` control
PartialPush	Indicates whether a button can show a partially-pushed appearance
Pushed	Indicates whether a button should appear pushed in
Rectangle	The bounding `Rectangle` for this button
Style	The style of this button; uses values from the `ToolBarButtonStyle` enumeration
Tag	The object that contains data about the control
Text	The text displayed on the Toolbar button
ToolTipText	The ToolTip text that should be shown when the mouse cursor rests over the button
Visible	Indicates whether the button should be shown

ToolTip

This control represents a pop-up window that appears when the user rests the mouse cursor over a control. This window should display helpful information on the use of the control. `ToolTip` does not inherit from the `Control` class. Table B.56 lists the properties and methods of this control.

TABLE B.56 Properties and Methods of the `ToolTip` Control

Property	Description
Active	Indicates whether the ToolTip is currently active
AutomaticDelay	The automatic delay in milliseconds for the ToolTip; this property automatically sets the `AutoPopDelay`, `InitialDelay`, and `ReshowDelay` properties
AutoPopDelay	The amount of time that the ToolTip will remain visible
InitialDelay	The amount of time that the mouse cursor must rest over the control before the ToolTip will appear
ReshowDelay	The time that must transpire between the disappearance of one ToolTip and the appearance of another
ShowAlways	Indicates whether the ToolTip should be displayed when the parent control is not active

TABLE B.56   continued

Method	Description
GetToolTip	Retrieves the Tool Tip associated with the specified control
RemoveAll	Removes the text associated with this ToolTip
SetToolTip	Sets the text associated with this ToolTip

TrackBar

This control represents a Windows trackbar; a scrollable control similar to ScrollBar. Table B.57 lists the properties, method, and events of this control.

TABLE B.57   Properties, Method, and Events of TrackBar

Property	Description
AutoSize	Indicates whether the trackbar is automatically sized
LargeChange	The value to be added to or subtracted from the Value property when the scroll box is moved a great distance (typically when the user clicks the scrollbar above or below the scroll box)
Maximum	The maximum value of the Value property
Minimum	The minimum value of the Value property
Orientation	Indicates the horizontal or vertical orientation of the trackbar; uses values from the Orientation enumeration
SmallChange	The value to be added or subtracted from the Value property when the scroll box is moved a short distance (typically when the user clicks the arrows on the scrollbar, or directly moves the scroll box)
TickFrequency	The value between ticks on the control
TickStyle	The style of ticks on the control; uses values from the TickStyle enumeration
Value	A numeric value that represents the current position of the scroll box

Method	Description
SetRange	Sets the minimum and maximum values for the trackbar

Event	Description
Scroll	Occurs when the scroll box has been moved
ValueChanged	Occurs when the Value property has changed

TreeView Controls

This control represents a hierarchical collection of labeled items. It can contain any number of nested `TreeNode` controls that represent each item. Table B.58 lists the properties, methods, and events of this control.

TABLE B.58   Properties, Methods, and Events of `TreeView`

Property	Description
BorderStyle	The border style for this control; uses values from the `BorderStyle` enumeration
CheckBoxes	Indicates whether check boxes should be shown next to each item in the `TreeView`
FullRowSelect	Indicates whether the selection highlight spans the entire length of the `TreeView`, or just the label of the node
HideSelection	Indicates whether a selected item should remain highlighted if the control goes out of focus
HotTracking	Indicates whether the items in the `TreeView` should change appearance as the mouse cursor moves over them
ImageIndex	The index of the image in the `ImageList` control associated with this `TreeView` that is the default image for items
ImageList	An `ImageList` control that contains images to display for each item in the `TreeView`
Indent	The distance in pixels to indent each node level
ItemHeight	The height of each item in the control
LabelEdit	Indicates whether the labels for each item are editable
Nodes	Returns a collection of `TreeNode` controls that represent the items in the `TreeView`
PathSeparator	The delimiter string that the tree node path uses
Scrollable	Indicates whether this control displays scrollbars as necessary
SelectedImageIndex	The associated `ImageList` index value of the image that is displayed for the currently selected item in the control
SelectedNode	The `TreeNode` that is currently selected
ShowLines	Indicates whether lines are drawn between the items in this control
ShowPlusMinus	Indicates whether plus and minus signs are displayed next to those items that have subitems
ShowRootLines	Indicates whether lines are drawn between items at the root level of the control

B

TABLE B.58   continued

Property	Description
Sorted	Indicates whether items should automatically be sorted
TopNode	The first fully visible item in the control
VisibleCount	The number of fully visible items in the control

Method	Description
BeginUpdate	Prevents the control from redrawing itself each time a new item is added until EndUpdate is called
CollapseAll	Collapses all expanded nodes in the list
EndUpdate	Resumes drawing for the control after BeginUpdate has been called
ExpandAll	Expands all collapsed nodes in the list
GetNodeAt	Retrieves the node that is nearest the specified Point
GetNodeCount	Retrieves the number of items in the list, optionally including all subtrees

Event	Description
AfterCheck	Occurs after a check box next to an item is checked
AfterCollapse	Occurs after an item is collapsed
AfterExpand	Occurs after an item is expanded
AfterLabelEdit	Occurs after an item's label is edited
AfterSelect	Occurs after an item is selected
BeforeCheck	Occurs before a check box next to an item is checked
BeforeCollapse	Occurs before an item is collapsed
BeforeExpand	Occurs before an item is expanded
BeforeLabelEdit	Occurs before an item's label is edited
BeforeSelect	Occurs before an item is selected
ItemDrag	Occurs when the user drags an item in the list

The TreeNode control represents each item in a TreeView control. Each TreeNode can have subnodes to form a hierarchical view. It does not derive from the Control class. Table B.59 lists the properties and methods of this control.

TABLE B.59   Properties and Methods of TreeNode

Property	Description
BackColor	The background color of the node
Bounds	The bounding Rectangle of the node

TABLE B.59   continued

Property	Description
Checked	Indicates whether the node is checked
FirstNode	Gets the first child node in the collection
ForeColor	The foreground color of the node
FullPath	The TreeView path from the root level to the current node
Handle	The handle for the node
ImageIndex	The index of the image in the containing TreeView's ImageList property to display for the current node
Index	The index of the current node in the list
IsEditing	Indicates whether the node is in an editable state
IsExpanded	Indicates whether the node is expanded
IsSelected	Indicates whether the node is selected
IsVisible	Indicates whether the node is currently visible
LastNode	Gets the last child node in the collection
NextNode	Gets the next node in the collection
NextVisibleNode	Gets the next fully visible node in the collection
NodeFont	The font used to display the text in the node
Nodes	A collection of the child TreeNode objects of this node
Parent	The parent TreeNode of the current node
PrevNode	Gets the previous node in the collection
PrevVisibleNode	Gets the previous fully visible node in the collection
SelectedImageIndex	Gets the index of the image in the containing TreeView's ImageList property that is to be used when the node is selected
Tag	The object that contains information about the node
Text	The text to display in the node
TreeView	Retrieves the containing TreeView control

Method	Description
BeginEdit	Attempts to put the node in a state where editing is allowed
Clone	Makes a copy the TreeNode and all of its child nodes
Collapse	Collapses the current node
EndEdit	Stops the edit-mode called by BeginEdit
EnsureVisible	Ensures that the current node is visible by scrolling and expanding the containing TreeView

B

TABLE B.59   continued

Method	Description
Expand	Expands the current node
ExpandAll	Expands all nodes in the collection
FromHandle	Gets the TreeNode associated with the specified TreeView control and handle
GetNodeCount	Gets the number of TreeNodes that belong to this node
Remove	Removes the current node from the collection
Toggle	Toggles the node to either the expanded or collapsed state

APPENDIX **C**

ADO.NET Controls: Properties and Methods

ADO.NET consists of two main parts: the DataSet and its related classes, and the Managed Providers that facilitate communication with data sources. This appendix describes the classes in each of these parts.

The DataSet and Related Classes

The following are the details for the DataSet and related items, such as DataRelation, DataTable, and so on.

Constraint and ConstraintCollection

This Constraint class represents a rule on a table that limits the data that can be modified. Table C.1 lists the properties of the Constraint class.

TABLE C.1 Properties of the Constraint Class

Property	Description
ConstraintName	The name of this constraint.
ExtendedProperties	Retrieves a collection of user-defined properties.
Table	Returns DataTable to which this constraint applies.

Table C.2 lists the property, methods, and event of the ConstraintCollection class.

TABLE C.2 Property, Methods, and Event of the ConstraintCollection Class

Property	Description
Item	Gets a constraint in the collection with either the name of the constraint or its index in the collection.
Method	**Description**
Add	Adds a constraint to the collection. This method is overloaded. See the .NET Framework SDK documentation for more information.
AddRange	Copies the elements from another ConstraintCollection object into the current one.
CanRemove	Indicates if a constraint specified by *Constraint* can be removed from the DataTable.
Clear	Clears the collection of all Constraint objects.
Contains	Indicates if the Constraint with the name *name* exists in the collection.
IndexOf	Retrieves the index of the specified constraint. This method is overloaded. See the .NET Framework SDK documentation for more information.
Remove	Removes the specified constraint from the collection. This method is overloaded. See the .NET Framework SDK documentation for more information.
RemoveAt	Removes the Constraint at the specified index.
Event	**Description**
CollectionChanged	Occurs when the collection is changed through additions or removals. Uses a CollectionChangeEventArgs object for the event parameter. This object contains the following properties:
	Action—Returns a value (Add, Remove, Refresh) indicating how the collection has changed.
	Element—Returns the instance of the collection that changed.

DataColumn and DataColumnCollection

A `DataColumn` represents a column of information in a `DataTable`. Table C.3 lists the properties and method of the `DataColumn` class.

TABLE C.3 Properties and Method of the `DataColumn` Class

Property	Description
AllowDBNull	Indicates if null values are allowed in this column.
AutoIncrement	Indicates if the value of the column automatically increments with the addition of a new row.
AutoIncrementSeed	The starting value for `AutoIncrement`.
AutoIncrementStep	The increment value used by `AutoIncrement`.
Caption	The caption for this column.
ColumnMapping	Returns a `MappingType` object indicating how the column is mapped when written as XML.
ColumnName	The name of the column.
DataType	The type of data stored in this column.
DefaultValue	The default value for this column when creating new rows.
Expression	A string expression used to filter rows, calculate the column's value, or create an aggregate column.
ExtendedProperties	Returns a `PropertyCollection` of custom user information.
MaxLength	The maximum length of a text column.
Namespace	The XML namespace containing the elements used in this column.
Ordinal	The position of this column in the `DataColumnCollection`.
Prefix	The prefix used for this column when represented as XML.
ReadOnly	Indicates if the column allows changes.
Table	Returns `DataTable` to which this column belongs.
Unique	Indicates if each value in the column must be unique.
Method	**Description**
ToString	Returns the `Expression` of this column, if one exists.

Table C.4 lists the property, methods, and event of the `DataColumnCollection` class.

C

TABLE C.4   Property, Methods, and Event of the `DataColumnCollection` Class

Property	Description
Item	Gets a `DataColumn` in the collection with either the name of the column or its index in the collection.

Method	Description
Add	Adds a column to the collection. This method is overloaded. See the .NET Framework SDK documentation for more information.
AddRange	Adds an array of `DataColumn` objects to the collection.
CanRemove	Indicates if a column specified by *Column* can be removed from the collection.
Clear	Clears the collection of all `DataColumn`objects.
Contains	Indicates if the `DataColumn` with the name *name* exists in the collection.
IndexOf	Retrieves the index of the specified column. This method is overloaded. See the .NET Framework SDK documentation for more information.
Remove	Removes the specified column from the collection. This method is overloaded. See the .NET Framework SDK documentation for more information.
RemoveAt	Removes the `DataColumn` at the specified index.

Event	Description
CollectionChanged	Occurs when the collection is changed through additions or removals. Uses a `CollectionChangeEventArgs` object for the event parameter. This object contains the following properties:
	`Action`—Returns a value (`Add`, `Remove`, `Refresh`) indicating how the collection has changed.
	`Element`—Returns the instance of the collection that changed.

DataRelation and DataRelationCollection

A `DataRelation` class represents the relationship between multiple tables in the `DataSet`. Table C.5 lists the properties of the `DataRelation` class.

TABLE C.5 Properties of the `DataRelation` Class

Property	Description
ChildColumns	Returns an array of `DataColumn` objects that represent the child columns of this relation.
ChildKeyConstraint	A `ForeignKeyConstraint` object for this relation.
ChildTable	Returns a `DataTable` representing the child table of this relation.
DataSet	Returns the `DataSet` to which this relation belongs to.
ExtendedProperties	Returns a `PropertyCollection` of custom user information.
Nested	Indicates if relations are nested.
ParentColumns	An array of `DataColumn` objects that represent the parent columns of this relation.
ParentKeyConstraint	A `UniqueConstraint` object for this relation.
ParentTable	Returns the `DataTable` representing the parent table of this relation.
RelationName	The name of this relation.

Table C.6 lists the property, methods, and event of the `DataRelationCollection` class.

TABLE C.6 Property, Methods, and Event of the `DataRelationCollection` Class

Property	Description
Item	Gets a `DataRelation` in the collection with either the name of the relation or its index in the collection.
Method	**Description**
Add	Adds a relation to the collection. This method is overloaded. See the .NET Framework SDK Documentation for more information.
AddRange	Adds an array of `DataRelation` objects to the collection.
CanRemove	Verifies whether the specified `DataRelation` can be removed from the collection.
Clear	Clears the collection of all `DataRelation` objects.
Contains	Indicates if the `DataRelation` with the name *name* exists in the collection.
IndexOf	Returns the index of the specified `DataRelation`.
Remove overloaded. See the	Removes the specified relation from the collection. This method is .NET Framework SDK Documentation for more information.
RemoveAt	Removes the `DataRelation` at the specified index.

TABLE C.6   continued

Event	Description
CollectionChanged	Occurs when the collection is changed through additions or removals. Uses a CollectionChangeEventArgs object for the event parameter. This object contains the following properties:
	Action—Returns a value (Add, Remove, Refresh) indicating how the collection has changed.
	Element—Returns the instance of the collection that changed.

DataRow and DataRowCollection

A DataRow represents a row of information in a DataTable, that is, an individual record of data. Table C.7 lists the properties and methods of the DataRow class.

TABLE C.7   Properties and Methods of the DataRow Class

Property	Description
HasErrors	Indicates if the data in the row contains any errors.
Item	Specifies the data contained in the specified column. The method is overloaded. See the .NET Framework SDK documentation for more details.
ItemArray	Specifies the data contained in the entire row, through an array.
RowError	The custom error description for the row.
RowState	The state of the row. Can be Detached, Unchanged, New, Deleted, or Modified.
Table	Returns DataTable to which this row belongs.

Method	Description
AcceptChanges	Commits all changes made to the row.
BeginEdit	Begins an edit operation on the row.
CancelEdit	Cancels an edit operation, repealing edits.
ClearErrors	Clears all errors for the row.
Delete	Deletes the row.
EndEdit	Ends the edit operation on the row.
GetChildRows	Returns an array of DataRow objects representing the child rows of this row, when using the specified DataRelation.
GetColumnError	Gets the error for a specified column in the row. This method is overloaded. See the .NET Framework SDK documentation for more information.

TABLE C.7 continued

Method	Description
GetColumnsInError	Gets an array of DataColumn objects that have errors.
GetParentRow	Returns a DataRow representing the parent of this row. This method is overloaded. See the .NET Framework SDK documentation for more details.
GetParentRows	Returns an array of DataRow objects representing the parent of this row using the specified DataRelation. This method is overloaded. See the .NET Framework SDK documentation for more details.
HasVersion	Indicates if a specified version of the row exists.
IsNull	Indicates if the specified column in the row contains a null value. This method is overloaded. See the .NET Framework SDK documentation for more details.
RejectChanges	Rolls back all changes made to the row.
SetColumnError	Sets the error description for the column. This method is overloaded.
SetParentRow	Sets the parent row of a given child row. This method is overloaded.

Table C.8 lists the property and methods of the DataRowCollection class.

TABLE C.8 Property and Methods of the DataRowCollection Class

Property	Description
Item	Gets a DataRow in the collection with either the name of the row or its index in the collection.

Method	Description
Add	Adds a row to the collection. This method is overloaded.
Clear	Clears the collection of all DataRow objects.
Contains	Indicates if the DataRow with the name *name* exists in the collection.
Find	Gets a specified DataRow. This method is overloaded.
InsertAt	Inserts a new DataRow at the specified location.
Remove	Removes the specified row from the collection. This method is overloaded.
RemoveAt	Removes the DataRow at the specified index.

DataSet

Table C.9 lists the properties, methods, and event of the DataSet class, which represents a disconnected data source.

TABLE C.9　Properties, Methods, and Event of the DataSet Class

Property	Description
CaseSensitive	Indicates if string comparisons in a DataTable are case-sensitive.
DataSetName	The name of this DataSet.
DefaultViewManager	Returns a DataViewManager that contains a customized view of the data in the DataSet.
EnforceConstraints	Indicates if constraint rules are followed when updating the data.
ExtendedProperties	A PropertyCollection object containing custom user information.
HasErrors	Indicates if the data in any of the rows of this DataSet contain errors.
Locale	The locale information used to compare strings. Returns a CultureInfo object.
Namsespace	Indicates the namespace of the DataSet.
Prefix	An XML alias for the namespace of the DataSet.
Relations	A DataRelationCollection object that represents all relations between tables in the DataSet.
Site	Returns an ISite interface for the DataSet (used to bind components to containers).
Tables	A DataTableCollection object representing all tables in the DataSet.

Method	Description
AcceptChanges	Commits all changes made to the DataSet.
Clear	Removes all rows in all tables in the DataSet.
Clone	Produces a DataSet identical to the current DataSet, without data.
Copy	Produces a DataSet identical to the current DataSet, with data.
GetChanges	Produces a DataSet that contains only the data that has changed.
GetXml	Returns the data in the DataSet in XML format.
GetXmlSchema	Returns the XML schema for the data in the DataSet.
HasChanges	Indicates if the data in the DataSet has changed at all.
InferXmlSchema	Builds the data structure from an XML data source. This function is overloaded; see the .NET SDK documentation for more details.
Merge	Merges the specified DataSet with the one specified.
ReadXml	Inserts data and schema information from an XML file in a DataSet.
ReadXmlSchema	Builds the data structure from an XML schema. This function is overloaded; see the .NET SDK documentation for more details.

TABLE C.9   continued

Method	Description
RejectChanges	Undoes all changes that have been made to this DataSet.
Reset	Resets the DataSet to its default properties.
WriteXml	Writes the content of the DataSet in XML format. This function is overloaded; see the .NET SDK documentation for more details.
WriteXmlSchema	Writes the structure of the DataSet in XML format. This function is overloaded; see the .NET SDK Documentation for more details.

Event	Description
MergeFailed	Occurs when a target and source DataRow have the same primary key value, and EnforceConstraints is true.

DataTable and DataTableCollection

A DataTable represents a table of information in a DataSet. Table C.10 lists the properties, methods, and events of the DataTable class.

TABLE C.10   Properties, Methods, and Events of the DataTable Class

Property	Description
CaseSensitive	Indicates if string comparisons in the table are case-sensitive.
ChildRelations	Returns a DataRelationCollection of the child relations of this table.
Columns	Returns a DataColumnCollection object representing the column in this table.
Constraints	Returns a DataRelationCollection object representing the data relations in this table.
DataSet	Returns the DataSet this table belongs to.
DefaultView	Returns a DataView representing a customized view of the data in this table.
DisplayExpression	A string expression that returns a value indicating how to display this table in the UI.
ExtendedProperties	Returns a PropertyCollection of custom user information.
HasErrors	Indicates if there are any errors in any of the rows of this table.
Locale	A CultureInfo object used to determine how strings are compared.
MinimumCapacity	The initial starting size for this table.
Namespace	The XML namespace containing the elements used in this table.

TABLE C.10   continued

Property	Description
ParentRelations	A DataRelationCollection of the parent relations of this table.
Prefix	The prefix used for this table when represented as XML.
PrimaryKey	An array of DataColumn objects that serve as the primary keys of the table.
Rows	A DataRowCollection object representing the rows belonging to this table.
Site	Returns an ISite interface for the DataTable (used to bind components to containers).
TableName	The name of the table.

Method	Description
AcceptChanges	Commits all changes made to this table.
BeginInit	Begins the initialization of this table.
BeginLoadData	Begins the data loading process.
Clear	Clears the table of all data.
Clone	Makes a copy of the DataTable's structure, including all its relations.
Compute	Computes the expression specified in the first parameter on the rows that pass the specified filter.
Copy	Copies both the structure and data contained in the DataTable.
EndInit	Ends the initialization process.
EndLoadData	Ends the data loading process.
GetChanges	Gets a copy of the DataTable that contains only the changes made to it since it was first created, or since AcceptChanges was called.
GetErrors	An array of DataRow objects that contain errors.
ImportRow	Copies a DataRow object into the DataTable.
LoadDataRow	Finds and updates a DataRow with the specified values. If a row is not found, a new one is created.
NewRow	Returns a blank DataRow with the same schema as the table.
RejectChanges	Rolls back all changes made to the table since it was first loaded or since AcceptChanges was last called.
Reset	Resets the DataTable to its default properties.
Select	Returns an array of DataRow objects. This method is overloaded.
ToString	Returns the TableName and DisplayExpression of this table.

TABLE C.10   continued

Event	Description
ColumnChanged	Occurs when a column has changed. Uses a DataColumnChangedEventArgs object for the event parameter. This object contains the following properties: Column—The column that changed. ProposedValue—The value to change to column to. Row—The DataRow to change.
ColumnChanging	Occurs when changes have been submitted for this column. Uses a DataColumnChangedEventArgs object.
RowChanged	Occurs when a row has changed. Uses a DataRowChangedEventArgs object for the event parameter. This object contains the following properties: Action—The action that occurred on the DataRow. Row—The DataRow to change.
RowChanging	Occurs when changes have been submitted for this column. Uses a DataRowChangedEventArgs object.
RowDeleted	Occurs after a row is deleted. Uses a DataRowChangedEventArgs object.
RowDeleting	Occurs before a row is deleted. Uses a DataRowChangedEventArgs object.

Table C.11 lists the property, methods, and events of the DataTableCollection class.

TABLE C.11   Property, Methods, and Events of the DataTableCollection Class

Property	Description
Item	Gets a DataTable in the collection with either the name of the table or its index in the collection.

Methods	Description
Add	Adds a table to the collection. This method is overloaded.
AddRange	Adds an array of DataTable objects to the collection.
CanRemove	Indicates if the table specified can be removed from the collection.
Clear	Clears the collection of all DataTableobjects.
Contains	Indicates if the DataTable with the specified name exists in the collection.
IndexOf	Retrieves the index of the specified table. This method is overloaded.

C

TABLE C.11 Property, Methods, and Events of the `DataTableCollection` Class

Methods	Description
Remove	Removes the specified table from the collection. This method is overloaded.
RemoveAt	Removes the `DataTable` at the specified index.

Event	Description
CollectionChanged	Occurs when the collection is changed through additions or removals. Uses a `CollectionChangeEventArgs` object for the event parameter. This object contains the following properties:
	`Action`—Returns a value (`Add`, `Remove`, `Refresh`) indicating how the collection has changed. `Element`—Returns the instance of the collection that changed.
CollectionChanging	Occurs before the collection is changed. Uses a `CollectionChangeEventArgs` object.

DataView

A `DataView` class represents a customized view of the data in a `DataSet`. Table C.12 lists the properties, methods, and event of the `DataView` class.

TABLE C.12 Properties, Methods, and Event of the `DataView` Class

Property	Description
AllowDelete	Indicates if deletes are allowed in this view.
AllowEdit	Indicates if edits are allowed in this view.
AllowNew	Indicates if new rows can be added in this view.
ApplyDefaultSort	Indicates if the default sort should be used.
Count	Returns the number of records in the `DataView`.
DataViewManager	The `DataView` that created this view (a pointer to the `DataSetView` that owns the corresponding `DataSet`).
Item	Gets a specified row of data from a table.
RowFilter	An expression used to filter which rows are added to the `DataView`.
RowStateFilter	Specifies which version of rows is added to the `DataView`. Can be `None`, `Unchanged`, `New`, `Deleted`, `ModifiedCurrent`, `ModifiedOriginal`, `OriginalRows`, and `CurrentRows` (default).
Sort	The columns to sort by.
Table	The source `DataTable` from which to pull data.

TABLE C.12 continued

Methods	Description
AddNew	Adds a new row to the DataView.
BeginInit	Begins the initialization of this DataView.
CopyTo	Copies items into an array.
Delete	Deletes a row at the specified index.
EndInit	Ends the initialization process.
Find	Finds a specified row in the DataView. This method is overloaded.
FindRows	Returns an array of DataRowView objects that match the specified criteria.
GetEnumerator	Returns an IEnumerator that can be used to iterate through this DataView.

Event	Description
ListChanged	Occurs when the list managed by the DataView changes. Uses a ListChangedEventArgs object for the event parameter. This object contains the following properties: ListChangedType—The way the list changed. NewIndex—The new index of the item that changed. OldIndex—The old index of the item that changed.

The Managed Providers

Managed providers allow ADO.NET to interact with any type of OleDB-Compliant data source. These providers are used to move data into the DataSet and its related classes, and can be used independently to modify data as well.

There are two managed providers: OleDB and SQL. The former deals with all OleDB compliant data stores, while the latter deals only with SQL Server. In nearly all cases, classes in one provider correspond exactly to classes in the other; the only difference is the use of a prefix: OleDb and Sql. For instance, both providers have a class that provides lightweight access to data, respectively named OleDbDataReader and SqlDataReader.

Because of the similarities of these two providers, only the OleDb managed provider is covered here. Where there are differences in the two, a note is made.

OleDbCommand

The OleDbCommand class represents a SQL statement to be made to a data source. Table C.13 lists the properties and methods of this class.

TABLE C.13   Properties and Methods of the OleDbCommand Class

Property	Description
CommandText	The SQL statement to execute.
CommandTimeout	The time limit in which the command must execute before termination.
CommandType	Specifies how the CommandText property is interpreted. Can be StoredProcedure, TableDirect, or Text (default).
Connection	Specifies an OleDbConnection used by this object.
DesignTimeVisible	Indicates if the command object should be visible in a custom Windows Forms designer control.
Parameters	Gets an OleDbParameterCollection object representing the parameters for use with this command.
Transaction	The OleDbTransaction used by the command.
UpdatedRowSource	The number of records affected by the command. Typically 1 if the command succeeds, and less than 1 otherwise.

Method	Description
Cancel	Cancels the execution of the command.
CreateParameter	Creates an OleDbParameter for use with this command.
ExecuteNonQuery	Executes an SQL statement that doesn't return any data.
ExecuteReader	Returns an OleDbDataReader filled with the data returned from the command.
ExecuteScalar	Executes the query, and returns values in the first column and first row of the returned results.
Prepare	Creates a compiled version of the command.
ResetCommandTimeout	Resets the CommandTimeout property to the default value.

OleDbCommandBuilder

The OleDbCommandBuilder class represents an easy way to generate commands for use against a data source. Table C.14 lists the properties and methods of this class.

TABLE C.14 Properties and Methods of the `OleDbCommandBuilder` Class

Property	Description
DataAdapter	The name of an `OleDbDataAdapter` for which the commands are generated.
QuotePrefix	Specifies a prefix to use when specifying data source object names (such as "tbl" for tables, "sp" for stored procedures, and so forth).
QuoteSuffix	Specifies a suffix to use when specifying data source object names.

Method	Description
DeriveParameters	Fills the `OleDbCommand`'s `Parameters` collection with values specified in the stored procedure.
GetDeleteCommand	Gets the automatically generated SQL statement to delete rows from the data source.
GetInsertCommand	Gets the automatically generated SQL statement to insert rows into the data source.
GetUpdateCommand	Gets the automatically generated SQL statement to update rows in the data source.
RefreshSchema	Retrieves the schema of the data source.

OleDbConnection

The `OleDbConnection` class represents a connection to a data source. Table C.15 lists the properties, methods, and events of this class.

TABLE C.15 Properties, Methods, and Events of the `OleDbConnection` Class

Property	Description
ConnectionString	The string used to open a database.
ConnectionTimeout	The time limit for establishing a connection to the database, after which an error will be generated.
Database	The name of the database to use once the connection is established.
DataSource	The name of the database to connect to.
Provider	The name of the database provider.
ServerVersion	A string containing the version of the server to which the client is connected.
State	The current state of the connection.

TABLE C.15   continued

Method	Description
BeginTransaction	Begins a database transaction. This method is overloaded.
ChangeDatabase	Changes the current database to another specified value.
Close	Closes the database connection.
CreateCommand	Returns an OleDbCommand object to execute commands against the database.
GetOleDbSchemaTable	Returns schema information from a data source specified by a GUID. (This method does not exist in the corresponding SqlConnection class.)
Open	Attempts to open the connection to the database.
ReleaseObjectPool	Indicates that the OleDbConnection object pooling can be cleared when the last underlying OLE DB Provider is released.

Event	Description
InfoMessage	Occurs when the provider sends a message. Uses an OleDbInfoMessageEventArgs object for the event parameter. This object contains the following properties:
	ErrorCode—An HRESULT value indicating the standard error. Errors—An OleDbErrorCollection of warnings sent by the provider. Message—The full text of the error message sent from the provider. Source—The name of the object that generated the error.
StateChange	Occurs when the state of the connection changes. Uses a StateChangeEventArgs for the event parameter. This object contains the following properties:
	CurrentState—The new state of the connection. OriginalState—The original state of the connection.

OleDbDataAdapter

The OleDbDataAdapter class represents a set of data commands and a database connection that are used to fill a DataSet. Table C.16 lists the properties, methods, and events of this class.

TABLE C.16 Properties, Methods, and Events of the `OleDbDataAdapter` Class

Property	Description
DeleteCommand	Returns an `OleDbCommand` object that contains a SQL statement for deleting data from the `DataSet`.
InsertCommand	Returns an `OleDbCommand` object that contains a SQL statement for inserting data into the `DataSet`.
SelectCommand	Returns an `OleDbCommand` object that contains a SQL statement for selecting data from the `DataSet`.
UpdateCommand	Returns an `OleDbCommand` object that contains a SQL statement for updating data in the `DataSet`.

Method	Description
Fill	Adds or changes rows in a `DataSet` to match the data source. This method is overloaded.
FillSchema	Adds a `DataTable` to the specified `DataSet` and configures the schema of the table. This method is overloaded.
GetFillParameters	Returns an array of `IDataParameter` objects that are used with the `SELECT` command.
Update	Updates the data source with the information in the `DataSet` using the `Delete`, `Insert`, and `UpdateCommand` properties. This method is overloaded.

Event	Description
FillError	Occurs when an error is returned during a `Fill` operation. Uses a `FillErrorEventArgs` object for the event parameter. This object contains the following properties: `Continue`—Indicates if the operation should continue. `DataTable`—The `DataTable` being updated when the error occurred. `Errors`—Returns an `Exception` object representing the errors being handled. `Values`—Returns an object representing the values for the row being updated when the error occurred.
RowUpdated	Occurs after an `Update` command has executed. Uses an `OleDbRowUpdatedEventArgs` object for the event parameter. This object contains the following properties: `Command`—Returns the `OleDbCommand` executed when `Update` is called. `Errors`—Returns an `Exception` object representing the errors that occurred. `RecordsAffected`—The number of records affected.

TABLE C.16   continued

Event	Description
	Row—Gets the DataRow used by Update.
	StatementType—The type of SQL statement being executed.
	Status—An UpdateStatus object representing the status of the command.
	TableMapping—Gets the DataTableMapping sent with the Update command.
RowUpdating	Occurs before an Update command has executed. Uses an OleDbRowUpdatingEventArgs object for the event parameter. This object contains the following properties:
	Command—Returns the OleDbCommand to execute when Update is called.
	Errors—Returns an Exception object representing the errors that occurred.
	Row—Gets the DataRow used by Update.
	StatementType—The type of SQL statement to execute.
	Status—An UpdateStatus object representing the status of the command.
	TableMapping—Gets the DataTableMapping sent with the Update command.

OleDbDataReader

The OleDbDataReader class represents a lightweight, streaming method for retrieving data from a data source. It is similar to a DataSet, but provides less functionality with increased performance. Table C.17 lists the properties and methods of this class.

TABLE C.17   Properties and Methods of the OleDbDataReader Class

Property	Description
Depth	The depth of the reader.
FieldCount	The number of fields within the current record.
IsClosed	Indicates if the data reader is closed.
Item	The value at the specified column in its native format. This method is overloaded.
RecordsAffected	The number of records affected by the command. Typically, this is 1 if successful—less than 1 otherwise.

TABLE C.17 continued

Method	Description
Close	Closes the OleDbDataReader object.
GetBoolean	Returns the value at the column specified as a Boolean value.
GetByte	Returns the value at the column specified as a Byte value.
GetBytes	Returns the value at the column specified as a Byte array.
GetChar	Returns the value at the column specified as a Char value.
GetChars	Returns the value at the column specified as a Char array.
GetDataTypeName	Returns the data type of the column specified.
GetDateTime	Returns the value at the column specified as a DateTime value.
GetDecimal	Returns the value at the column specified as a Decimal value.
GetDouble	Returns the value at the column specified as a Double value.
GetFieldType	Gets the Type that is the data type of the object.
GetFloat	Returns the value at the column specified as a Float value.
GetGuid	Returns the value at the column specified as a globally unique identifier value.
GetInt16	Returns the value at the column specified as a 16-bit signed integer.
GetInt32	Returns the value at the column specified as a 32-bit signed integer.
GetInt64	Returns the value at the column specified as a 64-bit signed integer.
GetName	Returns the name of the column specified.
GetOrdinal	Gets the column's index, given the column name.
GetSchemaTable	Returns a DataTable object that describes the column metadata for this object.
GetString	Returns the value at the column specified as a String value.
GetTimeSpan	Returns the value at the column specified as a TimeSpan value.
GetValue	Returns the value at the column specified in its native format.
GetValues	Returns all of the attributes for the current record, and places them in a specified array.
IsDBNull	Used to indicate nonexistent values.
NextResult	Advances the reader to the next result, when reading from the results of batch SQL statements.
Read	Moves the reader to the next record.

C

OleDbError and OleDbErrorCollection

The OleDbError class collects information about a warning supplied from the data source. Table C.18 lists the properties of this class.

TABLE C.18   Properties of the OleDbError Class

Property	Description
Message	A short description of the error.
NativeError	The database-specific error information.
Source	Gets the object that generated the error.
SQLState	Retrieves the five-character standard error code for the database.

Table C.19 lists the properties and method of the OleDbErrorCollection class, which represents a collection of OleDbError objects.

TABLE C.19   Properties and Method of the OleDbErrorCollection OClass

Property	Description
Count	The number of errors in the collection.
Item	Gets an OleDbError in the collection with the specified index.
Method	**Description**
CopyTo	Copies the entire collection to an array, starting at the specified index.

OleDbParameter and OleDbParameterCollection

The OleDbParameter class represents a value that is passed along with a database command to provide additional information or options. Table C.20 lists the properties and method of this class.

TABLE C.20   Properties and Method of the OleDbParameter Class

Property	Description
DbType	The data type of the data source.
Direction	Indicates how the parameter will be used. Can be: Input, InputOutput, Output, or ReturnValue.
IsNullable	Indicates if the parameter is allowed to contain a null value.
OleDbType	Specifies the Type of this parameter. (This property does not exist in the corresponding SqlParameter class.)

TABLE C.20   continued

Property	Description
Offset	The offset to the Value property. (This property only exists in the SqlParameter class.)
ParameterName	The name of the parameter.
Precision	The maximum number of digits used to represent the parameter.
Scale	The number of decimal places used to represent the parameter.
Size	The maximum size of this parameter.
SourceColumn	The name of the column in the data source mapped to the DataSet used for returning Value.
SourceVersion	Specifies the row version to use when loading data.
Value	The value of the parameter.

Method	Description
ToString	Returns the ParameterName.

Table C.21 lists the properties and methods of the OleDbParameterCollection class, which represents a collection of OleDbParameter objects.

TABLE C.21   Properties and Methods of the OleDbParameterCollection Class

Property	Description
Count	The number of OleDbParameter objects in the collection.
Item	Gets an OleDbParameter in the collection with either the name of the parameter or its index in the collection.

Method	Description
Add	Adds a parameter to the collection. This method is overloaded.
Clear	Clears the collection of all OleDbParameter objects.
Contains	Indicates if the OleDbParameter with the specified name exists in the collection.
CopyTo	Copies the entire collection to a specified array, starting at the specified index.
IndexOf	Retrieves the index of the specified parameter. This method is overloaded.
Insert	Inserts an OleDbParameter object at the specified index.
Remove	Removes the specified parameter from the collection. This method is overloaded.
RemoveAt	Removes the OleDbParameter at the specified index.

OleDbTransaction

The OleDbTransaction class represents a transaction that occurs at the data source. Table C.22 lists the properties and methods of this class.

TABLE C.22 Properties and Methods of the OleDbTransaction Class

Property	Description
Connection	The OleDbConnection object associated with this transaction.
IsoloationLevel	The isolation level for this transaction. Can be Chaos, ReadCommitted (default), ReadUncommitted, RepeatableRead, Serializable, or Unspecified.
Methods	Description
Begin	Starts the transaction. Subsequent commands and changes will all be stored in a transaction log pending committal, and can be rolled back at any time.
Commit	Commits all changes since calling Begin.
RollBack	Rolls back all changes that have been made to the data source since the Begin or Commit method was called.

INDEX

C